"*Fundamental Photoshop* provides a complete reference for the computer artist. More than just a 'glorified manual,' it gives the reader a comprehensive view of working with images ranging from basic skills, to explaining creative approaches, color theory, and calibration and output issues. Of particular interest is the 'Photoshop in Action' section, which uses real world examples to explain how Photoshop is used professionally."

*Bruce Wands, Chairman of the Computer Art Department*
*School of Visual Arts, New York City*

"As a photographer, I'm in awe of the incredible powers of Photoshop. As a Photoshop user, I'm in awe of the learning curve—all those layers, levels, nooks & crannies. What's a user to do?? When I hit a wall, I turn to THE best source of information available—*Fundamental Photoshop*! It's like having an expert instructor sitting on my keyboard, ready to help me navigate through complex waters.

When I need to get it done & I'm out of answers, *Fundamental Photoshop* pulls me through. It's extremely user-friendly, with clear, concise, well-organized and easy to use information plus great illustrations & step-by-step exercises.

Take my Nikon, take my Kodachrome—but don't take my *Fundamental Photoshop*!"

*Ira Wexler, Photographer/Author*
*The Business of Commercial Photography*
*(published by Watson Guptil/Amphoto, 1995)*

"*Fundamental Photoshop* is an informative text filled with practical and easily understood facts concerning every aspect of the program. A source worth its weight in gold! A must for every Photoshop owner!"

*Raymond A. Mastrobuoni, I.B.D. I.S.P, Vice President*
*Cartier Inc.*
*Visual Merchandising and Store Planning*

"When you start to understand the full power of Photoshop it can be overwhelming, until you fully understand how to use that power—and you will with this book."

*Homer Wright, VP Creative Director*
*Grey Advertising*

"Terrific...A boon for beginners and a bible for professionals. This book will become as indispensable to anyone in the graphic arts industry as a set of magic markers and a layout pad."

*Steve Alburty, MIS Director*
*Chiat/Day Inc. Advertising*

"This book should be a fundamental part of any computer artist's library. It covers all the essential ins and outs of Photoshop more succinctly and vividly than other books of its kind."

*Sally Face, Manager of Computer Systems*
*BBDO New York*

"Photoshop is one of the most powerful programs available to desktop publishers today, with a daunting array of features geared to varying areas of professional publishing. *Fundamental Photoshop* presents the features of the program in logically organized chapters and provides examples each step of the way. It is a well-organized, easy-to-follow guide to this sometimes difficult program."

*Wendy Allen, Director of Electronic Publishing Systems*
*New York Times Women's Magazines*

"Oh, no—not another Photoshop book! Oh, YES! If you only have time for one Photoshop book, *Fundamental Photoshop*, with its clarity, information, and pertinent examples, is the one to get."

*Donald Gambino, computer artist, consultant, and educator*

"*Fundamental Photoshop* is an unusually informative and highly readable introduction to the magic of Adobe Photoshop. It is of value to newcomers as well as experienced users in learning to effectively use Photoshop's power for image processing, photo retouching, and electronic painting. Particularly helpful are the clear illustrations, easy-to-understand explanations, and detailed step-by-step exercises. This is a truly comprehensive, single-source reference to Photoshop that will be of long-time value."

*Burton Holmes, President of Burton Holmes Associates*
*Corporate Marketing Communications*

# FUNDAMENTAL
## SECOND EDITION

PHOTOSHOP

# FUNDAMENTAL
## SECOND EDITION

PHOTOSHOP

Adele Droblas Greenberg
Seth Greenberg

Osborne **McGraw-Hill**

Berkeley   New York   St. Louis   San Francisco
Auckland   Bogotá   Hamburg   London   Madrid
Mexico City   Milan   Montreal   New Delhi   Panama City
Paris   São Paulo   Singapore   Sydney
Tokyo   Toronto

Osborne **McGraw-Hill**
2600 Tenth Street
Berkeley, California 94710
U.S.A.

For information on software, translations, or book distributors outside of the U.S.A., please write to Osborne McGraw-Hill at the above address.

## FUNDAMENTAL PHOTOSHOP, SECOND EDITION

1234567890 DOC 998765

ISBN 0-07-881093-6

Dedicated to our parents: Beatriz, Ben, Gloria, Max
brothers and sisters: Steven, Ginger, Gary, Josh, and Stacey
for their love and support

## About the Authors...

Adele Droblas Greenberg is a New York-based designer, retoucher, and desktop publishing/prepress consultant. She teaches at Pratt Institute in Manhattan and Columbia University. She is also the former training director at a New York City prepress house.

Seth Greenberg is a certified Apple Computer Consultant and a freelance writer. He has worked as a television producer and script writer, and has written for several computer magazines.

CONTENTS AT A GLANCE

A book as extensive as *Fundamental Photoshop* could not have been written without the help of numerous people.

Above all we'd like to thank the editorial and production staff at Osborne/McGraw-Hill, particularly Publisher Larry Levitsky, Editor-in-Chief Jeff Pepper, and Acquisitions Editor Scott Rogers. We owe a debt of gratitude to Scott for his dedication, perseverance, help, and enthusiasm during the writing, editing, and production stages of *Fundamental Photoshop*. We'd like to especially express our thanks and gratitude to Project Editor Wendy Rinaldi for her conscientiousness, and for all the long hours of hard work she put into *Fundamental Photoshop*.

For the second edition of *Fundamental Photoshop*, our special thanks to Graphic Designer Mason Fong, Technical Editor Sandee Cohen, Editorial Assistant Kelly Vogel, Production Supervisor Marcella Hancik, Production Manager Deborah Wilson, Managing Editor Cindy Brown, Illustrators Marla Shelasky and Lance Ravella, Copyeditor Carl Wikander, Proofreader Jeff Barash, and Indexer Richard Shrout. Thanks also to first edition Project Editor Janet Walden, Associate Editor Emily Rader, Computer Designer Mickey Galicia, Publicity Manager Lisa Kissinger, PR Assistant Patty Mon, Promotions and Marketing Coordinator Claudia Ramirez, Proofreader Charlotte Bagby, and Copyeditor Carol Henry. Thanks go to all of these people who spent many long hours helping us to ensure that *Fundamental Photoshop* would be the clear, concise, and attractive book that it is.

We'd also like to thank the many artists whose excellent work appears in the color inserts and the "Photoshop in Action" sections in this book. Special thanks are due to artist Dave McKean for seeing that his artwork was quickly and safely shipped from his home in England to the United States.

Thanks to everyone at Adobe Systems, especially Bryan Lamkin, Product Manager of Adobe Photoshop, for his support and help. We are especially grateful for the help provided by John Leddy, Macintosh Photoshop Product Manager, Technical Support Specialists Matt Brown and Eric Thomas, Beta Coordinator Tracy Wright and Adobe Deluxe CD-ROM Producer George Jardine. We'd also like to thank Adobe Photoshop Product Manager for Unix Jerry Granucci, Unix Platform Sales Administrator Becky Wilhelmsen, and LeVon Peck and Patricia Pane from

Adobe Public Relations. Above all, we'd like to thank the Photoshop programmers who created and developed such an outstanding product. Their hard work makes our work look like magic.

We'd also like to express our thanks to Martha Wells, Peter Faucetta, Maureen Beirne, Anthony Cozzolino, Joseph Burke, Ernie Migliaccil, Steve Kelsall, and the computer operators at Applied Graphics Technology who helped create the first color insert in this book.

We're grateful to our friends, clients, and students who kept asking us to put our consulting and training skills down on paper and provide a book for them. Special thanks are due to Mitch Rose, Richard Lombard, Ethan Ernest, Jurgen Wolff, David Peters, Richard Berenson, Dave Trooper, Ken Chaya, Bianca McGibny, Barbara Rietschel, Dolores Calafati, Joseph LaRezza, Dottie Gettelson, Won Chung, Emily Singer, Bill Lyon, Suzanne Arden, Richard DiLorenzo, Bill Glass, Dennis Green, Mary Kelly, Lisa McElroy, Eugene Hernandez, Meera Kothari, Jim Hamilton, Jamie Goldberg, Chris Thompson, Bruce Stark, Carol Chen, Miles Perkins, Lisa Smith, Jim Burris, Michael Boyle, Paul Lasaine, Michael Curtis, Lynda Freeman, Marian Powers, Alisa Hill, Joseph Favale, Phil Rose and Josephine Lapeyrade. We'd also like to thank our relatives, and everyone else who helped along the way.

We'd like to thank Rich Green of SyQuest Technology for seeing to it that we could easily send our color files back and forth across the country on SyQuest 270 cartridges.

We're grateful to Gary Stone of Lebanon Valley Offset for his assistance in tracking down the image we needed and sending it so quickly. We'd also like to thank many kind people at Quantas Airlines who helped ensure that the last chapters of our book made it to their destination.

We thank the many corporations who graciously provided assistance: Affinity, Agfa, Alias, Alien Skin, American Databankers Corp., Andromeda Software, Inc., Apple Computer, ArtBeats, ColorBytes, Corel, Dana Publishing, D'pix, DPA Software, Daystar, EFI, Elastic Reality, FWB, Flamenco Software, Gryphon Software, IBM, ImSpace, IN Software, HSC Software, Iris Graphics, Ken Hansen Photography, Knoll Software, Kodak, LetraSet, Light Source, Linotype-Hell, Logitech, 3M, Monaco Systems, Nikon, NIQ, PANTONE, PhotoDisc, Pixar, PixelCraft, Pre-Press Technologies, QMS, Radius, Second Glance, Scitex, Silicon Graphics, Specular, Strata, SuperMac, Sun Microsystems, SyQuest, Tektronix, Toshiba, TRUMATCH, Xaos Tools, Inc, and Wacom.

In the late 1980s, Thomas Knoll, a University of Michigan graduate student, created a computer program whose primary purpose was to open and display different graphics files on a Macintosh Plus. This was the humble beginning of the program that was eventually to become Photoshop.

Thankfully for Photoshop users, Tom found that working on a computer program proved to be much more fun than writing a thesis paper. With the encouragement of his brother John Knoll, a special effects supervisor at George Lucas' Industrial Light and Magic Company, Tom began adding image-editing capabilities to his program.

Adobe took Tom's creation under its wings. Soon Tom's brother John was creating filters for the program, and through the collaborative efforts of the Knoll brothers, Adobe's programmers, and the program's original project manager, Steve Guttman, Photoshop evolved into a software package that began revolutionizing the color publishing world.

As Photoshop grew in power and popularity, its users sought help. As consultants, trainers and Photoshop users, we were encouraged to write an easy-to-understand book that would cover the program's fundamentals, yet go well beyond the basics. The result is *Fundamental Photoshop*.

## About This Book

Whether you are a Photoshop beginner or an experienced user, we're sure you'll find *Fundamental Photoshop* to be both a unique instruction and reference book.

We not only cover virtually every command and dialog box in the program, but we also have you try them out. The book is filled with features, hints, tips, step-by-step tutorials, and full-fledged Photoshop projects that you can create with your own images or those provided by Adobe with the Photoshop package. As you read through the book, you'll learn how magazine and book covers, advertisements, and images for television series and film backgrounds were created by some of the top Photoshop artists in the country.

## How This Book is Organized

Chapters 1 through 6 are introductory chapters that guide you through the fundamental tools and basic features of the program.

Chapter 1 begins with an overview of the entire Photoshop design process, from digitizing images to outputting them at a prepress house. The chapter concludes with a guide to calibrating your monitor to ensure that you start your Photoshop work with the colors on your screen displayed as accurately as possible.

In Chapter 2, we enter the world of Photoshop by introducing you to the basics with a tour of the program's menus, tools, and palettes. The first tutorial emphasizes the importance of thinking like a painter and understanding the concepts and capabilities of a pixel-based program.

Chapter 3 provides an introduction to the selection tools. You may be surprised to see that even with the program's basic selection tools, you can create interesting and attractive montages, collages, and vignettes.

Chapter 4 provides an introduction to color theory. Understanding color theory is one of the prerequisites to successfully using Photoshop for color publishing. We'll take a look at the difference between the RGB (red/green/blue), CMYK (cyan/magenta/yellow/black), HSB (hue/saturation/brightness), and Lab color models.

Chapter 5 covers Photoshop's painting tools and shows you how to create custom brushes and use Photoshop's painting/editing modes.

Chapter 6, which concludes the first section of this book, is an introductory look at image-editing techniques. In this chapter you'll learn how to use the Blur/Sharpen, Dodge/Burn/Sponge, and Rubber Stamp tools.

Chapters 7 through 10 bring you to an intermediate level.

Chapter 7 covers digitizing images, cropping images and rotating, and changing brightness and contrast. We round out the chapter by covering image-editing commands, such as Perspective and Distort, so that you not only learn the basics of scanning, but can create a design project with the images you scan.

Chapter 8 teaches you how to apply various filters such as Unsharp Mask, Gaussian Blur, Motion Blur, Lighting Effects, Emboss, and Spherize. If you like special effects, you'll especially enjoy this chapter.

 Chapter 9 provides an in-depth discussion on switching modes—in particular, converting an RGB Color file to a CMYK Color file. This chapter will also lead you step-by-step through the process of creating a duotone and a mezzotint.

 Chapter 10 introduces you to Photoshop's powerful Pen tool. Here you'll be able to try your hand at creating paths and Bézier curves. You'll also learn how to create a clipping path, which is used to silhouette images that you place in other programs.

Chapters 11 through 14 lead you to more advanced levels.

 Chapter 11 provides an in-depth discussion of creating masks and using channels. You'll also learn how to save and load selections. The chapter ends with an overview of Photoshop's Apply Image and Calculations commands.

 Chapter 12 provides a thorough look at Photoshop's powerful layering features. You'll learn techniques for creating layers, and for working independently in different layers. You'll learn how to use Composite Controls, painting/editing modes, and Layer Masks to seamlessly blend layers together.

 Chapter 13 takes you step-by-step through the retouching and color-correcting processes. We show you how to correct old and damaged photographs. We also show you how to use the Curves and Levels dialog boxes. For many readers, this may be one of the most interesting chapters in the book.

 Chapter 14 explains the printing process and includes instructions for calibrating your system to a proof.

Appendixes A and B conclude *Fundamental Photoshop*.

 Appendix A provides a discussion of file formats and techniques for exporting and importing to Photoshop and other applications.

Appendix B shows you how to use Photoshop's File Info command which allows you to tag files according to the International Press Telecommunications Council standard.

Although this book concentrates on the Mac and PC versions of Photoshop, users with Silicon Graphics and Sun Computers can also take advantage of this book. The keyboard shortcuts for both of these computers are similar to those for the PC. Note, however, one exception: the Sun computer has a META key which is similar to the ALT key. See your Quick Reference card for more details on keyboard shortcuts.

# THE PHOTOSHOP STUDIO

Photoshop is truly magical. It can pluck a pyramid from the sands of Egypt and gently drop it down on the Champs-Elysées, looking so real that even a Parisian might not think anything is out of place. Photoshop can make the wrinkles of age vanish magically—or create them where they haven't yet appeared. It can transform a scan of a torn and discolored photograph so that it looks like a flawless image taken by a master photographer. And Photoshop can turn your blank computer screen into an artistic masterpiece—a blend of photorealistic images, fantastic designs, patterns, and colors.

As you'll see in the many professional art and design samples throughout this book, especially in the color inserts, the Photoshop design process can take many forms and can lead in a multitude of directions. Photoshop is an electronic passport to high-end color desktop publishing as well as prepress, multimedia, animation, digital photography, and painting.

Photoshop transports you to these ports of call in many different ways. Once an image is input into Photoshop from a scanner, digital or video camera, video recorder, or Photo CD image, it can be retouched, painted, color-corrected, sharpened, rippled, or distorted. An image can be cut apart, juxtaposed, or blended into another. It can then be output to a slide recorder, a video recorder, a black-and-white or color printer, or an imagesetter to create the final film, which is used to make plates for a printing press. Figure 1-1 illustrates the various input and output devices that cooperate in the Photoshop design and production process.

Although you undoubtedly are eager to jump right in and start turning your artistic visions into reality, take some time first to get acquainted with the Photoshop design process and the digital technology involved in computer image editing. This chapter provides a brief overview of the entire process—inputting, editing, and outputting images—and covers the basics of computers, storage devices, monitors, video display and accelerator cards, scanners, Photo CDs, digital and video cameras, and color printers.

You may want to consider purchasing much of the equipment reviewed in this chapter, but keep in mind that some of it is best left to the professional prepress houses, service bureaus, and electronic imaging centers that can afford state-of-the-art, high-end technology. For a fee, these electronic production companies will digitize your photos, slides, and artwork on drum scanners,

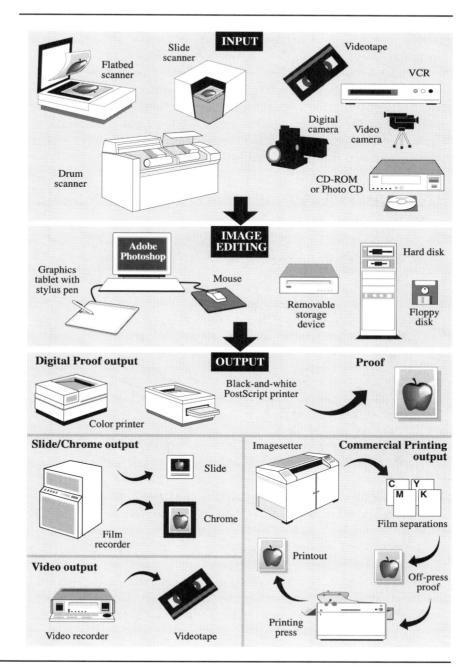

The Photoshop design and production process

**FIGURE** 1-1

providing you with high-quality images without your having to spend a fortune. A service bureau can also output your work to a color printer or imagesetter in preparation for the project's final destination, the printing press.

This chapter's overview of studio equipment begins with a discussion of computers and computer peripherals, and then branches out to input and output devices. Then you'll find a brief discussion of installing Photoshop and calibrating your monitor. Understanding Photoshop's equipment requirements will help guarantee that the program is running at optimum speed, so that you will be able to complete your design work efficiently.

## MACINTOSH AND PERSONAL COMPUTER SYSTEMS

The focal point of the Photoshop studio is your computer. To a significant degree, Photoshop's performance depends upon the speed and power of your computer.

The *minimum* system requirements recommended by Adobe for running Photoshop are

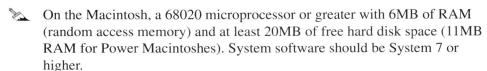 On the Macintosh, a 68020 microprocessor or greater with 6MB of RAM (random access memory) and at least 20MB of free hard disk space (11MB RAM for Power Macintoshes). System software should be System 7 or higher.

On the PC, an 80386 machine or greater with at least 8MB of RAM (for use with Windows 3.1; 16MB of RAM for Windows NT) and at least 20MB of free hard disk space.

If your computer meets these minimum requirements, you'll be able to run Photoshop and perform the exercises in this book. However, if your computer system barely squeaks by, be warned: Photoshop is a very enticing program. The more you learn about it, the more potential you'll see for its use. As you master Photoshop, you'll probably want to add more horsepower to your system to accelerate its performance and increase its ability to utilize Photoshop's power. And if you are buying a new computer just for Photoshop work, by all means consider purchasing the most powerful system you can afford, with the most amount of memory.

You might wonder why Photoshop is so demanding. The answer is that a large, high-quality color image can easily consume over 20 million bytes, or 20MB, of storage space. When such a large file needs to be loaded, color-corrected, and edited, a computer that typically is adequate for other tasks may bog down under the stress of working with Photoshop.

## The CPU

To evaluate Photoshop's performance on your system, or to decide what system to buy, you should have a basic knowledge of what controls a computer's operating speed. Perhaps the most important component is the computer's *microprocessor,* or *CPU* (central processing unit). The microprocessor is a chip that is often called the "brains" of a computer. Its job is to process the steps of a computer program and send instructions along the various data highways connected to its circuitry. In any microprocessor, regardless of whether it is driving a Macintosh or a PC, two main factors determine performance: the speed of the chip and the amount of data the chip can process.

Available CPUs run at various speeds and process various amounts of data. The primary CPUs for the Macintosh are the Power PC 600 series, 68040 and the 68030, all manufactured by Motorola. The Power PC, the most sophisticated of Apple's CPUs, can send information over 64 data channels at once—the equivalent of a 64-lane highway, with carloads of information running through the CPU. This highway is called a *64-bit data bus*. The bigger the data bus, the better the performance. The 68040 CPU in the Mac Quadra can process 32 bits of information at a time. The 68030, which powers older Macs, can process 16 bits at a time.

Apart from its 64-bit data bus, the Power PC RISC-based (Reduced Instruction Set Computing) architecture allows it to process instructions simultaneously and handle data more efficiently than the 68040.

The current version of Photoshop has been programmed to take full advantage of the Power PC chip. Mac users who upgrade to Power Macintoshes will see a significant performance boost when working in Photoshop.

*n*OTE: *RISC chips are often compared to CISC chips (Complex Instructions Set Computing). Instead of maintaining a set of complex instructions, RISC chips are programmed with fewer, simpler instructions—those that are most commonly used. When the RISC chip performs a task, it can do so at lightning speed because it breaks the chore into smaller, simple ones that it can perform simultaneously.*

Among PC-compatible computers, the Pentium chip is the fastest and most sophisticated. Although the Pentium is not considered a RISC chip, it does feature a 64-bit data bus and is very fast.

The speed of the microprocessor measures how quickly it handles a computer program's instructions. The speed of the microprocessor, usually called its *clock speed*, is measured in megahertz (MHz, which equals one million clock cycles). A

100 MHz Pentium chip is faster than a 66MHz one. But speed isn't everything. If you don't have a Pentium powered PC, you should realize that a 25MHz 486 chip will generally run programs faster than a 40MHz 386. This is because the 486 is a more sophisticated chip and can handle more instructions per second than the 386.

If you already own a computer, there are sometimes ways of improving the clock speed of your machine. Apple has traditionally provided motherboard upgrades (which should be installed by authorized Apple dealers) so that many of its older computers can be improved to function like the faster models. Apple's 040 line of computers is upgradable to its new line of lightning fast Power PCs. Many PCs sold today come outfitted with an empty microprocessor socket to allow an upgrade to the Pentium chip. If you are interested in investigating upgrades, contact an authorized Apple or PC vendor.

If you can't wait for an upgrade, or if none is available, a variety of manufacturers sell *accelerator cards* that take over the processing chores for slower computers. Many vendors and mail-order suppliers sell these cards (circuit boards), which generally are easily installed in a slot on your computer's motherboard.

**AUTION:** *Before buying any accelerator equipment, be sure to verify that it will run with Photoshop and any of the other peripherals connected to your system.*

Frequently, however, when you want to speed up your computer, you do not have to do anything as drastic as replacing its CPU. Instead, adding memory will often provide a noticeable increase in Photoshop performance.

## RAM

Much of Photoshop's speed is based upon how much work it can accomplish directly in your computer's RAM (random access memory). RAM is the area of memory your computer uses when you are first working on a file, before you store the data on your hard disk or on a floppy disk. Once a file is saved, when you reload it Photoshop will keep as much of the file in RAM as it can.

If you do not have enough RAM available for Photoshop's operations, it turns to your hard disk and grabs as much free space as it can to complete its chores. Memory accessed from the hard disk when RAM is insufficient is called *virtual memory*. Operations that take place purely in RAM are always going to be faster than those using virtual memory. The computer can interact faster with data it accesses from electronic chips than from a spinning mechanical disk.

As a rule of thumb for estimating RAM requirements, Adobe suggests having three to five times your file size available in RAM or on your hard disk. The more RAM available, the less often Photoshop will need to rely on virtual memory. Despite the safety net of virtual memory, you should be aware that certain Photoshop special effects will not operate at all unless sufficient RAM is available.

When upgrading your system's memory or purchasing a new computer, remember that not all computers are expandable to the same degree. The less expensive Macs and PCs generally will not allow as much memory expansion as the more expensive models. If you can't add any more RAM to your system, your hard disk becomes a crucial element in the Photoshop studio.

## Hard Disks

Since Photoshop must work with your hard disk when RAM is insufficient, the disk's speed and size have a direct effect on Photoshop productivity.

When Photoshop uses your hard disk in place of RAM, the speed of operations is directly related to the speed of your hard disk. In Photoshop, a hard disk used for virtual memory is called a *scratch disk*. If you don't have enough room on your hard disk, Photoshop may not be able to complete the command you are trying to execute. You will receive a screen alert with the message "Scratch Disk Full." It is imperative that you have sufficient hard disk space, or you may not have enough room to save the file you are working with.

If you are planning to add another hard disk to your system, purchase the largest and fastest one that you can afford. Usually, the larger the hard disk, the faster its *seek time*, the time it takes the drive's read/write head to jump to a specific spot on the disk's platter. Hard disk seek time is measured in milliseconds (ms). A 10ms hard disk is faster than a 20ms hard disk. Many new drives in the 200MB range have seek times in the neighborhood of 12ms or less. Gigabyte and two Gigabyte drives (1,000 MB) often feature seek times of less than 10ms, and usually can transfer several megabytes of data a second from the drive to the computer. For instance, FWB's Pockethammer 2050 has an 8ms seek time and a sustained transfer rate of 5.75MB per second. We used the Pockethammer to store the entire contents of this book, and still had lots of scratch disk space left for Photoshop.

## Removable Hard Disks

Before you add another hard disk to your system, you might consider offloading data to a *removable hard disk* to free up space on your system's internal hard disk. Removable hard disks are not only valuable for backing up data but have become essential to many Photoshop users because graphics files are often too large to fit on a floppy disk. When graphic designers need to send a large file out to a service bureau or deliver it to a client, they usually save it on a removable hard-disk cartridge. These cartridges slide in and out of a drive mechanism much as video cassettes do in a VCR, and thus are easily transported from computer to computer.

The most popular removable hard drives for Macs are manufactured by Syquest which also makes removable drives for the PC. Syquest's removable hard drives, shown in Figure 1-2, store from 44MB to 270MB and its cartridges are manufactured in two sizes: 5.25 and 3.5 inch.

If you are looking for speed, convenience, and a lot of storage at a reasonable price, consider Syquest's 270 removable drive. We used a Syquest 270 cartridge to store and ship many of the color images that appear in this book. The 270MB 3.5 inch cartridges cost from 75 to 100 dollars and are quite fast. Since the drive's speed is comparable to many mid-capacity hard drives, in a pinch you could probably get by using one as a scratch disk when working in Photoshop.

Iomega's Bernoulli drives and cartridges are another well-known family of removable hard disks. Current favorites among both Mac and PC users are Bernoulli's 90MB and 150MB removable drives.

If you are going to be purchasing a Syquest or Bernoulli drive that you will be sending to a printer, prepress house or service bureau, check to see that the service bureau can accept the type of drive you are going to buy. Most will accept 44MB and 88MB 5.25 inch Syquest cartridges.

SyQuest 105MB and 270MB External Removable Cartridge Disk Drives, courtesy of SyQuest Technology

**FIGURE 1-2**

## Optical and DAT Drives

When you need to store many large files for archival purposes, you may wish to purchase an *optical drive*. Although much slower than hard disks, optical drives often store between 500MB and 1,000MB (1 gigabyte). The chief appeal of opticals is that the cost per gigabyte is much lower than that of hard disks or removable hard disks.

Another economical choice for storing large amounts of data is a *digital audio tape (DAT) drive*. These tape drives store several gigabytes of data on tapes that cost approximately $10.00 each. Many DAT drives are available for under $2,000. Unlike hard drives, which can quickly access data anywhere on a spinning platter, the DAT has to wind and unwind to read and record data. This makes DAT drives inappropriate for most operations except archiving files.

## File Compression

If you are short on hard disk or archival storage space, one scheme for managing large files is to save them in *compressed format.* Various types of data compression exist. Some compression methods result in data loss; others compress without sacrificing picture quality. If you plan to compress your files, you should know whether your compression software will remove picture information during the compression process.

On the Mac, programs such as Stuffit Deluxe and Disk Doubler can compress files without losing data. On the PC, PKZIP and Stacker are two popular programs that offer compression without data loss. Stacker automatically compresses *every* file on a hard disk, as opposed to PKZIP, which compresses only files that you select for compression.

Photoshop can save files using JPEG and LZW compression formats. JPEG results in data loss; LZW does not. These options are discussed in more detail in Appendix A.

## COLOR VIDEO MONITORS

As you create and edit images, your window into the color digital world is your video monitor. Your monitor's screen size, sharpness, and color accuracy are all critical factors when working with Photoshop.

Although using a full- or two-page monitor is not a necessity in Photoshop, the larger your monitor, the more efficiently you'll be able to work. Even if you are working on small images, you're sure to want to magnify them. You will often want a palette of colors or brushes to be open while you paint or edit, or to have several images open at the same time. You may even wish to view the same image at various sizes in separate windows. All of these factors make screen real estate an important commodity.

If you think that 19- or 21-inch color monitors are beyond your budget, consider purchasing a 16- or 17-inch model. Many 17-inch monitors cost about half the price of 19-inch monitors and will probably pay for themselves in convenience and ease of use. The difference between 13- and 17-inch monitors may not seem like much, but because monitor size is measured diagonally, a 17-inch monitor actually provides approximately 85 percent more viewing area than a 13-inch one.

If you are planning to buy a new monitor, you'll find that many of the major desktop publishing vendors, such as Apple, NEC, SuperMac, Radius, RasterOps, and Sony, offer models that will suit your needs.

Most graphics monitors have a resolution of at least 72 pixels per inch (ppi). A *pixel* is the smallest visible element on screen. At 72 pixels per inch, the resolution on a 14-inch monitor is 640 by 480 pixels. Most 19-inch monitors display 1024 by 768 pixels. Radius' 20-inch IntelliColor for both PCs and Macs boasts a resolution as high as 1600 by 1200 pixels. The IntelliColor and most other newer monitors allow you to switch from one resolution to another. For instance, Apple's 17 Multiple Scan and SuperMac's 17T can match the resolution of a 19-inch display. This produces more pixels and thus increases the viewing area of images on screen (although the images are smaller).

A good monitor should not flicker. Most high-end models refresh the screen fast enough so that flicker is not a problem. Look for vertical scan rates (the *refresh rate*) on 14-inch monitors to be around 67 hertz (Hz, cycles per second). This means that the screen is scanned from top to bottom 67 times a second. Rates lower than 65Hz can cause flickering. Since more lines need to be scanned on larger monitors, refresh rates should be even higher.

Higher quality monitors are also *non-interlaced*, which means that lines of information are scanned one row after another, rather than the odd lines first, then the even. Non-interlaced monitors are sharper and produce less flicker. The dot pitch on monitors is also a factor governing image quality. *Dot pitch* is the distance between the red, blue, and green phosphor elements. The smaller the dot pitch, the sharper the monitor. You'll generally see graphics monitors featuring dot pitches of less than 29mm (millimeters).

When analyzing an image on a monitor, study the uniformity of the colors displayed. Different areas of the screen should generally appear at the same levels of brightness. Images should look sharp, not blurry. A straight line that traverses the screen should look straight, not bent. Circles should look like perfect circles.

Any new color monitor you buy should be capable of displaying over 16 million colors. The number of colors a monitor displays is closely tied to the video display card inside your computer, as explained next.

## VIDEO DISPLAY CARDS

The video display card, one of the circuit boards found in a computer, controls how many colors the monitor displays and often controls how fast the monitor redraws images on the screen. Some computers, including the newer models from Apple, have a video card built in, and no extra hardware is needed to drive the monitor.

The minimum number of colors displayed by Apple's color computers and most video display cards is 256. But for many Photoshop users, 256 colors just isn't enough. In order to view digitized images of color photographs on screen and see them as realistically as possible, millions of colors are needed. The reason so many colors are needed is simple: The human eye can discern millions of colors.

In order to view millions of colors, you will need a 24-bit video display color card. If you own one of Apple's high-end Quadras or a Power PC, you can add chips called video RAM to get 24-bit color on a 14- or 16-inch monitor. On Apple's top of the line Power PCs, you can add enough video RAM to view millions of colors on a 20-inch monitor.

If you're wondering how 24-bit color translates into 16 million colors, you need to know something about computer technology. This knowledge will be helpful because you will see the term *bit* used in several Photoshop dialog boxes. A bit is the smallest element the computer uses to describe data. The bit has two states: on or off. The total possible combinations for 8 bits of data yield 256 colors ($2\times2\times2\times2\times2\times2\times2\times2=256$).

A 24-bit color system divides the 24 bits into 8 bits for red values, 8 bits for green values, and 8 bits for blue values. This produces 256 possible values of red, 256 of green, and 256 of blue. By making combinations of all the possible values of red, green, and blue, the computer can create over 16.7 million colors ($256\times256\times256=16,777,216$).

If you do need to buy a 24-bit card, make your purchase carefully. Not all 24-bit cards will work with all monitor sizes. One 24-bit card may produce millions of colors on a 13-inch monitor, but not on a 19-inch monitor. One reason for this is that video cards need more memory to address larger screens.

### Accelerated Video Display Cards

If you decide you need a 24-bit video card, your next decision should be whether to buy an *accelerated video display card.* Acceleration is desirable because it reduces the amount of time required to update the thousands of pixels on a large color screen.

In addition to producing 16.7 million colors, accelerated 24-bit video cards speed up screen operations by adding an extra microprocessor, called a *coprocessor*, to your computer. This accelerates the entire procedure of working with graphic images. When your computer has a graphics coprocessor, its microprocessor can take a break from handling time-consuming screen processing operations.

Manufacturers of 24-bit cards for both PCs and Macs include Radius, RasterOps, SuperMac, TrueVision, and NEC.

*n***OTE:** *If you do plan to purchase an accelerated video card, be aware that it's hard to predict how much these will speed up screen display when you are working with Photoshop. They will undoubtedly accelerate screen redraw and scrolling, but they may not affect specific Photoshop functions.*

### Custom Photoshop Accelerator Cards

The demand for speed among Photoshop users has produced a market for cards whose sole purpose is to speed up various Photoshop operations.

Vendors such as Daystar, Mirror, Radius, SuperMac, and Spectral Innovations all manufacture Photoshop accelerator cards for the Macintosh. Storm Technology manufactures two Photoshop accelerator cards for the PC. Perhaps the best known of the custom cards is SuperMac's Thunderstorm. Thunderstorm and Daystar's Charger cards will work in most Macs that accept Nubus-specification cards. The Radius Photobooster will only work in Centris and Quadra models.

Many of the custom accelerator cards ship with special software that add to Photoshop's own feature set. For instance, Daystar's Charger Suites provide "power previews" which provide comparisons between before and after versions of an image *before* an effect is applied. The preview dialog box also allows push-button choices among different groups of effects.

*n***OTE:** *Before you purchase a custom accelator card, be aware that they do not speed up every Photoshop function. Most of the cards will improve the speed of resizing, rotating, compression, and many of the filters that you will learn about in Chapter 8. If you are using these features, the increase in speed can be dramatic.*

## GRAPHICS TABLET WITH STYLUS PEN

Often overlooked in the array of sophisticated graphic peripherals is the value of a graphics tablet and stylus pen. The stylus pen is a pressure-sensitive device that replaces the mouse. A stylus can simulate the pencil, pen, and paintbrush more accurately than the mouse, and thus many artists find it easier to use. The fine point of the stylus pen also enables you to more precisely retouch photographs in

Photoshop. Figure 1-3 shows artist C. David Piña using a Wacom tablet and stylus pen with Photoshop to work on the main title design for the 63rd Annual Academy Awards show.

The stylus must be used in conjunction with a graphics tablet. Wacom manufactures a tablet that includes a plastic overlay. Art can be slid under the overlay so that it can be traced much more accurately than would be possible with a mouse. Other manufacturers of tablets with stylus pens include CalComp and Kurta.

## INPUT DEVICES

*Input devices* digitize images so they can be edited and color-corrected in Photoshop. These devices include scanners, Photo CDs, digital cameras, and video cameras. Chapter 7 covers the digitizing process in detail.

Although the use of Photo CDs and digital photography is growing, the most common technique for digitizing images is with a scanner.

### Scanners

Scanners are used primarily to digitize photographs, flat art, and slides. Although the price of many scanners fits the budget for many Photoshop studios, the quality of low-cost scanners may not suit your needs. Depending upon the type of work you

A Wacom tablet and stylus pen, courtesy of Wacom Technology Corp.

■ FIGURE 1-3

do, you may find it necessary to send your files to a prepress house or service bureau to get the final quality you desire.

Even if you aren't going to purchase a scanner or actually do the scanning yourself, you should know the basics of how scanners work. This will give you an idea of what quality you can expect from various types of scanners.

## Flatbed Scanners

Most scanners sold today are flatbed scanners. In many ways, a flatbed scanner resembles a copy machine. Art or a photograph is placed under the scanner's cover, and the digital reproduction process begins. Some of the better-known manufacturers of flatbed scanners are Agfa, Hewlett-Packard, Howtek, La Cie, Microtek, Sharp, Nikon, and Umax.

Flatbed scanners are sometimes called *CCDs*. CCD stands for *charged coupled device*, a component in the scanner's head that sends thousands of beams of light across the object being scanned. Photoelectric cells on the head detect red, green, and blue components of light that are reflected back to the CCD. The reflected information produces high and low voltages depending upon the lightness and darkness of the image. This information is digitized so it can be saved to disk.

There are several factors to consider when evaluating what scanner to use or buy. The first is *resolution*, or how many pixels per inch (ppi) the scanner can create. The greater the number of pixels, the sharper the image. Many low-priced scanners will scan at at least 600 ppi. Some use an *interpolation* to make the resolution appear as high as 1200 ppi. When a scanner interpolates, it's not really a sharper representation of the actual scanned image. It merely adds more pixels and then colors the new pixels with the average color of surrounding pixels. For more information about scanning resolution, see Chapter 7.

One of the primary factors that determines scanned image quality is *dynamic range*. A scanner's dynamic range measures its ability to capture gradations from the lightest to darkest parts of an image. The greater a scanner's dynamic range, the sharper the image. To provide better dynamic range, the scanner needs to utilize more bits to store the information. Most low-end scanners scan at 8 bits per each red, green, or blue component. Technically, this should produce over 16.7 million colors; however, 2 bits are needed to handle noise and calibration, so this decreases the dynamic range.

Mid-range scanners are often 10-bit scanners. The Agfa Arcus II shown in Figure 1-4, which sells for about $3,500, is a 12-bit scanner. A high-end scanner such as the Scitex Smartscan sells for about $80,000. This scanner not only has a better dynamic range than lower-bit scanners but also has its own image-processing system. The Smartscan operator can make color adjustments before and during the scanning process.

Agfa's
Arcus II
scanner,
courtesy of
Agfa Corp.

**FIGURE 1-4**

## Slide Scanners

If you can obtain your images as slides, you're likely to improve the quality of your digital images. Slides are brighter than prints and have a higher dynamic range; thus the originating image for the scan is better than an opaque object.

In many slide scanners, the CCD is stationary, and light is redirected back to the photo sensors through a combination of mirrors and lenses. The optical system of slide scanners is often better than flatbeds; many slide scanners have resolutions in the 5,000-6,000 ppi range. Some of the better-known manufacturers of slide scanners are BarneyScan, Kodak, Nikon, and Polaroid.

Though slide scanners can be expensive, several models fall into the price range of flatbed scanners. Nikon's LS-10 Coolscan, shown in Figure 1-5, retails for about $2,000. The internal model will fit in a drive bay of various Macs and PCs.

## Rotary Drum Scanners

For most color professionals, the best way to ensure the highest digital quality is to scan with a drum scanner, shown in Figure 1-6. Instead of utilizing a CCD to emit light, the drum scanner uses a *photomultiplier tube,* often called a PMT. In PMT technology, the image being scanned rotates on a drum while a stationary source transmits light using photomultiplier tubes.

Nikon's LS-10 Coolscan slide scanner, courtesy of Nikon.

**FIGURE 1-5**

Dupont Crosfield drum scanner, courtesy of Dupont Crosfield

**FIGURE 1-6**

The rotary drum's sophisticated photoreceptors and advanced optics make the drum scanner much more sensitive to highlights and shadows than most CCD scanners. Service bureaus typically charge from $25 to $100 for images scanned on drum scanners. These scanners cost from $30,000 to several hundred thousand dollars and require trained operators to get the best scanning results.

If you need to digitize photographic images, you may be able to avoid scanning altogether and take advantage of the most recent and one of the more important developments in digitizing images: the Photo CD.

## Photo CDs

Since Eastman Kodak developed the Photo CD in 1992, it has become a serious and high-quality alternative to scanning. For a nominal fee per photo, a Photo CD service bureau can digitize your photographic film directly to a Photo CD disc. Kodak's Photo CD Master discs can hold 100 high-resolution 35mm images. Kodak's Pro Photo CD format allows the following film formats to be digitized on a Photo CD: 120mm, 70mm, 35mm, and 4-by-5 inch. The Photo CD image can be opened directly into Photoshop for image editing and color correcting.

If you are in the market for a CD-ROM player and wish to use Photo CD images, you must purchase a CD-ROM XA (extended architecture) such as the AppleCD 300e Plus, shown in Figure 1-7. Prices for CD-ROM players generally range from $200 to $900, with the fastest models generally being the most expensive. Speed is important because a large color image can take many times longer to load on a CD-ROM than on a hard drive. Some manufacturers, such as NEC, feature drives that can transfer data at different speeds. For instance, NEC's 3X Multispin drive can transfer data at 450KB (kilobytes) per second, approximately three times the standard CD-ROM data transfer rate of 150KB per second. NEC's Multispin 4X Pro transfers data at 600KB per second.

## Video and Digital Cameras

If your Photoshop work requires that you take your own photographs, you may want to investigate using a video or digital camera in order to digitize your images instantaneously. This eliminates delays caused by film processing, test shoots, and scanning prints or transparencies.

Many video cameras require that a video card be installed in your computer to digitize the video signal from the camera. There are also many systems that come with software that allows you to control the video digitizing process directly from within Photoshop.

AppleCD
300e Plus,
courtesy of
Apple
Computer,
Inc.
Photographed
by John
Greenleigh

**FIGURE 1-7**

Although capturing an image from video is both convenient and quick, the resolution of images produced on most video digitizing systems is not better than 640 by 480 pixels (72 ppi). This is because they use the NTSC (National Television System Committee) standard.

The alternative to a video camera is a digital camera. Many of these cameras look like standard 35mm cameras, but they store images to the camera's memory or to a small attached hard disk. Besides providing higher resolution than a video camera, the digital camera is extremely portable. Kodak, for instance, has released several models of the DCS 420 digital camera, shown in Figure 1-8, which uses a 35mm Nikon body as the optical power behind its digital camera system. The price for this camera runs from about $8,500 to $10,000.

Leaf Systems, a Scitex company, has developed a digital camera back that attaches to high-end cameras such as the Mamiya RZ 67 and Hasselblad's 500 EL and 553 RLX. Images taken by these cameras can then be downloaded to a Macintosh IIfx or Quadra.

## Video Capturing Cards

Another method for capturing video images is to use a video card, such as those manufactured by Diaquest and TrueVision. These allow you to use your computer

Kodak
Professional
DCS 420
digital
camera,
courtesy of
Eastman
Kodak
Company

**FIGURE 1-8**

to directly input from and output to video tape. Most cards allow you to capture directly from a video camera as well.

## OUTPUT DEVICES

Once you start working in Photoshop, you'll undoubtedly want to print your color images for final output or as a *proof*, a sample of your final printed version. Proofs created from the desktop before the film negative stage are often called *digital proofs*. To print a proof on paper, you can use either a black-and-white or color printer. Output devices generally used for producing color proofs include inkjet printers, thermal wax printers, dye-sublimation printers, color laser printers, and imagesetters. Most manufacturers of printers produce models that accept data from both Macs and PCs.

When outputting, it's always important to consider the quality of the color and the sharpness of the output. Printer resolution is usually measured in *dots per inch (dpi)*. The greater the number of dots, the better the quality.

**OTE:** *If your final output will be slides, you'll need to buy a film recorder or send your files to a service bureau that can output to a film recorder. If your final output will be videotape, you may need a special video card to output to a VCR.*

## Inkjet Printers

Low-end inkjet printers are the most inexpensive way of producing color files. These printers create colors by spraying ink from cartridges, usually using a process called *dithering*. The dithering process typically uses dot patterns of cyan, magenta, yellow, and often black inks (CMYK) to create the illusion of millions of colors. In many inkjet printers, the dot patterns are easy to see and the color is not always highly accurate. Cost per page for inkjet printers is usually less than thirty cents. Although many new inkjet printers output at 300 dpi, the dithering and color quality of most inexpensive inkjets is not precise enough to provide highly accurate representations of screen images.

On the high end of the scale for inkjet printers are the Scitex IRIS and IRIS Series 3000 printers. These printers cost from $40,000 to over $100,000 and are usually found at service bureaus and ad agencies. The IRIS produces near-photo-graphic-quality images by varying the dot size as it produces an image. In terms of color output, the IRIS provides higher quality than thermal wax and most dye-sublimation printers. The smallest printout from an IRIS printer is approximately 11 by 17 inches. The IRIS can also print poster-size images. The IRIS 3024 prints images as large as 24 by 24 inches; the 3047 prints images 34 by 44 inches.

## Thermal Wax Printers

Thermal wax printers are a large step up in quality from low-end inkjet printers, and thus are a popular choice for producing samples for clients or internal evaluation of layout and design. In the thermal wax printing process, ribbons coated with cyan, magenta, yellow, and black waxes are heated and transferred to paper. During the printing process, heat from the printer's head fuses dots of color to the page. The dot combinations produce the color. The cost per page averages from fifty cents to a few dollars.

If you're interested in a thermal wax printer, you might want to investigate the Tektronix Phaser III PXI. This printer prints on plain paper instead of coated, and the cost per page is about twenty-five cents. The printer will print on paper as large as 12 by 18 inches, thus allowing bleeds for work on 11-by-17-inch paper. Other well-known manufacturers of thermal wax printers include QMS and Océ.

## Dye-Sublimation Printers

Dye-sublimation printers produce stunning, photorealistic-quality images by printing colors created with dyes that *sublimate,* or turn into gas, when a heated printhead hits a colored ribbon. The gaseous colored inks are absorbed on special and expensive paper needed to output the print job. By properly controlling heat, the printhead applies pigments in specific amounts to produce many thousands of colors. Images are not created from a pattern of dots that produce an illusion of color; rather, the printer fills specific amounts of colored ink into each dot. The result is an image that is very detailed, with smooth transitions. Even though most dye-sublimation printers print at about 300 dpi, the quality resembles resolutions of 1,500 dpi.

Dupont, 3M, Kodak, SuperMac, and Tektronix all make dye-sublimation printers that cost from $6,000 to $20,000. The cost to output a print is from $3.00 to $5.00 when all consumables are added together.

Apart from the high cost of each printed page, the main disadvantage of dye-sublimation printers is that text can appear a bit fuzzy.

## Color Laser Printers

Perhaps the best-known color laser printer is the Canon ColorLaser copier, which doubles as a color copy machine. The laser technology uses toner colors of cyan, magenta, yellow, and black to create colored images. Although the quality is not as high as with dye-sublimation printers, color laser printers output faster and the price of consumables is less expensive.

Service bureaus and art departments that use the Canon often hook it up to a Fiery IPU (intelligence processing unit), allowing it to print PostScript images directly from the computer.

## Imagesetters

One of the last stops for the Photoshop design project that is headed for a commercial printer is the imagesetter. An imagesetter is a high-end output device used by prepress houses to record images on paper or film at resolutions from approximately 1,200 to 3,500 dpi. From film, the prepress house can provide a proof, giving an accurate preview of the final color output. The imagesetter output is then delivered to a commercial printer who creates printing plates from the film. These plates are used on the press to produce the final product.

**OTE:** *Chapter 14 takes you step by step through the process of printing composite proofs and separations with Photoshop.*

# INSTALLING AND OPTIMIZING PHOTOSHOP

Now that you've had a brief look at some of the important elements involved in the Photoshop design process, you're ready to start installing Photoshop. We won't repeat the thorough explanations provided by Adobe in the Photoshop package. Installation is simple and involves merely running the installation program from the installation disk.

If you haven't installed Photoshop, use the guide included with the software and begin the installation process.

If you are running Photoshop on a Mac, you must be using System 7.0 or greater. On the PC, you must be using Windows 3.1 or greater. In order for both programs to display type without jagged edges, Adobe Type Manager must be installed. Both Mac and PC versions of Adobe Photoshop come with complete instructions for installing Adobe Type Manager. Mac users should open the Calibration folder and move the Gamma control panel icon into the Control Panels folder in your System folder. You will use the Gamma control panel to calibrate your monitor later in this chapter. (If you have a third-party calibration utility, do not drag the Gamma control panel icon into your System folder.) After you install the Gamma control panel, you should restart your Macintosh.

If you have a hardware and software monitor calibration system created by a company such as Kodak, SuperMac, or RasterOps, follow those instructions for calibrating your monitor.

## The Read Me File

Before running Photoshop for the first time, double-click on the Read Me file that is installed along with the program. This file will explain any changes to the program that are not included in the Photoshop manual.

## Installing Plug-Ins

Your next step is to install any Photoshop plug-ins created by third-party software vendors. *Plug-ins* are programs that work within Photoshop, often created to run scanners or to output images to printers more efficiently. On both Mac and PC systems, all plug-ins that you wish to use in Photoshop should be copied to the Plug-ins folder (PC users: plugins).

**OTE:** *Photoshop automatically recognizes all plug-ins in the Plug-in folder (PC users: plugins). Photoshop will also recognize any plug-in that is in a folder within the plug-in folder. On the Mac, you can "hide" Plug-in subfolders so that Photoshop won't load its plug-ins. To hide a subfolder in the Plug-in folder, type¬ (OPTION-L) in front of the subfolder's name.*

## Allocating Memory for Photoshop on the Mac Using System 7

System 7 Mac users should be aware that Photoshop will not necessarily access all free memory in your computer unless you allocate it to Photoshop. Just because 20MB of RAM is available on your Mac doesn't mean Photoshop will grab extra memory when it needs it. You need to allocate the amount of memory you want to reserve for Photoshop. On the Mac, allocating memory is handled from the Finder.

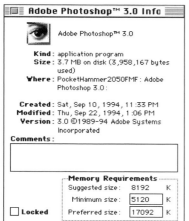

To allocate memory to Photoshop in System 7, first click on the Photoshop program icon, which is in the Adobe Photoshop folder. When you select Photoshop, the program's icon will turn darker. Then choose Get Info from the File menu. In the lower-right corner of the Adobe Photoshop Info window, you will see a number indicating the current size of memory allocated to Photoshop. The suggested size is 8192K, which is a little over 8MB. You should allocate as much memory as you can afford, but be sure to leave about five percent free for the Mac's operating system.

After you've set the memory allocation, close the Adobe Photoshop Info window. The next time you use Photoshop, it will open into the memory partition size that you designated.

Later in this chapter, the section, "Resetting the Scratch Disk" describes another memory allocation adjustment that can aid Photoshop's performance.

### Memory Control Panel Settings

Mac users should turn down the disk cache in their System folder as low as possible, because Photoshop does not take advantage of it. If you leave the disk cache on, you are only sealing off memory that Photoshop could use.

Access the disk cache by double-clicking on the Memory control panel in the Control Panels folder. In the Memory window that appears, as shown in the following illustration, make sure that the Off radio button for Virtual Memory is selected. Photoshop has its own virtual memory system. If you leave System 7's virtual memory on, the two systems may conflict.

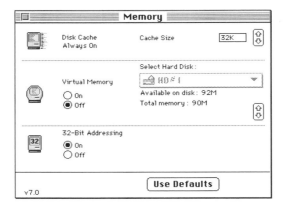

If you have more than 8MB of RAM, the 32-Bit Addressing On radio button should also be selected in this window to ensure that your Mac can access the extra memory beyond 8MB. If you have an older Mac, you may be able to use 32-bit addressing by installing a program called MODE 32. Contact your Apple dealer if you need a copy and for more details.

## Allocating Memory for Photoshop on the PC

For PC users, memory allocation is handled automatically from within Photoshop. Load Photoshop now to check the memory allocation. First start Windows, if it is not already running. In the Program Manager, double-click to open the Adobe group window. There you will see the Adobe Photoshop program icon. To load Photoshop, double-click on the Adobe Photoshop icon.

When Photoshop first loads, it will automatically allocate memory to itself. If you wish to change this allocation, choose Preferences in the File menu. From the Preferences submenu, choose Memory.

The Memory Preferences dialog box displays the currently allocated memory for Photoshop. If you think this will interfere with the operation of other programs, you can change the percentage of allocation by typing a number in the Used by Photoshop field or by clicking the down arrow to the right of the field.

**Memory Preferences**

Scratch Disks

Primary: Startup

Secondary: None

OK

Cancel

Help

Physical Memory Usage

Available RAM: 2616K

Used by Photoshop: 100 %

Photoshop RAM: 2616K

Note: Any changes will not take effect until the next time Photoshop is opened.

## Resetting the Scratch Disk

Your last installation step is to check the memory allocated to your scratch disk. In order to do this, you'll need to load Photoshop. To start Photoshop, double-click on the Adobe Photoshop icon in the Adobe Photoshop folder.

Adobe Photoshop™ 3.0

After the program loads, you may want to reset the scratch disk that Photoshop uses for virtual memory.

As mentioned earlier in this chapter, when Photoshop needs more memory than it can find in RAM, it will start using your hard disk as virtual memory. By default, Photoshop designates your startup drive as the scratch disk. If you have another hard disk connected to your computer that is faster or has more space available, you may want to set the scratch disk to this drive.

Mac users will need to enter a dialog box to set the scratch disk(s). If you wish to reset the scratch disk, choose Preferences from the File menu. From the Preferences submenu, choose Scratch Disks.

**Scratch Disk Preferences**

Scratch Disks

Primary: HD#1

Secondary: Untitled

OK

Cancel

Note: Any changes will not take effect until the next time Photoshop is opened.

PC users will already be in the Memory dialog box if you checked Memory allocation in the procedure outlined in the previous section. If necessary, choose Preferences from the File menu, then choose Memory from the Preferences submenu.

In the Memory Preferences dialog box that appears, click on the Primary or Secondary pop-up menu and choose the desired drive. Your primary scratch disk should be the fastest and emptiest hard drive connected to your system.

**OTE:** *When setting scratch disks and allocating memory, you should have at least as much free disk space as RAM allocated to Photoshop. Otherwise, you may receive a Scratch Disk Full error, even though you have enough memory to complete the command you execute.*

If you wish to boost the performance of Photoshop, be sure that the free space on your hard disk is as contiguous as possible. If you've been accessing your hard disk frequently during your computer sessions, available free space may be spread over many different sectors. Packages such as Norton Utilities, PC Tools, and Mac Tools include optimization programs that will reallocate the files on your hard disk so the free space is as contiguous as possible.

**IP:** *If you are not going to be copying and pasting to other applications, you can free up a bit more memory if you turn off the Export Clipboard option. You can access this by selecting General Preferences in the File menu, then clicking on the More button.*

## MONITOR CALIBRATION

In order for the colors you see on screen to match as closely as possible those on the printed page, your system needs to be properly calibrated. The first step is to calibrate your monitor.

Every monitor has preset color intensity levels called gamma. *Gamma* is the relationship between the picture data input from your software and the color values that are output on screen. For example, if the stored color values saved to disk for an image are set for a light shade of yellow, the screen may display it darker despite the fact that the values are correct on disk. Adjusting a monitor's gamma can help you distinguish between light and dark shades in an image. Many color monitors also display *color casts* and *color shifts* toward red or blue. These color shifts can be corrected by calibrating your monitor.

Another variable that must be factored into the calibration equation is room lighting. Bright light, shifts in sunlight, and even color reflection from objects near a monitor can change the way color is perceived on screen.

## Preparing for the Calibration Process

Before you begin to calibrate your monitor

1. Make sure that your computer's screen display has been turned on for a half hour or more. This stabilizes your monitor.

2. Adjust the room lighting, if necessary, so it is at the level you will maintain while working on the computer. Remember that if you are working near a window, colors may appear different depending upon the amount of sunlight entering your room.

3. Adjust your monitor's brightness and contrast controls to the desired levels. Once the brightness and contrast are set, you may wish to put tape across the monitor's knobs so they can't be changed.

4. Set your monitor's background color to gray. This will prevent background colors from altering your color perception while you are calibrating and while working in Photoshop. For instance, if the background color on your screen is blue, yellows might appear to have a greenish shade around them.

   General Controls

   Mac users: Use the General Controls control panel device to change your background screen to gray.

   Windows 3.1 users: Double-click on the Color icon in the Control panel.

5. Once your monitor's background color has been set to gray, you need to access the calibration program.

   Gamma

   Mac users: Open the Control Panels folder by choosing Control Panels from the Apple menu, and then double-click on the Gamma icon to open the Gamma control panel. Make sure that the On button in the lower-left corner is selected.

   PC users: The calibration program is directly accessible from within Photoshop. Make sure Photoshop is loaded, and then choose Preferences from the File menu. In the Preferences submenu, choose Monitor Setup, and click on the Calibrate button.

6. Set the target gamma.

# Photoshop in Action

The windows in the second floor needed to be removed.

Some of the windows on the side needed to be removed.

Artist: Yusei Uesugi
Client: Lucasfilm Ltd.

The images on these two pages will give you an idea of the image-editing power of Photoshop.

Yusei Uesugi of Industrial Light & Magic, a division of Lucasfilm, creates mattes (backgrounds) for films. Often he must take a dull vintage image, such as the one shown above used for a scene in the television program "Young Indiana Jones" and transform it into a lively background. This image was captured on film, transferred to video, and then digitized into Photoshop, where the image-editing process began.

# Photoshop in Action

Photoshop was used to delete the
windows and create the movie
marquee and the awning.

The windows on the side were deleted.
More light was added to the center of the
image, and the movie posters were added.

A new wall was painted in to separate
the theater from its surroundings.

In Photoshop, Yusei removed the windows on the side of building and on the second floor. He also created the marquee and movie posters near the entrance with Photoshop's painting tools.

After the editing was completed, a printout of the image was used by a model maker to create a model. Yusei then took photographs of the model, which provided him with various angles and light settings so that versions of the image could be created for different scenes.

The versions of the image were digitized into Photoshop for some touching up and so that more details could be added. The result shown above appears to be a photograph taken of an actual location.

Mac users: In the Gamma dialog box, the 1.8 Target Gamma radio button should be selected (the default setting for Macintosh displays). This is your target gamma. If you are outputting to video or slides, Target Gamma should be set to 2.2. A lower gamma results in lower contrast and darker images; a higher gamma results in higher contrast and lighter images.

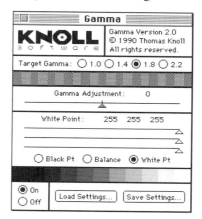

PC users: You don't need to set a target gamma in the Calibrate dialog box. (You will set it in the Monitor Setup dialog box.)

## The Calibration Process

After you've followed all the preparatory steps outlined in the previous section, you're ready to begin the actual calibration process.

The first step will be to make an adjustment to help eliminate color casts that appear in most monitors. For instance, a bluish color cast is produced by many 13-inch monitors, and a reddish color cast often appears in larger monitors. To adjust for unwanted color casts, you need to match the white on your monitor to a sample of the paper stock you will be using when printing. Hold the paper up beside the screen. In the Gamma control panel (PC users: Calibrate dialog box), select the White Pt radio button. Then drag the red, green, and blue slider controls (just above the White Pt radio button) until the monitor matches the white paper as closely as possible.

Next, you'll adjust the gray levels of the monitor. To do this, click on the control for the Gamma Adjustment slider (located at the top of the dialog box). Drag the control left or right until the solid and patterned grays in the dialog box match one another as closely as possible. When you're done, the strip should look as much as possible like one tone of gray.

Monitor calibration can also help eliminate red, green, and blue color casts that result from one of your monitor's red, green, or blue color components being out of balance. To eliminate these types of color casts, click on the Balance button, then drag the red, green, and blue slider controls so that no color tints are visible in the gray strip at the bottom of the dialog box. Next, click on the Black PT radio button to begin setting the black point. This calibrates your monitor so that the darker, or shadow areas will be properly displayed on your monitor. To set the black point, adjust the three sliders so that no tint appears in the lower gray bar, while making sure that a definite gradation between each swatch is visible. If you notice that the Gamma setting has shifted, readjust it; then close the Gamma control panel. (PC users: Click on the Preview button to see the changes.)

If you are using a variety of paper stocks, it's advisable to save various calibration settings for the different papers. If you need to reuse a calibration setting, return to the Gamma control panel (PC users: Calibrate dialog box) and load the settings.

When you are finished adjusting the Gamma settings, close the Gamma control panel by clicking on the Close box (the small square located in the upper-left corner of the window). (PC users: Click OK.) Mac users will next need to load Photoshop to open the Monitor Setup dialog box. PC users will now be in the Monitor Setup dialog box, where you will continue calibrating your monitor.

## The Monitor Setup Dialog Box

The final stage of monitor calibration is to set the options in Photoshop's Monitor Setup dialog box. The Monitor Setup dialog box allows Photoshop to set display output depending upon the type of monitor being used, the room lighting, and the gamma setting.

If Photoshop is not loaded, load it now by double-clicking on the Adobe Photoshop icon. Open the Monitor Setup dialog box by choosing Preferences in the File menu. From the Preferences submenu, choose Monitor Setup. (PC users: You will already be in this dialog box if you just completed the previous calibration steps.)

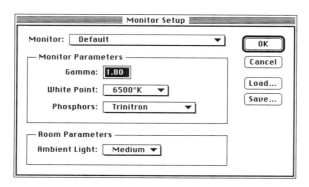

*OTE:* *The settings in the Monitor Setup dialog box are used by Photoshop during conversion between RGB and CMYK color modes. CMYK mode is used for printing four-color process separations. These subjects are covered extensively in Chapters 4 and 9. If you plan to convert from RGB to CMYK mode, it is vital that the settings in the Monitor Setup dialog box be correct.*

In the Monitor Setup dialog box, click on the Monitor pop-up menu and select your monitor from the list.

Enter a target gamma in the Gamma field. This gamma should be the same as that entered in the previous calibration settings procedure. PC users should enter 1.8 or 2.2 if outputting to slides or video. PC and Mac users who are sharing data files should keep their gammas set to identical values.

Leave White Point set at 6500°K (K stands for Kelvin, a temperature measurement scale). The white point is the color measure of white when the intensities of red, green, and blue are equal. The setting 6500°K is used because it is the color temperature of cool daylight. If you are using a third-party calibration device, use the setting recommended for it. If that setting is not in the pop-up menu list, choose Custom from the list and enter the appropriate value.

From the Phosphors pop-up menu, choose the listing that matches the phosphors arrangement in your monitor. (Note that many manufacturers, such as Apple, use Sony monitors that take the Trinitron setting.) If your monitor is not on the list, obtain the proper red, green, and blue chromacity coordinates from your monitor manufacturer. These can be entered by choosing Custom in the Phosphors pop-up menu.

Next, choose a setting from the Ambient Light pop-up menu. Medium is the default, which means the monitor's brightness is about the same as the room lighting. Choose the High setting if the room lighting is brighter, or the Low setting if the room lighting is not as bright as the screen's.

If you will be using various levels of lighting or several different monitors, retain your settings by using the Save button. You then can access these settings with the Load button.

When you are finished entering the information in the Monitor Setup dialog box, click OK.

Now that you've completed the program's installation and calibrated your monitor, you're ready to proceed to the next chapter for your first tour of Photoshop.

# 2

# GETTING STARTED IN THE WORLD OF PHOTOSHOP

If you begin to use Photoshop, mouse in hand but without any "basic training," it won't take long for you to figure out how to fill your screen with assorted shapes, text, and rainbows of brilliant colors. But without a foundation of knowledge about Photoshop's simple tasks and operations, your creativity will soon give way to frustration: How do you move an object from one place to another? How do you edit a word on screen? How do you delete everything from the screen?

Although it's tempting to dive right into Photoshop and start grabbing every tool in sight, the best way to learn how to use this powerful program is to start with the basics. You need to get acquainted with the overall structure of the program and find out how the program works. That's the goal of this chapter. You'll begin with an introductory tour of the program's menus, windows, and palettes; then you'll create a new file and try out several of the tools in the Toolbox. By the end of the chapter, you'll have a good idea of what's going on behind the scenes in Photoshop.

What's behind the scenes in Photoshop? Pixels. Every Photoshop image is comprised of a grid of tiny squares called pixels. When you paint, retouch, cut, paste, or alter any image in Photoshop, you are changing pixels. A *pixel* is the smallest picture element in your image—in fact, the word was created from the two words picture and element. In an image with a *resolution* of 72 pixels per inch, there are 5,184 pixels in every square inch of the image (72 pixels per row in an inch x 72 pixels per column in an inch =5,184). Generally, the more pixels per square inch, the sharper an image is, and the smoother the blend between colors.

Drawing programs such as Adobe Illustrator, Freehand, ClarisDraw, and CorelDRAW utilize lines to create shapes; each shape you draw and each letter you type is an object, separate from other objects. In these programs, when you want to move or resize an object, you can often simply click on it and drag it with the mouse.

Not so in Photoshop. When you work in Photoshop, you have to think like a painter. When you draw a line, create a shape, or type text, you are filling in pixels on screen, painting on an electronic canvas. After you create an object or text, it "dries" on the canvas, almost as if it's embedded on the screen. If you wish to move the object, you'll need to use the proper tool, which essentially cuts the object out of its background so it can be lifted and moved to replace other pixels. To delete the object, you have to paint over it—usually with a white background color.

**OTE:** *In Chapters 3, 5, and 12 you'll learn how layers can provide you with more freedom to move images on screen.*

**2**

Once you begin to think like a painter, what once may have seemed to be a Photoshop peculiarity will begin to feel more natural. By the end of this chapter, we promise you'll be thinking like a painter.

## TOURING PHOTOSHOP

When you are ready to begin your tour of Photoshop, launch the program by double-clicking the Photoshop icon.

After Photoshop is loaded, its menu bar, Toolbox, and three palette groups (Brushes/Options, Picker/Swatches/Scratch, Layers/Channels/Paths), appear on the screen. Unlike many programs, Photoshop does not automatically open a new document for you to work in. You'll learn how to do this later in the chapter, in the section "Creating a New File."

Photoshop has seven pull-down menus available in the menu bar (PC users have an eighth, Help). The more familiar you are with how Photoshop divides up its power, the more likely you are to take the right path when you begin to work with the program.

### A Tour of Photoshop Menus

Most of the commands in the File menu are for storing, loading, and printing files. The New, Open, Save, Save As, Page Setup, Print, and Quit (PC users: Exit) commands work very much as they do in other Macintosh and Windows applications. Revert is covered later in this chapter as is the Save a Copy command. The Acquire command allows you to digitize images from scanners, digital cameras and video capture boards directly into Photoshop. Acquire is also your pathway to Photoshop's Quick Edit command which allows you to load a portion of your file for image editing. Quick Edit is covered in Chapter 6.

The Edit menu is generally used for duplicating or moving parts of images to other areas of a document or to other files. The Edit menu also features an Undo command that allows you to void the action of your last command. Mac and Windows users will recognize standard Edit menu commands: Undo, Cut, Copy, and Paste.

Photoshop's Edit menu also allows you to define a custom pattern that can be used in place of a painting color. The Take Snapshot command allows a version of your file to be held in the computer's memory, so you can revert to it, if necessary, after making changes. The Paste Into command allows you to paste an image into a selection. The Paste Layer command allows you to paste an image into a layer. This command is covered in Chapter 12. The Take Snapshot and Define Pattern commands are discussed in Chapter 6.

The Mode menu allows you to change a color image to grayscale and then from grayscale to black and white. The Mode menu also allows you to convert a file from RGB (red/green/blue), the standard computer color monitor display mode, to CMYK (cyan/magenta/yellow/black), the mode used for four-color process printing. Changing modes is covered in Chapter 9.

The Image menu is primarily used to manipulate the shape of an image, and analyze and correct its color. For example, you can rotate an image, distort it, change its size, and adjust its color balance, brightness, or contrast. Image menu commands are covered in Chapters 7, 11, 13 and 14.

The Filter menu creates effects similar to a photographer's filter that is placed in front of a lens to produce a special effect. By applying a Photoshop filter in one of the Filter submenus, you can sharpen, blur, distort, stylize, and add lighting effects and noise to an image or part of an image. Photoshop features over 40 different filters. The Filter menu is covered in Chapter 8.

The Select menu allows you to modify a selection or select an entire image. (In Photoshop, before you can change any part of an image, you often need to isolate or *select* it.) Select/Grow expands a selection, and Select/Inverse reverses a selection so that everything that isn't selected will be selected. The Select/Modify submenu commands allow you to turn a selection into one that borders the previous selection, smooths a selection, or expands or contracts a selection. Select/Feather blurs the edges of a selection. The Select commands are covered in Chapter 3.

The Window menu allows you to move from one document on the screen to another, to zoom in/out, and to show or hide Photoshop's rulers. You can also create a new window to view the same image simultaneously at different magnifications; when an image is being edited, both windows get updated. The Window menu will also allow you to open and close Photoshop's various palettes. The Window menu will be discussed later in this chapter.

The Help menu is only available in the Windows version of Photoshop. From this menu you can quickly access information about Photoshop features and commands. In many respects, the Help menu is like having the Photoshop User manual a few mouse clicks away.

## CREATING A NEW FILE

In this section, you'll create a new file so that you can explore and get familiar with the Photoshop document window, and get started using the Toolbox. Without a document on screen, you won't be able to use Photoshop's palettes or any of its tools. You'll be creating a document 7 inches wide by 5 inches high, which will provide a comfortable working area on most monitors.

1. To create your new document, select New from the File menu. The New dialog box appears. The settings in the New dialog box will either be Photoshop's default settings or the settings that were last used.

    As you work in Photoshop, you'll find that the program often retains the dialog box settings that were last used.

**OTE:** *If you copy or cut a selection, the dimensions of the selection will appear in the New dialog box. If you wish you can override this by pressing* OPTION *(PC users:* ALT*) when choosing File/New.*

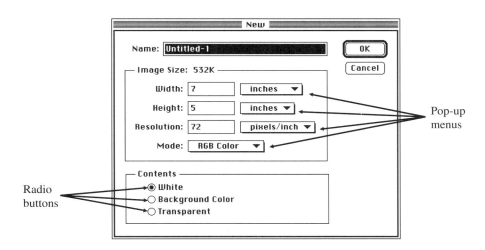

2. In the Name field, you can enter a window title name for your document before you save it. Naming your document before it is saved can be helpful when you have more than one unsaved document on screen. At this point, leave your document untitled.

**3.** If the Width and Height measurement units are not set to inches, change them by selecting inches in the pop-up menus to the right of the Width and Height fields. Pop-up menus are represented by a box containing a down-pointing arrowhead and are outlined with a drop shadow. To access the pop-up menus, Mac users can click anywhere in the pop-up menu but must keep the mouse button pressed in order to drag down and select inches from the list. PC users must click on the down arrow in the pop-up menu and then choose inches.

Width: [7]

| pixels |
| ✓inches |
| cm |
| points |
| picas |
| columns |

**4.** If Width is not set to 7 and Height is not set to 5, enter these values now. Click on the Width field to select it, and type **7**. Press TAB to move to the Height field and type **5**. (Note that you can move among the fields in a dialog box by either clicking on the field or pressing the TAB key to move the cursor from one field to the next.) If you make a mistake, press DELETE (PC users: BACKSPACE) and then retype your entry.

Notice that the Resolution field is set to 72 pixels per inch. Photoshop uses 72 as the default ppi because most monitors display 72 pixels for every inch of screen area. In other words, you are setting the resolution of your document to be the same as the resolution of your monitor.

**5.** If necessary, change the Resolution setting to 72. Press TAB to move to the Resolution field, and type **72**. If you make the Resolution, Height, or Width settings larger, the size of your image file will grow. Try to avoid large images when practicing; they're cumbersome to work with and they slow down your computer.

You should only raise the Resolution setting when necessary. For instance, when creating a file that will be printed on a commercial printing press, resolution should generally be twice the *screen frequency*. For more information about screen frequency, see Chapter 7.

*n* **OTE:** *If a file has a resolution higher than your monitor's 72 pixels per inch, Photoshop will display the image larger than actual size, because it needs the extra screen area to display the extra pixels. For example, on a 72-ppi monitor Photoshop will display a 300-ppi file approximately four times larger than its actual size, because there are about four times as many pixels on the 300-ppi grid than on a 72-ppi grid. In other words, since your monitor can only display 72 dots per inch, Photoshop stretches the image across a wider screen area in order to display it.*

The Mode option should be set to RGB Color (red/green/blue). Photoshop uses RGB Color as the default display mode because RGB is the standard color model used by video monitors to display colors. In RGB mode, colors are created from red, green, and blue values. When Mode is set to RGB Color, all painting and editing features of Photoshop are available. For a full discussion of the different file modes in Photoshop, please refer to Chapter 9.

6. If necessary, set the Mode option to RGB Color by clicking on the Mode pop-up menu, and choosing RGB Color from the Mode list. (PC users can also choose the mode by typing the first letter of the Mode name.)

7. To assure that the background contents of your new document is white, click on the White radio button in the Contents group. If you choose the Background Color option instead, the background color that was last used in Photoshop will be used for your new document. If you choose Transparent, the background of your image will be clear, without any color values. A checkerboard pattern will represent the clear area.

8. Click OK to close the dialog box.

*n* **OTE:** *If you're confused about the difference between a white background and a transparent background, think of a transparent background as a clear layer above your electronic canvas. Assume you created a black doughnut-shaped object on a transparent background. If you copy the doughnut with the transparent background into a document that has a colored background, the color will show through the doughnut hole. Had you created the same doughnut with a white background, you would see white in the middle of the doughnut hole even after copying it into a colored document.*

A new Untitled document window appears. If you wish to magnify the screen, select Zoom In from the Window menu or, on the keyboard, press the key combination COMMAND-PLUS (PC users: CTRL-PLUS). To zoom out, select Zoom Out from the Window, or press COMMAND-MINUS (PC users: CTRL-MINUS). You can press the PLUS and MINUS keys either on the keyboard or the numeric keypad (with NUM LOCK on).

## THE PHOTOSHOP WINDOW

The Photoshop window, shown in Figure 2-1, conforms to Mac and Windows conventions. You can scroll, zoom, resize, and close it as you would in most Windows or Mac applications. You can move the window by clicking and dragging in the title bar. In the window's title bar are the document's filename, mode, and magnification ratio. In the bottom-left corner of the window is the file size indicator. The numbers show you how much memory you are using and whether or not Photoshop needs to use a scratch disk.

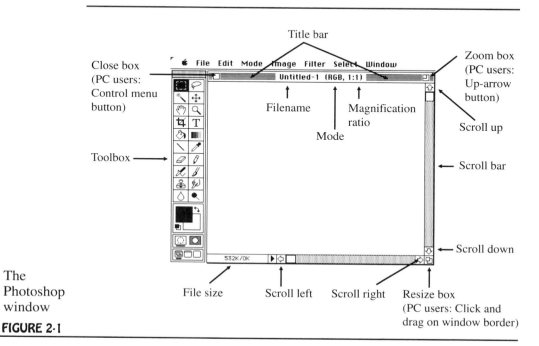

The Photoshop window

**FIGURE 2-1**

Take a moment to see how this setting can be changed by clicking on the arrow to the right of the two numbers. When you click on the arrow, a pop-up menu appears. If the pop-up menu is set to Document Sizes, the left number indicates the document size without any layers. You can also think of this number as the size of the image when all layers are flattened. The number on the right indicates the file size when layers are added to the image.

When the pop-up menu is set to Scratch Sizes, the first number indicates how much memory all open documents are consuming. The second number reveals the amount of RAM available. When the first number is larger than the second number, Photoshop needs to rely on your scratch disk because additional memory is needed.

A magnification ratio of 1:1 indicates that you are viewing the file at its actual size; 2:1 means you are viewing the file at 200% magnification (two times actual size); and 1:2 is a 200% reduction, or half the size. If you wish to see Photoshop's magnification powers in action, you can choose Zoom Factor from the Window menu. In the Zoom Factor dialog box, enter a magnifcation factor from 1 to 16 or a reduction factor from 1 to 16.

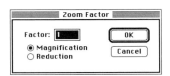

No matter what magnification ratio you're working in, it's generally a good idea to display Photoshop's horizontal and vertical rulers on screen. That way, you won't lose sight of how large or small your file's dimensions and images are. To make the rulers visible if they're not already on screen, choose Show Rulers from the Window menu.

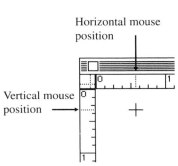

Horizontal mouse position

Vertical mouse position

The rulers continually indicate your position in the window with a mark that glides along each ruler as you move the mouse. If you haven't noticed the marks, focus on either the horizontal or the vertical ruler and move the mouse diagonally across the screen until you see each of them.

Along the left side of the window is Photoshop's Toolbox. The Toolbox contains the essential tools for painting, selecting, and editing graphics. Each tool is depicted by an icon. Understanding the purpose and power of each tool is the key to learning Photoshop. Just as an artisan must know the right tool to use for each job, so must the Photoshop user.

# THE PHOTOSHOP TOOLBOX

There are over 22 tools in the Photoshop Toolbox, shown in Figure 2-2, each providing a specific utility to aid you when you're creating, editing, and color correcting images. The first time you load Photoshop after it is installed, the Marquee is the selected tool. Thereafter, when you load Photoshop or create a new file, the last tool used remains selected. When a tool is selected, its Toolbox location turns black and its icon turns white. This section introduces you to the tools as well as the other icons that share the Toolbox.

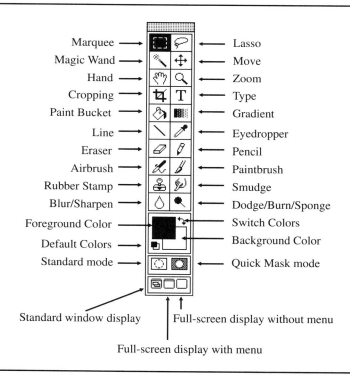

Marquee → ← Lasso
Magic Wand → ← Move
Hand → ← Zoom
Cropping → ← Type
Paint Bucket → ← Gradient
Line → ← Eyedropper
Eraser → ← Pencil
Airbrush → ← Paintbrush
Rubber Stamp → ← Smudge
Blur/Sharpen → ← Dodge/Burn/Sponge
Foreground Color → ← Switch Colors
Default Colors → ← Background Color
Standard mode → ← Quick Mask mode

Standard window display
Full-screen display without menu
Full-screen display with menu

The Photoshop Toolbox

**FIGURE 2-2**

## The Selection Tools

The first three tools in the Toolbox are the selection tools: Marquee, Lasso, and Magic Wand. If you wish to make changes to an object, you'll usually need to select it with one of these tools first.

The Marquee tool allows you to make rectangular and elliptical selections. It also allows you to create one pixel wide vertical and horizontal selections. To choose a marquee shape, open the Marquee Options palette by double-clicking on the Marquee tool. After the palette opens, click on the Shape pop-up menu arrow to choose Rectangular, Elliptical, Single Row, or Single Column.

```
Shape: ● Rectangular
        Elliptical
        Single Row
        Single Column
```

If you choose the Elliptical option, the Marquee in the toolbox changes to a circle. When using all other Marquee shapes, the icon in the toolbox remains a rectangle.

If you wish to toggle between the Rectangle or Elliptical Marquee tool, press OPTION (PC Users: ALT), and click on the Marquee in the toolbox. You can also toggle between the tools by pressing M on your keyboard.

The Lasso tool can be used as a freehand tool; you use it to outline irregularly shaped selections. The Lasso tool can be activated by pressing L. The Magic Wand selects according to similarity of colors. It can be activated by pressing W.

Several of the selection tools also allow you to create shapes. You will learn how to do this in Chapter 3.

## The Move Tool

The Move tool is used to move selections or layers. If you're working in a layer, you can click and drag with the Move tool to move all objects in a layer at one time. You can activate the Move tool by pressing V on your keyboard.

## The Cropping Tool

The Cropping tool is used to cut out a portion of an image and remove the rest. It can also be used to resize an image. The Cropping tool is covered in Chapter 7. You can activate the Cropping tool by pressing C on your keyboard.

## The Type Tool

With the Type tool, you can add text to your document as well as choose different fonts and type sizes. You will use the Type tool in this chapter and in the exercises throughout this book. You can activate the Type tool by pressing Y on your keyboard.

## The Hand Tool and Zoom Tool

The Hand and Zoom tools are often used in conjunction with each other. The Hand tool allows you to scroll through a document to view areas that don't fit in the Photoshop window. It allows more control than the window's scroll bars because you can click on the document and scroll in any direction. You can activate this tool by pressing H on your keyboard. When any tool is activated, you can temporarily access the Hand tool by pressing and holding the SPACEBAR on your keyboard.

The Zoom tool increases or decreases the magnification of an image. Activate this tool by pressing Z on your keyboard. To zoom out, you can temporarily access the Zoom tool by pressing COMMAND (PC users: CTRL) and holding down the SPACEBAR. Pressing OPTION (PC users: ALT) and holding down the SPACEBAR allows you to zoom out. After zooming, you may need to use the Hand tool to reposition the area you zoomed into. You will use the Hand and Zoom tools in this chapter and throughout the book.

## The Painting Tools

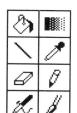

The painting tools are the Paint Bucket, Gradient, Line, Eyedropper, Eraser, Pencil, Airbrush, and Paintbrush. In Photoshop the painting color is called the foreground color, and the background color (usually white) is the color often used for erasing parts of an image or deleting an entire object.

The Paint Bucket, Line, Paintbrush, and Airbrush all paint with the foreground color. The Eraser paints with the background color and can erase parts of an image so that a transparent background can show through the image. The Pencil tool simulates drawing with a pencil, in either the foreground or background color. The Gradient tool can create blends with both the foreground and background colors and create a blend from a transparent background to the foreground color and vice versa. The Eyedropper picks up colors from your image and changes the foreground or background color to the Eyedropper color. The painting tools are covered in Chapter 5. The keys for activating the different painting tools are listed here:

| Tool | Key |
| --- | --- |
| Paint Bucket | K |
| Gradient | G |
| Line | N |
| Eraser | E |
| Pencil | P |
| Airbrush | A |
| Paintbrush | B |
| Eyedropper | I |

## The Editing Tools

The editing tools are the Rubber Stamp, Smudge, Blur/Sharpen, and Dodge/Burn/Sponge.

The Rubber Stamp is a cloning tool. With it you can sample an area and *clone* (copy) it elsewhere, pixel by pixel, by clicking and dragging the mouse. You'll use this tool frequently when retouching images or creating special effects. Press S to activate the Rubber Stamp tool.

The Smudge tool allows you to create a watercolor effect. It smudges a color to make it look as if water has been applied to it. Press U to activate the Smudge tool.

Blur and Sharpen are two tools that appear under one roof; the icon in the Toolbox changes to reflect which tool is selected. To choose between Blur and Sharpen, double-click on the Blur/Sharpen icon. The Focus Tool Options palette will open. The Tool pop-up menu in the palette allows you to choose between the two tools. Blur softens hard edges, and Sharpen brings out more detail. You can toggle between the Blur and Sharpen tools by pressing OPTION (PC users: ALT), clicking on either tool, or by pressing R on your keyboard.

The Dodge, Burn, and Sponge tools change the color and/or gray tones in an image. Like Blur and Sharpen, Dodge/Burn/Sponge also share a toolbox location. To choose the tools, double-click on the Dodge/Burn/Sponge icon. This opens the Toning Tools Options palette. The tool choices appear in the Tools pop-up menu.

After you select Dodge, Burn, or Sponge, the toolbox icon changes to display the selected tool. Dodge and Burn, traditional darkroom tools, are used to correct exposure by lightening and darkening specific areas. Sponge allows you to saturate or desaturate (intensify or de-intensify) the color in an image. You can activate and step through Dodge/Burn/Sponge by pressing OPTION (PC Users: ALT) and clicking on the active Toning tool in the Toolbox, or by pressing O.

## The Color-Control Icons

Just below the Blur/Sharpen and Dodge/Burn/Sponge tools are several color-control icons that allow you to view and switch colors.

The Foreground Color or Background Color icons display the current foreground and background colors. If you click on either icon, Photoshop's Color Picker dialog box will appear, allowing you to change either the foreground or background color. The Color Picker is explored in Chapter 4.

Clicking on the Switch Colors icon changes the color of the Foreground Color icon to the Background Color icon and vice versa. Pressing X on the keyboard will also switch between foreground and background colors.

The Default Colors icon restores the default colors for the foreground color (black) and the background color (white). Pressing D on the keyboard will also restore the default colors.

## The Mode Icons

The right-hand icon represents the Quick Mask mode, which allows you to easily create, view, and edit a mask. This lets you view your work through a colored tint overlay and edit areas in a cutout (similar to a *rubylith*—a red film that is used to shield objects in print production). The area outside of the cutout is normally protected; the area inside is unprotected. If you're unfamiliar with the concept of a mask, think of a painter laying down masking tape so he or she can paint without ruining surrounding areas. In Photoshop, working in the cutout allows you to refine your work without affecting areas beyond the cutout.

Clicking on the Quick Mask mode icon (or pressing Q on the keyboard) turns the masking function on. Once you enter the Quick Mask mode, you can create and edit a mask's shape with the selection tools as well as the painting tools. The left-hand Standard mode icon, the default, takes you out of the Quick Mask mode. Creating Quick Masks is discussed in Chapter 12.

## The Screen Display Icons

The three Screen Display icons at the bottom of the Toolbox change the window display modes. The left-hand icon represents the standard window. Clicking on the middle icon zooms the window out to occupy all of the video screen. Clicking on the right-hand icon also zooms out to full-screen size and hides the menus, as well. The keyboard shortcut for switching from one screen display to another is F.

# TOURING PHOTOSHOP'S FLOATING PALETTES

Now that you're familiar with the Toolbox, take a quick look at Photoshop's floating palettes. Unlike other windows, palettes always float above your active window. This means that they are always accessible and will never drop behind any open document. (Windows that are not palettes can drop behind other documents.) When more than one document is open, clicking on a Photoshop window will cause it to jump in front of all other windows on the screen.

Photoshop's palettes are accessed by first clicking on the Windows menu, then choosing Palettes. In the Palettes submenu you select a specific palette by choosing Show Brushes, Show Options, Show Picker, Show Swatches, Show Scratch, Show Layers, Show Channels, Show Paths, Show Info, or Show Commands. The design of Photoshop's palettes and their ability to lock together into specific groups provide quick and easy access to commands and options that are used frequently. Each palette can be moved by clicking and dragging in its title bar. This lets you keep specific palettes handy at all times.

By default, many Photoshop palettes are organized into palette groups. A *palette group* is essentially one window with several palettes in it. For instance, the Brushes and Options palettes open together in one palette group. The Picker, Swatches, and Scratch palettes appear in another; the Layers, Channels, and Paths palettes appear in another. The Command and Info palettes always appear separately on screen. The individual palettes in each group are easily distinguished by a palette tab with the palette's name on it.

**OTE:** *By default palettes for Photoshop tools appear in the Brushes/Options group. If the Brushes/Options palette group isn't open, you can open a palette for a specific tool by double-clicking on the tool.*

To bring a palette to the front of a palette group, you merely click on its tab. You can also click and drag on a palette tab to move the palette from one group to another group, as shown in Figure 2-3. By dragging on a palette's tab you can also pull it out of a group to use it alone on screen. Custom palette groups can also be created. For instance, if you wish to use the Picker and Brushes palettes together in a palette group, you can drag the Picker palette out of its palette group, then drag the Brushes palette out of its palette group. Once the two palettes are separated, you can drag one palette into the other to create the new group. The next time you choose Show Paths or Show Picker from the Palettes submenu, your new palette group (with both palettes in it) will open.

**OTE:** *The Layers, Channels, and Paths palettes can be resized. To resize a palette on the Mac, click and drag on the Resize box in the lower-right corner of the palette. On the PC, click and drag on the palette's border.*

Certain features are common in all the palettes. In Figure 2-4a you can see the palette tabs of the Brushes and Options palettes; the palette group's Close box, which closes the palette (PC users can double-click on the Control icon); its title bar, which you click on to move the palette; and the Expand/Collapse box. The Expand/

(a)

(a) Click and drag on a palette tab to move a palette from one group to another; (b) the Brushes palette moved to another palette group

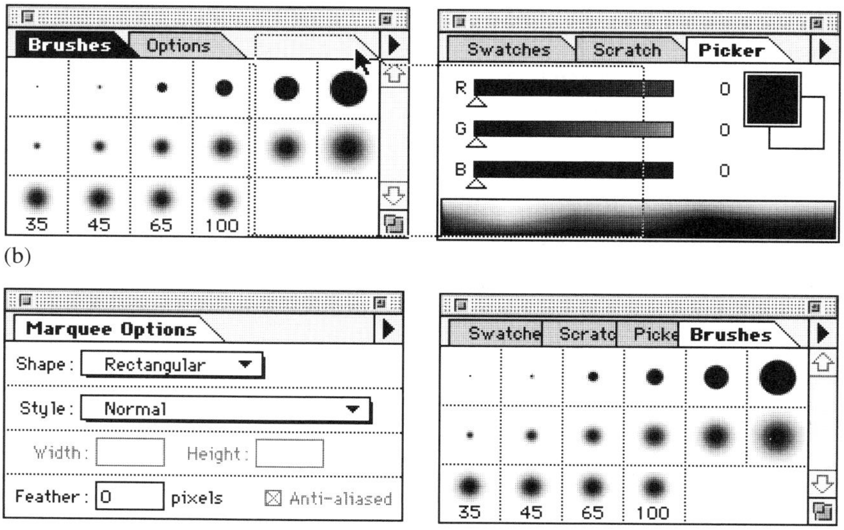

(b)

**FIGURE 2-3**

Collapse box allows you to shrink a palette so that it occupies less room on screen, thus letting you view more of your image. To shrink the palette to its smallest size, press OPTION (PC Users: ALT), then click on the Expand/Collapse box, or double-click on the palette's tab. After a palette shrinks, you can expand it by clicking once again on the Expand/Collapse box or by double-clicking on the palette's tab. Below the Expand/Collapse box is the palette's pop-up menu arrow. When clicked, it displays a menu of options for that palette, as shown in Figure 2-4b.

Let's start our examination of the palettes by looking at one of the most frequently used palettes, the Brushes palette.

## The Brushes Palette

You'll use the Brushes palette, shown in Figure 2-4a, primarily to choose the size of a brush and whether it will be soft- or hard-edged.

In the Brushes palette pop-up menu are commands for loading, saving, creating, and deleting brushes. To see these commands, click on the pop-up menu arrow in

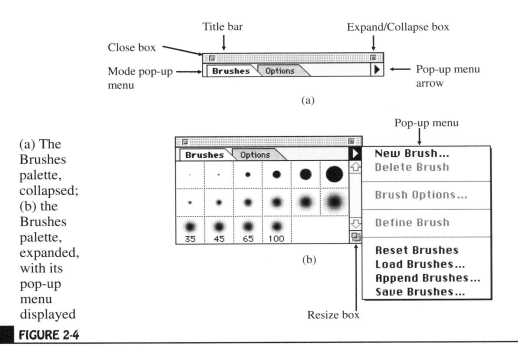

(a) The Brushes palette, collapsed; (b) the Brushes palette, expanded, with its pop-up menu displayed

**FIGURE 2-4**

the Brushes palette. Using the commands in the Brushes palette's pop-up menu is covered in Chapter 5.

## The Options Palette

The Options palette provides options for the currently selected tool. For instance, the Options palette for the Paintbrush tool allows you to set the opacity of the painting color and to choose a painting/editing mode, which controls how one color paints over another. By default, the Options palette opens in a group with the Brushes palette. If the Options palette isn't open on screen, you can double-click on any tool to open the palette for that tool.

The Options palette pop-up menu allows you to reset the palette's tool or all tools to their defaults.

## The Picker Palette

In the Picker palette you can change foreground and background colors by using sliders based upon color models such as RGB and CMYK, or by clicking on the color spectrum bar at the bottom of the palette. The Picker palette pop-up menu can be used to switch to sliders based upon different color models. This topic is discussed in Chapter 4.

## The Scratch Palette

The Scratch palette is used as a floating scratch pad for testing painting and editing effects. For instance, before you create a blend on screen, you can create the blend in the Scratch palette to preview its effect. You can also mix paint in the Scratch palette before applying it to your document. The Scratch palette pop-up menu allows you to copy, paste, lock, and reset the palette. It also enables you to save and load other Scratch palettes. The Scratch palette is discussed in Chapter 5.

## The Swatches Palette

The Swatches palette is used for quickly picking a foreground or background color by clicking on a swatch. The Swatches palette pop-up menu allows swatches to be added to the palette, saved on disk, and reloaded. This topic is discussed in Chapter 4.

## The Layers Palette

A *layer* is like a clear plastic overlay that can be placed over the background electronic canvas. Objects in one layer can be easily moved independently of objects in another layer. This provides an extremely efficient means of compositing images together and previewng their effects.

The Layers palette allows you to create new layers, move from layer to layer, rearrange layers, and group and merge layers. The Opacity slider in the Layers palette provides a simple means of blending one layer with another layer. The palette's Mode pop-up menu provides special effects for blending layers together. For instance, using the Darken mode, you can replace lighter image areas in one layer with darker image areas from another layer.

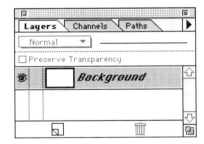

Layers are covered in detail in Chapter 12.

In the Layers palette, the word Background appears as your base layer if you create a new file with the Contents radio button set to White or Background Color. If you choose the Transparent Contents radio button instead, "Layer 1" appears at the top of your palette. In all layers other than the Background, areas without color are transparent.

## The Info Palette

The Info palette displays the x-coordinate (horizontal) and y-coordinate (vertical) of the mouse pointer. Move the mouse pointer across the screen, and you'll see the X and Y values in the palette change. If you wish to change the measurement units for the mouse coordinates displayed in the Info palette, access the Info palette's pop-up menu. The mouse coordinates can be displayed in inches, points, pixels, or centimeters.

If you move the mouse pointer over colored or gray areas, the Info palette functions as a *densitometer* (an instrument used by printers to measure color density), displaying color values as you move over them.

For instance, if you position the pointer over an area painted with 60% magenta, the Info palette will display 60% in the M (for magenta) readout.

## The Paths Palette

The Paths palette allows you to access Photoshop's Pen tool, which can be used to create Bézier curves and straight lines. The Paths palette contains its own set of tools that enable you to adjust and edit the shapes, called *paths*, that the Pen tool creates. The Arrow tool in the palette allows you to select paths so they can be moved and edited. The Pen+ and Pen- tools allow points to be added and subtracted from paths. The Corner tool can change a soft curve into a sharp corner or vice versa. The Paths palette's pop-up menu can be used to outline or fill paths with colors and change paths into selections. Press T to access the Paths palette and activate the Pen tool. Press T again to activate the Arrow tool in the Paths palette. The Pen tool and Paths palette are covered in Chapter 10.

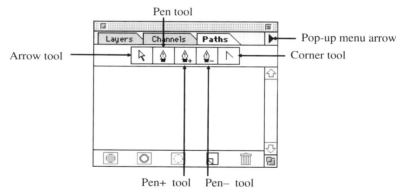

## The Channels Palette

A *channel* is similar to a plate in commercial printing. The Channels palette allows you to easily view a channel or edit an image in a channel.

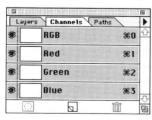

The Channels palette will display different channels depending upon the file Mode of the image. If you are working in an RGB Color file, the Channels palette displays the separate channels for each of the Red, Green, and Blue color components of the image along with the RGB composite. If you are viewing a CMYK Color file on screen, the Channels palette displays the separate channels for Cyan, Magenta, Yellow, and Black along with the CMYK composite. If you wanted to alter only the Yellow component of a CMYK image, you could click on Yellow in the Channels palette and then make your changes.

The Channels palette pop-up menu allows you to create and name *alpha* channels to use as masks. See Chapter 12 for an in-depth discussion on using channels and masks.

## The Commands Palette

The Commands palette allows you to execute a Photoshop command with a click of the mouse or press of a key. The palette lists function key assignments, allowing you to execute commands by either pressing a function key or by clicking on the command in the palette. The Commands palette also allows you to edit function key assignments as well as display them in multiple columns. You can even save and load different combinations of function key groups.

```
┌─────────────────────────────────────────────┐
│ Commands ▶   New Command...                  │
│ Image Size  F1   Edit Commands...            │
│ Canvas Size F2 ································│
│ Scale       F3   Reset Commands              │
│ Free        F4   Load Commands...            │
│ Feather     F5   Append Commands...          │
│ Defringe    F6   Save Commands...            │
│ Fill        F7                               │
│ New Layer   F8                               │
│ Hide Brushes F9                              │
│ Show Picker F10                              │
│ Show Layers F11                              │
│ Show Info   F12                              │
└─────────────────────────────────────────────┘
```

When you install Photoshop, a folder called Command Sets is copied to your hard disk. Within the folder are different command palette settings specifically grouped for prepress work, retouching, design work, etc. These commands can be loaded by choosing Load Commands from the Commands palette's pop-up menu.

If you'd like to change a command, display the Commands palette options by clicking on the palette's pop-up menu arrow. From the list of options, choose Edit Commands.

In the Edit Commands dialog box, pick the function that you want to change by clicking on it, then click on the Change button. Next, click on a Photoshop menu choice to change the command. Edit the text that appears in the Name field, and select the Shift check box if you wish to use the SHIFT key and a function key to execute the command. Click on OK to complete the editing process.

*n***OTE:** *Like Photoshop's Commands palette, Daystar's Photosmatic and Tempo II Plus can streamline your Photoshop work. Both programs can be used to record and playback keystrokes from within Photoshop.*

*T***IP:** *To temporarily clear the screen of all palettes, press TAB. Press TAB again to redisplay the palettes.*

# USING PHOTOSHOP TOOLS TO EXAMINE AND EDIT PIXELS

Now that you're familiar with the Photoshop window and have an understanding of how to use the palettes, you're ready to try out a few tools and start exploring the fundamentals of a pixel-based program. The following exercise demonstrates how to use the Type tool to enter text, the Zoom tool to examine pixels, and the Eraser tool to edit pixels. Let's start with the Type tool; this is a comfortable bridge to the Toolbox because many users are already familiar with the concept of placing text on a screen.

## Entering Text with the Type Tool

Even though the Type tool is not complex, you may be surprised when you first try to enter text, because Photoshop (unlike many other programs) does not allow you to type directly on screen. Text must be typed into a dialog box. In the following exercises, you'll learn how to activate the Type Tool dialog box, enter text, and edit it with the Eraser tool.

*n***OTE:** *Before beginning this next series of exercises, check to see what colors are displayed in the Foreground Color and Background Color icons in the Toolbox. If black is not the foreground color and white is not the background color, click on the Default Colors icon or press D on your keyboard. This will ensure that your text is black and the Eraser tool erases with white. You should also have a new 7-by-5-inch RGB file with a resolution of 72 ppi on screen and the background Contents set to White.*

 **1.** Before you can create any text in Photoshop, you must first activate the Type tool in the Toolbox. To do this, simply point to and click on the Type tool, or press Y on the keyboard.

**2.** Move the mouse pointer toward the document window. As you do, notice that the pointer changes. This pointer is called the *I-beam*.

**3.** To enter text in the upper-left corner of the window, move the I-beam to this part of the screen.

**4.** Click the mouse to open the Type Tool dialog box, shown in Figure 2-5.

In the Type Tool dialog box, you can pick a font by choosing from a list in the Font pop-up menu. You can also change point size, *leading* (space between lines), spacing (space between the letters), text style, and alignment. The left group of alignment radio buttons allows you to align text left, center, and right. The right group of choices places one character of text below the previous character. The icons preview how the vertical text will be displayed: aligned at the top, in the center, or at the bottom. For leading settings to be visible on screen, you need at least two rows of text.  Also, Photoshop does not allow you to choose more than one font or point size, or more than one leading or spacing setting for a text selection.

Before you begin to enter text, change the font and point size.

The Type
Tool dialog
box with
entered text

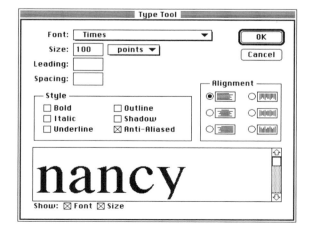

**FIGURE 2-5**

5. Click on the Font pop-up menu and choose Times or any other font from the list provided.

6. Press TAB to move to the Size field and type **100**. (Make sure points has been selected from the pop-up menu.) This sets your font size to 100 points, about 1.5 inches high. Make sure alignment is set to left. Leave the Anti-aliased check box selected. You'll learn about this option later in this chapter.

7. Click on the text box at the bottom of the dialog box. A blinking cursor will appear; this is where you enter your text. To see a preview of the font and size, make sure that the Show Font and Show Size check boxes are selected. Type **nancy** (or your own name) in the text box, as shown in Figure 2-5.

8. Check to make sure you haven't made any typos. If you made a mistake, this is your chance to fix it. The simplest way to replace a character is to position the cursor to the right of the character you want to change, and press DELETE (PC users: BACKSPACE). Then type the correct character.

9. When you're done, click the OK button. Your text appears in the document window surrounded with a marquee (represented by a series of dotted lines):

# nancy

The marquee surrounding your text indicates the object is in *Floating* mode. (Think of this as the text being suspended in air above the electronic canvas.) Take a moment to examine the Layers palette. If the palette isn't open, choose Show Layers from the Window palette's submenu. Notice that the word "Floating" appears at the top of the palette. This is because the floating text is in a temporary layer above the Background. Note also the Opacity slider in the palette. If Opacity is set to less than 100%, your text will be translucent.

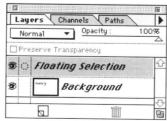

**2**

Only when the text is floating can it be deleted or moved around in the window as an individual object. In a sense, Floating mode gives you one last chance to delete the text and retype it before the paint has dried on the electronic canvas. Don't deselect. Continue to the next section to learn how to move a floating selection.

## Moving and Locking Text into Position

To see Floating mode in action, move your text to a new position on screen, using either the keyboard arrows or the mouse.

**OTE:** *In order to perform the following exercise, you must keep the text selected. Don't click away from your text. If you do, the marquee will disappear and the text will no longer be floating. If this happens, immediately select Undo from the Edit menu.*

1. Press the UP ARROW on your keyboard two or three times. Each time you press it, your text will move up one pixel at a time.

2. To move the text by clicking and dragging the mouse, first position the I-beam over any letter. When the I-beam changes to an arrow, click and drag the text to a new position about an inch lower. (Do not move the text too far down because you're going to use the lower part of the screen later.) Notice that as you drag the mouse, a second version of the text is moved, though Photoshop still shows the text's original position on screen.

When you release the mouse, the skeleton version of the text turns black, and the text that was seen in the original position disappears.

**IP:** *Floating text can be deleted from the screen by pressing DELETE (PC users: BACKSPACE). Even though the text is deleted from the screen, Photoshop retains it in the Type Tool dialog box. This is helpful because you can then edit your text in the dialog box. To do this, click again in the document with the Type tool to open the Type Tool dialog box. The text you last entered will be displayed in the dialog box. After you change the text, click OK and the edited text will appear in the document window.*

3. When you're satisfied with the placement of your text, lock it into position to prevent it from being inadvertently moved or deleted. To do this, you must first exit Floating mode. Click above, below, to the left, or to the right of your text. The marquee disappears, indicating that the text is no longer floating. In the Layers palette, the word "floating" disappears.

When text is not floating, it becomes locked down on the screen's grid of pixels, like dried paint on a canvas. The only way to change the locked text is to do what a painter would do—paint over it with white (the color of the canvas), and then re-create the text. In the next section, you'll examine the pixels that make up the text, to see what you'll eventually be painting over.

## Examining Pixels with the Zoom Tool

In this section, you'll zoom in to text on screen so that you can see the matrix of pixels that combine to make the letters you typed. The Zoom tool allows you to point to an area in the document window and magnify it. Each time you click the Zoom tool, magnification grows by a factor of two. For instance, the first time you zoom, your image will grow to twice as large as the original. The next time you zoom, it will be four times as large; the next, eight times as large, and so on.

1. To activate the Zoom tool, click on it. The mouse pointer changes to a magnifying glass. (Notice that the Options palette now displays Zoom Tool options.)

2. Position the Zoom tool pointer over the letter n (or the first letter of your name), and click. The screen image doubles. Notice that the magnification ratio in the title bar has changed to 2:1. Keep clicking the mouse until the magnification ratio is 8:1 (16:1 is the limit).

3. To ensure that the zoomed letter is in view, use the scroll arrows at the lower-right and lower-left of the screen to reposition the letter if necessary. Instead of scrolling, you can also use the Hand tool. Click on the tool and drag to reposition the screen. (You may need to click and drag on the Resize box in the lower-right corner to enlarge the document window. PC users can click and drag on the window border to resize.) Your screen will look similar to Figure 2-6.

Notice that your zoomed text looks jagged; this is because the letters are made of pixels. The jaggies are the pixel edges. Notice how different combinations of pixels form the various letters. As stated earlier, all images in Photoshop are basically created the same way, from pixels. You might notice that some of the hard edges in the zoomed text are blurred or partially filled in. Photoshop tries to eliminate the jaggies as much as possible; this blurring effect is called *anti-aliasing*.

**OTE:** *Since you created your file at a resolution of 72 pixels per inch, each linear inch of your image is comprised of 72 pixels. As mentioned at the beginning of this chapter, at this resolution there are over 5,000 pixels in every square inch of your image.*

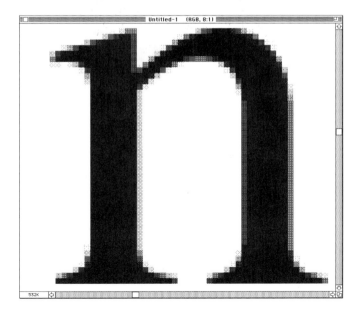

Jagged
edges
displaying
pixels in
text

**FIGURE 2-6**

## Editing Pixels with the Eraser Tool

Since the letters in Photoshop are not individual objects but rather locked together on a grid of pixels, there's no way of slipping a cursor between them to delete or edit them. To delete and edit in Photoshop, you'll need to white out the pixels of any letter you wish to remove, and then make your changes.

In this exercise you'll use the Eraser tool to white out the lowercase n from the word nancy, and then replace it with an uppercase N. (You can do the same with the first letter of whatever text you typed on the screen.)

1. Click the Eraser tool in the Toolbox. The mouse pointer changes to a small eraser and the Options palette displays Eraser options. By default the Eraser Options palette is set to erase by painting with a paint brush stroke. In order to better see the Eraser's pixel-by-pixel erasing effects, switch tool types in the Eraser Options palette by clicking on the pop-up menu and choosing Block. When you erase with a Block, you do not use a paint brush stroke and you erase with 100% of the background color (in this case, white).

2. Position the Eraser over any part of the n in nancy (or the first letter of your name). Click the mouse, and Photoshop replaces the black in that pixel with white.

3. Click over different parts of the letter to create a speckled effect.

   At first glance it seems the Eraser is merely removing black from each individual pixel. You are, however, actually painting with the default background color of white. This may seem like a slow way of deleting, but it's actually one of the strengths of Photoshop: You can edit any object at the smallest possible level: the pixel. In most other programs, you can edit text, but not pieces of type.

4. Continue whiting out the lowercase n until you have deleted it. To work a little faster with the Eraser tool, keep the mouse button pressed as you move the Eraser back and forth over the letter, much the same as you would use a rubber eraser on paper.

**IP:** *If you accidentally erase part of another letter in your text, choose the Undo command from the Edit menu. This will cancel your last action.*

Now that you've removed the lowercase n, you'll use the Type tool to enter a capital N and move it to the left of the letters currently on screen. It will be easier to perform this task if you can see all the letters of the name on the screen. Instead of zooming out and scrolling, here is a shortcut you can use to make an image fit on screen: Double-click on the Hand tool. The magnification ratio will change to 1:1. (You can also double-click on the Zoom tool or click on the Zoom 1:1 button in the Hand or Zoom Tool Options palette.)

**2**

1. To enter the capital N, activate the Type tool and then click below the letters on screen. The Type Tool dialog box will open.

2. In the Type Tool dialog box, type **N** and click OK. The letter appears in the document window in Floating mode.

**EMEMBER:** *Because the letter is still floating you can move it with either the keyboard arrows or the mouse.*

3. While the letter is still floating, move the I-beam over the letter. When the I-beam changes to the arrow pointer, click and drag the letter to the left of the other letters, so your screen looks like this:

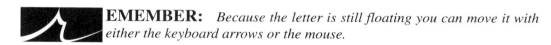

4. When you're happy with the position of your new capital letter, move the pointer away from the image and click. The letter stops floating and locks down on the screen.

This concludes your introduction to pixel editing. You have seen how to access tools in Photoshop's Toolbox, and have had an introduction to "thinking like a painter" when you're using Photoshop.

## STORING AND RETRIEVING FILES

Although Photoshop requires you to think like a painter, it doesn't allow you to work *exactly* like one. Unlike a painter, when your work is done you can't just turn out the lights to the studio and go home for the day. If you wish to return to your Photoshop work for another session, you need to save your file.

## Saving a File

Although your file so far is merely a practice document, save it anyway so that you can practice storing and retrieving it later. The next exercises will help you become familiar with the steps involved in saving your document.

1. To save your work, select Save from the File menu. The Save As dialog box appears the first time you save your file. In the text box labeled Save this document as, you'll see the highlighted word "Untitled-1." This is the text box where you name your document.

2. Type **MyType**. (Since "Untitled-1" is highlighted, as soon as you start typing you replace it with the name of your file.)

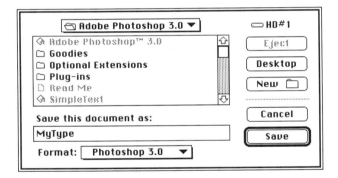

Notice that Format displays as "Photoshop 3.0"; this is the default file format. If this field contains another format name, you or someone else changed it while working.

3. To change file formats (if necessary), click on the Format pop-up menu and choose Photoshop 3.0.

Look at the folder icons in the dialog box to see where you're saving your file. (PC users: Folders are visual representations of your directories.) Make sure you are saving it in a location that you will remember.

**4.** When you're ready to save, click the Save button (PC users: OK). After Photoshop saves your file, the filename, MyType in this case, appears in the title bar of your document window.

 **OTE:** *As you work on any Photoshop file, you can save as often as you like by choosing Save from the File menu or by pressing COMMAND-S (PC users: CTRL-S). Be aware, though, that the Save command always replaces the previous version of your file. If you wish to make a copy of your file, you should use the Save a Copy command or the Save As command.*

**AUTION:** *System crashes, however rare, do occur. To avoid losing hours of your hard work in the electronic void, save your work frequently.*

## Using Save As

The Save As command reopens the Save As dialog box so that you can save the file you are in under a new name. This lets you create different versions of a file or save it to another hard drive or storage device as a backup.

**1.** To save another version of your MyType file, choose Save As from the File menu. The Save As dialog box appears, where you see MyType waiting to be renamed (PC users will see mytype.psd).

**2.** Position the I-beam immediately after the letter e in MyType, and click the mouse. The cursor is now blinking after the letter e (PC users: Make sure your cursor is blinking between the e and the period in front of psd).

**3.** Type the number **2**. The filename changes to MyType2 (PC users will see mytype2.psd).

**4.** To save a copy of your document with the name MyType2, click the Save button (PC users: OK).

When the dialog box closes, you are in the document MyType2. The previous version of the file is no longer open, but remains on your hard disk still saved as MyType. You can continue to work in MyType2, knowing that MyType is still intact on your hard disk.

# Photoshop in Action

The highway was pasted using an 80% opacity.

The rectangle was created using the Marquee tool's Rectangular shape.

The ellipse was created using the Marquee tool's Elliptical shape.

Artist: Josh Gosfield

Book cover for St. Martins Press

This image was pasted using a 70% opacity.

Josh created this book cover by first filling in the background with color. He then used different selection tools to select images from other files to copy and paste in the book cover file. After an image was pasted, he lowered the Opacity setting in the Layers palette to create a blending effect between the pasted image and the background. Once the images were in position, he added the rectangle and ellipse. After these areas were filled with color, the text was then placed over them.

Most artists add text to an image by using Photoshop's Type tool or by creating the text in a drawing or page-layout program. In this case, the publisher supplied Josh with the typeset book title and author's name on paper. This was scanned in and selected with the selection tools, then copied and pasted over the rectangle and the ellipse. Josh was also able to rotate and shrink the text to place on the spine by using the Rotate command in the Image menu and the Scale command in the Image/Effects submenu.

As you work on new versions of your practice file, you can continue to use Save As to rename your file MyType3, MyType4, and so on. This way you can always return to any previous version of your file.

**N**OTE: *If you use the File/Save a Copy command to save your file under a new name, Photoshop leaves you in your original document, not the copy. As you'll learn later in this book, File/Save a Copy allows you to flatten layers (Chapter 12) and save a file without its alpha channels (Chapter 11).*

## Using the Revert Command

A command almost as beneficial as Save As is the File menu's Revert command. While Save As can be used to save different versions of your file, Revert always returns you to the last saved version. When you use the Revert command, you automatically load your previous version, without using the File/Open command.

To get to know the value of the Revert command, you'll need to make some changes to MyType2. Start by adding Nancy's last name, Smith. (Of course, you can do all of this next exercise using your own name if you wish.)

1.  Click on the Type tool to activate it.

2.  To display the Type Tool dialog box, click on the middle of your screen below the word "Nancy."

3.  Type **Smith** into the text entry field and click OK. Smith appears under Nancy.

4.  Position the I-beam over Smith. When it becomes an arrow, click and drag Smith away from Nancy.

5.  Click away from the text to deselect it and drop it out of Floating mode.

6.  To save this version of your file, select Save in the File menu.

**R**EMEMBER: *It is a good idea to save your file before you start experimenting with new ideas.*

Now that you've edited and saved your file, make a few more changes before you use Revert to get the last saved version. Try experimenting with the Eraser tool to see if you can create some interesting typographic effects.

**1.** Click on the Eraser tool. Move the eraser pointer over into the middle of the N in Nancy, and click and drag to the right to create a white swath through all of the letters. Create another white swath through Smith, like this:

**2.** You're not impressed, so you want to undo your changes. Choose Undo from the Edit menu.

Note that Undo cancels only the last change you made: Smith has returned to its original state, but not Nancy. Fortunately, you saved before beginning your Eraser experiment. You can now return to the last saved version of your file using Revert.

**3.** From the File menu, select Revert. The Revert alert box appears.

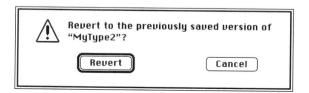

**4.** If you wish to revert to the last saved version, click Revert. In a few seconds, your screen returns to the way it was before you began to erase.

**AUTION:** *The Revert command is irreversible. Once you revert, you can't Undo it.*

Once you decide that the image on screen is exactly the way you want it, you'll probably want to output it to your printer. The next section covers printing and Photoshop's page preview feature.

## PAGE PREVIEW AND PRINTING

Before you print, it's often a good idea to preview your output, particularly because graphic images usually take a long time to be processed by most printers. Although Photoshop does not provide a print preview of your image, it does let you preview page orientation and other specific printing options, such as crop and registration marks. For a detailed discussion of the options in the Page Setup dialog box, see Chapter 14.

To preview your file, click on the file size number in the lower-left corner of the Photoshop window. A preview of your page's orientation—landscape or portrait—pops up in the lower-left corner of the window.

The preview can also show labels, crop marks, registration marks, calibration bars, negatives, and emulsion type. These are all options that can be selected in the Page Setup dialog box accessed through the File menu.

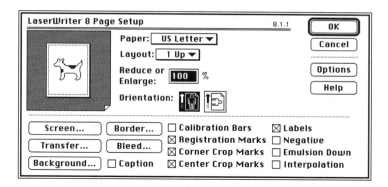

**OTE:** *If you aren't using Apple's Print Driver 8.1.1, your Page Setup dialog box will not look exactly the same as the one shown here.*

If you click on the file size number with the OPTION (PC users: ALT) key pressed, Photoshop will display information about your file's size, resolution, and number of channels.

```
Width: 504 pixels (7 inches)
Height: 360 pixels (5 inches)
Channels:   3 (RGB Color)
Resolution:  72 pixels/inch
```

To print your document, select Print from the File menu. The Print dialog box appears and contains standard Mac/Windows print options. In addition, Photoshop allows you to print a color image as a Grayscale, RGB, or CMYK image. The Print Selected Area option will only print an area that is selected on screen. If no area is selected, this option will be dimmed. For more information about printing, see Chapter 14.

You may be surprised at the low quality of the printed MyType2 file. The jagged edges are the result of the 72-ppi file resolution. Since Photoshop is a pixel-based program, the print quality of text is dependent upon the file's resolution, not the output resolution of your printer. Users who need high-quality printed text often export their files into drawing programs such as Adobe Illustrator and Freehand. In these programs, the quality of type does not depend on image resolution.

## USING PREFERENCES TO CHANGE THE DEFAULTS

Before quitting Photoshop, let's take a look at how to change some of the program's default settings. Changing the defaults lets you customize your Photoshop environment to make it more comfortable for you to use, and possibly to save you some time. The defaults can be accessed from the Preferences command in the File menu.

### Unit Preferences

To change the Photoshop ruler measuring units, select Units from the File/Preferences submenu. Then click on the Ruler Units pop-up menu; here you can change the measuring units to pixels, inches, centimeters, points, or picas.

If you are using points, you can choose either the PostScript (72 points/inch) or Traditional (72.27 points/inch) setting, by clicking on the appropriate radio button in the Unit Preferences dialog box, shown in Figure 2-7.

 **EMEMBER:** *To display the rulers in your document window, select Show Rulers from the Window menu.*

The Column Size settings allow you to specify a column width and gutter as a measuring unit. This measuring unit is named Columns. In the New, Image Size, Canvas Size, and Cropping Tool dialog boxes, Columns can be used in place of inches, points, pixels, or centimeters. This can be helpful when working with images that will be placed in columns in page-layout programs such as QuarkXPress and Aldus PageMaker.

# Photoshop in Action

The circles in the background were created using the Paintbrush and a custom brush.

The rectangle was created using the Marquee tool.

The text was created using Photoshop's Type tool. To make the text appear vertically, the Type tool alignment was set to vertical and center.

The speckled effect was created using the Airbrush tool with a small soft-edged brush.

Artist: Pamela Hobbs          Promotional poster for the Limelight

Pamela created this poster by starting with a photograph of KEDA, the musician, wearing jeans, and with a sketch of the costume he would wear the night of his performance at the Limelight in New York City.

After the photograph was scanned in, Pamela began painting over it with the painting tools, using the costume sketch as a guide. Once the image of KEDA in his costume was completed, the background was created and the text applied.

To create the fire in the background, the Paintbrush, Airbrush, and Blur/Sharpen tools were used with different foreground colors, brushes, opacities, and pressures. Next, the two rectangles on both sides of the image were created and filled with color. The text was then added, and the finishing touches were applied with the Airbrush tool.

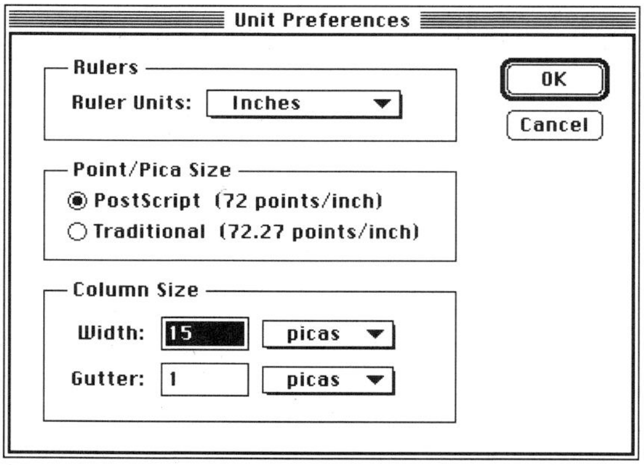

Unit
Preferences
dialog box

**FIGURE 2-7**

## General Preferences

The bulk of Photoshop's Preferences options are found in the General submenu. These general preferences cover a wide variety of settings, from how the screen displays imported images to whether your computer beeps when it has completed a task.

Although most preferences are simple in concept, some might be confusing until you've had a chance to work more with Photoshop. Don't worry—these options will be covered in detail as you work through the other chapters in this book.

**OTE:** *If you would like all palettes and dialog boxes to return to the positions you left them in, make sure that the Restore Palettes & Dialog Box Positions option is selected in the More Preferences dialog box. To access the dialog box, choose General from the File/Preferences submenu. In the General Preference dialog box, click the More button.*

**OTE:** *If you wish to ensure that Adobe Photoshop 3.0 files can be read by Adobe Photoshop 2.5, the Photoshop 2.5 Compatibility check box must be selected in the More Preferences dialog box.*

## CONCLUSION

By now you should have a sense of the fundamentals of Photoshop. In Chapter 3, you'll build on this foundation, taking a thorough look at how to use the selection tools. Chapter 3 will set you on your way to creating shapes, separating images from their background, and cutting, pasting, moving, and filling objects.

If you wish to exit Photoshop now before going ahead to Chapter 3, select Quit (PC users: Exit) from the File menu. If you made changes to a file that you haven't saved, an alert box will appear asking if you wish to save the changes. Click the Save button if you do, or Don't Save if you don't. Click Cancel if you change your mind and want to go directly on to the next chapter.

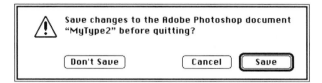

# 3

# SELECTING AND CREATING SHAPES

It's virtually impossible to complete any Photoshop project without using at least one of the three *selection tools:* the Marquee, Lasso, and Magic Wand. These tools, which can be found at the top of Photoshop's Toolbox, are used primarily for outlining and isolating specific areas in images so they can be moved, copied, retouched, or color corrected.

The selection tools are integral to the creation of *photomontages* (multiple photographs from different images) and *collages* (various images and graphics blended together). These tools also allow you to quickly turn scanned images into line art and to create special effects such as *vignettes* (pictures that gradually fade off into the surroundings).

In this chapter you'll have a chance to try each of the selection tools. More importantly, you'll be introduced to the concept of selections and why they're so important in Photoshop. Along the way, you'll learn how to fill and *stroke* (outline or frame) a shape with the foreground and background colors. As you work through the chapter you'll use many of the commands in Photoshop's Select menu, as well as create three simple collages and a vignette.

The first image you create will be the flag collage shown in Figure 3-1. The flag image was assembled primarily by using the Marquee selection tool. The highway in the upper-left corner of the flag was taken from a larger scanned image by selecting it with the Marquee tool; once selected, it was then copied and pasted over the flag graphic.

You might be surprised to learn that the flag was *created* with a selection tool, but you'll soon see that all of Photoshop's selection tools provide a dual function: They can be used to select as well as create shapes.

The exercises in this chapter use shapes as stepping stones to image creation and editing. The first exercises will help you understand what a selection is and how *floating* applies to selected objects. You'll get to practice working with simple images before you move on to more complicated ones.

Before proceeding, it's important to remember that you are using a pixel-based (sometimes called *raster*) program, not an object-oriented (sometimes called *vector*) drawing program. As discussed in the previous chapter, in object-oriented drawing programs you can select an object with the mouse and delete it. In Photoshop, your electronic canvas is either filled with colored pixels or "transparent" pixels. To delete a selected object on a white or colored background, you have to paint over it with the background color (usually white), in much the same way you use a liquid

The flag
collage

**FIGURE 3-1**

white-out product to correct typing mistakes. If, however, you are working on a layer (other than the Background), selecting an object and deleting it causes the transparent background or the layer beneath it to show through the hole you've created in your electronic canvas. (For a complete discussion of layers, see Chapter 12.)

Because Photoshop is pixel-based, you need to take special care when selecting and moving objects. If you don't understand the fundamentals of these actions, you may get some surprising and often unwanted results. But once you've learned the basics of how to create and use selections, you'll be on your way to creating successful Photoshop design projects.

## THE FLAG COLLAGE

Before beginning to work with the selection tools, start by creating a new document to work in. You'll use this document for the following introductory exercises and for composing the flag collage.

1. Select New from the File menu.

2. When the New dialog box appears

**a.** Check to see that the Width and Height measurement units are set to inches. If they aren't, click on the pop-up menu for each field and change the units to inches.

**b.** In the Width field, type **5.5**, and in the Height field, type **3.75**. These dimensions will make the flag fit snugly in the document window.

**c.** Resolution should be set to 72 pixels/inch. If it isn't, press TAB to move to the Resolution field and enter **72**.

**d.** If Mode is not set to RGB Color, click on the pop-up menu and change the setting. Since having a white background will make it easier to create the white stripes of the flag, set the background Contents radio button to white.

**REMEMBER:** *When you create a new file with the Contents radio button set to White or Background color, Photoshop creates a base layer called the Background. When you choose the White Contents radio button, working in the Background is like painting on a white colored canvas. If you choose the Background Color Contents option, working in the Background is like painting on a colored canvas. If you choose the Transparent option in the New dialog box, Photoshop creates a base layer called Layer 1. Working in this layer is equivalent to painting on a sheet of clear acetate, rather than on a white or colored canvas.*

**e.** Click OK to open the new document window.

**TIP:** *It is a good idea to add Photoshop's rulers and Info palette to the window before you start learning to create selections on screen. These features help you judge the size of the selections that you create.*

**3.** To make the rulers visible, select Show Rulers from the Window menu.

**4.** To open the Info palette, select Show Info from the Window/Palettes submenu.

## Introductory Exercises: Creating, Filling, Moving, and Floating a Selection

It doesn't matter what shape a selection is; Photoshop treats them all the same. Once you select an area on the screen, Photoshop points its attention to the selection. You can execute virtually any image-editing command, and only the selected area will be affected.

Let's start with the Marquee tool, since it is primarily used to create the flag in the collage. Besides allowing you to create rectangular selections, the Marquee tool can create elliptical selections, one-pixel-wide selections. These options will be discussed later in this chapter.

 **OTE:** *The selections you create with the Marquee tool share the same characteristics as all selections, no matter what selection tool created them.*

 ### Creating a Selection with the Rectangular Marquee and Normal Option

The Marquee tool's Rectangular option allows you to create and select squares and rectangles.

1. Before you create a selection, double-click on the Marquee tool to open the Marquee Options palette. If the Options palette is already active, you can also click on the Marquee Toolbox location, or press M on your keyboard.

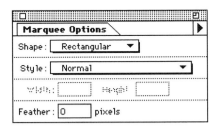

2. In the Marquee Options palette, the Shape pop-up menu controls the shape of the selection the Marquee tool creates. Click on the pop-up menu to see the list of choices: Rectangular, Elliptical, Single Row, and Single Column. If Rectangular isn't selected, select it now.

**3.** In the Marquee Options palette, check to see that Normal is selected in the Style pop-up menu; if it isn't, click on it.

With Shape set to Rectangular, the Normal setting allows you to create rectangular selections of any size. This is the default setting, and it will be selected unless you've previously changed it. If another option is selected, such as Fixed Size, the tool will create rectangles that are always the same size. The Constrained Aspect Ratio forces the width and height of a selection to be created at a specific ratio. Don't worry about the other options in the Marquee Options palette; they'll be covered later in this chapter.

 **EMEMBER:** *The Options palette settings for all of the tools in Photoshop retain the last settings used. They do not automatically return to their default settings. To reset a tool palette to its default settings, click on its pop-up menu arrow and choose Reset Tool. To reset all tools to their default settings, choose Reset All Tools from the pop-up menu.*

 **4.** Move the mouse pointer to the document window. Notice that when the pointer moves over the document area, it changes to a crosshair, as shown here. Now you can start using the Rectangular Marquee to create a selection.

**5.** Position the crosshair at the 1-inch mark both vertically (x-axis) and horizontally (y-axis). To make sure you are positioned at 1 inch both vertically and horizontally, refer to the Info palette. As you move the mouse, the X and Y readings next to the crosshair icon show your horizontal (X) and vertical (Y) positions. The X and Y readings next to the anchor icon indicate your original X and Y positions.

 **OTE:** *You can change the measurement units in the Info palette by first clicking on its pop-up menu arrow, then choosing Info Options. In the Info Options palette, click on the Ruler Units pop-up menu and choose Inches.*

**6.** When the Info palette shows both X and Y reading 1, click and drag diagonally down from left to right to make a rectangular selection about 2 inches by 2 inches, as shown in Figure 3-2. Refer again to the Info palette; notice the width (W) and height (H) readings of the selection you are creating. When your selection looks like Figure 3-2, release the mouse.

**7.** Your selection is represented on screen by a blinking *marquee,* which appears as a series of dashed lines. Your selection is now an isolated area that you can work with as an independent object, separate from the rest of the screen.

**8.** Click again anywhere in your document outside your rectangular selection. Photoshop thinks you're finished working with the selection or that you want to create another selection, so it *deselects* your original selection, and the marquee disappears.

A marquee created by a selection tool is really nothing but tiny, blinking lines on the screen. The marquee is used to isolate part of an existing onscreen image or to *create* a shape. The next sections will introduce you to techniques for creating shapes by filling selections with foreground and background colors and by moving and duplicating selections.

## Filling a Selection with the Foreground or Background Color

If you wish to create an object with Photoshop's selection tools, you can't just draw it. You must first create a selection, and then make it come to life by either filling it with a color (either the foreground or background color) or stroking it (putting an outline around it). You'll see how to do this in the following exercise.

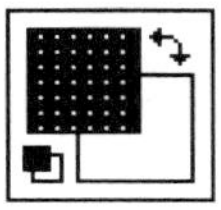

To make it easier to follow the instructions in this exercise, start with the foreground and background colors at their default settings (black foreground and white background). Check the Foreground Color and Background Color icons in the Toolbox. If the foreground color is not black and the background color is not white, click the Default Colors icon to reset the colors to their defaults.

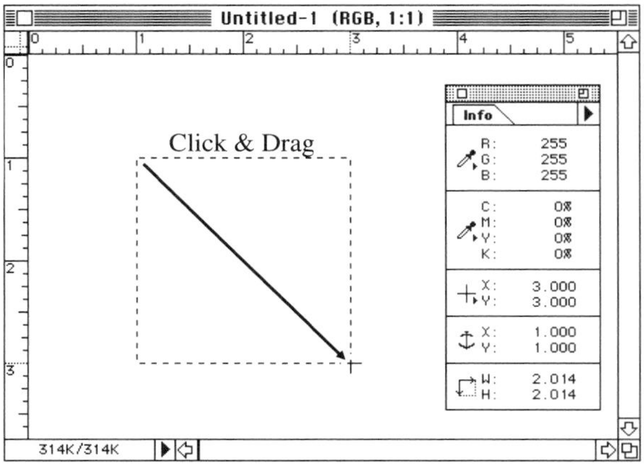

Clicking
and
dragging
with the
Marquee
tool to
make a
rectangular
selection

**FIGURE 3-2**

> **OTE:** *Until you've become familiar with Photoshop, you might find it helpful to refer back to Figure 2-2 in Chapter 2 for the locations and names of all Toolbox icons.*

To fill a selection with the foreground color, you can either choose Fill from the Edit menu or hold down the OPTION key (PC users: ALT) and press DELETE (PC users can also press BACKSPACE). To fill a selection with the background color, press DELETE or choose Edit/Clear. When you fill selections using these commands, you apply opaque foreground and background colors. The Edit/Fill command also allows you to fill with the foreground or background color, allowing opacity and painting/editing modes to be changed. These and other Edit/Fill options will be discussed in Chapters 5 and 6.

Start by creating a rectangular selection and filling it with the foreground color, then with the background color.

1. Notice that the Marquee tool is still selected—it's the last tool you used and Photoshop keeps it active. To create the rectangular selection, click approximately 1 inch from the upper-left corner of the screen and drag down diagonally approximately 2 or 3 inches. Release the mouse button.

2. To fill the selection with the foreground color, press the OPTION (PC users: ALT) key. Hold it down, and press DELETE.

   Your rectangular selection immediately turns black. Notice that the selection marquee still surrounds your rectangle.

3. Now fill with the background color by pressing DELETE.

The rectangle disappears but the selection remains. This often gives Photoshop beginners the mistaken impression that the DELETE key deletes objects. Actually, however, the DELETE key fills with the background color and could therefore be considered a painting tool. You have just painted your black rectangle white. (If you're still skeptical about this concept, be patient. When you press DELETE with a background color other than white, you'll be convinced.)

> **OTE:** *If you were in a layer other than the Background, DELETE would cut a hole in the layer allowing either the layer below or the transparent background to show through the deleted area.*

## Changing the Foreground and Background Colors

Photoshop provides a variety of ways to choose colors for the foreground and background. At this stage, since all you need are red and blue to create the flag collage, you can pick colors using the simplest method: from the color bar spectrum found at the bottom of the Picker palette.

**NOTE:** *If you don't see a spectrum of colors at the bottom of the Picker palette, click on the Picker palette's pop-up menu arrow and choose Color Bar. When the Color Bar dialog box opens, choose RGB Spectrum or CMYK Spectrum in the Style pop-up menu. Then click OK.*

**NOTE:** *While working in a document with no selection on screen, pressing OPTION-DELETE (PC users: ALT-DELETE), fills the entire document with the foreground color.*

1. To display the Picker palette, select Show Picker from the Window/Palettes submenu.

2. Notice the two squares in the upper-right corner of the Picker palette. The top square is the Foreground selection box and represents the foreground color. It overlaps a second square, the Backgound selection box, which represents the background color. A white band surrounding the selection box indicates that that color is active and ready to be changed. Click on the Foreground selection box so you can change the foreground color. (At this point, don't worry about any other items in the Picker palette. These will be introduced to you in Chapter 4.)

3. To change the foreground color to red, position the mouse pointer over a red area in the color bar. The mouse pointer changes to an eyedropper. Click on the red area. The Foreground selection box changes to red, and the Foreground Color icon in the Toolbox changes to the same red color.

4. Now change the background color to blue. Point to and click on the Background selection box, which is currently white. The white band jumps to and surrounds this box.

5. Point to the color bar and click on a blue area. Again, notice the change in both the Background selection box in the Picker palette and the Background Color icon in the Toolbox.

   Now you're ready to create an object and fill it with the new backgound and foreground colors.

6. Using the Marquee tool, create a rectangular selection. To apply the background color, press DELETE. The rectangle fills with blue.

7. To apply the foreground color, press OPTION-DELETE. The rectangle changes to red.

8. To remove the marquee from the selection, position the crosshair anywhere inside the document window and click.

The marquee disappears, indicating that the rectangle is no longer selected. If you wish to continue experimenting with the colored rectangle on screen, you must select it again, as described in the following exercise.

## Selecting a Rectangle with the Rectangular Marquee

To select the rectangle on screen, position the Marquee crosshair so that it touches the top-left corner of the object, as shown here.

Click and drag diagonally down to the bottom-right corner, and release the mouse button. Now that the rectangle is selected, you can change it—by filling it with either the foreground or background color, or by moving it to another location, as described in the next section.

## Moving a Selection

Once a selection is created, you may want to move it to the perfect location on screen. In this exercise you'll learn how to move a selection using the mouse.

1. Make sure your rectangle is selected.

2. To move the rectangle with the mouse, start by positioning the crosshair over the middle of the rectangle. The crosshair changes to an arrow pointer.

3. Once the arrow pointer appears on screen, click and drag it to move the rectangle about 1 inch to the right and about .5 inches down.

*n* **OTE:** *Clicking away from a selection causes it to be deselected. If this occurs, you can reselect it by immediately choosing the Undo command from the Edit menu. This undoes your last action. You can also execute the Undo command by using a keyboard shortcut: press COMMAND-Z (PC users: CTRL-Z).*

As you move the object, you'll see that Photoshop leaves a duplicate of the rectangular selection in its original position, filled with the background color, as shown in Figure 3-3.

You may find it annoying that Photoshop leaves the background color on screen where an object was moved from. (If you are working in a layer other than the Background, moving a selection causes the transparent background or the layer beneath it to show through.) Most of the time when you move an object, you won't

Moving an object leaves the current background color in the object's original position

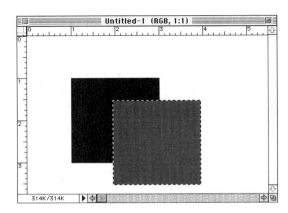

**FIGURE 3-3**

want a hole left behind filled with the current background color. Figure 3-4 shows the effects of moving a rectangular selection in a scanned image. Here, too, Photoshop has cut a hole in the image.

A simple way to avoid this is to make your selection float. In the previous chapter, you were introduced to the concept of floating when you created and moved text. When an object floats, Photoshop essentially places it in a temporary layer above the background plane of pixels. A floating object can be deleted and moved without disturbing the underlying pixels.

Fortunately, Photoshop often automatically puts an object in Float mode after that object has been moved. Photoshop notifies you that a selection is floating by placing the words "Floating Selection" in the Layers palette. You can see this now by examining the Layers palette. If the Layers palette is not open, choose Show Layers from the Window/Palettes submenu. You can test Float mode by moving the rectangle you created in the foregoing exercise. This time, try moving it using the keyboard: Press any directional arrow key three or four times. With each keypress, the object will move one pixel up, down, left, or right. This time, Photoshop does not rip a hole out of the background.

**EMEMBER:** *When you move an object that is not floating, Photoshop creates a "hole" in your image. You can use the Edit/Undo or File/Revert command to restore your original image.*

Cutting and
moving a
portion of
an onscreen
image
leaves the
background
color behind

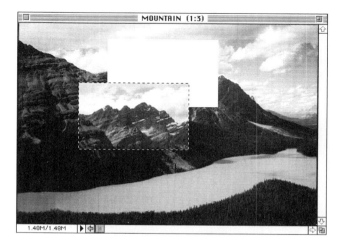

**FIGURE 3-4**

In the next exercise, you'll learn how to turn the Float mode on *before* you move and fill, so that no underlying pixels are affected. Before proceeding, let's clear the clutter from your screen so you'll have more room in which to work.

## Clearing the Screen

In Photoshop, one method of clearing the screen is to execute the Select/All command, which selects the entire screen. Once the entire screen is selected, it can then be "erased" by filling it with white. The Select/All command is also helpful when you wish to apply a Photoshop command to everything on screen.

1. Change the background color back to white by clicking once on the Default Colors icon.

2. To select the entire screen, choose All from the Select menu.

3. Press DELETE. The entire screen fills with the background color, white.

4. Notice the marquee surrounding your screen, indicating that the entire screen is still selected. To deselect it, choose None from the Select menu.

## Using the Float Command

In this exercise you'll create a rectangular selection and then use the Select/Float command to put it into Float mode, so it floats above the background pixels. Once the object is in Float mode, you can move it or delete it without affecting the underlying pixels.

1. Start by resetting the foreground color to red and the background color to blue. If you don't change the background color, you won't see the effects of using the Float command.

2. Click in the upper-left corner of your window and drag diagonally about two or three inches to the right to create a rectangular selection. Do not deselect.

3. To put the object into Float mode, choose Float from the Select menu. Notice that the words "Floating Selection" appear in the Layers palette, verifying that you have a floating selection.

4. Fill the object with the foreground color by pressing OPTION-DELETE (PC users: ALT-DELETE).

**5.** Position the pointer in the middle of the rectangle and drag about 1 inch down and to the right. Don't deselect.

This time, when you moved the selection, the background did not change. When you switched to Float mode, Photoshop lifted the selection over the underlying pixels. In addition to the Layers palette, you can also confirm that the object is in Float mode by clicking on the Select menu. In the menu, you'll see the word Defloat, rather than Float. This means that the object is floating. (Don't select Defloat; this will drop the object out of Float mode.)

**6.** When an the object is floating, you can delete it by pressing DELETE. Do this now.

**EMEMBER:** *In Float mode, pressing DELETE will delete the object, **not** fill it with the background color.*

Now that you know how to create a selection, fill it and float it, you are almost ready to create the Flag collage. In the Flag exercise, you will need to copy a selection from one image and paste it into another. Thus, before you begin, you should understand how the Copy and Paste commands work in Photoshop.

## WORKING WITH COPY & PASTE

In the upcoming exercises in this chapter, you will use the Edit/Copy and Edit/Paste commands to copy a selection from one file into another.

**OTE:** *When using the Paste command to work with text, bear this in mind: Unlike most Mac and Windows programs, you cannot paste text from another application directly into a Photoshop document. Instead, you must paste it into the Type Tool dialog box.*

### Temporarily Storing the Contents of a Selection in the Clipboard

Before you begin to experiment with Photoshop's Paste commands, you need to understand how Photoshop handles memory when you Cut or Copy the material you want to paste. When Photoshop's Edit/Cut and Edit/Copy commands are executed, Photoshop automatically copies the contents of a selection to an area of the computer's memory called the *Clipboard*. The Clipboard is a temporary storage area for copied or cut items. Every time a selection is copied into the Clipboard, that selection replaces any existing Clipboard contents; only one item at a time can be stored in the Clipboard. When the Paste command is executed, the contents of the Clipboard is copied into the active document.

 **OTE:** *If you wish to copy an image from Photoshop's Clipboard to another Mac or Windows application, you must first select the Export Clipboard option in the More Preferences dialog box. To open the dialog box, choose General from the File/Preferences submenu. In the General Preferences box, click the More button.*

It's important to realize that when the contents of a large selection is being held in the Clipboard, there is less memory available for Photoshop to use. In this situation, you might receive an unexpected out-of-memory message. To prevent this from happening, make sure that you allocate as much RAM as possible to Photoshop and that your scratch disk's storage capacity is as large as possible. Ideally, of course, the best solution is to purchase more RAM or a larger hard disk. For more information about allocating memory, RAM, and hard disks, see Chapter 1.

If you think the contents of the Clipboard is consuming too much memory (and you no longer need to store that information), there's an easy way to reduce the amount of memory used by the Clipboard. Make a small selection—even just one pixel—then select Cut or Copy from the Edit menu. Your small selection will replace the memory-hungry one currently in the Clipboard.

## Handling Different Resolutions During Paste Operations

When you paste a selected area from one Photoshop file into another file with a different resolution, you may be surprised at the consequences. The contents of the selection you paste will take on the resolution of the file into which you paste. Thus, if the selection's resolution is higher than that of the target file, the selection will enlarge when pasted. If you paste a selected area with a low resolution into a higher-resolution file, the selection will shrink when pasted.

To understand this phenomenon, remember that there are more pixels per square inch in a high-resolution file than in a low resolution file. For example, if you select an area 72 pixels by 72 pixels in a file that has a resolution of 72 pixels per inch, the selection is one inch. But if you paste the selection into a file with a resolution of 300 pixels per inch, the selection shrinks to about a quarter of an inch in the new file. The selection is still composed of 72 pixels by 72 pixels, but the pixels must diminish in size when they are placed in an image where 300 pixels by 300 pixels comprise an inch.

**NOTE:** *If an image's size increases or decreases after pasting, you can resize the selection using the Image/Effects/Scale command. (See Chapter 7 for more information.)*

## Composing the Flag

Now you are ready to create the flag portion of the image shown in Figure 3-1.

For the following project you will need a 5.5-by-3.75-inch file on screen. If you don't have the original practice file open, create a new one with these dimensions and set the background Contents to White. Make sure all objects are cleared from your screen.

Bear in mind that the resolution of your file is set to 72 ppi. This resolution will be fine for practicing and producing *comps* (samples or simulations of the completed art design) to test designs and techniques. 72 ppi is also suitable for most on screen and video presentations. For professional output of the collage, you may want to use a higher resolution, such as 300 ppi. If you do this, make sure you have enough memory to handle the file. A 5.5-by-3.75-inch RGB color file at 300 ppi will consume 5.31MB, versus 314K at 72 ppi. Remember, as mentioned in Chapter 1, Photoshop generally requires memory at least three times your file size to be free on either your hard disk or in RAM.

If you do create the flag collage or any of the other projects in this chapter at a resolution higher than 72 ppi, you will need to convert the pixel measurements in order to compensate for the fact that more pixels per inch will be used. For instance, in the next exercise the height of the flag stripes is 21 pixels at 72 ppi. To convert to 300 ppi, divide the 21 pixels by 72 (72 pixels = 1 inch), to get the precise size of the object in inches. Then multiply by 300 to calculate how many pixels there will be at 300 pixels per inch, $(21 \div 72) \times 300$.

**TIP:** *Use the following formula to convert a measurement from one resolution to another:* (Measurement in ppi ÷ Original ppi) × New ppi.

### Creating the Red Stripes

To create rectangles with specific measurements, use the Fixed Size option from the Style pop-up menu in the Marquee Options palette. This option allows you to type in specific measurements for rectangular objects.

**TIP:**   *The Fixed Size option in the Style pop-up menu is a time-saver because objects can be created at precise sizes with one mouse click. It's much easier to use Fixed Size than to create shapes with the Normal option while checking against the ruler and/or the Info palette.*

**1.** To specify the size of the stripes, first double-click on the Marquee tool if the Marquee Options palette is not open.

**2.** In the Marquee Options palette, choose Fixed Size from the Style pop-up menu.

Notice that the Fixed Size option only allows measurements to be entered in pixels. Since a pixel is the smallest element possible on screen, it is the most precise way of measuring.

**3.** The red stripes you are creating are approximately .3 by 5.5 inches. To set the length of the stripe to approximately 5.5 inches, type **396** (72×5.5 = 396) in the Width field of the Fixed Size option. (Remember that there are 72 pixels per inch in a file that has a resolution of 72 ppi.)

**4.** To set the Height of the stripe to approximately .3 inches, type **21** (72×.3 = 21.6). Click OK.

**5.** To create the selection, click on the middle of the screen. A rectangular selection appears, 5.5 inches long; this is the first stripe.

**6.** Change the foreground color to red and the background color to white. You'll use the red foreground color to fill the stripes.

**7.** To color the stripe red, press OPTION-DELETE (PC users: ALT-DELETE).

**8.** To create the top of the flag, drag the stripe to the very top of your document, as shown in Figure 3-5. Don't deselect.

Since the background color of your file is white, you won't need to create a white stripe. What you need is the ability to create a duplicate of the red stripe's selection to use as a white placeholder between the red stripes. Photoshop provides a keyboard trick that can do this for you. The keyboard trick allows you to move a selection marquee without grabbing the underlying pixels. Before the selection is moved, a temporary duplicate selection appears.

**9.** Press OPTION-COMMAND (PC users: ALT-CTRL), and click on the selection that surrounds the red stripe. Drag down slowly. A copy of the selection marquee—but not the red stripe—moves as you drag.

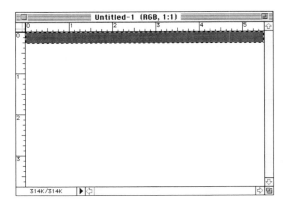

Creating
the first
stripe of the
flag

**FIGURE 3-5**

 **EMEMBER:** *Pressing OPTION-COMMAND (PC users: ALT-CTRL) while clicking and dragging moves the selection marquee without moving the selected area.*

10. Move the marquee down, so the top of it touches the bottom of the red stripe. When your screen looks like Figure 3-6, release the mouse button. The blinking marquee jumps to the copy of the selection, creating a placeholder which will act as the white stripe.

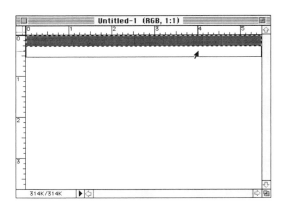

Moving the
selection
marquee to
create a
placeholder
for the
second
stripe

**FIGURE 3-6**

**11.** Now duplicate the selection you just created, but use this duplicate as a stripe, not as a placeholder. Press OPTION-COMMAND (PC users: ALT-CTRL) again, and click on the middle of the marquee on screen. Drag the selection down. Again, when the top of the selection touches the bottom border of the white stripe, release the mouse.

**12.** Fill the selection with the red foreground color.

Now that you have three stripes created, you can speed things up by selecting a white and red stripe together (since the flag ends on a red stripe) and then duplicating them using the Float command.

**13.** To select both the second (white) and third (red) stripes, switch from Fixed Size to Normal in the Marquee Options palette by choosing Normal in the Style pop-up menu.

**14.** With the Rectangular Marquee activated, select the second and third stripes.

**15.** From the Select menu, choose Float. Photoshop copies your selection into a layer above the underlying pixels.

**IP:** *Here's a shortcut for duplicating a selected object and automatically putting it into Float mode. After selecting an object, press and hold OPTION (PC users: ALT) while you click on the middle of the object and drag. As you drag, Photoshop duplicates the object without changing the background pixels.*

**16.** Drag the duplicated stripes into position under the first set of stripes. Click away from the object to deselect. When you deselect the rectangle, it drops back to the background layer, creating your fourth and fifth stripes.

**17.** To save your work, choose Save from the File menu. Name your file **Flag**. Then click Save (PC users: OK).

**18.** Continue creating stripes by duplicating them with the Float command until you have created seven red stripes and six white ones. The first and last stripes should be red.

**19.** Save your work again.

**OTE:** *Throughout the next sections, you'll save your file after you've successfully finished each segment of the collage. If you keep saving, you'll always be able to use the Revert command to return to the last correct version of the file.*

## Creating the Blue Rectangle of the Flag

Next you'll use the Marquee tool's Rectangular Shape and Fixed Size option to create a blue rectangle and move it to the top-left corner of the screen.

1. In the Marquee Options palette, click on the Style pop-up menu and choose Fixed Size.

2. The blue rectangle you are creating is approximately 2.5 by 2 inches, so enter **180** (2.5×72) in the Width field, and **144** (2×72) in the Height field.

3. Click the mouse on screen, but *do not* click and drag to move the selection. You need to use the Float command to move the selection without affecting the stripes beneath it.

4. To put the selection in Float mode, choose Float from the Select menu.

5. Now click in the middle of the rectangular selection and move it to the upper-left corner of your screen.

6. Change the foreground color to blue, then press OPTION-DELETE (PC users: ALT-DELETE) to fill the selection.

7. Choose None from the Select menu to deselect and lock the blue rectangle into place, as shown in Figure 3-7.

You have now completed the flag. Save your work. Your next step is to place a scanned image into the flag's blue rectangle.

## Placing a Photograph into the Flag File

In this section, you'll learn how to copy an image in one file and paste it into another. This example uses a scanned image of a highway that will be placed in the Flag file. If you do not have a similar image, you can pick any scanned image or even choose one from the Frames file (PC users: frames.jpg) located in the Tutorial folder. The Tutorial files are copied to your hard disk when you install Photoshop.

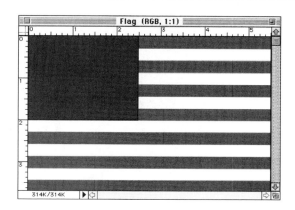

Adding the
blue
rectangle to
the flag

**FIGURE 3-7**

**C**AUTION:  *No matter what digitized image you use, its resolution should match the resolution of your Photoshop collage file. The digitized image you place into the collage will enlarge if its resolution is higher or shrink if its resolution is lower.*

1. To open a digitized image in Photoshop, choose Open from the File menu. If you don't see the file you are looking for, try selecting the Show All Files check box. Select the filename, and then click Open (PC users: OK). The image will load on screen.

2. If the Marquee Options palette isn't displayed on screen, double-click on the Marquee tool. To create a selection that is the proper size for the blue rectangle of the flag, make sure that the Shape pop-up menu in the Marquee options palette is set to Rectangular and the Style pop-up menu is set to Fixed Size. Enter **168** in the Width field and **134** in the Height field. Then click on screen to make the selection appear.

   Don't try to move the selection by clicking and dragging with the mouse. The easiest way to move the selection on the screen is with the same technique you used to create the placeholder when working on the flag stripes earlier.

3. Press OPTION-COMMAND (PC users: ALT-CTRL). Click and drag the selection to the part of the image that you wish to copy into the Flag file, as shown in Figure 3-8.

Selecting
an image
from a
photograph
to be
copied and
pasted in
the flag's
blue
rectangle

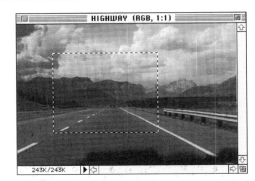

**FIGURE 3-8**

4. To copy the area into memory so you can paste it into the Flag file, choose Copy from the Edit menu. Photoshop stores the selection in the Clipboard.

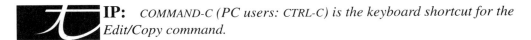

**IP:**   *COMMAND-C (PC users: CTRL-C) is the keyboard shortcut for the Edit/Copy command.*

5. Close the image file; the Flag file will still be open.

6. To paste the selection from the Clipboard into your Flag file, select Paste from the Edit menu.

**IP:**   *COMMAND-V (PC users: CTRL-V) is the keyboard shortcut for the Edit/Paste command.*

7. When you use the Paste command, Photoshop automatically puts the pasted image into Float mode, so you can click and drag it without worrying about altering the underlying pixels. To move the image, click and drag it into position in the top-left corner of the flag, as shown in Figure 3-9.

8. Choose None from the Select menu to deselect the pasted selection.

**OTE:**   *Instead of copying and pasting, you can also drag a selection from one file directly to another. You'll do this later in this chapter.*

3

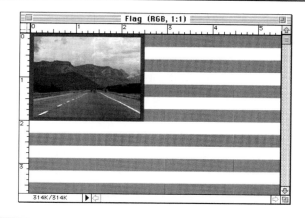

Pasting and
moving the
photograph
into position

**FIGURE 3-9**

## Placing Text on the Flag

In Chapter 1, the issue of type quality was discussed, and here it's worth repeating that type quality in Photoshop is dependent upon file resolution. If you work in a file with a resolution of 72 ppi, sending it as output to a high-resolution printer will not improve the quality. If you need to produce a Photoshop project with very high-resolution text, it's often best not to create the text in Photoshop. Save the file so it can be exported to a drawing program such as Adobe Illustrator, or a page-layout program such as QuarkXPress. In these programs, text is created as a separate object that is printed at the resolution of the output device. If you wanted Photoshop's text to match the quality of text as output from these programs, you'd need to create an image at an extremely high resolution. For example, if you wanted your text output at 1,270 ppi, your file's resolution would need to be 1,270 ppi. Obviously, the file size would be gigantic. Saving files so they can be output to other programs is covered in Appendix A.

In this exercise, high-resolution text isn't necessary, so you'll just use Photoshop's Type tool to generate the words for the flag collage.

1.  Select the Type tool.

2.  Click about an inch above the middle of the screen.

3.  If you wish to make the text appear as it does in the example in Figure 3-1, enter the following specifications:

Click on the Font pop-up menu and change the font to Times. If Times is not installed on your system, pick another font. In the Size field, type **70** points. In the Leading field, type **125**. In the Spacing field, type **2**. In the Alignment group, click on the align right radio button (the last button in the first column). In the text box, type **USA's** and press RETURN (PC users: ENTER). Then type **HIGHWAYS** (underneath USA's). In the Style options, make sure the Anti-aliased check box is selected. Click OK.

4. When the text appears on screen, click and drag "USA's" and "HIGHWAYS" into position, as shown in Figure 3-1. As you move the type, the underlying pixels will not be affected because the text is floating.

 **EMEMBER:** *As discussed in the section "Entering Text with the Type Tool" in Chapter 2, Photoshop automatically puts the text you create in Float mode.*

5. When you are satisfied with the position of the text, click away from it to deselect, and save your file.

**IP:** *When you save your file, Photoshop can create a thumbnail image preview that is displayed in the Open dialog box. To have Photoshop create the thumbnail, make sure that the Thumbnail check box is selected in the More Preferences dialog box. If the Icon check box is (Macintosh only) also selected, Photoshop creates a preview of the image seen in the file's icon. To access the dialog box, choose General from the File/Preferences submenu. In the General Preferences dialog box, click on the More button.*

That's it! You've just completed the Flag collage.

In the next section, you'll create another collage and will learn more about the options available in the Marquee Options palette. You'll also begin to explore the other selection tools—the Elliptical Marquee, the Lasso, and the Magic Wand.

## THE TRUCK COLLAGE

Your next Photoshop project, the truck collage shown in Figure 3-10, will give you additional experience with the selection tools and their Options palettes. This collage project is divided into two parts. In the first part, you will create a truck on which you'll paste a scanned image of some fruit. In the second part, you'll outline and fill

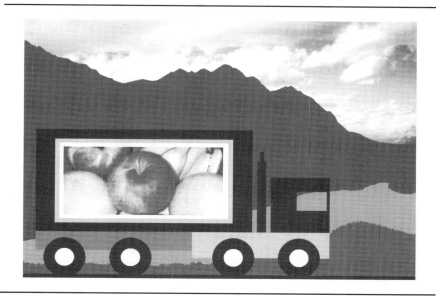

The truck
collage

**FIGURE 3-10**

parts of a scanned image to create a landscape background. Each project section begins with a few introductory exercises designed to introduce you to the selection tools and options that you'll be using for the first time.

## Introductory Exercises: Filling and Stroking Selections in a Layer

The first introductory exercises of the truck collage will teach you how to create perfect squares and circles. You'll be using these shapes to produce the cab and wheels of the truck. To build these objects you'll use the Constrained Aspect Ratio option found in the Marquee Options palette. When you create a border for the fruit poster and generate the truck wheels, you'll learn how to stroke, or outline, selections. Before beginning the exercises in this section, close the Flag file or any other documents you might have open on screen. This will keep memory usage to a minimum.

In this section, you'll work in a layer that has a transparent background. This means any layers beneath the layer you are working in can be seen through areas in your file that are not filled with color. You'll see this feature in action when you create the truck collage later in this chapter.

# Photoshop in Action

The boxers were selected with the Lasso tool so that they could be pasted into the image.

Parts of the letter *M* were selected with the Magic Wand tool and then moved.

Artist: Marc Yankus

Client: Data Communication

The Perspective command in the Image/Effects submenu was applied to the circuit board.

Marc started this image by creating a rectangular selection with the Marquee tool. Once the selection was on screen, he filled it with a blend using the Gradient tool. His next steps were to scan in a circuit board, select it with the Marquee tool, and then paste it into the image. While the circuit board was still selected, he applied the Perspective command from the Image/ Effects submenu. This created a sense of depth in the image.

Once the circuit board was placed, the boxers were scanned in, selected with the Lasso tool, copied, and pasted into the image. Finally, the letters IBM were scanned, copied, and pasted into the image. Then Marc used the Magic Wand tool to select parts of the letter *M* and break them away from the rest of the letter.

**3**

1. Start by creating an RGB Color file 7 inches wide by 5 inches high to use for the introductory exercises. This size will give you sufficient room to practice.

    In the New dialog box, choose the Transparent radio button in the Contents group. After you click OK, notice that the screen is filled with a checkerboard-like pattern. This indicates that the background of your file is transparent. Notice also that the title bar of your document window includes the words "Layer 1." If the Layers palette isn't open, open it now by choosing Show Layers from the Window/Palettes submenu. As mentioned earlier the words "Layer 1" appear in the Layers palette, instead of the word "Background," if you choose the Transparent Contents radio button in the New dialog box.

**nOTE:** *The color and size of the grid which indicates you are working in a layer with a transparent background can be modified. To change the transparent background, choose Transparency from the File/Preferences submenu. To change the size of the checkerboard pattern, choose a size from the Grid group radio button. To change colors, click on the Set pop-up menu or click on either of the color swatches to open the Color Picker.*

2. From the Window menu, select Show Rulers and Show Info. Use the rulers and the Info palette to help you measure when completing the exercises in this section.

3. Use black as the foreground color and white as the background color. Check to see that these are your current settings; if they aren't, click on the Default Colors icon in the Toolbox.

## Using the Rectangular Marquee and Constrained Aspect Ratio Option

Start by exploring the Constrained Aspect Ratio option, which creates selections according to proportions specified in the Marquee Options palette.

1. To open the Marquee Options palette, double-click on the Marquee tool. In the Style pop-up menu, choose Constrained Aspect Ratio. Leave both Width and Height field set at 1, the defaults.

    These settings will constrain the mouse selection so the width and height are always drawn at a 1:1 ratio—in other words, you'll be creating a square. The width and height of the rectangular selection will always be equal to each other.

2. To create the square, move the crosshair to the upper-left corner of your document. Click and drag down diagonally from left to right. As you drag, notice that your selection is a square. Release the mouse.

   Now try creating another rectangular selection. No matter how hard you try, you won't be able to create anything other than a square selection. The selection can be any size, but it will always be a square because the width to height proportions have been *constrained* to a 1:1 ratio.

   Although the Constrained Aspect Ratio option is often used to create squares, you can use it to create rectangles at other proportions. For instance, if you need to make rectangles in which the height is twice as long as the width (1:2), you can set the aspect ratio accordingly.

3. To make a rectangle with a 1:2 ratio, leave Width set to 1, and change Height to 2 in the Marquee Options Palette.

4. Click and drag to create a selection.

No matter how large your selection, the height will always be double the width. Here are some rectangles with 1:1, 1:2, and 2:1 ratios:

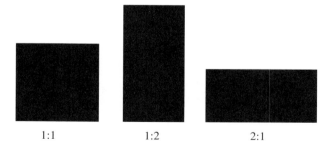

1:1        1:2        2:1

## Using the Elliptical Marquee

The Elliptical Marquee functions similarly to the Rectangular Marquee, except it creates round rather than rectangular shapes. To use the Marquee tool's Elliptical shape, choose Elliptical from the Shape pop-up menu in the Marquee Options palette. Alternatively, you can OPTION-click (PC users: ALT-click) on the Rectangular Marquee icon in the Toolbox. In the Toolbox, you'll now see the

Elliptical Marquee icon. In the Marquee Options palette's Style pop-up menu, the Normal, Constrained Aspect Ratio, and Fixed Size options work exactly as they do with the Rectangular Marquee.

**THE ELLIPTICAL MARQUEE AND THE NORMAL OPTION**   The Marquee tool's Elliptical shape allows you to create elliptical selections. Since you haven't used the Elliptical Marquee before, start with it set to the Normal option so that you can see how the tool works without any constraints.

**3**

1. Start by checking to see that Normal is selected in the Style pop-up menu. If it isn't, select it now.

   Drawing an ellipse with the mouse is not too different from drawing a rectangle, primarily because you can click and drag diagonally to create the shape. The perimeter of the ellipse starts where you click, and the shape grows according to the size of the angle and distance you drag.

2. To draw an ellipse, click in the upper-left corner of your screen and slowly drag diagonally toward the lower-right corner. When you have an elliptical selection on the screen, release the mouse button.

3. To practice a bit more, try drawing another ellipse. This time, drag only about one-half inch down and then drag across to the right, almost to the edge of the screen. This produces a cigar-shaped ellipse.

**THE ELLIPTICAL MARQUEE AND CONSTRAINED ASPECT RATIO OPTION**   As with the Marquee tool's Rectangular shape, you can utilize the Style pop-up menu's Constrained Aspect Ratio to create selections according to specific proportions. With this option selected and a 1:1 ratio specified, the Marquee tool's Elliptical shape creates a perfect circle.

Try creating a circular selection with the Elliptical Marquee:

1. In the Marquee Options palette, select the Constrained Aspect Ratio in the Style pop-up menu. If Width and Height aren't set to 1, type **1** in both the Width and Height fields.

2. Click and drag diagonally down from the upper-left corner of your screen toward the bottom-right corner. Your selection will be a perfect circle.

3. Try creating another selection, but this time use different ratios. Here are some ellipses with 1:1, 1:2, and 2:1 ratios:

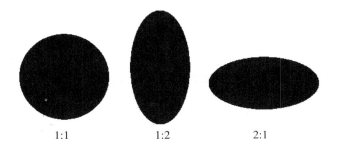

1:1          1:2          2:1

**IP:** *If the Constrained Aspect Ratio option is not activated, you can still create a perfect square or perfect circle by clicking and dragging with the SHIFT key pressed. If you click and drag with the OPTION key (PC users: CTRL) pressed, you create a square, rectangle, ellipse, or circle from the center out.*

## Using Edit/Fill and Edit/Stroke

For the truck collage, you will create circles for the wheels of the truck by using the Marquee tool's Elliptical and Constrained Aspect Ratio option. Instead of creating white circles within black circles to create the tires, you'll fill each circular selection with white and then stroke it with black.

To fill the circular selection with white, you'll use the Edit/Fill command which allows you to fill with the background color as well as the foreground color. The Fill command also allows you to fill a selection with black, 50% gray, white, a pattern, the last saved version of your file, or a Snapshot of your file. The Pattern, Saved, and Snapshot Fill options are covered in Chapter 6. The Fill dialog box also provides settings for changing Opacity and painting/editing modes. Changing Opacity and using the painting/editing modes are covered in Chapter 5. After using the Edit/Fill command, you'll use Edit/Stroke.

The Stroke command in the Edit menu allows you to put a border or outline, using the current foreground color, around a selection. You can't stroke with the background color. The Stroke dialog box allows you to enter the stroke width in pixels; acceptable values are integers between 1 and 16, inclusive. You can designate whether you wish the stroke to be along the outside of the selection marquee, inside it, or in the middle. You can also create a stroke with a *tint* (a percentage of the foreground color). Working with tint is discussed in Chapter 5.

In this exercise, you will fill a selection with white, then stroke the selection.

1. Before you fill or stroke an object, you need to create a selection on screen. Select the Marquee tool's Elliptical option from the Shape pop-up menu, then click and drag to create a circle about 2 inches in diameter.

2. If the foreground and background colors are not set to black and white, click on the Default Colors icon to change them.

3. To fill the selection with white, open the Fill dialog box, shown here, by choosing Fill from the Edit menu. In the Use pop-up menu, choose either Background Color or White. Leave Opacity set to 100% and Mode to Normal. Do not select the Preserve Transparency check box; otherwise, the transparent area in the selection (in this case, the entire selection) will not be affected.

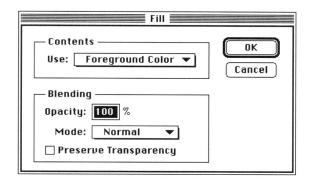

**IP:**   *Press and hold SHIFT, then press the DELETE key to open the Fill dialog box.*

4. To stroke the selection, open the Stroke dialog box, shown here, or choose Stroke from the Edit menu.

```
┌──────────────────────── Stroke ════════════════════════┐
│  ┌─ Stroke ──────────────────────────────┐  ┌─────────┐ │
│  │  Width: [ 1 ]  pixels                  │  │   OK    │ │
│  │                                        │  └─────────┘ │
│  └────────────────────────────────────────┘  ┌─────────┐ │
│  ┌─ Location ─────────────────────────────┐  │ Cancel  │ │
│  │ ○ Inside   ● Center   ○ Outside        │  └─────────┘ │
│  └────────────────────────────────────────┘             │
│  ┌─ Blending ─────────────────────────────┐             │
│  │ Opacity: [100] %   Mode: [ Normal  ▼]  │             │
│  │ □ Preserve Transparency                │             │
│  └────────────────────────────────────────┘             │
└──────────────────────────────────────────────────────────┘
```

**5.** To set the size of the stroke, type **5** in the Width field. Leave Location set to Center, Opacity set to 100%, and Mode set to Normal (these are the defaults). Then click OK. The circle appears, with a 5-pixel outline. In the middle of the circle's 5-pixel stroke, you'll see the selection marquee still blinking. The stroke was created in the center of the selection. Click away to deselect and to see the stroke.

Before closing this file, take a look at some aspects of working in a layer. In a layer, you can move all of its contents by clicking and dragging with the Move tool. Try this out by activating the Move tool, then clicking and dragging with the Move tool on the circle. The circle moves, but you didn't have to select it. This doesn't mean you don't need the selection tools anymore. If you had two circles on screen and wanted to move them independently of one another, you would need to select the one you wanted to move first.

Now, delete the circle by first selecting it using a keyboard shortcut that selects all non-transparent areas of a layer (other than the Background). Press COMMAND-OPTION-T (PC users: CTRL-ALT-T). Then press DELETE, or choose Edit/Clear. After you press DELETE, the transparency checkerboard replaces the circle, indicating that you have erased the circle. If you didn't have a transparent background, pressing DELETE would have filled the selection with the background color.

Now that you've covered all the tools and commands you'll need to create the truck collage, you can close this practice file.

## Creating the Truck

Start by creating a new file designed to tightly fit the truck you're creating.

1. To create a new file, choose New from the File menu. Set the dimensions of the file to Width **5** and Height **3.5**. Set Mode to RGB Color and 72 ppi for the resolution. Before clicking OK, set the Contents radio button to Transparent. When the new document appears, you'll see the words "Layer 1" in the Layers palette, rather than the word "Background."

**EMEMBER:**  *If you wish to create this collage at a resolution higher than 72 ppi, you'll need to convert pixel measurements to compensate for the higher resolution change. See the Tip in the section "Composing the Flag" earlier in this chapter for the conversion formula.*

2. Since the file's dimensions are small, you'll probably want to zoom in so your work area is bigger. To magnify the document window, press COMMAND-PLUS (PC users: CTRL-PLUS), the keyboard equivalent of the Zoom In command found in the Window menu. The magnification ratio in the Window title bar now reads 2:1.

3. You'll be needing both the rulers and Info palette for measuring, so open them. From the Window menu, select Show Rulers and then Show Info from the Window/Palettes submenu.

   When the Info palette opens, notice that a new readout appears. The letters "Op" stand for Opacity. The Opacity readout appears because you are working in a document that does not have a white or colored Background layer visible. The opacity of the entire transparent background is controlled by the Layers palette. However, not until you create more than one layer in your document will changing opacity have an effect.

## Moving the Zero Point

When you create the truck, give yourself some breathing room by creating it one-half inch from the top and one-half inch from the left side of your document. You will measure distances from the *truck's* origin, not from the *zero point*, or origin, of the rulers. To aid you in measuring in these situations, Photoshop allows you to move the zero point of both vertical and horizontal screen rulers so you can measure from anywhere on screen.

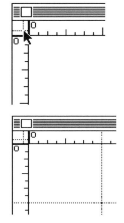

Before moving the zero point, make sure that the 0 and half-inch marks appear on both the horizontal and vertical rulers. In order to move the zero point, you'll need to be able to view this part of the ruler. If you can't see it, scroll left and/or up until you can see these marks on both rulers.

To move the zero point, select the crosshair at the intersection of the horizontal and vertical rulers in the top-left corner of your screen, as shown in the top illustration here. Click and drag diagonally down to the half-inch mark on the vertical ruler and the half-inch mark on the horizontal ruler. As you drag, horizontal and vertical guides will appear at what will be the new zero point, as shown in the bottom illustration here.

Check the Info palette to make sure that the X and Y positions of the mouse both read .5 inch. When they do, release the mouse button to set the origin of both horizontal and vertical rulers.

If you released the mouse at the wrong point, you can return the zero point to its original position and try again; just double-click on the crosshair in the top-left corner of the screen.

To see the effects of the relocated zero point, move the mouse across the screen and watch the X and Y coordinates in the Info palette. Notice that the values read zero when you are at one-half inch from the top and the left side of the screen. You'll start creating the trailer of the truck at this new zero point.

## Creating the Truck Trailer

Both the truck trailer and the poster area within it will be created using the Marquee tool's Rectangular shape. Later in this exercise you will paste an image into the poster area.

To make the truck's trailer, you'll need to create a rectangle that is twice as wide as it is high.

1. Double-click on the Marquee tool to display the Marquee Options palette. In the Shape pop-up menu, choose Rectangular. In the Style pop-up menu, choose Constrained Aspect Ratio. In the Width field type **2**, and in the Height field type **1**.

2. Use the rulers and Info palette as guides to position the crosshair so that the X and Y coordinates both read 0. Click and drag diagonally to the right until the X coordinate is 2.75 inches. The width of the trailer will be

set automatically to be a rectangle with a width of 1.375 inches because you are using a Constrained Aspect Ratio of 2:1.

3. At this point, release the mouse button.

4. Next fill the selection with the foreground color (black) by pressing OPTION-DELETE (PC users: ALT-DELETE).

5. Click away from the truck to deselect, so you don't inadvertently move it.

6. Before continuing to create the poster border on the truck's trailer, save your file. By doing so, you can use the Revert command if you make a mistake in the upcoming steps. Name the file **Truck**.

   Now you are going to create a smaller rectangle inside the truck's trailer. This rectangle will be used as a border for the fruit image you'll be pasting into the file.

7. Move the crosshair so that the x-axis is at approximately .250 inches, and the y-axis is at about .125 inches. Click and drag diagonally so the X coordinate in the Info palette is 2.500 inches and the Y coordinate is at 1.250 inches. This creates a rectangle with a width of approximately 2.250 inches and a height of about 1.125 inches.

8. To create a placeholder for the poster on the trailer, fill this rectangle with the background color, white. Don't deselect, because you're going to add a finishing touch by filling the area with white and then stroking the selection with a 4-pixel-wide gray border.

9. To fill the selected area with white, open the Fill dialog box by choosing Fill from the Edit menu or by pressing SHIFT-DELETE. In the Fill dialog box, choose White in the Use pop-up menu. Leave Opacity set at 100%, and the Mode set to Normal. Then click OK.

10. Since the Stroke command paints with the foreground color, you need to start by setting the foreground color to light blue. If the Picker palette is not on screen, open it by choosing Show Picker from the Window/Palettes submenu. Set the foreground color to a light blue by clicking on a blue area in the color bar.

11. To create the stroke, select Stroke from the Edit menu. In the Stroke dialog box, type **4** in the Width field. In the Location group, click on the Inside radio button—you want the stroke to be placed on the *inside* of the selection marquee (extending 4 pixels in from the selection), not on the outside of the selection (extending 4 pixels out from the selection) and not centered (placed directly on the selection marquee). Click OK.

12. Save your work before continuing.

Before pasting the fruit into the poster area, proceed to create the chassis, cab, and wheels of the truck.

## Creating the Chassis and the Cab

The chassis will consist of two, long, filled rectangles as shown below. Use the Marquee tool's Rectangular Shape to create the rectangles, and fill them with shades of blue. To make the cab, create a square selection and fill it with black. To add a transparent window to the cab, create a rectangular selection with the Marquee tool, then press DELETE or choose Edit/Clear. The truck should now look like this:

 **EMEMBER:** *If you need to move a selection, press COMMAND-OPTION (PC users: CTRL-ALT) so that you only move the selection and don't affect any underlying pixels.*

## Creating the Smoke Stack

To make the truck's smoke stack, use Figure 3-10 as a guide. Create two rectangles, a large one on the bottom (standing on its end) with a smaller one on top. Fill both with black.

## Creating the Wheels

Now you are ready to create the first back wheel. After you create one wheel, you'll duplicate it to make the other three wheels.

1. In the Marquee Options palette, set the Shape pop-up menu to Elliptical. Then set the Style pop-up menu to Constrained Aspect Ratio. Type in **1** for both the Width and Height fields.

2. Position the crosshair in the back of the truck chassis where you want the midpoint of the wheel to be. To draw a circle from the midpoint out, press OPTION (PC users: ALT) and hold the key while you click and drag to create a small circle. Fill the selection with the background color, white, by choosing Fill from the Edit menu. In the Use pop-up menu, choose Background Color or White. Then click OK.

3. To create the black tire, you will stroke the circle with the foreground color. Make sure that the foreground color is black, and then choose Stroke from the Edit menu. In the Stroke dialog box, set the width to **9** pixels. The Opacity should be **100%**. Click OK. The circular selection will now look like a wheel.

    Now you'll duplicate the wheel three times and drag each duplicate into position. Before you start to drag, you'll press the SHIFT key to constrain the wheel to moving in a straight line.

4. With the wheel selected, press OPTION (PC users: ALT) then click and drag to duplicate it. Next, press SHIFT. With SHIFT still pressed, drag to the right. As you drag, the wheel is constrained on a horizontal plane. Position the wheel using Figure 3-10 as a guide. Repeat this procedure to create and position two more wheels.

5. Before continuing, save your work.

You've just finished creating the truck. Now you're ready to paste an image of some fruit in the poster placeholder.

## Creating the Poster

To create the proper selection size for the poster, use the Fixed Size option in the Marquee Options palette.

1. In the Marquee Options palette, set the Shape pop-up menu to Retangular.

2. In the Style pop-up menu select Fixed Size, and type **145** in the Width field and **65** in the Height field. Click OK.

3. Click on the truck's trailer to make the selection marquee appear. This is the selection size you will eventually use for the scanned image.

4. If you need to reposition the selection, just move the mouse to the upper-left corner where you want the selection to start and click again. You could also use the OPTION-COMMAND (PC users: ALT-CTRL) key combination and then click and drag the selection into the middle of the poster area of the truck, as shown here:

Keep this portion selected, because later you will copy a fruit image into this area. Notice that the selection was made slightly smaller than the poster area to provide a white border for the scanned image.

To select the fruit image to copy into the poster, you can create a selection from the fruit plate in the Frames file that is included with Photoshop (PC users: frames.jpg) or use any suitable image. The image you see on the truck in Figure 3-10 is one that was scanned from a photograph of fruit.

**EMEMBER:** *The resolution of your scanned image should match the resolution of your file.*

3

**5.** To open the Frames file, choose Open from the File menu. Locate the Frames file in the Tutorial folder (PC users: frames.jpg file), and double-click the filename.

**6.** Once the image opens on screen, you'll only need to click to create a selection because the Fixed Size option is in effect. Click in the middle of the screen to create the 145-by-65-pixel selection. Adjust the position of the selection over the fruits by pressing OPTION-COMMAND (PC users: ALT-CTRL), and clicking and dragging the mouse until you've framed a selection of fruits.

**7.** To copy the selection, choose Copy from the Edit menu.

**8.** Select Close from the File menu.

**9.** You are now back in the Truck file; notice the selection marquee is right where you left it, in the border area of the truck's trailer. When you paste, you will be pasting the image directly into the selection marquee. Choose Paste from the Edit menu. Your image will look like this:

**10.** Save your work and close the Truck file.

Next you'll perform several introductory exercises before you move on to the second part of the truck collage, where you create a background landscape from a scanned image and then paste the truck over it.

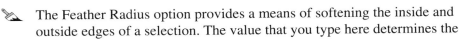 

## Introductory Exercises: Using the Lasso and Magic Wand Tools and Various Select Commands

To create the landscape, you will be converting a photograph of a landscape to colored line art. You'll use the Lasso and Magic Wand tools to select various parts of the landscape and fill them with a color.

In order to complete the next exercises, you'll need a new document open on screen. Create a new file, 7 by 5 inches, to give you sufficient room to practice with these tools. You can set the background Contents to either White or Transparent.

### Using the Lasso Tool

The Lasso tool is used for selecting irregularly shaped objects. It allows you to create a selection by drawing in a freehand mode, somewhat like drawing on screen with a pencil.

The Lasso can also be used to create *polygons*. To create these, you must press and hold OPTION (PC users: ALT) while you click the mouse at various points on the screen. As you click, the Lasso tool connects the points where you clicked to create a selection.

No matter what shape you draw, the Lasso always closes your selection. It will not allow you to leave an open curve or angle on screen.

Before you test the Lasso, take a look at the Lasso Options palette. As usual, you can open the palette by double-clicking on the tool. If the Options palette is open on screen, you can also click on the tool in the Toolbox or press L on your keyboard.

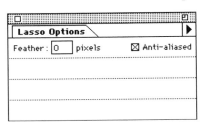

The Anti-aliased check box is selected by default. Leave it selected, because this option softens the hard edges of pixels by partially selecting them. This will cause selection edges to appear less jagged when filled with a color. (Review Chapter 2 for a discussion on pixels.)

The Feather Radius option provides a means of softening the inside and outside edges of a selection. The value that you type here determines the width in pixels of the feathered edge. You won't use feathering in this exercise, but you will later in this chapter when you create a vignette. If this value is not currently set to 0, type **0** in the field now.

**CREATING FREEFORM SHAPES WITH THE LASSO**    In this section, you'll try your hand at the Lasso tool by creating a freeform, kidney-shaped selection.

1. With the Lasso tool active, move the pointer into the middle of the document window. As you move the mouse, the pointer changes to a Lasso icon. Position the Lasso in the upper-left corner of the screen.

**OTE:**    *If you press the CAPS LOCK key, the mouse pointer will turn into a crosshair. The crosshair is provided as an alternative to the Lasso pointer because it allows you to select more precisely. The crosshair will also appear if the Tool Cursors settings for Other Tools is set to Precise in the General Preferences dialog box.*

2. To create the kidney shape, click and drag as shown in Figure 3-11. As you drag the mouse, be careful not to release the mouse button. If you do, the Lasso tool will finalize the selection by connecting the starting and ending points. If this happens, click outside the selection to deselect it and start over again.

3. When you've completed the kidney shape, release the mouse button.

Next you'll try out the Lasso's constraining mode, which you'll need later to select a mountain range for the landscape.

**CONSTRAINING THE LASSO SELECTION**    The Lasso's constraining option allows you to create polygons by clicking at different points on the screen. As you click, the Lasso connects the points with selection lines. To make the Lasso work in this mode, press OPTION (PC users: ALT) while you use the tool.

**OTE:**    *While selecting with the Lasso constraining option, it's often a good idea to use the crosshair pointer to make more accurate selections.*

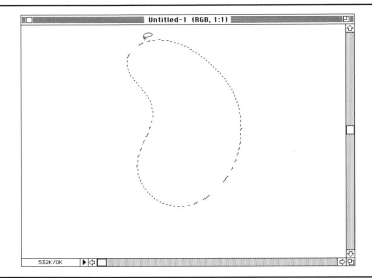

Creating a
freeform
selection
with the
Lasso tool

**FIGURE 3-11**

Try out the Lasso's constraining option by creating a simple triangle.

1. With the Lasso tool activated, press CAPS LOCK to activate the crosshair. Press OPTION (PC users: ALT) to constrain your selection. Keep OPTION (PC users: ALT) pressed as you create the triangle.

2. Move the crosshair about 1 inch down from the left side of your file and 4 inches directly across to the right. Click the mouse button. Next, move the pointer diagonally, about 2 inches to the right and about 3 inches down. Click again.

   You now have a straight line connecting your first and second mouse clicks.

3. Move the mouse horizontally to the left about 4 inches and click. Now return to your original starting point and click again. Release OPTION (PC users: ALT). Your screen will look like Figure 3-12.

   Don't deselect yet, because you'll need to use this triangular selection in the next exercise, where you'll be introduced to the Magic Wand. In order to see the Wand's color-selecting capabilities in action, you'll need to fill the triangle you just created with a color.

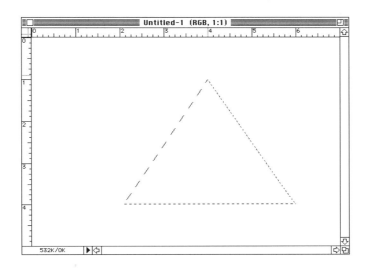

Constraining
a selection
with the
Lasso tool

**FIGURE 3-12**

**4.** If the Picker palette is not on screen, open it by choosing Show Picker from the Window/Palettes submenu. Change the foreground color to orange by clicking on an orange area in the color bar in the Picker palette. Fill the selection by pressing OPTION-DELETE (PC users: ALT-DELETE). Click away from the object to deselect, and release CAPS LOCK.

**5.** Use the Marquee tool's Elliptical Shape option to create a circle in the middle of the triangle. Set the style to Normal in the Marquee Options palette, if necessary. Change the foreground color to yellow, and fill the circle with yellow.

You now have two shapes and two colors with which to test the Magic Wand tool's powers.

## Using the Magic Wand

Of all Photoshop's selecting tools, the Magic Wand is usually considered the most powerful because it can create selections that would be nearly impossible to reproduce by hand. This tool works by selecting a color range with one click of the mouse. It is normally used to select areas according to similarity of color.

Before you begin to use the Wand with a scanned image in the landscape exercise, examine the Magic Wand Options palette. Open it in the usual way, by double-clicking on the Magic Wand in the Toolbox. If the Option palette is already open, you can click on the Wand in the Toolbox instead, or press W on your keyboard.

```
┌─────────────────────────────────────────┐
│ □                                       ⊡ │
│ ┌─────────────────────────────┐         ▶ │
│ │ Magic Wand Options          \           │
│ ├─────────────────────────────┘           │
│ Tolerance: │ 32 │        ⊠ Anti-aliased   │
│                                           │
│ □ Sample Merged                           │
│                                           │
│                                           │
│                                           │
└─────────────────────────────────────────┘
```

Notice that Anti-aliased is also an option in the Wand's dialog box. It functions exactly as it does in the Type and Lasso Options dialog boxes.

The value you see in the Tolerance field controls the color range that the Wand will select. The greater the Tolerance setting, the broader the color range. The smallest value you can enter is 0; the largest is 255. The default value is 32. If the Wand's Tolerance is set to 0, it will select an area of contiguous pixels that are only the same color as the pixel that you click on. If you increase the Tolerance setting, the Wand will expand the selection to include a greater range of color, using the color you clicked on as its starting point. A very high Tolerance setting will create a selection over a color range that can vary greatly from the color originally clicked on.

If Sampled Merged is selected the Magic Wand tool analyzes not only the pixels you click on but the pixels in all visible layers. For more information about layers, see Chapter 12.

Change the Tolerance setting in the Magic Wand Options palette so you can begin testing the Wand. For this exercise, you should have the yellow circle and orange triangle from the previous exercise on screen. If you don't, create an orange triangle, then create a yellow circle over it.

1. In the Tolerance field, type **0**.

2. Point to the yellow circle you just created. Notice that the mouse pointer changes to a wand icon when you move it over the document area. (If the mouse pointer is a crosshair and not a wand icon, CAPS LOCK is on.)

3. Click on the circle. The Wand selects only the circle. Click on the triangle and the Wand selects only the orange area of the triangle. Since the Tolerance value is set to 0, in both cases the Wand only selects one color.

4. Now change the Tolerance setting in the Magic Wand Options palette to see how it affects the selection. Type **255** in the Tolerance field.

5. Click again on the yellow circle. This time the Wand selects both the circle and triangle because the high Tolerance setting allowed more colors to slip into the selection.

Even with this less-than-intricate selection, the Wand still proves to be a time-saver: If you had to reselect the triangular selection on screen, you'd have to use the Lasso tool to click precisely over your original mouse clicks.

 **OTE:** *The Select Menu's Color Range command provides another means of creating a selection based on color. This advanced selection command is covered in Chapter 11.*

## Using the Select/Matting Commands

When using the Magic Wand you might encounter a mysterious halo of color that seems to tag along with your image. When you select an area with the Magic Wand, Lasso, or Elliptical Marquee, Photoshop may include extra colored pixels along the edges of the selection; these can become noticeable when a selection is pasted or moved. It is especially apparent when a light image is moved over a dark background or a dark image is moved over a light background. The extra colored pixels are often the result of Photoshop's Anti-aliasing feature, which partially blurs fringe pixels. In the process, extra pixels around the perimeter are added to the selection. Photoshop's Select/Matting command allows you to remove the unwanted pixels.

### Defringing a Pasted Image

With the Select/Matting Defringe command, you can remove the unwanted color from fringe pixels. Defringe replaces the colors on the fringes of a selection with a color that is closest to the fringe from within the selection. In order for the Defringe command to be accessible, the area you want to defringe must be floating. When you select Defringe, a dialog box appears, allowing you to specify the pixel width of the fringe area to be colored. The following illustration (a) shows an image that was copied and pasted without Defringe. Illustration (b) shows the same image after the Defringe command was applied.

(a)                                     (b)

If you wish to try out the Defringe command, open the Flower file (PC users: flower.jpg) from the Tutorial folder. Activate the Magic Wand tool, and set the Tolerance in the Wand Options palette to 150. Make sure the Anti-aliased check box is selected. Click on a petal of the flower. This will select the perimeter of the flower. Now, copy and paste the flower into a new file with a white background. Don't deselect. To see the extra fringe pixels, hide the Selection Edges by pressing COMMAND-H (PC users: CTRL-H). You'll see a thin border of green surrounding the flower. To remove the green edge pixels, choose Defringe from the Select/Matting submenu. In the Defringe dialog box, enter 3 as the pixel width. After you click OK, the green fringe will be gone. Now deselect.

## Using Black-and-White Matte

If you select an image in a black background, choose Black Matte from the Select/Matting submenu to remove extraneous black fringe pixels. If you select an image in a white background, choose White Matte from the Select/Matting submenu to remove the extraneous white fringe pixels.

If you'd like to experiment more with the Magic Wand, try filling various selections with different colors and then testing the Wand's selections. When you're finished, proceed to the next section, where you'll learn several very helpful selection tips for all of the program's selection tools.

## Adding to and Subtracting from Selections

Even though you've learned to use all of Photoshop's selection tools, your selection knowledge won't be complete until you know how to change your selections by adding to them, subtracting from them, and intersecting them.

If you've used other Mac or Windows programs, you can probably guess that you add to a selection by SHIFT-*clicking*. Just hold down the SHIFT key when you make a new selection, and Photoshop adds to a previous selection. However, unlike many Mac and Windows programs, you cannot subtract from a selection by pressing SHIFT and clicking on a selection.

Suppose you want to remove part of a selection from the screen but leave other areas selected. To subtract from a selection, press and hold COMMAND (PC users: CTRL) while you click and drag over or within a selection.

Try removing a corner from a rectangular selection, using the Lasso tool. First create a rectangular selection on screen. Then activate the Lasso tool. While holding down COMMAND (PC users: CTRL), click and drag to create a curved selection over any corner of the rectangle on screen. When you release the mouse, the corner is subtracted from the selection.

You can also create a selection that is the intersection of two selections. To try this, press both COMMAND and SHIFT (PC users: CTRL and SHIFT); then click and drag to make a selection that overlaps the rectangular selection on screen. Fill with the foreground color, and you'll see that Photoshop paints the intersection—that is, only the common areas of the two selections.

## Using Select/Grow and Select/Similar

The Select menu includes two commands that can help when you are selecting with the Magic Wand. Execute the Select/Grow command, and the selection on screen will expand as if you had doubled the Tolerance range in the Wand's dialog box. Execute the Select/Similar command, and the selection will jump over areas beyond the Wand's tolerance to select areas that fit within its tolerance. For instance, if an image contained a black bridge over a river, which prevented the Wand from selecting the entire river, the Select/Similar command would cause the selection to jump over the bridge and select the rest of the water.

## Using Select/Modify/Expand and Contract

The Select menu has two other commands that can help you manage selections. The Select/Modify/Expand and Select/Modify/Contract commands allow you to make a selection grow or shrink by a specified number of pixels. Like Select/Grow and Select/Similar, these commands are used after a selection is created. For instance, if you selected an area, and wish to expand it by one pixel, choose Select/Modify/Expand. The Expand Selection dialog box opens. Enter **1** in the Pixel field. After you click OK, the selection will grow one pixel outward.

To shrink a selection by one pixel, choose Select/Modify/Contract. The Contract Selection dialog box opens. Enter **1** in the Pixel field. After you click OK, the selection will decrease one pixel inward.

## Using Select/Modify/Border and Smooth

The Border command is another Select/Modify menu option that changes a selection. Select/Border replaces a selection with a border selection surrounding the area of the original selection. The size of the border is specified in the Border dialog box. If you wish to see the Border command in action, create any selection, then choose Select/Modify/Border. In the Border dialog box, enter a pixel width for the border, then click OK. Fill the new selection with a color. You'll see that the border around the selection is filled, not the original selection.

The Smooth command is another Select/Modify menu option that alters selections by adding to or deleting from the original selection. Like Expand, Contract, and Border, Smooth allows you to type in a pixel value to control the effect. The Smooth command, however, uses the pixel value as a radius. For instance, when you type in a pixel value of 8, Photoshop radiates out from a central location evaluating 8 pixels in each direction. Thus, the actual distance examined for smoothing is 16 pixels. The Smooth command evaluates whether most of the pixels in the radius area are selected; if they are, it selects the unselected pixels. If most of the pixels in the radius area are not selected, it deselects the selected pixels.

The Smooth command can be helpful when you are trying to combine selections, blend a selection into its surroundings, or smooth the sharp edges of a selection.

To try out the Smooth command, create a star-shaped selection with the Lasso tool. Connect the points of the star by pressing OPTION (PC users: ALT) and clicking. Once you've created the star, execute Select/Modify/Smooth. Enter **5** pixels in the dialog box, then click OK. The edges of your rectangular selection will be smoothed.

For a more dramatic look at the Smooth command, create a rectangular selection. Press SHIFT and create two other rectangular selections directly above the first, about a quarter of an inch apart. Execute the Smooth command with a high pixel value. The Smooth command will join all three selections into one selection.

In the next section, you may need to add to or subtract from a selection when you use the Magic Wand to create the background landscape in the truck collage.

## Creating the Landscape for the Truck

Now that you've been introduced to the Lasso and the Magic Wand, and you know how to add and subtract from selections, you're ready to create the landscape for

the background of the truck collage. You'll use both these tools to select areas in a scanned image and fill them with colors.

In order to create the landscape, open any suitable image that provides shapes and colors that you can select. For this example, a scanned image of the Rocky Mountains was used. Once the image is on screen, you'll want to zoom in to your work area. This will make it easier to select intricate areas when you use the Lasso tool. Press COMMAND-PLUS (PC users: CTRL-PLUS) to magnify your work area.

Once you've selected an area, fill it with a color. Try experimenting with different selection tools and fill the areas with different colors. Our completed landscape is shown in Figure 3-13.

### Creating the Highway

Before you paste the truck created earlier in this chapter into its setting, create a highway for it. The easiest way to create the highway is to use the Single Row shape in the Marquee Options palette, which will create a 1-pixel-wide selection the entire width of the document window. (Single Column creates a 1-pixel-wide selection the entire height of the document window.) You'll stroke the selection with gray to pave this roadway with color.

The completed landscape

**FIGURE 3-13**

1. Access the Marquee Options palette and select Single Row from the Style pop-up menu.

2. Create a selection by positioning the crosshair just above the bottom of the document window and clicking the mouse. A 1-pixel-wide horizontal selection appears.

3. Next, select a black or gray foreground color.

4. Stroke the selection by choosing Stroke from the Edit menu. In the Width field box, type **4**; choose the Center option in the Location group; keep Opacity at 100%; and leave Mode set to Normal. Click OK, and then save your work.

Once you've created the highway, you're finished with the landscape portion of the collage. Now it's time to tie it all together by placing the truck into the landscape.

## Placing the Truck into the Landscape

Before you can add the truck into the landscape, you need to reopen both the Truck and Landscape files in order to place the truck into the landscape. If you had created the truck on a white background, you'd now be faced with a problem; how do you select the truck so it can be copied into the file containing the landscape? Luckily, since you created the truck on a transparent background, you can easily use the Move tool to drag and drop it into the Landscape file without selecting.

Before doing this, here's how you would have solved the problem of selecting the truck if it had been on a white background: Using the Magic Wand, you would first select the white area that surrounds the truck. Next, you would execute the Select/Inverse command. This would change the selection so everything except the white area would be selected. On screen only the truck would be surrounded by the blinking marquee. Then, you could copy and paste it into the Landscape file. Once in the Landscape file, you might need to remove extraneous white pixels with the Select/Defringe command.

Here are the steps for dragging and dropping the truck that is in Layer 1 into the Landscape file.

1. Open the Truck file.

2. Open the Landscape file.

**3.** When both files are on screen make sure that you can see them. Either position them side-by-side or so that they overlap with the Truck file on top of the Landscape file.

Instead of copying and pasting the truck, use a shortcut. Drag the truck and drop it over the Landscape file.

 **EMEMBER:** *You can also select all non-transparent areas of a layer by pressing COMMAND-OPTION-T (PC users: CTRL-ALT-T).*

**3**

**4.** Select the Move tool and position the mouse pointer over the truck. Click and keep the mouse button pressed. Next, drag the truck over the Landscape file. The pointer will change to a tiny grabbing hand. When you see a black border surrounding the Landscape file, release the mouse. The truck is now in the Landscape file. Notice that you can now see through the transparent window of the truck.

To understand exactly what happened when you moved the truck, examine the Layers palette. If the Layers palette isn't open, open it by choosing Show Layers from the Window/Palettes submenu. Notice that Photoshop created a new layer in the Landscape file. The "Background" of the file is the landscape, and "Layer 1" is the truck. Also notice that the area surrounding "Layer 1" is gray. This means that this is the selected, or target layer. The target layer is the layer being edited. There is no gray area surrounding the Background section of the Layers palette, meaning if you make any changes to the file now, only the Truck layer will be affected. The eye icons next to the Truck and the Background mean that both Layer 1 and the Background are visible.

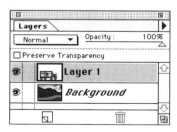

**5.** Since the truck is still in a layer, you can still reposition it with the Move tool. Use the Move tool, now to position the truck as shown in Figure 3-10.

Before you save your file, notice that the memory indicator in the lower-left corner of the screen shows two different numbers. The number on the right indicates that the memory size of the file has grown due to the new layer. When you save the file, you can flatten it to preserve memory. This will not change the image in the file but it will merge all the layers into the Background.

6. To flatten the file when you save it, choose Save a Copy from the File menu. Select the Flatten Layers check box, then name the file Truck Collage (PC users: trcklage). If you wish to save the file with the Layer, you must save it in Photoshop 3.0 format. You can use the standard File/Save As command to save the file under a new name so that the Landscape file remains intact, or you can use File/Save a Copy without flattening the file.

That's it. You have successfully created a truck and a landscape and placed the two together into a collage.

*n***OTE:**  *When creating collages, you might wish to create all objects in separate layers so that you can view them together, yet move and edit each layer independently. Be aware that each layer you create will increase the file size. If you wish to learn more about layers, see Chapter 12. If you are going to be creating many collages, you might wish to investigate Specular's Collage. This program does not increase file size as you create your layers. The program builds the file and increases file size when you are done editing.*

## FEATHERING THE EDGES OF A SELECTION

The last selection tools exercise shows you how to create a vignette using the Feather option available for the Marquee and Lasso tools.

To take a look at how the Feather option works, start by creating a new file, 5 by 5 inches, to use as a practice document. Click on the Default Colors icon to reset the foreground and background colors.

Let's start with the Marquee Tool's Feather option with the Shape pop-up menu set to Rectangular; it allows you to soften the edges of a rectangle. The value that you type in the Feather field determines the width of the feather edge. This value defaults to 0 pixels; the maximum value allowed is 250. Since the feather edge extends both inside and outside the selection, the actual feather will be twice the pixel value.

# Photoshop in Action

Elements for the image were selected with the Lasso tool using different Feather settings to create soft-edged effect when pasted.

Areas of the background were selected with the Magic Wand and colored with the Edit/Fill command.

Artist: Josh Gosfield        A Time Warner Annual Report

Josh first created the background of the image by scanning a photo he took of a television screen with interference. Once the photo was scanned, different areas were selected with the Magic Wand tool and then painted with the Edit/Fill command.

After the background was completed, Josh scanned various images and selected them using the Lasso tool with different Feather settings. This created a soft-edged effect when he pasted them into the final image.

Double-click on the Marquee tool. In the Marquee Options palette set the Shape pop-up menu to Rectangular and set the Style pop-up menu to Normal. In the Feather field type **15**. This value will give you a Feather edge of 30 pixels. Now click and drag to make a rectangle. Press OPTION-DELETE (PC users: ALT-DELETE) to fill the rectangle with the foreground color. The feathered rectangle will look like this:

Notice what has happened: The edges in the object have been softened 30 pixels; the feathering begins 15 pixels within the selection and extends 15 pixels beyond the selection. The outer edges of the black rectangle have a *gradient* effect; they start out black and then turn gray, until they blend into the white background. This effect, called a vignette, is also sometimes called a *halo* or *glow*.

## Creating a Vignette

The Feather option for the Elliptical Marquee was used to create the vignette shown in Figure 3-14. If you wish to try creating this type of special effect, start by opening an image on your screen. If you don't have an image, you can use the Portrait file (PC users: portrait.jpg) in Photoshop's Tutorial folder.

1. Set the Shape pop-up menu in the Marquee Options palette to Elliptical. Leave the Style set to Normal, and set the Feather field to **10**.

2. Click and drag to create an ellipse surrounding the area where you want to add the vignette effect. (The vignette will not appear until after you copy and paste the selection.)

3. From the Edit menu, choose Copy.

Creating a
vignette

**FIGURE 3-14**

4. Create a new file where you will paste your selection. From the File menu, choose New, and change the Width and Height settings to make them larger, if desired. Click OK.

5. From the Edit menu, choose Paste. The image is pasted with the feathering effect that creates the vignette.

*𝓃* **OTE:** *Depending upon the resolution and dimensions of your image, you may wish to experiment with different Feather values.*

The vignette exercise is the last of the selection tools design projects in this chapter. Here's one more simple exercise that illustrates how selections can be used to create special effects. This exercise uses the Select/Modify/Border command, which changes the blinking marquee so that it borders the original selection. Also used in this exercise is the Select/Feather command which feathers, or blurs, the edge of a selection. Select/Feather works just like the Feather option in the Lasso Options palette and the Marquee Options palette.

## Creating Glowing Text

In this exercise, you will learn how to create a glowing, or backlit, effect for text by copying, pasting, and using the Select menu's Modify/Border and Feather commands. The Border and Feather commands control the width and intensity of the glow.

Although this example creates a glowing background for text, you can produce the same effect on any selection instead of text. Here are the steps:

1. Create a new file, 6 inches by 4 inches, in RGB mode at 72 ppi. Set the background Contents to either Transparent or White.

2. You're going to create yellow text with a red glow, and you'll create the text first. Change the foreground color to red and the background color to white.

3. Activate the Type tool.

4. Click on the center of your document. When the Type Tool dialog box appears, type **GLOW** in the text box. Set the font to Helvetica. Enter **120** in the Size field and type **-10** in the Spacing field. In the Style group, choose Bold and turn on the Anti-aliased option. Click OK to place the text in your document. Make sure the Opacity slider in the Layers palette is set to 100% and the Mode to Normal. If Opacity is not set to 100%, your text will not be opaque.

*𝓃* **OTE:** *The value entered in the Spacing field in the Type Tool dialog box controls the spacing between letters (kerning). Entering a negative number decreases the spacing between letters (a positive number would increase spacing). The Spacing value is in points or pixels, depending upon the measurement unit set for font size. Values can be from -99.9 to 999.9.*

5. Once the floating text is on screen, move it into the center of the document window; you can do this by pressing the arrow keys or by clicking and dragging on the text. *Don't deselect.*

6. Next you will place the text into the Clipboard so that it can be copied back into the image after you've bordered, feathered, and filled it. From the Edit menu, choose Copy, and keep the text selected.

7. Now place a border selection around each letter of the text. From the Select menu choose Modify/Border, type **20** in the Width field, and click OK.

8. To soften the edges of the newly created border, choose Feather from the Select menu. Type **6** and click OK. The 20-pixel border now has a 6-pixel feather beyond its edges. (The Feather command feathers 6 pixels within the selection and six pixels beyond the selection.)

9. Now fill the selection on screen with the foreground color (red), to start creating the glow effect. Choose Fill from the Edit menu. In the Fill dialog box, set Opacity to 100% and Mode to Normal. You will see the soft edges of the feathered border.

10. To make the text sharper and more readable, paste the text from the Clipboard back onto the soft-edged glow. To do this, select Paste from the Edit menu. Keep the text selected.

11. Now you will fill the text with yellow; the combination of yellow text with a red feathered border will provide the glowing text effect. Start by changing the foreground color to yellow. Keep the text selected.

12. Choose Fill from the Edit menu or press OPTION-DELETE (PC users: ALT-DELETE). Click away from the text to deselect. Your text is now glowing.

If you'd like, you can use one or more of Photoshop's filters to create a more dramatic effect. Here we applied the Spherize filter. (For more information about filters, see Chapter 8.)

# Photoshop in Action

The bricks intersecting the circle were created by defining a pattern and then selecting and filling the areas with the pattern.

The glowing circle was created by applying the Select/Feather command to a circular selection and then filling it with black.

The hands and arms were created in Adobe Illustrator and then placed into the final image.

The Select/Feather command was used to soften the edges of the globe and the segmented circle beneath it.

Artist: Louis Fishauf, Reactor Art + Design Limited      Client: Digital Equipment

Louis created this image for a quarterly publication for Digital Equipment. To produce the glow around the circle, he created a circular selection with the Marquee tool and then softened its edges by using the Select/Feather command. Once the feathering was applied, he filled the circle with black.

Next, inside the glowing circle he created another circle where he could paste the face using the Edit/Paste Into command. While the face image was still selected, he applied the Spherize filter.

After the face was completed, he created the hands and arms in Adobe Illustrator and used Photoshop's File/Place command to put them into the image. To create the four brick walls, Louis selected a digitized image of bricks, then executed the Edit/Define Pattern command. He filled the four walls with the brick pattern using Edit/Fill.

## CONCLUSION

If you've read through and completed all the exercises in this chapter, you are now prepared to move on to more advanced topics, particularly those involving the use of color in your Photoshop work. The next chapter lays the groundwork for painting and image editing by covering the fundamentals of color theory. It will also provide a thorough discussion of how to use the colors in the Picker and Swatches palettes, as well as help you understand the differences between RGB and CMYK colors.

**3**

**FIG 4-2**

The primary (additive) colors and their components. When all three primary colors are mixed together, they create white.

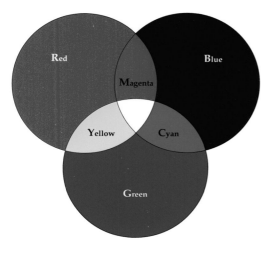

**FIG 4-3**

The secondary (subtractive) colors and their complements. When all three secondary colors are mixed together, they create a muddy brown.

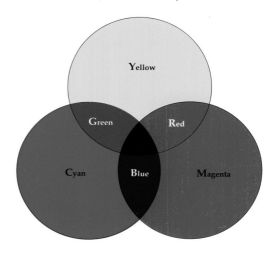

**FIG 4-4**

Each color in the color wheel is opposite its complement and between the two colors that create it.

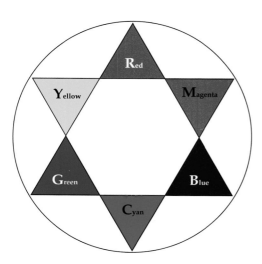

**FIG 4-8**

The Hue, Saturation, and Brightness color model. (Courtesy of Agfa Corporation)

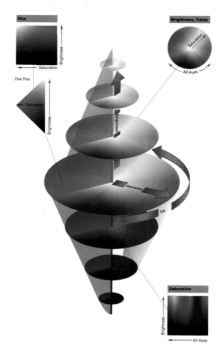

# The Photoshop Portfolio

**1**  This photograph (also shown in Chapter 13) of a beautiful New England town was taken by Gene Ahrens for the cover of a proposed Reader's Digest book titled *Back Roads of America*. The image was almost perfect, however, the power lines and telephone wires running through the town marred the landscape. The art director of Reader's Digest General Books, David Trooper, felt that areas of the sky were too dark and would conflict with the color of the book's title. He also wanted the road signs in the foreground removed. To make the changes, the image was scanned and saved as a CMYK file, then retouched and color-corrected by Adele Droblas Greenberg.

**2**  This image (also shown in Chapter 13) shows the final cover for the proposed book after retouching and color-correcting. To remove the road signs, telephone wires, and power lines, Adele used the Rubber Stamp tool's Cloning option. Before color-correcting, several masks were created using the selection tools and the Quick Mask mode. To make the water bluer, she added cyan using the Levels command in the Image/Adjust submenu. The clouds behind the title were lightened using the Curves command in the Image/Adjust submenu. The colors on the hills across the water were made to look more autumn-like and the foliage in the town was made more vibrant. For a full discussion of the steps involved, see Chapter 13.

**3**  This photograph (also shown in Chapter 13) was taken in the late 1800s of a 24-year-old French nobleman who came to the United States in hopes of fulfilling his dream of raising cattle. The photograph was selected for the Reader's Digest book, *Discover America's Past*, where it appears as a sepia. Notice that the lower part of his left leg and his left foot are badly faded and barely noticeable. In addition to restoring the leg and foot, the book's art editor, Ken Chaya, asked Adele Droblas Greenberg to paint in the left elbow, add tone to the pistol, and enhance the detail in the rifle and hat.

**4**  Here is the image (also shown in Chapter 13) after retouching. Adele began restoring the lower left leg and left foot by copying, pasting, and flipping part of the right leg and foot into a new file. She then used the Rubber Stamp tool's Cloning option to clone the foot back into the image, and the Airbrush tool to provide a seamless transition between the restored and original areas. Before painting the left elbow, Adele used the Eyedropper tool to set the foreground color so it matched the tone of the original. Next, she used the Airbrush and Paintbrush tools to paint in the left elbow. For complete details on how this image was retouched, see Chapter 13.

**1**

**2**

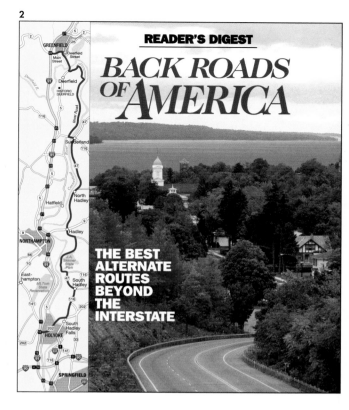

READER'S DIGEST

# BACK ROADS OF AMERICA

THE BEST
ALTERNATE
ROUTES
BEYOND
THE
INTERSTATE

**3**

**4**

**1**
Image before retouching
and color-correcting
Photograph courtesy of Gene Ahrens

**2**
Image after retouching
and color-correcting
**Artist:** Adele Droblas Greenberg
**Client:** Reader's Digest General Books

**3**
Image before retouching
Photograph courtesy of Library of
Congress

**4**
Image after retouching
**Artist:** Adele Droblas Greenberg
**Client:** Reader's Digest General Books

# The Photoshop Portfolio

**5**     This fantastic image won the 1991 APA Gold Award for Special Effects and Kodak's VIP Image Search '91 awards for Best in Show and Best in Digital Photography. The image was created as a self-promotion piece for R/GA Print, a division of R/Greenberg Associates, which is well known for its creation of a Diet Coke television commercial featuring Paula Abdul dancing with Gene Kelly.

    The dove, the parrot, and the sky in this image were photographed by Ryszard Horowitz. The cone was created using R/GA Print's own proprietary 3-D computer software and was rendered twice, once with the sky and once with "wild" colors. In order to create the opaque blue sky and the clear sky, a linear blend was applied using the Gradient tool in an alpha channel. All of the images were then composited together using the Image/Calculate (Image/Apply Image in Photoshop 3.0) and Edit/Paste commands. The mirrored image of the cone was created by copying, pasting, and then changing Composite Control settings.

    Alpha channels and the Apply Image commands are covered in Chapter 11. Composite Control settings are covered in Chapter 12.

**6**     Josh began creating this inspirational campaign image by selecting parts of a scanned photograph of a crowd at a Clinton/Gore rally and pasting them into a new file. He also scanned an American flag, then selected, copied, and pasted it several times into the new file using different opacity settings. He flipped and rotated the flag using the commands in the Image menu.

    After a few flags were pasted, he scanned pictures of Clinton and Gore. He selected each image using the Lasso tool with a Feather setting so that both would blend into the background when pasted. Next, using a very low opacity setting, he again pasted the flag image—this time on top of Clinton, so that his face would appear through the flag's stripes. As a finishing touch, he selected, rotated, and pasted a Clinton banner over several parts of the background with a low opacity setting.

**7**     This collage, created for a Time Warner annual report, was begun by scanning an old wedding album, movie images, the Warner Brothers logo, and the number one. Josh then selected different areas of the digitized album and, using the Edit/Fill command, filled them with color. Next he selected, copied, and pasted the movie images provided by Time Warner into the final file. To make the images and the background blend together, he used Select/Feather and changed Composite Control settings. After all the elements were placed, he created the lines using Photoshop's Line tool.

**5**

**6**

**7**

**5**
**Artist:** R/GA Print
**Client:** R/GA Print
(promotional materials)

**6**
**Artist:** Josh Gosfield
**Client:** Newsweek Magazine

**7**
**Artist:** Josh Gosfield
**Client:** Time Warner Inc.

# The Photoshop Portfolio

**8** This image was created from a set designed by Santa Barbara Studios for the movie, "500 nations" (from Pathways Productions; Jack Leustig, owner and producer; Kevin Costner and Jim Wilson, executive producers), which will air on CBS as a miniseries. Christopher started creating this image by scanning a slide of the sky. After retouching the image, he added rays of light using the Airbrush and Gradient tools and the Rubber Stamp tool's Cloning option. He also used the Airbrush tool to create the sky's haze. To paint the trees, he used the Paintbrush tool with a one-pixel-wide brush. Based upon the staff archaeologist's design, he created an oil painting of the pyramids on canvas. He photographed it and then scanned and synthesized it into the final image. The images of the Indians, who were actors in costumes, were digitized using a video camera, then frame-grabbed. Christopher then scaled down the actors in Photoshop using the Image/Effects/Scale command, and color-corrected the images using various commands in the Image/Adjust submenu. Image/Effects commands are covered in Chapter 7.

**9** The concept of Ted Turner's global village is perfectly conveyed in photographer Greg Heisler's cover for *Time* magazine's 1992 Man of the Year issue. To begin the project, Greg had approximately 100 video images frame-grabbed and converted to slides. He digitized them and chose 42 for the final image. Using Photoshop's Image/Adjust submenu commands, he color-corrected the images and assembled them in a grid of seven rows by six columns. To create the globe effect, he applied Photoshop's Spherize filter. The highlight on the right side of the globe was created by first photographing a plastic sphere with a spotlight pointed towards it. Then the Composite Control settings were used with the Lighten mode selected to blend the sphere with the globe image.

To produce the gap in the middle of the globe, Greg created a selection with the Elliptical Marquee and filled it with black. Next, he used the Elliptical Marquee to create a selection in the middle of the gap and, with the Paste Into command, pasted a digitized image of his photograph of Ted Turner.

**10** This imaginative magazine cover for *Sports Illustrated for Kids* is comprised of a variety of photographs which were scanned and placed into one file. The first image to be digitized was the wide-eyed child at the table. After the three images of the standing players were scanned, they were outlined using the Pen tool, converted to selections, then scaled using the Image/Effects/Scale command. The player images were also rotated using the Image/Rotate command. Then they were copied and pasted into the file with the child, and their shadows were created using the Pen tool and the Image/Adjust/Levels command.

The players on the cards were also outlined with the Pen tool, converted to selections, then filled with white. For the finishing touch, a football was scanned in, selected, scaled, copied, and then pasted into the final image. Finally, the Motion Blur filter was applied to the football to make it look like it was flying through the air.

8

**8**
**Artist:** Christopher Evans
**Client:** Pathways Productions

**9**
**Artist:** Greg Heisler
**Client:** Time Magazine

**10**
**Artist:** Nik Kleinberg
**Client:** Sports Illustrated for Kids

9

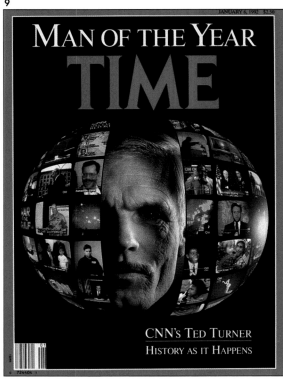

JANUARY 6, 1992   $2.50

MAN OF THE YEAR
TIME

CNN'S TED TURNER
HISTORY AS IT HAPPENS

724404

10

# The Photoshop Portfolio

**11** Anne created this montage for the front and back covers of a J.P. Morgan financial brochure by scanning different images, selecting them, and placing them into one file. She first worked on the background; the pavement, blue sky, and water. Then she began the process of selecting and pasting the images using primarily the Lasso tool, and the Pen tool to create paths and change them into selections. Anne created the montage as a low-resolution file and then had it printed on a color printer for the client's approval. Once it was approved, the image was re-created as a high-resolution file at a prepress house. When the image was finally printed, a screen frequency of 200 lpi was used.

To learn more about the selection tools, see Chapter 3. To learn more about the Pen tool, see Chapter 10.

**12** This image was used as the cover illustration for an issue of the *Washington Post* magazine which featured an article titled "What's Wrong with Newspapers." To digitize the image, Rico and Mauricio used a camcorder. After the pens were digitized, they were individually scaled and distorted using commands in the Image/Effects submenu. The artists then created the target by scanning different newspapers and applying tinted rings using circular selections filled at a low opacity setting. The borders of each separate ring were enhanced with the Select/Modify/Border, Select/Feather, and Edit/Fill commands. The shadows were created with the Lasso tool's Feather option and the Edit/Fill command. Finishing touches were applied with the Airbrush and other painting tools. Finally, the Dodge and Burn tools were used to balance specific areas of shadow, textures, and light sources.

The Dodge and Burn tools are discussed in Chapter 6.

**13** Rico created this intriguing image as a cover for the *Boston Globe* magazine to illustrate the article, "New World Borders, Madness for Mapmakers." Using a flat-bed scanner, Rico digitized different maps and objects such as a Band-Aid, tacks, a tape measure, thread, and yarn. Before assembling the elements together on screen, he used the Gradient tool to achieve a linear blend from dark to light for the background. The globe was created with a circular selection that was then saved to an alpha channel. Next, he applied the Spherize filter to the different scanned elements and pasted them into the circular selection. Using the Elliptical Marquee with the Feather option set to 25 pixels, Rico created the elliptical shadow below the globe and filled it with black. The smooth shadow on the underside of the globe was created with Adobe Illustrator.

To learn how to`use the Spherize filter and other powerful Photoshop filters, see Chapter 8.

**11**
**Artist:** Anne Wren
**Client:** J.P. Morgan & Co. Incorporated

**12**
**Artists:** Rico Lins and Mauricio Nacif
**Client:** Washington Post Magazine

**13**
**Artist:** Rico Lins
**Client:** Boston Globe Magazine

# The Photoshop Portfolio

**14** Adobe Photoshop and StrataVision, a photo-realistic 3-D program, were used to produce this sci-fi image. George created the earth, moon, and stars in Photoshop. To produce the glow around the earth, he created a Pen path that was stroked with the Airbrush tool.

Once the earth, moon, and stars were created, George used Photoshop's Airbrush tool with a Wacom stylus and tablet to paint the woman. The 3-D spaceship cabin and futuristic laptop computers were created in StrataVision.

**15** From photographs taken by Mark Sokol of the water, fire, sky, circuit board, and the rock on a sandy beach, Daniel created this surrealistic image for a California service bureau. In order to work efficiently, he first produced the entire image as a low-resolution comp. As he worked, he created masks for the various elements in the image which allowed him to isolate and edit each area without affecting surrounding regions.

To create the CMYK page edges, he used Freehand and then imported the image into Photoshop to add color and shadows. Once he perfected the various design elements, he reloaded the masks and high-resolution versions of the images, and used Photoshop's painting tools to blend them together.

**16** Marc created this intriguing cover for *Art Direction* magazine by first scanning a circuit board. With green selected as the foreground color and lavendar as the background color, he used the Gradient tool to fill the circuit board with a linear blend. To produce the bottom part of the background, he made a rectangular selection using the Rectangular Marquee, then filled the area using the Gradient tool to create a black-to-purple linear blend.

Marc then scanned a black-and-white picture of a jar from an old medical catalog and an engraving of a man's face. Once the face was scanned, Marc colorized it using the Edit/Fill command's Darken mode. The Darken mode painted only the white areas and left the black areas untouched. He then selected the face and saved it to an alpha channel.

Using the Magic Wand tool, Marc selected two different portions in the jar and filled one with blue. He pasted the face inside the other selection by using the Edit/Paste Into command. When the jar was completed, he selected and pasted it into the final image. To create the reflection of the face, Marc returned to the original scanned image and loaded the selection from the alpha channel. He then copied and pasted it into the final image using a 50% Opacity setting. While the face was still selected, he applied the Ripple filter. This same technique was used on the reflection of the pen. To achieve the blend from yellow to pink in the pen, the Gradient tool was used with the Darken mode selected so that the black areas were not affected.

14

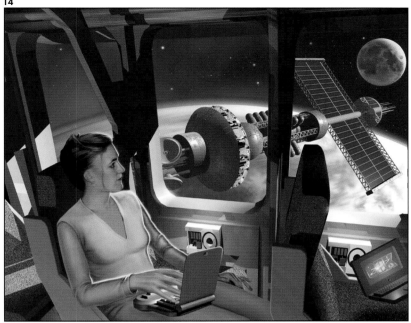

14
**Artist:** George H. Krauter
**Client:** ANALOG Science Fiction
and Fact Magazine

15
**Artist:** Daniel Clark
**Client:** Raging Fingers

16
**Artist:** Marc Yankus
**Client:** Art Direction Magazine

15

16

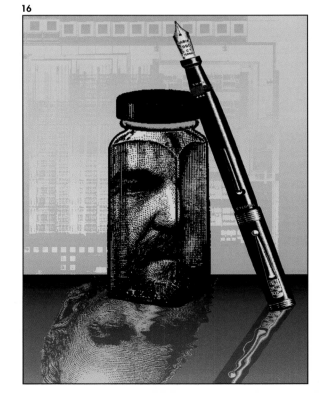

# The Photoshop Portfolio

**17**
Paul created this intricate three-dimensional image of a space station for the museum in Ontario, Canada, using both StrataVision and Photoshop. Since the size of the final file was fairly large, Paul selected and copied individual areas and pasted them into new files where he could work more efficiently. After he completed work on one area, he reselected it, and then copied and pasted it back into position in the original file.

He created the 3-D renderings in StrataVision. The StrataVision file was saved in TIFF format and then imported into Photoshop. In Photoshop, he touched-up the 3-D renderings, adjusted colors, and added details. He also used Photoshop to create the texture maps that were applied to the 3-D shapes in StrataVision.

**18**
This humorous animal balancing act was created from several photographs taken by Howard Berman. With the assistance of a professional animal handler, Howard took at least two photographs each of the dog and the cat in different positions. Separate photos were taken of the fish and the fish bowl. The fish were shot in a calm, stable fish tank and the fish bowl was shot while water was being splashed in it. The two birds that look like parrots are actually one bird, a canary, that was enlarged in the computer to look like a parrot. The bird and the wheel, which was made by a model maker, were photographed separately. The ball under the dog was shot and then enlarged in Photoshop. After the photographs were taken, they were scanned, then copied and pasted by Bob Bowen and Frank Lance at R/GA Print using the selection tools and alpha channels. The shadow was created using the selection tools and the Image/Adjust submenu's Levels and Curves commands.

**19**
Ruth Kedar, former art director of Adobe Systems, created this surreal image as a promotional piece to demonstrate filter effects for Andromeda Software. Ruth started by creating a new CMYK Color file. To create the background, she used the Gradient tool to produce several vertical color blends. She then created an alpha channel in which she applied an Andromeda Designs filter. Next, Ruth scanned a grayscale photograph of a child. She used various selection tools and the Quick Mask mode to separate the child from its background, then copied and pasted the image into the CMYK Color file. To colorize the child's hair, Ruth selected it, feathered it with the Select/Feather command, and then filled it with a reddish-brown color. The bubbles were created using the Andromeda cMulti filter. They were selected using the Elliptical Marquee, then duplicated and scaled using the Image/Effects/Scale command. Each bubble was colorized using the Image/Adjust/Color Balance command. Next, the Andromeda Prism filter was applied to create the look of multiple floating bubbles. Ruth's final touch was to paste one of the bubbles on top of the child's hand. When she pasted the bubble, she used a 60% Opacity setting to create the illusion that the child is indeed blowing bubbles.

**17**

**17**
**Artist:** Paul Cosby
**Client:** National Museum of
Science and Technology

**18**
**Artist:** R/GA Print
**Client:** Computer Associates

**19**
**Artist:** Ruth Kedar
**Client:** Andromeda Software

**18**

**19**

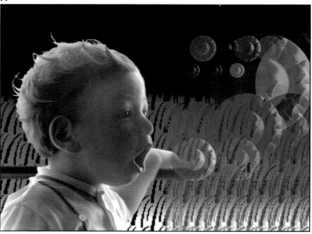

# The Photoshop Portfolio

**20** José created this image by first using a scratchboard and a blade to create black-and-white line art. He scanned it into Photoshop and then used the Pencil tool to touch up the black lines. In order to paint the image, he converted the black-and-white file into a CMYK Color file. Next, he selected the image with the Rectangular Marquee and used the Lighten mode in the Edit/Fill dialog box to fill only the black lines with red. To complete the colorization, he used the Paint Bucket tool to fill the various white areas.

The Pencil and Paint Bucket tools are covered in Chapter 5.

**21** Pamela created this appealing image using both Photoshop and Freehand. She first scanned a photograph of an Absolut vodka bottle and then selected one side of it with the Rectangular Marquee. Using the Image/Map/Invert command, she inverted the selection which turned the light portions of the bottle dark and the dark portions light. After the bottle image was completed, the file was saved in an EPS format and then imported into Freehand. Using Freehand, she began painting all of the images around the bottle.

Saving in different file formats so you can export Photoshop files to other programs is covered in Appendix A.

**22** Adele began this image by creating a black-and-white still life with pencils and markers. She scanned the image in as a color file and then applied color to the plants using the Paintbrush tool and a Wacom stylus and tablet. Then she selected the window area with the selection tools and created a mask using the Quick Mask mode. Once the area was masked, Adele saved the selection to an alpha channel. She then loaded the selection and pasted a digitized photograph of a sky and mountains into the masked area using the Edit/Paste Into command. The Image/Effects/Scale command was then used to slightly distort the perspective.

To add depth to the image, Adele used StrataVision to create the cubes and textures, which were saved as TIFF files. The two cubes were positioned into the final image using the Rubber Stamp tool's Cloning option. Selections of the wall and vase were created, saved to alpha channels, and then loaded before the textures were pasted into them. The shadow of the vase was produced by converting a Pen path into a selection, then filling it with 20% black.

**20**

**21**

**22**

**20**
**Artist:** José Ortega
**Client:** Money Magazine

**21**
**Artist:** Pamela Hobbs
**Client:** Carallion Importers

**22**
**Artist:** Adele Droblas Greenberg
**Client:** AD. Design and Consulting

# The Photoshop Portfolio

The color separations for this insert were produced by the New York City office of Applied Graphics Technologies, Inc. (AGT), a prepress house with offices throughout the United States. The authors asked them to create the separations because of AGT's reputation for high-quality output and extensive experience with Photoshop.

The layout with the high-resolution images was created in QuarkXPress and proofed by the authors on a Tektronix Phase IISDX dye-sublimation printer. Once the layout was approved, it was supplied to AGT. Since many of the color images were RGB Color files, AGT needed to convert them to CMYK Color. When converting, AGT used its own customized separation table. Images that were supplied as chromes were digitized on a Dupont Crosfield drum scanner.

Once all of the images were digitized and the RGB Color files converted to CMYK Color, AGT created proofs using its Kodak Approval Digital Color proofing system. After the proofs were analyzed, several were color-corrected. The final separations were output on a Scitex Dolev 400 imagesetter at a resolution of 2,540 dpi, and then proofed with 3M matchprints.

If you would like to contact Applied Graphics Technologies, the company has offices in Foster City, Glendale, and Los Angeles, CA; Boulder, CO; Washington, DC; Detroit, MI; Carlstadt and Moonacie, NJ; and New York City, Oceanside, and Rochester, NY.

*color evokes a mood*

*creates contrast*

*enhances the beauty*

*can make a tired image*

*suddenly sparkle with life*

# UNDERSTANDING
# COLOR THEORY

Color evokes a mood; it creates contrast and enhances the beauty in an image. It can make a dull scene vibrant and a tired image suddenly sparkle with life.

To the graphic designer, painter, artist, or video producer, creating the perfect color is essential. When the colors aren't correct, the concept isn't complete; the image may fail to convey its information and the artistic experience may be lost. If the rich green that should radiate from a forest setting is too yellow and sickly, the magnificence of nature is not portrayed, and the "healthy" feeling of the great outdoors is lost. If the forest's reds that should glow with fire and vibrance turn dull, a sense of decay and rust is conveyed, rather than excitement.

Producing the perfect color is no easy task. A painter must mix and remix paint, blending to get the perfect shades to match images seen or imagined. Photographers and filmmakers must spend hours testing, refocusing, and adding lights until the proper scene is created. In many respects, working with color on the computer is no different. The computer creates its own set of special complications and technical difficulties. How can you ensure that the colors you see on your screen match the colors of nature or your artistic vision? And then how do you get the same colors you see on screen to appear in your printed image?

Producing the right colors in Photoshop requires a knowledge of color theory. Once you understand the basics of color theory, you'll begin to recognize the color terminology used throughout Photoshop's dialog boxes, menus, and palettes. You'll also understand the process of adding and subtracting colors when you're doing color correcting. With a knowledge of color theory, you'll know how to paint the sky a richer, fuller blue. You'll be able to pick colors so that the same luscious emerald green you create in Photoshop appears in the forest on your printed page.

To be successful in choosing the right colors in Photoshop, you must first understand color models. *Color models* were created to provide a way of translating colors into numerical data so that they can be described consistently in various media. For instance, referring to a color as "greenish-blue" leaves it open to interpretation based largely on personal human perception. On the other hand, assigning that color specific values in a color model—in the CMYK model it would be 100% cyan, 3% magenta, 30% yellow, and 15% black—makes it possible to reproduce that color the same way, again and again.

As you use Photoshop's color features, you'll work with several different color models: RGB, CMYK, HSB, and Lab. The RGB and CMYK color models are a constant reminder that the colors of nature, the colors on your monitor, and colors on the printed page are created in completely different ways. Your monitor creates colors by emitting red, green, and blue beams of light; it uses the RGB (red/green/blue) color model. To reproduce the continuous-tone effect of color photographs, printing technology uses a combination of cyan, magenta, yellow, and black inks that reflect and absorb various wavelengths of light. Colors created by overprinting these four colors are part of the CMYK (cyan/magenta/yellow/black) color model. The HSB (hue/saturation/brightness) color model provides an intuitive way to translate the colors of nature to the colors your computer creates because it is based on the way humans perceive colors. The Lab color model provides a means for creating "device-independent" color, meaning that Lab colors shouldn't vary, regardless of the monitor or printer used.

## WHAT IS COLOR?

Color exists because of three entities: light, the object being viewed, and the viewer. Physicists have proven that white light is composed of wavelengths of red, green, and blue. The human eye perceives color as various wavelengths of red, green, and blue that are absorbed or reflected by objects. For example, assume you are at a picnic on a sunny day, ready to reach for a red apple. Sunlight shines on the apple and the red wavelength of light is reflected off the apple back to your eyes. The wavelengths of blue and green are absorbed into the apple, as shown in Figure 4-1. Sensors in your eye react to the reflected light, sending a message that is interpreted by your brain as the color red.

Your perception of the red color depends upon the apple, the light, and you. One apple will absorb more green and blue than another, and thus its color will appear redder. If clouds cover the sun, the apple's red will appear darker. Your interpretation of the apple will also be affected by your own physiology, by your experience as an apple eater, or by the fact that you haven't eaten all day.

The apple absorbs the green and blue wavelengths; the red wavelength is reflected back to the eye

**FIGURE 4-1**

The red, green, and blue wavelengths that allow you to see the apple are the basis for all colors in nature. That is why red, green, and blue are often called the *primary colors* of light. All colors of the spectrum are created by different intensities of these wavelengths of light. Figure 4-2 (reproduced on the "Color Theory" page of the first color insert in this book) is a simple example of how different colors can be created with the primary red, green, and blue wavelengths. When the three primary colors overlap, they create the secondary colors: cyan, magenta, and yellow. The primary and secondary colors are complements of one another. *Complementary colors* are colors that are most unlike each other. In Figure 4-2 you can see that yellow is made up of red and green. Blue is the missing primary color; therefore, blue and yellow are complements. The complement of green is magenta, and the complement of red is cyan. This explains why you see other colors besides red, green, and blue. In a sunflower, you see yellow because red and green wavelengths of light are reflected back to you, while the blue is absorbed by the plant.

Figure 4-2 also shows that all primary colors combine to create white. You might think that adding these colors together would produce a darker color, but remember that you are adding *light*. When light wavelengths are added together, you get lighter colors. This is why the primary colors are often called *additive* colors. By adding all of the colors of light together, you obtain the lightest light: white light. Thus, when you see a white piece of paper, all of the red, green, and blue wavelengths of

The primary (additive) colors and their complements. When all three primary colors are mixed together, they create white

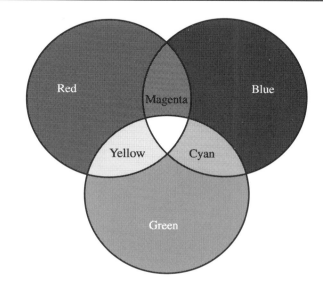

**FIGURE 4-2**

light are being reflected back to you. When you see black, all of the red, green, and blue wavelengths of light are being completely absorbed by the object; thus no light is reflected back to you.

## THE RGB COLOR MODEL

The system of creating colors on your monitor is based on the same fundamental properties of light that occur in nature: that colors can be created from red, green, and blue. This is the basis of the RGB color model.

Your color monitor creates colors by emitting three light beams at different intensities, lighting up red, green, and blue phosphorescent material overlaying the inside of your monitor's screen. When you see red in Photoshop, your monitor has turned on its red beam, which excites red phosphors, lighting up a red pixel on your screen. Thus, seeing a scanned image of an apple on screen is different from seeing the apple that sits on top of your computer, waiting to be eaten. If you turn off the lights in your room, you won't see your red snack; but you'll still see the scanned apple, because light is being emitted from your monitor.

In Photoshop's RGB color model, pixel colors can be changed by combining various values of red, green, and blue. Each of these three primary colors has a range of values from 0 to 255. When you combine the 256 possible values of red, 256 values of green, and 256 values of blue, the total number of possible colors is approximately 16.7 million (256×256×256). This may seem like a lot of colors, but remember that these are only a portion of the visible colors in nature. Nevertheless, 16.7 million colors is sufficient to reproduce crystal-clear digitized images on a monitor connected to a computer equipped with 24-bit color.

### Using RGB Colors in the Picker and Swatches Palettes

In this section, you'll experiment with RGB color in the Picker and Swatches palettes. You'll see how colors are created from RGB color values, and learn how to set RGB color values to mix colors. If the Picker and Swatches palettes aren't open, open the Picker/Swatches/Scratch group now by choosing Show Picker from the Window/Palette submenu. Since you will need to see both palettes open at the same time, separate the Picker palette from the Picker/Swatches/Scratch group by clicking on the Picker palette tab and dragging it away from the palette group. If the Swatches palette isn't in the palette group with the Picker palette, choose Show Swatches from the Window/Palette submenu.

By default, the Picker palette will display the RGB color model palette, unless it was changed in a previous session. You should see three bars, called *color sliders*, labeled R, G, and B. If you do not see the letters R, G, and B, you are in another color model's palette. To change to the RGB palette, click on the Picker palette pop-up menu arrow. A list of Photoshop's color models will appear. Select RGB Sliders from the list, and the palette with the three RGB sliders will load. Beneath each slider is a triangular-shaped slider *control*. Using the mouse, you can click and drag on the slider controls to change the values of red, green, and blue in the foreground or background color. The foreground and background colors are indicated in the selection boxes (the overlapping squares in the upper-right corner of the Picker palette).

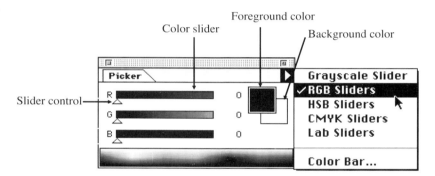

Notice that the Picker palette also displays a horizontal color bar along the bottom of the palette. By default the bar displays the spectrum, or *gamut*, of RGB colors. Check to see that the bar is set to the RGB spectrum by clicking on the palette's pop-up menu arrow and choosing Color Bar. The Color Bar dialog box appears.

The Style pop-up menu in the dialog box allows you to choose between RGB and CMYK color spectrum bars. You can also make the Color Bar display gray shades from black to white or a gradient from the foreground to background color. If the Style menu is not set to RGB Spectrum, reset it now by choosing RGB Spectrum from the list of choices.

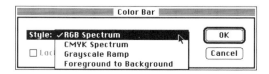

The Color Bar can be used to quickly pick a foreground or background color. All you have to do is click on the bar. However, in the next section, you'll pick colors more precisely by using the Swatches palette.

**OTE:** *Selecting the Foreground to Background Style in the Color Bar dialog box activates the Lock to Current Colors check box. When this option is selected, the Foreground to Background color bar in the Picker palette won't change when a new foreground or background color is selected.*

## Using Swatches to Pick Colors

Start by clicking on the red, green, and blue color squares, or swatches, in the Swatches palette, and examine the color values of the primary colors. This will demonstrate the full range of each color component in the RGB color model. When you click on a swatch, Photoshop displays the swatch color in either the Foreground or Background selection box, as well as displaying its R, G, and B values to the right of the sliders, in the Picker palette.

**OTE:** *In order to see the foreground or background colors in each slider, Photoshop's Dynamic Sliders option must be activated. When the Dynamic Sliders option is activated, each slider displays the current foreground or background color above the slider control. Also, each slider shows the range of colors available when you click and drag the slider control left or right. If the Dynamic Sliders option is not enabled, each slider will only show color values for red, green, or blue color components. To enable Dynamic Sliders, choose General from the File/Preferences submenu. In the General Preferences dialog box, click on the More button. In the More Preferences dialog box, select the Dynamic Sliders check box.*

In this exercise, you will only work with Photoshop's foreground color. Before you begin, make sure that the Foreground selection box (the top overlapping square to the right of the sliders in the Picker palette) is activated. If the white band is not surrounding the Foreground selection box, click on that box to activate the foreground color.

To see the RGB values of the primary color red, position the mouse pointer over the red color swatch in the upper-left corner of the color swatches, in the first row. When the pointer turns into an eyedropper, click on the red swatch.

In the Picker palette, notice that the R slider control jumps to the far right. The number to the right of the slider indicates the red value of the color swatch you just clicked. (If you clicked the correct shade of red, the value will be 255.) The active color in Photoshop (the foreground color) has now changed to this value of red. Take a look at the sliders for green and blue; they are both at 0, because the shade of red you clicked contains no green or blue.

To see the RGB values of the primary color green, click on the green swatch (the third from the left in the first row in the Swatches palette). The G value in the Picker palette jumps to 255, and the values of blue and red drop to 0. To see the values of the primary color blue, click on the fifth swatch from the left in the first row in the Swatches palette. Pure blue's value is 255, with no red and no green.

You can see from the foregoing color swatch tests that each primary color has a range of values from 0 to 255, to produce 256 separate color values.

## Using Sliders to Create RGB Colors

Now that you've seen the color values of pure red, green, and blue, take a look at some colors created from the primaries. Click on any swatch in the Swatches palette, and you'll see its combination of RGB color values. Try the yellowish color, the one four rows down and four rows across. Notice the combination of values: R 255, G 236, and B 103. Click on a few of the other color swatches, and notice the combinations of the three primary colors.

The palette swatches obviously can't contain all 16.7 million colors, but by adjusting the slider controls with the mouse, you can create every one of the 16.7 million colors Photoshop can display.

All three sliders work in the same manner. When you click and drag a slider control to the right, you are adding more color. When you drag left, you are subtracting color. With any color swatch selected, try dragging the G slider control from left to right. Notice that as you drag to the right, the green values increase, and the foreground color you are creating in the Picker palette grows brighter. Now drag left; as you do, the color values decrease and the green gets darker.

To create black, drag all of the slider controls to the left, setting them to 0. Watch as the foreground color in the Picker palette grows darker. When all of the values reach 0, the foreground color displays black. If red, green, and blue are equal in value but are not 0 or 255, a shade of gray is created. To create white, move the slider controls in the opposite direction. By doing this you are adding light. Set each slider to its full value of 255, and you'll create white.

## Using the Sliders to Display RGB Complements

If you are using the Dynamic Sliders option, you'll see a range of colors displayed in each slider when all of the RGB sliders are set to 255. The R slider displays white turning to cyan; the G slider displays white changing to magenta; and the B slider displays white changing to yellow.

Why do the sliders change colors? The designers of Photoshop are shrewdly reminding you about color theory. In each slider, you see the opposite of each primary color (its *complement*). The color towards the left end of each slider is showing you what happens if you subtract a primary color from white (by dragging the slider control all the way to the left). Remember the discussion earlier in the chapter of why you see yellow when you look at a sunflower? The sunflower absorbs (subtracts) the blue wavelength of light. When red and green are reflected back to you, you see yellow.

You can easily demonstrate this with the sliders. To create yellow, which is the complement of blue, drag the B slider control back to 0, and leave the R and G sliders set to 255. Thus yellow is created by subtracting blue from white.

To create cyan, which is red's complement, first set all the sliders back to 255, and then drag the R slider control to 0. By subtracting the red value from the primary colors, you have created cyan.

To create magenta, the complement of green, drag the R slider control back to 255 and the G slider control to 0. Magenta is created by subtracting green from the primary colors.

This concept of subtracting colors is the foundation of the CMYK color model, described in the following section.

# THE CMYK COLOR MODEL

The CMYK color model is based not on adding light, but on subtracting it. In the RGB model, colors were created by adding light; the monitor (or a television) is a light source that can create colors. But a printed page doesn't emit light; it absorbs and reflects light. So when you want to translate the monitor's colors to paper, another color model, CMYK, must be used. The CMYK color model is the basis for *four-color process* printing, which is used primarily to print continuous-tone images (such as digitized photographs) on a printing press. In four-color process printing, colors are reproduced on a printing press by using four different printing plates; C (cyan), M (magenta), Y (yellow), and K (black—black is represented by the letter K because B might also stand for blue).

Because the printed page cannot emit light, a press cannot use RGB colors to print; instead, it uses inks that can absorb specific wavelengths of light and reflect other wavelengths. By combining inks of cyan, magenta, and yellow, a commercial printer can reproduce a significant portion of the visible spectrum of colors. In theory, 100% cyan, 100% magenta, and 100% yellow should combine to produce black. However, because of the impurity of inks, the cyan, magenta, and yellow colors produce a muddy brown rather than black. Therefore, printers often add black to cyan, magenta, and yellow to produce the darker and gray portions of images. Figure 4-3 (reproduced on the "Color Theory" page of the first color insert in this book) shows the subtractive colors overlapping to create a muddy brown. Notice that each two subtractive colors creates a primary color.

## Using CMYK Colors in the Picker Palette

To introduce you to the CMYK color model, start by switching to the CMYK color spectrum. To do this click on the Picker palette's pop-up menu arrow, then choose Color Bar from the pop-up list. When the Color Bar dialog box opens, choose CMYK Spectrum from the Style pop-up menu. You'll probably notice that the CMYK colors are a bit duller than the RGB colors.

The secondary (subtractive) colors and their complements. When all three secondary colors are mixed together, they create a muddy brown

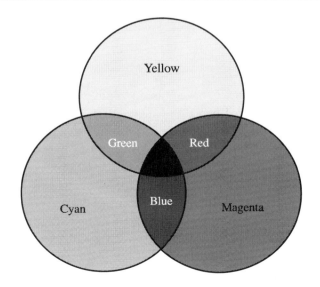

**FIGURE 4-3**

Now take a look at how to change colors using the CMYK sliders in the Picker palette. First you'll need to switch to the CMYK color sliders by clicking on the Picker palette's pop-up menu arrow. Mac users drag to the CMYK Sliders choice (PC users: click on CMYK Sliders).

In the Picker palette you'll also see some differences between the RGB and CMYK palettes. First, CMYK utilizes four sliders, not three. There is a slider for each *subtractive* color: C for cyan, M for magenta, Y for yellow, and K for black. Also, the colors are measured in percentages. The percentages provide a standard way of conveying various ink values from the design studio to the printing press.

Using CMYK percentages can be confusing, but it helps to understand that you can produce the primary colors using CMYK percentages. When you know how to produce red, green, and blue from CMYK values, you'll be better able to orient yourself when mixing colors or correcting color in this color model. To aid you in creating these colors, it's helpful to have a color wheel at hand. The color wheel shown in Figure 4-4 (reproduced on the "Color Theory" page of the first color insert in this book) is a simplified version of the color wheels professional color correctors use to help them add and subtract colors.

In a color wheel, colors are arranged in a circle to show the relationship between each color. The primary colors are positioned around the circle equidistant from one another. Each secondary color is situated between two primary colors. In this

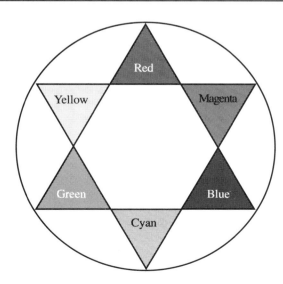

The color wheel

**FIGURE 4-4**

arrangement, each color is directly opposite its complement, and each color on the wheel is situated between the two colors that are used to create it.

By studying the wheel, you can see that adding yellow and magenta creates red. If you subtract both yellow and magenta, you remove red. Thus, if you want to subtract red from an image, you decrease the percentages of yellow and magenta. Another point to realize about the color wheel is that when you are adding color to an image, you are subtracting its complement. For instance, when you are making an image redder, you are decreasing the percentage of cyan (which is red's complement, directly opposite it in the color wheel).

## Using Sliders to Create CMYK Colors

Now you'll practice using both the color wheel and the CMYK sliders to create red, green, and blue. This simple exercise will demonstrate how CMYK inks absorb different light waves and reflect others to produce colors, as shown in Figure 4-5.

To create red, drag magenta and yellow to 100%, and leave cyan and black at 0%. Notice that red is between yellow and magenta on the color wheel. When you see red in an image printed using four-color process printing, this indicates that yellow and magenta inks have combined to absorb the blue and green wavelengths of light. The result is the color red.

To create green, drag yellow and cyan to 100%, and put magenta and black at 0%. Green is between yellow and cyan on the color wheel. When you see green in an image printed using four-color process printing, yellow and cyan inks have combined to absorb the blue and red wavelengths of light.

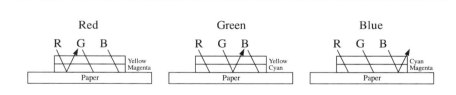

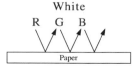

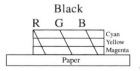

Wavelenths of light, absorbed and reflected

**FIGURE 4-5**

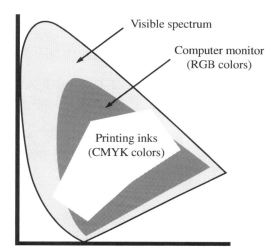

Visible spectrum

Computer monitor
(RGB colors)

Printing inks
(CMYK colors)

Visible
color
spectrums
(gamuts)
for the
RGB and
CMYK
color
models

**FIGURE 4-6**

**4**

To create blue, drag cyan and magenta to 100%, and yellow and black to 0%. Blue is between cyan and magenta on the color wheel. When you see blue in an image printed using four-color process printing, cyan and magenta inks have combined to absorb red and green wavelengths of light.

Now try experimenting with the sliders to create additional CMYK colors. If you have a swatch book displaying CMYK percentages and the colors they produce, use the sliders to re-create a few of these colors, and see how close the screen color comes to the real thing.

**OTE:** *If you're interested in creating and printing four-color separations, your file mode must be CMYK Color. See Chapters 9 and 14 for more information.*

### The Out-of-Gamut Alert

Before you leave the CMYK color model and move on to the next section, it's important to realize that the color spectrum of the RGB and CMYK color models are different. The professional term for the visible color range of a color model is *gamut*. The gamut of RGB is larger than that of CMYK, as shown in Figure 4-6.

Therefore, if you only work with RGB color on your computer, be aware that you may be designing and editing with onscreen colors that cannot be printed.

 Fortunately, Photoshop provides a warning when you overstep the bounds of printable colors. You may even have already noticed this warning: it's a small Alert symbol—a triangle with an exclamation mark inside—that appears in the Picker palette. Even when you are working with CMYK sliders, you can still activate the Alert feature by clicking on any of the first six color swatches from the left in the top row.

For example, click on the red swatch in the top row of the Swatches palette. The Alert will immediately appear, indicating that this color is beyond the CMYK gamut. If you click on the Alert, Photoshop will select the nearest printable color. Try clicking the Alert now; the closest printable red will be displayed as the foreground color. But even though Photoshop is showing you that the red is printable, it is only displaying an RGB monitor's simulation of red. Never assume that the color you see on screen is an exact representation of the printed color.

**NOTE:** *If you are in a CMYK color file and try to paint with an out-of-gamut color, Photoshop will convert it to the nearest printable color. Photoshop can also preview all out-of-gamut colors before an RGB color image is converted to CMYK colors. See Chapter 9 for more information.*

**NOTE:** *If you are outputting your work to slides or video, you needn't worry about the out-of-gamut Alert, because slides and video use RGB colors. The Alert indicates that the color cannot be created by commercial printers' inks.*

## THE HSB COLOR MODEL

Although both RGB and CMYK are essential color models for computer graphics and printing, many designers and graphic artists find it unnecessarily complicated to try to mix colors using values or percentages of other colors. Using a color wheel helps, but neither RGB nor CMYK is very intuitive. The human mind doesn't divide up colors into models of red/green/blue or cyan/magenta/yellow/black. To make such choices easier, a third color model—HSB (hue/saturation/brightness)—was created.

HSB is based on human perception of colors, rather than the computer values of RGB or printers' percentages of CMYK. The human eye sees colors as components of hue, saturation, and brightness.

Think of hues as the colors you can see on a color wheel. In technical terms, *hue* is based upon the wavelength of light reflected from an object, or transmitted through it. *Saturation*, often called chroma, is the amount of gray in a color. The higher the saturation, the lower the gray content and the more intense the color. *Brightness* is a measure of the intensity of light in a color.

## Using HSB Sliders in the Picker Palette

Let's take a look at how to choose colors using the HSB color model. In the Picker palette, click on the pop-up menu arrow and choose HSB Sliders. You'll see three sliders: H for changing hue values, measured in degrees; S for saturation, and B for brightness, both measured in percentages. As with the sliders in the other two color models, you move through the different hue, saturation, and brightness values by clicking and dragging the slider controls.

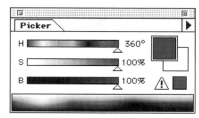

Try this now by clicking and dragging the H slider control to the right. As you move through different degrees of hue, the Foreground or Background selection boxes in the Picker palette will display the same colors that you would see if you were traveling the perimeter of a color wheel. When you reach 360 degrees, you'll see the same red that is displayed when you are at 0 degrees because you are traveling around the circumference of a circle.

The major color values of hue, with saturation and brightness set to 100%, are as follows:

| Color | Hue Setting |
|-------|-------------|
| Red | 0 or 360° |
| Yellow | 60° |
| Green | 120° |
| Cyan | 180° |
| Blue | 240° |
| Magenta | 300° |

Now we'll experiment with changing saturation and brightness to other percentages and see how they affect the color red.

### Changing Saturation and Brightness

To follow along with the next steps in this exercise using the HSB color model, start by selecting the red color swatch in the first row of the color swatches in the Swatches palette.

Let's begin by observing the effects of changing the saturation percentage for the red color. Move the S slider control. The intensity of the red will diminish as you decrease saturation by dragging the slider control to the left. Try it, and you'll move from red to light red to pink. When you reach 0%, the red will have changed to white.

**n OTE:**  *You cannot create white and black with the hue slider. To create white, the saturation slider control must be set to 0% and the brightness slider control to 100%. To create black, the saturation slider control must be set to 0% and the brightness slider control to 0%.*

Before you test the brightness slider, click and drag saturation back to 100%, to give you a reference point for observing the effects of changing brightness. Dragging the brightness control to the left will decrease the percentage of color brightness, dragging to the right will increase the brightness.

Try it now: Drag the B slider control to the left, and you'll see that red gradually darkens. When you reach 0%, the red will have turned to black. To bring brightness back to the red, drag the control back toward 100%.

If you wish, continue to experiment with the HSB color sliders by picking a hue and then adjusting its saturation and brightness. It probably won't take long before you agree that HSB is the easiest of the color models to use, because it's the most intuitive. There's less guesswork involved in color creation when you don't have to worry about mixing other colors together. You may even decide to do all of your work in the HSB model—particularly if you're going to use Photoshop as a painting program and will not be creating output for four-color printing.

## THE LAB COLOR MODEL

One more color model remains to be explored. Though it's not used as frequently in Photoshop as the RGB, CMYK, and HSB color models, the Lab color model is worth investigating, particularly because it may prove helpful in certain color editing situations. When you learn about changing modes in Chapter 9, you'll see that Lab color can be used when editing Photo CD images and when outputting to PostScript Level-2 printers.

Although you may never need to use Lab color, this color model is vital to Photoshop. Lab is the internal color model that Photoshop uses to convert from one color mode to another. In Chapter 9, you'll learn how to change modes from RGB to CMYK so that you can produce a four-color separation. When Photoshop converts from RGB to CMYK, it first converts to Lab color, then from Lab to CMYK. One reason why it uses Lab is because the Lab color gamut encompasses both the color gamuts of RGB and CMYK.

The Lab color model is based upon the work of the Commission Internationale de l'Eclairage that was formed in the early 1900s to try to standardize color measurement. The commission designed a color model based upon how color is perceived by the eye. In 1976, the original color model was refined and called CIE Lab. It was created to provide consistent colors, no matter what monitor or printer is being used; this is called *device-independent color*. Device-independent color isn't affected by the characteristics or idiosyncrasies of any piece of hardware.

## Using Lab Sliders in the Picker Palette

You might wonder why you should know anything about the Lab color model, if Photoshop uses it internally. The reason is that Lab divides colors using an approach different from that of RGB, CMYK, and HSB, and gives you another perspective to editing colors: the Lab model comprises a lightness, or luminance, factor and two color axes.

Take a look at Lab color in the Picker palette. Click on the pop-up menu arrow and switch to Lab Sliders. You'll see three sliders, labeled L, a, and b. The L slider allows you to change a color's lightness, in values from 0 to 100. The a slider represents an axis of colors ranging from green to magenta; and the b slider is an axis of colors ranging from blue to yellow. The values accessible from both axes are −120 to 120. 100 at L, a at 0, and b at 0 create white.

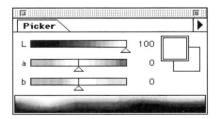

Lab is useful if all you wish to do is change the lightness of a color. Also, if you need to change only the red and green components of a color, or the blue and yellow components, you can click and drag on the Lab slider controls to do this.

To see how the Lab sliders affect color, start with the L slider control set all the way to the right at 100. This provides the brightest levels for the colors you will be creating.

To see how the a slider changes colors from green to magenta, set the b slider to 0. Then, click and drag on the a slider control, moving first to the right, then to the left. As you drag the a slider control to the left, the color will turn to green. Now drag the a slider control to the right to see the color change to magenta. When you are done, leave the control in the middle of the a slider (set to 0). This will best enable you to see the effects of changing the b slider.

Now observe how the b slider changes colors from blue to yellow by clicking and dragging the slider control. First drag it to the right, and the color will turn to yellow. Drag to the left to see the color change to blue.

If you wish to keep experimenting, try clicking and dragging on the L slider control to see how lowering the L value darkens colors.

## THE COLOR PICKER DIALOG BOX

Now that you've examined each of the color models in the Picker palette, take a look at Photoshop's Color Picker dialog box. The Color Picker provides another tool for picking foreground and background colors. The chief differences between the Color Picker dialog box and the Picker palette are that the Color Picker allows you to see the values of all four color models (RGB, CMYK, HSB and Lab) at the same time, and you can enter specific values for most color settings. The Color Picker also lets you access color-matching systems such as PANTONE and TRUMATCH.

To access the Color Picker, click on the Foreground Color or Background Color icon in the Toolbox. You may also open the Color Picker from the Picker palette, by clicking on either the Foreground or Background selection box. If the Foreground selection box is activated, changing settings in the Color Picker will affect the foreground color. If the Background selection box is selected, your settings change the background color.

Take a look at the Color Picker in action. Start by accessing the Color Picker dialog box from the Picker palette to change the foreground color. Here's how: Make sure the Picker palette is set to change the foreground color; a white band should surround the Foreground selection box in the upper-right of the palette. If the white band surrounds the Background selection box instead, click the Foreground selection box to activate it. Then click it again to display the Color Picker dialog box, as shown in Figure 4-7.

**OTE:** *The Color Picker will not appear if you have switched to either the Apple or Windows color picker in the General Preferences dialog box. If you use either the Apple or the Windows color picker, be aware that neither alerts you when you are picking unprintable colors. To switch back to Photoshop's Color Picker, select Preferences in the File menu and then click General from the submenu. In the Color Picker pop-up menu, click and choose Photoshop.*

## Exploring the Color Picker

You'll notice that all of the color models—RGB, CMYK, HSB, and Lab—are included in the Color Picker dialog box, with entry fields where you can type values for the various color components. Thus, if you know the precise CMYK values you

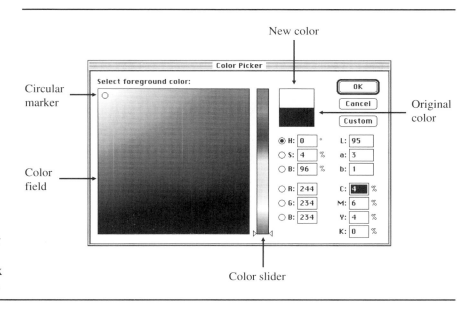

New color

Circular marker

Color field

Original color

Color slider

The Color Picker dialog box

**FIGURE 4-7**

want for an image, you can just type them in, rather than having to nudge the CMYK slider controls into position in the Picker palette.

**TIP:** *Before you start experimenting with the settings in the Color Picker dialog box, notice the color in the bottom half of the small box next to the top of the color slider. This box displays your original color. As you work, the top part of the box will change to show you the new color currently being edited (see Figure 4-7). The bottom portion of the square always remains the same. If you wish to return to the original color, you can click on the bottom of the square. This is a very handy "undo" feature.*

As you choose or edit colors, you can choose the color model that best suits your needs. For instance, suppose you need to add more green to an image that must be output in CMYK for process printing. If you were working in the CMYK model in the Picker palette, you might have to refer to a color wheel or try to figure out which sliders would add green. With the Color Picker, however, you can add green by simply entering a higher value into the G field of the RGB values.

Though the Color Picker doesn't provide sliders for all color models, it does offer one vertical slider that can be used for any of the RGB or HSB color components. You convert the slider's role by clicking on one of the radio buttons that appear to the left of the HSB and RGB value fields. For instance, if you click on the R radio button, the vertical slider lets you move through red values in the RGB color model. Click on the H radio button, and you can move through hue values.

The large colored square that occupies the entire left half of the Color Picker dialog box is called the *color field*. A small circular marker in the color field allows you to change color components by clicking on it and dragging the mouse. For instance, if you click on the H radio button, the vertical slider changes hue values; now clicking and dragging on the marker in the color field changes saturation and brightness. (Dragging the circle horizontally changes saturation; dragging vertically changes brightness.)

If you don't click and drag the circle, but instead click anywhere in the color field, the circular marker will jump to the new position. The values in the dialog box and the foreground or background color displayed will change accordingly.

If the Color Picker is confusing to you at first, imagine yourself in a three-dimensional version of the color model you are using. This is often called a color model's *color space*. Figure 4-8 (reproduced on the "Color Theory" page of

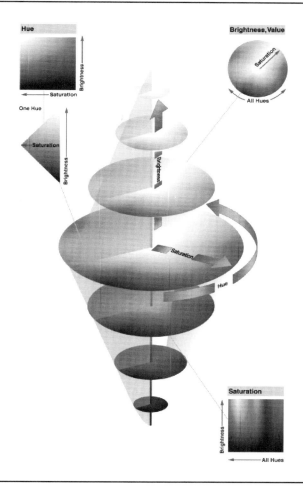

4

The HSB color model, in 3-D (courtesy of Agfa Corporation)

**FIGURE 4-8**

the first color insert in this book) illustrates a three-dimensional view of the HSB color model. As you are swimming in this three-dimensional pool of HSB colors, the hue levels change around the perimeter of the pool. The saturation levels change as you swim out to the middle of the pool. The brightness levels change as you dive deeper into the pool.

As you move along the edges of the pool, you pass through various hues. This is the equivalent of clicking and dragging on the vertical slider control with the Hue radio button selected, while viewing saturation and brightness in the color field. As you look across the water of the pool, you see the saturation and brightness values of each hue you pass through.

If you dive straight down along the edge of the pool, you pass through various levels of brightness. From your vantage point, you see the saturation and hue values of the colors according to your brightness depth. This is equivalent to clicking on the Brightness radio button while viewing saturation and hue in the color field.

Now imagine that you're swimming out to the middle of the pool, moving through the saturation levels of colors. Dive deeper and view the colors around you. The colors you see are similar to those in the color field when you clicked on the Saturation radio button.

## Changing Colors Using the Color Picker

Now try the Color Picker and see how you can use the combination of radio buttons, vertical slider, and value fields to change colors. Assume that you wish to edit a color by adding more green to it. First set the vertical slider to change green RGB values, by clicking on the G radio button.

When you drag the control for the vertical slider, you'll see that it functions much the same way as the horizontal sliders do in the RGB model. Dragging the slider control upward raises the green value, and dragging downward lowers it. Try this now: Click on the control and drag toward the top of the slider. As you drag higher, the green color value grows. Drag up to 255, and then back down. The highest value that appears in the G entry field is 255, and the lowest is 0.

When you clicked on the G radio button, the circular marker in the color field is set to change the R and B values of the RGB model. (If you had clicked on the R radio button, instead, the color field marker would change the G and B values of RGB; clicking on the B button makes the marker control the G and R values.) When the G radio button is selected, dragging the marker upward adds red to the color you are creating, and dragging to the right adds blue.

Experiment with the marker to see how the color field controls the R and B values. Click and drag the circular marker up. As you drag, notice that the value in the R field increases. As you drag down, it decreases. Now drag to the right; this causes blue levels to increase. Drag left, and the levels decrease. You can probably guess what happens if you drag diagonally—you can change both R and B values at the same time.

Now that you have oriented yourself in the Color Picker, can you guess how to create pure green? Drag the slider control all the way up to 255, and then drag the color field marker to the bottom-left corner of the color field. When your color changes to green, you'll see the same Alert sign that you saw in the Picker palette, again warning you that you are viewing an unprintable color. If you click on the Alert, Photoshop will choose the closest printable color for you.

If you'd like, you can continue to experiment with the Color Picker. As you grow accustomed to it, you may find yourself beginning to prefer it to the Picker palette. But don't give up on the Picker palette; you'll find more uses for it later in this chapter.

## ACCESSING CUSTOM COLORS FROM THE COLOR PICKER

An important feature in the Color Picker dialog box is the Custom button. This button allows you to choose colors using color-matching systems to make printed colors more predictable.

As you've worked through this chapter, you've become aware that it is often difficult to precisely translate colors displayed on your computer screen to the printed page. The problem is compounded by the fact that not all monitors are the same, not all inks are the same, and a printed page cannot completely reproduce the color sensation of the video monitor. Video colors often look brighter than their counterparts on the printed page.

One way to obtain a better idea of how the colors on your screen will print, or at least to better predict color output, is to pick colors not by how they look on the computer screen but by their appearance in a color swatch book—a book of many color samples printed on paper, used to label or classify colors.

Suppose you wish to print a blue border around an image. You could pick a blue from a swatch book and then choose that same blue color from Photoshop's Custom Colors dialog box. During the printing process, your commercial printer will be able to match the swatch's custom color when producing your image.

 **OTE:** *To accurately match colors, make sure that the colors in your swatch book have not faded.*

In deciding which swatch book to use, consider the following:

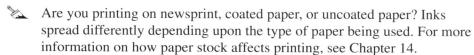

- Are you printing on newsprint, coated paper, or uncoated paper? Inks spread differently depending upon the type of paper being used. For more information on how paper stock affects printing, see Chapter 14.

- Are you using spot color (explained below) or four-color process colors?

The most commonly used color-matching system was created by PANTONE. It's important to understand that PANTONE has traditionally been used for *spot*-color printing, not in four-color separation work. Spot color is similar to printing an overlay, separate from any other color; this is quite different from four-color separation, where cyan, magenta, yellow, and black combine to create a color. In spot color, the printer mixes inks to create a matching color and prints that one color on an individual plate. This is fine for one or two colors but would be very expensive for multiple colors.

Spot colors can be used as "fifth" colors; this is a term used when a job is printed with the standard four-color process and needs a fifth color picked for a specific match of a certain color. Fifth colors are used to create silvers, coppers, golds, deep blues, and certain greens, because they can't be created with four-color inks. Although Photoshop does not directly support spot color, a technique for creating and printing spot colors is discussed in Chapter 11.

 **OTE:** *Second Glance of Laguna Hills, California, produces spot-color separation software for Photoshop called PhotoSpot.*

## Using Color-Matching Systems

In this section you'll learn how to use color-matching systems. Then you'll add a custom color to the Swatches palette and save the edited palette.

If the Color Picker isn't open, click on the Foreground Color icon in the Toolbox. The Color Picker dialog box will open. Click on the Custom button to open the Custom Colors dialog box.

**IP:** *Photoshop can search for a custom color that matches a color you have created with sliders or the Color Picker. First, the color you wish to match must be active in either the Foreground or the Background selection box. Then, access the Book pop-up menu from within the Custom Colors dialog box and select which swatch book (e.g., PANTONE, TRUMATCH) you want the match to come from. The Custom Colors dialog box then displays the custom color that most closely matches the color you created.*

### Selecting a Color-Matching System and a Color

To access a custom color, you first have to access the Book pop-up menu and choose an ink-matching system, as shown in Figure 4-9:

 *ANPA Color*   These colors are used for printing to newsprint.

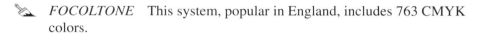

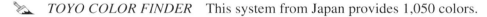

> *FOCOLTONE*   This system, popular in England, includes 763 CMYK colors.

> *PANTONE Coated, PANTONE Process, PANTONE ProSim, or PANTONE Uncoated*   Even though PANTONE is known primarily for its spot-color swatches, it also produces a process-color swatch set, PANTONE Process, with 3,006 CMYK combinations. PANTONE ProSim is a process-color simulation of spot (solid) colors. PANTONE Coated consists of spot (solid) colors printed on coated paper, and PANTONE Uncoated consists of spot (solid) colors printed on uncoated paper; uncoated colors are more muted than the coated colors.

**NOTE:** *PANTONE Color Systems Cross Reference is a stand-alone software utility that matches a chosen color from one PANTONE Color System to another. Pick a color, and Cross Reference finds the best match for spot-color and four-color process printing, plastics and textiles. The software even shows if a PANTONE by Letraset Color Marker and/or PANTONE by Letraset Color Paper can match the color you've selected.*

> *TOYO COLOR FINDER*   This system from Japan provides 1,050 colors.

> *TRUMATCH*   The TRUMATCH system uses strictly CMYK process colors. It has approximately 2,000 process colors, arranged according to hue, saturation, and brightness.

Once you've selected the color-matching system you want to use (for this exercise, choose PANTONE Process), you can select a color. To find a color you can either click the up or down arrow in the vertical slider of colors, or click anywhere within the slider, or type in a number on your keyboard. In Figure 4-9 we chose a reddish PANTONE color, number 73-1 by quickly typing 73 on our keyboard. Do this on your own computer, then click on PANTONE Process color 73-1 which will be selected on screen in the list of custom colors and in the swatch box. The vertical slider on screen will also be set to the custom color. (You can, however, select any color you want).

Click OK to close the Custom Colors dialog box. Notice that your foreground color has been changed to the PANTONE color (or the custom color) you selected. If you position the mouse pointer over the Foreground selection box in the Picker palette (without clicking), the title bar of the Picker palette tab will display the name of the PANTONE (or custom) color you picked.

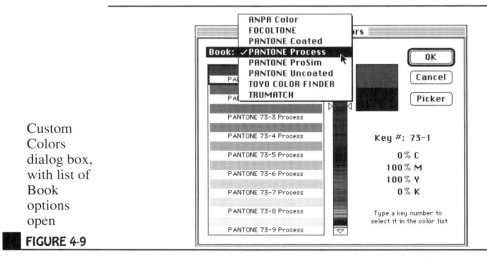

Custom
Colors
dialog box,
with list of
Book
options
open

**FIGURE 4-9**

**NOTE:** *If you intend to export your Photoshop file to any program that uses short PANTONE names, choose Short PANTONE names in the More Preferences dialog box before you select any PANTONE colors. To access the More Preferences dialog box, choose General from the File/Preferences submenu; then click on the More button.*

### Saving Custom Colors in the Swatches Palette

If you want to keep this custom color handy, you can add it to the swatches that appear in the Swatches palette.

To add a custom color, or any color, to the Swatches palette, position the mouse pointer in the white area to the right of the last color swatch in the Swatches palette. When the pointer turns into a paint bucket, click to create a swatch of your active color. To insert the custom color between two existing swatches, press and hold down SHIFT-OPTION (PC users: SHIFT-ALT) while you click on a swatch or between two swatches to insert the active custom color. To replace an existing swatch with the current foreground color, press SHIFT, then click on the swatch. Note that if the Background selection box (in the Swatches palette) is active, you will add a swatch of your background color to the Swatches palette.

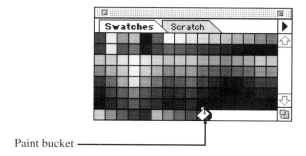

Paint bucket

**4**

To delete a swatch, position the mouse pointer over a swatch and press COMMAND (PC users: CTRL). When the pointer turns into a scissors, click and the swatch will be deleted.

## Saving Cutomized Palettes

You can continue to add your own custom colors to the Swatches palette and then save the palette so that you can access it at a later time. Just click on the pop-up menu arrow in the Swatches palette and choose Save Colors to open the Save dialog box.

It might be a good idea to save your custom palette in Photoshop's Color Palettes folder (PC users: palettes), so that all of your palettes are in the same place. For the filename, type **MyColors**, and then click Save (PC users: OK). You are now working in the Swatches palette called Mycolors.

| ⬆️ Color Palettes ▼ | 🖴 HD#1 |
|---|---|
| 🗋 ANPA Colors | Eject |
| 🗋 FOCOLTONE Colors | Desktop |
| 🗋 PANTONE Colors (Coated) | |
| 🗋 PANTONE Colors (Process) | New 🗀 |
| 🗋 PANTONE Colors (ProSim) | |
| 🗋 PANTONE Colors (Uncoated) | Cancel |

Save swatches in:

MyColors

Save

**IP:** *If you'd like, you can create your own color swatch book. Open a new file, and using the Rectangular Marquee tool, create a small rectangular selection. Fill the rectangle with a swatch color by using the Fill command in the Edit menu. With the Type tool, label the selection by typing in the name of the swatch color. Continue to create and label rectangles until you have applied all the color swatches from your palette to the new file. Save the file and print it to whatever output device you will be using with this collection of swatches. Then use the printout of the color swatches as a guide for what the swatch color will look like when printed from your output device.*

## Loading and Appending Swatches Palettes

If at any time you want to open a Swatches palette, you can do so by clicking the pop-up menu arrow in the palette and choosing Load Swatches.

Click on the Swatches palette you wish to load from within the Color Palettes folder (PC users: palette), then click Open (PC users: OK). After you load the color palette, it will replace the current palette on screen.

**OTE:** *To return the default swatches to the Swatches palette, choose Reset Swatches from the palette's pop-up menu.*

As you continue to experiment with the various palettes, you may wish to append a saved palette to the Swatches palette on screen. To do this, choose Append Colors from the pop-up menu. A dialog box will appear, allowing you to load a palette from your hard disk.

## CONCLUSION

In this chapter we've laid the foundation for further exploration into Photoshop's color spectrum. As you progress to more advanced topics, you'll see that it's vital to understand the differences between the color models. In future chapters you'll be introduced to such topics as converting from RGB Color to CMYK Color mode, calibrating your system for RGB to CMYK conversions, color-correcting in CMYK Color mode, and printing spot colors and four-color separations.

Next, in Chapter 5, you'll go one step further into the world of color as you begin to explore the painting tools, painting/editing modes and Brushes palette.

**4**

color evokes
creates co
enhances
can make a fixed image
suddenly sparkle with life.

# 5

# INTRODUCTION TO
# PAINTING TECHNIQUES

E ven if you're not an artist, the scope, power, and rich diversity of Photoshop's painting capabilities are certain to inspire the creativity within you. You'll marvel at the realistic and electronic effects within your grasp. At times, you might even expect to see the paint dripping down your screen, or sparks flying from your electronic brushes. In this chapter, you'll try your hand at being a painter, using electronic versions of a paintbrush, pencil, eraser, paint bucket, and airbrush. These tools, along with the Line, Gradient, and Eyedropper tools, and Photoshop's Brushes, Picker, Swatches, Scratch, and Options palettes, will open a world of infinite artistic possibilities for you.

If you're not interested in Photoshop's painting features and are using the program more for its image-editing and photo-retouching capabilities, don't skip this chapter. You'll need to know the tools and techniques covered here because they are a fundamental part of electronic composition. As you continue to read this book, you'll see the need for these tools and techniques arise again and again.

The chapter is primarily divided into short introductory exercises and projects. Although the focal point is primarily the Toolbox's painting tools, you'll also use the Brushes palette and learn how to change brushes, to create, save, and load custom brushes, and the Options palette to change the opacity of colors. At the conclusion of the chapter you'll explore Photoshop's painting/editing modes, accessed through the Options palette, which can change an image based on the color being applied, the color over which it is painted, and the mode that is chosen.

## INTRODUCTION TO THE LINE, ERASER, AND PAINT BUCKET TOOLS

The best way to learn the painting tools is to start with the easiest ones—the Line, Eraser, and Paint Bucket. Creating artistic effects with these tools requires only a click or a click-and-drag of the mouse, and knowledge of how to use the Options and Brushes palettes.

## Preparation for the Exercises

When working with the Line tool (and all other painting tools), you'll make extensive use of the Picker, Swatches, and Scratch palettes to change colors. In the exercises in this chapter, you'll be using the HSB color model because it's the most intuitive one. Switch to the HSB color model by selecting the pop-up menu in the Picker palette and choosing HSB Sliders.

In preparation for the introductory exercises in this section, make sure that the Options palette is visible on your screen. If necessary, open it now by choosing Show Options from the Window/Palettes submenu. The name and appearance of the palette changes depending on which tool is selected in the Toolbox.

Now click on the Line tool in the Toolbox. The Line Tool Options palette controls the opacity and painting/editing mode of the lines you create. The Options palette also controls the opacity and painting/editing mode of the Pencil, Paint Bucket, Paintbrush, Gradient, and Rubber Stamp tools. After you set the opacity and mode of a tool, they stay set for that tool until you change them.

**OTE:** *The element controlled by the slider in the Options palette depends on which tool you are using. When you use the Line, Pencil, Paint Bucket, Paintbrush, Gradient, and Rubber Stamp tools, the slider sets opacity. For the Airbrush, Smudge, and Blur/Sharpen tools, the slider sets pressure. For the Dodge/Burn/Sponge tool, the slider sets exposure. (You will be introduced to the Rubber Stamp, Smudge, Blur/Sharpen, and Dodge/Burn/Sponge tools in Chapter 6.)*

If you examine the settings in the Line Tool Options palette you'll see the Mode and Opacity settings are either the default settings or the last settings used for that tool.

If Opacity is set at less than 100%, you will not be painting with an opaque color, but rather a *tint*—a transparent version of a color. Painting with a tint can create a transparent effect and different shades of colors. When you lower the opacity percentage, you make a color more translucent; when you raise it, you make the color more opaque.

Later in this section, you'll lower the opacity to create tinted lines. For now, though, start with opaque lines. If Opacity is not 100%, reset it by clicking and dragging the Opacity slider control all the way to the right.

Before continuing, look at the Mode pop-up menu in the Line Tool Options palette to see which painting/editing mode is in effect. You will see one of the following words: Normal, Dissolve, Multiply, Screen, Overlay, Soft Light, Hard Light, Darken, Lighten, Difference, Hue, Saturation, Color, and Luminosity. If you are working in a layer other than the Background layer, you will also be able to use the Behind and Clear modes. (For more information on layers, see Chapter 12.) These are the painting/editing modes, and they control how Photoshop applies one color over another.

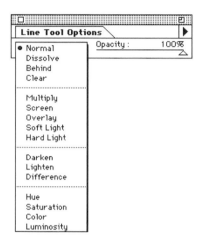

For now, you will work in Normal mode (the default). When you paint in Normal mode, you paint all of the underlying pixels with the foreground or background color that is set in the Picker palette or Color Picker dialog box. If the painting/editing mode is not Normal, change it now by clicking on the pop-up menu and selecting Normal from the list that appears.

Now that the Line Tool Options palette options are set, you can create a new file to begin working with the Line tool. Choose New from the File menu. Set both Width and Height to 5 inches. Set Resolution to 72 pixels/inch, use RGB Color for Mode, and set the background Contents by clicking on the White radio button in the Contents group. These settings will create a practice file that does not consume too much memory. Click OK. Once the new file appears, display the rulers and open the Info palette by selecting Show Rulers from the Window menu and select Show Info from the Window/Palette submenu. You'll be using the Rulers and the Info palette as measuring guides in the Line tool exercise.

## Using the Line Tool to Create Lines and Arrows

As you can probably guess, the Line tool is used to create lines. You can create vertical or horizontal lines, or slanted lines drawn on a diagonal in increments of 45 degrees. The Line Tool Options palette allows you to control the thickness of a line, as well as create arrowheads at the beginning and end of a line. In this section, you'll be using the Line tool to create lines at various thicknesses, angles, and shades, with and without arrowheads, as shown in Figure 5-1.

As with most other tools, the Options palette for the Line tool provides its various options. Let's examine the Line Tool Options palette. In the palette, the Line Width field allows you to change the pixel width of the lines you create; the default width is 1. In the Arrowheads section you can choose to have arrowheads at the start and/or at the end of a line. You can specify the size of arrowheads to appear at either or both ends of a line by clicking on the Shape button and typing in values in the Arrowhead Shape dialog box that appears.

**5**

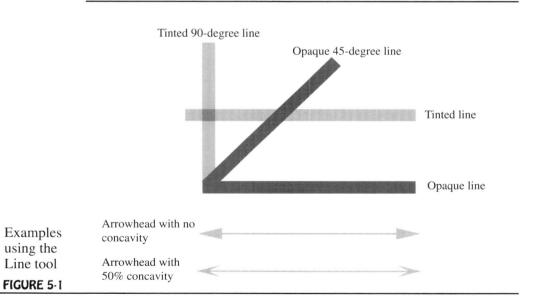

Tinted 90-degree line

Opaque 45-degree line

Tinted line

Opaque line

Arrowhead with no concavity

Arrowhead with 50% concavity

Examples using the Line tool

**FIGURE 5-1**

```
┌─────────────────────────────────────────┐
│ □                                      ◪ │
├─────────────────────────────────────────┤
│  Line Tool Options ╲                  ▶  │
│  ┌──────────┬──┐  Opacity:        100%   │
│  │ Normal   │▼ │  ─────────────────△     │
│  └──────────┴──┘                         │
│  Line Width: │1    │ pixels  ⊠ Anti-aliased│
│                                          │
│  Arrowheads: □Start □End  │ Shape.. │    │
│                                          │
└─────────────────────────────────────────┘
```

Use the Line tool now to create a wide, red line. In the Line Tool Options palette, type **16** in the Line Width field. Make sure the Anti-aliased option is selected. This helps ensure that line edges appear smooth. Before creating the line, use the Picker palette to change the color in the Foreground selection box. Move the H (hue) slider control so that it is set to red (either 0 or 360 degrees). The S (saturation) and B (brightness) sliders should be set to 100%.

**OTE:** *Don't worry about setting the background color in the Picker palette, because the Line tool only paints with the foreground color.*

## Creating a Line

Drawing a line is simple. Once you've set your Line Tool options, move the mouse pointer toward the middle of your document. As you move the mouse, the mouse pointer will change to a small crosshair. To create the line, all you need to do is click and drag.

**OTE:** *If a selection exists on screen, you will only be able to use a painting tool in the selected area. To remove a selection from the screen, click away from it, or press COMMAND-D (PC users: CTRL-D)—the keyboard equivalent to choosing None from the Select menu.*

1. Position the crosshair about 1 inch from the left side of the screen and 2.5 inches from the top of the screen; then click and drag to the right. As you drag, Photoshop creates an outline of the line that will appear on screen.

Notice that as you drag the mouse, the values in the Info palette change. In addition to the X and Y coordinates that appear next to the crosshair icon, look at those adjacent to the icon of the square with arrows. These X and Y coordinates, which have a triangle in front of them, indicate the distance moved horizontally or vertically from one position to another. Next to the angle icon are A and D coordinates—the A coordinate shows the angle that you are dragging the mouse, and the D coordinate indicates the distance.

2. When you get near the right edge of the document window, release the mouse button. Not until you release the mouse will Photoshop use the foreground color to fill the linear outline it has drawn on screen.

*n* **OTE:** *Look carefully at the line you just created, and notice that it has a soft edge. This is because you created the line with the Anti-aliased option.*

### Drawing Lines to Create Angles

The Line tool allows you to draw lines in increments of 45 degrees; to do this, press SHIFT as you're drawing a line. Since you'll be using this *constraining* technique in the File Manager with File Cabinet project later in the chapter, practice it now by drawing a line at a 45-degree angle from the left endpoint of the one already on your screen.

1. Move the crosshair to the left edge of the existing line. Press and hold SHIFT, and click and drag diagonally up and to the right.

   You'll see that your movement is constrained to a 45-degree angle. When you've dragged about 3 inches, release the mouse, and Photoshop will draw a diagonal line at 45 degrees to the original one.

   Next, you'll press the SHIFT key while clicking and dragging to draw a 90-degree angle, but this time you'll change the Opacity setting in the Line Tool Options palette to create a tinted line.

2. In the Line Tool Options palette, click and drag the slider control to the left, decreasing the Opacity percentage. (You can also use the keyboard to

change the Opacity value in increments of 10 percent. For instance, type **3** and Opacity will jump to 30%.) Before you draw the next line, use the keyboard now to set Opacity to 50% by typing **5**.

The next line you paint, at a 90-degree angle, will illustrate the effect of placing a translucent color over an opaque color. Once again, you'll start painting the line at the left endpoint of the first line you drew.

3. Position the crosshair on the left endpoint of the horizontal red line, press and hold SHIFT, and click and drag up to constrain the line to a 90-degree angle.

When you release the mouse, you'll see that the new line is 50% red. Notice that even though you drew the 50% red line on top of the opaque line, the opaque line's color has not changed to the tinted shade. It's as if the intensity of the 100% red burns through the translucent version of the same color.

For an example of painting a translucent color over another translucent color, click and drag to create a horizontal line that intersects both the 90-degree red-tinted line and the 45-degree opaque red line, as shown in Figure 5-1. Where the two translucent colors intersect, a square appears with a more intense red. But once again, when the red with the 50% opacity is painted over the opaque red, only the opaque version of the color shows.

**IP:** *If you set the width for the Line tool to zero pixels, you can use the tool as a screen-measuring device and to tell whether an image is straight or not. When you click and drag, Photoshop creates an electronic tape measure, a thin line on screen that you can use to drag over items that you wish to measure. The linear dimensions and angle of the object will appear in the Info palette. When you release the mouse, the measuring line will disappear.*

## Creating Lines with Arrowheads

Next, try the Arrowheads options. This time, you'll create a thinner line so the effects of the arrowhead settings will be clearly visible.

1. In the Line Tool Options palette, type **2** in the Line Width field.

2. In the Arrowheads section, click on the At Start and At End check boxes. When these options are selected, the Line tool will create arrowheads at both ends of the next line you create.

You can also control the width and the length of the arrowhead, using the Width and Length fields in the Arrowhead Shape dialog box. To open the dialog box, click on the Shape button. The Width field accepts values between 10 and 1000%. The Length field accepts values between 10 and 5000%.

```
▦▦▦▦▦ Arrowhead Shape ▦▦▦▦▦
     Width: [500  ] %        ( OK )
    Length: [1000 ] %      ( Cancel )
  Concavity: [0    ] %
```

**5**

**a.** To create an arrowhead that is twice as long as it is wide, you can use the default settings. If they've been changed, type **500** in the Width field and **1000** in the Length field. The Width of the arrowhead will be 5 times larger than the Line width. The Length of the arrowhead will be 10 times larger than the Line width.

If you wish, you can also change the shape of the arrowhead by setting its *concavity*. Concavity determines the curve on the back of the arrowhead, as shown in some examples in Figure 5-1.

**b.** Set Concavity to 0 if it is not already set to 0, so you can see how an arrowhead looks without concavity.

**3.** Click OK to accept the Arrowhead Shape settings.

**4.** To see the arrowheads, draw a line from left to right below the other lines on your screen. This time, the line features arrowheads at both ends.

Take a look at how concavity changes the arrowhead. First, you'll need to reopen the Arrowhead Shape dialog box and change the concavity of the arrow to 50% (values can be between -50% and 50%) and click OK. Then click and drag to create another line below the last one you created. Your screen will now look like Figure 5-1. Notice that the back of the 50% concavity arrowhead has a very distinctive curve.

If you wish to continue experimenting with the Line tool, try creating one more line below the others with Concavity set to a negative number. This will create a line with an arrowhead that looks like a diamond.

After you've finished testing the Line tool, you can proceed to the next section, where you'll learn how to paint and fill using the Paint Bucket.

## Using the Paint Bucket Tool to Paint and Fill

 The Paint Bucket tool lets you quickly fill areas of an image with the foreground color. The area painted by the tool is determined by how similar in color the adjacent pixels are to the pixel that you click on.

The Paint Bucket and Magic Wand tools work in a similar way, by first analyzing the color of the pixel that is clicked and then using the Tolerance settings in the tools' Options palette to determine the range of pixels affected. As with the Magic Wand, the greater the Tolerance, the larger the pixel range affected; the lower the Tolerance, the smaller the pixel range.

There is a clear difference between the two tools, however, that you need to understand: The Magic Wand *selects* according to the Tolerance setting, but the Paint Bucket *paints over image areas* according to the Tolerance setting. The Magic Wand selects; the Paint Bucket paints. (To review the properties of the Magic Wand tool, see "Using the Magic Wand" in Chapter 3.)

In this section, you'll observe how various Tolerance settings determine how the Paint Bucket fills the four adjoining red lines created in the previous section. Double-click on the Paint Bucket tool to open the Paint Bucket Options palette. Start by examining the Tolerance setting; by default, it is set to 32. Like the Magic Wand, the Paint Bucket's Tolerance range is 0 to 255. If you type a low number in the Tolerance field, Photoshop will apply the foreground color to contiguous areas that are very similar in color to the pixel you click on. If you enter a large number in the Tolerance field, Photoshop applies the foreground color over contiguous areas that vary greatly from the pixel you click on.

| Paint Bucket Options | | |
| --- | --- | --- |
| Normal ▼ | Opacity : | 100% |
| Tolerance : 32 | | ☒ Anti-aliased |
| Contents : Foreground ▼ | | |
| ☐ Sample Merged | | |

Click on the Contents pop-up menu. You'll see that the Paint Bucket tool paints with either the foreground color or a pattern. (You'll be creating and using patterns in Chapter 6.) The Anti-aliased option ensures that the paint applied with the Paint Bucket tool will appear smooth, without jagged edges. The Sample Merged option applies the Tolerance setting to the layer you are in based upon a sample of the colors in all visible layers. Since you are not working in a file with layers, this option will have no effect.

Start by testing the effects of a low Tolerance setting.

1. Change the value in the Tolerance field to 0.

2. In order to see the Paint Bucket tool in action, you'll need to change the foreground color. Do this by picking a swatch from the Swatches palette or moving the HSB slider controls in the Picker palette. In the Swatches palette, click on a bright blue color, like the first blue square in the first row of swatches. In the Picker Palette you can set H to 240°, and S and B to 100%. To fill with an opaque blue, make sure that Opacity is set to 100% and that Mode is set to Normal in the Paint Bucket Options palette.

3. Now move the mouse pointer to the first red horizontal line that you drew in the previous section. As you move into the document window, the mouse pointer changes to a paint bucket. Position the paint bucket directly over any part of the thick, horizontal red line and click.

*n* **OTE:** *If you want to use a crosshair instead of the paint bucket, turn on CAPS LOCK before you use the Paint Bucket tool, or choose Precise in the Painting Tools options in the Tool Cursors group in the General Preferences dialog box. To access the dialog box, choose File/Preference/General.*

With a zero Tolerance setting, the Paint Bucket tool fills only the two opaque red lines with blue. When you clicked the paint bucket (or crosshair) on the horizontal opaque red line, Photoshop hunted down only the adjacent opaque red pixels and filled them with the blue color, but not the pixels painted at a lower opacity (the 50% tinted lines).

To force the Paint Bucket tool to spread its paint over all the red lines, opaque and tinted, you'll need to increase the Tolerance setting.

4. Before testing this, choose Undo from the Edit menu to reset the line's color back to red. Then change Tolerance to 200 in the Paint Bucket Options palette.

5. Once again, move the paint bucket (or crosshair) over the horizontal opaque line and click. This time the Paint Bucket tool paints all of the adjoining lines, including the tinted ones. The higher Tolerance level causes the Paint Bucket tool to paint over pixels that have a color range that is broader than just opaque red.

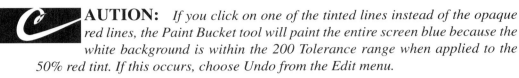

**AUTION:**   *If you click on one of the tinted lines instead of the opaque red lines, the Paint Bucket tool will paint the entire screen blue because the white background is within the 200 Tolerance range when applied to the 50% red tint. If this occurs, choose Undo from the Edit menu.*

**6.** Before continuing, save your work and name it **Bucket.**

You'll be using the Paint Bucket tool throughout this chapter, primarily to paint over areas that have been outlined with either the Paintbrush or Pencil tools, or that have been previously painted. The Paint Bucket tool can also be used to fill a selection. When a selected area exists on screen, the Paint Bucket, like all painting tools, will only paint within the selection.

Next you'll work with the Eraser tool you learned about in Chapter 2 and try out the Magic Eraser.

## Using the Eraser Tool to Erase and the Magic Eraser to Revert

Now that you've finished learning about the Line and Paint Bucket tools, you might want to erase everything on screen so you have room to experiment. One of the fastest ways to clear the screen is to paint the screen with the background color using the Eraser tool's Erase Image button. Recall that the Eraser tool erases (paints) with the background color. However, if you are working in a layer, the Eraser tool ignores your background color, and wipes away your image by replacing it with a transparent background.

Before you erase the entire screen, examine the different choices available in the Eraser Options palette. Open the Eraser Options palette by clicking on the Eraser tool in the Toolbox. (If the Options palette isn't displayed on screen, you'll need to double-click on the tool.) In the palette, you'll see a Mode pop-up menu that allows you to control how the Eraser tool erases.

Click on the Mode pop-up menu in the Eraser Options palette to examine the choices: Paintbrush, Airbrush, Pencil, Block. By selecting one of these, you can erase as if you were using the Paintbrush, Airbrush, or Pencil tool. As discussed in Chapter 2, the Block option allows you to erase pixels as if it were an electronic version of a rubber eraser. When using the Pencil, Paintbrush, or Airbrush option, you can change the Opacity and use the Fade and Stylus Pressure features. When using the Paintbrush option, an additional choice, Wet Edges, is available. With all three of these options you can choose a brush size in the Brushes palette. You'll learn how to use these features when the Pencil, Paintbrush, and Airbrush tools are covered later in this chapter.

To use the Eraser to clear everything on screen, first make sure your background color is white. Now click the Erase Image button in the Eraser Options palette. (If you are working in a layer, the Erase Image button is replaced by the Erase Layer button.) An alert will appear, asking you to confirm that you wish to erase the entire image or layer. Click OK to confirm.

**TIP:** *To quickly switch from one Eraser tool type to another, press OPTION (PC users: ALT) while clicking on the Eraser tool.*

Now that you've cleared the entire screen, let's assume you acted too rashly and shouldn't have erased the lines that have arrowheads. A handy feature of the Eraser tool, called the Magic Eraser, will put a smile on your face in this situation. The Magic Eraser works like the File menu's Revert command, except that the Magic Eraser only reverts the part of your document that you click and drag over. As you can imagine, the Magic Eraser is an extremely handy feature for any Photoshop project.

Although you can use any of the eraser modes as a Magic Eraser, select the Block option because it isn't affected by opacity settings in the Eraser Options palette or by the brush size in the Brushes palette.

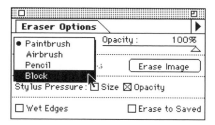

To try out the Magic Eraser, choose Block in the Eraser Options palette's Mode pop-up menu. Then click on the Erase to Saved check box and move the pointer back over your image. Notice that the icon changes to show a dog-eared page over the Eraser block ( ). If you are erasing using the Paintbrush, Airbrush, or Pencil option, the Magic Eraser icon looks like this: ( ). Now, click and drag over the bottom portion of your screen. At first nothing will happen—but be patient—Photoshop is loading the previously saved version of the file (the one you named Bucket). In a few moments, you'll see parts of two lines reappearing. Keep clicking and dragging until you at least see the arrowheads. Notice that the Magic Eraser tool is not really erasing, but rather is reverting part of the image back to your last saved version.

**IP:** *If you don't wish to use the Erase to Saved option in the Eraser Options palette, you can activate the Magic Eraser by pressing OPTION (PC users: ALT) while clicking and dragging over previously saved image areas with the Eraser tool.*

**AUTION:** *If you change resolution or if you change color modes using the Mode menu, the Magic Eraser will not be able to revert to the saved version of your image.*

When you are ready to proceed to the next section, close the file on screen. You don't need to save the changes because you won't use this file anymore.

## INTRODUCTION TO THE PENCIL, PAINTBRUSH, AND EYEDROPPER TOOLS

In this section you will be introduced to the painting tools—the Pencil, Paintbrush, and Eyedropper. If you wish to create the File Manager with File Cabinet project in this chapter, these are the tools you'll use. The Pencil and Paintbrush tools let you paint with brushes from the Brushes palette. The Eyedropper tool aids you in changing foreground and background colors. Since you will be using both the Brushes palette and the Options palette, you'll be able to work more efficiently if you separate the palettes so you can see both on screen at the same time. To separate the Brushes palette from the Options palette, click on the Brushes palette's tab and drag it out of the Options palette.

Since you will be using different size brushes in the following exercises, you may wish to switch preference settings so that the painting tool pointer is the same size as the brush with which you are painting. This can help give you a preview of how a brush stroke will affect an image before painting. To set the painting tool pointer to reflect your brush size, choose General from the File/Preferences submenu. In the General Preferences dialog box, click on the Brush Size radio button in the Painting Tools group, in the Tool Cursors section. If you choose the Precise option, the tool pointer will appear as a crosshair which can allow more precise alignment while working with the painting or other tools. The Standard option keeps the painting tool pointer set to the default settings. If you'd like, pick a setting, then click OK; otherwise, click Cancel.

For the following exercise, you'll create a file with a transparent background where you will paint the word ART using the Pencil tool's Auto Erase feature. By working in a file with a transparent background, you'll be able to drag and drop the word ART into another file, without needing to select the letters. Also, when ART is dropped into another file, the ART file's transparent background will allow color from the destination file to show through the letters. Start by creating a new file large enough for the next few practice exercises. Set both Width and Height to 5 inches, the resolution to 72 pixels/inch, and Mode to RGB Color. To make the background transparent, click on the Transparent radio button in the Contents group. When you are ready to begin, click OK to display a new, untitled document. When the new document appears, notice that the document title bar displays the word Layer 1. If the Layers palette isn't open on screen, choose Show Layers from the Window/Palettes submenu. In the Layers palette, you'll also see the word "Layer 1" listed in the palette. When you create a new file with the Contents set to Transparent, Photoshop automatically creates a new layer with a transparent background as the base layer. For more information about working with layers, see Chapter 12.

## Using the Pencil Tool to Draw and Erase

Photoshop's electronic Pencil tool is unlike any pencil you've ever used before. It not only emulates a real pencil but can also draw lines between mouse clicks and erase by painting with the background color. It also allows you to pick different "lead" sizes from the Brushes palette.

You may be surprised to learn that the Pencil tool's "lead," or stroke, is controlled by a brush chosen in the Brushes palette. This gives the Pencil tool tremendous versatility. When you use the Pencil tool, the stroke can be thick, thin, round, or square. The tool's smallest stroke is one pixel wide, which is handy for retouching images one pixel at a time.

Apart from retouching individual pixels, the Pencil tool can be used for freehand sketching. When you click and drag on the screen with the Pencil tool, it paints with the foreground color, using a stroke set in the Brushes palette, and opacity and mode determined by the Pencil Options palette. No matter what the brush size or shape, the Pencil tool will always paint with a hard-edge brush—unlike the Paintbrush and Airbrush tools, which can paint with soft edges. To see this in action, activate the Pencil tool and draw a line by clicking and dragging on screen. The line is created with the foreground color and is the width of the currently active brush.

Now take a look at the features in the Pencil Options palette. If the Options palette is open click on the Pencil tool to view the Pencil options; otherwise, double-click on the tool. Notice the Fade, Stylus Pressure, and Auto Erase options. (Fade and Stylus Pressure also appear in the dialog boxes for the Paintbrush and Airbrush tools.) The Fade options work similarly for the Pencil, Paintbrush, and Airbrush tools, and are covered later in this chapter when you learn how to use the Paintbrush and Airbrush tools.

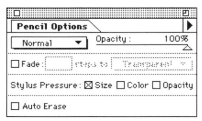

## The Stylus Pressure Options

The Stylus Pressure options can only be activated if you have a stylus and graphics tablet connected to your computer. If you do have a stylus, these options are invaluable: You can control the size, color, and opacity of your painting by applying different amounts of pressure to the stylus.

Here are brief explanations of the Stylus Pressure options available for the Pencil, Paintbrush, and Airbrush tools:

*Size*   When this check box is selected, you can control the size of your brush strokes by applying different pressure with the stylus. Light pressure creates a small brush stroke; heavy pressure creates a large brush stroke. (The Stylus Pressure options for the Airbrush tool do not include size.)

*Color*   When this check box is selected, you can apply either the foreground color, the background color, or an *intermediate color*—a blend of the foreground and background colors. Applying heavy pressure administers the foreground color, applying light pressure administers the background color, and applying a medium amount of pressure administers an intermediate color.

*Opacity*   When this check box is selected, you can use stylus pressure to control how opaque or transparent your brush strokes will be. The heavier the pressure, the more opaque the color; the lighter the pressure, the more translucent the color.

The various Stylus Pressure options shown in the following illustration were created with a Wacom stylus with the Pencil tool activated.

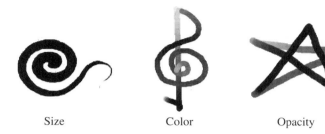

Size                    Color                    Opacity

## The Auto Erase Option

The Auto Erase option in the Pencil Options palette allows the Pencil tool to work as an eraser. Remember, "erasing" in Photoshop means painting with the background color. Turning on the Auto Erase option triggers the Pencil tool to automatically switch to the background color when you paint over the foreground color.

Take a look at the Auto Erase feature in action.

1. If the Auto Erase option isn't selected, click on the check box in the Pencil Options palette.

   Next, select a vivid color for the foreground color and its complement for the background color from the Picker palette. For instance, try blue as the foreground color and yellow as the background color.

2. If the Foreground selection box is not active in the Picker palette, click on it. To choose a blue foreground color, you can either click on the first blue swatch in the first row of the Swatches palette, or move the hue (H) slider control to 240 degrees, with saturation (S) and brightness (B) set to 100%.

3. Click on the Background selection box in the Picker palette. To choose a yellow color, click on the yellow swatch in the first row of the Swatches palette, or move the H slider control to 60 degrees, with the S and B sliders set to 100%.

   After you've chosen your colors, the next step is to select a brush from the Brushes palette to set the brush stroke the Pencil tool will use.

4. Start with a large brush size, so the Pencil tool's stroke will be dramatic. Click on the largest brush in the first row of the Brushes palette. After you click, the brush will be outlined, indicating it is the active brush for the Pencil tool.

**OTE:** *Brushes that are too large to be depicted by icons in the Brushes palette are represented by a brush with a number below it, representing the pixel width of the brush's diameter.*

Now, with the Pencil tool's Auto Erase option enabled, create the word *ART*, using capital letters.

5. Begin by clicking and dragging to start creating the left, slanted side of the capital letter *A*. As you drag, the Pencil tool paints with the foreground color. When you finish the stroke, release the mouse button. To begin creating the right side of the letter A, position the mouse at the top of the stroke you just produced. Then click and drag diagonally to the right. Notice that as soon as the mouse detects the foreground color, the Auto Erase option causes the Pencil tool to paint with the background color. Now, connect the two slanted lines by drawing the crossbar of the A. If you start the bar by touching the left slant, your bar will be yellow. If you start painting by touching the right slant, the crossbar will be blue.

When you've completed the letter *A*, start drawing the letter *R*. Immediately, the Pencil tool returns to the foreground color. As you draw the *R*, the Auto Erase feature causes the Pencil tool to switch to the background color whenever a stroke begins on the foreground color.

To create the letter *T*, try a different painting technique as a special effect: Instead of dragging with the mouse, create the *T* with mouse clicks. Begin by clicking once to create a foreground-colored spot, then move the mouse halfway into the colored spot and click again. This creates a background-colored spot. Keep using overlapping mouse clicks to gradually create the letter. When you've finished, the letter will be entirely created from Pencil marks alternating between the foreground and background colors.

### Dragging and Dropping ART into Another File

After you've finished creating the word ART, you are ready to drag and drop the image over another file. Open a file in which you wish to place the word ART. If you don't have an image, use the Fruit (PC users: fruit.jpg) file in the Tutorial folder. When the file is open, place the two images either side by side, or so that they overlap.

To move ART into the other file, activate the Move tool. Using the Move tool, click anywhere in the ART file. With the mouse button still pressed, drag ART over the image you just opened (over the Fruit file, if you are using the Tutorial image). When the Move tool icon ( ⊞ ) is replaced by a tiny grabbing hand icon ( ✋ ), you can release the mouse. The word ART will drop onto the file. Since ART was created in a file with a transparent background, you can see through the letters R and A as if they had been created on a clear acetate over the Fruit file. In the Layers palette notice that Photoshop automatically created a new layer for the ART image. The two eye icons in the Layers palette next to the Background and Layer 1 indicate that both layers are being viewed. The gray area surrounding Layer 1 indicates that you are currently working in this layer. Since you are working in a layer, you can reposition the entire layer without having to use a selection tool to select it, and move it without affecting the Background. Try using the Move tool to move ART into another position on screen.

If you wish to save the Fruit file with its new layer, you must save it in Photoshop 3.0 format. Use the Save As command to save it under a new name, so you do not replace the original file. If you don't need to preserve the layer, use the File/Save a Copy command. When you do, the Flatten Image check box will be selected automatically. This indicates that all layers in the file will be merged into a Background layer. Another way of removing layers from an image is to choose the Flatten Image or Merge Layers command from the Layers palette pop-up menu. To learn about merging and flattening layers, see Chapter 12.

## SHIFT-Clicking with the Pencil Tool

Now that you've completed your penmanship exercise, turn off the Pencil tool's Auto Erase option and experiment with the SHIFT key and the Pencil tool. Before you begin, create a new file to practice in. Make the file a 5-by-5-inch RGB Color file with the background Contents set to White.

Once the file opens, click on screen with the Pencil tool; then move the mouse to another area, press and hold SHIFT, then click again. The Pencil tool connects your mouse clicks.

If you wish, keep experimenting with the SHIFT and Pencil tool. When you're ready to move on to the next section and explore the Paintbrush tool, you'll need to clear your screen. To do this, first reset your background color to white. If the Options palette is still displayed on screen, click once on the Eraser tool; otherwise double-click. In the Eraser Options palette, click on the Erase Image button. When the alert appears, click OK.

**EMEMBER:** *If you are working on an image that does not have a transparent background, the Eraser tool paints with the background color. When working in a layer other than the Background, the Eraser tool clears pixels as if wiping colors off of a clear acetate, leaving a transparent background.*

## Painting with the Paintbrush Tool

The Paintbrush tool is Photoshop's electronic version of an artist's paintbrush. The Paintbrush tool paints with the foreground color, using your choice of brush strokes. Using the tool's Fade options, you can also create colors that *fade,* or dissolve, as you paint.

Like the Pencil tool, the Paintbrush tool allows you to connect painted brush strokes by pressing SHIFT while clicking the mouse. Unlike the Pencil tool, though, the Paintbrush tool offers soft brush strokes that simulate paint applied with a paintbrush. When you activate the Paintbrush, take a moment to examine the Brushes palette; it includes a row of soft-edged brushes that weren't available when you were using the Pencil tool.

Double-click on the Paintbrush tool to open the Paintbrush Options palette. You'll notice that the Paintbrush's options are almost identical to those of the Pencil tool, except that the Paintbrush does not have an Auto Erase feature. Instead, it has a Wet Edges option. The Wet Edges option produces the effect of painting with watercolors or markers, rather than acrylic or oil. The colors created have a fully saturated appearance at stroke edges but not in the center of the stroke. If you paint an image using wet edges in a layer, underlying layers will show through the brush strokes. Both the Paintbrush and Pencil tools have the same Stylus Pressure controls, and both feature the Fade option. The choices in the Fade option allow you to create effects where the stroke you are painting gradually disappears (Fade to Transparent) or gradually turns into the background color (Fade to Background). In the Fade field you specify how many pixels the Paintbrush tool will paint before the fade-out begins. In the pop-up menu you choose whether to fade to Transparent or to the background color.

```
┌─────────────────────────────────────────┐
│ □                                     回  │
│ ┌───────────────────────────────────────┐│
│ │ Paintbrush Options ╲              ▶    ││
│ │ ┌─────────────┬──┐  Opacity :   100%  ││
│ │ │   Normal    │ ▼│                     ││
│ │ └─────────────┴──┘              △      ││
│ │ ─────────────────────────────────────  ││
│ │ □Fade:│      │ steps to │Transparent ▼│││
│ │ ─────────────────────────────────────  ││
│ │ Stylus Pressure: ⊠Size □Color □Opacity ││
│ │ ─────────────────────────────────────  ││
│ │ □Wet Edges                              ││
│ └───────────────────────────────────────┘│
└─────────────────────────────────────────┘
```

## Beginning the Painter's Palette Exercise

As you work through the next few sections, you'll be performing the steps of an exercise to create a painter's palette like the one shown in Figure 5-2. Your experimentation with the Paintbrush tool's Fade options will be the start of the exercise. Since you'll begin by painting without a Fade option chosen, check to see that there is a value currently in the Fade field. If there is, delete it now.

Before you start painting open a new 5 x 5 inch RGB Color file on screen. Set the background Contents to White.

1. Set the foreground color to a dark gray. In the Brushes palette, choose a medium, hard-edged brush from the second row of brushes. In the Paintbrush Options palette, click and drag the Opacity slider control to 100%, or press **0** on your keyboard.

2. Position the Paintbrush tool about .5 inch from the top of your screen, and click and drag to create a kidney shape, representing the palette. Refer to

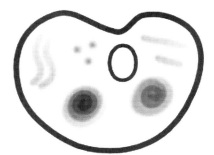

The
Painter's
Palette
exercise

**FIGURE 5-2**

Figure 5-2 as a guide. To paint the handle hole in the middle of the palette, click and drag again with the Paintbrush in a circular motion.

To create the paint dabs in the palette, use the Paintbrush's Fade to Transparent feature.

**3.** Double-click on the Paintbrush to activate the Paintbrush Options palette. Click in the Fade check box, then type **75** in the steps field. If Transparent isn't selected, choose it by clicking on the pop-up menu. These settings will cause the painting color to fade out after 75 pixels.

**4.** Create a couple of circular paint dabs in the painter's palette. Pick a foreground color, and choose a medium, soft-edged brush in the Brushes palette. Again using Figure 5-2 as your guide, click and drag with the Paintbrush tool in a circular motion in the palette. As you click and drag, the paint will gradually fade out. Do this one more time with another color to create another paint dab.

To paint the small, waved lines in the upper-left part of the palette, you'll need to reset the Fade field so the paint fades before you finish creating the lines.

**5.** In the Paintbrush Options palette, type **35** in the Fade field. Set the foreground color, and then click and drag to create the two waved lines at the top-left side of the palette. You'll notice that the fade-out occurs as you're drawing these lines.

**6.** Click three times to apply three soft-edged dots adjacent to the handle hole. To finish up, draw two more short, straight lines at the top-right side of the palette. Your painter's palette should look similar to Figure 5-2.

Now assume that you want to add a few more artistic touches to the palette, with the same colors that you used to paint the lines and circles. For this, you need to use the Eyedropper tool.

## Sampling Colors with the Eyedropper Tool

 The Eyedropper tool doesn't paint, but is an invaluable tool in the painting process; it is used to *sample,* or read, an image's color so it can be used as the foreground or background color. With one quick click of the Eyedropper tool, the foreground or background color can be changed to the color of the pixel you clicked on with the tool. For example, it would be a lot of work to mix colors in the Picker palette to obtain a particular flesh tone that appears in a scanned image. With the Eyedropper tool, on the other hand, you need only click on that colored portion of the image, and Photoshop's foreground color instantly changes to the flesh tone you need. This technique is a tremendous time-saver when you are color correcting and retouching scanned color images.

Before trying out the Eyedropper tool, take a look at its options. Click on the Eyedropper tool to open the Eyedropper Options palette, and then click on the Sample Size pop-up menu.

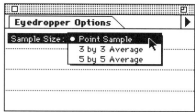

All of the Eyedropper options reside in the Sample Size pop-up. The default Sample Size setting is Point Sample, which narrows the Eyedropper's sample to the color value of the pixel on which you click. The 3 by 3 Average option reads the average color value of a 3-pixel-by-3-pixel area, and the 5 by 5 Average option operates similarly. To test the Eyedropper tool at its default setting, make sure the Sample Size option is set to Point Sample.

## Changing the Foreground and Background Colors with the Eyedropper

Move the mouse pointer toward the first paint dab you created in the painter's palette. As you move the mouse into the document window, notice that the pointer changes to an eyedropper. (If CAPS LOCK is on or if the Other Tools Cursor group in the General Preferences dialog box is set to Precise, the pointer will be a crosshair, but it will still function as the Eyedropper tool.) Position the pointer over the first paint dab you created, but don't click the mouse yet. First, examine the color value readings in the Info palette.

The Info palette displays the color values of the pixels underlying the Eyedropper tool, using various color models. You can display one or two color model values at a time. If you will be sending your file to a printing press, it can be helpful to view CMYK colors at the same time as RGB or HSB colors are displayed. When CMYK colors are displayed in the Info palette, an exclamation point appears next to CMYK percentages that are out of gamut. If you are color correcting, it's very helpful to

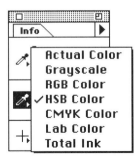

have both RGB and CMYK colors on screen because you will have a readout of the primary colors and their complements.

You can also change to RGB, CMYK, HSB, Lab, or Grayscale by clicking on either of the eyedropper icons in the Info palette. When you click, the pop-up menu will appear, shown here, allowing you to choose the Color model of your choice or to display the percentage of ink coverage when working with CMYK or Duotone images. Ink coverage is discussed in Chapter 9.

*n*OTE: *If you set both eyedropper icons in the Info palette to the same color model, the bottom eyedropper and color model readout will disappear. To return both eyedroppers to the Info palette, click on the eyedropper icon, and choose another color model. You can also click on the pop-up menu arrow and choose a second color model in the Info Options palette. Once two different color models are chosen, both color model readouts will appear in the Info palette.*

With the Eyedropper tool pointer positioned over the first paint dab that you created, click the mouse. Notice that the foreground color immediately changes to match the color you clicked on. To further test the Eyedropper's sampling power, move it to the outer edge of the paint dab circle, and click the mouse. The foreground color changes to a lighter shade, reflecting the color created by the Fade to Transparent option you used with the Paintbrush tool to make the paint dab.

**OPTION-CLICKING (PC USERS: ALT-CLICKING) WITH THE EYEDROPPER**    From time to time, you may wish to use the Eyedropper tool to change the background color when the Foreground selection box is activated in the Picker palette, or to change the foreground color when the Background selection box is activated. If the Foreground selection box is activated, you can change the background color by pressing OPTION (PC users: ALT) while clicking on a color in the image with the Eyedropper tool. If the Background selection box is activated, you can change the foreground color by pressing OPTION (PC users: ALT) while clicking on a color in the image with the Eyedropper tool.

Try this. Change the background color by pressing OPTION (PC users: ALT) and clicking with the Eyedropper tool on any colored element in the painter's palette you created.

**IP:** *The designers of Photoshop recognized the tremendous value of the Eyedropper tool and made it readily available for changing the foreground color. Press OPTION (PC users: ALT) while using the Pencil, Line, Paintbrush, Paint Bucket, Airbrush, or Gradient tools, and that tool will change to the Eyedropper tool. Many experienced Photoshop users take full advantage of this feature by using it with the Scratch palette, as explained in the following section.*

## Using the Eyedropper Tool and the Scratch Palette Together

The Scratch palette allows you to test colors, brush strokes, blends, and special effects without altering your document. You can also use the Scratch palette in conjunction with the Eyedropper tool as a holding area for colors you wish to keep readily accessible.

Before you use the Scratch palette, make sure it isn't locked. If the palette is locked you will not be able to change it. To check if the palette is locked, click on its pop-up menu. If the palette is locked. you'll see a check mark next to the word Locked. If so, select the word Locked, which will remove the check mark and unlock the Scratch palette.

Since you will soon be painting in the Scratch palette, it will be easier to view your work if you remove the Scratch palette's default color spectrum. To clear the Scratch palette, first set the background color to white, then choose Clear from the palette's pop-up menu. The Clear command always paints the Scratch palette with the background color.

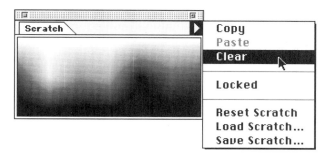

**IP:** *You can clear the Scratch palette by setting your background color to white, then dragging the Scratch palette contents out of view with the Move tool. If you drag the contents of the Scratch palette into your document, Photoshop will create a new layer in your document and place the Scratch palette contents in the layer.*

Suppose you wish to use a few of the colors from the painter's palette over and over again. One way to facilitate this is by first transferring a color into the Foreground selection box using the Eyedropper tool, and then dropping the color into the Scratch palette with the Paintbrush tool. Here's how to do this without having to go to the Toolbox more than once. Click on the Paintbrush tool to activate it. Then press and hold OPTION (PC users: ALT), which switches you to the Eyedropper tool, and move the eyedropper to the edge of one of the paint dabs on the palette. To change the foreground color to the color of the paint dab, continue to hold OPTION (PC users: ALT) and click. Next, to place that color in the Scratch palette, first release OPTION (PC users: ALT) so that the Paintbrush pointer returns. Position the Paintbrush pointer over the Scratch palette and click the mouse. You have now copied a color from your image into the Scratch palette. To practice, try the same technique with another color.

While you work on a project, you can add more colors into the Scratch palette. You can even drop colors of varying opacities into the Scratch palette to mix and test them. You can then easily access any of them when you need to by changing the foreground color to one of the "custom" colors, as described next.

To change the foreground color to a color from the Scratch palette, first press OPTION (PC users: ALT) to turn the Paintbrush tool into the Eyedropper tool. Position the eyedropper over the desired color in the Scratch palette and click. The foreground color changes to the color you clicked in the Scratch palette.

If you'd like, you can save different palettes to use with different projects. To save the current Scratch palette choose Save Scratch in the Scratch palette pop-up menu. To load a Scratch palette, choose Load Scratch from the pop-up menu. When the dialog box appears, click on the palette you would like to load, then click Open (PC users: OK). To lock a Scratch palette to prevent it from being changed, choose Locked from the Scratch palette pop-up menu. To reset the Scratch palette to its default settings, choose Reset Scratch from the pop-up menu.

*η* **OTE:** *You can copy and paste items from one Scratch palette into another. To do this, first open the Scratch palette that has the item you wish to copy. Next, select the area you wish to copy with a selection tool. Choose Copy from the Edit menu. Now, open the Scratch palette that you wish to copy into. From the Edit menu, choose Paste.*

Close the painter's palette image now, and save it with an appropriate file name if you wish to use it again.

## Using the Paintbrush's Wet Edges Option

In this section you'll use the Paintbrush's Wet Edges option to create a flower, as shown in Figure 5-3. In order to help you create the flower, you'll add a new layer over an existing flower image, then use the underlying flower image as a type of tracing guide. Before beginning this exercise, make sure that the Layers palette is open on screen. If it isn't choose Show Layers from the Window/Palettes submenu.

1. Start by scanning a flower, or scan the flower image in Figure 5-3. If a scanner is not available, load the Flower (PC users: flower.jpg) file from the Tutorial folder. This is the background you will use to paint over.

2. In order to use the flower as a tracing guide, you'll need to create a new layer to use like a plastic acetate. To create the layer, click on the Layer palette's pop-up menu and choose New Layer. The options in the New Layer pop-up menu will be discussed in detail in Chapter 12. For the time being, make sure that Opacity is set to 100%, Mode is set to Normal, and Group With Previous Layer is not selected. In the Name field type **Painted Flower**, then click OK to create the layer.

Flower
created
using the
Wet Edges
option

**FIGURE 5-3**

Notice that the name of the layer you just created is now in the Title bar and in the Layers palette. The two eye icons in the Layers palette next to the Background layer and Painted Flower layer indicate that both layers are being viewed. The gray color surrounding Painted Flower in the Layers palette indicates that it is the target layer. This is the layer in which you will be painting.

3. Next, activate the Paintbrush tool and select the Wet Edges option in the Paintbrush tool's Options palette.

4 Choose a foreground color, a brush size, and if you'd like—a Fade option. Start painting over the flower. Notice that as you paint, the colors look as if they are slightly diluted with water with the edges less diluted. Try painting one color over another. If you release the mouse and then reapply paint over areas you've already colored, the paint grows darker.

Try painting with different brushes, both soft and hard, and at different opacities. If you'd like to test the effects of different colors and brushes, try them out in the Scratch palette first before painting your image.

5. Finish the flower by adding a stem and a few leaves around the stem.

After you've finished painting, place the flower into another image with an interesting background. If you don't have an image, use the Seasons file (PC users: seasons.jpg) in the Adobe Photoshop Tutorial folder.

6. Open a file over which you wish to place the flower you just painted.

Since you created the flower in a layer, you can drag and drop or copy and paste the flower into another file without having to use the selection tools to select it.

7. Place the two files on screen side by side, or so that they overlap. Then use the Move tool to drag the Painted Flower layer into the Seasons file.

When the Painted Flower layer is in the Seasons file you'll see that there is now a layer in the Layers palette called Painted Flower. Also, notice that you can see through the translucent areas of the Painted Flower. Move the Painted Flower into position using the Move tool. Since you are in a layer, the flower moves above the Seasons Background layer. If you wish to save your file with the Painted Flower layer, use the File/Save As command and save your file in Photoshop 3.0 format. Save the file under a new name so that you do not replace the tutorial image. If you wish to save your file but do not wish to preserve the layer, use the File/Save a Copy command to flatten the image and save it.

## THE FILE MANAGER WITH FILE CABINET PROJECT

Before proceeding to learn about more painting tools, you may wish to practice using the painting tools that have been covered so far. Using the Line, Paintbrush, Pencil, and Paint Bucket tools, you can create the image shown in Figure 5-4. You'll start by creating the file cabinet first, then create the file manager character in another file, which will then be pasted into the file cabinet file. Although the steps are detailed as follows, feel free to improvise and experiment as you work.

1. Create a new file, 7 inches wide and 5 inches high. (This size will accommodate both the file cabinet and the file manager character.) Set the resolution to 72 ppi and Mode to RGB Color. Since the images you will be creating will be white, set the Contents radio button to White.

The File
Manager
with File
Cabinet
project

**FIGURE 5-4**

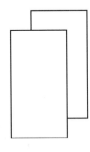

**n**OTE: *If you wish to use this or any of the other images in this chapter as the basis for a project that you will output professionally, you'll probably want to use a resolution higher than 72 ppi. Make sure that you have enough memory to handle the file size—a 5-by 7-inch RGB file at 300 ppi consumes 9MB as compared to 532K at 72 ppi.*

**2.** Your first step is to use the Marquee tool and the Edit/Stroke command to create a rectangle. In the Stroke dialog box, set Width to 2 pixels and Location to Inside. After the first rectangle is stroked, don't deselect. Duplicate the rectangle by pressing OPTION (PC users: ALT) while you click and drag on a selection edge. Drag downwards and to the left so that your image looks like the illustration shown here. When the rectangle is in the desired location, deselect it by clicking away from the selected area.

**3.** Use the Line tool with a 2-pixel width to connect the two offset rectangles to create a three-dimensional effect. Next, use the Paint Bucket tool to fill the side of the file cabinet. Make sure that no gaps appear in the outline of the area you are filling; otherwise the Paint Bucket tool will spread paint over the entire image. Clean up the image by removing any unwanted lines with the Eraser tool.

**4.** Once you have the basic structure of the cabinet created, use the Marquee tool and the Edit/Stroke command to create two rectangles for the file cabinet drawers. Duplicate the top drawer rectangle and offset (as you did with the rectangles to create the file cabinet).

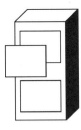

**5.** Use the Line tool to create a three-dimensional effect for the top drawer, and fill with the Paint Bucket tool to create a shadow along the side. Again, use the Eraser tool to remove any unwanted lines. Experiment with the different Modes and Opacities in the Eraser Options palette. Also, use different brush sizes. Then use the Line tool with a 75% opacity to create the drawer handles. To create the file folders in the cabinet, draw lines with a 50% opacity setting. Your image should look similar to this:

6. When you've completed the filing cabinet, save the file and name it **Cabinet**.

## Creating the File Manager Character

Follow these steps to create the file manager character shown in Figure 5-4.

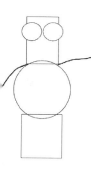

1. Create a new RGB Color file, with the Width and Height both set to 5 inches. This should provide enough room to work with the file manager character, which will be about 4 inches by 4 inches.

2. Use the Marquee tool and the Edit/Stroke command to create simple shapes, as shown here, to use as a rough guide for the file manager. Use the Pencil tool with a small brush to sketch a rough outline for the arms.

3. After creating the foundation for the character, use the Paintbrush tool to paint in details. Use the Eraser tool to erase any of the unwanted foundation lines that remain. When erasing you may wish to experiment with the different modes and opacities in the Eraser Options palette. If you use any other Mode besides Block, don't forget to check the brush size you're using in the Brushes palette. Choose the color you want for the mouth, nose, eyes, ears, and hair.

4. Use the Pencil tool to create details in the shirt—the buttons, cuffs, and cuff links. Then, use the Pencil tool with your choice of colors to add the pocket, pencil, and bow tie.

5. Use the Paintbrush tool to paint in the hands. Create the disk with the Pencil tool, then continue using the Pencil tool to outline the character's pants.

6. Fill in the pants using the Paint Bucket tool. Again, when you fill them in, make sure that no gaps appear in the outline of the area you are filling; otherwise the Paint Bucket will spread paint over the entire image.

When you are satisfied with the file manager's appearance, save your work. Name the file **Manager**. Now you're ready to copy the file manager character into the file cabinet document.

## Pasting the File Manager into the File Cabinet File

In this section, you'll use the Magic Wand tool to select the white background of the file manager character and then invert the selection so that you can copy the image.

1. With the file manager character on screen, double-click on the Magic Wand tool. To ensure that you will only select the white background, type **0** in the Tolerance field in the Magic Wand Options palette. Next, click on the white background; only the background should be selected. Choose Inverse from the Select menu; now only the file manager character should be selected.

2. From the Edit menu, select Copy. Close the Manager file and open the Cabinet file.

3. Select Paste from the Edit menu, and the file manager character will appear in the Cabinet document.

**OTE:** *You can also drag and drop a selection from one file to another, rather than copy and paste.*

4. While the character is still floating, click and drag it to a suitable position, as shown in Figure 5-4. Lock the character into position by choosing None from the Select menu.

5. To save your work, use the Save As command and name your file **FileMan** so you can keep the original Cabinet file intact.

You now have three files on your disk: the original file, Cabinet; the original file, Manager; and the final project file, FileMan. By keeping the original Cabinet and Manager files, you can always edit them and then re-create the final project.

Now that you've mastered Photoshop's basic painting tools, you are ready to progress to more advanced painting tools and techniques.

## INTRODUCTION TO THE AIRBRUSH TOOL

The Airbrush tool is an electronic version of the mechanical airbrush that artists use to create three-dimensional shading effects. The tool is also used to soften images with a hint of color. In retouching and painting work, the Airbrush tool is often the best tool for adding highlights and shadows.

The Airbrush tool paints in much the same manner as the Paintbrush tool, except the Airbrush colors with a softer edge. Like the Pencil and Paintbrush, the Airbrush allows you to pick from a variety of brushes from the Brushes palette. Unlike the other tools, however, the Opacity slider in the Airbrush Options palette is not available with the Airbrush; instead, you have a Pressure slider. The greater the pressure setting, the more paint that gets sprayed when you click and hold down the mouse button.

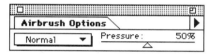

In this section you will experiment with the Airbrush tool and its Fade options. In order to perform the exercises, create a new file 6 inches wide by 4 inches high. Set the background Contents to Transparent. When you click OK, you will be in a new layer. All non-painted areas in the layer are transparent. This is the size you will need to accommodate the Summer Sale Postcard project (shown in Figure 5-5) after the introductory exercises.

Click now on the Airbrush tool to activate it. For the foreground color, choose any color swatch in the Swatches palette or create a color using the slider controls in the Picker palette. From the Brushes palette, pick a large, soft-edged brush. In the Airbrush Options palette, examine the Pressure slider; if it is not set to 100%, click on the slider control and drag all the way to the right. Make sure Mode is set to Normal.

Now move the mouse pointer toward the document area. As you move, the pointer changes to an airbrush. (If CAPS LOCK is on or if the Painting Tools Cursor group is set to Precise, your pointer will be a crosshair, but the tool will still work as the Airbrush.)

Move the Airbrush pointer anywhere in the document. Click the mouse and keep it pressed for a second or two. Notice that paint keeps spilling out. Now click and drag slowly for a few inches to see the soft, diffused spray created by the tool.

The
Summer
Sale
Postcard
project

**FIGURE 5-5**

To observe the effects of painting with a lower pressure, click and drag the Pressure slider control in the Airbrush Options palette to 50%. Move the Airbrush pointer back into the document, and click and hold the mouse button. This time, less paint is sprayed by the brush onto the screen.

Continue experimenting with the Airbrush tool, choosing various brush sizes and pressure settings. When you're ready, continue to the next section and explore the Airbrush's Fade options.

## The Airbrush Fade Options

To open the Airbrush Options palette, double-click on the Airbrush tool or click once on the tool if the Options palette is open on screen. Notice that the palette options here are very similar to those for the Paintbrush and Pencil tools. The Fade options for the Airbrush work exactly as they do with the Paintbrush and Pencil. You'll remember them—they are Transparent and Background. When one of these options is selected, painting starts with the foreground color and fades out to either a completely transparent color or to the background color. The Fade field controls how much paint appears before the fade occurs. For both Fade options, the brush size you choose in the Brushes palette controls the width of the fade.

To try out the Fade options, type **100** in the Fade field of the Airbrush Options palette. Click on the pop-up menu and choose Transparent, if it is not already set to this option. Set the Pressure to 100%. In the Brushes palette, choose a medium, soft-edged brush. Change the foreground color, if you wish. To see the fade, click and drag in a spiral motion. As you drag you'll see a soft-edged brush stroke that gradually fades out after 100 pixels of paint have been applied.

Next, try the Background Fade option. This time, choose Background from the pop-up menu in the Airbrush Options palette. Leave the Fade field set to 100. This will make it easier to compare the difference between the Transparent and Background fade options.

Before you begin to paint, set the foreground color to green and the background color to yellow. These two colors are near each other on the color wheel, and so there won't be a great contrast as one switches to the other. The fade effect will appear smoother and more realistic. Keep Brightness and Saturation set high to ensure that the colors will be bright. Now click and drag to create another spiral on screen. This time, the green, soft-edged brush stroke will gradually dissolve into the yellow you picked as the background color.

If you wish to keep experimenting, use a few other color pairs. Try working with colors that are near each other on the Hue slider, and then compare the effects to what you get when you pick a color and its complement, such as blue and yellow.

Before you continue to the next section, clear the screen by double-clicking on the Eraser tool and then clicking on the Erase Layer button. The Erase Layer button appears in the palette because you are in a layer that is not the Background layer. When a prompt appears, click OK to confirm.

## THE SUMMER SALE POSTCARD PROJECT

If you'd like to practice using the Airbrush tool, try your hand at creating the Summer Sale postcard, shown in Figure 5-5. This project was designed to convey a feeling of lightness and delicacy to match the type of clothes people buy in the summer. In

# Photoshop in Action

The flaring light effect was created by applying the Lens Flare filter in the Filter/Render submenu.

The Airbrush tool was used to create the glow effects in the planet and in the arm.

©ER/VEGA

Artist: Enrique Rivera-Vega                                Promotional Material

Enrique began this image by creating two rectangular selections. He filled the bottom selection with color, then applied the Add Noise filter to create a gravelly texture in the foreground. He filled the top selection with black, then used the Airbrush tool to create the lighter areas in the dark background. Next, Enrique created a circular selection for the planet, then used the Airbrush again to create the different lighting effects within it.

The robot was first sketched with the Pencil tool, then filled using the Paintbrush and Airbrush tools. All of the glow effects were created with the Airbrush tool.

order to create this mood, a very soft brush stroke was needed, one that would taper off. The Airbrush tool is perfect for the job.

## Creating the Sun

The first step in this project is creating the sun. You'll use the Airbrush tool with both the Fade to Background and to Transparent options. Using both Fade options adds variety and realism, as they are perfect for giving a soft edge to the sun and for blending its colors from yellow to orange.

1. Double-click on the Airbrush tool. In the Airbrush Options palette, make sure the Fade option is selected, then type **200** in the Fade field. Choose the Background option in the pop-up menu next to the words "steps to."

2. In the Brushes palette, pick any small, soft-edged brush.

3. In the Picker palette, choose an orange foreground color and a yellow background color.

4. Now create the spiral that is the center of the sun by clicking and dragging in a spiral motion.

5. In the Airbrush Options palette switch to the Fade to Transparent option to create the rays of the sun. Type **10** in the Fade field.

6. In the Brushes palette, pick a medium, soft-edged brush.

7. Position the mouse at the edge of the sun's spiral, and click and drag outward to create several rays, as shown in Figure 5-5.

8. Save your work and name the file **Summer.**

## Creating the Butterfly

In this section, you'll continue using the Airbrush to create the butterfly on the Summer Sale postcard.

1. Since you will be painting a sketch of the butterfly, make sure that the Fade option is no longer active in the Airbrush Options palette. If it is, deselect the Fade check box. In the palette, set Pressure to 25%.

2. Click on the Default Colors icon to reset the foreground to black and the background to white. In the Brushes palette, choose a small brush.

3. Use the Airbrush to sketch an outline of a short ellipse and a long ellipse for the butterfly's body. Then create the outline of the wings.

4. Once you've sketched the outline of the butterfly, paint the wings using various shades of blue. Use different Pressure settings and different Fade options in the Airbrush Options palette.

5. When you have finished coloring the wings, you are ready to fill in the body of the butterfly. Use the Fade to Transparent option with Pressure set to 30%, but change the foreground color to black and choose a medium, soft-edged brush.

6. Now apply the finishing touches. Create the black strokes for texture in the butterfly's body, wings, eyes, and antennae by airbrushing with a small, hard-edged brush and Pressure set to 90%.

Feel free to continue to experiment with different colors and effects in the butterfly. If you try something and don't like the results, use the Undo command. Also, don't forget that you can activate the Eraser tool's Erase to Saved option to revert a portion of your document to the last saved version. Try using the different modes and opacities in the Eraser Options palette.

## Creating the Text and Clothing Items

The next step in the postcard project is using the Type tool to add the words, SUMMER SALE. Remember, when you use the Type tool, Photoshop paints using the current foreground color and current opacity and painting/editing mode settings in the Layers palette.

1. Activate the Type tool and click in the upper-left side of your document window.

2. In the Type dialog box, choose Times (or another typeface) in the Font pop-up menu. Type **40** in the Size field. Make sure the Anti-aliased check box is selected. In the text field, type **SUMMER SALE.** To have Photoshop drop the type into your painting, click OK.

Notice that the Layers palette shows you that a floating selection exists. This indicates that this is a temporary layer.

3. While the text is floating, move it into position by clicking and dragging in the middle of the text. Do not deselect.

4. Try creating a special effect in the text by changing the foreground color and using the Airbrush tool to apply another color. When you paint over selected text, Photoshop applies the color to the text only, not to the underlying pixels. With the Airbrush tool, dab a bright color over the SUMMER SALE letters to create highlights.

5. To finish off the project, create the clothes and the hangers. Draw the hangers with the Pencil tool, and then paint the clothes over them; use the Airbrush and Paintbrush tools with whatever colors you like. If you wish, add more items.

When you're satisfied with your work on the Summer Sale postcard project, save and close the file.

# INTRODUCTION TO THE GRADIENT TOOL AND CUSTOM BRUSHES

In this section, you'll learn how to create blends and custom brushes. A *blend* is a gradual transition from one color to another. A *custom brush* is a brush you create by specifying its size, shape, and other characteristics. After you create a custom brush, Photoshop automatically adds it to the Brushes palette.

To get started, create a new file 6 inches wide by 4 inches high. You'll use this file for both the introductory exercises and for the final project. The file resolution should be set to 72 and the Mode to RGB Color.

## Using the Gradient Tool to Create Blends

The Gradient tool allows you to fill the screen or a selection with a blend that gradually changes from the foreground color to the background color, or from the foreground color to a transparent background, or from a transparent background to the foreground color. Blends are frequently used to produce shading and lighting effects, as well as to quickly create visually pleasing backgrounds. By changing opacity and/or painting/editing mode settings, you can create interesting effects by applying blends over images and over other blends.

To access the Gradient Tool Options palette, double-click on the Gradient tool icon in the Toolbox.

```
┌─────────────────────────────────────┐
│ □                                 ⊡ │ ▶
│ ┌─────────────────────┐             │
│ │ Gradient Tool Options \           │
│ ┌───────────────┐  Opacity:   100% │
│ │ Normal      ▼ │                   │
│                              △      │
│ Style: │ Foreground to Background ▼│
│ Midpoint:   50%   Radial Offset    │
│            △                        │
│ Type: │ Linear  ▼ │      ⊠ Dither  │
└─────────────────────────────────────┘
```

**C**AUTION:  *Be aware that various factors may affect the way a blend prints. The blend's printed output will depend on the colors you use, the length of the blend, the file mode you are in, and the resolution at which you are printing. For more information about printing blends, see Chapter 14.*

**T**IP:  *If you keep the Dither check box selected when creating a blend, Photoshop smoothes the foreground and background using a process called dithering. This should help prevent banding when outputting a blend. When banding occurs, steps or breaks are seen in the blend.*

## The Gradient Tool Style Options

The Style options in the Gradient Tool Options palette determine how colors are used in the blend. If Foreground to Background is selected, Photoshop will blend the colors, creating a smooth transition between the foreground and background colors. The next two options, Foreground to Transparent and Transparent to Foreground, create a blend from the foreground color to a transparent background or from a transparent background to the foreground color. Clockwise Spectrum and Counterclockwise Spectrum alter the blend so the colors change from foreground to background, using the colors in the color wheel in either a clockwise or counterclockwise direction.

## The Linear Gradient Option

The Linear option for the Gradient tool creates a blend along a straight line. The blend is created from the point where you start clicking and dragging the mouse and ends where you release the mouse.

The Midpoint Skew slider in the Gradient Tool Options palette determines where the blend begins to change from the foreground to background color, or to or from Transparency. The default Midpoint Skew value is 50%; if you move the slider to a larger number, the blend will be produced with more foreground color than background color. Set the slider to a smaller number, and the blend will be created with less foreground color and more background color.

You can specify where you want the blend to occur by selecting an area on screen with one of the selection tools before you create the blend. You can even create a blend inside text by clicking and dragging with the Gradient tool over floating text. If you don't designate a selection or create the blend over floating type, the entire screen will be filled with the blend.

Try creating a blend that will simulate a change in lighting. To produce a blend for a lighting effect, you don't want to pick colors that contrast too much. Choose a yellow foreground color (the first yellow color swatch in the Swatches palette). For the background color, lower the Hue slider about 20 degrees. This will produce an orange color.

1. You'll create the blend in a rectangular selection, so activate the Marquee tool and set the Shape pop-up menu to Rectangular. Click and drag to create a rectangle about 2.5 inches wide by 2 inches high.

2. Double-click on the Gradient tool, and make sure that Style is set to Foreground to Background in the Gradient Tool Options palette. Click on the Type pop-up menu and set it to Linear. Set the Midpoint slider to 50%.

3. Now create a gradient that starts on the left with the foreground color and blends to the right into the background color. Position the crosshair about .5 inch inside the selection. Click and drag from left to right—the direction in which you want the blend to go. As you drag, Photoshop will create a line on screen indicating where the blend will be created. To

5

produce the blend, release the mouse about .5 inch away from the right side of the selection.

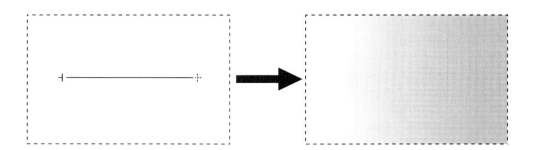

Notice that the blend appears between the two endpoints of your mouse selection. Photoshop fills the area directly before the blend with the solid foreground color and the area after the blend with solid background color. To get a sense of how Photoshop fills in the intermediate colors, open the Info palette (if it isn't already open), slowly move the mouse pointer over the blend from left to right, without clicking, and watch the color values gradually change.

If you'd like to experiment with a few more linear blends, clear your screen first; then try adjusting the Midpoint setting in the Gradient Tool Options palette, and create another blend. You also might want to try some *angled blends*. This is easily done by clicking and dragging at an angle with the Gradient tool. You can even hold down the constraining SHIFT key to create blends at a 45-degree diagonal. After you've created a few more blends, continue on to the next section to create a radial gradient.

**IP:** *If you wish to test a blend without altering your document, create it in the Scratch palette. After setting the foreground and background color and the Gradient Tool Options palette, click and drag with the Gradient tool in the Scratch palette.*

## The Radial Gradient Option

The Radial option for the Gradient tool produces an effect similar to a linear blend, except the radial blend radiates outward from a central starting point. In this exercise, you'll see the effects of creating a radial blend using the Transparent to Foreground option.

Try creating a radial blend in a circular selection.

1. Create a new RGB Color file, 3 inches by 3 inches. Set the background contents to Transparent.

2. Set the foreground color to yellow.

3. To create the circular selection, double-click on the Marquee tool. In the Marquee Options palette set the Shape pop-up menu to Elliptical and the Style pop-up menu to Normal.

4. Double-click on the Gradient tool. In the Gradient Tool Options palette, click on the Type pop-up menu and choose Radial. Set the Style to Transparent to Foreground.

To create the blend, position the mouse in the center of your elliptical selection. Click and drag in any direction toward the edge of the elliptical selection. This time Photoshop creates the blend radiating out from the center, instead of in a straight line.

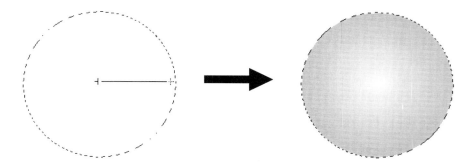

Notice that you can see right through the lightest area of the blend. This is because you used the Transparent to Foreground option.

5. Before opening the file that you will place the blend into, deselect.

6. Open the Flower (PC users: flower.jpg) file in the Tutorial folder. Activate the Move tool and drag the blend over the Flower file. You'll see that the flower shows through the transparent part of the blend. The same effect could also have been produced by creating a new layer in the Flower file, then creating the Transparent to Foreground blend in the new layer.

At this point you'll probably want to do some experimenting with radial blends. If you wish, you can also try out various settings for the Radial Offset option. The Radial Offset percentage controls the distance from the start of the blend, where the foreground color is displayed as a solid color. For example, a radial offset of 25% makes the solid foreground color appear for 25% of the distance from the starting point to the end of the blend.

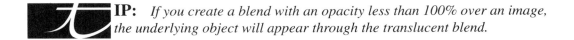

**IP:** *If you create a blend with an opacity less than 100% over an image, the underlying object will appear through the translucent blend.*

**CREATING A GLOWING PLANET EFFECT**  Here's how you can use the Gradient tool's Radial Offset option with the Elliptical Marquee's Feather Radius option to create a glowing planet effect.

1. Start by choosing a reddish foreground color and a reddish-yellow background color.

2. Double-click on the Gradient tool. Set the Style to Foreground to Background. Choose the Radial option. Leave Midpoint set at 50%. Change Radial Offset to 60%.

3. Activate the Marquee Tool palette by double-clicking on the tool. Set the Marquee to the Elliptical shape. Click on the Constrained Aspect Ratio radio button, and set Width to 1 and Height to 1. Set the Feather field to 15. Click OK.

4. Now click and drag on screen with the Marquee tool to create the circular selection.

5. Activate the Gradient tool and position the crosshair in the center of the selection. Click and drag toward the edge of the circular selection. When you release the mouse, the blend will be created with a large central red area. The Radial Offset setting of 60% is responsible for creating this red mass in the circle. The Feather setting creates the soft edge of the blend.

Before continuing, reset the Marquee tool to Normal and change the Feather field to 0.

# Photoshop in Action

The light beams were created with linear blends

The lighting effects under the plane were created with blends

The Airbrush tool was used to create the the movie marquee lights

**Artist: Leslie Carbaga**  **Art Director: Ron Kellum**  **Client: Vision Cable of South Carolina**

Leslie created this image for a pay-per-view advertisement. The outline for the image was sketched in Adobe Illustrator, then placed in Photoshop.

Using the Pen tool, Leslie created paths to outline each part of the image, then converted each path into a selection. Most of the lighting effects were created using the Gradient tool to produce blends in the different selections.

Leslie then touched up the image by using the Airbrush tool to paint the lights in the movie marquee and to fill the area under the marquee.

## Creating and Using Custom Brushes

Thus far in this chapter, you've been using the default brushes that appear automatically in Photoshop's Brushes palette. But it's likely you will want to create your own custom brushes to add more variety and style to your work, and this section tells you how. You'll also learn how to save a palette of custom brushes and load it from your hard disk.

### Examining the New Brush Dialog Box

You'll start by creating a new brush based on one of the brushes already in the Brushes palette. You'll use a large brush as the model because its diameter, hardness, and roundness attributes will be more noticeable than those of a smaller one. Click once on the largest, hard-edged brush in the first row of the Brushes palette.

Your next step in creating a new brush is to choose the New Brush command in the Options menu of the Brushes palette. The New Brush dialog box will appear, with the settings for the brush that was selected in the Brushes palette. In the dialog box you'll see there are sliders for controlling Diameter, Hardness, and Spacing, and boxes for entering Angle degrees and Roundness percentages.

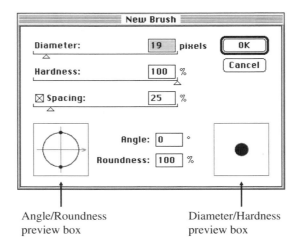

Angle/Roundness          Diameter/Hardness
preview box              preview box

**DIAMETER**   Start by exploring the Diameter setting, which determines the size of the brush. To change this, click and drag the slider control, or type a value (in pixels) into the Diameter field. Try clicking and dragging the slider control to the right. As you drag, watch the preview box in the lower-right corner of the dialog box. It may take a moment or two, but eventually a preview of the new brush size will appear.

As you drag the slider to the right, the brush's diameter grows. Change the diameter to 29. If you make it any larger, the brush's representation in the Brushes palette will be replaced by a number.

**HARDNESS**   Now test the Hardness slider, which controls whether the brush paints with a soft or hard edge. This value is a percentage of the center of the brush. The best way to visualize this is to gradually drag the Hardness slider to the left and stop at every 25% interval to watch the changes in the preview box. As you drag, you'll see a light shade surrounding the brush gradually grow. This shading indicates the soft area of the brush. Drag all the way to 0% to see the preview of the softest setting. In the Hardness field, 0% produces the softest brush, 100% the hardest.

**5**

**SPACING**   Next, test the Spacing option, which controls the distance the brush paints as make you make a stroke. The Spacing option is turned off or on with a check box.

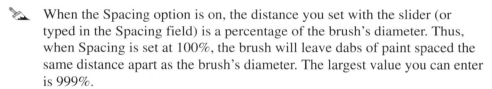

When the Spacing option is on, the distance you set with the slider (or typed in the Spacing field) is a percentage of the brush's diameter. Thus, when Spacing is set at 100%, the brush will leave dabs of paint spaced the same distance apart as the brush's diameter. The largest value you can enter is 999%.

When the Spacing option is off, the brush's stroke is controlled by your mouse or stylus dragging speed. Drag slowly, and more pixels on screen are absorbed with paint; drag quickly, and the brush jumps over pixels.

Turn the New Brush Spacing option on and set the value to 300%, a change that will be easily seen when you start painting with your custom brush.

**ANGLE AND ROUNDNESS**   The next two options in the Brushes palette, Angle and Roundness, work together. The Angle setting changes the brush shape only if Roundness is *not* set to 100%. (A roundness setting of 100% produces a circular brush.) Therefore, start by changing the brush shape from a circle to an ellipse.

You can change the roundness by either typing a value in the Roundness field or by clicking and dragging either of the two dots in the preview box in the lower-left corner of the dialog box. So, to create an elliptical brush, you would click and drag one of the two dots toward the other one. As you drag, you will decrease the percentage of roundness. The lower the percentage of roundness, the more elliptical your brush will be.

Once you've created the elliptical brush, you can change the Angle setting; you either type in a value between -180 and 180 degrees, or click and drag on the arrowed axis line in the preview box.

Now try this out: Change the Angle value to create a brush that will be dramatically different from the original one. Set the Angle to 45 degrees and the Roundness to 40%. Notice that both preview boxes reflect the changes. Before closing the New Brush dialog box, examine all the settings of your custom brush. Diameter should be 29 pixels, Hardness 0%, Spacing 300%, Angle 45%, and Roundness 40%. Click OK to accept the settings.

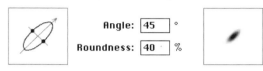

Your new brush appears in the bottom row of the Brushes palette.

Experiment with your custom brush using the Paintbrush tool. Click on the tool, and then activate the custom brush in the Brushes palette. Click and drag on screen to test it. You'll see that the brush paints a stroke at an angle of 45 degrees and creates a dotted effect, as shown here, because of the Spacing setting in the New Brush dialog box. This brush stroke was created with the following settings: Hardness 0%, Spacing 300%, Angle 45 degrees, and Roundness 40%.

Now return to your new brush's settings and change the Spacing and Hardness options. To do this, double-click on the Brushes palette on the brush you just created. Change Spacing to 25% and set Hardness to 100%. To accept the new settings, click OK. To see the change, try painting once again with your custom brush. As you paint, you'll see the brush now has a hard-edged stroke, and the white spaces between the brush strokes have disappeared. This brush stroke was created from these settings: Hardness 100%, Spacing 25%, Angle 45 degrees, and Roundness 40%.

If you wish to continue experimenting, try turning off the Spacing option by deselecting the Spacing check box in the New Brush dialog box. Try a few quick brush strokes and then a very slow brush stroke. You'll see that when you paint slowly, more paint is absorbed by the pixels on screen. When you paint faster, fewer pixels are filled in.

## Defining a Custom Brush

With Photoshop you can design unusual custom brushes, something only an electronic painting program could produce. In this next example, you'll create a brush using the Type tool. Instead of using the New Brush command in the Brushes palette pop-up menu, you'll use the Define Brush command, which turns a selection or floating text into a brush. To demonstrate this, try creating a custom brush out of the dollar sign character on the keyboard. This will allow you to paint dollar signs on the screen with the painting tools.

1. To begin, activate the Type tool and click anywhere in your document. In the Type Tool dialog box, choose any font from the pop-up menu; then type **24** in the Size field and type **$** in the text box. Click OK to make the text appear on screen.

2. While the dollar sign is floating, choose Define Brush from the pop-up menu in the Brushes palette. A $ (dollar sign) should appear in the Brushes palette.

3. Double-click on this brush in the Brushes palette. Notice that your options for altering the brush have been changed: Spacing and Anti-aliased are the only choices available. (The Anti-aliased option is only available for small brush sizes.) Before you close the Brush Options dialog box, feel free to change the settings if you wish.

4. To use your new brush, activate either the Paintbrush or Airbrush tool and then select the $ (dollar sign) brush. All you need to do now is just click on the screen, and the dollar sign will appear in the current foreground color.

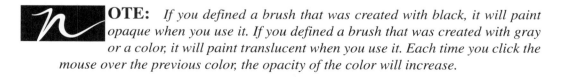

**OTE:** *If you defined a brush that was created with black, it will paint opaque when you use it. If you defined a brush that was created with gray or a color, it will paint translucent when you use it. Each time you click the mouse over the previous color, the opacity of the color will increase.*

You can purchase different typefaces that are symbols and/or ornaments and use them to create different custom brushes. (These typefaces include Dingbats, Carta, Sonata, Wood, and Wingdings.) For example, if you are using the Dingbat font, you can create star (★ ✫), snowflake (✳), sun (☼), flower (✿), and heart (♥) brushes. To create stars, press SHIFT-H or SHIFT-P. Press the letter f to create a snowflake Dingbat. Press the letter b to create a sun. To create a flower, press SHIFT-MINUS. To create a heart, press OPTION-2 (PC users: ALT and type **0164** on the numeric keypad).

**TIP:** *In addition to using the Type tool to create custom brushes, you can create custom brushes from any selected object on screen. It doesn't matter what tool you use to create the object, or whether the image was created from scratch or digitized.*

You can also create, select, and define brushes in the Scratch palette. Just type a letter, or paint an object, or copy an item into the Scratch palette. If the item isn't selected, use a selection tool to select it. While the item is selected in the Scratch palette, choose Define Brush from the Brushes palette pop-up menu.

Continue experimenting, creating various custom brushes using the techniques described in this section. If you want to delete a brush, move the pointer over the brush that you want to delete, press and hold COMMAND (PC users: CTRL); when the Scissors icon appears, click. You can also use the Delete Brush command in the Brushes pop-up menu to delete the currently selected brush. When you are done, proceed to the next section to learn how to save your custom brushes.

## Saving and Loading Custom Brushes

If you like the custom brushes you create and wish to use them again, you can save the entire Brushes palette to disk. When you need it again, you can load the palette from the disk.

To save your Brushes palette, including all the custom brushes you have designed, select Save Brushes from the Brushes palette pop-up menu. To keep all of your custom brushes together, it might be a good idea to save them in the Brushes & Patterns folder (PC users: brushes). When you install Photoshop, the Brushes & Patterns folder (PC users: brushes) is automatically installed. Once you've located the folder, name your brush palette **MyBrush** and click Save.

**OTE:** *If you wish to add custom brushes that already exist in a saved brushes file to the current Brushes palette on screen, use the Append Brushes command in the Brushes palette pop-up menu.*

Incidentally, since you've opened Photoshop's Brushes & Patterns folder, take a look at the custom brushes Adobe includes with Photoshop. Within this folder are three different brush files: Assorted Brushes, Drop Shadow Brushes, and Square Brushes (PC users: custom.abr, shadows.abr, and square.abr files).

Any time you wish to load any of these or other custom brushes, just select Load Brushes from the Brushes palette pop-up menu. For example, choose Load Brushes from the Brushes palette pop-up menu. Open the Patterns & Brushes folder (PC users: brushes). Click on the Assorted Brushes file (PC users: custom.abr) and open it. The brushes in the Brushes palette have now changed. Your Brushes palette should now look like this:

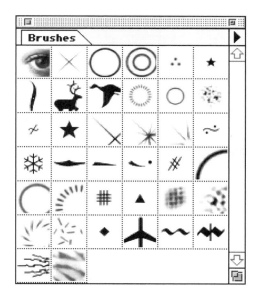

Take a few moments to experiment with the various brushes.

**OTE:** *Whenever you wish to return the default Brushes palette to the screen, load the Default Brushes file (PC users: default.abr) from the Brushes & Patterns folder (PC users: brushes), or choose Reset from the Brushes palette pop-up menu.*

This concludes the exercises and projects for the painting tools and techniques. In the next section, you'll learn about changing painting/editing modes.

## PAINTING/EDITING MODES

In the Options palette, you can choose from a wide range of color-painting modes, also called editing modes. These modes are generally used to change colors and create special effects when painting, or when pasting or blending previously colored areas. How those areas are affected depends upon the painting/editing mode, the color being applied, and the range of pixels that are painted or pasted over. For instance, if you apply a red color to an image in Darken mode, only the underlying pixels in the image that are lighter than red will be darkened with the red color. If you paint in Lighten mode, only pixels darker than your red will be lightened by the red color.

In addition to the Options palette, painting/editing modes appear in the Layers palette, and in several dialog boxes for Fill, Stroke, Fill Path, Apply Image, Calculations and New Layer.

This section describes the fundamental purpose of each mode. As you work through this book, you'll gain experience with all the modes and see how they can produce effects from simple to startling. At the conclusion of this section, you'll have a chance to create some special effects using the Lighten and Darken modes.

Here are basic descriptions of the painting/editing modes:

***Normal***   This painting mode modifies every underlying pixel with the color being applied. In Normal mode, with Opacity set to 100%, underlying pixels will be completely replaced with the color being applied. If Opacity is less than 100%, the color of underlying pixels will show through the color being applied.

***Darken***   Only colors lighter than the color you are applying are affected, causing them to be darkened by the painting color.

***Lighten***   This mode is the opposite of Darken mode. Only target pixels darker than the color you are applying are modified. The darker colors are lightened by the painting color.

***Hue***   When you paint or edit in Hue mode, you paint with only the hue of the painting color. Thus, only the hue of the affected pixels is modified by the painting color, but not their Saturation and Luminosity values. Applying colors to black or white pixels in Hue mode has no effect.

***Saturation***   When you edit or apply color in Saturation mode, you paint with the Saturation value of the painting color. Thus, only the Saturation values of underlying pixels will change. Applying colors to black or white pixels in Saturation mode will have no effect.

***Color***   In this mode, you paint with the Hue and Saturation of a painting color. Thus, the Hue and Saturation values of underlying pixels change, but not Luminosity. The Color mode is frequently used to colorize gray or monochrome images because underlying shadows and contours will show through the color that is being applied. The effect is similar to colorizing old black-and-white movies. This technique is demonstrated in Chapter 9.

 **OTE:**   *If you wish to colorize a grayscale file, you must convert the file to a Color mode such as RGB Color, using the Mode menu. For more information about changing modes, see Chapter 9.*

***Luminosity***   Luminosity measures a color's brightness. When you paint in Luminosity mode, you paint with only the luminance value of a color. In Luminosity mode, the lightness and darkness values of an underlying color's pixels will change, but the color values won't. The Luminosity mode is the opposite of the Color mode.

Photoshop's internal formula for computing a pixel's luminosity is

30% of Red value + 59% of Green value + 11% of Blue value

This formula always produces a number between 0 and 255. The closer a number is to 255, the closer the luminosity is to white; the lower the number, the closer the luminosity is to black. When you apply color in Luminosity mode over black or white, all RGB color values will switch to the luminosity value produced by the formula, which will apply a gray shade to your image.

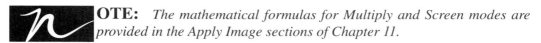

**OTE:** *The Hue, Saturation, Color, and Luminosity modes are based on a Hue/Saturation/Luminosity (HSL) color model. This color model is slightly different from the Hue/Saturation/Brightness (HSB) color model. Thus, if you try to evaluate the effects of painting in these modes using the HSB readouts in the Info palette, it may seem that the modes do not work exactly as specified. For instance, when you paint over a color using Hue mode, the HSB readout in the Info palette may show that the color's saturation as well as its hue have changed.*

**Multiply**   This mode multiplies color values, causing underlying pixels to darken. Each time a color is applied, pixels will receive more of the painting color's values. Painting with black in Multiply mode produces black. Painting with white has no effect. Painting in Multiply mode can be somewhat similar to applying colored markers over an image.

**Screen**   This mode whitens underlying pixels, leaving them in a tint of the color being applied. If you repeatedly apply color in Screen mode, pixels grow lighter and lighter. The Screen mode is the opposite of the Multiply mode. Thus, painting with white in Screen mode produces white; painting with black has no effect.

**OTE:** *The mathematical formulas for Multiply and Screen modes are provided in the Apply Image sections of Chapter 11.*

**Dissolve**   When colors are applied in Dissolve mode, the painting color randomly replaces underlying pixels. The resulting color is a mixture of painting color and the color of the original underlying pixels. Results depend upon the opacity of the painting color and the opacity of the underlying colors. This can produce anything from a speckled paint to a sandpaper effect. For more dramatic results, use Dissolve mode with a large brush and experiment with different opacities.

**Behind**   This mode is only available when working in a layer (other than the Background). Behind simulates the effect of painting behind an image on screen. Painting over non-transparent areas (colored areas) has no effect, but the paint applied appears over the transparent areas. When working in Behind mode, think of it as painting on the back of a clear plastic acetate rather than on a painter's canvas.

***Overlay*** When painting in Overlay mode, underlying pixels are either screened or multiplied to blend with the painting color. When you paint, darker underlying colors cause the painting color to be multiplied; lighter underlying colors cause the painting color to be screened. When painting over images, highlights and shadows are maintained. Overlay produces no effect when painting over white or black pixels.

***Soft Light*** This mode produces the effect of pointing a soft spotlight on an image. If your painting color is lighter than underlying pixels, the image is lightened. If your painting color is darker than underlying pixels, the image is darkened. The effect is one of diffuse, not harsh, light being applied.

***Hard Light*** This mode produces the effect of pointing a harsh spotlight on an image. If your painting color is lighter than underlying pixels, the image is lightened. If your painting color is darker than underlying pixels, the image is darkened. Painting with black in Hard Light mode produces black; painting with white produces white.

**IP:** *To quickly see the difference between Soft and Hard light modes, open an image on screen. Set the foreground color to yellow or yellow orange. Select the entire screen by choosing Choose All. Use the Edit/Fill command to fill using Soft Light mode; undo, then use the Edit/Fill command to fill in Hard Light mode.*

***Difference*** This mode subtracts the brightness or luminance values of the painting color from the brightness values of the underlying pixels. When using Difference it's helpful to remember that the pixel value of black is 0, and the brightness value of white is 255. Painting with black in Difference mode has no effect on underlying pixels. Painting over black in Difference mode produces the color you are painting with (because you are subtracting a color value from zero). Thus, if you had a black stripe against a green background, and filled the entire image using Difference mode with green, the result would be a green stripe with a black background. Painting over white in Difference mode produces the complement of the color you are painting with.

If you wish to compute the exact resulting brightness value produced when using Difference, use the formula above to compute the luminosity value of two colors, then subtract the two luminosity values.

***Clear*** This mode only appears when working in a layer (other than the Background). It appears in the Line and Paint Bucket Options palette Mode pop-up menu, in the Edit/Fill Mode pop-up menu, and in the Mode pop-up menu of the Fill

Path or Fill Subpath dialog box. Editing in this mode is similar to using the Eraser tool while working in the layer. Clear mode wipes away color, making pixels transparent.

*Threshold*   This mode only appears when working in Bitmap mode files. It indicates that you will be painting with black if the foreground color is set to 50% black or greater; otherwise you will be painting with white.

## Color Mode Exercises

In this section, you'll try using the Darken, Lighten, and Behind modes with the Type and Gradient tools to see how these modes completely change how a blend is applied. First you'll create a radial blend behind some text; then you'll create a linear blend within the letters of the text.

1. Begin by opening a new file, 5 inches by 5 inches. Set the mode to RGB and the resolution to 72 ppi. In the New dialog box, set the Contents radio button to White.

2. Click on the Default Colors icon to reset the foreground and and background colors. This will ensure that the text you create is black.

3. Select the Type tool and click on the screen. When the Type Tool dialog box appears, click on the Font pop-up menu and choose Times (or the font of your choice). In the Size field box, type **100**. Leave the Leading and Spacing fields empty. In the Style group, check to see that Anti-aliased is selected. In the Text field, type **BLEND**. When you are finished, click OK.

4. While the text is still floating, move it to the center of your document, using the mouse or the keyboard arrow keys. While the text is still selected, make sure Opacity is set to 100% in the Layers palette. To open the Layers palette, choose Show Layers from the Window/Palettes submenu. Now, deselect the text by choosing None from the Select menu.

5. Next, create the blend. Double-click on the Gradient tool to open the Gradient Tool Options palette. Select the Clockwise Spectrum option, leave Midpoint set to 50%, and select the Radial option from the Type pop-up menu. Click on the Mode pop-up menu and choose the Darken mode. Set Opacity to 100%.

6. Pick a yellow foreground color and a blue background color.

7. Now create the radial blend. With the Gradient tool activated, click and drag diagonally from the top-left corner of your document to the bottom-right corner. The blend appears with the text over it. Because you used the Darken mode, only the areas lighter than the painting color were affected, not the darker areas. Thus, even though you created the blend over the entire screen, only the white pixels were affected, not the black text.

   Now, you'll work with the Lighten mode, the opposite of Darken.

8. In the Edit menu, select Undo to remove the effects of the blend that was created in Darken mode.

9. In the Gradient Tool Options palette, click on the Mode pop-up menu and change the mode to Lighten. Before creating another blend, choose Linear from the Type pop-up menu.

10. To create the blend, position the mouse to the left of the word *BLEND,* and click and drag to the far-right side of the screen. When you release the mouse, you'll see that the blend is created inside the text, without affecting the white background. The Lighten mode only lightens areas darker than the painting color. Thus, the black text was lightened by the blend, and the background white area was not affected. By switching to Lighten mode, you were able to change the text without first selecting it.

Next, try an exercise which demonstrates how the Behind mode simulates painting behind your image.

1. As you did in the previous exercise, create a new 72 ppi RGB file, 5 inches by 5 inches. This time, however, set the background Contents to Transparent before clicking OK.

2. Set the foreground color to Red.

3. With the Type tool selected, click in the middle of your document. In the Type Tool dialog box pick a font, type **100** in the Size field, make sure the Anti-aliased option in the Style group is selected, and type the word **Paint**. Click OK for your type to appear in your document. Deselect the text.

4. Double-click on the Gradient tool. In the Gardient Tool Options palette, set the Type pop-up menu to Linear, the Style pop-up menu to Clockwise

**5**

Spectrum, and set the Mode to Behind. Now, use the Gradient tool to click and drag from left to right over the entire image.

The resulting image will appear as if you had painted behind the word on screen. The transparent background is filled with the gradient; the word is not affected.

You have just seen several very clear examples of how powerful the painting/editing modes can be in your Photoshop work. You now have new options at your disposal that edit pixels not according to whether they are selected but according to their color values.

## CONCLUSION

All the exercises in this chapter have offered but a taste of the features and special effects that await you in Photoshop. In Chapter 6, the electronic magic will continue as you learn the basics of image editing.

# 6

# INTRODUCTION TO
# IMAGE EDITING

Image editing is where the magic of Photoshop truly comes alive. With Photoshop's image-editing tools at your command, objects once hidden in darkness will suddenly emerge from the shadows. Images almost lost in the distance will gradually sharpen into focus. Images that are bland, barren, or unbalanced can be populated with just the right objects in exactly the right place. In short, Photoshop's image-editing tools allow you to produce or improve an image to look the way you want it to look.

The goal of this chapter, though, is not to concentrate on the fantastic and amazing, but rather to provide you with an introduction to the basics of image editing. We'll begin here by performing a little image-editing magic with the Blur/Sharpen, Dodge/Burn/Sponge, Rubber Stamp, and Smudge tools. As you did in Chapter 5, you'll use these tools from the Toolbox in conjunction with the Brushes and Options palettes.

You'll begin the exercises in this chapter by opening a digitized image. With this image on screen, you will use the Dodge and Burn tools to lighten overexposed and darken underexposed areas. You'll use the Sponge tool to saturate (intensify) and desaturate (weaken) the colors in your image. Once you've improved the image's exposure levels, you'll use the Blur and Sharpen tools to soften and clarify certain areas. With the Smudge tool, you'll blend small parts of the image to create watercolor and finger-painting effects. You'll also use the powerful Rubber Stamp tool to clone areas of the image, create impressionistic effects, and apply a pattern to the digitized image. Finally, you'll explore Photoshop's Quick Edit command which enables you to load only a portion of an image when you need to edit it.

When you are ready to begin, open any digitized image as your practice document. If you don't have a digitized image available, open the Frames (PC users: frames.jpg) file in the Adobe Photoshop Tutorial folder.

The examples in this chapter use a scanned image of an oriental fan. Figure 6-1 shows the original scanned image of the oriental fan with its imperfections. You can see that light areas needed to be darkened, and shadowed areas needed to be lightened. The flowers needed to be sharpened and their colors intensified so that they would stand out. The edges of the fan also needed to be softened, so that the fan would blend into a background photograph. Figure 6-2 shows the corrected fan as part of a completed project. Notice that the fan now has more flowers than in the original image—these flowers were *cloned*, or copied, to make the fan look more interesting. The translucent effect of the type was created by using the Type tool to add the text, then setting Opacity to 50% in the Layers palette.

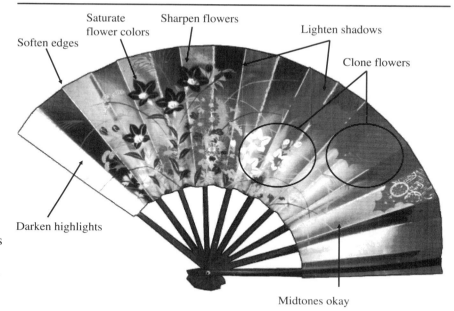

Soften edges

Saturate
flower colors

Sharpen flowers

Lighten shadows

Clone flowers

Darken highlights

Midtones okay

Corrections
needed for
the oriental
fan image

**FIGURE 6-1**

6

Oriental
fan and text
added to
the image
(Background
setting
photograph
courtesy of
Stacy
Kollar
Photography)

**FIGURE 6-2**

## USING THE DODGE AND BURN TOOLS

The Dodge and Burn tools are two tools that have begun enticing photographers out of the darkroom and into the Photoshop studio. These tools are simulations of traditional darkroom techniques. Photographers can often improve even their best work by using Dodge and Burn to block out or add light from a negative in order to enhance image definition. In photography, dodging is usually employed to lighten *shadow areas* (the darkest portions of an image), and burning is employed to darken *highlights* (the brightest parts of an image)—both techniques increase the detail in a photograph. Photoshop's Dodge and Burn tools produce the same effects in a digitized image.

As discussed in "The Editing Tools" section in Chapter 2, the Dodge, Burn, and Sponge tools share one location in the Toolbox, with only one icon visible at a time (Dodge is the default tool). You can switch tools using the Tool pop-up menu that appears in the Toning Tools Options palette. (The Sponge tool will be discussed in the next section.)

When either Dodge or Burn is activated, the slider in the Toning Tools Options palette measures exposure. In photography, an *overexposed* image is one that is too light; an *underexposed* image is too dark. By clicking and dragging on the slider control, you can set the exposure level from 1% to 100%. By typing a number on your keyboard, you can step through exposure settings in intervals of 10% (typing **0** sets exposure to 100%). Increasing the exposure while using the Dodge tool intensifies the Dodge tool's lightening effect. Increasing the exposure while using the Burn tool intensifies the Burn tool's darkening effect.

When you use Dodge or Burn, the Mode pop-up menu in the Toning Tools Options palette displays the following options: Shadows, Midtones, and Highlights (shown in the following illustration). Highlights are the brightest components of an image; midtones are halfway between the highlights and shadows; and shadows are the darkest components of an image. By selecting one of these options, you can apply the Dodge or Burn tool to correct either shadows, midtones, or highlights. For instance, if you select Highlights, only highlight areas will be affected.

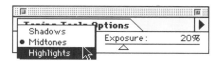

The width of the area you edit is determined by the size of the brush you pick in the Brushes palette and whether it is hard-edged or soft-edged. By allowing you to choose a brush size, an exposure level, and an image's highlights, midtones, and shadows, Photoshop provides tremendous control over brightness and darkness levels. Using a soft-edged brush with a low exposure creates a subtle effect; a hard-edged brush with a high exposure rate produces a more dramatic effect.

As you see in Figure 6-1, the light areas on the left side of the fan are too light, almost white. The dark areas on the top of the fan are almost the same color as the flowers, causing the flowers to fade into the background and appear less visible.

In the image that you have on your screen, look for areas that are too bright and too dark. These are the areas to focus on when you put the Dodge and Burn tools to work. Before you begin, however, use the File/Save As command so that you don't alter the original image. Name your practice file **Editing**. If you are using the Frames file, the JPEG Options dialog box will appear displaying four Image Quality options, after you click Save (PC users: OK). This is because the file was saved using a compression format called JPEG. Click OK to save the file in a compressed format. (For more information about JPEG and other file formats, see Appendix A.)

## Using the Dodge Tool to Lighten Image Areas

Start by using the Dodge tool to lighten shadow areas, so that more detail is visible in the dark areas of your image. If the Dodge tool is not shown as the active tool in the Toolbox, double-click on the Burn or Sponge tool icon. In the Toning Tools Options palette, click on the Tool pop-up menu and select Dodge.

Now use the Dodge tool to lighten shadow areas that are too dark.

1. First, in the Brushes palette, pick a soft-edged brush to make subtle changes. In the Toning Tools Options palette, set Exposure to 20% and click on the Mode pop-up menu and select Shadows.

2. Move the mouse pointer over a dark area of your image. (The mouse pointer changes to the Dodge tool when it enters the document window, unless CAPS LOCK is depressed.) Click and drag with a few short mouse

movements. As you do, you'll see that the darkest areas that you are clicking and dragging over become lighter. In Figure 6-3, you can see that the Dodge tool has lightened shadowed areas to add tonal balance to the fan.

3. Continue using the Dodge tool to lighten all of the unwanted dark areas in your image. You might need to change the brush size, exposure, and mode to produce the desired effect.

**OTE:** *Using a stylus and digitizing tablet provides even more control when editing images with the Dodge, Burn and Sponge tool. If you turn on the Size and/or Exposure check boxes in the Stylus Pressure section of the Toning Tools Options palette, you can change the exposure and size of the area you are editing by applying more or less pressure to the stylus pen.*

## Using the Burn Tool to Darken Image Areas

To switch to the Burn tool, click the Tool pop-up menu in the Toning Tools Options palette and select Burn.

1. With the Burn tool active, change the settings in the Brushes palette. To create a subtle effect, use a soft-edged brush. In the Toning Tools Options

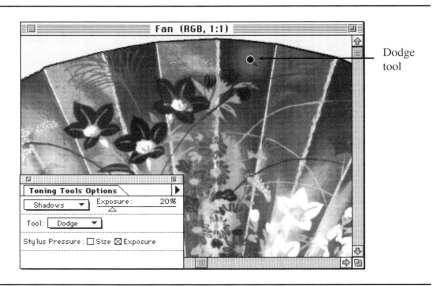

Lightening
shadows
with the
Dodge tool

**FIGURE 6-3**

palette, set Exposure to 20%. Since you only want to darken the brightest areas of the image, choose Highlights in the Mode pop-up menu.

2. In your image, look for a bright portion to start working on, and then position the Burn tool pointer over this area. (As you move the mouse pointer over the document area of the screen, the pointer changes to the Burn tool.)

**IP:** *If you wish to zoom in, use the keyboard shortcut: Hold down COMMAND-SPACEBAR (PC users: CTRL-SPACEBAR) and click over the area that you wish to zoom. To zoom out, click the mouse while pressing OPTION-SPACEBAR (PC users: ALT-SPACEBAR).*

3. When you are ready to begin, click and drag several times over the area using short strokes. As you drag, the lightest part of the image turns slightly darker. Now you can see how the rate of the darkening reflects the brush size and exposure setting you are using. Because the exposure setting is low and you are using a soft-edged brush, the darkening progresses slowly.

Figure 6-4 shows an example where the Burn tool is adding tone to an overexposed area of the fan.

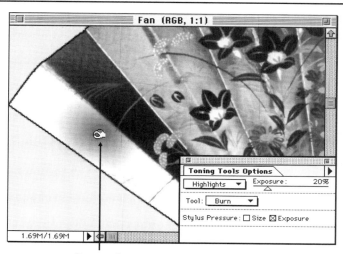

Darkening
highlights
with the
Burn tool

**FIGURE 6-4**

Burn tool

**IP:**  *If an image area requires you to lighten or darken in a straight line or at 45-degree increments—for example, if you're lightening or darkening the edges or corners of a book—press SHIFT while clicking and dragging with either the Dodge or Burn tool activated.*

4.  If you wish to darken shadow or midtone areas that are too light, you will need to change mode settings in the Toning Tools Options palette first. Continue editing by changing to Shadows or Midtones and using various brush sizes and exposure percentages.

When you've finished darkening the light areas of your image, move on to the next section, where you will use the Sponge tool.

## USING THE SPONGE TOOL

As mentioned earlier, the Sponge tool shares a toolbox location with the Dodge and Burn tools. When you choose the Sponge tool from the Tool pop-up menu in the Toning Tools Options palette the slider displays Pressure rather than Exposure, and you can choose either Desaturate or Saturate from the Mode pop-up menu.

The Sponge tool is used to increase the *saturation* or intensity of a color. When saturation is added to a color, the gray level of a color diminishes; thus it becomes less neutral. The Sponge tool can also be used to *desaturate* or diminish the intensity of a color. The Sponge tool's Desaturate option can be quite useful when an RGB Color image displays CMYK out-of-gamut colors. By rubbing the Sponge tool over these out of gamut colors, you can gradually dilute them so that they drop into the CMYK spectrum of printable colors.

*n***OTE:**  *For more information about using the Sponge tool to correct out-of-gamut colors, see Chapter 9.*

### Using the Sponge Tool to Saturate and Desaturate Image Areas

Start by using the Sponge tool to intensify colors in your image. In order to help you prevent over-saturating the colors, open the Info palette. If you make your colors too intense, the Info palette's CMYK out of gamut alarm will appear.

1. Open the Info palette by choosing Show Info from the Window/Palettes submenu.

   The out of gamut alarm only appears when the CMYK readouts are displayed in the Info palette. If you don't see the CMYK readouts in the Info palette, click on one of the eyedroppers in the palette and choose CMYK Color.

2. Move the Sponge tool to an area of your image where the colors look dull. Before you begin to saturate the area, notice the CMYK Color readouts in the Info palette.

3. In the Toning Tools Options palette, pick Saturate from the Mode pop-up menu and set the pressure to 30%. This will produce a slow and gradual saturation. If pressure were set to 100%, the colors would saturate very quickly. In the Brushes palette pick a medium, soft-edged brush. Start saturating by clicking and dragging the Sponge tool over the dull-colored areas in your image.

4. After you've saturated the colors in an image area, look at the CMYK Color readouts in the Info palette.

   If there is an exclamation point after the CMYK Color readouts, you've overstepped the CMYK Color gamut, which means the colors on screen cannot be printed on a commercial printing press. If you are outputting to slides or video, you do not have to worry about out of gamut CMYK colors.

5. If you've saturated too much and want to desaturate, choose Desaturate from the Mode pop-up menu in the Toning Tools Options palette. Use the Sponge tool to lower the intensity of the colors so that they are not out of gamut. Don't desaturate too much; otherwise, your colors will turn gray.

**IP:** *A quick way to switch between the Dodge, Burn and Sponge tools in the Toolbox is to press the OPTION key (PC users: ALT) while clicking on either tool. (You can also press O on your keyboard to toggle between Dodge, Burn and Sponge.) This same technique also works with the Blur and Sharpen tools. (Press R on your keyboard to toggle between Blur and Sharpen.)*

When you are finished using the Sponge tool, proceed to the next section to learn about using the Blur and Sharpen image-editing tools.

**OTE:** *If you wish to completely desaturate an image or selection, use Photoshop's Image/Adjust/Desaturate command. This will change all colors to shades of gray.*

## USING THE BLUR AND SHARPEN TOOLS

The Blur tool softens parts of an image by, as you probably guessed, blurring it. Its counterpart, the Sharpen tool, makes image areas sharper and more distinct. Photoshop's Blur tool works by decreasing the contrast among the pixels you drag over; the Sharpen tool works by heightening contrast in neighboring pixels.

Like the Dodge and Burn tool combination, Blur and Sharpen are often used to enhance the quality of digitized images. You may wonder, though, why anyone would want to make an image more blurry. It's because scanners sometimes accentuate edges too much, causing images to look too harsh. These edges can be softened with the Blur tool. The Blur tool can also be used to help soften the jagged edges of an image that is pasted into a document, so that it blends more smoothly into its surroundings. It can also be used to create subtle shadow effects.

The Blur and Sharpen tools share one location in the Toolbox, as do Dodge and Burn. By default, when Photoshop is first loaded, only the Blur tool appears in the Toolbox. Again, as with Dodge/Burn/Sponge, you can switch between the Blur and Sharpen tools by using the Tool pop-up menu in the Options palette. You can also press the OPTION key (PC users: ALT) and click on the active tool in the Toolbox or press R on your keyboard. Try holding the OPTION key (PC users: ALT) and clicking to switch between the Blur/Sharpen tools.

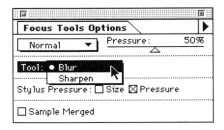

Now take a look at the Focus Tools Options palette. If the Options palette is already open, click once on the Blur/Sharpen tool. If it isn't open, double-click on the tool to display the Focus Tools Options palette. Click on the Mode pop-up menu to view the different modes. When the Blur or Sharpen tool is activated, the modes available to you in the palette are Normal, Darken, Lighten, Hue, Saturation, Color, and Luminosity. Also, notice that the slider in the palette now controls Pressure. (See Chapter 5 for a discussion of the different painting/editing modes.)

The Pressure slider controls the amount of sharpening and blurring that these tools produce. The greater the Pressure percentage, the greater the effect of the sharpening or blurring. As usual, the size of the area that changes is determined by the brush size you are using—smaller brushes affect smaller areas, larger brushes affect larger areas.

 **OTE:** *If you have a stylus and digitizing tablet, you can also take advantage of the two Stylus Pressure options for the Blur and Sharpen tools: Size and Pressure.*

When using Blur/Sharpen, the Rubber Stamp, and the Smudge tool, the Sample Merged check box option is available. When this option is not selected Photoshop analyzes pixel values only in the layer you are currently working in. If the check box option is selected, Photoshop samples and edits using pixel values from all visible layers, when the tool is used. Since you are working in only one layer, selecting the Sample Merged check box will have no effect when image editing. See Chapter 12 for more information about layers.

## Using the Sharpen Tool to Increase Contrast

Because it's easier to recognize the need for sharpening image areas rather than for blurring them, start by experimenting with the Sharpen tool first. If the Sharpen tool is not active, switch to it.

Before you begin sharpening your own image, pick a brush size in the Brushes palette and a Pressure value in the Focus Tools Options palette. Leave Mode set to Normal. By switching modes, you can control which image areas will be affected; for instance, if you choose Darken, only lighter pixels will be changed. If you use a medium-sized, soft-edged brush and a low Pressure setting, the sharpening effect will be barely noticeable. A large, hard-edged brush with a high Pressure value will produce a more intense effect.

Be aware of sharpening too much. If you overdo it, the colors will break up and become pixelated, as shown in Figure 6-5. Here the Sharpen tool is being used to heighten the contrast in the fan's flowers. To avoid oversharpening, use the Zoom tool to zoom in and keep a close eye on the pixels being affected.

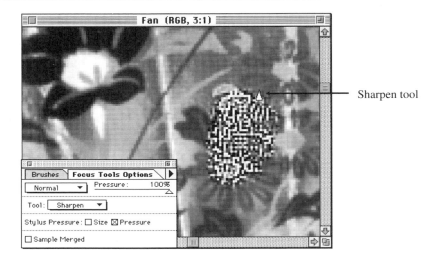

Sharpen tool

Pixelation
occurs
if you
oversharpen

**FIGURE 6-5**

Now decide which area you want to work on, move the Sharpen tool over that area, and click and drag the mouse to begin increasing contrast. Try moving to other areas in the image to see the results of sharpening with different Pressure settings.

 **EMEMBER:** *Oversharpening will cause pixelation.*

## Using the Blur Tool to Soften Hard Edges

 You can use the Blur tool to soften hard edges in an image and to correct any pixelation caused by oversharpening.

Press and hold OPTION (PC users: ALT) while clicking on the Sharpen tool to switch to the Blur tool. Look for areas in your image that are too sharp or that have hard edges that need to be softened. Work these edges first with a low-pressure setting in the Brushes palette, so you don't blur your image too much.

Figure 6-6 shows the Blur tool being used to correct the pixelation that occurred when the fan's flowers were being sharpened (in Figure 6-5). The Blur tool was also used to soften all of the hard edges of the fan, including the ridged perimeter after it was pasted into the final photograph.

 **OTE:** *In addition to using the Blur and Sharpen tools, you can apply filters to make entire images more or less distinct. Filters are discussed in Chapter 8.*

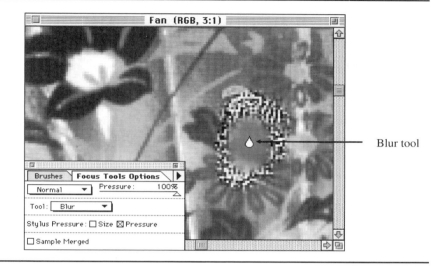

Using the
Blur tool
to soften
pixelated
area of
image

Blur tool

6

If you wish, continue to experiment with the Blur and Sharpen tools. When you're done, save your work and close the practice file. Then proceed to the next section to try your hand at more image-editing techniques with the Smudge tool, which can make your image look as though it is hand painted.

## USING THE SMUDGE TOOL TO MIX COLORS AND CREATE WATERCOLOR EFFECTS

The Smudge tool lets you blend colors as if you had smudged them together with your finger. When you use the Smudge tool, Photoshop starts with the color you clicked on and mixes it with the colors you drag over. Besides blending colors and mixing paint, the Smudge tool can be used to produce a watercolor effect in your image.

*n*OTE: *The Smudge tool cannot be used on Indexed Color or Bitmap images.*

In this section, you'll have a chance to experiment with the Smudge tool by transforming a digitized image into a watercolor painting. You'll also learn how to add colors to an image by activating the Smudge tool's Finger Painting option.

1. Before proceeding, open any scanned image file, or reopen the Frames (PC users: frames.jpg) file you started with at the beginning of this

chapter. Use Save As to create another copy of your file. Name your file WaterPainting (PC users: WaterPtg). By using Save As, your original file will not be affected by the changes you are going to make in the following exercises.

 **EMEMBER:** *Saving different versions of your file enables you to experiment with various designs and keep them as you are working on a project.*

2. Double-click on the Smudge tool to examine the Smudge Tool Options palette; you'll begin by using the Smudge tool without the Finger Painting option. If necessary, deselect this option by clicking on the check box.

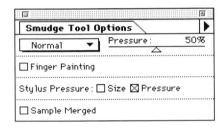

To control how the colors are smudged together, you can pick a brush size and a mode in the Brushes palette, and a Pressure value in the Smudge Tool Options palette. If you use a large brush with a high pressure value, you will create a large smudge that will completely distort your image. A lower pressure value with a small- or medium-sized brush will decrease the size of the smudge and create a less dramatic effect.

 **OTE:** *The Smudge tool can be used to soften unwanted wrinkles and blemishes in fleshtones. This technique is discussed in Chapter 13.*

The modes that are available in the Smudge Tool Options palette are the standard choices (as discussed in Chapter 5). These can provide further control of your smudge. For example, if you use Hue mode, only the hue values will be smudged (not the saturation or the luminosity values). Similarly, use Saturation mode to change only the saturation values, and Luminosity mode to smudge only the luminosity values. If you have more than one layer on screen, you can also choose to smudge using sampled pixel values from all visible layers. To do this, click on the Sample Merged check box.

Smudge tool

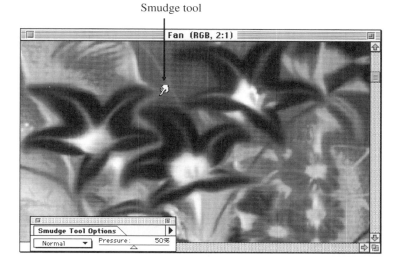

Creating a watercolor effect using the Smudge tool

**FIGURE 6-7**

**6**

3. Pick a medium-sized, soft-edged brush from the Brushes palette. In the Smudge Tool Options palette, set the Pressure to 50% and Mode to Normal. Move the smudge pointer anywhere in your document, and click and drag the mouse in one direction. You'll see that a small smudge of colors appears on screen. Zoom in to see a close-up view of the smudge. If you create a few more smudges, your image will start looking more like a watercolor painting, as in Figure 6-7.

Experiment with various brush sizes. Also, try switching modes a few times before smudging different parts of your image.

## The Smudge Tool's Finger Painting Option

To this point, you have created a watercolor effect by smudging the colors of your image together. What if you want to create a watercolor effect and add new color to your image at the same time? You can do this by activating the Smudge tool's Finger Painting option, which smudges using the foreground color, at the beginning of each click and drag of the mouse.

1. Double-click on the Smudge tool, select the Finger Painting check box in the Smudge Tool Options palette. Leave Pressure set to 50%.

2. For this exercise, set the foreground color to a bright color so you can easily view the Finger Painting effects.

3. In the Brushes palette, continue to use a medium-sized, soft-edged brush.

4. Click and drag over an area on your document, and notice how the Smudge tool smudges with the selected foreground color each time you click and drag. Continue to experiment using other foreground colors. When you're finished, close the file and save it, if you wish.

In the next section, you'll learn about one of Photoshop's most versatile tools, the Rubber Stamp.

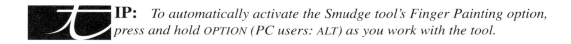

**IP:** *To automatically activate the Smudge tool's Finger Painting option, press and hold OPTION (PC users: ALT) as you work with the tool.*

## USING THE RUBBER STAMP TOOL

 The Rubber Stamp is a multipurpose tool. Although it can be used for reverting, applying a pattern, or creating an impressionistic effect, its most valuable feature is undoubtedly its cloning capability. *Cloning* means choosing parts of an image and duplicating them to areas in the same file or in another file. This is quite different than copying and pasting. During the cloning procedure, Photoshop *samples,* or reads, a source area and clones it to a target area. As you click and drag in the target area in the file, a clone of the sampled area gradually appears. This process can produce an undetectable blend of old pixels and new. When executed properly, the cloning effect is often seamless and—even to the experienced Photoshop user—frequently amazing.

To see the Rubber Stamp tool's options, double-click on the tool in the Toolbox. In the Rubber Stamp Options palette, the Option pop-up menu displays the currently selected option. Click on the Option pop-up menu to see what the tool has to offer. The choices are numerous: Clone (aligned or non-aligned), Pattern (aligned or non-aligned), From Snapshot, From Saved, and Impressionist.

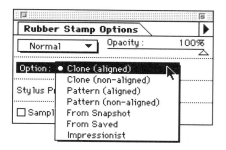

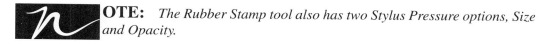

**OTE:** *The Rubber Stamp tool also has two Stylus Pressure options, Size and Opacity.*

In the next sections, the oriental fan image will be used to demonstrate the basics of the Rubber Stamp tool. To follow along, open the file you named Editing (earlier in this chapter), or load any digitized image.

## Using the Clone Options to Duplicate Image Areas

Cloning can be tremendously helpful when you edit an image or retouch a photo. For example, one of the authors of this book retouched a cover for a proposed Reader's Digest travel guide. The picture that the book's art director wished to use was a photograph of a small New England town. Everything in the photo was beautiful—except for the telephone wires criss-crossing through the scene. Using the Rubber Stamp tool's Clone option, parts of the trees that surrounded the wires were easily cloned over the wires to make them disappear. You'll see this example in Chapter 13, where advanced retouching techniques are introduced.

The Clone (aligned) option allows you to clone different parts of an image to different areas of the same file or another file. When you clone using the aligned option, Photoshop retains the same distance and angle relationship between the source area that you are sampling and the target area where the clone appears. Say, for instance, you wish to clone an image two inches directly above the original sample. After you finish cloning, if you move the mouse to another area of the file and then click and drag, Photoshop will clone whatever is two inches directly above the mouse pointer.

The Clone (non-aligned) option automatically keeps sampling the original source area, so you can clone the same sample in many places after you release the mouse. For the completed fan image in Figure 6-2, the Clone (aligned) option was

# Photoshop in Action

New sky was created with the painting and editing tools.

The Rubber Stamp tool's cloning option was used to help blend the characters into the mountain.

Artwork by: R/GA Print

Client: Acclaim Entertainment

The characters were combined with a scan of Mount Rushmore.

R/GA Print gave artist David Mattingly photographs of the characters that would appear in this final image. David then created a painting of the characters to make it look as if they were created from stone.

Karen Sideman at R/GA Print scanned an image of Mount Rushmore, then scanned Dave's painting and combined the two together. To blend the images together, she used the Rubber Stamp tool's cloning option. To create a brilliant blue sky in the background, Karen used Photoshop's painting and editing tools.

Mount Rushmore will never be the same.

used to duplicate different flowers in various areas of the fan. Had the designer wanted to clone the same flower in many parts of the fan, the Clone (non-aligned) option would have been used instead.

**OTE:** *If you are cloning in a file that has layers, you may wish to select the Sample Merged check box in the Rubber Stamp Options palette. This allows you to clone from all visible layers, rather than just the layer you are working in.*

1. To start the exercise, choose Clone (aligned) from the Option pop-up menu in the Rubber Stamp Options palette.

2. Pick a large brush in the Brushes palette and a high opacity setting in the Rubber Stamp Options palette. With a large brush and a high opacity setting, the cloning will happen faster and its effect will be more obvious.

3. To clone part of your image, move the rubber stamp pointer so that it's over the area you wish to duplicate. Press and hold the OPTION key (PC users: ALT) and then click the mouse to sample the area. Notice that the small black triangle at the base of the rubber stamp (⬚) turns white (⬚). This indicates that an area has been sampled. Once you've sampled an area, release the OPTION key (PC users: ALT) and move the rubber stamp pointer to the area where you wish the clone to appear.

4. To begin cloning, click and drag the mouse, moving the rubber stamp pointer over the target area. As you move the mouse, the clone will begin to appear in that area. Notice that a crosshair in the source area follows the movements of your rubber stamp pointer in the target area. The crosshair always remains the same distance and the same angle from the rubber stamp pointer, as shown in Figure 6-8. Continue clicking and dragging the mouse. The greater the area that you click and drag over, the greater the area that is cloned.

When you use the Clone (aligned) option, it's important to remember that the distance and the angle between the sampled area and the area where the clone is placed are always the same. To verify this, release the mouse button and then move the rubber stamp pointer to another area on the screen. Click and drag—Photoshop resamples and starts cloning again. Notice that when you clone the new area, the distance and angle between the crosshair and the rubber stamp pointer are the same as in the previous sample/clone pair. If you want to reset the distance between the source area and the target area, move the rubber stamp pointer to another area that

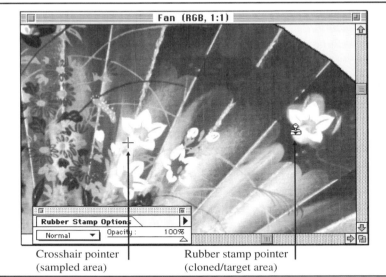

Using the
Rubber
Stamp
tool's
Clone
(aligned)
option to
clone a
flower

**FIGURE 6-8**

Crosshair pointer      Rubber stamp pointer
(sampled area)         (cloned/target area)

you wish to sample, then press OPTION (PC users: ALT) and click the mouse. Now you can move the Rubber Stamp tool to the other area where you wish to clone the new sample. Subsequent sample/clone pairs will then be separated by this new distance and angle. The cloning will begin as soon as you click and drag.

If you wish to clone the same sample to different areas in your image, use the Clone (non-aligned) option. Try this now. In the Rubber Stamp Options palette choose Clone (non-aligned) from the Option pop-up menu. When you are ready to begin, pick an area that you wish to clone. Once again, press OPTION (PC users: ALT) and click the mouse to sample. Move the Rubber Stamp tool to the area where you want to apply the clone, then click and drag. After you've created the clone of the image, release the mouse button. Move to another area of the screen where you wish to duplicate the sample, and click and drag again. As you click and drag, another clone of the first sampled area will be created.

**IP:** *You can press the CAPS LOCK key to turn the rubber stamp pointer into a crosshair (or choose Precise from the Painting Tools option in the Tool Cursors group in the General Preferences dialog box). It's easier to use the middle of the crosshair than the rubber stamp icon as a guide to judge the specific area that you are cloning. When you use this technique, you'll have two crosshairs on screen—one indicating the sample area and the other indicating the target area where the clone appears. (You can distinguish between the two crosshairs because the one indicating the target area has a dot in the middle.)*

As you work, you'll want to make the cloned image look as natural as possible. You don't want the clone to stand out from its surroundings. To make your clone blend in, experiment using the Rubber Stamp tool with different brushes, opacities, and modes. In the fan example, a soft-edged brush was used. This helped blend the new flower at the top of the fan to look as though it has always been there.

When you've finished cloning, save your file and proceed to the next section, where you'll experiment with more Rubber Stamp options.

**IP:**  *You can also clone an image from one file to another. To do this, open the two files side-by-side on screen. Press OPTION (PC users: ALT) and click over the area you wish to sample; then activate the target file. Position the rubber stamp pointer over the area where you wish to place the clone, then click and drag. If you are working with layers, you can sample in one layer and create the clone in another layer.*

## Reverting Using the From Saved and From Snapshot Options

The Rubber Stamp tool's From Saved and From Snapshot options work much like the Erase to Saved option of the Eraser Options palette. Recall from Chapter 5 that the Erase to Saved option allows you to click and drag to revert, or unerase—that is, to resurrect parts of images that have been changed. You can also revert with the Rubber Stamp's From Saved and From Snapshot options. With these options you can choose *how* you want to revert, by specifying a mode, opacity, and brush in the Brushes palette. The From Saved option allows you to revert to the last saved version of your file. The From Snapshot option allows you to revert to a *snapshot,* a version of the file captured using the Edit menu's Take Snapshop option, which is temporarily stored to an area of memory called the *image buffer.*

Reverting using the Rubber Stamp tool allows you to resurrect just a part of the previous version of an image by painting it on the screen. You can use the Brushes palette to choose a brush type, and the Rubber Stamp Options palette to set the opacity percentage and the mode. These options—for example, using a soft-edged brush or lowering the opacity—can prove valuable for blending the reverted part of a file into the image on screen.

### Using the From Saved Option

In this exercise, you're going to alter a file by coloring the entire screen with the background color. After you have changed the screen, you'll use the From Saved option to return part of the file to its original form.

1. Open the Frames (PC users: frames.jpg) file or any other digitized image.

2. Double-click on the Eraser tool and click on the Erase Image button in the Eraser Options palette. When the prompt appears, click OK to erase the entire screen by filling it with the background color.

3. Double-click on the Rubber Stamp tool. In the Rubber Stamp Options palette choose From Saved in the Option pop-up menu. Set Opacity to 100%. The Mode should be Normal.

4. Before you start reverting, pick a large brush from the Brushes palette. When you start using the Rubber Stamp tool, these settings will return your file to its original form using a large brush stroke and its original opacity.

5. Now move the rubber stamp pointer to an area that you want to revert, and click and drag over the area. Photoshop takes a few minutes or moments, depending upon how fast your computer is, to read the file information of the saved version. As you move with the brush, you'll see parts of your image being restored; they will match the size and shape of your brush.

6. Before you finish, change Opacity to 50%, and then click and drag in the document window. Now the image is being restored with a 50% opacity. Keep this technique in mind. It might come in handy when you wish to create special effects.

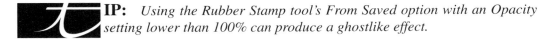

**IP:** *Using the Rubber Stamp tool's From Saved option with an Opacity setting lower than 100% can produce a ghostlike effect.*

Continue experimenting with the From Saved option. Keep Opacity set to 50% and the large, soft-edged brush selected, but switch modes from Normal to Dissolve. Dissolve, as mentioned in the "Painting/Editing Modes" section of Chapter 5, randomly changes the colors of pixels. The results of this effect will vary according to the image's original color. When you're done, keep your file on screen and proceed to the next section.

## Blending Using the From Saved and From Snapshot Options

Before you begin exploring the From Snapshot option, you must take a "snapshot" of your work. A snapshot saves your file's image in an area of memory called the *image buffer*, rather than to your hard disk. If you change an image that has already been saved and then take a snapshot, you have a choice between reverting to the disk (saved) version or the snapshot version of the image.

To see how this works, you'll blend two images together using both the Rubber Stamp's From Saved and From Snapshot options. In order to see the two options in action, you'll need to open two images, a source and a target image. You'll drag the source image over the target image to create a new layer, then blend the two images together. If you don't have two images available, either use two of the images on the CD-ROM that comes with Photoshop or use the Frames and Flower images in the Photoshop Tutorial folder. Figure 6-9 shows the effects of blending Figure 6-10 with Figure 6-11.

1. Once you have two images open on screen, place them either side by side or so that they overlap.

2. Activate the source file. If you're using the Tutorial files, activate the Flower file so that you can select it and then place it over the target (Frames) file.

3. Next, you'll use the Marquee tool to select part of the source file. Before you use the Marquee tool, you'll need to change some of the options in the Marquee Options palette. If the Options palette is already on screen click once on the Marquee tool; if it isn't, click twice on the Marquee tool. In the Marquee Options palette, set the Shape pop-up menu to Rectangular, the Style pop-up menu to Normal, and type **5** in the Feather field. (Using the Feather option softens the edges of the source file when it is moved to the target file and therefore helps blend the two images together. Review Chapter 3 for more information about Feathering.) Using the Marquee tool, click and drag over the area you want to select in the source file.

4. Once the source image is selected, activate the Move tool. Place the Move tool in the center of the selected image, drag and drop it over the target file (if you're using the Tutorial files, the Frames file). This creates a new layer in the target file.

5. When the source image is in the target file, move it to the desired location. When the source image is in position, take a snapshot of your image so that you can recall this version of your file if you need to. To take a snapshot of your image on screen, select the Take Snapshot command from the Edit menu, then deselect the image on screen.

The doll and fan images blended together using the Rubber Stamp's From Saved and From Snapshot options

 **FIGURE 6-9**

The doll image before blending it with the fan

 **FIGURE 6-10**

The fan image before blending it with the doll

**FIGURE 6-11**

**OTE:** *Photoshop can hold only one snapshot in memory at a time. When Take Snapshot is executed, any previous snapshot is replaced by the current snapshot.*

Now you can start blending the two images together. You'll use the From Saved version of the source file so that it blends into the target file and looks like it was always there.

> **6.** In the Rubber Stamp Options palette, choose From Saved from the Options pop-up menu, set Opacity to 75% and leave the Mode set to Normal. In the Brushes palette pick a medium, soft-edged brush.

Now you're ready to revert your image to 75% of the saved version.

> **7.** Position the Rubber Stamp pointer over the edges of the source image (if you're using the Tutorial files, the Flower file), and click and drag. As you move the mouse, you'll see the Rubber Stamp tool return the image to the saved version of the file.
>
> If you take away too much of the source image and want to bring it back, use the Rubber Stamp's From Snapshot option.

> **8.** In the Rubber Stamp Options palette, choose From Snapshot from the Options pop-up menu. If you wish, change the Opacity, Mode in the Options palette, and Brush size in the Brushes palette. Next, position the Rubber Stamp pointer over the area where you want to bring back the source image, then click and drag. As you move the mouse, you'll see that the Rubber Stamp tool gradually returns the image to the snapshot version of the file.

You have now seen how Photoshop gives you the ability to blend two files together using the saved and/or snapshot version. If you wish, continue experimenting with From Saved and From Snapshot, using different Opacities, Modes, and Brushes. When you're finished, use the Save As command in the File menu to save your file on screen, then close the file.

 **OTE:** *Using Edit/Fill, you can revert a selection to either the last saved version or to the snapshot version. To revert using Edit/Fill, first select an area. From the Edit menu, choose Fill. From the Use pop-up menu, choose either Saved or Snapshot.*

Your next stop is the Rubber Stamp tool's Impressionist feature.

## Using the Impressionist Option

Another of the Rubber Stamp tool's many specialties is its ability to take a scanned photograph and transform it by applying the characteristics of an impressionist painting. The Impressionist option takes the pixels from the last saved version of the file and blends them into the pixels of the current version of the file.

The Impressionist effect will vary depending upon the brush, opacity, and painting/editing mode used. If you use either a large, hard-edged brush or a small, soft-edged brush with a low Spacing value, you will produce a very spotted effect, making it difficult to decipher what the image is supposed to be. If you wish to produce a more realistic, less impressionistic effect, use a small brush with a high Spacing value. (See "Creating and Using Custom Brushes" in Chapter 5 for a discussion on brush attributes.)

1. Start with a fresh file. If you don't have an image, use the Fruit file from the Photoshop Tutorial folder.

2. For this first experiment, in the Rubber Stamp Options palette set Opacity to 100% and Mode to Normal. To use the Impressionist option, click on the pop-up menu and choose Impressionist.

3. To set the Spacing value of a brush, click on any brush in the Brushes palette. Then click on the pop-up menu arrow in the Brushes palette and choose New Brush from the list that appears. In the New Brush dialog box, set the Spacing to 300%, Hardness to 50%, and Diameter to 19 pixels. If you want your strokes to be round, keep Roundness at 100%. For strokes that look more elliptical than round, set Angle to 50 degrees and Roundness to 40%. Click OK to accept the changes.

4. Click and drag over any area of your file. It will take a few moments for the last saved version of the file to be read. As you drag, you'll see the pixels appear to smear together, as shown in Figure 6-12, almost as if Renoir had taken control of the painting.

An effect
created
with the
Rubber
Stamp
tool's
Impressionist
option

**FIGURE 6-12**

Additional effects can be created by using painting/editing modes: Normal, Dissolve, Multiply, Screen, Overlay, Soft Light, Hard Light, Darken, Lighten, Difference, Hue, Saturation, Color, Luminosity, and Behind. The Behind option is only active if you are working in a file on a layer other than the Background layer. (See Chapter 12 for more information about Layers.) Continue experimenting with various modes and opacities. When you are done, make sure to use either the Save or the Save As command if you wish to save your file. Before proceeding to the next section, close the file.

## Using the Pattern Option

The other options for the Rubber Stamp tool are Pattern (aligned) and Pattern (non-aligned). To experiment with these options, you need to create and define a pattern. Patterns can be used to create special effects, background textures, and fabric or wallpaper designs. In this section you'll learn how to create a pattern and then use the Rubber Stamp tool to apply it.

## Using Adobe Photoshop's Patterns

When you install Photoshop, a Brushes & Patterns folder (PC users: patterns) is created. This folder contains PostScript patterns that were created in Adobe Illustrator for you to use in Photoshop.

To access one of Adobe's patterns, choose Open from the File menu. In the Open dialog box, locate the PostScript Patterns folder (PC users: patterns) and open it. In this folder you will see a long list of files. Select the Mali Primitive file (PC users: mali.ai) and open it. In a few moments, Photoshop's EPS Rasterizer dialog box will appear. Since the pattern was created in Illustrator, which is a vector program, Photoshop needs to convert it to Photoshop's native format, bitmap. You do not need to change any of the dialog box settings if you have the default settings activated (Width: 1.25 inches; Height: 0.625 inches; Resolution: 72; Mode: Grayscale; and Anti-Aliased and Constrain Proportions selected). Just click OK. (The rasterizer options are discussed in Appendix A.)

```
┌──────── Rasterize Adobe Illustrator Format ────────┐
│                                                     │
│  ┌ Image Size: 4K ─────────────┐   ┌──────────┐     │
│  │                             │   │    OK    │     │
│  │  Width:  [1.25]  [inches ▼] │   └──────────┘     │
│  │                             │   ┌──────────┐     │
│  │  Height: [0.625] [inches ▼] │   │  Cancel  │     │
│  │                             │   └──────────┘     │
│  │  Resolution: [72]  [pixels/inch ▼]               │
│  │                             │                     │
│  │  Mode:  [Grayscale ▼]       │                     │
│  └─────────────────────────────┘                     │
│                                                     │
│   ☒ Anti-aliased   ☒ Constrain Proportions          │
└─────────────────────────────────────────────────────┘
```

When the file appears, you are ready to define it as a pattern. In order to define any image or part of an image as a pattern, it must first be selected. In this example, you'll select the entire image.

1. Choose All from the Select menu. To define the pattern, choose Define Pattern from the Edit menu. The pattern has now been defined, and you can proceed to use the Rubber Stamp or Paint Bucket tool, or the Fill command to apply it to your file.

2. With the pattern defined and in memory, you no longer need the pattern file (Mali Primitive) open, so close it.

3. Create a new 5-inch-by-5-inch RGB file, which you'll use to see the effects of painting with a pattern using the Rubber Stamp tool.

**4.** When you have a new file on screen, double-click on the Rubber Stamp tool. From the Option pop-up menu, select Pattern (aligned), set Opacity to 100% and change the mode to Normal.

The Pattern (aligned) option allows you to apply a continuous pattern, no matter how many times you stop and start. If you pick the Pattern (non-aligned) option instead, the pattern will restart every time you release the mouse button and click and drag again in your image.

**5.** In the Brushes palette, choose a large brush size.

**6.** Click and drag with the Rubber Stamp tool to start painting. As you paint, the Rubber Stamp tool applies the selected pattern. If you wish, test out other brush sizes and opacity settings.

As you work, you might decide that the pattern would look better with a little color, perhaps some green. One easy way of doing this is to paint the entire screen green and then use the painting/editing modes and the Rubber Stamp tool to help paint the pattern back into the picture.

**7.** Change the background color to green, or to any color that you want to add to your pattern (other than black or white). Then double-click on the Eraser tool. In the Eraser Options palette, click on the Erase Image button to erase your document with this color.

**8.** Once the document has become the background color, activate the Rubber Stamp tool. Pick a large brush and set Opacity to 100%.

Establish a reference point on screen by painting a few brush strokes with the mode set to Normal, and then switch to the Lighten mode. This will only lighten areas that are darker than the pattern you are painting with. Thus, when you paint the pattern with the Rubber Stamp tool in Lighten mode, the white part of the pattern will paint over the green colors on the screen. The black part of the pattern is not painted because it is darker than the green color on screen. Try painting several brush strokes on the screen to see the effect.

If you wish to reverse the colors in the previous example, choose the Darken mode. Now, only the black part of the pattern is applied because black is darker than the underlying green color. Figure 6-13 shows the Mali Primitive pattern applied with the Normal, Lighten, and Darken modes.

**6**

Applying a
pattern
with the
Rubber
Stamp tool
using
Normal,
Lighten,
and Darken
modes

**FIGURE 6-13**

Normal mode

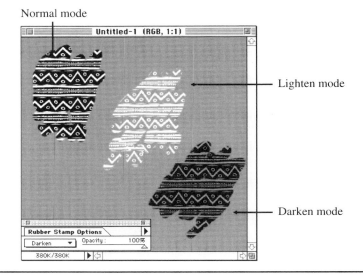

Lighten mode

Darken mode

 **OTE:** *You can add colors to one of Photoshop's pattern files after you open the file and choose RGB Color or CMYK Color from the Mode menu.*

### Creating, Defining, and Applying Custom Patterns

Now that you know how to apply one of Adobe Photoshop's patterns, you're ready to learn how to create one of your own. Although you can create a pattern in any file, it's probably best to make one in a new file. If you create each pattern in a separate file that you name and save, you'll have an easier time accessing your patterns when you wish to use them again. Since these files will be used solely to hold the design of your pattern, they don't need to be very large.

To create a pattern, follow these steps:

1. Open a new file, 2 inches by 2 inches. If you will be applying your pattern over an image, you may wish to choose Transparent from the contents group in the New dialog box. This will allow you to see the underlying image through the non-colored areas of your pattern.

2. Use any of Photoshop's tools to create a pattern.

**IP:** *You can also select a portion of a digitized image to use as a pattern.*

**3.** Select with the Marquee tool Rectangular Shape option the area you wish to include in your pattern file, as shown in the following illustration. If the background of your pattern file is white and you select any white background area with your pattern, that white area will be included when you paint with the pattern.

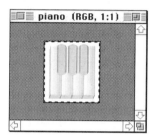

**4.** While the pattern is selected, choose Define Pattern from the Edit menu.

**OTE:** *If you select an area using a Feather, the Define Pattern command will be dimmed. The area you select cannot have a feathered edge in order to use the Define Pattern command.*

**5.** Save your file and close it.

**OTE:** *Photoshop, unfortunately, can only remember one pattern at a time. The defined pattern is stored in memory until you either define another pattern or quit the program. Thus, if you want to use a pattern again, you must save the file that the pattern was created in.*

**6.** To apply your pattern, create a new file, 5 inches by 5 inches, or open a file you wish to apply the pattern to.

**7.** When the file appears, you can use either the Rubber Stamp or Paint Bucket tool, or the Fill command to apply the pattern. For this exercise, use the Rubber Stamp tool. Double-click on the Rubber Stamp tool, and from the Option pop-up menu, choose Pattern (aligned).

**8.** Click and drag in the document to paint with the pattern using the Rubber Stamp tool.

Try experimenting by applying your pattern with the Pattern (non-aligned) option, with the Paint Bucket tool, or with the Edit/Fill command. To make your pattern more interesting, you may wish to create a custom brush and apply it to different areas in the image. The music notes shown in this illustration were created with a custom brush from the Sonata typeface. (See Chapter 5 for more details on creating a custom brush.)

## RENOVATING A KITCHEN

Here's a tip for architects, interior designers, or anyone who might be involved in a renovation project. This project demonstrates how to take a scanned image of an old, dusty kitchen and transform it into a clean, modern one.

Certainly, one of the major advantages of a computer is that you can experiment with various interior and scenic designs without paying anyone to lift a hammer or a paint brush. If you wish to use Photoshop for this type of project, you will need to scan (or have a service bureau scan) photographs of the rooms that you wish to renovate. (You'll learn more about digitizing your images in Chapter 7.) If you are thinking of using different wallpaper or colors, take photographs that include the wallpaper samples. This way, you can easily create a pattern in Photoshop from the wallpaper, and it will be at the proper proportions. Of course, you can also create your own patterns for wallpaper and floor tile designs.

Once you have digitized an image of a room, with its wallpaper and floor patterns, load your file. Figure 6-14 is a digitized image of a photograph of a kitchen before image editing in Photoshop. Notice the wallpaper samples hanging on the wall. Figure 6-15 displays the same digitized image after the electronic renovation. In this example, the Rubber Stamp tool's cloning powers were used to remove unwanted items such as the dishes, bottles, old-fashioned light fixture, paper towel holder, and pots and pans. The Edit/Fill command was used to fill a pattern created from a

The kitchen
before
image
editing

**FIGURE 6-14**

6

The kitchen
after image
editing

**FIGURE 6-15**

wallpaper sample taped to the wall. The Burn tool dissipated the highlights, and the Sharpen tool made certain areas of the image more distinct.

This example should give you an idea of how money can be saved and mistakes avoided by first visualizing (via computer) various wallpaper designs, floor coverings, and cabinet treatments.

## USING QUICK EDIT

Now that you've covered the basics of image editing, you're ready to apply your knowledge to Photoshop projects. As you work, though, you may find that editing large, high-resolution images can be quite cumbersome. You may even find that, from time to time, you run out of memory. The solution to this problem may be to use Photoshop's Quick Edit command, which allows you to load part of an image rather than the entire file.

The only disadvantage to using Quick Edit is that it does not work with files saved under Photoshop's native 3.0 format. This means that it will only work with files that have a Background and no additional layers. Quick Edit only loads files saved in Scitex CT format and uncompressed TIFF formats. (For more information about Scitex CT and TIFF file formats, see Appendix A.)

To use Quick Edit with an image that is not in the correct file format, use the File/Save As or File/Save a copy command to save it in Scitex CT or TIFF format. If you'd like to test Quick Edit, try saving one of your files or a Tutorial file in Scitex CT or TIFF format.

Start by opening any file that has a background and no additional layers, then choose Save As from the File menu. In the Save As dialog box, click in the Format pop-up menu and choose either TIFF or Scitex CT. If you choose TIFF, do not choose LZW compression because Quick Edit will not read compressed TIFF files. After you've saved your file, close it.

To use the Quick Edit command, choose Quick Edit from the Acquire menu. In the Open dialog box, you will only see Scitex CT or TIFF files. Select the file that you wish to edit. Then click Open (PC users: OK). The Quick Edit dialog box opens with a preview of your image in it.

Before you can edit a portion of the file, you must select the area that you want to edit. To make selecting easier, you can have Photoshop create a grid. When you click in the grid, Photoshop automatically selects the area of the grid that you clicked in.

Try clicking on the Grid check box. Use the + icons and/or - icons to change the number of rows and columns in the grid. Next click in one of the grid cells. A blinking marquee surrounds the portion of the grid that you clicked on, as shown in Figure

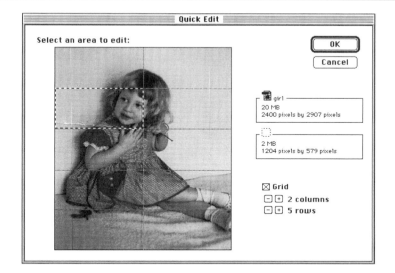

Clicking in a grid cell selects the portion of the image to be used with Quick Edit

**FIGURE 6-16**

6-16. Notice that Photoshop also indicates the file size of the portion that is selected. To load the selection on screen for editing, click the OK button.

After the section of your file opens on screen, use one of the painting or editing tools to edit it. You're sure to notice that editing is much faster on a small piece, rather than the entire image. To save your editing changes to the original file, choose Export from the File menu. In the Export submenu choose Quick Edit Save. Close the Quick Edit document, then reload your file using File/Open. On screen, you'll see your image with the changes you made using Quick Edit.

## CONCLUSION

From the examples and exercises in this chapter, you can see that Photoshop provides numerous possibilities when editing an image. Now that you've seen the potential of image editing, you'll probably want to learn more about digitizing images so they can be edited with Photoshop. That's the subject of the next chapter.

# DIGITIZING and
# MANIPULATING IMAGES

Digitized images are at the core of most Photoshop design projects. When you digitize a visual image, you are translating it into digital signals so it can be broken down into pixels and loaded into the computer. Assuring that images are digitized correctly is crucial to the success of your work. If the digitization process is not conducted properly, image quality will likely be unacceptable and colors may be flawed. Images that are digitized at too low a resolution may look jagged or blurred, and too high a resolution may cause the file size to increase to the point where the file can't even be edited on your computer.

Since scanning is the most widely used digitizing process, this chapter focuses on using a scanner to digitize an image directly through Photoshop. In addition, you'll experiment with some simple commands that are generally used right after scanning, including those that allow you to manipulate, correct, resize, and create special effects. You'll put your skills to work on a design project, as well as learn about other digitizing alternatives rapidly gaining popularity, such as Photo CD.

Before you can begin digitizing any image, you must first decide what equipment is necessary to properly digitize an image. For digitizing flat art, slides, or photographic prints, you will undoubtedly use a scanner. If your images are on film, you can have them digitized through Kodak's Photo CD process and then view the results in Photoshop with the aid of a CD-ROM XA (extended architecture) player. If you don't already have photographs or slides to work with, you may want to use a digital or video camera to digitize your images at the time you are shooting them. You can also digitize a still frame from videotape by using a video capture card connected to a video recorder.

## SCANNING

The most important point to remember about scanners is that different scanners provide different quality output, just as different types of cameras produce photographs of various quality. An expensive camera with a sophisticated optical system will produce sharp, crisp images with a full range of accurate colors. Images produced from a cheaper camera will, of course, be of lower quality.

Using a low-end scanner is much like shooting a picture with an inexpensive camera. A low-end desktop scanner may well suit your needs for newspaper work and other low-resolution printing. Low-end desktop scans can also be placed in documents to test layout and design concepts; this is often called *FPO* ("for position only"). After the design has been finalized, the FPO image is replaced with a high-end scan before the project starts its journey to the printing press.

High-end digitizing is the domain of the service bureau. A service bureau will scan your image on expensive prepress equipment, such as Scitex's flatbed scanner, or a rotary drum scanner manufactured by DuPont Crosfield, Linotype-Hell, or Optronics. All of these scanners employ sophisticated optical and color-correcting systems to make your images crisp and sharp. Most will also digitize an image directly as a CMYK Color file.

**CAUTION:** *Be aware that any image editing you do in Photoshop to FPO images cannot automatically be converted to the high-resolution scan. The work will need to be re-created on the higher-quality image. Most service bureaus and prepress houses will do this work for you if your own computer system cannot handle the file size of the high-resolution scans.*

You may be able to avoid the expense of high-end equipment by using a midrange scanner. These produce highly acceptable images because they can process more color information than low-end scanners, and they are more sensitive to the color range of an image. See Chapter 1 for more information on scanning hardware.

Before you begin scanning, you should know the dimensions of your final image and calculate the correct scanning resolution. Like monitor resolution, scanning resolution is measured in pixels per inch. More pixels in an image means it contains more information. Thus, in general, the more pixels you can pack into an image, the sharper it will be. If you scan at too low a resolution, your image may be blurry, or you may see the individual pixel elements in the image.

Notwithstanding the value of high-resolution images, it's generally unnecessary to scan at the highest possible resolution, because eventually a point of diminishing returns is reached. Printing presses can only produce images at a limited number of lines per inch, so the extra resolution will be wasted and may even result in images that look flat. The same holds true if your scans will be output for television, which has a top resolution of 640 by 480 pixels (72 ppi)—the NTSC (National Television System Committee) standard. Since television cannot produce images at a quality higher than that standard, it is generally unnecessary to scan at a higher resolution.

Why not scan everything at a high resolution, just to be safe? Consider that file size is directly related to an image's resolution. Images that are scanned at higher resolutions produce larger file sizes than images scanned at low resolution. For instance, if you take a 72-ppi image and rescan it at twice the resolution (144 ppi),

7

the new file will be approximately four times as large as the original 72-ppi image. Thus, if you scan at too high a resolution, an image's file size may become so large that it overwhelms your computer's memory capacity.

**EMEMBER:** *File size is directly related to an image's resolution. It's advisable to have at least three to five times your image's file size available in RAM or on your hard disk.*

## Calculating Resolution and Image Size

If you are producing output for a printing press, calculate the image's resolution based upon the printing resolution.

The resolution of a printing press is measured in lines per inch (lpi), often called *line screen* or *screen frequency.* Your scanning resolution (measured in ppi) is directly related to the screen frequency. In the electronic printing process, screen frequency is determined by rows of cells composed of *halftones.* These halftones are built from the tiniest dots that can be produced by printers—from lasers to imagesetters. (Imagesetter dots are sometimes called *rels,* or raster elements; laser printer dots are frequently called pixels.) The following illustration shows how a halftone is built from a grid of pixels. Different-sized halftones combine to produce the illusion of continuous tones of grays and colors in photographs. Halftones will be discussed in greater detail in Chapter 14.

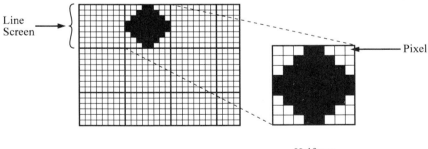

Halftone

When scanning, use this as a general rule: Two image pixels are needed for every halftone to produce high-quality output for images that will be printed on a printing press. Thus, the process of calculating the correct scanning resolution can often be reduced to the simple formula of doubling the screen frequency:

scanning resolution = 2 × screen frequency (lpi)

*OTE: When an image is printed, a file scanned at two times the line frequency actually has four times as much information, compared with the same file scanned at one times the line frequency. The number of pixels is quadrupled because pixels are added for each horizontal and vertical line screen.*

If you don't know what screen frequency will be used to print your work, ask your printer. When discussing printing resolution with your printer, you should also know what type of paper will be used. Generally, newspapers are printed at 85 lpi. Most magazines are printed on an offset press using 133 or 150 lpi. Some art books printed on coated paper use 200 lpi. Once you know what lpi you'll be using, you can calculate the resolution, or how many pixels per inch (ppi), you will need when you scan.

If you'd like, you can have Photoshop calculate the scanning resolution for you, as explained next. When Photoshop calculates the resolution, it will also reveal the file size of the image that you will be scanning.

## Letting Photoshop Calculate Image Size and Resolution

In this section, you'll have Photoshop calculate both the file size and resolution for a grayscale or color image. Later in the chapter you'll read about calculating resolution for black-and-white line art and for images that will be enlarged.

Start by creating a new file. Select File/New, and in the dialog box enter the dimensions of the image you will be scanning. For the example here, use 3.5 inches for the Width and 5 inches for the Height. For now, leave the resolution set to 72 ppi. (Eventually Photoshop will change this value.) If you are scanning a color image, leave the mode set to RGB Color, because both your monitor and scanner produce colors from red, green, and blue values. If you are scanning a grayscale image, switch to Grayscale mode.

*OTE: If you are scanning in Grayscale mode, your file size will be smaller than in RGB Color mode because Photoshop will not need to store as much information. Rather than 24 bits per pixel of information to create colors, Photoshop uses only 8 bits per pixel for grayscale.*

At this point, notice that Photoshop has already calculated a file size. At 3.5 by 5 inches and Mode set to RGB Color, the dialog box displays 266K as the file size. Before continuing, make sure that the Contents radio button is set to White, then click OK.

After the new file appears, select Image Size from the Image menu. Notice that the Image Size dialog box, shown in Figure 7-1, contains all of the information you entered in the New dialog box: Width and Height are set to the size of your image, Resolution is set to 72 ppi, and the file size is the same as it was in the New dialog box. You'll also see the Constrain option check boxes called Proportions and File Size; these options will be discussed later.

Now you're ready to have Photoshop calculate your scanning resolution. In the Image Size dialog box, click the Auto button to display the Auto Resolution dialog box.

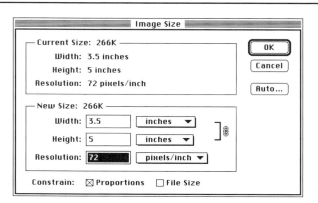

In the Screen field, type in the screen frequency that you'll be using (if you don't know this, type **150**). Then click on one of the three Quality radio buttons to designate how you want Photoshop to calculate image resolution. If you click Best, Photoshop will multiply the screen frequency by 2 to compute the resolution; for Good, Photoshop will multiply the screen frequency by 1.5. If you pick Draft and your screen frequency is not less than 72, Photoshop will enter 72. If you enter a screen frequency less than 72 in the Screen field, Photoshop will use that number as your scanning resolution. Click OK, and Photoshop will calculate your resolution and return you to the Image Size dialog box.

The Image Size dialog box lets you tell Photoshop how to calculate file size and scanning resolution

**FIGURE 7-1**

When the Image Size dialog box reappears, notice that the New Size and Resolution values have changed. Resolution now displays the desired resolution, according to your screen frequency (if you used a screen frequency of 150, your new resolution will be 300 ppi). New Size displays the size of the file you will be working with. Now you can compare the anticipated file size to your computer's memory capacity.

## Changing Image Dimensions and Resampling

If the new file size is too large for your system to handle, you can reduce the file size by decreasing the dimensions of the image in the Image Size dialog box.

Before you start making changes in the Image Size dialog box, note whether the Constrain Proportions check box is selected. If it is, the width-to-height ratio will remain constant no matter what values you enter (that is, altering the Width field will cause a proportional change in the Height field). The chain-link icon next to these two fields indicates that the two values are linked.

```
percent
pixels
✓ inches
cm
points
picas
columns
```

If you know the percentage of enlargement or reduction for the file to be digitized, you can change the measurement units in the New Size fields from inches to percent. To do this, click on the pop-up menu to the right of either Width or Height and choose percent. (You'll also see a columns measurement unit in this menu, which can be used if you will be exporting your file into a desktop publishing program that has multicolumn page-layout capability. The columns measurement uses the units specified in the Unit Preferences dialog box, discussed in the "Unit Preferences" section of Chapter 2. In this dialog box you can set the column width and the gutter size as well.)

If you don't want a proportional change, deselect the Constrain Proportions check box. Be aware, however, that if you turn off the Proportions option and then change the dimensions of an image, you will distort it.

The other Constrain option in the Image Size dialog box is for File Size. When this option is *not* selected, Photoshop reduces the file size when the New Size Height and Width values are decreased. It will also decrease the file size if you lower the Resolution value. If you increase Resolution or Width and Height, the file size will grow. If the File Size check box is selected now, deselect it so you can experiment; then type a smaller number into the Width or Height field. Notice that the New Size value decreases.

When Photoshop increases or decreases the file size, it adds or subtracts pixels in your image. Adding or subtracting pixels is called *resampling*. It's important to realize that when you resample, Photoshop must make some sacrifices in image quality. If you decrease the dimensions of your image size, Photoshop must subtract pixels; if you increase your image size, Photoshop must add pixels. When Photoshop adds pixels, it *interpolates*. During interpolation, Photoshop attempts to smooth the difference between the original pixels and the ones it adds. This can result in a somewhat blurred image.

If you resample down (that is, decrease file size) and then later resample back up, the final image will not be as sharp as the original. This is because Photoshop must remove pixels, and when you resample back up Photoshop interpolates and cannot add the original pixels that were subtracted earlier.

## Changing Image Dimensions Without Resampling

At this point, you may be wondering whether it's possible to change an image's size or resolution without resampling (adding or subtracting pixels). You can—using the Constrain File Size option. When the File Size check box is selected, the file size of your image will not change when you modify its dimensions or resolution. In order to keep the file size constant, though, Photoshop must compensate by changing the resolution when you change dimensions, or changing dimensions when you change the resolution. To avoid adding or subtracting pixels, Photoshop decreases the resolution if you increase the dimensions of your image. If you decrease the dimensions of your image, Photoshop increases the resolution.

**NOTE:**  *If you resize without resampling, the display of your image on screen will not change because you have not added or subtracted pixels. If Photoshop's rulers are displayed, they will indicate any change in image dimensions.*

Take a moment and try this out—it's important to understand how file size, image dimension, and resolution are related because they all affect your work. Select the Constrain File Size check box. Notice that the chain-link icon now shows that the image dimensions and resolution are linked. Enter a higher value for either Width or Height, and you'll see that Resolution drops. This makes sense: If you want to make an image larger, but you don't add any information to it, the resolution will be lower.

The inverse is true when you change the Resolution setting. Increase it, and Photoshop decreases the image dimensions; decrease Resolution, and Photoshop increases the image dimensions. Try entering a higher value into the Resolution field, and watch the file's dimensions drop. If you want more pixels per inch and you don't want the file size to change, the image dimensions will have to decrease.

If this concept seems confusing, here's an analogy: Assume that you have a balloon with a painted image on it, consisting of many tiny dots of paint. If you stretch the balloon out to make the image size greater, the space between each dot grows, and you have fewer dots per square inch. This is the same as decreasing resolution when file dimensions are increased. Squeeze the balloon to make the image smaller, and the dots get closer together. Similarly, an image's resolution increases when the file dimensions are decreased. In both cases, whether you stretched or compressed the balloon, the actual mass of rubber or the number of dots did not change. Likewise, the file size and number of pixels in your image always remain the same even if you change its dimensions or resolution with the Constrain File Size check box selected.

The following chart summarizes how the Constrain File Size option affects your image, when working in inches:

| | Increase Dimensions | Decrease Dimensions | Increase Resolution | Decrease Resolution |
|---|---|---|---|---|
| File Size check box OFF (resampling) | Increases file size | Decreases file size | Increases file size | Decreases file size |
| File Size check box ON (no resampling) | Decreases resolution; file size is unchanged | Increases resolution; file size is unchanged | Decreases dimensions; file size is unchanged | Increases dimensions; file size is unchanged |

At this point, you should have a good idea about how you can control Photoshop image dimensions, file sizes, and resolutions. You can even test how fast Photoshop will operate on your computer at different image sizes and resolutions. If you'd like to "test-drive" your computer at your digitized image's size and resolution, return the settings in the Image Size dialog box to those needed by your image. (In our example, width is 3.5 inches, height is 5 inches, and resolution is 300 ppi.) Click OK to continue.

After you click OK in the Image Size dialog box, you'll probably see your document window enlarge—because you have increased the file's resolution over its previous setting of 72 ppi. The new window size reflects the fact that more pixels are consuming each inch of the image. Remember, if you are working on any file that has a resolution higher than your monitor's (often 72 ppi), your image will be displayed larger than actual size. (For more information, see "Creating a New File" in Chapter 2.)

Now you can test to see how fast your computer will work with the anticipated file size of your soon-to-be-scanned image. Try painting with a couple of different tools to see how Photoshop responds. You don't need an image in the file to do this. Remember, even though the file has no image, pixels are pixels; it doesn't matter whether they're white, black, or colored.

## Calculating Resolution for an Enlarged Image

Now that you have calculated your scanning resolution and image size, you are just about ready to scan your image. But there are two more issues you might need to consider—whether the image will be enlarged during scanning or in Photoshop, and whether black-and-white line art will be scanned.

If you are going to enlarge the scanned image dimensions (likely if you are scanning slides, for instance), you'll need to increase the scanning resolution before you scan. Increasing the number of pixels in the image will ensure that the quality is maintained when the image is enlarged. If you don't boost the resolution, image clarity will suffer, and the image may become pixelated (the individual pixels in the image become evident when the image dimensions are enlarged).

To calculate the correct scanning resolution for an image that will be enlarged, use the following formula:

longest dimension in final image × screen frequency (lpi) × pixel-to-line screen ratio ÷ longest dimension of original image

As an example, assume you scan an image of 2 inches by 3 inches and want to enlarge it to 4 inches by 6 inches. (Also assume your screen frequency is 150 lpi.) Here's a step-by-step explanation of how to apply the formula:

1. Multiply the longest dimension (height or width) of the final image by the screen frequency (lpi). This produces the minimum number of pixels necessary to produce the longest dimension of the image. In our example, $6 \times 150$ equals a total of 900 pixels.

2. As discussed earlier in the chapter, to produce a high-quality image 2 pixels are needed for every line-screen inch (or per halftone dot); thus, 2 is the pixel-to-line screen ratio. In our example, 2 times 900 equals 1,800, the optimum number of pixels necessary to produce the longest dimension of the image.

**3.** To obtain the scanning resolution, divide the optimum number of pixels needed to produce the longest dimension by the longest dimension of the original image. In our example, 1,800 divided by 3 equals 600 ppi, the final scanning resolution.

After you've calculated the correct resolution and scanned your image at that resolution, you would then use the Image Size dialog box with the Constrain File Size check box selected to enlarge your image.

**OTE:** *If you are uncertain about what screen frequency or pixel-to-line screen ratio you should use, check with your service bureau and/or commercial printer.*

As previously mentioned, the foregoing calculation is extremely important when scanning slides. For example, let's say you are enlarging the longest dimension of a slide to 5 inches. Since the longest dimension of a 35mm slide is 1.375 inches, you would use the following calculation (if your screen frequency is 150): $5 \times 150 \times 2 \div 1.375$, and your scanning resolution would be a little less than 1,100 ppi.

## Choosing a Resolution for Black-and-White Line Art

Black-and-white images such as line art, logos, and text are frequently referred to as *bitmap* images. This term is used because only 1 bit is necessary to make each pixel of the image black or white. As discussed in "Video Display Cards" in Chapter 1, a bit can be either off or on. If the bit is on, the pixel is black; if it is off, the pixel is white.

If you are scanning bitmap images, you may be surprised to learn that resolution must sometimes be set higher than when working with color. In color and grayscale images, gradations of colors and grays can hide edges and make an image blend into its background. In black-and-white images, on the other hand, the stark contrast between black and white draws the eye's attention to outlines.

Many printing professionals suggest scanning at a resolution as high as your output device. As mentioned in "Output Devices" in Chapter 1, resolution for both printers and imagesetters is measured in dots per inch (dpi). If you are producing output for an imagesetter with a resolution of 1,200 dpi, you should scan at 1,200 ppi. If you are printing to a laser printer that outputs 300 dpi, you may as well scan at 300 ppi. Even if you scan at a 1,000 ppi, your 300-dpi printer cannot add any more resolution to the image.

## Using File/Acquire to Scan an Image

After you've decided which scanner to use and have calculated your scanning resolution, you are ready to start scanning. This section takes you step by step from previewing your image to scanning it from within Photoshop.

TWAIN

In order to scan, you will need to install the plug-in (driver) that is provided by your scanner's manufacturer, which allows you to operate the scanner from within Photoshop. To install the plug-in, copy it into the Plug-ins folder of the Acquire/Adjust folder (PC users: plugins). If you are using a scanner that supports the TWAIN standard—such as the Hewlett-Packard Scanjet—you will need to install the TWAIN software that comes with your scanner. PC users might need to update scanning software that was released earlier than the Windows version of Photoshop.

**OTE:** *If your scanner did not come with a Photoshop plug-in, you may need to scan using the software that came with your scanner.*

If you install the plug-in while you have Photoshop open, you'll need to Quit and restart Photoshop before you continue.

Once your scanner plug-in is installed, and before you begin digitizing an image, read the instructions that come with your scanner. In particular, find out whether your scanner allows you to set the *white point* (sometimes called *highlight point*) and the *black point* (sometimes called the *shadow point*). From these two endpoints, your software may be able to create a tone curve to ensure that the scanner captures the widest density or dynamic range.

**OTE:** *Scanning software, such as PixelCraft Color Access, Light Source Ofoto, and Flamingo Bay ScanPrep, may provide features not found in your scanning software.*

FotoLook PS 1.1

The explanations in this section are based on the Agfa Arcus II scanner, a midrange scanner available for both Mac and PC users, using the Agfa FotoLook PS 1.1 plug-in. The steps described here are similar to those you'll perform for most desktop scanners.

When you're ready, turn on the scanner (if it isn't already on). Place the image facedown on the scanner's glass plate. Try to get the image placed as straight as possible; otherwise, the scanned image will appear crooked. If you are using a slide scanner, place the slide in the slide holder. The Arcus II scanner scans reflective objects, such as photographs and line art, as well as transparencies, such as slides. In this procedure, we will use the reflective option.

To begin the scanning process within Photoshop, select Acquire from the File menu. If your scanner has a plug-in, you will see it in the Acquire submenu. Select your scanner driver from the Acquire submenu.

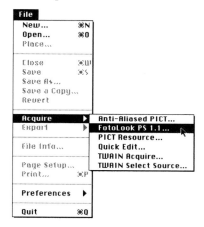

If you have a TWAIN-compatible scanner, the first time you use your scanner you must select it as the scanning source. In the Acquire submenu, choose TWAIN Select Source, and then select your scanner in the dialog box that appears. To start the scanning process, choose File/Acquire again, and choose TWAIN Acquire.

Your next step is to preview the scanned image and choose a specific area of the image to scan. If you don't do this, the final image will be as large as the scanner's entire scanning area and you'd wind up with a very large file size. Another reason for previewing is to make sure you haven't put the image in the scanner upside down. To begin the preview, click on the Preview button. In a minute or so the preview will appear on screen.

After the miniature image appears, select the specific area to scan, as shown in Figure 7-2. Most scanner selection controls work similarly; typically you only need to click and drag over the specific part of the previewed image that you wish to scan. Don't worry about selecting too precisely. Once the image has been scanned, you can crop out extraneous portions in Photoshop. Notice, as shown in Figure 7-2, that the Agfa FotoLook scanner dialog box produces a handy readout of the image dimensions, image size (5587K).

Next, after selecting the area to be scanned, you're ready to choose a mode and scanning resolution for the digitized image. Click on the Mode pop-up menu and choose either Color, RGB, Gray-Scale, or Lineart (sometimes called Bitmap), then

The Agfa
scanner,
FotoLook
plug-in
previews
an image
and its file
size, and
allows the
dynamic
range to
be set
automatically

**FIGURE 7-2**

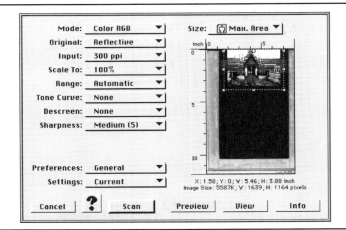

choose a resolution. In this example, the Input pop-up menu will be used to change
the resolution to 300 ppi. (Agfa's FotoLook plug-in allows you to scan using input
resolution in ppi or output resolution in lpi.)

Before scanning, examine the controls in your own scanning window. If you
don't know the purpose of each option, consult your scanner's manual. Notice that
the Agfa FotoLook scanning window includes a Range setting. When Range is set
to Automatic, the scanner will automatically set its *density range,* or *dynamic range.*
A scanner's dynamic range is the range of colors it can identify, from the brightest
to the darkest. With Range set to Automatic, the scanner prescans the image to
measure the brightest highlight and the darkest shadow. This helps the scanner
capture the broadest dynamic range possible.

The Agfa FotoLook plug-in also features commands to eliminate *color casts,*
shifts in color toward red, green, or blue. If an image displays too much of any of
these colors, the cast can be eliminated by choosing Color from the Preferences
pop-up menu. This opens the Color Preferences dialog box where you can adjust
the sliders for red, green, and blue values. Notice that the Agfa FotoLook scanning
plug-in also provides a Sharpness setting which can be used to enhance image edges.
The Descreen option can help eliminate moiré patterns when scanning images that
have been printed using screens.

Many scanners allow you to change exposure settings before you scan. If you
wish, you can experiment with these settings, or make adjustments to your image
later in Photoshop.

When you're ready to scan the image, click the Scan button. In a few minutes,
the scan will be completed and the image will appear in a Photoshop window.

**AUTION:** *When working with digitized images, make sure you secure all rights before using them.*

## ROTATING AND FLIPPING A SCANNED IMAGE

When the scanned image appears in Photoshop, you may see that, despite your best efforts, the image is tilted. The Rotate commands in Photoshop's Image menu help you fix this. These commands can also be used to rotate an image that had to be scanned sideways so that it would fit on the scanner flatbed, or to turn over an image that was inadvertently scanned upside down.

If you wish to rotate your entire image, you need not select it (except when using the Image/Rotate/Free command). If you rotate a selected portion of the image or select the entire image, Photoshop may crop part of it when you execute one of the Rotate commands. This can occur because Photoshop allows you to rotate an image so that parts of it extend beyond the document window. If you rotate the entire image without first selecting it, Photoshop will change the size of the window, so no part of the image will be cropped.

**OTE:** *If you want to follow along with these steps, but you don't want to rotate or change your scanned image on screen, you can load one of the images from the Frames file (PC users: frames.jpg) in the Tutorial folder.*

To rotate the image, choose Rotate from the Image menu. The Rotate submenu provides you with several choices, as shown here. Each option will rotate your image according to the angle indicated (CW means clockwise and CCW means counterclockwise). The Arbitrary option allows you to specify a particular degree of rotation. Since this command is more flexible than the others, it's a good place to start, so select Arbitrary.

In the dialog box that appears, you will enter the rotation degree that you wish to use and specify clockwise or counterclockwise rotation. In the Angle field you can enter values from −359.99 to 359.99 degrees. So you can easily see the results of this test, enter **45**. Click the CCW radio button to rotate counterclockwise. Click OK.

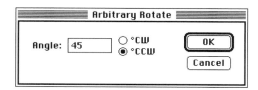

You'll see that the entire screen image rotates 45 degrees counterclockwise. To return the screen to its original position, rotate the image again, this time 45 degrees clockwise.

Before moving on, try one more test, using the Rotate submenu's Free option. This option allows you to click and drag with the mouse to control the rotation. When you rotate with the Free option, it's often helpful to have the Info palette on screen; this palette will display your rotating angle as you are working.

Now try this out. Select part of your image with the Rectangular Marquee. Select Image/Rotate and choose Free. Handles will appear at the corners of the selection marquee. To rotate, position the mouse pointer over any handle, and click and drag it in any direction. The selection marquee will provide you with a preview of your selection. When you are happy with the rotation, position the mouse over the selection, and the pointer will change to a gavel ( ☞ ). This indicates that Photoshop will hammer down the selection when you click the mouse.

**IP:** *After rotating an image, you can check to see whether it is crooked or not by aligning the edges of an image with the edges of a palette.*

## Flipping an Image

The Flip commands in the Image menu let you flip an image to face it in a different direction. The Flip, as well as the Rotate, commands can be applied to a selected area in an image to create special effects.

If you wish to flip the entire image, you do not have to select it. (However, if the image you are working with now is large and you wish to test this command, it's 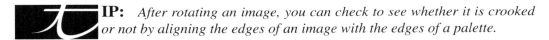wise to use the Rectangular Marquee to create a small selection to flip. Otherwise, you may be waiting some time for Photoshop to finish its task.) If you wish, you can continue to use the Frames file or any digitized image to experiment with.

To flip your image horizontally, choose Flip from the Image menu, and choose Horizontal. Your image will flip along a vertical plane and face in a new direction. Return to the Flip submenu and choose Vertical to see the image flip along a horizontal plane, turning it upside down. Flip your image again to make it right-side up.

Now that you've rotated your image so it's straight and flipped it to face in the direction you want, you might wish to crop it, as explained next.

## USING THE CROPPING TOOL

*Cropping* is very similar to taking a pair of scissors and cutting an image so that only a portion of the original is visible. You can also crop to remove unwanted border areas left over from a scan. Removing unwanted border areas is also a good way to keep the size of your file under control.

Before you begin to crop, double-click on the Cropping tool to display the Cropping Tool Options palette.

```
┌──────────────────────────────────────────────┐
│ □                                          ▣ │
├──────────────────────────────────────────────┤
│  Cropping Tool Options                     ▶ │
│  ☒ Fixed Target Size      [ Front Image ]    │
│       Width : [        ]  [ inches    ▼ ]     │
│      Height : [        ]  [ inches    ▼ ]     │
│  Resolution : [        ]  [ pixels/inch ▼ ]   │
└──────────────────────────────────────────────┘
```

The Cropping Tool Options palette contains dimension settings that are by now familiar to you. In order to activate the dimension settings, the Fixed Target Size option must be selected. If it isn't, click on it to select it. You can specify Width and Height measurement units in inches, centimeters, points, pixels, or columns. Notice that you can also change the resolution of the cropped area. If you change the width and height measurements and you want to maintain your image's current resolution, it's important to type that resolution into the Resolution field. If you don't, Photoshop will change the resolution to compensate for the change in width or height when you eventually execute the crop.

The Cropping tool also works somewhat like the Image Size dialog box. If you don't enter a resolution, it's the same as telling Photoshop to readjust the file dimensions without changing the number of pixels in the image. So if you reduce the width or height, Photoshop will increase the resolution proportionally.

Conversely, if you enter a resolution without changing the height or width, Photoshop will change the image dimensions proportionally. If you increase the resolution, Photoshop will decrease the image size; decrease the resolution, and Photoshop will increase the image size.

If you don't set any values in the Cropping Tool Options palette, you can crop freely with the mouse, and the resolution of the image will remain unchanged. You can also crop freely by deselecting the Fixed Target Size option. For this experiment, deselect the Fixed Target Size option.

7

**IP:** *If* CAPS LOCK *is on or if the Tool Cursors for Other Tools in the General Preferences dialog box (choose General from the Field/Preferences submenu) is set to Precise, the pointer will be a crosshair instead of the cropping tool icon. The crosshair pointer is more precise, because you can set the starting point of the cropping area to be exactly at the intersection of the crosshair.*

With the Cropping tool selected, click and drag over the image area that you want to retain. The area *outside* the selection is the portion that will be cropped. When you are satisfied with the selection, release the mouse button. Notice that the selected area on screen now includes one handle at each corner. If you need to make any adjustments to the crop, click and drag any of the handles to resize the selected area. To move the entire selection marquee, press COMMAND (PC users: CTRL), click on one of the four handles, and drag with the mouse.

If you crop your image incorrectly or accidentally, it's easy to undo the crop by immediately choosing Edit/Undo.

**IP:** *You can also use the Cropping tool to rotate a selection. Press* OPTION *(PC users:* ALT*) and click and drag on any of the selection handles.*

You'll probably notice that if you move the mouse outside the selected cropping area, the pointer will change to a circle with a bar through it ( ⊘ ). This indicates you can cancel the selected cropping area by clicking the mouse. If you move the mouse inside the selected area, the pointer will change to a scissors icon ( ✂ ). The scissors icon indicates that you can crop the image by clicking the mouse.

When you have selected the area you wish to crop, move the Cropping tool into the middle of the selection. The scissors icon will appear, as shown in Figure 7-3. At this point, click the mouse to crop the area.

**IP:** *To crop an image, you can also use the Rectangular Marquee to select an area and then choose the Crop command from the Edit menu.*

Now that you have the image cropped exactly the way you want it, you may want to make some simple adjustments to your image's brightness and contrast.

Crop line ⟶

The scissors icon shows that the area selected with the Cropping tool can be cropped by clicking the mouse

Crop handle          Scissors icon

■ **FIGURE 7-3**

## ADJUSTING BRIGHTNESS AND CONTRAST

*Contrast* is the difference between the lightest and darkest parts of an image. *Brightness* is the degree of light that is reflected from an image or transmitted through it.

Some scanners have a tendency to darken images, causing them to lose contrast. Images frame-grabbed from videotape also may have a tendency to darken when loaded into Photoshop. When you need to make simple adjustments to the brightness and contrast levels of your image, you'll find that the Brightness/Contrast command in the Image/Adjust submenu may solve the problem. (If your image needs more extensive color correction and retouching, refer to Chapter 13.)

To use the Brightness/Contrast controls, first select an area to be adjusted, or don't select in order to adjust the entire image. Choose Adjust from the Image menu, and then Brightness/Contrast. The Brightness/Contrast dialog box is a simple one: It contains a Preview check box and sliders for adjusting Brightness and Contrast.

```
┌─────────────────────────────────────────┐
│ ════════════ Brightness/Contrast ════════│
│ ┌───────────────────────────────────────┐│
│ │                                       ││
│ │ Brightness:        [ 0 ]   ┌─────────┐││
│ │            ────────△───────│    OK   │││
│ │                            └─────────┘││
│ │ Contrast:          [ 0 ]   ┌─────────┐││
│ │            ───────────△────│ Cancel  │││
│ │                            └─────────┘││
│ │                            ⊠ Preview  ││
│ └───────────────────────────────────────┘│
└─────────────────────────────────────────┘
```

First, make sure the Preview check box is selected so you can watch the results of your adjustments, and then begin by testing the Brightness slider. Drag the slider control to the right to brighten your image, or to the left to darken your image. Take a few moments now to adjust Brightness to the best level for your image. Be careful not to overexpose or underexpose the image.

When you are satisfied with the brightness level, try adjusting the contrast. Moving the slider control to the right adds more detail; this increases the difference between the lightest and darkest portions of the image. If you drag the slider control to the left, the lightness and darkness levels will begin to merge.

If the image doesn't look as good as it did when you started, you can either drag both sliders back to their zero points or click Cancel. Once you are satisfied with the new brightness and contrast levels, click OK.

## RESIZING AN IMAGE

You may need to increase or decrease the size of a digitized image so that it will fit in a specific area when you print it. To resize an image, you'll use the Image Size command in the Image menu, which is fully explained earlier in this chapter.

Remember, if you increase image dimensions (with the Constrain File Size check box deselected), Photoshop must interpolate. By default, Photoshop uses its best possible interpolation method. As you can probably guess, the best method is also the slowest.

### Changing Interpolation Methods

To view the interpolation choices, select Preferences in the File menu, and choose General. Click on the Interpolation pop-up menu to see the choices. Nearest Neighbor is the fastest but least exact interpolation method. If you use this method, your image will

probably look jagged after rotating or using other manipulation commands. With Bicubic, the best interpolation method, Photoshop attempts to improve contrast while interpolating. Bilinear is the middle ground between Nearest Neighbor and Bicubic.

If you wish to change interpolation methods now, select one from the list, click OK in the General Preferences dialog box, and continue.

## Changing the Image Dimensions

To change the dimensions of the image, enter a new value in either the Width or Height field (under New Size) in the Image Size dialog box. If the Constrain Proportions check box is selected, Photoshop will automatically change the other value. If the Constrain File Size option is off, your resolution will remain the same, but the new file size in bytes will change.

Later in this chapter, in the "Working with the Image/Effects Commands" section, you will work through a design project in which the example image will be reduced by one half-inch. Go ahead and lower the width and height dimensions of your own image now, if you wish. But before you click OK, remember that when you decrease the size of your image (with the Constrain File Size check box deselected), Photoshop removes pixels from it. Thus, if you later try to resample up, the image will not look as sharp as the original. Once Photoshop removes the pixels, they're gone for good; Photoshop cannot re-create them. When Photoshop resamples up, it resamples based upon the contents of the current file. When you are ready to have Photoshop resample your image, click OK.

## INCREASING THE CANVAS SIZE

Now that you have the image the size you want, you may wish to increase your work area on screen. You can do this by changing the *canvas size* of your image. When you increase the canvas size, you extend the perimeter of your document. This puts a border of the background color around the image. Later in this chapter, you'll see how you can utilize this border as an area for adding text and extra images to a document.

When a border is added, Photoshop uses the current background color as the canvas color. Before you change the canvas size, pick a background color that you like. If you want the canvas color to match one of the colors in your image, you can use the Eyedropper tool and OPTION key (PC users: ALT) to switch background colors (as long as the Foreground selection box is activated in the Picker palette). Activate the Eyedropper by clicking on it, press OPTION (PC users: ALT), move the eyedropper pointer over the color you wish to use as your background color, and click.

To change the canvas size, choose Canvas Size from the Image menu. In the Canvas Size dialog box, notice that your image's current dimensions appear in the Width and Height fields. At this point, they are the same as those for the canvas.

you increase these values in the Width and Height fields for New Size, the perimeter or surrounding canvas will grow. This will produce a border around the image in the current background color.

The Canvas Size dialog box also allows you to indicate the placement of your image in the canvas. At the bottom of the dialog box is the Placement area, a grid of nine boxes. The selected box represents the position of your image in relation to the canvas. If you select the center box, Photoshop will center your image in the Canvas. If you click on the lower-middle box, Photoshop will drop your image to the bottom-middle part of the canvas. This is the placement chosen for the design project, shown in Figure 7-6, presented later in this chapter. Also, 1 inch was added to both the Width and Height, as shown in Figure 7-4. The result is a half-inch border on the left and right sides of the image, and a one-inch canvas area on top.

To create a canvas background for your image now, increase the Width and Height settings in the New Size area of the Canvas Size dialog box. Try adding 1 inch to both. If you wish your image to appear as shown in the design project, choose the bottom-middle Placement box. Click OK to see the results.

At this point you have learned how to rotate, flip, crop, change brightness and contrast, resize, and border your digitized image. We'll look now at some special effects that will add variety to your image. You will use these techniques to create a sample design project.

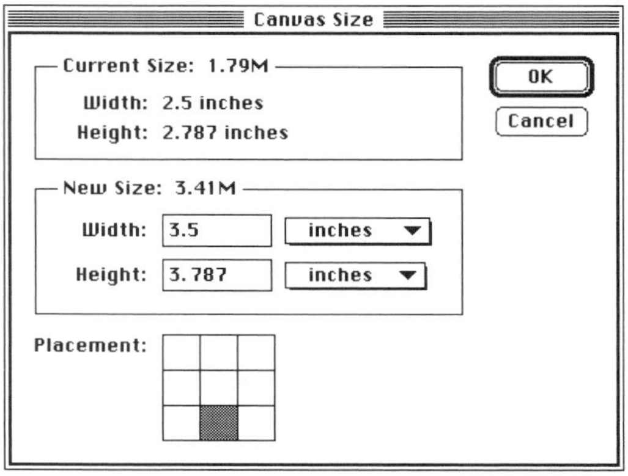

One inch was added to the Width and Height to increase the canvas (work area)

**Canvas Size**

Current Size: 1.79M
 Width: 2.5 inches
 Height: 2.787 inches

OK
Cancel

New Size: 3.41M
 Width: 3.5    inches ▼
 Height: 3.787    inches ▼

Placement:

**FIGURE 7-4**

## WORKING WITH THE IMAGE/EFFECTS COMMANDS

The commands available in Photoshop's Image/Effects submenu allow you to scale, skew, change perspective, and distort floating text or any selected part of an image. Use the Scale command to resize part of an image, Skew to slant an image, Perspective to create the appearance of depth in an image, and Distort to stretch an image in different directions.

To try any of these commands, you must first create a selection, and then choose either Scale, Skew, Perspective, or Distort from the Image/Effects submenu. These commands work similarly to the Rotate/Free command. After you choose an Image/Effects command, Photoshop adds handles to the selection. With the mouse,

you click and drag on the handles to preview the effect. Once you position the mouse over the selection, the gavel icon appears, and when you click inside the selection, Photoshop executes the command.

 **AUTION:** *Be aware that when you execute any of the Image/Effects menu commands, Photoshop interpolates. Thus, image quality depends upon the interpolation method set in the General Preferences dialog box.*

Take a few moments to try out each Image/Effects command. If you don't wish to apply the commands to your current image, open a new file and create some text that you can experiment with. Remember, these commands can only be applied to selections or to floating text. Here are some guidelines for using Image/Effects commands:

 To scale an object in proportion, press the SHIFT key while you use the Scale command.

 When you use the Perspective command, try dragging one handle up and the opposite one down or diagonally in and out. As you drag one handle, another one will move in the opposite direction, to create depth or dimensionality. Figure 7-5 illustrates the effect of the Perspective command applied to a text selection. Here, clicking and dragging downward on the lower-right handle caused the top-right handle to move upward.

When you skew a selection, click and drag on any handle. All handles will always move along a horizontal plane as the object is slanted.

# Photoshop in Action

The sphinx was scanned and then selected with the Lasso tool. It was pasted into the monitor, then shrunk with the Image/Effects/Scale command.

The monitor was selected and then stretched using the Image/Effects/Scale command.

Artist: Marc Yankus                                      Client: Computer World

Marc started by scanning black-and-white images of various pyramids. These were selected with the selection tools and filled with color using the Edit/Fill command. In the Fill dialog box, Marc set the mode to Darken, so that only the light areas would be painted and not the dark areas. Then he scanned a picture of a computer. Once the computer was scanned, he selected it with the Lasso tool and pasted it into the final image.

With the Perspective command, dragging a handle distorts the image and creates depth

**FIGURE 7-5**

You can distort a selection by clicking and dragging on any handle in any direction. With Distort you can create effects that look like Perspective and Skew, except you have more control over the selected area.

After you've finished experimenting, you may want to use the Revert command to retrieve the last saved version of your file before you continue to the next section, where you'll see the image effects demonstrated in a design project.

**N OTE:** *If you paste or drag an image into a layer that is smaller than the image, Photoshop will not crop the offscreen areas when executing Image/Effects commands or Image/Rotate. If you wish to see the offscreen areas, you can increase the Canvas size.*

## Image Effects Design Project

If you wish to complete a project like the one shown in Figure 7-6, load any digitized image, or the image you used in the "Increasing the Canvas Size" section earlier in the chapter (and skip step 1).

A design
project
created
using the
Image/Effects
commands

**FIGURE 7-6**

1. Choose a background color and then use the Image/Canvas Size command to add 1 inch to both the Width and Height of your image. Set Placement in the Canvas Size dialog box so that the bottom-middle box is selected. This will create a .5-inch canvas border area on the left and right or your image, and a 1-inch canvas border area above your image.

2. Next, to fill the half-inch border on the right and left sides with a duplicated portion of your image (see Figure 7-6 as an example), use the Marquee tool to create a rectangular selection. It doesn't matter whether the selection is bigger than the half-inch canvas border because you can scale it to fit.

3. With the image area selected, duplicate it by pressing OPTION (PC users: ALT) while you click and drag the selection toward the upper-left canvas border area. *Don't deselect.* (You can also create a duplicate by choosing Select/Float and then clicking and dragging the selection.)

4. Choose Scale from the Image/Effects submenu. Scale the image by clicking on one of the four corners. If you wish, press SHIFT to constrain proportionally.

Gavel icon ———

BANGKOK (RGB, 1:2)

The Scale
command
is used to
shrink a
selection
that was
created by
duplicating
part of the
image

■ **FIGURE 7-7**

3.41M/3.41M

**7**

5. When you are satisfied with the scaling, move the mouse pointer into the center of the scaled image. When the gavel icon appears, as shown in Figure 7-7, click the mouse. After the scaled image has been hammered down on your screen, *do not deselect it.*

6. Keep the scaled image selected so that you can reproduce it several times in order to cover the entire left and right borders. While pressing OPTION (PC users: ALT), click and drag to duplicate the image. Do this as many times as needed to cover the borders.

   Once you've assembled the border, you are ready to start creating the distorted text. Before you begin, make sure that the foreground color is set to the color you wish to use for the text (we used white).

7. Select the Type tool and click on the top canvas area. When the Type Tool dialog box appears, pick an appropriate font and size. So that the text does not appear jagged, select the Anti-Aliased option.

8. Type the heading you want to appear in your image. In our example, we used BANGKOK. Click OK. Don't deselect.

9. Your next step is to distort the type. While the text is still selected, choose Distort from the Image/Effects submenu. (If you prefer, you can create a

different effect by choosing Perspective or Skew.) When the handles appear, click and drag on them to create the look you want. In this example, all four handles were dragged to create the distortion.

10. When you are ready to apply the effects of your adjustments, move the mouse into the center of the selection. When the gavel appears, as shown in Figure 7-8, click to seal in your changes.

11. Move the distorted text into position. If you'd like, duplicate the text, fill it with another color (we used black), and offset it; this effect can be seen in Figure 7-6.

If you wish to execute any more image effects, feel free to experiment. In the next section, you'll learn how to use the Image/Map commands.

## WORKING WITH THE IMAGE/MAP COMMANDS

The Map commands in the Image menu are used to remap, or reassign, pixel values

in a selection or in an entire image. The Map commands quickly let you alter your digitized images to evenly distribute tone and color, or they can be used to create special effects that drastically change brightness values. For

With the Distort command, selection handles can be adjusted to create the distortion

**FIGURE 7-8**

instance, you can transform a color or grayscale image into a high-contrast, black-and-white image or invert all of the color values in an image to produce a negative of the original.

## Creating a Negative Using Invert

The Image/Map/Invert command reverses your image, turning it into a negative of the original: All black values become white, all white values turn black, and all colors are converted to their complements. Pixel values are inverted on a scale of 0 to 255. A pixel with a value of 0 will be inverted to 255; a pixel with the value of 10 will be change to 245; and so on.

You may invert a selection or an entire image; if no area is selected, the entire image is inverted.

In the example in Figure 7-9, black text was entered on screen first; then the bottom half was selected using the Rectangular Marquee. When the Image/Map/Invert command was applied to the rectangular selection, the black text within the selection turned white, and the white area between the letters turned black.

## Expanding Tonal Range with Equalize

The Equalize command distributes light and dark values evenly and can be used to adjust dark scans and make them lighter. When the Equalize command is executed, Photoshop remaps light and dark values over the full tonal range from black to white. The darkest areas in the images are darkened as much as possible, and the lightest are lightened as much as possible. All other values are distributed according to the new tonal range. Images will often look brighter, exhibiting more balance and contrast.

The Invert command can be used to create a reverse (negative) effect

**FIGURE 7-9**

If an image area is selected and you execute Image/Map/Equalize, the Equalize dialog box will appear. Choose the Selected Area Only radio button to Equalize only the selectIf you choose Entire Image Based on Area, Photoshop equalizes the entire image based upon the lightness and darkness values of the selected area.

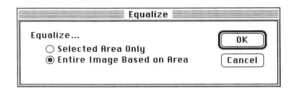

Figure 7-10a shows the original scanned image of a wine glass and bottle. Figure 7-10b displays the results after the Equalize command was applied.

## Converting an Image to Black and White Using Threshold

The Image/Map/Threshold command converts a color or grayscale image into a high-contrast, black-and-white image. The Threshold dialog box allows you to pick a Threshold Level—a dividing line between black and white pixels. All pixels lighter

Scanned image before (a) and after (b) the Image/Map/ Equalize command is applied (photograph courtesy of Stacy Kollar Photography)

(a)

(b)

**FIGURE 7-10**

than or equal to the Threshold Level value become white; all pixels darker than the Threshold Level are converted to black.

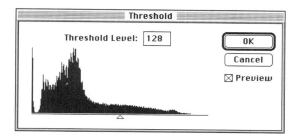

In the dialog box, you see a *histogram*, which graphically presents the brightness, or luminance, values of the pixels in the current image or selection. The histogram plots the number of pixels at each tonal level of the image. Darker values are plotted on the left side of the histogram, lighter values are plotted on the right side. You'll read more about using histograms when retouching and color correcting in Chapter 13.

Clicking and dragging on the Threshold dialog box slider control changes the Threshold Level (dragging right raises the value; dragging left lowers it). Or you can enter a value between 1 and 255 in the Threshold Level field (the default is 128). If the Threshold command is executed at the default settings, all pixels with values greater than or equal to 128 will turn white, and all pixels with values less than 128 will turn black. If the Preview check box is selected, Photoshop will show you the results of the Threshold command.

Figure 7-11 shows the wine bottle image after the Threshold command was applied.

The results of applying the Threshold command to the image from Figure 7-10a

**FIGURE 7-11**

## An Exercise Using Threshold and Paste Behind

The following exercise shows you how to create an interesting artistic effect by decreasing the number of colors in an image.

1. Open any color image. If you don't have one to use, load the Portrait file (PC users: portrait.jpg) from the Tutorial folder.

2. Select the entire image by pressing COMMAND-A (PC users: CTRL-A).

3. Choose Copy from the Edit menu.

4. Paste the image over itself by choosing Paste from the Edit menu. (The Select/Float command can also be used instead of Paste.)

5. To convert the floating selection to black and white, choose Threshold from the Image/Map submenu.

6. In the Threshold dialog box, make sure the Preview check box is selected, and then drag the slider control to choose a level that creates an attractive black-and-white image. If you are using the Portrait file, try setting the Threshold to **95**. When you like what you see, click OK. Don't deselect.

   In order to create the decreased colors effect, you'll need to blend the pixels of the floating image with the underlying image. To do this you'll need to activate the Layers palette.

7. If the palette isn't on screen, choose Show Layers from the Window/Palettes submenu. To add the image's original color back into the dark areas of the image, choose Lighten from the Mode pop-up menu in the Layers palette.

   The result will be a composite image with color in what was once the darker areas, and white in the lighter areas.

8. If you wish, continue to experiment with different opacities and modes such as Screen and Overlay. When you are ready to continue to the next section, save your file, if desired, and close it.

## Reducing Gray Levels Using Posterize

In this next exercise you will reduce the gray levels in an image using the Posterize command. This command can create some unusual special effects, because the gray contours in an image disappear and are replaced by large flat-color or gray areas.

Load any color image on screen, then select Image/Map/Posterize to open the Posterize dialog box. In the Levels field, enter the number of gray levels you wish to have appear in the image or selected area. Acceptable values range from 2 to 255. The lower the number, the fewer the gray levels. When the Preview check box is selected, Photoshop will preview the results of applying the Posterize command.

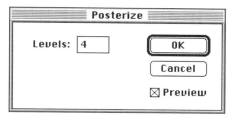

For a dramatic effect, try **4** in the Levels field. Then raise the number of gray levels a few increments at a time to see the different effects. Figure 7-12a shows a scanned image of South America's Iguaçu Falls; Figure 7-12b shows the results after applying the Posterize command with Levels set to 4.

The remaining sections of this chapter discuss some alternative digitizing methods for use with Photoshop; these options require hardware other than scanners.

## PHOTO CD

If you need to have your images photographed first before digitizing them, you might be able to avoid scanning altogether. Eastman Kodak's Photo CD process transforms a roll of film into a CD-ROM disc filled with digitized images. Each disc stored in Kodak's standard Master format can hold 25 to 100 35mm images. The images are stored at five different resolutions, from 128 by 192 pixels to 2,048 by 3,072 pixels. Expect the low-resolution color images to be about 72K in size; high-resolution images will be around 18MB.

Kodak's Pro Photo CD format allows film sizes of up to 4 inches by 5 inches and a top resolution of 4,000 by 6,000 pixels. For a 4-by-5-inch image, this would provide you with a resolution of approximately 1,200 ppi. Thus, you easily could enlarge to an 8-by-10-inch image without sacrificing quality.

In order to use the Photo CD images, you need a CD-ROM player that incorporates XA (extended architecture), which most new CD-ROM players have. You'll also want to get a multisession drive, because it will let you add photos to CD-ROMs that are not filled to the 100-picture capacity. Once you've connected

(a)

Iguaçu
Falls before
(a) and
after (b)
applying
Image/Map/
Posterize
with a
Levels
setting of 4

(b)

**FIGURE 7-12**

your CD-ROM to your computer, you can load the images into Photoshop using the File/Open command. When you load the file, you will be able to choose a file format and a resolution.

Kodak sells a plug-in (driver) for Photoshop. After choosing the Photo CD plug-in from the File/Acquire submenu, you see the dialog box shown in Figure 7-13, in which you choose an image and a resolution. You can see that there is a preview of the image, and a Sharpening option. There are also a variety of Metric options, which give you a choice of importing the file into Photoshop as a Video RGB, Grayscale, or Photo YCC image (Kodak's own color space model). The Metric

# Photoshop in Action

This child was scanned, resized, and then rotated using the commands in the Image/Effects submenu.

The background is a piece of textured paper that was moved as it was being scanned.

Artist: Pamela Hobbs

Client: Children's TV/Pentagram Design

7

Pamela created the image above for the Children's TV magazine, Sesame Street. All of the above images were scanned. First the background was scanned. It was a piece of textured paper that was moved as it was being scanned to give the appearance of motion. To soften the transition of the move affect, the Motion Blur filter was applied. After the background was created the children were scanned.

Each child was scanned separately and then placed into the final document. Later some of the images of the children were scaled and rotated using the commands in the Image/Effects submenu.

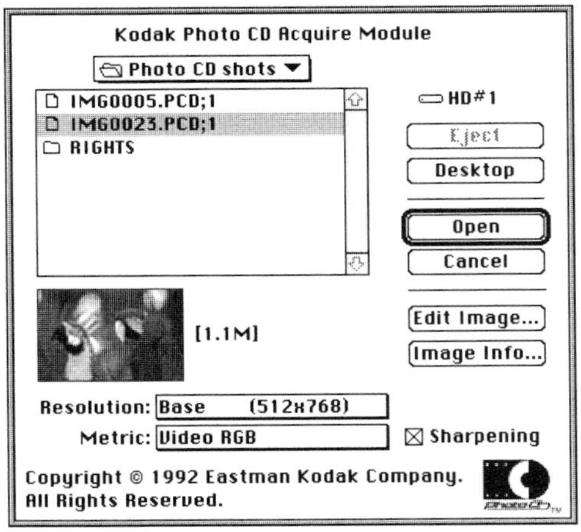

Photo CD images can be loaded and their resolution chosen using the Kodak Photo CD Acquire Module

**FIGURE 7-13**

option also allows you to change gamma levels for the midtones of the image. A gamma setting higher than 1 brightens; a gamma setting lower than 1 darkens.

If you select Video RGB or a gamma level, and then click on the Edit Image button, you can change the color balance of the image by clicking and dragging on slider controls for Saturation, Cyan/Red, Magenta/Green, Yellow/Blue, and Dark/Light. For more information about loading Photo CD images, see Appendix A.

## DIGITAL AND VIDEO CAMERAS

Digital and still-video cameras provide even more versatile alternatives to scanning. With these cameras, you don't have to wait for film to be developed and then scan or convert to Photo CD. By digitizing with a still-video or digital camera, you can quickly see the results by shooting in a studio with the camera connected to a computer. If the image doesn't please you, you can usually change your lighting setup and reshoot.

Still video cameras are video cameras primarily used for taking still pictures. Many cameras require that a video capture board be installed in the computer so that images can be stored on a hard drive. Digital cameras immediately digitize an image which can usually be downloaded directly as a digital file to the computer through a serial or SCSI connection.

Still-video and digital photography are growing in popularity—particularly in catalog work, where many products need to be digitized quickly. Many digital cameras provide Photoshop plug-ins, so you can use the File/Acquire command to load the image directly into Photoshop. Many also feature on-board disks, memory cards, or hard disks. To download files to a computer, some cameras require an interface card to be installed in the computer; others, such as Kodak's DCS 420, can be plugged into a computer via a SCSI port.

## Kodak's DCS 420 Digital Camera

Combining high resolution and excellent optics, Kodak's DCS 420 digital camera is becoming a favorite with professional photographers for both news and catalog work. The DCS 420 consists of an electronic back connected to a Nikon N90 camera. The camera accepts all F-Mounted lenses manufactured for the N90 and includes nearly all of the standard SLR (Single Lens Reflex) features, including automatic exposure, flash, and self-timing.

Unlike its predecessor, Kodak's DCS 200, the 420 does not incorporate a built-in hard drive. It uses hard disks that conform to the PCMCIA-ATA standard for portable computers. Images can be downloaded to both PCs and MACs via a SCSI

**7**

A Photoshop screen shot of an image digitized by Kodak's DCS camera

**FIGURE 7-14**

connection. (The MAC has a built-in SCSI port; most PC users will need to purchase a SCSI interface card.)

Kodak digital cameras come with a plug-in that is accessed using the File/Acquire command. The Acquire dialog box provides a preview of the image. Using the mouse, you can click on a white area of the preview to set the image's *white point*—the lightest part of the image. Once the white point is captured, the image can be opened into Photoshop at the proper dynamic range.

The example you see in Figure 7-14 was digitized by Image Technologies, Inc., a New York City prepress house, using a Kodak digital camera. In the image, notice there is a Kodak Gray Scale alongside the art being digitized. After the image was digitized, Photoshop's Eyedropper tool was used to click on the various gray levels to analyze whether pure gray was being produced. This test ensured that no color cast (excess of any color) was being produced during the digital photography session.

## Apple's QuickTake and Logitech's FotoMan Plus

If you don't need high-resolution color images but you still want to save time and avoid the cost of film and processing, Apple's QuickTake 100 or Logitech's FotoMan Plus might be the option for you. Both cameras sell for less than $800.

Apple's QuickTake 100 camera can save eight 24-bit color images at a resolution of 640 by 480 pixels and 32 images at 320 by 420 pixels. QuickTake's output makes it great for comping purposes. Its photos may even be acceptable for some catalog and newsletter work.

The FotoMan Plus saves up to 32 grayscale photos in its internal memory with an image resolution of 496 by 360 pixels. Images from both the QuickTake 100 and FotoMan Plus can be downloaded to both Macs and PCs via a serial port connection.

# VIDEO CAPTURE

Photoshop's plug-in capabilities allow still-frames to be captured from videotape. To capture video, a card must be installed in your computer to convert the television signals (NTSC) to RGB so the images can be input to Photoshop. The plug-in and video card combination also allows the RGB signals to be converted to an NTSC television signal for output back to videotape. One of the best-known manufacturers of video cards for both PCs and Macs is TrueVision. TrueVision makes the Targa board for the PC and the NuVista board for the Mac. If you are using a Mac, you should investigate Apple's Power PC AV computer models, which have video input and output capabilities built in.

To obtain frame-accurate control over the input and recording of the video signal, most multimedia systems require a video card that controls a videotape recorder.

Figure 7-15 shows two dialog boxes that appear in Photoshop when used with DiaQuest's video controller card and plug-in. The dialog box options allow you to control a videotape player and pick a frame from the tape.

Microcomputer Publishing Center (a video and prepress service bureau) in New York digitized a variety of Effie-award-winning TV commercials for *BRANDWEEK* magazine. The images appeared as part of a special color insert featuring freeze frames from the commercials. All images were digitized and enhanced in Photoshop. A few of the images are reprinted in the following figures (with permission of *BRANDWEEK* and Microcomputer Publishing Center)—Figure 7-16 shows an image from a commercial for Andersen Consulting (with permission also from the company), Figure 7-17 is from a commercial for Rhone-Poulenc's Buctril Corn Herbicide (with permission also from the company and Rhea & Kaiser Advertising), Figure 7-18 is from a commercial for Little Caesars Pizza (with permission also from the company and Cliff Freeman & Partners).

**7**

DiaQuest video controller dialog boxes allow videotape control directly from Photoshop (images courtesy of Microcomputer Publishing Center)

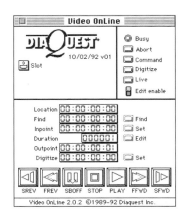

**FIGURE 7-15**

Digitized
video
frames
from a
commercial
advertising
Andersen
Consulting

**FIGURE 7-16**

## DIGITIZED STOCK PHOTOS

If your image needs are not specific, and you don't need to scan or photograph images, numerous sources of stock digital images are available. Several stock photo collections are now sold on CD-ROM discs for both the PC and the Mac. Many collections allow unlimited usage, and some contain images that are scanned on high-end drum scanners in 24-bit color. Before purchasing stock photos, check to see that the resolution and size of the images meet your needs. Also, find out whether the images are compressed, and if they are, whether a lossy or lossless compression method was used. Lossless compression means that no loss of picture quality occurs during compression.

Digitized
image
from a
commercial
for Buctril
Corn
Herbicide

**FIGURE 7-17**

Digitized video frame from a commercial advertising Little Caesars pizza

**FIGURE 7-18**

Here are the names of companies that provide digitized images: ColorBytes, American Databankers Corp., COREL, PhotoDisc, Gazelle Technologies, Aztech New Media Corp., and Dana Publishing. These companies provide digitized backgrounds: Pixar (One Twenty Eight), Xaos (Artist Residence), ArtBeats (Marble & Granite, Marbled Paper Textures, and Wood and Paper), and D'Pix.

Another option for obtaining images is downloading them over the telephone with a modem. Kodak's Picture Exchange allows you on-line access to a variety of major image collections. The Picture Exchange software allows you to search for the type of image you want, browse through contact sheets, and download design proofs. When you wish to use the original image, you order through an onscreen order form. Fees are charged for on-line time and for picture use by the image provider.

## IMAGE DATABASE SOFTWARE

If you start building a library of digitized images, you'll soon long for an efficient means to keep track of them. If you are storing many files on disk, consider purchasing image-management software that will help you catalog, archive, and find images. Examples of these programs include Fetch, Kudo from Imspace Systems, Kodak's Shoebox, and Nikon's Image Access. Both Shoebox and Image Access are available for both Macs and PCs.

Perhaps the chief advantage of most of these programs is that the actual images in the database do not need to be on the same hard disk as the image cataloging

# Photoshop in Action

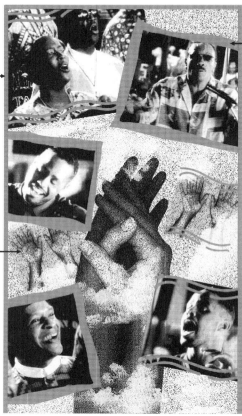

The different musicians were scanned separately and then pasted into the final image.

All of the hands were scanned, scaled, and then placed into the final image.

After all the musicians and hands were in place, the file was converted from Grayscale to Duotone mode. It was then saved in EPS format so that it could be placed into Adobe Illustrator where the line art was created.

**Artist: Lynda Kusnetz**        **Client: Columbia House**

Lynda created this spirited image for a Columbia House mail-order catalog of inspirational music. She started by scanning a photograph of a sky with clouds to use for the background. Then she scanned her hands in different positions by placing them under the scanner lid with the help of a co-worker who controlled the scanner. Once the hands were scanned, they were scaled using the Image/Effects/Scale command. Then the Add Noise filter was applied to create the textured background effect.

After the background was created, the photographs of the different musicians were scanned and pasted into the image (clockwise from top are Tramaine Hawkins and Alvin Chea, Quincy Jones, Mervyn Warren, Al Jarreau, and Mervyn Warren). Next, the Mode menu was used to change the image into a Duotone. The file was saved as an EPS file so it could be placed into Adobe Illustrator, where the frames around the images were created.

software. The programs maintain low-resolution images for quick access, and the high-resolution files can be stored on removable media. Virtually all cataloging software lets you sort your images and search by title or keyword.

## CONCLUSION

Now that you've learned the basics of digitizing images, you're ready to explore further into the world of image enhancement and editing. In the following chapter, you will learn how Photoshop's electronic filters can sharpen your images, blur them, and apply special effects that make them ripple, twirl, and even melt before your very eyes.

7

# FILTERS

Photoshop's magical filters are designed to do what your scanner can't do: enhance an image and disguise its defects. A filter can turn soft, blurred contours into sharp, crisp edges, or it can soften an image with jagged or harsh edges. Filters can also remove dust and scratches in digitized images. They can also help eliminate *color banding,* abrupt changes in color values, and *noise,* randomly colored pixels that can appear in a scanned image.

Although many filters are designed to subtly improve scanned images, others will create dramatic alterations, for example, twisting, bending an image, or spinning it into motion. Some filters can grab a continuous-tone or painted image and make it appear to be made of three-dimensional blocks or pyramid shapes. Many filters create unusual, eerie, or humorous effects. Digitized images, as well as original images created in Photoshop, can be spherized, zigzagged, or twirled into a digital "soup."

The complex digital effects produced by Photoshop's filters have their roots in photography. Photographic filters are used to filter out light, to enhance images, and to create special effects. But the photographic filter can't match Photoshop's digital filters in effects or versatility. In Photoshop, filters can be applied again and again, one after another, until just the right effect is achieved for the entire image or within selections in the image. For instance, one filter might be applied to enhance the edges of an image and another to give it an embossed effect. The possibilities are endless.

## HOW A FILTER WORKS

Each of Photoshop's filters produces a different effect. Some filters work by analyzing every pixel in an image or selection and transforming it by applying mathematical algorithms to create random or predefined shapes, such as tiles, three-dimensional blocks or pyramids. Many filters, though, achieve their effects by first sampling individual pixels or groups of pixels to define areas that display the greatest difference in color or brightness. Once it zeroes in on one of these transitional areas, the filter starts changing color values—sometimes replacing one pixel's color with that of an adjacent pixel, sometimes substituting pixel colors with the average color value of neighboring pixels. The result, depending upon the filter, can be a sharpening of the image, a softening of harsh edges, or a complete transformation.

Many filters invite you to be an active participant in determining the outcome of the filter's effects. Before these filters begin their work, a dialog box is presented to you, where you can control the magnitude of the filter's effects and often specify the *radius* (range) in which changes will occur.

## HOW TO APPLY A FILTER

Despite the differences among Photoshop's numerous filters, the process of applying each one is virtually the same. Start by opening, or activating, the image you will

| Filter |
| --- |
| Last Filter ⌘F |
| Blur ▶ |
| Distort ▶ |
| Noise ▶ |
| Pixelate ▶ |
| Render ▶ |
| Sharpen ▶ |
| Stylize ▶ |
| Video ▶ |
| Other ▶ |

be changing. If you wish to apply the filter to only a portion of the image, select that area with one of the selection tools; otherwise, Photoshop will apply the filter to the entire image. If you are working in a layer, Photoshop only applies the filter to colored, not transparent areas of the layer. It will not apply a filter to more than one layer at a time.

From the Filter menu, choose one of the filter groups: Blur, Distort, Noise, Pixelate, Render, Sharpen, Stylize, Video, or Other. From the submenu that appears, select the filter that you wish to apply. Several of the filters are applied immediately when you select them. For others, you'll need to set dialog box options to control the filter's results.

**OTE:** *Filters cannot be applied to Bitmap or Indexed Color images. If you are working on a Bitmap or Indexed Color image and wish to apply a filter, change modes first by choosing either Grayscale or RGB Color in the Mode menu. Indexed Color and Bitmap images and changing modes are discussed in Chapter 9.*

Sometimes the effect of a filter on an image will be so subtle that you won't notice it, and you may wish to apply the filter again to enhance the results. To facilitate the process of reapplying filters, Photoshop copies the name of the last filter used from a submenu and installs it at the top of the Filter menu. To reapply the filter, just click on the first menu item in the Filter menu or press COMMAND-F (PC users: CTRL-F). If the filter requires dialog box settings, you can press OPTION-COMMAND-F (PC users: ALT-CTRL-F) to open the dialog box before reapplying the filter.

Many of the filter dialog boxes provide invaluable image previews which allow you to see the filter effect on the image before it is applied. The previews can appear in a preview box as shown on the following page.

By clicking on the + or – icon, the image in the preview box can be enlarged or reduced by specific ratios. For instance, clicking on the + icon to change the image ratio to 2:1 would double the image size in the preview box; clicking on the – icon to change it to 1:2 would make it half the size.

If the preview box doesn't show the specific area you wish to view, you can adjust the image by clicking and dragging on the miniature image in the preview box. When you move the mouse over the preview box a tiny hand icon appears, alerting that you can click and drag to move the image. If you want the preview box to display an image area that is far outside the range of the preview box, you can click outside the dialog box on the image area you wish to see in the preview box.

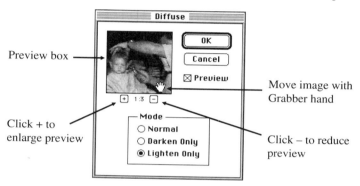

Because many Photoshop filters are sophisticated and require extensive computer processing, they may take some time to execute, particularly in a large image or selection. If you apply a filter and wish to halt it before it is finished processing, you can usually press COMMAND-PERIOD (PC users: CTRL-PERIOD) to cancel.

If you'd like to try out the filters as you work through the discussions in this chapter, open the scanned image you used in Chapter 7, or choose one of the files available in the Tutorial folder.

**n**OTE: *Some filters do not use your scratch disk while executing, so you must have sufficient RAM to complete the entire filter operation. If you do not, you may still be able to apply the filter to the image one channel at a time. See Chapters 9 and 11 for more information.*

## THE BLUR FILTERS

The five Blur filters are often used to smooth areas where edges are too sharp and contrast is too high. They soften image edges by removing contrast. Blur filters can also be used to blur the background of an image so the foreground stands out, or to create a soft shadow effect.

**BLUR**    The Blur filter creates a light blurring effect that can be used to decrease contrast and eliminate noise in color transitions.

**BLUR MORE**    The Blur More filter blurs about three to four times more than the Blur filter.

**GAUSSIAN BLUR**    The Gaussian Blur allows you to control the blurring effect, creating anything from a slight softening of image edges to a thick haze that blurs the image beyond recognition. This filter is named because it maps pixel color values according to a Gaussian bell-shaped curve.

In the Gaussian Blur dialog box, you specify a value from .1 to 250 in the Radius field to control the range of the blur from transitional areas. The higher the number, the greater the blur.

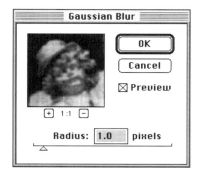

By experimenting with different Radius values, you can often eliminate moiré patterns in scanned images. A *moiré* pattern is an unwanted mottled effect that sometimes occurs during the scanning of printed photographs or when an image is printed at an incorrect screen angle. Figure 8-1a shows a photograph, scanned from a Pratt Manhattan Art School's course catalog, of Puck standing on top of New York City's Puck building; notice the moiré pattern over the entire image. Figure 8-1b shows the same image after the Gaussian Blur filter was applied. As you can see, after applying the filter, the pattern is hardly noticeable.

**MOTION BLUR**    The Motion Blur filter creates the illusion of motion. It imitates the effect of photographing a moving object using a timed exposure.

The Motion Blur dialog box allows you to control the direction and strength of the blur. To set direction, type a degree value from –360 to 360 in the Angle box, or

(a) Image
showing a
moiré
pattern, and
(b) after
applying
Gaussian
Blur
(courtesy
of Pratt
Manhattan
and
photographer
Federico
Savini)

(a)

(b)

**FIGURE 8-1**

use the mouse to click and drag on the radius line in the circle. To control intensity, enter a pixel value from 1 to 999 in the Distance field.

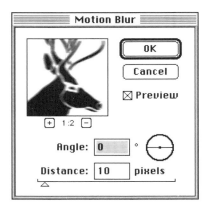

If you experiment with Motion Blur, zoom in on the pixels after blurring, and you will easily see how the filter works. It copies the image using the number in the Distance field as a guide, then offsets (shifts) the duplicate according to the Angle value, and overlays the copy of the image over the original as it lowers the opacity of the duplicate.

The next illustration shows the results of Motion Blur. In order to prevent the deer image itself from appearing blurred, the original image was selected with the Magic Wand

and copied into the Clipboard before the blur was applied. In the Motion Blur dialog box, Distance was set to 60 pixels; Angle was set to 45 degrees to match the deer's jumping angle. Then the copy of the deer from the Clipboard was pasted over the blurred image. While the pasted image was floating, it was offset about a quarter of an inch away from the blur.

**RADIAL BLUR**   The Radial Blur creates numerous interesting effects. It can spin an image into a circular shape or make it radiate out from its center.

When you activate Radial Blur, a wireframe preview appears in the filter's dialog box, providing a skeletal view of the blur's effect. This is extremely helpful because the Radial Blur often takes a long time to execute.

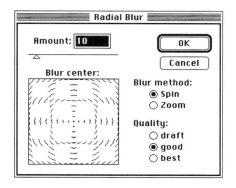

In the Radial Blur dialog box, you can select either Spin or Zoom as the blur method. If you select Spin, the blur is created in concentric circles, often making your image look as if it were spun on a potter's wheel. With Zoom, blurred image lines zoom out from the image's center point.

To control the intensity of the blur, enter a value between 1 and 100 in the Amount field, or drag the Amount slider control until the blur in the preview box shows the effect you desire. The higher the value, the more intense the blur. To change the center of the blur, click and drag on the dot in the center of the Blur center box.

The Radial Blur dialog box also allows you to specify the quality of the blur. The Best option produces the smoothest blur, but it takes the longest to execute. With the Draft option, Photoshop completes the blur faster, but the results will be grainy. The Good option will produce a level of quality between Best and Draft, although for large files, there may be little noticeable difference between Best and Good.

In the following illustration, the Radial Blur filter was applied to the wheel graphic at the left to produce the spinning wheel at the right. The filter was applied with an Amount setting of 30; Spin was selected as the blur method; and Quality was set to Best.

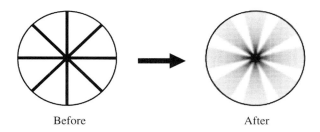

Before                              After

## THE NOISE FILTERS

*Noise*, randomly colored pixels, is occasionally introduced during the scanning process. The Noise filters will blend noise to make it less apparent. Or you can use Add Noise to drown an image with so much noise that it is completely transformed into colored pixel patterns; this effect can be used to quickly create interesting and unusual textured backgrounds.

**ADD NOISE**   The Add Noise filter adds noise to an image, blends noise into an image, and helps diffuse color banding that can occur in blends. This filter is sometimes used to help blend images created with painting tools into their surroundings, or to create interesting patterned backgrounds. When you use it to create background patterns, experiment with different file resolutions because the pattern will change depending upon the resolution.

Use the Add Noise dialog box to indicate the amount of noise you wish to add to an image. Enter a value from 1 to 999 in the Amount field; the greater the amount, the greater the noise effect.

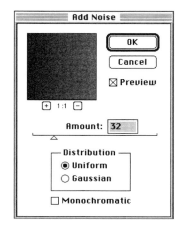

# Photoshop in Action

The kids were photographed with the table and balloons.

Shaquille O'Neal from the Orlando Magic was photographed with a tray in his hand.

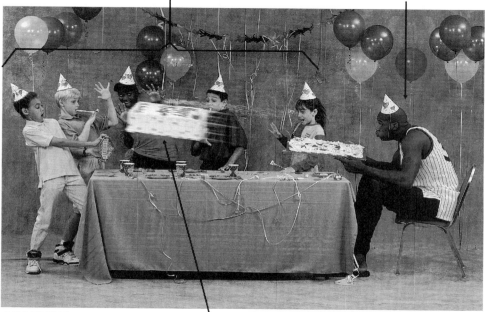

Artist: Nik Kleinberg

With the cake selected, the Motion Blur filter was applied.

Client: Sports Illustrated for Kids

**8**

It's a bird, it's a plane, it's a birthday cake! Covers for *Sports Illustrated for Kids* are always creative, unusual, and playful. This cover began when George B. Fry III photographed the children and balloons around the table. Later he photographed basketball star Shaquille O'Neal holding a tray beside the table, while an assistant held the cake over the middle of the table at the angle seen above. For an added effect, a photograph was taken of smoke created by candles that were blown out.

After the photographs were scanned, Nik selected, then copied and pasted Shaquille into the image with the kids. Next, he selected the cake with the Rectangular Marquee tool's Feather option, and then copied and pasted it into the image with the kids. After the cake was pasted and moved into position, the Motion Blur filter was applied to it. To create the streams of smoke trailing the cake, Nik pasted the digitized photograph of the smoke. Then he pasted a portion from the original children's image over the smoke. Next, he used the Rubber Stamp tool's From Save option with a low opacity and a soft-edged brush to bring the smoke back into the image. Nik also used the Airbrush tool's Fade option and a low opacity with a soft-edged brush to create more streams of smoke trailing from the cake.

There are two Distribution options in the Add Noise dialog box. When you select Uniform, Photoshop generates the noise randomly, using the Amount field value to calculate the random values. For instance, if you enter 5 in the Amount field, Photoshop will calculate random color values between –5 and 5 for each pixel's color. With the Gaussian distribution option, the noise is mapped along a bell-shaped curve. This often produces a noisier effect than that of the Uniform setting. The Gaussian option also tends to produce a greater number of light pixels than the Uniform setting. If you select the Monochromatic check box colors will not be added to the image when noise is created. It is like adding noise to the luminance values of your image.

The following illustration shows a pattern created with the Add Noise filter. This effect was generated by first creating a dark-to-light linear blend horizontally (left to right) on the screen. Then the Add Noise filter was applied once with the Gaussian option selected and an Amount value of 100.

**DESPECKLE**   The Despeckle filter seeks out areas of greatest color change in an image and blurs everything except transitional edges; thus detail is not lost. Use this filter when you need to reduce noise or to blur areas that have been pixelated due to oversharpening. The Despeckle filter can sometimes help reduce moiré patterns that can occur after scanning images that have been printed.

**DUST & SCRATCHES**   The Dust & Scratches filter hunts down small imperfections in an image or selection and blends them into the surrounding image.

Before opening the Dust & Scratches filter, select the area that includes the imperfections you wish to eliminate. When you open the filter, the selected area will appear in the preview box. In the Dust & Scratches dialog box, click on the + control to zoom in to view the dust and/or scratches you wish to eliminate.

In the Dust & Scratches dialog box, Photoshop uses the value entered in the Threshold field to determine which pixels to analyze when cleaning up the image. When you enter a Threshold value, the filter uses it to analyze the difference between the pixel values of the scratches and the pixel values of the surrounding pixels. If you type in 0, the filter analyzes all pixels in an image. By typing in a number you begin to restrict the area the filter evaluates. For instance, assume you have an image area with a brightness value of 100, and in that image area you have a 1 pixel gray scratch with a brightness value of 150. If you type 49 in the Threshold field, the scratch will disappear. If you type 50 or any number over, the scratch will not disappear.

Once the filter homes in on a scratch or imperfection, it uses the Radius value to determine how large of an area to clean up. The Radius value controls the range in the scratch or dust area that is cleaned up. If you enter too large of an area, your image could begin to look blurry.

Try to maintain a balance between the Threshold and Radius so that defects are removed, but the sharpness of your image is maintained.

The Dust & Scratches filter, with a little help from the Rubber Stamp tool was applied to the image in Figure 8-2a. The result is shown in Figure 8-2b.

**MEDIAN**  The Median filter also reduces noise by blending the brightness of pixels within a selection. It's called the Median filter because it replaces the center pixel in a radius area with the median brightness value of the pixels in the area. In the Median dialog box, you may enter a Radius value between 1 and 16 pixels. The Radius value is the distance the filter searches from each pixel to analyze brightness.

(a) Image
before
applying
the Dust &
Scratches
filter
(b) Image
after
applying
the Dust &
Scratches
filter

(a)    (b)

**FIGURE 8-2**

# THE SHARPEN FILTERS

The four Sharpen filters clarify images by creating more contrast and are often used to enhance the contours of scanned images. It is often helpful to apply these filters after reducing or distorting images that have been edited with Image/Effects submenu commands; the Sharpen filters will reduce the blurring that can occur after interpolation.

**AUTION:** *Be careful not to sharpen too much, otherwise distinct pixels will begin to show through, causing the image to look pixelated.*

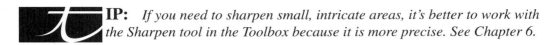**IP:** *If you need to sharpen small, intricate areas, it's better to work with the Sharpen tool in the Toolbox because it is more precise. See Chapter 6.*

**SHARPEN**   The Sharpen filter sharpens by increasing the contrast between neighboring pixels.

**SHARPEN EDGES**   The Sharpen Edges filter works like the Sharpen filter, except it sharpens only the edges of an image (smooth areas are unaffected).

**SHARPEN MORE**   The Sharpen More filter provides a stronger sharpening effect than the Sharpen filter.

**UNSHARP MASK**   The Unsharp Mask filter exaggerates the sharpness of an image's edges. It is often helpful to apply this filter after converting an image from RGB to CMYK, or after any other Photoshop operation that involves interpolation. Unlike the other Sharpen filters, Unsharp Mask lets you control the amount of sharpening when you apply it.

The name of the Unsharp Mask filter is based on a traditional photographic masking technique in which a negative and blurred positive of an image are combined to make the image stand out.

You can control the intensity of this filter's effect by entering a percentage from 1 to 500 in the Amount field of the Unsharp Mask dialog box. The greater the percentage, the greater the sharpening. A percentage of 150 usually provides good results with 300-ppi color images. Higher resolution images will often require a higher percentage. In the Radius field, you can specify the distance (in pixels) out from transitional edges that you want sharpened. If you enter a low Radius number, the sharpening occurs closer to image edges. The higher the Radius number, the greater the distance sharpening will occur beyond image contours.

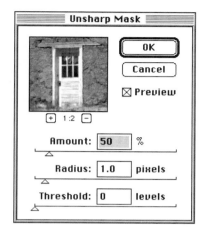

The Threshold field allows you to specify a comparison between neighboring pixels for sharpening. It allows you to prevent sharpening unless contrast between pixels is above the Threshold value. For instance, if the brightness values of neighboring pixels differ by 5, typing in a Threshold of 4 will cause sharpening to occur. Enter 5 or larger in Threshold, and Photoshop will ignore the pixels. Thus, the Threshold value can be used to prevent oversharpening in the entire image or a selected area. If you keep Threshold set at the default level, 0, the filter will change the most pixels possible. The higher you set Threshold, the fewer number of pixels are affected.

Figure 8-3 shows a Santa Fe landscape with part of the image sharpened. The Unsharp Mask filter was applied three times, with Amount set to 50%, Radius set to 1, and Threshold set to 0.

## RENDER

The Render filters primarily create lighting effects in your images. The filters run from the uncomplicated to the complex. For instance, the Cloud filter simply creates cloud-like effects on your screen. On the other end of the scale, the Lighting Effects filter allows you to point up to 16 different light sources at your image. The filter can even apply a texture to your image to make it look as if it were a lunar landscape.

 **OTE:** *The Lighting Effects filters can only be applied to RGB Color images. The Lens Flare filter and the Lighting Effects filters require a co-processor (FPU) chip, unless you have a Power PC.*

Area sharpened

Unsharp
Mask
applied to
a portion
of a
Santa Fe
landscape
(photograph
courtesy of
Stacy
Kollar
Photography)

**FIGURE 8-3**

## TEXTURE FILL

The Texture Fill filter allows you to load a grayscale image into an alpha channel so it can be utilized as a texture for the Lighting Effects filter. The Texture Fill filter will also allow you to load a grayscale image directly into a selection or over the image on screen.

If you are using the filter to create a Texture for the Lighting Effects filter, you must first create an alpha channel, then choose Texture Fill from the Filter/Render submenu. (See the Lighting Effects filter for instructions on using the Texture Fill filter as a texture map. Also, see Chapter 11 for more information on alpha channels.) When you execute the filter a dialog box will appear prompting you to load the grayscale image as a Texture Fill.

## LIGHTING EFFECTS

The Lighting Effects filter allows you to apply different light sources, types, and light properties to an image. The Lighting Effects filter allows you to add depth to an image and spotlight image areas, as well as change moods. The Lighting Effects filter can also be used to create texture maps from grayscale images. This can add a three-dimensional effect to flat images by making it appear as if light is bouncing off bumps in the texture.

**OTE:**  *The Lighting Effects filter can only be applied to RGB Color images.*

## Choosing a Style and Light Type

In the Lighting Effects dialog box, choose a Style in the Style pop-up menu. The default style provides a medium- to full-strength spotlight with a wide focus. Later in this section, you'll learn how to name and save your settings so that they appear in the Style pop-up menu.

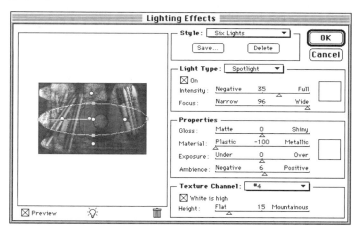

To create new lights, click on the Light Bulb icon (  ) and drag it into the image preview area in the dialog box. Press OPTION and drag if you wish to duplicate a light. If you wish to delete a light, drag the light's circle icon into the Trash icon ( 🗑 ) in the dialog box. For each new light, you can choose a light type from the Light Type pop-up menu.

When the On check box is selected, the light is on. When the check box is selected, you can choose a light type from the Light Type pop-up menu. The following list describes the different types of lights.

*Spotlight*   Casts the light in a long elliptical shape. To see the effects of the Spotlight, choose Spotlight from the Light Type pop-up menu. Notice that the preview box includes an ellipse and four boxes.

In the preview box, you can move the Spotlight by clicking and dragging the center circle. You can change the angle and length of the light by dragging the line to make it larger or smaller. Change the focus of the light by dragging on any of the four boxes on the ellipse. Dragging the boxes away from the center will increase the area that is lit.

**IP:** *When altering the Spotlight with the mouse, you can change the size of the ellipse without affecting the angle by pressing* SHIFT *and dragging. Press* COMMAND *(PC users:* CTRL*) and drag to change the angle but not the size of the ellipse.*

If your light type is Spotlight, you can change the focus of the light which determines the amount of light that fills the elliptical area.

*Omni*   Casts light in all directions as if the light were above the image. To see the effects of the Omni light, choose Omni from the Light Type pop-up menu. Notice that the preview box includes a circle and four boxes.

To move the light, drag the center circle in the Preview box. To give the appearance that the light is closer to the image, drag one of the four boxes closer towards the image. Dragging a box further away makes it appear as though the light is further away.

*Directional*   The Directional light casts light in one straight direction. To see the effects of the Directional light, choose Directional from the Light Type pop-up menu. Notice that the Preview box does not include an ellipse.

Directional only allows you to change the direction and angle of the light. To move the light, drag on the center of the circle. To change the height, drag the square at the end of the line. The longer the line, the further away the light. Decreasing the size of the line creates an intense light.

When using Omni, Directional, or Spotlight, drag the Intensity slider to control the strength of the light. The slider ranges from 100 (brightest), to −100 (pure black). A value of 50 is considered normal intensity. A negative value produces an effect similar to a black light.

The Focus slider is only available when using the Spotlight. Dragging the slider towards Widen broadens the scope of the light within the ellipse area. Dragging the slider towards Narrow produces the effect of a thinner light beam being applied to an image.

If you wish to change the color of the light, click on the rectangular swatch in the Light Type section. This will open the Color Picker dialog box where you can pick a lighting color. (If the Apple or Windows Color Picker is selected in the General Preferences dialog box, the Apple/Windows Color Picker will appear instead.)

**OTE:** *If a style contains several Light Types and Settings, pressing* TAB *will move you from one Light Type and its settings to another.*

## Choosing a Property

Each light has a set of properties. The following is a summary of each property.

Gloss determines how light reflects off an image. Use the slider to vary the surface from matte to glossy.

Material controls whether the light, or the object the light is shining on has more reflectance. The slider allows you to drag from Plastic to Metallic. Plastic reflects the light's color. Metallic reflects the color of the image on screen.

Exposure either lightens or darkens the shining light.

Ambience allows you to create the effect of blending light from the light source with the room light in an image.

Before experimenting with the Ambient slider, note the swatch to the right of the Properties group. Clicking on the swatch allows you to pick a color for the Ambient light. If you drag the Ambient slider to 100 (to the right), Ambient light intensifies so it is not diffused with the light from the Light Type section. Drag the slider to the left and the Ambient light gradually diminishes.

## Using the Texture Channel

The Texture Channel allows you to use a grayscale image as a texture map. To use this feature a grayscale texture must be chosen in the Texture Channel pop-up menu. When chosen, Photoshop will bounce lights off contours in the image that correspond to the grayscale texture. Use this to create terrain and embossed effect out of your image as shown in Figure 8-6. To create this effect, the flower shown in Figure 8-4 was used as a Texture Channel when the Lighting Effects filter set to the Six Lights style was applied to Figure 8-5.

You must set up the Texture channel with the Texture Fill filter. This must be done before opening the Lighting Effects dialog box. Once the Texture Fill is applied to an alpha channel, choose the channel from the Texture Channel pop-up menu. In the list of choices you'll see the RGB Channels of your image, as well as any alpha channels you added to the image. (See the steps that follow for adding a channel to your image.) If you are working in a layer, the Texture Channel pop-up menu allows you to select a Transparency choice for your layer. You can use this option to add a black or colored edge to the perimeter of a non-transparent area of your layer.

If you wish to create an emboss effect, select the White is High check box. This creates the appearance of light being emitted from the image surface. Turn off this

**8**

Image
before
applying
the
Lighting
Effects filter

**FIGURE 8-4**

option if you want light to shoot down into the depths of your texture. To create a more bumpy texture, drag the slider towards Mountainous. A less bumpy texture will be produced if you drag the slider towards Flat.

Image used
as basis for
texture fill

**FIGURE 8-5**

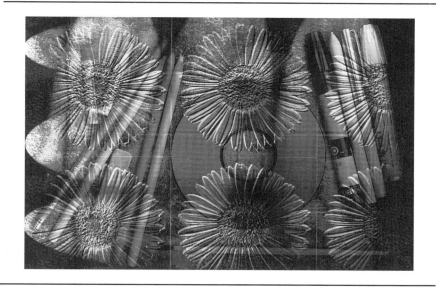

Image after
applying
Lighting
Effects
filter with
a texture
channel

**FIGURE 8-6**

## Creating a Lighting Effect with a Texture Fill

The CD ROM that accompanies Photoshop includes a variety of textures to try out with the Lighting Effects filter. If you don't have a texture map to use, here are step-by-step instructions for converting a color tutorial image to grayscale and then using the grayscale image as a texture with the Lighting Effects filter. In the following example the texture map will be created out of the Leaf tutorial file. It will then be applied to the Fruit tutorial file.

First, you will load the leaf image and convert it to Grayscale mode.

1. Load the Leaf (PC users: leaf.psd) image from the Tutorial folder. Since you will be converting it to grayscale, use the File/Save As command to save it under the name Leafgray. This ensures you do not overwrite the original tutorial file.

2. To change the image into a grayscale file, choose Grayscale from the Mode menu. When prompted to "Flatten layers?", click OK. Next, another alert will appear asking whether you wish to "Discard color information." Click OK.

3. The file on screen will now be a grayscale image. Choose File/Save, then close the file.

**4.** Open the Fruit file (PC users: fruit.jpg) from the Tutorial folder.

Next you will create a new channel in the Fruit file and load the grayscale leaf image into the new channel using the Texture Fill filter.

**5.** Open the Channels palette by choosing Show Channels from the Window/Palette submenu.

**6.** Click on the Channels palette pop-up arrow. In the list of choices choose New Channel. (To create a new channel, you can also click on the dog-eared page icon in the Channels palette.) If desired, enter a name in the dialog box to name the filter. Then click OK. Notice that the new channel (#4) is selected in the Channels palette. This indicates that it is the target channel, the channel currently being edited.

**7.** To load the texture into the new alpha channel, choose Texture Fill from the Filter/Render submenu. When the Open dialog box appears, choose the Leafgray image. Notice that a pattern filling the screen is created out of the grayscale leaf alpha channel.

**8.** To return to the RGB composite channel and the composite view of your image, click on the letters RGB in the Channels palette.

**9.** Open the Lighting Effects dialog box by choosing Lighting Effects from the Filter/Render submenu.

**10.** In the Filter dialog box, load the leaf texture by choosing Channel #4 in the Texture Channel pop-up menu. If you named your channel in step 6, select the Channel name.

You should see the textures loaded into the Fruit image, as if parts of the leaf image were embossed into the Fruit file. To intensify the effect, move the Height slider to Mountainous. Before clicking OK to close the dialog box, experiment with different lighting effects.

## Saving Lighting Styles

The Lighting Effects dialog box also allows you to save your own lighting styles to disk. When you save a style, settings for all lights in the Lighting Effects dialog box are saved, and the style's name appears in the Style pop-up menu. To save the settings on screen as a style, click the Save button. In the dialog box that opens, enter a name for your style, then click OK.

If you are using Texture channels, it's important to note that the named style reads the channel's number, not its contents. This means that when you open the image, the texture you need must be loaded in the Channels palette. If you need to make the style appear in another document, you must duplicate the channel to that document. For information about duplicating a channel, see Chapter 11.

If you wish to delete a style, select it in the Style pop-up menu, then click the Delete button.

## CLOUDS

The Clouds filter transforms your image into soft clouds using random pixel values that fall between the foreground and background colors. If you wish to create a less-diffused cloud effect, press SHIFT when you choose the Clouds command.

To try out the Clouds command, create a new 5-inch-by-5-inch RGB Color file. Set the foreground color to blue and the background color to white. Apply the Clouds filter by choosing Clouds from the Filter/Render submenu.

## DIFFERENCE CLOUD

The Difference Cloud filter inverts your image, blending it into a cloud-like background. The effect is very much like a combination between the Clouds command and the Difference painting/editing mode. When the filter is applied, a cloud-like effect is first generated from random pixel values that fall between the values of the foreground and background colors. Next, the filter subtracts the pixel values of the cloud data from the pixel values of your image. If you keep running the filter a marbleized version of your image will be created.

If you'd like to test the effect, open the Tools file (PC users: tools.jpg) from the Tutorial folder. Set the foreground color to blue and the background color to yellow, then run the Difference Clouds filter.

**LENS FLARE** The Lens Flare filter creates an effect similar to a bright light shining into the lens of a camera, as demonstrated in Figure 8-7.

The Lens Flare dialog box allows you to set the brightness of the light, the center of the light source, and the lens type. In the Brightness field, type in or use the slider control to enter a value between 10% and 300%. Click anywhere on the image icon to

The highway image after applying the Lens Flare filter

**FIGURE 8-7**

choose a center point for the light source. After you click, a crosshair indicates the center point. Before executing the filter, choose one of the Lens type radio buttons.

Crosshair ———

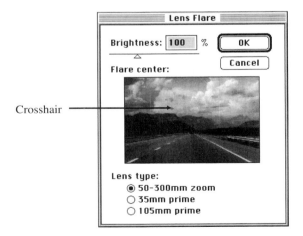

**OTE:** *The Lens Flare filter only works on RGB files. Also, the filter does not work in computers without a math coprocessor (FPU chip).*

# PIXELATE

The Pixelate filters break your image down into pieces to make them look as if they were created from large blocks and squares. Besides making your image more mosaic-like, the Pixelate filters generally flatten them as well.

**COLOR HALFTONE**    The Color Halftone filter makes an image appear to be created from large halftone dots. Photoshop creates this effect by dividing the image into rectangular grids and then filling each rectangular grid with pixels to simulate the halftone dots. The Width and Height of the grid is controlled by the Max. radius field.

**CRYSTALLIZE**    The Crystallize filter sharpens images by moving similarly colored pixels together into a polygonal grid of pixels. The size of the polygon is controlled by the value entered in the Cell Size field. Figure 8-8 shows the effect of the Crystallize filter applied to the Santa Fe landscape photo with a cell size of 10 pixels.

**FACET**    The Facet filter gives a hand-painted look to an image, by grouping and changing sampled pixels into blocks of similarly colored pixels. When this filter is applied, solid and similar colors are emphasized.

The
Santa Fe
landscape
after
applying
the
Crystallize
filter

**FIGURE 8-8**

**FRAGMENT**   The Fragment filter creates an unfocused effect by copying an image's pixels four times, averaging them, and then offsetting them. This filter will quickly create an unfocused background over which you can paste objects to make them stand out.

**MEZZOTINT**   The Mezzotint filter recreates your image out of dots, lines, or strokes.
In the Mezzotint dialog box, choose from the Type pop-up menu to pick the desired effect. The Fine Dots choice will often provide a mezzotint that looks closest to your original. To see the effects of the filter, load any image, then click on each choice in the Type pop-up menu to see the results. If you don't have an image to use, try applying the filter to the Flower (PC users: flower.jpg) image from the Tutorial folder.

**MOSAIC**   The Mosaic filter gives your image a mosaic effect. If you are using Photoshop to create video animation, you can use the Mosaic filter to replicate a technique commonly used in television, where an image gradually breaks up into pieces and then disappears. Enter a number between 2 and 64 pixels in the Cell Size field or click and drag on the slider. The filter creates the mosaic effect by making all pixels in a cell the same color.

**POINTILLIZE**   The Pointillize filter breaks up an image into random dots, producing an effect much like a pointillist painting. To control the size of dots in the filtered image, you can enter a cell value between 3 and 300. When the Pointillize filter is applied, Photoshop uses the current Background color as the background.

## THE DISTORT FILTERS

The Distort filters are used to create distortions that vary from rippling an image to twirling and twisting it. How you use them is up to you. If you are creating original art with Photoshop's tools, you'll find that many of the Distort filters can help save you time when you are creating unusual effects.

**DISPLACE**   Of all the filters in Photoshop's varied collection, the Displace filter is probably the most difficult to understand and the hardest to predict. The results seem unpredictable because the filtered image's pixels can be shifted in different directions, and the shift is based not only on dialog box settings but also on a *displacement map,* which can be any Photoshop file saved in a 2.0, 2.5 or 3.0 format that is not a Bitmap file.

The Displace filter also works differently from any other Photoshop filter. After the Displace dialog box settings are accepted, the filter doesn't immediately begin processing. Instead, an Open dialog box appears, allowing you to select a file to use as the displacement map. After the displacement map file is chosen, the Displace filter shifts image pixels according to color values in the displacement map.

Color values in the displacement map are measured on a scale from 0 to 255. Low values (darker colors) produce a displacement down and to the right in the filtered image. Midrange values (near 128) produce little displacement. High values (lighter colors) produce a displacement up and to the left.

If you wish to experiment with the Displace filter, you can use a variety of displacement maps included with the Photoshop package, in the Displacement Maps folder in the Plug-ins folder (PC users: dispmaps in the plugins folder).

**PRACTICE WITH THE DISPLACE FILTER**    The best way to get a feel for the Displace filter is to first use one of Photoshop's displacement maps, and then analyze the effects.

1. Before you begin, load the displacement map, Crumbles, to take a look at how the light and dark areas are dispersed in the image. After examining the Crumbles file, it's a good idea to close it (so you don't inadvertently apply the Displace filter to it, rather than to your image).

2. Open an image on screen that you wish to apply the filter to. If you'd like, you can choose any file from the Tutorial folder.

3. From the Filter menu, choose Distort. From the Distort submenu, choose Displace.

   In the Displace dialog box, you can enter values that control the degree of horizontal and vertical displacement. By entering a value in the Horizontal Scale field, you specify how much the filter will shift your image left or right according to the color values in the displacement map. The value in the Vertical Scale field specifies the amount the filter will shift your image up or down according to the color values in the displacement map. The highest allowed percentage, 100, displaces your image 128 pixels in areas corresponding to black or white in the displacement map.

```
┌─────────────────── Displace ───────────────────┐
│                                                  │
│   Horizontal Scale: [10]      ┌──────────┐      │
│   Vertical Scale:   [10]      │    OK    │      │
│                               └──────────┘      │
│   Displacement map:   Undefined Areas:          │
│     ● Stretch to fit    ○ Wrap Around           │
│     ○ Tile              ● Repeat edge pixels     │
│                                                  │
└──────────────────────────────────────────────────┘
```

4. For this exercise, you'll use low displacement values. (Higher values would displace your image so much that you wouldn't be able to decipher the results.) Enter **20** for the Horizontal Scale and **20** for the Vertical Scale.

There are two choices for handling displacement maps that are not the same size as the area you are applying the filter to. The Stretch to Fit option transforms the size of the displacement map to match the image. The Tile option uses the displacement map as a repeating pattern.

You can also control the destiny of pixels that would normally be outcast from the screen by the displacement effect. Under Undefined Areas, the Wrap Around option will wrap the image so that it appears on the opposite side of the screen. The Repeat Edge Pixels option disperses the extra pixels over the edges of the image; this can sometimes create distinct color bands if the color of the extra pixels is different from the rest of the edge.

5. To keep your image from becoming too distorted, select the Tile and Repeat Edge Pixels options, and click OK.

6. An Open dialog box appears, where you will choose a file to use as a displacement map. Open the Crumbles file from the Displacement Maps folder (PC users: dispmaps in the plugins folder).

The progress indicator on the screen now indicates that the filter is being applied. In a few moments, your image will be displaced according to the Crumbles displacement map.

Now that you know how to run the filter, you can begin to analyze how the Displace filter works. Perhaps the most complicated factor about this filter is that its behavior depends on the number of channels in the displacement map. As mentioned in Chapter 2, a channel is somewhat similar to a color plate in printing.

RGB and Lab images consist of three channels, a CMYK file has four channels, and a Grayscale image has one channel.

In one-channel displacement maps, the Displace filter displaces along x- and y-axes. Darker values in the displacement map displace pixels downward according to the Vertical Scale value in the dialog box, and to the right according to the Horizontal Scale value. White values are displaced upward according to the Vertical Scale value and to the left according to the Horizontal Scale value.

When the displacement map has more than one channel, the filter displaces according to the first two channels only: horizontally according to the first channel and vertically according to the second channel. In the first channel, darker areas will cause displacement to the right, and lighter areas will cause displacement to the left, according to the dialog box values. In the second channel, dark areas displace the image downward and white areas displace upward, according to the dialog box values. Thus, to predict the outcome of the filter, you not only need to think in different dimensions but you must also try to figure out how the color range in the displacement maps will affect the image.

If the Displace filter seems confusing to you, try creating your own simple one-channel displacement map and analyze the results. Follow these steps:

1. Create a new Grayscale file, and set the width and height to be about the same size as the image that you will be applying the filter to.

2. Create a radial blend from black to white in the middle of the screen. Save the circle file in Photoshop's native 3.0 format. This will be your displacement map.

3. Open the image or one of the Tutorial files that you wish to apply the filter to. From the Filter menu choose Distort, and select the Displace filter.

4. In the Displace dialog box, type **50** in the Vertical Scale field, and type **0** in the Horizontal Scale field. Choose both the Stretch to Fit and Repeat Edge Pixels options. Click OK.

5. When the Open dialog box appears, select the file that contains your radial blend.

   After the filter is finished processing, you will see that the image pixels corresponding to the darkest areas of the displacement map area have moved down. Pixels corresponding to the white displacement areas have moved up.

6. Now undo the changes so that you can analyze the horizontal displacement. Select Edit/Undo.

7. Select the Displace filter again. This time, type **50** in the Horizontal Scale field, and **0** in the Vertical Scale field. Click OK. Use the same displacement map that you used before.

This time, when the filter is applied, the darker areas displace your image to the right; white areas are displaced to the left.

The Displace filter was applied to the car image shown in Figure 8-9a using the white-to-black radial blend shown in Figure 8-9b as the displacement map. A 25% radial offset was used to enlarge the white area (foreground color) of the blend. When the filter was applied, 70 was the value for both Horizontal Scale and Vertical Scale in the Displace dialog box. The result is shown in Figure 8-9c. The car was bent up and slightly to the left in the areas corresponding to the light areas in the displacement map, and bent down and to the right in areas corresponding to the dark portions of the displacement map.

(a)

(b)

(a) The original car image; (b) the displacement map; (c) the image after applying the Displace filter

(c)

**FIGURE 8-9**

**PINCH**   The Pinch filter is used to squeeze an image inwards or outwards. Figure 8-10a shows a clock graphic before the Pinch filter was applied; Figure 8-10b shows it after applying an outward pinch at –100% (100% results in an inward pinch). Before the Pinch filter was applied, it was selected with the Rectangular Marquee. By leaving more space in the marquee selection on the right side of the clock, a slight leftward tilt in the pinch effect was produced.

**POLAR COORDINATES**   The Polar Coordinates filter converts an image's coordinates from Rectangular to Polar or from Polar to Rectangular.

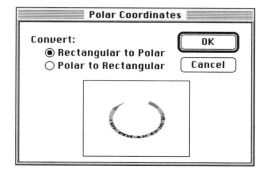

This filter can take a rectangular object and bend it into a circular shape. Figure 8-11a shows a pencil graphic before using the Polar Coordinates filter with Rectangular to Polar selected; in Figure 8-11b the pencil has been bent by the filter. When the filter was applied, no selection was made on screen. If the pencil had been

(a) The clock graphic before and; (b) after applying the (outward) Pinch filter

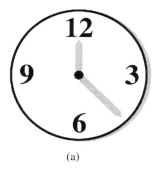

(a)

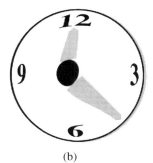

(b)

**FIGURE 8-10**

The pencil graphic before and after applying the Polar Coordinates filter using the Rectangular to Polar option

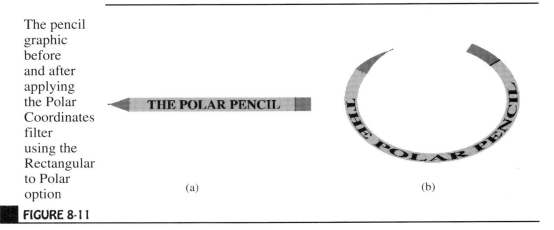

(a)                                          (b)

**FIGURE 8-11**

selected, the filter would have made it look somewhat like a round pie with a wedge cut out of the top.

When you select the Polar to Rectangular option in the dialog box, the Polar Coordinates filter will take a circular object and stretch it. The following illustration shows the effects of applying this filter to the clock graphic from Figure 8-10a using the Polar to Rectangular option. The snaking line at the bottom was created because a rectangular selection was made around the clock before the filter was applied.

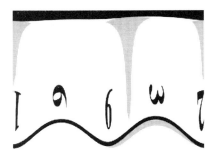

**RIPPLE**    The Ripple filter transforms an image by displacing its pixels to create a ripple effect. The following illustration shows what happened to the Polar Pencil from Figure 8-11a after the Ripple filter was applied. To create this effect, the Ripple Amount was set to 100 and the Ripple Frequency to Large.

**SHEAR**   The Shear filter bends an image according to a curve established in the Shear filter's dialog box. The effect can be used to bend and elongate an object.

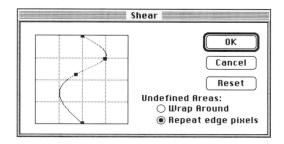

To establish the curve in the Shear dialog box, you click and drag on the vertical band in the dialog box grid. Each click will produce another control point that can be dragged to create the curve. If you need to reset the curve back to its starting position, click the Reset button. When the filter is applied to an object, it will bend along the curve you have established in the dialog box.

Here is the clock graphic that was shown in Figure 8-10a, this time with the Shear filter applied:

**SPHERIZE**   The Spherize filter transforms a selection into a spherical shape. Use it to give text or an object a three-dimensional or bloated effect. In Figure 8-12, the Spherize filter has been applied to the truck (from Chapter 3) with a grid background. To create this effect, the Amount field in the Spherize dialog box was set to 100%, and the Mode was set to Normal. To view more examples of the Spherize filter in action, see the *Time* magazine (image 9) and *Boston Globe* magazine (image 13) covers in the first color insert in this book.

**TWIRL**   The Twirl filter creates swirling pinwheel effects, with the rotation focused toward the center of the object. When you apply it at maximum strength, the Twirl

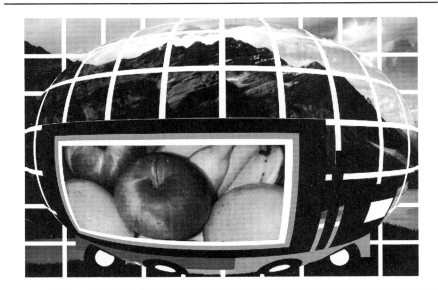

The truck image from Chapter 3 after applying the Spherize filter

**FIGURE 8-12**

filter will make your image look as if it were whipped by a blender. Here once again is the clock graphic, showing the Twirl filter's effect when set to 150 degrees:

**WAVE**   The Wave filter helps you create many different undulating effects by providing various wavelength options to distort an image. In the filter's dialog box values can be entered by clicking and dragging on slider controls or by typing numbers into fields.

In the Number of Generators field you can control the number of waves generated, from 1 to 999. The more waves you generate, the more distorted the effect because the peaks and dips of the wavelengths begin to intersect, causing more and more havoc in your image. Creating multiple waves is somewhat analogous to one ocean wave crashing into others: The more waves that crash together, the greater the turbulence.

You can specify the distance between wave crests by entering a minimum and maximum Wavelength value. The height of each wave is controlled by the value specified for the minimum and maximum Amplitude values. Wavelength and Amplitude values can be from 1 to 999.9.

You can select a wave Type of Sine (curved), Triangle, or Square. The Scale percentages determine the degree of the distortions horizontally and vertically; values can be from 0% to 100%.

**CAUTION:**  *If you wish to replicate your wave results on other images, do not click the Randomize button because it creates a random starting point for the wave effect.*

When using the Wave filter, the image can sometimes blend and twist off the screen. The Undefined Areas options allow you to control the destiny of these outcast pixels. If you select Wrap Around, images will wrap to the opposite side of the screen. The Repeat Edge Pixels option disperses the extra pixels over the edge of the image;

this can sometimes create distinct color bands if the color of the extra pixels is different from the rest of the edge.

Figure 8-13b shows the Wave filter applied to Figure 8-13a to create a tidal wave effect.

**ZIGZAG**  This filter can be used to create ripples-in-a-pond and twirling effects. This effect is controlled by the value entered in the Amount and Ridges field and whether you choose the Pond Ripples, Out from Center, or Around Center options in the Zigzag dialog box. Figure 8-14 demonstrates how the Zigzag filter's Pond Ripples option can be used to create pond ripples out of almost anything. In this case, the ripples were created in the Santa Fe landscape image shown earlier in Figure 8-3.

## THE STYLIZE FILTERS

The Stylize filters are used to create the look of impressionist paintings and other painterly effects. Many of these effects are so dramatic you may hardly recognize your original.

A dock in New Zealand before and after applying the Wave filter

(a)                                                  (b)

**FIGURE 8-13**

The
Santa Fe
landscape
after
applying
the Zigzag
filter using
the Pond
Ripples
option

**FIGURE 8-14**

**DIFFUSE**    The Diffuse filter creates an unfocused effect that breaks up an image as though seen through frosted glass. The effect is created by shifting pixels at random (Normal option), by replacing light pixels with darker ones (Darken Only option), or by replacing dark pixels with lighter ones (Lighten Only option).

**EMBOSS**    The Emboss filter creates a raised effect by outlining the edges in a selection and lowering surrounding color values. This filter is often used for designing raised type or creating a relief effect.

In the Emboss dialog box, the direction of the embossing is controlled by the Angle field. Values can range from −360 to 360 degrees. You can type in the value or click and drag the angle indicator in the circle; dragging clockwise increases the angle, and dragging counterclockwise decreases the angle.

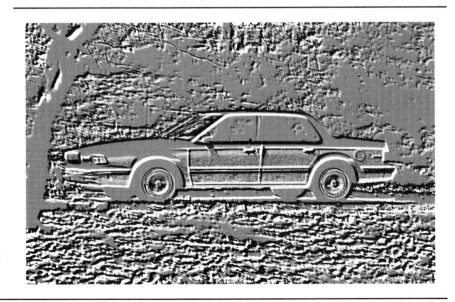

The height of the embossing is controlled by the value in the Height field, which can range from 1 to 10 pixels. To raise or lower the color values in the embossed image, enter a value from 1% to 500% into the Amount field. The lower the percentage, the lower the amount of color; the higher the percentage, the more color is applied to edges.

Figure 8-15 shows the effects of the Emboss filter applied to the car image from Figure 8-9a. In the Emboss dialog box, the Angle was set to 135, the Height was set

The car image after applying the Emboss filter

**FIGURE 8-15**

# Photoshop in Action

The Centurion character was lightened so that the message would be readable.

The text was embossed using various filters and alpha channels.

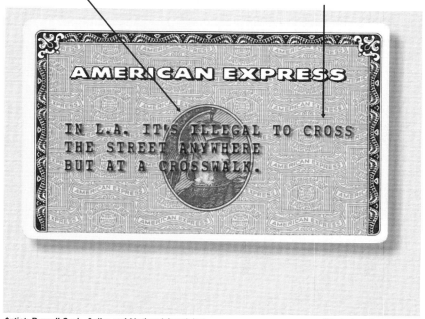

Artist: Russell Cook, Ogilvy and Mather Advertising                    Client: American Express

Russell Cook, an artist at Ogilvy and Mather Advertising, created the above image as a public service sign for American Express. Variations of the sign have appeared in many airports around the world. After an American Express card was digitized, Russell used the Rubber Stamp tool to clean up the scan.

The type was imported from Adobe Illustrator. Once the type was in Photoshop, an alpha channel was created for it. The alpha channel was duplicated and the Emboss filter was applied. The embossed alpha channel was duplicated and inverted so that one alpha channel could be used for the highlights and the other for the shadows. Russell then used the Image/Map/Threshold command to isolate highlight and shadow areas. The Gaussian Blur and Motion Blur filters were applied to the shadowed text alpha channel.

Once the card was perfected it was laid over a textured background where a shadow was added. When the card was complete it was imported into QuarkXPress, where the following text was added: "Welcome to Los Angeles. We're here to help."

8

to 10 pixels, and the Amount was set to 200%. Before the filter was applied, the contrast of the image was increased with the Brightness/Contrast command in the Image/Adjust submenu. This emphasized the edges in the image, thereby enhancing the effect of the Emboss filter.

**EXTRUDE**   The Extrude filter transforms an image into a series of three-dimensional blocks or pyramids depending upon the option set in the dialog box. Use it to distort images or create unusual 3-D backgrounds. Figure 8-16 shows the Extrude filter Pyramids option applied to a radial blend grading from a dark color to a lighter one.

In the Extrude filter dialog box, you can set the size of the base of the blocks or pyramids by typing a value from 2 to 255 in the Size field. Enter a value from 0 to 255 into the Depth field to control how far the objects extrude from the screen. Choose the Random radio button if you wish the depth of each extruding object to be set to a random value.

If you want brighter parts of the image to protrude more than darker parts, select the Level-Based radio button. This option links the pyramid or block depth to color values. If you choose the Solid Front Faces check box, the face of the block is filled with the average color of the object, rather than the image. To ensure that no extruding object extends past the filtered selection, choose the Mask Incomplete Blocks check box.

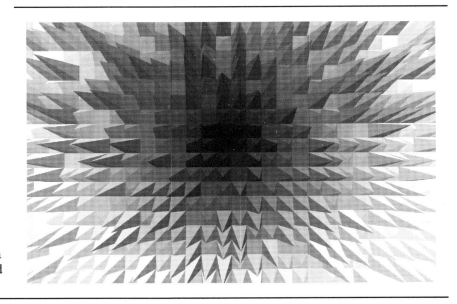

The effects of the Extrude filter applied to a radial blend

**FIGURE 8-16**

**FIND EDGES**    The Find Edges filter searches for image areas that exhibit major color changes and then enhances transitional pixels. It can make an image look as though it were outlined with a pencil. In Figure 8-17, the Find Edges filter has been applied to the car image. First, though, the contrast of the image was increased, using the Brightness/Contrast command in the Image/Adjust submenu. This enhanced the effect of the filter by adding more edges for the filter to outline.

**TRACE CONTOUR**    The effect of the Trace Contour filter is similar to that of the Find Edges filter, except Trace Contour draws thinner lines around edges and allows you to specify a tonal level for transition areas. In the Trace Contour dialog box, you can enter a value between 0 and 255 in the Level field. Darker pixels correspond to lower numbers; lighter pixels to higher numbers. The Upper and Lower options allow you to choose whether you want contours traced above or below the Level value.

**SOLARIZE**    The Solarize filter creates the effect of a positive and negative of an image blended together. In photography, you accomplish similar results by adding light during the developing process. See Chapter 13 to learn how to create a solarized effect using the Image/Adjust/Curves command.

**8**

The car image after applying the Find Edges filter

**FIGURE 8-17**

**TILES**    The Tiles filter divides an image into tiles according to values specified in the filter's dialog box. Figure 8-18 shows the effect of the Tiles filter when it is applied to the Santa Fe landscape using the default settings. In the Number of Tiles field, enter the minimum number of tiles you wish to appear in each row and column of tiles. In the Maximum Offset field, enter the maximum distance (as a percentage) that you want the tiles offset from their original positions. If you want the area between the tiles filled with color, choose the Background Color or Foreground Color radio buttons in the Fill Empty Area With section. Choosing the Inverse Image radio button causes a reverse color image of your original image to appear through the tile cracks. Choosing the Unaltered Image radio button makes the tiles appear over the original image.

**WIND**    The Wind filter creates a windblown effect by adding small horizontal lines. The Wind filter dialog box allows you to choose how strong the wind is and what direction you wish the wind to blow. In the Wind dialog box, select the Wind radio button to create a wind effect. To create a stronger wind effect, choose Blast. If you choose the Stagger option, the wind lines will be offset from one another. In the Directions group, choose Left or Right to set the wind direction. In Figure 8-19, the Wind filter was applied to the car image, first with the filter's Blast option selected,

The
Santa Fe
landscape
after
applying
the Tiles
filter

**FIGURE 8-18**

The car
image after
applying
the Wind
filter

**FIGURE 8-19**

and then with the Wind option selected. The Direction was set to Right, rather than
Left (the default).

## VIDEO FILTERS

Photoshop's Video filters were designed for images that will be input from video or
output to videotape.

**NTSC COLORS**   These filters reduce the color gamut of the image to acceptable
levels for television.

**DEINTERLACE**   This filter smooths video images by removing odd or even
interlaced lines. This filter is needed when a video frame is captured between an odd
and even field, and a blurred scan line becomes visible. The filter's dialog box gives
you a choice of substituting the line by duplication or interpolation.

## THE OTHER FILTERS

The filters in this menu are a diverse group that don't fit into any other major
category. Perhaps the most interesting is the Custom filter choice, which allows you
to create your own filter.

## Custom

If you would like to try your hand at creating your own filters, select Custom from the Other submenu. You won't be able to create filters as sophisticated as Photoshop's filters, but you can design your own sharpening, blurring, and embossing effects.

In the Custom dialog box, you can control the brightness values for all pixels that will be filtered. Each pixel evaluated is represented by the text field that is in the center of the matrix of text fields in the dialog box (in the following illustration, it's the one with the 5). The value entered in this box is the number by which Photoshop multiplies the current pixel's brightness. You can enter between –999 and 999.

By typing numbers in the surrounding text fields, you control the brightness of adjacent pixels in relation to the pixel represented in the center box. Photoshop multiplies the brightness value of adjacent pixels by this number. In other words, with the Custom dialog box's default settings, the brightness value of the pixel to the left of the central pixel will be multiplied by –1.

In the Scale field, you can enter a value that will be used to divide the sum of the brightness values. In the Offset field, you can enter a value that you wish to have added to the Scale's calculation results.

When the filter is applied, Photoshop recalculates the brightness of each pixel in the image or selected area, summing up the multiplied values used in the dialog box matrix. It then divides this result by the Scale value and adds the Offset value, if there is one.

- To create a sharpening filter, you'll need to increase the contrast between neighboring pixels. If you balance a set of negative numbers around the central matrix pixel, you will sharpen your image.

- To create a blur filter, surround the central matrix pixel with positive numbers. The positive numbers reduce the contrast between pixels as the matrix formula passes over the images.

- To create an embossing filter, balance positive and negative values around the central matrix area.

Figure 8-20 shows an image before and after increasing contrast and applying a custom emboss filter.

Try your hand at creating a filter or two, using the foregoing suggestions and examples as a guide. You can save and reload your custom filters by using the Save and Load buttons in the Custom dialog box.

**HIGH PASS**    The High Pass filter suppresses areas that contain gradual increases in brightness and preserves portions of the image that exhibit the sharpest transitions in color. When you apply this filter, it removes shading and accentuates highlights. In the High Pass filter dialog box, you can control the size of the transition edge by typing a pixel value from 1 to 100 in the Edge field. A large value leaves more of the image's pixels near transitional points. A lower value preserves only the edges of the transition areas.

When the filter is applied, it analyzes each pixel from the pixel to a specified Radius distance. When the Maximum filter is applied, the current pixel's brightness value is replaced by the maximum brightness of surrounding pixels. When the Minimum filter is applied, the current pixel's brightness value is replaced with the minimum brightness values of surrounding pixels. The distance of the surrounding pixels can be specified entering a value from 1 to 10 in the Radius field.

Before
and after
applying
a custom
emboss
filter
(photograph
courtesy of
Stacy
Kollar
Photography)

(a)

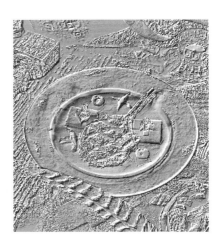
(b)

**FIGURE 8-20**

**HSL&HSB**    This filter does not come with Photoshop 3.0, but if you have version 2.5.1 you can drag this plug-in into your Photoshop 3.0 Plug-ins folder in order to use this filter. The HSL&HSB filter was added to version 2.5.1 of Photoshop to allow users of previous versions to work in the HSL (Hue/Saturation/Lightness) and HSB (Hue/Saturation/Brightness) modes. (In Photoshop 2.5, HSL and HSB were removed from the Modes menu, and Lab Color was added.)

When the HSL&HSB filter is applied, a dialog box appears allowing conversion from RGB to HSL or to HSB. You can also return from HSL or HSB to RGB. When this filter is applied, the RGB components of an image are converted to HSL and HSB components, and vice versa.

When you convert an RGB file to either HSB or HSL, RGB's red channel becomes the hue channel, the green channel becomes the saturation channel, and the blue channel becomes the brightness or lightness channel. Once the filter is applied, you can make changes to each separate channel and then use the filter to convert the image back to RGB as well.

**OTE:**    *See Chapter 9 for information about viewing images in separate channels; see Chapter 11 for information about editing images in channels.*

**MAXIMUM**    The Maximum filter expands light areas and diminishes dark areas. The filter can be used in an alpha channel to increase the light area in the channel. (*Alpha channels* can be used for masking out parts of an image so they can be edited in an isolated area, as discussed in Chapter 11.)

**MINIMUM**    This filter is similar to the Maximum filter except that it expands *dark* areas and diminishes *light* areas. The Minimum filter can be used in an alpha channel to increase the dark areas.

**OFFSET**    The Offset filter moves the filtered image according to values entered in the Offset dialog box. You can use this filter to create a shadowed effect.

```
================== Offset ==================

  Horizontal: [0        ]  pixels right      ( ( OK ) )

    Vertical: [0        ]  pixels down        ( Cancel )

  ┌─ Undefined Areas ─────────┐     ☒ Preview
  │  ◉ Set to Background       │
  │  ○ Repeat Edge Pixels      │
  │  ○ Wrap Around             │
  └───────────────────────────┘
```

    In the Offset filter dialog box, specify whether you wish the image to move horizontally and/or vertically. In the Vertical and Horizontal fields, you can enter values between –30,000 and 30,000. Positive values offset right and up, negative values offset left and down. If you wish to have the background of the image filled with the current background color, select the Set to Background radio button.

    The Offset filter also includes options for handling pixels that would be offset out of the screen area. The Wrap Around option wraps these pixels so they appear on the opposite side of the screen. The Repeat Edge Pixels option disperses the extra pixels along the edges of the image.

## USING FILTER FACTORY

If you'd like to try your hand at creating filters that are quite a bit more fancy than those allowed by Photoshop's Custom filter, you should investigate Filter Factory which is included on the Adobe Photoshop Deluxe CD-ROM. When you create a filter with Filter Factory, a plug-in filter is produced that contains an image preview and slider controls, if desired. When the plug-in is moved into Photoshop's Plug-ins folder (PC users: plugins), Photoshop treats it like plug-ins created by third-party software companies. The plug-in appears in the Filter menu, and its name and copyright information appear in the About Plug-ins dialog box.

Included in this section are step-by-step instructions for creating a simple filter with Filter Factory. If you'd like to delve deeper into creating filters, print out the instructions that accompany Filter Factory from the Adobe Deluxe CD-ROM. Although you don't have to be a computer programmer to create filters with Filter Factory, the instructions will probably be easier to understand if you've had some programming experience or have written formulas with applications like Microsoft Excel or Lotus 1-2-3.

In order to use Filter Factory, copy the Filter Factory plug-in from the Adobe Photoshop Deluxe CD-ROM into your Plug-ins folder (PC users: plugins). In order to load Filter Factory, you must restart Photoshop. Once you reload Photoshop, open any RGB Color image on screen.

To use Filter Factory, first click on the Filter menu. In the menu you'll see a new menu choice called "Synthetic." Click on the Synthetic submenu and choose Filter Factory. The Filter Factory dialog box opens.

In the dialog box, you'll see a preview box, sliders, and an area for creating an *expression*, or formula, for the Red, Green, and Blue channels of your image. As you can probably guess, this means that Filter Factory only affects RGB Color images. The formula that you enter into the R text field changes color values for pixels in the Red channel. Green and Blue channels are changed by expressions entered in the G and B text fields.

Before you create a filter in Filter Factory, you should have some idea about what you want your filter to do. Then, you need to figure out the expression that needs to be typed into the R, G, and B fields. When you write your expression, you must remember that all R, G, B pixels can have a value from 0 to 255. Dark pixels have lower pixel values; light pixels have higher pixel values.

If you start delving into Filter Factory, you'll learn that Filter Factory also addresses pixels in terms of a two-dimensional grid system. For instance, the second pixel in the fifth row of your image in the channel would be addressed as (2,5). Filter Factory also has its own set of functions that can return the values of slider controls, return the color value of any pixel on screen, and generate random values. The example picked in this section can add a solarized and/or negative look to your image. It was chosen to demonstrate how easy it is to create a simple filter, and to show you how to integrate slider controls into a filter.

The filter you are going to create subtracts the value that the user sets with three sliders from the color values in each Red, Green, and Blue channel.

Type the following in the R field: **ctl(0)-r**. ctl is a function whose purpose is to return to Filter Factory the number generated by clicking and dragging on a slider. The 0 in the ctl function represents the first slider in the dialog box. Thus, the expression in the R field tells Filter Factory to subtract the slider value from the color value in the Red channel. Note that all expressions must be typed in lowercase. Also, if you make a mistake, a yellow alert sign appears below the field label. To find the error in the expression, click on the yellow alert sign.

In the G channel, type **ctl(1)-g**. In the B field, type **ctl(2)-b**.

At this point you can try out your filter by dragging the first three sliders in the Filter Factory dialog box as shown here:

If you're happy with the results, you can save the text expression in the R, G, and B fields by clicking on the Save button. The expression can later be reloaded into Photoshop using the Filter Factory Load button, or it can be loaded into a word processor as a text file.

To save your filter as a plug-in, click the Make button. In the Make dialog box, text entered into the Category field will appear in Photoshop's Filter menu as a choice alongside Blur, Sharpen, Pixelate, etc. Text entered into the Name field appears as a choice when the Category word in the Filter menu is selected. If you name several filters using the same Category name, the names will appear as choices in your Category submenu.

Enter the data for the text fields as shown next. Type the appropriate information into the Copyright and Author fields.

| | |
|---|---|
| Category: | Fundamental Photoshop |
| Title: | Do Something Cool |
| Copyright: | Copyright © 1994 Your Name Here<br>All Rights Reserved. |
| Author: | Your Name Here |

☐ Map 0    Map 0:

Red          ☒ Control 0
Green        ☒ Control 1

☐ Map 1    Map 1:

Blue         ☒ Control 2
Control 3:   ☐ Control 3

☐ Map 2    Map 2:

Control 4:   ☐ Control 4
Control 5:   ☐ Control 5

☐ Map 3    Map 3:

Control 6:   ☐ Control 6
Control 7:   ☐ Control 7

[ Cancel ]    [ OK ]

After you've entered data in the text fields, name your sliders. Click on the check boxes adjacent to Control 0, Control 1, and Control 2. Clicking on the check boxes generates three sliders in your filter. Text entered into the Control text boxes will appear adjacent to the sliders. Type **Red**, **Green**, and **Blue** into the appropriate fields. You do not need to change the Map check boxes. These can be used if you wish to set up your sliders in groups of two. To save your filter plug-in, click OK. In the dialog box that appears, set the target directory so that you save your filter into the Plug-ins folder (PC users: plugins) or the Filter folder.

Before you try out your filter, you must restart Photoshop. After Photoshop reloads, run your filter by first clicking on the Filter menu. In the Filter menu, you should see the Fundamental Photoshop submenu. Click on Fundamental Photoshop, and the Do Something Cool filter choice will appear.

**Fundamental Photoshop** ▶ Do Something Cool...

Select Do Something Cool to open the Filter dialog box. In it, you'll see a preview box with three sliders labeled Red, Blue, and Green. Now test the filter. If you find that the slider controls are somewhat sticky, just click on the slider bar, rather than trying to drag the slider triangles.

As you can see, it's not too difficult to create a custom filter with Filter Factory. If you'd like to try creating another custom filter, here's a more sophisticated expression primarily designed to give you an idea of how different Filter Factory functions work. The expression averages each pixel with the pixel two columns to its left and two columns to its right. It then adds a random value based upon the slider settings to the average of the three pixels. The result is a noise filter in which color values can be controlled by sliders.

If you'd like to create the filter, enter the following expressions into the R, G, and B text fields in the Filter Factory dialog box:

In the R text box: **src(x-2,y,0)+src(x,y,0)+src(x+2,y,0))/3+rnd(-ctl(0),ctl(0))**

In the G text box: **src(x-2,y,1)+src(x,y,1)+src(x+2,y,1))/3+rnd(-ctl(0),ctl(0))**

In the B text box: **src(x-2,y,2)+src(x,y,2)+src(x+2,y,2))/3+rnd(-ctl(0),ctl(0))**

Here's a brief explanation of the expressions. The src function returns pixel values from separate channels according to specified coordinates. For instance, src(5,6,0) returns the value of the fifth pixel in the sixth row of the Red channel. Channel 0 is red. Channel 1 is the Green channel, channel 2 is the Blue channel. rnd(-ctl(0),ctl(0)) instructs Filter Factory to generate a random number between plus or minus the value returned by the first slider in the dialog box. Thus, if the slider were set to 150, random numbers could be between -150 and 150 inclusive.

For a complete list of Filter Factory functions and more details about how to use them, see the documentation provided on the CD-ROM. Who knows? With Filter Factory, you may be the next Kai Krause.

## FILTERS FROM THIRD-PARTY MANUFACTURERS

Now that you've seen the tremendous capabilities of Photoshop filters, you may feel that you have more than enough filters to meet your image-editing needs. However, if you ever grow tired of Photoshop's filters, you'll be happy to know that there's a small industry of third-party manufacturers of plug-in filters. For example, Alchemy by Xaos Tools, Inc., and Gallery Affects by Aldus offer filters that add more painting effects to a scanned image. Xaos Tools, Inc. also sells a filter called Terazzo that allows you to create patterns out of selections. And if you want more in the way of startling and unusual effects, investigate Andromeda Software Inc. and Kai's Power Tools. Andromeda Software Inc. also creates a filter called Series 2 that allows you to

# Photoshop in Action

The shadow was created by applying Gaussian Blur filter, to the alpha channel with the selection of the shadow. When the blurred selection in the alpha channel was loaded it was darkened using the Image/Adjust/Levels command.

After one of the TVs was copied, then pasted several times at different opacities and offset, the Motion Blur filter was applied to give the appearance of motion.

The linear blend in the background was created using the Gradient tool. After the blend was created the Add Noise filter was applied to reduce the chance of banding when the image was printed.

**Designer: John Brown    Electronic Retouching: Jaime Ordoñez    Client: HBO TV**

This image was created as a promotion for HBO. The concept began with a sketch created by Designer, John Brown. Then Jaime recreated the image in Photoshop. Jaime started by creating the background from a blue to white linear blend using the Gradient tool. After he created the blend, he applied the Add Noise filter to reduce the chance of banding when the image was printed.

Photographer Craig Blankenhorn shot various images of model Tony Melovia with the TVs so that Jaime could select the best shots and paste them into the final image. After the photographs were digitized, Jaime silhouetted Tony and the televisions, using selection tools and the Pen tool. He copied Tony's head from one image, his stomach, hands, legs, shoes from other images. The shadow was created by selecting Tony with the TV. He then offset the selection of Tony and the TVs in an alpha channel. Next, he applied the Image/Effects/Skew and Perspective commands to the alpha channel. Jaime blurred the alpha channel using the Gaussian Blur filter, then loaded the blurred selection and darkened the selection using the Image/Adjust/Levels command. (For more information about using alpha channels, see Chapter 11.)

The HBO logo in the TVs was first created in Illustrator then placed into an alpha channel in Photoshop. After the alpha channel was loaded as a selection, it was feathered and then colorized with the Color Balance command. This created the glow around the logo. The selection in the alpha channel was loaded again and filled with black to create the logo. To give the appearance of motion to the falling TV first, one of the TVs was copied, then pasted several times at different opacities and offset. Afterwards, the Motion Blur filter was applied.

convert 2D images into 3D. An example of the effects of an Andromeda filter is shown in image 19 in the first color insert in this book.

Here are a few other plug-ins and stand-alone software that will help you bend, twist, and texturize images. Knoll Software's CyberMesh allows you to create 3-D models out of grayscale images. This plug-in is extremely useful for creating terrain maps that consist of many polygons. With The Black Box, by Alien Skin, you can create drop shadows, glow effects, and emboss instantly.

Stand-alone software that allows you to transform one image into another as if they were made of rubber include Morph, by Gryphon software, Digital Morph, by HSC, and Elastic Reality.

If you're specifically interested in creating 3-D models and textures, check out Strata Studio Pro, Alias Sketch, Specular Infini-D, Pixar Showcase Renderman, RayDream Designer, and Adobe Dimensions. If you're looking for unusual landscapes and terrain, HSC's KPT Bryce will do the trick. If you'd like to create 3-D walk-through effects, investigate Strata's Virtual 3D.

## CONCLUSION

In future chapters of *Fundamental Photoshop*, you will frequently need to apply filters, particularly sharpening and blurring filters. As you work, remember not to overdo the effects of filters. Often, the subtlest changes are the best.

8

# 9

# CONVERTING FROM
# ONE MODE TO ANOTHER

Throughout this book you've been working primarily in RGB Color mode, Photoshop's default image mode. Although RGB Color allows you to access the full range of Photoshop image-editing menus and commands, many Photoshop projects will require that you convert images from RGB Color to another mode. For instance:

- To output a file for four-color process printing, you will need to convert to CMYK Color mode.

- When you need to work with a display of 256 (or fewer) colors, you can switch to Indexed Color mode.

- To add color to a grayscale image, you'll need to convert from Grayscale mode to one of Photoshop's color modes (RGB Color, Indexed Color, CMYK Color, or Lab Color).

- For other projects, you may need to remove all color from an image. In this case, you can convert from any color mode to Grayscale mode, and from Grayscale you can convert to Bitmap (black and white) mode.

Switching modes also allows you to create special printing effects such as duotones and mezzotints. A *duotone* is a grayscale image in which two inks, usually black and another color, are printed over each other. The resulting extra color can add interest and depth to a grayscale image. A *mezzotint* is a bitmap image created from randomly shaped dots.

In this chapter, you'll have a chance to explore Photoshop's eight modes: Bitmap, Grayscale, Duotone, Indexed Color, RGB Color, CMYK Color, Lab Color, and Multichannel. You'll learn how to switch between one mode and another and, most importantly, from RGB Color to CMYK Color.

**ℕOTE:** *If you change modes in an image that has layers, Photoshop will allow you to choose whether or not to "flatten" the image before the mode change. If you flatten the image, its file size will be reduced but all layers will be merged into the Background.*

## RGB COLOR MODE

RGB Color is Photoshop's native color mode. As discussed in Chapter 4, in RGB Color mode, all colors are created by combining different values of red, green, and blue. In Photoshop's RGB Color mode, over 16.7 million colors are available to you. You can view and edit each of the red, green, and blue color components, called *channels,* individually. Viewing an image's channels can help you better understand the difference between one mode and another.

In order to see the RGB channels that make up an RGB Color image, open any RGB Color file on your screen. (If you don't have an RGB image, load the Portrait file (PC users: portrait.jpg) from the Tutorial folder. With your file displayed, open the Channels palette by choosing Show Channels from the Window/Palettes submenu.

### Using the Channels Palette

When the Channels palette opens, you'll see the three RGB channels listed. There's also a composite channel, where all channels combine to produce one color image. The eye icon (👁) indicates that the components of a particular channel are being viewed. The gray area in the channel means that the channel is selected and its contents will be affected if the image is edited. When a channel is selected, it is often referred to as the *target channel.* The thumbnail image in the channel is a miniature version of the image on screen. You can change the size of the palette's thumbnail by choosing the Palette Options command in the Channels palette's pop-up menu.

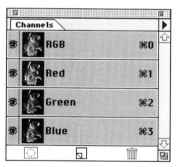

You'll have a better sense of how RGB colors combine to create an image if you take a look at each channel. To do this, click on the name of the channel in the Channels palette. For instance, to view only the Red channel, move the mouse over the word Red in the Channels palette. When the hand icon ( 🖑 ) appears click on Red, or use the keyboard shortcut COMMAND-1 (PC users: CTRL-1). In the image on your screen, you will only see the Red channel.

*n* **OTE:** *You'll probably see the channel as a grayscale image; Photoshop does not display the individual channels in color unless you change one of the default General Preferences settings. To see the channels in color, open the File menu and select Preferences and then General from the submenu. In the General Preferences dialog box, select the Color Channels in Color option. Click OK.*

Take a look at each one individually. Press COMMAND-2 (PC users: CTRL-2) to view the Green channel, and then COMMAND-3 (PC users: CTRL-3) to view the Blue channel. Notice that the eye icon next to the Blue channel in the Channels palette is visible and that the Blue Channel section in the Channels palette is gray. This means that the Blue channel is the only channel in view and the only channel that can be edited. If you'd like, you can view and edit two channels together, independently of the third. While viewing the Blue channel, press and hold SHIFT while you click on Green in the Channels palette. You will see both Blue and Green channels together on screen. Now you can begin to see how the colors combine to create the image. If you wish to deactivate and hide a channel, you can SHIFT-click on the channel name in the palette. To return to the composite view, click on the RGB composite channel, or press COMMAND-0 (PC users: CTRL-0).

Besides viewing the RGB channels, you can also edit within them to create special effects. For example, you could click on a channel name so it will be the only channel that can be viewed and edited, then apply a filter to it. In addition, you can apply paint to each channel separately. If you paint with white in a channel, you will be painting with that channel's color (red, green, or blue); if you paint with black, you add that channel's complementary color to the image.

## Switching from RGB to Other Modes

The three RGB channels and the millions of colors that can be produced in RGB images will provide you with the proper colors for output to slides and video or for printing to an RGB color printer. But as you work with Photoshop, your design goals or the output requirements of a project may necessitate switching modes. The following chart lists the modes to which you can convert from RGB Color, with a brief explanation of each one.

**OTE:** *From RGB Color, you cannot convert directly to Bitmap (black and white) or Duotone; you must convert from RGB Color to Grayscale mode first.*

| Mode | Description |
|---|---|
| Grayscale | 256 shades of gray. (From Grayscale you can switch to Bitmap to work in black and white, or to Duotone.) |
| Indexed Color | Restricts number of colors to 256 or fewer. |
| CMYK Color | Allows you to produce color separations. |
| Lab Color | Encompasses both RGB and CMYK color gamuts. Used by Photo CDs and PostScript Level 2 printers. |
| Multichannel | No composite channel is created. Channels are viewed separately. When you delete a channel from RGB, Lab, or CMYK modes, Photoshop automatically switches to Multichannel. |

When you convert from RGB Color to another mode (except Multichannel), Photoshop changes the color data in the image's file. If you save the file after converting, you will not be able to return to the original color data, unless you are converting between RGB and Lab Color. Thus, before converting from RGB Color to another mode, it's wise to use the File/Save As command to create a second copy of your file. That way you can always return to your original RGB file, if necessary.

In the next section, you will convert your RGB Color image to a CMYK Color image. Before proceeding, use the Save As command to save a copy of your image, and rename the new file **ModeTest**.

## CMYK COLOR MODE

The CMYK Color mode is used for viewing and editing images for output by a commercial printer. If you are working with an RGB Color file and need to produce four-color separations, you should convert the image from RGB Color to CMYK Color. CMYK Color images are divided into four channels, one for each of the process colors used to create four-color separations: Cyan, Magenta, Yellow, and Black. From the four channels, a prepress house produces the four pieces of film needed by a print shop to create the cyan, magenta, yellow, and black printing plates. When the image is printed, the tiny colored ink dots from each plate combine to create countless varieties of color.

If your images are digitized on a high-end scanner, they will probably be saved as CMYK files. These scanners can convert from RGB to CMYK "on the fly"—during the process of digitizing the image. When the scanned image is loaded into Photoshop, it will open as a CMYK image in CMYK Color mode. Photo CD "profiles," available from Kodak, can convert Photo CD files directly to CMYK Color when the images are opened.

**OTE:** *If you are working with a CMYK Color file, it is not advisable to convert it to RGB Color and then back to CMYK Color. When you convert to RGB Color, you lose color data that will not be restored when you convert it back to CMYK Color.*

When you work in CMYK Color mode, you have a choice as to how the CMYK colors are displayed. In the General Preferences dialog box (File/Preferences/General), you can change the CMYK Composites option from Faster (the default) to Smoother. Photoshop will then display the colors as accurately as possible. The disadvantage of the Smoother option is that it slows down the screen display.

## Converting from RGB Color to CMYK Color

Before you convert a file from RGB Color to CMYK Color, bear in mind that CMYK Color files are larger than RGB Color files, due to the addition of the fourth channel. Thus, working in RGB Color mode is generally quicker, particularly if your computer is not fast. It's often advisable not to convert a file to CMYK Color until all image editing is complete. If, however, you are color correcting an image that you will be printing on a printing press, you may want to convert to CMYK Color before you complete a project. This will allow you to edit using the same colors that will be used when the image is printed. When you edit in CMYK Color, you'll be able to color correct and edit in the four individual channels.

Although converting an RGB Color file to CMYK Color is a simple process, it's vital to understand the steps Photoshop goes through to complete the conversion. If you don't, you may not be happy with the color quality of the printed image. To begin the conversion process, you simply select CMYK Color from the Mode menu. The conversion process can take several minutes. When it's done, the RGB colors will be converted to CMYK equivalents, and you will have a larger file because of the fourth channel.

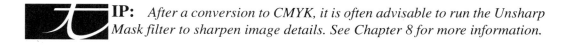

**IP:** *After a conversion to CMYK, it is often advisable to run the Unsharp Mask filter to sharpen image details. See Chapter 8 for more information.*

When the conversion begins, Photoshop first uses the information in the Monitor Setup dialog box (accessed from the File/Preferences submenu) to *internally* convert from RGB Color to Lab Color. Thus, if your monitor is not properly calibrated, you could be on your way to a separation that will produce unsatisfactory colors in the printed image. If you need to, review the section on monitor calibration in Chapter 1.

Next, Photoshop analyzes the settings in two dialog boxes that will be discussed in later sections of this chapter: Printing Inks Setup and Separation Setup, both of which are accessed via the File/Preferences command. Using the information in these two dialog boxes and the Monitor Setup dialog box, Photoshop creates the CMYK Color file.

**OTE:** *Once a file is converted to CMYK Color, changing the settings in the Monitor Setup and Printing Inks Setup dialog boxes will only affect the CMYK Color image's onscreen display. It will not affect the color data in the file. Thus, if you convert a file with incorrect settings, you will then need to change the settings, return to the original RGB Color file, and again convert to CMYK Color.*

## Printing Inks Setup Dialog Box

The primary purpose of the Printing Inks Setup dialog box is to provide Photoshop with information about the ink and paper your commercial printer will be using. Photoshop uses this information to fine-tune the conversion so that the CMYK colors are the most appropriate for your particular print job. When you change the settings in the dialog box, only the display of a CMYK Color image will be affected—not the display of an RGB Color image.

To access the Printing Inks Setup dialog box, choose Preferences from the File menu, and select Printing Inks Setup from the submenu. The Printing Inks Setup options allow you to choose from various printers and printing inks.

```
┌─────────────────────── Printing Inks Setup ───────────────────────┐
│                                                                    │
│   Ink Colors:  │ SWOP (Coated)              ▼│    ┌─── OK ───┐      │
│                                                   └──────────┘      │
│   Dot Gain: │20│ %                                ┌── Cancel ──┐    │
│                                                   └────────────┘    │
│   ┌─ Gray Balance ──────────────────────┐        ┌── Load... ──┐    │
│   │  C: │1.00│    M: │1.00│              │        └─────────────┘    │
│   │                                      │        ┌── Save... ──┐    │
│   │  Y: │1.00│    K: │1.00│              │        └─────────────┘    │
│   └──────────────────────────────────────┘                          │
│                                                                    │
│   ⊠ Use Dot Gain for Grayscale Images                              │
│                                                                    │
└────────────────────────────────────────────────────────────────────┘
```

When the dialog box appears, open the Ink Colors pop-up menu to view the choices available. The default setting is SWOP (Coated). The SWOP (Specifications Web Offset Proofing) organization has published specifications for web offset printing. Choosing one of the SWOP settings means you are choosing inks and papers according to these specifications. Notice the other choices: SWOP (Newsprint), QMS, NEC, and Tektronix printers, as well as Canon laser copiers.

When you make a choice in the Ink Colors pop-up menu, the value in the Dot Gain field, explained next, is updated automatically.

## Understanding Dot Gain and Gray Balance

The Dot Gain percentage indicates the percentage of dot gain expected on a printing press. *Dot gain* is the bleed or spreading of the ink that occurs on paper when an image is printed on a printing press. Dot gain is caused by halftone dots that print larger or smaller than their actual size on film or on the printing plate. This unavoidable phenomenon is most noticeable in midtones and shadow areas of printed images, where the halftone dots are the largest. The degree of dot gain is primarily determined by the printing paper. When Photoshop converts to CMYK Color, it adjusts CMYK percentages in the converted image to compensate for dot gain.

At first glance, the number in the Dot Gain field may seem frighteningly large—but it's really not as bad as it seems. The percentage is measured in terms of the ink increase beyond the size of midtone halftone dots in the film output from the imagesetter. Photoshop then takes the dot gain value and creates a "power" curve which it uses to calculate dot gain in other areas beside midtones.

Since the dot gain value is entered automatically when you change the Ink Colors selection, there's generally no need to enter a number in the Dot Gain field. As long as you know the printing process you will be using, you won't need to change the value in the Dot Gain field. You may, however, wish to change the Dot Gain setting when you calibrate your system to a proof (or sample printout). This subject is covered in Chapter 14.

**𝓃 OTE:** *When the Use Dot Gain for Grayscale Images check box is on, display of grayscale images is changed in order to compensate for dot gain. For more information, see the section "Converting from Any Color Mode to Grayscale" later in this chapter.*

The Printing Inks Setup dialog box also allows adjustment of gray balance settings. The four fields here allow you to control the levels of CMYK colors to compensate for color casts. For instance, a color cast may appear if one of the process inks has a higher dot gain than the others.

Usually, the Gray Balance fields are only changed when you're recalibrating your system to a proof (or sample printout) while you are in a CMYK Color file. In an RGB Color file, changing these values affects the separation settings but not how colors are displayed. In a CMYK Color image, *increasing* the value of any of the Gray Balance fields will lighten that color's display on screen, and vice versa. Chapter 14 tells you how to use a proof as a guide for adjusting for the Gray Balance fields.

The Printing Inks Setup dialog box also includes Save and Load buttons, which allow you to save your settings and reload them to use again in another file.

If you are working with an image on screen, and you are certain of the correct Printing Inks Setup settings for your project, go ahead and select the appropriate choice in the Ink Colors pop-up menu and click OK. Otherwise, if you made changes to the Printing Inks Setup dialog box while working through this section, click Cancel now so that the default settings remain intact. Next, take a look at the Separation Setup dialog box, which is also used during CMYK conversion.

## Choosing a Separation Setup

To open the Separation Setup dialog box, choose Preferences from the File menu and then select Separation Setup. The Separation Setup dialog box controls how the black plate is created during the separation process. In most cases, the default dialog box settings should provide good results. The Save and Load buttons allow you to save and reload the settings you make here; this is helpful when you need to return to a particular set of print settings or wish to reload the Black Generation custom curve (explained next).

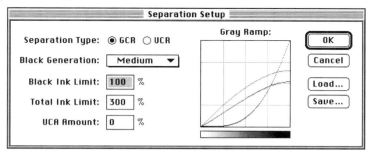

**CAUTION:** *If you experiment with the Separation Setup dialog box settings as you work through this section, be sure to change them back to the defaults. These settings should only be changed on the advice of your commercial printer or prepress house.*

As discussed in Chapter 4, cyan, magenta, and yellow can theoretically produce all of the colors needed for commercial printing. Unfortunately, however, when the three colors overprint, ink impurities produce a muddy brown color instead of pure black. To remedy this, a black plate is added to increase contrast and produce blacker blacks. When black is added, levels of cyan, magenta, and yellow can be reduced to enhance printing quality. The two primary techniques used to substitute black for CMY colors are UCR (Under Color Removal) and GCR (Gray Component Replacement).

The decision to use either GCR or UCR in Photoshop is often determined by paper stock and printing requirements. GCR is generally used for coated stock and UCR for uncoated stock.

For the UCR separation type, levels of cyan, magenta, and yellow are subtracted from gray and shadow areas and replaced with an appropriate amount of black. For the GCR separation type (Photoshop's default), levels of cyan, magenta, and yellow are subtracted from both gray and colored areas. To compensate for the removal of one or all three of the these colors, when GCR is chosen, an appropriate amount of black is added. The degree of black replacement can be specified in the Black Generation pop-up menu of the Separation Setup dialog box.

Most of you won't need to delve deeply into the inner workings of GCR; the basic theory is that one of the three process inks (CMY) often is the gray component of a color. The gray component is the ink that lightens or darkens; the other two inks provide most of the color. When GCR is applied, the gray component ink is reduced and black is added. For instance, consider a digitized image of green grass that is primarily composed of cyan and yellow, with a small percentage of magenta darkening the image. During the separation process with the GCR option selected, a portion of the magenta can be reduced and replaced with black. Theoretically, GCR can result in better gray balance and better reproduction of saturated colors.

**𝓃OTE:** *Despite what you read or are told about the advantages of GCR over UCR (or vice versa), don't make any choices without contacting your print shop.*

In the Separation Setup dialog box you'll also see a grid where a slope portraying the *gray ramp* is displayed. The Gray Ramp grid provides a visual representation of how the process inks produce neutral or gray colors based upon the settings in the dialog box. The x-axis charts the color value from 0% to 100%. The gray bar depicts the actual shade of gray from white to black. The y-axis charts the ink that will be used to produce the gray value.

**GCR AND THE GRAY RAMP**    The best way to understand how the Gray Ramp works is to see what happens when you turn off the black plate with the GCR option enabled. To turn off the black plate, select None in the Black Generation pop-up menu. This menu controls the amount of black substituted in the image when the GCR option is used.

As soon as you click None, the Gray Ramp changes, showing you that the grays will be produced with approximately equal amounts of cyan, magenta, and yellow, but not black. Now click on Medium in the Black Generation pop-up menu. The Gray Ramp now shows that CMY levels are reduced, with black used to help produce grays starting in areas just lighter than the image's midtones. Switch among the choices in the Black Generation menu, and you'll see that as more black is added, the CMY inks are reduced; when black is reduced, the CMY levels are increased.

The Custom selection in the Black Generation pop-up lets you manually control the generation of the black plate. When you choose Custom, a Black Generation dialog box appears, where you can customize black generation by clicking and dragging on a curve. After you adjust the curve and click OK, the cyan, magenta, and yellow levels are changed according to the black curve.

When you choose the GCR separation type, the UCA (Undercolor Addition) Amount field at the bottom of the Separation Setup dialog box allows you to add cyan, magenta, and yellow back into the areas that contain the highest percentage of black in an image. When you add cyan, magenta, and yellow, black is not subtracted. This results in more intense blacks, which can help prevent shadow areas from appearing too flat. Acceptable values in the UCA Amount field are between 0 and 100%. Once again, if you change settings, you will see the results in the Gray Ramp. And remember: *Any value entered in this field should also be approved by your commercial printer or prepress house.*

Before continuing, if you have changed the Black Generation menu selection, return it now to the default setting, Medium. In most situations, Medium will provide good results when you convert from RGB to CMYK.

**UCR AND THE GRAY RAMP**    To see how the UCR option affects the Gray Ramp, click on the UCR radio button in the Separation Setup dialog box. Notice that the black ink increases in the dark shadow areas while the appropriate CMY colors are decreased in this area.

**SETTING INK LIMITS**    The Black Ink Limit field in the dialog box allows you to tell Photoshop the maximum ink density that your commercial printer's press can support; the default value is 100%. This means that the darkest black (K) value in

your converted CMYK Color image can be 100%. The default setting for the Total Ink Limit is 300%. This means that the total percentage of your CMY inks together will not be over 200% (300%-100%=200%, the 100% being the Black Ink Limit). If you lower the values in these fields, you'll see that the maximum values for the CMYK inks will drop in the Gray Ramp. The same warning applies here: *Do not change any values without consulting your print shop.*

**N** OTE: *To view the total percentage of CMYK inks in the Info palette, set one of the Eyedropper readouts to Total Ink.*

To close the Separation Setup dialog box and exit without changing the default settings, click Cancel.

## Separation Tables

If you are going to be printing Photoshop projects with various inks or printing systems, the settings you choose in the Printing Ink Setup and Separation Setup dialog boxes can be saved together, as a *separation table.* If you save a separation table, you do not need to save the individual settings in these dialog boxes. Saving the table essentially saves the settings in both the Printing Inks Setup and Separation Setup dialog boxes on disk.

When you want to convert an image that needs a particular group of settings, you just load the settings from the Separation Tables dialog box, instead of having to reenter the settings in the Printing Inks Setup and Separation Setup dialog boxes. Using a separation table also results in a speedier completion of the RGB-to-CMYK conversion because the separation table Photoshop will use in that conversion will have already been created.

Once you have established the settings in the Printing Inks Setup and Separation Setup dialog boxes, you can have Photoshop build a separation table. To do this, choose Preferences from the File menu and then select Separation Tables to display the Separation Tables dialog box. Click the Save button, and wait for Photoshop to build a separation table. Next, when a dialog box appears, name your table and save it on your disk. After you name your separation table, load it by clicking on the Load button and choosing the table file from the list of files in the dialog box.

When a separation table is loaded, the Separation Tables dialog box displays the name of the table alongside the Use Table radio button. When the Use Table radio button is selected, it means that the table will be used when you convert to CMYK and that the table will be used to display the CMYK color values on your RGB monitor. If you wish to use the settings in the Printing Inks Setup dialog box instead of the separation table, select the Use Printing Inks Setup radio button.

```
╔══════════════════ Separation Tables ══════════════════╗
║  ┌─ To CMYK ──────────────────────────┐   ┌──────────┐  ║
║  │  ○ Use Separation Setup            │   │    OK    │  ║
║  │  ⊙ Use Table:   Fundamental Photoshop │  └──────────┘  ║
║  │                                    │   ┌──────────┐  ║
║  └────────────────────────────────────┘   │  Cancel  │  ║
║  ┌─ From CMYK ────────────────────────┐   └──────────┘  ║
║  │  ○ Use Printing Inks Setup         │   ┌──────────┐  ║
║  │  ⊙ Use Table:   Fundamental Photoshop │  │  Load... │  ║
║  │                                    │   └──────────┘  ║
║  └────────────────────────────────────┘   ┌──────────┐  ║
║                                            │  Save... │  ║
║                                            └──────────┘  ║
╚════════════════════════════════════════════════════════╝
```

The Separation Tables dialog box is also used if you are loading separation tables created by third-party software vendors such as EFI (Electronics for Imaging). EFI has created a variety of separation tables designed to work with specific printers and printing systems. For more details about using EfiColor Works, see Chapter 14.

**OTE:**  *When you load a separation table, the Separation Setup dialog box will be disabled. Also, if you try to open the Printing Inks Setup dialog box, an alert message will appear, warning you that the Printing Inks Setup dialog box will not affect the CMYK conversion because a separation table has been selected.*

## CMYK Preview

Now that you have an understanding of what goes on behind the scenes, you're just about ready to convert your image from RGB Color to CMYK Color.

### Gamut Warning and CMYK Preview

Before converting from RGB Color to CMYK Color, you can have Photoshop check to see if any RGB colors are beyond the CMYK Color gamut. You can also have Photoshop create a preview of the CMYK colors.

**OTE:**  *For more information about the CMYK Color gamut, see Chapter 4.*

To see if any of your colors are beyond the CMYK gamut, choose Gamut Warning from the Mode menu. In a few moments, Photoshop will turn any out-of-gamut colors in your image to a deep gray tone. If you wish, you can change the opacity or color of the Out of Gamut warning by choosing Gamut Warning from the File/Preferences submenu. In the Gamut Warning Preferences dialog box enter a new opacity, or click on the gray swatch to open the Color Picker.

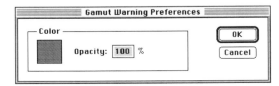

If you wish to select the out of gamut colors so that you can edit only within the out of gamut colors, choose Color Range from the Select menu. In the Color Range dialog box, choose Out of Gamut from the Select pop-up menu. To ensure that you can see your entire image, leave the Selection Preview pop-up menu set to None. After you click OK in the Color Range dialog box, only the out-of-gamut colors will be selected.

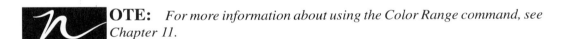

**OTE:** *For more information about using the Color Range command, see Chapter 11.*

The easiest way to correct your out of gamut colors is to use the Sponge tool. To activate the Sponge tool, double-click on the Dodge/Burn/Sponge tool. In the Toning Tools Options palette choose Sponge from the Tool pop-up menu. Set the Mode pop-up menu to Desaturate. Now you can click and drag over the out of gamut areas displayed on your screen. As the Sponge tool desaturates, the gray Out of Gamut warning color will gradually disappear; colors will return to your image, but these colors will be within the CMYK Color gamut. As you continue to work, be careful not to desaturate too much. This can cause your colors to turn gray. You may also wish to use a color process swatch book as a reference guide (as described in Chapter 4), in conjunction with the Info palette readouts.

**IP:** *As you desaturate you might find it helpful to view your image with and without the out of gamut gray warning colors. This will make it easier to check your progress as you remove the out of gamut colors. To do this, open a duplicate window on screen by choosing New Window from the Window menu. Turn the Gamut Warning on in one window; leave the menu command deselected in the other.*

To see a CMYK preview, select CMYK Preview from the Mode menu. When Photoshop previews the colors, it does not convert the image to CMYK Color mode, but displays the RGB colors in their CMYK equivalents.

**IP:** *You can view the RGB colors of an image and their CMYK equivalents simultaneously in two windows. To do this, choose New Window from the Window menu in your RGB Color file. This will create a duplicate window of your RGB file. In the duplicate window, select CMYK Preview from the Mode menu.*

To turn off the Preview, choose Preview again in the Mode menu. Now you're ready to start the conversion from RGB Color to CMYK Color.

### Completing the CMYK Conversion

Once you're satisfied that all out-of-gamut colors have been removed from your RGB Color image, you're ready to convert to CMYK Color. First, if you haven't already backed up your file, use the Save As command to create another version of your image. Then, to begin the conversion, choose CMYK Color from the Mode menu. When the conversion is completed, the mode in the title bar will change from RGB to CMYK. After converting, it is often advisable to run the Unsharp Mask filter, as explained in Chapter 8, to sharpen the image.

After the file has been converted, open the Channels palette and notice that it now comprises four channels. If you look at the File Size indicator (towards the bottom left-hand corner of your screen), you'll see that the extra channel has increased the size of the image file. Take a moment to click on each of the channels to see how the image is created from the four process colors: cyan, magenta, yellow, and black.

One of the advantages of working in a CMYK Color file is that Photoshop will not allow you to paint with out-of-gamut colors. Also, you can edit in the four individual channels or in any combination of the four channels. This is helpful when you want to color correct in the individual channels or when you are creating interesting special effects.

Here's a design tip for adding color to a black-and-white (bitmap) image, without affecting the underlying black color. This technique is possible because you can turn off editing in the black channel while you paint in the CMY channels. First, convert the black-and-white line art to CMYK Color. If you have a bitmap image, you will need to use the Mode menu to convert from Bitmap to Grayscale, then from Grayscale to CMYK Color. Once the image is in CMYK Color mode, deactivate the Black channel so that the black plate will not be affected. To do this, position the pointer over the Black channel in the Channels palette. Press and hold SHIFT as you click the mouse. Now turn on the eye icon so the contents of the Black channel are visible. Do this by clicking in the eye column to the left of the Black channel. Now you can see the Black channel, but any editing changes you make won't affect it. Then use Photoshop's painting tools to add color to your image. When you're done painting, click on CMYK in the Channels palette to see the Composite image.

After converting to CMYK, you'll probably want to save the file so it can be output for proofing purposes. Often this means saving the file in EPS, TIFF or Scitex CT format before sending it to a service bureau or prepress house. Before you send the file to the service bureau, you may need to export your EPS or TIFF file to a page-layout program such as QuarkXPress. For more information about saving Photoshop files in EPS, TIFF, and Scitex CT formats, see Appendix A.

## INDEXED COLOR MODE

The Indexed Color mode is used to create and edit files that only require a maximum of 256 colors. Converting to Indexed Color is often necessary when editing files that will be exported to programs that only support 256 colors. The Indexed Color mode can also be used if you are creating applications or silkscreens that only require a few colors.

When you convert a file to Indexed Color, Photoshop reduces the channels in the image to one and creates a color table that is essentially a palette of colors that is tied to the document. This table is called a *color lookup table* (CLUT), and it acts as a type of index for the colors in the image.

You can convert to Indexed Color from RGB Color, Grayscale, or Duotone mode. In this section, you'll learn how to convert an RGB Color file to Indexed Color and edit the related color table. If your RGB Color file contains more than 256 colors, you will lose color information when you convert to Indexed Color. Although you can convert from Indexed Color back to RGB Color, Photoshop will not return the original colors to the file. Thus, you should always keep a backup copy of your original color file before converting.

 **OTE:** *Once you convert to Indexed Color mode, Photoshop's filters and the Image/Effects submenu commands will not be available. You must execute these before converting to Indexed Color.*

## Converting from RGB Color to Indexed Color

If you wish to experiment with Indexed Color, choose Revert from the File menu to return to the RGB Color version of the ModeTest file you created at the beginning of this chapter. If you wish to use another file, you can load any RGB Color file. Make sure that you use the Save As command first to rename the file, so you can later return to the original version.

### The Indexed Color Dialog Box

To convert an RGB Color file to Indexed Color, choose Indexed Color from the Mode menu. In the Indexed Color dialog box, you can choose the desired number of colors, a color palette, and a dithering pattern, if you wish.

```
╔══════════════ Indexed Color ══════════════╗
║  ┌─ Resolution ──────────┐   ┌────────┐   ║
║  │  ○ 3 bits/pixel        │   │   OK   │   ║
║  │  ○ 4 bits/pixel        │   └────────┘   ║
║  │  ○ 5 bits/pixel        │   ┌────────┐   ║
║  │  ○ 6 bits/pixel        │   │ Cancel │   ║
║  │  ○ 7 bits/pixel        │   └────────┘   ║
║  │  ◉ 8 bits/pixel        │               ║
║  │                        │               ║
║  │  ○ Other: ▢▢▢ colors   │               ║
║  └────────────────────────┘               ║
║                                            ║
║  ┌─ Palette ──┐  ┌─ Dither ──────┐        ║
║  │ ○ Exact    │  │ ○ None         │        ║
║  │ ○ System   │  │ ○ Pattern      │        ║
║  │ ◉ Adaptive │  │ ◉ Diffusion    │        ║
║  │ ○ Custom...│  └────────────────┘        ║
║  │ ○ Previous │                            ║
║  └────────────┘                            ║
╚════════════════════════════════════════════╝
```

Use the Resolution options to specify the number of colors in the Indexed Color file. In this case, resolution refers to the bit resolution of the image. If you choose 8 bits/pixel, 256 ($2^8$) colors can be displayed; choose 4 bits/pixel, and 16 ($2^4$) colors can displayed. If you know the exact number of colors that you wish in an image, you can enter it into the Other field. The Other field will only accept values less than or equal to 256.

The Palette options provide a variety of color choices for the Indexed Color file. Read the following descriptions; then, if you wish, take a look at what happens to your image with each Palette option. Click on a radio button and then click OK. After you've seen the effects of a palette on your image, choose Undo from the Edit menu and then test the next palette.

*Exact*   This option is only available if the image contains 256 or fewer colors. When Exact is chosen, Photoshop will build a table using the same colors that appear in the original RGB Color image. When this option is selected, the number of colors in the image is changed according to the resolution setting. No dithering is necessary because no new colors need to be simulated.

*System*   This option uses the Mac or Windows default system palette. If you designate fewer than 8 bits/pixel for Resolution, Photoshop replaces the System option with the Uniform option to indicate that the full System palette is not available.

*Adaptive*   This option generates a color table from the most commonly used colors in the image being converted. If you wish to have more control over the Adaptive palette conversion process, first select an area of the image that includes the colors you wish to retain. In the conversion to Indexed Color, Photoshop will choose colors based more upon the selection than on all of the colors in the image.

*Custom*   This option allows you to create your own custom color table for the file. When you select this option, the Color Table dialog box appears, in which you can edit, save, and load color tables. You can also choose from several predefined color tables. When you choose a predefined table or edit a table, the colors of the image on screen will change to those in the color table when it is applied to your image. The colors are applied to the image when you click OK in the Color Table dialog box. For a description of each predefined table, see the section "Viewing the Predefined Colors" that follows.

*Previous*   This option converts using the palette from the previous conversion, which is useful when you are converting several images at a time.

To the right of the Palette group are the Dither options. *Dithering* combines different colored pixels together to give the appearance of colors that are not actually in the image. Choosing a dithering option may be advisable because the color table that is created may not contain all of the colors in your image. Here are descriptions of the Dither options:

*None*   Choose None if you do not wish dithering to occur. When this option is chosen, Photoshop picks the closest match it can find in the Color Table to replace a missing color in the converted image. This usually results in sharp color transitions.

*Pattern*    This option uses a pattern of random dots to simulate a missing color. This option is only available if the System or Uniform palette option is selected.

 *Diffusion*    When you choose Diffusion, Photoshop diffuses the difference between the original pixels and the pixels in the converted image to simulate the missing colors.

## Viewing the Predefined Colors

There are two ways to access the Color Table dialog box in order to choose a predefined color table. If you have already converted to Indexed Color, you can choose Color Table from the Mode menu. If you haven't yet converted, first choose Indexed Color from the Mode menu, and then select Custom in the Palette group of the Indexed Color dialog box.

In the Color Table dialog box, the predefined tables are accessed by clicking on the Table pop-up menu. Here's a brief description of these tables; you may want to select each one to view the colors produced.

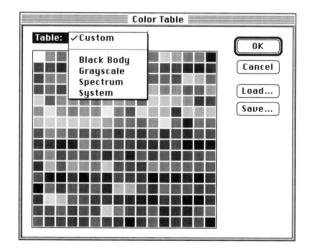

 *Black Body*    This option transforms the color table based on colors produced when a blackbody radiator is heated. You'll see a range of colors from black to red, as well as orange, yellow, and white. This table can be used for scientific applications or to produce a hot, glowing effect.

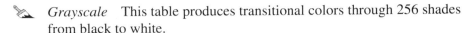 

*Grayscale* This table produces transitional colors through 256 shades from black to white.

*Spectrum* This table produces the colors in the color spectrum.

*System* This table is the standard Mac or Windows color palette.

## Editing the Indexed Color Table

If you'd like, you can open the color table used by your image and edit the colors. To do this, your image should be converted to Indexed Color.

Once you have an Indexed Color file on screen, select Color Table from the Mode menu; the color table for your file will be displayed. Now you can edit any color in the table by clicking on the color. After you click, Photoshop's Color Picker will appear, allowing you to change the colors. Use the dialog box options to pick a color that is not already in the color table, and then click OK. Photoshop will return to your document, where each pixel that contained the color you clicked in the Color Table dialog box is converted to the new color.

Photoshop's Indexed Color also allows you to change a range of colors in the table at one time. This can be helpful if you want to prevent the color changes in your image from being too dramatic. To change a range of colors, select Color Table from the Mode menu. In the Color Table dialog box, click and drag through a row of colors. When you release the mouse, the Color Picker will appear with the message "Select first color." Choose a color and click OK. The Color Picker will reopen with the message "Select last color." When you click OK, a gradient of colors—from the first color you specified to the last color—will appear in the color table. Click OK in the dialog box to see the effects in your image.

## Saving and Loading Indexed Color Tables

If you wish to create a custom color table to use with other documents, you can return to the Color Table dialog box and click the Save button to name the table and save it on disk. When you wish to apply it to a document, use the Load button to load it. After the table is loaded, click OK in the Color Table dialog box to have the colors from the table appear in the document on screen.

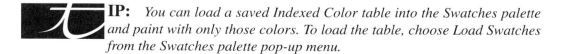 **IP:** *You can load a saved Indexed Color table into the Swatches palette and paint with only those colors. To load the table, choose Load Swatches from the Swatches palette pop-up menu.*

# CONVERTING FROM ANY COLOR MODE TO GRAYSCALE

If for design purposes you need to convert your digitized color image to grayscale or black and white, you will need to first convert your file to Grayscale mode. From Grayscale, you can convert to a Duotone or Bitmap file. (Duotones and bitmap images are discussed later in this chapter.)

Grayscale files are 8-bit images that can be composed of up to 256 shades of gray. When a color file is converted to grayscale, all color information is removed from the file. Although the Mode menu allows you to convert a grayscale file to a color mode file, you will not be able to return the original colors to a file that has been converted to grayscale. Thus, before converting a color image to grayscale, it's advisable to use the Save As command to create a copy of your color file so that you have a backup.

If you don't have a color file on screen, load one now so that you can convert it to grayscale (try the ModeTest file that's been used throughout this chapter). Then select Grayscale from the Mode menu. An alert box will appear, warning that you will be discarding the color information in the file. After you click OK, your file will be converted to a grayscale image, and the Channels palette will display only one channel, Black.

For a grayscale image, the Picker palette displays only one grayscale slider, labeled K (Black). You can change the percentage of gray by clicking and dragging on the slider control. The lower the percentage, the lighter the shade of gray; the higher the percentage, the darker the shade of gray.

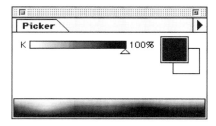

When working with Grayscale mode images, keep in mind that the Dot Gain percentage in the Printing Inks Setup dialog box is automatically applied by Photoshop, based on your selection in the Ink Colors pop-up menu. The Dot Gain setting changes the display of a grayscale image to compensate for dot gain that can occur on press. Before editing a grayscale image, open the Printing Inks Setup dialog box (choose Printing Inks Setup from the File/Preferences submenu) and verify that the Ink Colors selection is correct. If you want the Dot Gain setting to affect the display, make sure that the Use Dot Gain for Grayscale Images option at the bottom of the dialog box is selected.

When Photoshop converts to grayscale, it uses a formula to convert the color information to gray values. Notwithstanding the formula's accuracy, you still may decide that the grayscale version needs some tonal corrections. If this is the case, you can make simple tonal adjustments using the Brightness/Contrast command in the Image/Adjust submenu. To learn more advanced techniques for making tonal adjustments to grayscale images, see Chapter 13.

## CONVERTING FROM GRAYSCALE TO ANY COLOR MODE

While working with an image in Grayscale mode, you cannot add color to it. If you wish to add color to a grayscale image, convert the image to one of the color modes (RGB Color, CMYK Color, Lab Color, or Indexed Color) by selecting that mode from the Mode menu. After you convert, you can colorize the image.

**C AUTION:** *When converting a Grayscale image to CMYK Color, the Dot Gain for Grayscale Images check box in the Printing Inks dialog box should be deselected. If the check box is selected, Info palette readings will be incorrect because Photoshop will correct for dot gain once when it converts from Grayscale to Lab Color mode, then once more when it converts from Lab Color to CMYK Color.*

*If you convert an image from Grayscale to a color mode and wish to edit in individual color channels, select the Dot Gain for Grayscale Images check box. This ensures that Info palette readings will be correct because when you edit in a channel of a color image, you are essentially working in a grayscale image.*

### Colorizing Grayscale Images

Using the computer to colorize a grayscale image is similar to the process of adding color to old black-and-white movies. Like the process of creating colorized movies, transforming a grayscale image into color allows the image's shadows and contours, and definition beneath the color to show through.

To start colorizing, you will need to load a grayscale image. (As usual, to ensure that you will be able to return to the original grayscale image, it's always advisable to use the Save As command and rename the file.) Then open the Picker palette by choosing Show Picker in the Window/Palette submenu. Select the Mode menu, and convert your file from Grayscale to RGB Color or CMYK Color. This will allow you to add colors to your image.

Set the foreground color and choose the Paintbrush tool in the Toolbox. If the Brushes palette isn't open, choose Show Brushes in the Window/Palette submenu. In the Brushes palette, select a medium, soft-edged brush size.

You'll start painting the image with the Paintbrush tool, but before you do, double-click on the Paintbrush to open the Paintbrush Options palette. In the palette, set Opacity to 100% and in the Mode pop-up menu, select Color as the painting mode. Notice the result: The portion you paint changes color, but you can still see the underlying shadows and textures. This is because you are painting in Color mode. When you paint using Color mode, Photoshop paints with only the hue and saturation of a color. This allows the underlying brightness values to show through your painting color. If you were painting in Normal mode at 100% Opacity, the opaque color would completely cover the image.

If there are large areas that you wish to color in your image, use the Pen tool or a selection tool to create a selection. Then choose Fill from the Edit menu, and set the Mode in the Edit menu to Color. After you click OK, color will be applied to your image, but again, the underlying lightness and darkness levels will show through the color.

You may wish to experiment with the Darken, Lighten, Multiply, Overlay, Soft Light, and Screen painting modes. Lighten and Darken, in particular, can be used to add various color tones to areas already colorized. (For a review of Darken, Lighten, Multiply, Overlay, Soft Light, and Screen, see "Painting/Editing Modes" in Chapter 5.) Also, you may wish to activate the Blur or Smudge tools to blend colors together. You can use the Sharpen tool to enhance detail by increasing contrast as well.

## Using the Colorize Option in the Hue/Saturation Dialog Box

Photoshop also allows you to adjust colors from a variety of dialog boxes accessed from the Image/Adjust submenu. You'll be using these commands extensively when retouching and color correcting (in Chapter 13). Only the Hue/Saturation command is discussed here because it includes an option specifically designed to colorize.

# Photoshop in Action

The white areas of the
image were colored.

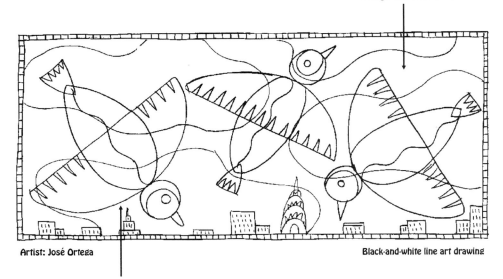

Artist: José Ortega

Black-and-white line art drawing

The black marker lines of the
image were colored.

José began this project for New York's Metropolitan Transit Authority (MTA) by first using a marker to make this line drawing. He then scanned the image as black-and-white line art. Once the image was digitized, he removed any dust spots with the Eraser tool and closed white gaps in the marker lines with the Pencil tool.

Photoshop in Action

The white areas no longer exist.
They were filled using the
Darken painting/editing mode.

Artist: José Ortega

Client: Metropolitan Transit Authority

The black marker lines no longer
exist. They were colored by using
the Lighten painting/editing  mode.

After the black-and-white line art drawing was digitized, José converted it to a color image by choosing RGB Color from the Mode menu. He colored the white areas of the image by using the Paint Bucket tool with different Tolerance settings and the Darken painting/editing mode. By using the Darken painting/editing mode, José prevented the black marker lines from being affected. After filling the white areas, he colored the black marker lines by using the Lighten painting/editing mode.

To complete the project, he selected the entire image with the Marquee tool and created a black frame around it using the Edit/Stroke command.

Before experimenting with the Hue/Saturation command, select an area in your image that you wish to colorize. Choose Hue/Saturation from the Image/Adjust submenu. In the dialog box, click on the Preview check box. This lets you see the changes in your image as you colorize. Then click on the Colorize check box, and the selection you've just made will turn red. Don't worry—this is supposed to happen. Notice that the Hue setting on your screen is set to 0 degrees, as shown in this illustration; this is the value assigned to red in Photoshop's HSB Colors palette. When you turned on the Colorize option, Photoshop applied this setting to your selection.

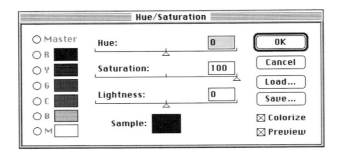

**NOTE:** *When the Colorize option is on in the Hue/Saturation dialog box, the radio buttons for the various RGB and CMY colors, at the left of the dialog box, are dimmed. When you are color correcting an image with the Colorize option turned off, these radio buttons become accessible. They will be discussed in Chapter 13.*

Adjusting the Hue slider will change the color of the image. Adjusting the Saturation slider will change the amount of gray in a color. When you are colorizing a grayscale image, the more saturation you add, the stronger the colors will be and the less gray they will contain. Adjusting the Lightness slider allows you to control how light or dark the color will be. The Sample swatch previews the color you are creating.

Now try working with the Hue/Saturation sliders. To move through the color spectrum, drag the Hue slider control right or left. Drag it all the way to the left to −180, and you'll see the color in the Sample box change from red to magenta to blue and eventually to cyan. Drag to the right from 0 to 180 degrees, and you'll see red, yellow, green, and cyan again. If you find it confusing that you returned to cyan, think of the slider as the linear equivalent of a color wheel. When you move in a positive direction from red along the wheel, you eventually reach cyan; when you move in a

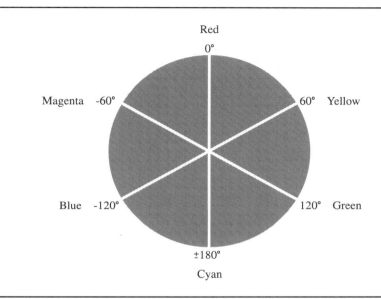

Hue slider
values
arranged on
a color
wheel

**FIGURE 9-1**

negative direction, you arrive at the same color. Figure 9-1 shows how the Hue slider values and their corresponding colors would appear if arranged on a color wheel.

If you wish, you can change the Saturation setting. If you drag the Saturation slider control to the right, saturation increases; dragging left decreases saturation. Moving the Lightness slider control to the right toward 100 lightens your color; sliding it left toward -100 darkens it. With Lightness set to 100, the color changes to white; -100 changes it to black. By adjusting the Lightness slider control, you can even add color to pure white and pure black image areas.

After you decide what combination of Hue, Saturation, and Lightness you wish to apply to an image area, you can save your settings so that they can be applied to other files. Click the Save button, and a dialog box appears, allowing you to enter a name for the settings. After naming your settings, click Save (PC users: OK) to return to the Hue/Saturation dialog box. When you wish to use these color settings again, select another area of the image or open another image; then return to the Hue/Saturation dialog box and load your color settings by clicking the Load button and opening your Hue/Saturation settings file. If you wish to exit the Hue/Saturation dialog box and apply the settings now, click OK; otherwise, click Cancel.

**IP:**   *After you have finished colorizing, you may wish to create special effects by applying any of Photoshop's filters from the Filter menu. See Chapter 8.*

## CONVERTING FROM GRAYSCALE TO A DUOTONE

Printing a grayscale image with an extra gray or colored ink can make it more interesting and dramatic by adding depth and dimension. These enhanced grayscale images are called *duotones.* In Photoshop's Duotone mode you can create monotones, duotones, tritones, and quadtones—grayscale images to which you add one, two, three, or four colors. This printing technique lets you create interesting images less expensively than printing four-color images.

In order to create a monotone, duotone, tritone, or quadtone image, you must start with a grayscale image or convert a color image to a grayscale image. Only while in Grayscale mode can you access the Duotone mode.

In this section, you will create a duotone from a grayscale image. Start by loading any color file and converting it to Grayscale mode. If you wish, you can use the ModeTest file that was converted to Grayscale earlier in the chapter, or use the Hands file (PC users: hands.jpg) in the Tutorial folder.

1. Select Duotone from the Mode menu. In the Duotone Options dialog box, Type is set to Monotone by default. When the Monotone option is selected, notice that Ink 1 is active. Next to Ink 1 are two squares. The square with the diagonal line represents the ink density curve. The second square is the color swatch box. This represents the color you are applying to your image. To activate another Type option, click on the Type pop-up menu and make your selection. Select the Duotone option, since that is the option most commonly used.

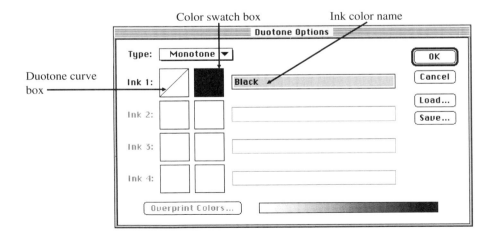

When you choose Duotone from the Type pop-up menu, Ink 1 and Ink 2 are active, but not Ink 3 and Ink 4. This is because duotones are composed of only two colors. The number of inks that appear depends upon the option you select in the Type pop-up menu.

**OTE:** *When Photoshop prints a duotone, it prints the inks in ascending order. Thus, the darkest ink is usually the first ink and the lightest ink is the last ink in the Duotone Options dialog box.*

2. Notice that for the Duotone option, you will need to pick a second ink color. Click once on the white color swatch box to the right of Ink 2. The Custom Colors dialog box appears.

    In the Custom Colors dialog box, you can either pick a custom color or click on the Picker button to access the Color Picker dialog box and then enter CMYK percentages to pick a process color.

3. To pick a PANTONE Coated color in the Custom Colors dialog box, click on the Book pop-up menu and choose PANTONE Coated if it is not already displayed. To choose a color, type **2645**. Notice that PANTONE 2645 CV (or PANTONE 2645 CVC if the Short PANTONE Names option in the General Preferences dialog box isn't selected) becomes the active color. Click OK to confirm the change and return to the Duotone Options dialog box.

**OTE:** *If Photoshop does not find the correct color, try quickly retyping the Custom Color number on your numeric keypad.*

4. To see the effects of your changes, click OK in the Duotone Options dialog box. When your image appears on screen, you will see that it contains two colors: black and PANTONE 2645 CV.

## Controlling Duotone Ink

After you have selected the second ink color for a duotone, you may want to control ink density in shadow, midtone, and highlight areas. You do this by adjusting that ink's curve. Usually in duotone images, black is applied to the shadow areas, and gray or another color is applied to the midtone and highlight areas. To change the way an ink is applied to an image, follow these steps:

**OTE:** *Before and after you make adjustments in the Duotone Curve dialog box, you may want to open the Colors palette to see the different shades of Ink 1 and Ink 2.*

1. Return to the Duotone Options dialog box by choosing Duotone from the Mode menu. In the Duotone Options dialog box, click on the box with the diagonal line in it for Ink 1 or Ink 2. The Duotone Curve dialog box appears, containing a graph depicting the ink coverage over different image areas.

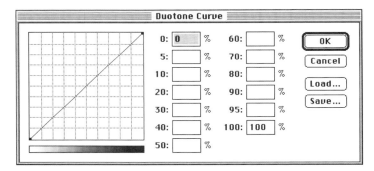

In the Duotone Curve dialog box, observe the graph on the left and the percentages on the right. In the graph, the x-axis represents the tonal range in the original image, from highlights to shadows. The y-axis represents the ink density values. The default settings of the graph are always represented by a diagonal line. The diagonal indicates that the printing ink percentage matches the black percentage value of every pixel in the image. This means if the image contains black values of 100%, they will print with a 100% density (a 100% dot of the specified ink color) for the specified ink. A 50% midtone pixel will be printed at a 50% density (a 50% dot of the specified ink). The diagonal line can be adjusted by clicking and dragging it, or by typing percentage values in the entry fields on the right. The numbers entered into the fields represent ink density. The 0% field represents highlights (the lightest portions of the image) and the 100% field represents shadows (the darkest portions of the image). The 50% field represents the midtones. Thus, if you enter 80 in the 100% box, it means an 80% dot of the specified ink will be used to print the darkest shadow areas.

2. Click on the middle of the diagonal line and drag downward. When you click, a small dot (control point) is added to the curve, and a value is entered into the 50% field. (If you didn't click exactly on the middle of curve, Photoshop enters a value in the field corresponding to the point were you clicked.) The value entered is the percentage of ink density for midtone areas.

3. Try making some adjustments in the curve by clicking and dragging and by typing percentages into the fields. When you drag the curve upward, you add more of the ink to the image; drag the curve downward, and you use less ink. If you type a percentage into the field, a corresponding control point appears on the curve.

4. When you're finished experimenting with adjustments to the curve, click OK to return to the Duotone Options dialog box. Click OK again to see the adjusted curve's effects on your image.

## Viewing the Duotone's Readouts in the Info Palette

Once you've examined your duotone image on screen, you may decide to make adjustments to the curve or change the color of the inks. Before you do, it's often a good idea to analyze the true colors in your image by viewing the Eyedropper's readouts in the Info palette. Viewing these readouts of the ink percentages ensures that you don't rely totally on how the image looks on your monitor.

If the Info palette is not open, select Show Info from the Window menu. If the Info palette readout does not display two inks, click on the Info palette's pop-up menu arrow. In the following Info Options dialog box, select Show First Color Readout, and then choose Actual Color from the corresponding pop-up menu. Since all duotone colors are displayed in the first readout, you can hide the second readout by also setting it to Actual Color. Click OK to confirm the settings. The image's actual color values in percentages for both inks will appear in the Info palette.

9

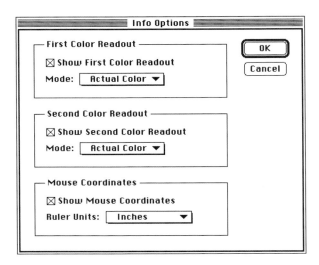

**IP:** *For a shortcut to changing the First and/or Second Color Readout settings in the Info Options dialog box, click on the first and/or second Eyedropper in the Info palette.*

Now move the mouse pointer over different areas of your image. Notice that the Info palette displays the percentage of each individual duotone ink. This can help you judge the degree of change if you edit the curve in the Duotone Curve dialog box, as well as give you a sense of how the image will print, regardless of the brightness settings on your monitor.

## Saving and Loading Duotone Settings

Use the Save and Load buttons in the Duotone Options dialog box to save duotone curves, ink settings, ink colors, and overprint colors (colors printed on top of each other). To save your settings, reopen the Duotone Options dialog box (select Duotone in the Mode menu), then click on the Save button. In the dialog box, name the file and click Save (PC users: OK). Once you have saved a setting, it can be loaded and applied to other grayscale images that you wish to convert to duotones.

OTE:   *Clicking the Overprint Colors button allows you to adjust screen display so you can see how colors will look when ink combinations are output. When adjusting the overprint colors, it's best to use a printed sample of the overprint colors as a guide.*

## Photoshop's Preset Duotone Curves

If you're hesitant about picking your own colors for creating duotones, you can use Photoshop's preset inks and curves for duotones, tritones, and quadtones. These ink and curve samples are loaded on your hard disk during the Photoshop installation. You can find them in the Duotone Presets (PC users: duotones) folder.

To access the sample set, click the Load button in the Duotone Options dialog box. In the Open dialog box, use the mouse to move to the Duotone Presets (PC users: duotones) folder and open it. Inside it you will see three folders: Duotones, Quadtones, and Tritones (PC users: duotone, quadtone, and tritone). Inside each of these folders are other folders for Gray, PANTONE, and Process (CMYK Color) files. Select and open a Gray, PANTONE, or Process file from within its folder. After you have opened a file, you will be returned to the Duotone Options dialog box. Click OK to apply the settings to your image.

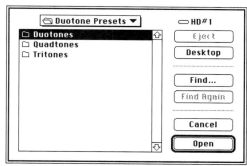

## Creating a Sepia

In the Process Tritones (PC users: process) folder, accessed by opening the Tritones (PC users: tritone) folder found in the Duotone Presets (PC users: duotones) folder, Photoshop has included four different sepia settings for you to use. A *sepia* is a light reddish-brown tone applied to a photograph to give it an aged effect. Try creating a sepia, using the same file you used in the previous section.

1. Open the Duotone Options dialog box by choosing Duotone from the Mode menu.

2. To load one of Photoshop's Sepia settings, click on the Load button in the Duotone Options dialog box. Then open the Duotone Presets (PC users: duotones) folder, and from there select the Tritones (PC users: tritone) folder.

3. From within the Tritones folder, open the Process Tritones (PC users: process) folder.

4. In the list of files, notice BMY Sepia 1, BMY Sepia 2, BMY Sepia 3, and BMY Sepia 4 (PC users: mysepia1.ado, mysepia2.ado, mysepia3.ado, mysepia4.ado). Select and open any one of these Sepia files. Instantly, the settings appear in the Duotone Options dialog box.

5. To preview the changes to your image, click OK in the Duotones Options dialog box.

After you've previewed the settings, you may want to try another sepia setting. Just repeat the above steps to do so.

**n**OTE: *This book's first color insert shows an example of a sepia (image 4). Also, in the Photoshop "User Guide" there are printed samples of several of Photoshop's duotone, tritone, and quadtone curves, including Process Tritone BMY Sepia 1.*

After you've created a sepia image, you may wish to add other objects or images to your document that contain more colors than the ones in your tritone file. In order to do this, you must convert the tritone file to Indexed Color, RGB Color, Lab Color, or CMYK Color.

## Viewing Duotone Colors in Multichannel Mode

Although duotones are one-channel images, Photoshop will let you view the duotone as if you were viewing the two printing plates involved in the printing process. It will also allow you to view tritones and quadtones as if you were viewing three or four printing plates.

In order to view the printing plates, you convert the duotone image to a multichannel image (from the Mode menu, choose Multichannel) for viewing purposes only. You'll then be able to view each duotone ink used in a separate channel in the Channels palette. Once you've examined the channels, choose Undo from the Edit menu to reconvert the image back to Duotone mode.

## Printing a Duotone

Before you print your duotone (or tritone or quadtone) image, you need to specify settings for halftone screen angles, printing resolution, and screen frequency. For more information about these printing options, see Chapter 14.

To print the file, choose Print from the File menu. If you wish to print a composite image, click OK; otherwise, select the Print Separations option and then click OK.

To print a duotone from QuarkXPress or Adobe Illustrator, save the Photoshop file in EPS format, as explained in Appendix A. If you are using PANTONE or any spot colors in your image, you will need to have the same PANTONE names in QuarkXPress and Adobe Illustrator as you do in Photoshop. Since QuarkXPress and Illustrator use "short PANTONE names," the Short PANTONE Names option must be selected in Photoshop's General Preferences dialog box. (Select Preferences from the File menu and then choose General.) If the Short PANTONE Names option wasn't activated when you chose your PANTONE colors, you must return to the Duotone Options dialog box and choose them again or you could type in the correct name.

If you will not be outputting your duotone (or tritone or quadtone) files yourself, consult with your prepress house or print shop to ensure that the images will be output properly.

## CONVERTING FROM GRAYSCALE TO BITMAP

In order to convert an image to black and white, the image must be converted to Bitmap. In Bitmap mode, many of Photoshop's editing options are not available; thus it is often preferable to edit in Grayscale mode and then convert to Bitmap. In this section, you'll learn the different options available when you convert to Bitmap, as well as how to create a mezzotint.

Only grayscale and multichannel images can be converted to Bitmap mode. When you convert from Grayscale mode to Bitmap mode, a dialog box will appear, where you set the Output Resolution of the file and the conversion method. After

## Photoshop in Action

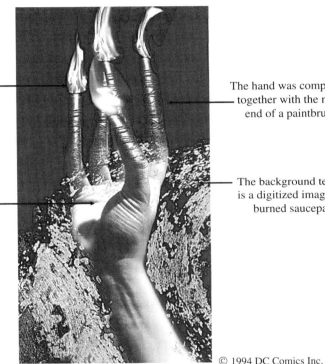

The flame was stretched and distorted using the Image/Distort command.

The hand was composited together with the metal end of a paintbrush.

The hand was tritoned, using the Duotone mode.

The background texture is a digitized image of a burned saucepan.

© 1994 DC Comics Inc.

Artist: Dave McKean     Client: Vertigo/DC Comics

This version of the "Five of Wands" tarot card is one image from a completely digital 78-card Tarot deck, all created by the artist.

Dave began by scanning a photograph of his wife's hands. He composited the hand with the metal end of a paint brush and a digitized image of flames. Using the commands in the Image menu, Dave twirled and stretched the flame to enhance the fire effect. He then created a Tritone out of the hand by converting it to Duotone mode and then selecting three inks to create a tritone. The tritone effect changed the color of the hand to better match the color of the metal paintbrush handle.

The unusual background texture was created in an unorthodox manner—by scanning the bottom of a burned saucepan.

you make your choices, click OK to apply them to your image. Following are descriptions of the five conversion methods.

```
┌─────────────────────── Bitmap ═══════════════════════╗
│ ┌─ Resolution ──────────────────┐  ┌──────────┐      │
│ │                               │  │    OK    │      │
│ │   Input: 72 pixels/inch       │  └──────────┘      │
│ │                               │  ┌──────────┐      │
│ │   Output: [72]  [ pixels/inch ▼] │  │  Cancel  │      │
│ │                               │  └──────────┘      │
│ └───────────────────────────────┘                   │
│ ┌─ Method ──────────────────────┐                   │
│ │   ○ 50% Threshold             │                   │
│ │   ○ Pattern Dither            │                   │
│ │   ◉ Diffusion Dither          │                   │
│ │   ○ Halftone Screen...        │                   │
│ │   ○ Custom Pattern            │                   │
│ └───────────────────────────────┘                   │
└───────────────────────────────────────────────────────┘
```

**50% THRESHOLD**　This conversion creates high-contrast black-and-white images. When the conversion is executed, Photoshop sets the threshold level at 128 pixels. All pixel values in the grayscale image below 128 are converted to black; all pixel values of 128 and greater are converted to white.

**PATTERN DITHER**　In this conversion, the gray levels are changed into geometric patterns composed of black and white dots.

**DIFFUSION DITHER**　This conversion uses a diffusion process to change a pixel to black and white. This diffuses the error between the original grayscale pixels and the black-and-white pixels. The result is a grainy effect.

**HALFTONE SCREEN**　This conversion makes the image appear as if it is a grayscale image printed using a halftone screen. Halftone Screen is typically used to print images on non-PostScript printers.

In the Halftone Screen dialog box, you choose a Frequency, Angle, and Shape for the halftone pattern.

 Acceptable values for the screen frequency (often called "line screen") are from 1.000 to 999.999 for lines per inch, .400 to 400 lines per centimeter. Decimal values are acceptable. Newspapers often use a screen frequency of 85; magazines, 150. If you do not know the correct screen frequency, check with your print shop.

✎   Screen angles from -180 to 180 may be entered.

✎   Shape choices are Round, Diamond, Ellipse, Line, Square, and Cross.

Halftone Screen settings may be saved and loaded using the Save and Load buttons in the dialog box.

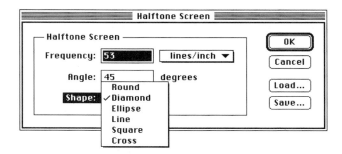

**CUSTOM PATTERN**   This conversion method allows you to apply a custom pattern to a bitmap image. This option will be dimmed unless a custom pattern is defined.

## Creating a Mezzotint

A mezzotint is a black-and-white image that appears to consist of randomly shaped dots. Mezzotints are used to create special effects from black-and-white images. Traditionally, mezzotints were created with halftone screens designed to produce random or unusual dot effects. In Photoshop, composing a mezzotint is fairly easy and can be accomplished in just a few steps.

**OTE:**   *Photoshop's Mezzotint filter can also be used to create mezzotints. For more information, see Chapter 8.*

Before you can create a mezzotint, you must first define a pattern. After you convert from Grayscale mode to Bitmap mode, you apply the pattern to the bitmap image to create the mezzotint. For this exercise, load a pattern from the PostScript Patterns folder (PC users: patterns) in the Brushes & Patterns folder (PC users: brushes).

1. Select File/Open. Mac users: Open the PostScript Patterns folder located in the Brushes & Patterns folder, and open the Mezzotint-shape file. PC users: Open the patterns folder, and load the mezzodot.ai file.

2. After you have opened the mezzotint pattern file, the EPS Rasterizer dialog box appears, containing settings for the Width, Height, Resolution, and Mode of the pattern. Click OK to accept the default settings, and the pattern will appear.

3. Choose Select/All to select the entire pattern. Then choose Define Pattern from the Edit menu and close the file.

**IP:** *Before defining the pattern, you might wish to use the Blur or Blur More command from the Filter/Blur submenu to blur the pattern you will be using in the conversion process, so that the edges of the pattern blend together.*

4. Load the file to which you want to apply the mezzotint. (If the file isn't a grayscale image, you'll need to convert it by choosing Grayscale from the Mode menu. If you wish, you can use the Hands (PC users: hands.jpg) file in the Tutorial folder.

5. Convert the grayscale image to bitmap by choosing Bitmap from the Mode menu.

**IP:** *Before you convert your grayscale image to a bitmap image, there are a few steps you can take to enhance or alter the effect of the mezzotint. Use the Brightness/Contrast command in the Image/Adjust submenu so that the converted bitmap image will display more contrast. This will produce fewer dots and more solid blacks and whites.*

6. When the Bitmap dialog box appears, select the Custom Pattern option. (It will no longer be dimmed because you defined a pattern in steps 2 and 3.) Enter an Output Resolution (the higher the Output Resolution, the better the image pattern quality). The Input Resolution is the resolution of the original file. Click OK.

You should now have a mezzotint on screen. Figure 9-2 shows an image before a mezzotint was applied (Figure 9-3).

Before
creating a
mezzotint
(photograph
by Bob
Barber,
courtesy of
ColorBytes
Inc.)

**FIGURE 9-2**

Bitmap
mezzotint
effect
applied to
photograph
shown in
Figure 9-2

**FIGURE 9-3**

After you've created a mezzotint, you may wish to add color to enhance the image, or create some special effects. To add color to a bitmap image, you must first convert to Grayscale and then to a color mode.

## CONVERTING FROM BITMAP TO GRAYSCALE

When you convert from Bitmap mode to Grayscale mode, the Grayscale dialog box appears, allowing you to enter a Size Ratio from 1 to 16. The Size Ratio is the

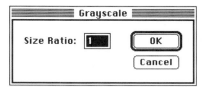

multiple by which you wish to decrease an image's size. For instance, if you enter 2, the final image will be one-half its original size. Enter 3, and the image will decrease to one-third its original size.

## USING SEVERAL MODES TO CREATE A COLORED MEZZOTINT EFFECT

Here's a design tip utilizing a combination of mode changes to create a colored mezzotint effect. To produce the effect, start with a color file, then select your entire image and choose Copy from the Edit menu. Next, create a mezzotint by first defining a pattern, then converting the color image to Grayscale mode, and then from Grayscale to Bitmap mode using the Custom Pattern method. After the mezzotint is created, convert from Bitmap to Grayscale and then to a color mode.

After you've converted from Bitmap to a color mode, make sure a selection tool is activated, then paste the copied colored image. While the pasted image is still floating, use the Lighten mode in the Layers palette to blend the black-and-white mezzotint image with the colored image.

When you paste an image with a selection tool activated and the Lighten mode selected in the Layers palette, only darker pixels in the underlying image are pasted over with corresponding light pixels from the floating image.

## USING THE LAB COLOR MODE

As mentioned earlier in this book, Lab Color is the internal format Photoshop uses while making mode conversions. For instance, when Photoshop converts from RGB Color to CMYK Color, it first converts the RGB colors to Lab Color and then converts from Lab Color to CMYK Color.

# Photoshop in Action

Design Director: Michael Grossman    Art Director: Mark Michaelson

Before converting to Bitmap mode, the Brightness/Contrast command in the Image/Effects submenu was used to increase contrast in the image.

After the image was converted from Bitmap mode to CMYK Color, it was filled with color (yellow) using the Paint Bucket tool.

When converting to Bitmap mode, the Diffusion Dither option was chosen to create the black-and-white dot patterns.

Production: Carlos Lema    Client: Entertainment Weekly

When *Entertainment Weekly* decided to publish an article on the movie "JFK," design director Michael Grossman and art director Mark Michaelson decided to include an image of John F. Kennedy on the magazine's cover. Michael and Carlos Lema worked with a grayscale photo of JFK. To make the grayscale image more interesting, they slightly distorted it using the Skew command in the Image/Effects submenu. Carlos then converted the image to black and white by choosing Bitmap in the Mode menu. From Bitmap mode, the image was converted back to Grayscale and then to CMYK Color, so color could be added and separations created from the image.

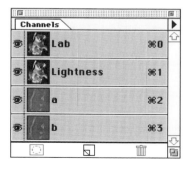

Lab mode images have three channels: a Lightness (or luminance) channel, and two color channels designated as channel a (green to magenta) and channel b (blue to yellow). Use Lab Color mode if you wish to edit an image's lightness independent of its color values. To do this, click to activate the Lightness channel in the Channels palette. In the Lightness channel, you can edit the Lightness values of an image or even select the entire image and paste it into a new file. The copied image in the new file will be a gray version of your original because you copied and pasted only the Lightness component of the image.

As discussed in Chapter 4, Lab is a device-independent color model used to help provide consistent color on various output devices. Thus, Lab Color is also the model used for transferring files between different color systems. For instance, Kodak's Photo CD uses YCC for its images. YCC is Kodak's own version of the Lab Color model; Y is the lightness, or luminance, value, and the two C channels are similar to Photoshop's channels a and b. Thus, when you load a Photo CD image into Photoshop, there should be little or no loss of color data. Since PostScript Level 2 takes advantage of Lab's device-independent color model, Lab is the recommended mode for printing to PostScript Level 2 printers.

## CONCLUSION

As you've read in this chapter, the color modes in Photoshop are vital to producing CMYK separations, duotones, and mezzotints. In upcoming chapters, you'll add alpha channels to an image in order to create masks and special effects. You'll also learn how various dialog boxes allow you to adjust colors in individual channels.

9

Toto je moje babička
na jej chalúpka.

Na stranu je moj dom.

# 10

# CREATING PATHS
# WITH THE PEN TOOL

When you create objects with Photoshop's Pen tool, it's almost like being in two programs at once: a painting program and a drawing program. Unlike Photoshop's painting tools, which paint directly onto the electronic canvas, the Pen tool creates wireframe shapes that exist *above underlying pixels*. This allows the Pen tool in Photoshop to create Bézier curves and intricate objects in much the same way as pen tools in programs such as Adobe Illustrator and Freehand. As in Illustrator and Freehand, objects created by the Pen tool are called *paths*.

## ABOUT PATHS

A path can be a point, a line, or a curve, but usually it's a series of line segments or curve segments, connected by their endpoints. Because they don't lock down onto the background pixels on screen, paths can easily be reshaped, reselected, and moved. They can also be saved and exported to other programs. Thus, paths are unlike any object created with Photoshop's painting tools and unlike any selection created by Photoshop selection tools. Undoubtedly, this is one reason that the Pen tool is not included in the Toolbox and can only be accessed by opening the Paths palette.

Once you open the Paths palette, you'll see that it is not like Photoshop's other palettes. Not only does it function as a miniature toolbox just for the Pen tool, it also provides access to a set of commands that only work with paths. These commands allow paths to be filled, stroked, and turned into selections. Without these commands, the intricate and precise shapes you create with the Pen tool would be useless because most of Photoshop's menu commands and tools have no effect on paths.

Before you can begin to turn paths into artwork and into Photoshop selections, you need to learn some fundamentals. Since most paths created with the Pen tool consist of lines and/or curves, this chapter begins with an explanation of how to create straight and curved path segments, and how to join them together. You'll learn how to change a smooth corner into an angled corner, and how to change a path into a selection (and vice versa).

Then you'll be introduced to the Fill, Stroke, Make Selection, and Save Path commands in the Paths palette. Once you learn how to save paths, you'll be able to reload them when you reload your saved images. If need be, you can convert the paths to selections so that the selections can be used like *masks*. A mask allows you

to protect an area on screen so that you can edit, paint, or apply a filter within it—without affecting surrounding portions of the image.

At the end of the chapter, you'll learn how to create another type of mask, called a *clipping path*. Clipping paths are typically used to silhouette an area and mask out the background image areas, so that only the area within the clipping path will appear when the file is placed into other programs, such as Illustrator, PageMaker, and QuarkXPress.

## PEN TOOL FUNDAMENTALS

In order to use the Pen tool, you must first open the Paths palette by choosing Show Paths from the Window/Palettes submenu.

At first glance, you may find the Paths palette a little confusing because it contains three Pen tools, not one. The first Pen tool—the one with the pen-point icon alone—creates straight or curved paths. The Pen with the plus sign is used to add points to a path, and the Pen with the minus sign is used for subtracting points from a path. The Corner tool lets you turn a smooth corner of a path into a sharp corner, and vice versa. You use the Arrow tool to select and deselect paths and points on paths. The icons at the bottom of the Paths palette are shortcuts for commands that appear in the palette's pop-up menu.

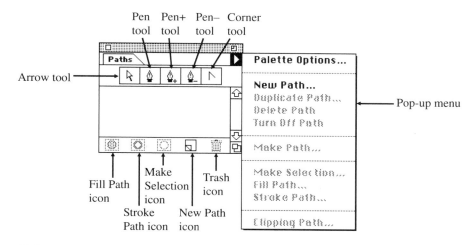

Take a moment to click on the pop-up menu arrow now, and examine the choices offered. Notice the commands Fill Path and Stroke Path. When you wish to fill or stroke a path, you must access these commands from the Paths palette, *not* from the Edit menu.

Another important point to remember is that Photoshop's tools and many of its menu commands will not affect a path you create, unless you convert a path to a selection first.

Before you begin to use the Pen tool, click on the Paths pop-up menu and choose Palette Options. When the Paths Palette Options dialog box appears, click on the second radio button next to the second starfish ( ). This will allow you to see a small thumbnail of your path in the Paths palette (using a large thumbnail could slow down screen display). If you choose None, the thumbnail preview will be turned off. Click OK to close the dialog box. Next, take a look at the Pen Tool Options palette. Open it by double-clicking on the Pen tool (the first pen icon in the Paths palette).

The sole option in the palette is the Rubber Band check box.

```
Pen Tool Options                    ▶
☐ Rubber Band
```

When this option is selected, a path segment trails the Pen tool after an anchor point is created. As you move the Pen tool on screen, the segment is displayed from your last mouse click to the current pen position, as if you were stretching a rubber band. If you don't turn the Rubber Band option on, each path segment appears only after you click the mouse to connect anchor points, rather than as you move the mouse.

Select the Rubber Band option now to turn it on; then click on the palette's Close box (PC users: double-click on the Control icon) to close the palette. In the next sections, you'll see how the Rubber Band previews path segments as you create them.

## Drawing Straight Paths

When you use the Pen tool to create a straight path, you first click to establish a starting point, then move the mouse to another position and click again to establish the endpoint. Each time you click the mouse to establish a starting or ending point, you create an *anchor point*.

In this section, you will learn how to create straight paths by connecting anchor points. To begin, create a new file, 5 inches by 5 inches. To make it easier to execute the following steps, select Show Rulers from the Window menu.

1. If the Pen tool isn't activated, click on it and move it into your document about 2 inches from the top and 1 inch from the left, then click. A small gray or black square appears on screen; this is the first anchor point. In the Paths palette, notice that a Work Path is created.

**OTE:** *If CAPS LOCK is on or if the Tool Cursors Other Tools Precise option is selected in the General Preferences dialog box, the pen pointer will turn into a crosshair. The effects of using the Pen tool are the same whether you work with the pen pointer or the crosshair.*

2. Move the Pen tool to the right, about 1.5 inches away from the first anchor point, and click. This creates a second anchor point, connected to the first anchor point with a straight path segment. Notice that the second anchor point is gray or black and the first one is now hollow. The gray or black anchor point is the one that is currently selected; the hollow anchor point is no longer selected. Also notice that the Work Path thumbnail in the Paths palette updates as you make changes to the Work Path on screen.

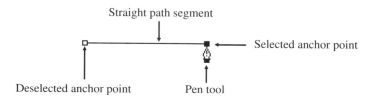

Straight path segment

Selected anchor point

Deselected anchor point

Pen tool

**AUTION:** *When drawing straight paths, don't click and drag the mouse when you click to create an anchor point or you will create a curve rather than a line.*

**3.** Press and hold SHIFT while you create a third anchor point anywhere on your screen.

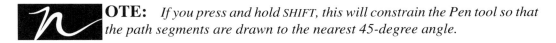

**OTE:** *If you press and hold SHIFT, this will constrain the Pen tool so that the path segments are drawn to the nearest 45-degree angle.*

The path you have just created is called an *open path*. An open path has two endpoints, a beginning and an end. As long as you have an open path and the Pen tool is activated, the Rubber Band will keep stretching from your last anchor point to the Pen tool's current position. Thus every time you click the mouse, you will be extending the open path. To stop Photoshop from extending an open path every time the Pen tool is clicked you can save a path or close a path. You can also click again on the Pen tool in the Paths palette or switch to the Arrow tool and deselect. You'll learn how to save, close, and deselect paths later in this chapter.

If you make a mistake while creating your first path, press DELETE (PC users can also press BACKSPACE) once to erase the last path segment. Be careful not to press DELETE twice; if you do, you will erase the entire Work path. If you press DELETE three times, all paths on the screen will be erased.

If you wish to continue experimenting with the Pen tool, move on to the next section, where you will learn how to deactivate the Pen tool in order to move a segment of a path or the entire path.

## Selecting, Manipulating, Copying, Joining, and Deselecting Paths

After you have created a path, you might want to adjust it by moving an anchor point or the entire path. Or you may need to duplicate the path so you can use it elsewhere in the document.

To complete the following exercise, you will need to have a path created on screen. Either use the path from the previous exercise or create a new path. After you have a path on screen, you'll select an anchor point by first deactivating the Pen tool and then activating the Arrow tool in the Paths palette.

**1.** In the Paths palette, click on the Arrow tool to activate it so you can select an anchor point.

**2.** Position the Arrow tool over the anchor point you wish to adjust, and click to select it. The selected anchor point turns black.

If you don't see anchor points on your path, click anywhere on the path to display the anchor points. If all anchor points on your path are selected, you first need to deselect the path by clicking away from the path. Then click on the path again.

**3.** Drag the selected anchor point to a new location. When you click and drag, the path's angle and size are adjusted according to the angle at which you drag the anchor point and how far you move it. Notice that the path moves as if it were floating on another layer above the background pixels. Also notice that the Work Path in the Paths palette is updated.

**4.** Anchor points can also be moved using the directional arrow keys on your keyboard. Try this: Press the UP, DOWN, LEFT, and RIGHT ARROW keys a few times. The selected anchor point moves in the direction of the keys you press in 1-pixel increments. If you press and hold SHIFT while you press one of the directional arrow keys, the selected anchor point moves in 10-pixel increments.

To move the entire path as a single entity, every anchor point in the path must be selected. One technique for selecting additional anchor points is to SHIFT-click on each unselected anchor point. If the path you need to select is large, press OPTION (PC users: ALT) and click on any segment or anchor point to select the entire path. You can also select an entire path by clicking and dragging over the entire path with the Arrow tool pointer.

**5.** Select the entire path on your screen by pressing OPTION (PC users: ALT) and clicking on any segment or anchor point of the path. All the anchor points turn black or gray when the path is selected. Then click on any segment of the path and drag the path to a new location.

Once a path is selected, you can copy it.

**6.** To copy the path, press and hold OPTION (PC users: ALT) while you click and drag the path with the Arrow tool to a new location. A duplicate of the path will appear. After the duplicate appears, release OPTION (PC users: ALT) and the mouse button.

When you copy a path or create new path segments, Photoshop considers the segments to be subpaths. On screen, you now have two subpaths. To Photoshop, you still have one path on the screen, but the path is composed of the two subpaths. This distinction becomes important

**10**

later in this chapter when you begin to use Paths palette pop-up menu commands, such as Save Path, Fill Path, and Duplicate Path.

7. Now try joining the two subpaths on screen. First reactivate the Pen tool. Click on the endpoint of one subpath, and then click on the endpoint of the second subpath. The two subpaths become one path.

8. To deselect the path, activate the Arrow tool and then click away from the path. All of the anchor points will disappear. Note that the anchor points will reappear when the path is reselected.

After you deselect, you can create another subpath if you'd like.

Now that you understand the basics of drawing and adjusting straight paths, you are ready to learn about working with smooth curves, one of the features for which the Pen tool is best known. Before continuing, delete the path currently on your screen by pressing DELETE once if no anchor points on the path are selected. Press DELETE twice if any anchor point is selected.

## Drawing and Adjusting Curves

The Pen tool's ability to draw smooth curves with precision makes it an invaluable aid when you need to create any curved shape or selection. Drawing a curve with the Pen tool does, however, take some getting used to. You can't just draw a curve on screen as you would with the Lasso tool or one of the painting tools. As you'll see in the next exercise, drawing curves, which slope in different directions, with the Pen tool requires a moving, "seesaw" motion with the mouse.

If you do not have a document open, create a new one now; make it a 72-ppi file, 5 inches by 5 inches. If the rulers and Info palette are not already displayed, select Show Rulers from the Window menu and Show Info from the Window/Palettes submenu to turn these features on.

1. With the Pen tool selected, move the Pen's tip about 1 inch from the left side of your screen and about 2 inches down from the top. Click (an anchor point will be created) and drag down about 1.5 inches to begin the process of creating a curve that faces down. As you drag, the Pen pointer changes to an arrowhead, indicating that you are specifying a direction for the curve.

As you drag, a *direction line* extends in opposite directions from the anchor point, as shown in Figure 10-1. Later, you'll see that the size and angle of the direction line determine the length and slope of the curve. The two endpoints of the direction lines are called *direction points*. By clicking and dragging on either of the direction line's direction points, you can move the direction line, and thus change the shape of a curve. Once the curve is created and deselected, the direction lines and points will disappear.

2. Now create the second anchor point for the curve. Move the Pen tool horizontally to the right about 1 inch from the first anchor point. To create a curve, click and drag straight up, as shown in Figure 10-2. Notice that the curve ends at the new anchor point. As you drag, the curve takes shape and a new direction line appears. Release the mouse after dragging up about 1.5 inches.

Don't worry if you are feeling a little overwhelmed by the all of the lines, points, and other items on your screen. At this stage, the most important concept to remember is that *the curve slopes in the direction in which you drag the mouse.* The first part of the curve you drew slopes

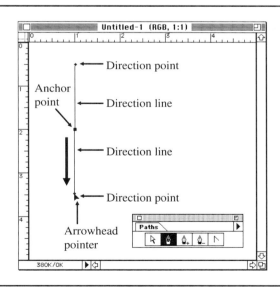

Clicking and dragging downward starts the process of creating the lower part of the curve

**FIGURE 10-1**

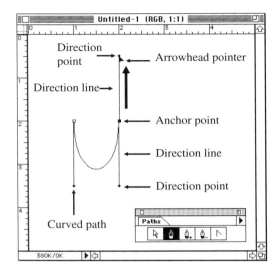

Clicking
and
dragging
upward
creates the
upper part
of the curve

**FIGURE 10-2**

downward (the direction in which you originally dragged the mouse). The second part of the curve slopes upward, the direction in which you dragged in step 2.

*n* **OTE:** *The curve you see on the screen is called a Bézier curve, named after the French mathematician Pierre Bézier, who defined the shape of a curve in mathematical terms with four direction points. By adjusting the direction points, you have complete control of the size and shape of the curve.*

**3.** To adjust the curve, you need to switch from the Pen tool to the Arrow tool. In the Paths palette, click on the Arrow tool. Then click on the bottom-left direction point of the curve and drag to the right. Now click on the bottom-right direction point of the curve and drag to the left. Notice that the curve gets more pointed. If you wish to flatten the curve, drag both bottom direction points in opposite directions.

Another way to adjust the shape of a curve is to click on the curve segment itself with the Arrow tool, and then click and drag. When you do this, both direction lines will adjust themselves according to how you move the curve. You can also change the height and depth of the curve by

clicking and dragging on the direction points to make the direction line larger or smaller. Try these techniques now, in the next step.

4. Click and drag on the bottom left, then bottom right direction points to make both direction lines smaller and thus reduce the size of the curve. After you have experimented with changing the direction lines, click and drag on the direction points to return the direction lines to their original length of about 1.5 inches from the anchor point.

5. Select the Pen tool again and click on the last anchor point you created so that you can create another curve segment.

6. To begin creating the next curve, move the Pen tool 1 inch directly to the right of the last anchor point you created. Then click and drag straight down approximately 1.5 inches, as shown in Figure 10-3.

Notice the smooth transition between the two continuous curves that you have created. The point between the two curves is called a *smooth point*. When the direction line that intersects a smooth anchor point is adjusted, the curves on either side of the smooth point change.

Besides changing the slope of a curve, you can also change its width by moving either one of its anchor points. Try this next.

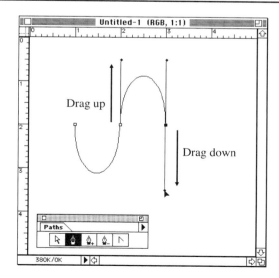

Creating a continuous curved path with the Pen tool

**FIGURE 10-3**

7. Before changing the width of a curve, you must activate the Arrow tool. Here's a shortcut: With the Pen tool selected, press and hold COMMAND (PC users: CTRL) to change the pen pointer (or crosshair) to the Arrow tool.

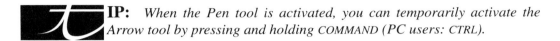

**IP:** *When the Pen tool is activated, you can temporarily activate the Arrow tool by pressing and holding COMMAND (PC users: CTRL).*

8. Change the width of the curve you just drew by clicking on the last anchor point with the Arrow tool and then dragging to the left about .5 inch. Release the mouse to return to the Pen tool.

9. Continue creating curves, alternating between clicking and dragging up, then down. To practice some more, you may want to first press DELETE twice and delete the path currently on screen; then you can start all over again. If you create your first anchor point by dragging up, the first curve will slope upward.

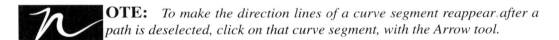

**OTE:** *To make the direction lines of a curve segment reappear after a path is deselected, click on that curve segment, with the Arrow tool.*

10. When you are done practicing, clear the screen by pressing DELETE twice. If you have more than one subpath on screen, press DELETE three times.

## Drawing Scalloped Curves

You can also draw curves so that they all point in the same direction. These *scalloped curves* can be used to create curved border effects around images. Scalloped curves cannot be drawn like the continuous curves you just created. When you create scalloped curves, you create a *corner point* in order to change the direction in which the curve is drawn. As you'll see in the following exercise, the direction lines that stem from corner points do not work the same as direction lines that bisect smooth points: A corner point's direction line controls only one side of one curve.

1. To create the first curve, begin by positioning the Pen tool about .5 inch from the left side of your document window and about 2 inches from the top. The first curve you create will point upward, so start by clicking and dragging straight up about 1 inch.

2. Move the mouse horizontally to the right about 1.5 inches from the last anchor point. Click and drag straight down about 1 inch.

   The next curve you create will point in the same direction as the first curve. To accomplish this, you need to create a corner point between the curves.

3. To create a corner point, press and hold OPTION (PC users: ALT) while you click on the anchor point that you created in step 2. Notice that one of the direction lines disappears. Continue to keep OPTION (PC users: ALT) pressed while you drag diagonally up to the right about 1 inch from the anchor point, to create a new direction line. Release OPTION (PC users: ALT). This direction line will allow you to draw the next curve in the same direction as the line you just created.

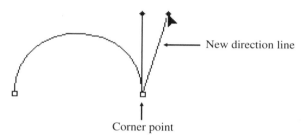

New direction line

Corner point

4. To create the second curve, move the Pen tool directly to the right about 1.5 inches away from the last anchor point. This will be the endpoint of the curve that you are about to create. Click and drag straight down about 1 inch, and a curve will appear.

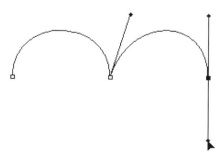

**10**

5. To create the third scalloped curve, repeat the technique in steps 3 and 4. Position the mouse over the last anchor point you created, press OPTION (PC users: ALT), and click and drag diagonally up to create a new

direction line. Move the mouse about 1.5 inches to the right of the anchor point, and then click and drag down about 1 inch to create the curve.

6. When you are ready, delete the path currently on screen by pressing DELETE twice.

Creating a corner point to control the direction of a curve also enables you to create paths in which straight segments are joined to curves, as explained next.

## Connecting Curves and Straight Paths

When you are using the Pen tool and working with paths, you'll often need to connect a line to a curve or a curve to a line. Shapes made of both curves and lines are all around you: vases, bottles, paddles, and so on. When you want to trace any of these shapes with the Pen tool or create them from scratch, you'll need to master the Pen tool techniques described in the following exercise.

Start by creating a curve and connecting a line segment to it.

1. If the Pen tool is not activated, select it in the Paths palette. Position the Pen tool about 1 inch from the left side of the screen and about 2 inches from the top. To begin, click and drag straight up about 1 inch.

2. To create the curve, move the mouse 1 inch to the right from the first anchor point; then click and drag downward about 1 inch.

3. Next, create the corner point that will allow you to connect this curve to a line. Press OPTION (PC users: ALT) and click once on the last anchor point you created. Notice that the bottom direction line disappears. Release the mouse and OPTION (PC users: ALT).

4. To create a line that connects to the curve, move the Pen tool to the right horizontally about 1 inch from the curve's second anchor point, and click. Remember, if you want to create a line at an angle of 45 degrees (or

increments thereof), you can press and hold SHIFT while you click. The curve is now connected to a line.

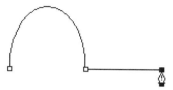

**5.** Now clear your screen by pressing DELETE twice, and try creating a line that connects it to a curve.

**6.** Create a line segment about 1 inch long by connecting two anchor points. If you need to review the steps to create line segments, refer to the earlier section "Drawing Straight Paths."

**7.** Use the OPTION (PC users: ALT) key to create a corner point so the line can be connected to a curve. Press and hold OPTION (PC users: ALT) while you click on the last anchor point you created and then drag diagonally upward to the right about 1 inch. When the direction line is created, release the OPTION (PC users: ALT) key and the mouse button.

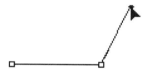

**8.** Now, to create a curve that connects to the line, move the Pen tool horizontally about 1 inch to the right of the corner point. Then click and drag straight down about 1 inch. If you need to adjust the curve, use the Arrow tool.

**10**

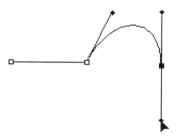

**9.** When you are finished practicing, clear the screen by pressing DELETE twice. If you have more than one path on screen, press three times.

## Creating a Closed Path

The next technique you will learn is how to close a path. A *closed path* is a path that ends at its starting point. Once a path is closed, you can move the pen pointer away from it and create other paths. In this next exercise, you will create a closed path in the shape of a triangle by connecting three anchor points.

If you don't have a document open on screen, create a new one, 5 inches by 5 inches. Make sure that the rulers and Info palette are displayed.

1. Activate the Pen tool in the Paths palette, and move the Pen tool up toward the top-middle part of the document. Using the ruler and Info palette as guides, position the Pen tool about 2.5 inches from the left side of the document window and about .5 inch down from the top. Click the mouse to create the first anchor point of the triangle.

2. To create a second anchor point, move the Pen tool diagonally down and left about 2 inches (in the Info palette, the x-axis is approximately 1.00 and the y-axis is approximately 2.5) and then click. This creates a line segment from the first anchor point to the second anchor point.

3. To create a third anchor point, move the Pen tool horizontally to the right of the second anchor point about 3 inches, and click. This creates a line segment from the second anchor point to the third anchor point.

4. To close the path, you must return to the starting point of the triangle. Move the Pen tool to the first anchor point. You will see a small loop at the bottom-right side of the Pen tool; this indicates that you have returned to your starting point. Click the mouse and the path will be closed. When you click on the last anchor point notice that the Info palette displays angle and distance readouts.

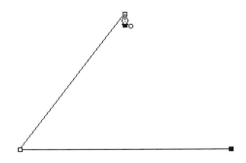

Leave the triangle displayed on your screen and proceed to the next section, which explains how adding, subtracting, and editing points on a path can change its shape.

## Adding/Subtracting Points and Switching Between a Smooth Point and a Corner Point

You've learned how to adjust a path by moving anchor and direction points. Paths can also be reshaped by adding or subtracting anchor points, and by converting smooth points to corner points, and vice versa. By combining these techniques with your Pen-drawing skills, you will be able to edit the shape of most any path.

In this next exercise, you will transform the triangular path you created in the previous section into a diamond shape, and then back to a triangle. If you do not have the triangle from the previous section on screen, create one in the middle of your document window now. You'll start by activating the Pen+ tool, which adds anchor points.

1. With the triangular path displayed, activate the Pen+ tool in the Paths palette.

2. To transform the triangle into a diamond, you need to add an anchor point to the base of the triangle. Position the Pen+ tool in the middle of the base of the triangle. Click the mouse, and a new anchor point is added to the path at the point where you clicked.

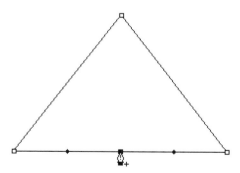

**10**

3. To move the new anchor point down to begin creating the diamond shape, you need switch from the Pen+ pointer to the Arrow tool. Rather than doing this by clicking in the Paths palette and switching tools, you can use the keyboard shortcut: Press and hold COMMAND (PC users: CTRL), and the Pen+ tool changes to the Arrow tool.

**4.** Once you've switched from the Pen+ pointer to the Arrow tool, click on the new anchor point you created in step 2 and drag it downward about 2 inches, so that the triangle begins to look like a diamond.

**5.** Notice that the new point is a smooth point. You can turn the round edge into a corner point by using the Corner tool in the Paths palette. Select the Corner tool, and then click on the smooth point, as shown in Figure 10-4a. The smooth corner point changes to a sharply angled corner point, as shown in Figure 10-4b.

**OTE:** *With any of the Pen tools activated, Mac users can press OPTION-CONTROL and click to change a smooth point to a corner point, and vice versa. When the Arrow tool is activated (instead of a Pen tool), Mac users can press the CONTROL key and click to switch between smooth and corner points.*

Your diamond is now finished. Suppose, though, that you've changed your mind and want the diamond switched back into a triangle. To do this, you will need to subtract the last anchor point you created.

**6.** To delete the last anchor point you created, click on the Pen- tool. Then click on the anchor point you used to create the diamond. The corner point disappears, and the diamond shape immediately snaps back into a triangle.

(a) Use the Corner tool to convert a smooth point to a corner point; (b) The path after the smooth point is converted to a corner point

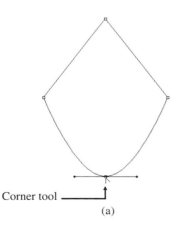

Corner tool

(a)

(b)

**FIGURE 10-4**

**IP:**   *When the Arrow tool is activated, there is a keyboard shortcut for adding and deleting anchor points. To add an anchor point, press and hold* COMMAND-OPTION *(PC users:* CTRL-ALT*) while you click on a segment. To delete an anchor point, press and hold* COMMAND-OPTION *(PC users:* CTRL-ALT*) while you click on the anchor point you want to delete. Mac users: When the Pen tool is activated (not the Arrow tool!), you can also add or delete anchor points from a path by pressing* CONTROL *and clicking.*

The ability to convert from smooth points to corner points and corner points to smooth points allows you to quickly edit paths and change their shapes. For example, you can outline a curved object by first connecting straight segments, and then generate the necessary curves by changing corner points into smooth points.

The following exercise demonstrates how you can transform a sharply cornered wedge into a heart shape by changing corner points to smooth points. Before proceeding, delete the triangle you now have on screen, by pressing DELETE twice.

1. Using the Pen tool, create and connect four anchor points to create a wedge shape. To make the wedge, start by creating an anchor point in the upper-left corner of your screen. Create the next anchor point at the bottom of your screen, then create another one in the upper-right corner. Continue creating the closed path so that it looks like this one:

2. Now transform the two top corner points of the wedge to smooth corner points. Start by activating the Corner tool in the Paths palette.

**3.** Position the Corner tool on the top-left corner point, and click and drag downward to the left until a curve is created. Notice that as you drag, the Corner tool changes to an arrowhead pointer because a direction line for the curve is being created.

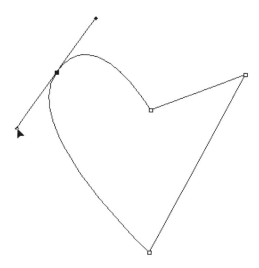

**4.** To create a curve out of the top-right corner point, click and drag upward to the left on this corner point with the Corner tool. Stop when a curve is created.

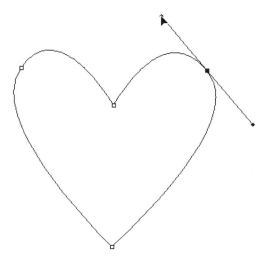

**5.** If you wish to make adjustments to the curves of the heart, click and drag on the curves' direction points, using the Arrow tool.

**6.** At this point, you may wish to fill, stroke, or save the heart path that you just created. If so, turn to the section, "Filling and Stroking Paths and Subpaths" or to the section, "Saving, Hiding, Loading, and Deleting Paths" later in this chapter. Otherwise, delete the heart path from the screen and proceed to the next section to learn how to convert a path into a selection.

## Converting a Path into a Selection

As you work with paths, you'll often need to convert them to selections. Once a selection border is created from the path, you'll be able to use all of Photoshop's commands that affect selections.

In this exercise you'll learn how to a turn path into a selection and to merge both a path and a selection together into one selection. To start, if you don't have a blank document on screen, create a new file, 5 inches by 5 inches.

**1.** Start by using the Pen tool to create a rectangular *path*, approximately 2.5 inches by 2 inches.

**2.** Use the Marquee tool to create a circular *selection* that overlaps the rectangular path.

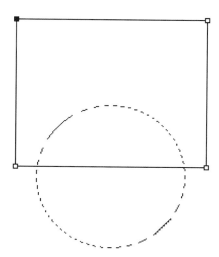

3. Open the pop-up menu in the Paths palette, and choose Make Selection. This opens the Make Selection dialog box, where you specify the type of selection you want to create from any paths or selections on screen. You can also open the Make Selection dialog box by pressing OPTION (PC users: ALT) and clicking on the Make Selection icon ( ⬚ ) in the Paths palette.

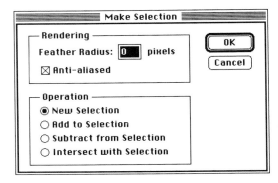

In the Make Selection dialog box, the Feather Radius and Anti-aliased options function exactly as they do with Photoshop's selection tools. Use the Operation options to specify how you want the selection to be created. The Operations options are as follows:

*New Selection*   Creates a selection from the path only. In the example here, only the rectangular path would be turned into a selection.

*Add to Selection*   Adds the area specified by the path to the current selection on screen. In the example here, a selection would be created from both the rectangle and circle together.

*Subtract from Selection*   Removes a path from a selection. In the example here, the rectangular area that overlaps the circle would be removed from the circular selection border.

*Intersect with Selection*   Creates a selection from the area where the path and selection overlap. In the example here, the selection would be transformed into one selection, including only the overlapping areas of the rectangle and circle.

Try each of these options with the example on your screen. First select the New Selection radio button and then click OK. Photoshop creates a selection from the rectangle only. Choose Edit/Undo to remove the selection. Now return to the Make Selection dialog box to try out any of the other options.

*n* **OTE:** *Press ENTER on the numeric keypad to quickly create a selection out of a path. You can also convert a path into a selection by clicking on the Make Selection icon in the Paths palette or by clicking and dragging the path name over the Make Selection icon. When the Make Selection icon changes color, release the mouse.*

## Converting a Selection into a Path

Now that you've seen how Photoshop creates a selection out of a path, let's take a look at how to transform a selection into a path. Occasionally, it's easier to create a path from a selection, rather than constructing it from scratch with the Pen. For example, you might wish to create a path from an intricate Magic Wand selection that would take too much time to create using the Pen tool. To convert a selection into a path, you use the Make Path command in the Paths palette.

The following exercise demonstrates how Photoshop creates anchor points when converting a selection border into a path. You can change any selection into a path, but in this exercise you'll work with a figure eight because the path will require numerous anchor points. Begin by clearing the screen of all selections by choosing None from the Select menu. Then remove all paths by pressing DELETE three times.

1. Activate the Lasso tool; then click and drag to create a figure eight.

2. To turn the figure-eight selection border into a path, select Make Path from the pop-up menu in the Paths palette.

**10**

The Make Path dialog box contains a field for setting the Tolerance value, which determines the number of anchor points the path will include. The default Tolerance value is 2 pixels; you can specify from .5 to 10 pixels. If you enter a high Tolerance value, fewer anchor points will be used and the resulting path will be smoother. Select a low Tolerance, and more anchor points will be used, resulting in a bumpier path.

```
╔═══════════════════════════════════╗
║          Make Path                ║
║                                   ║
║   Tolerance: [2.0] pixels   ┌──────┐ ║
║                             │  OK  │ ║
║                             └──────┘ ║
║                             ┌──────┐ ║
║                             │Cancel│ ║
║                             └──────┘ ║
╚═══════════════════════════════════╝
```

**3.** In the Make Path dialog box, type **1** in the Tolerance field and click OK. When the path appears, click on it with the Arrow tool (from the Paths palette) so you can examine the number of anchor points that were created. Count the number of anchor points.

**4.** Now try a higher Tolerance setting and observe the results. First, return to a selection on screen by clicking on the Make Selection icon in the Paths palette. Then reopen the Make Path dialog box. Enter **10** as the Tolerance setting and click OK. When the path appears, click on it with the Arrow tool and count the number of anchor points. Observe that the higher Tolerance value results in fewer anchor points.

**C**AUTION: *Converting selections to paths sometimes creates paths that are too complicated for printers to print. In this situation, your best bet is to delete some anchor points with the Pen- tool or re-create the path using a higher Tolerance setting.*

**T**IP: *A shortcut for converting a selection into a path is to make a selection on screen, then click on the Make Selection icon at the bottom of the Paths palette and drag this icon over the New Paths icon.*

You've now learned the fundamental techniques required to work with the Paths palette, the Pen tools, and the Arrow tool. In the next section, you'll learn how to fill or stroke a path with a color or pattern.

## FILLING AND STROKING PATHS AND SUBPATHS

Photoshop allows you to fill a path with the foreground color or with a pattern, and from a Snapshot or the last saved version of the file. When you stroke a path or fill a path, Photoshop strokes or fills the entire path, including all subpaths— non-contiguous joined segments. When you stroke a path, the stroke width is determined by the current brush size of the stroking tool.

**Artist:** Robert Bowen and Ryszard Horowitz
**Client:** Horowitz+Bowen Studio

1

This fantastic image was created as an experiment to explore digital design possibilities. The idea for the image came from the collaborative efforts of both Ryszard and Bob, who carefully plan and execute each image they create so it cohesively reflects a uniform idea. Before starting in Photoshop, several pencil sketches were first created by Ryszard and Bob.

The image is comprised of various digitized images from photographs taken by both

artists. The fish, mountains, moon, and baby were all photographed separately. The eagle is a digitized image of a live eagle taken in a studio. The splash is an image taken of water being pumped into an aquarium. A photograph of a Plexiglas tray pouring water is the basis of the cuboidal block pouring water into the lake.

To create the final image, Bob worked in Photoshop on a Silicon Graphics Indy and an Apple Macintosh computer. He used Alias' Power Maker on the Indy to map the mountains and the lake to the cuboidal cube. With Ryszard's collaboration, Bob created several low-res versions until they decided on the final image. Next, Bob enlarged the low-res image. He carefully used the Info palette with the Line tool as a measurement instrument to measure angles and distances in the low-res image so he could replicate them in the high-res version.

When creating the image, Bob used the Pen tool to outline the eagle. To blend images together, Bob often used the Select/Border command to place a selection border around an image. Then he would blend the selection into its surroundings with the Gaussian Blur filter and Photoshop's Lighten or Darken modes. Another blending technique Bob used was to paint using the Rubber Stamp tool's From Saved option.

# The Photoshop Portfolio

**2** Although it may not be apparent, much of the power of this fascinating image comes from placing one layer on top of another, then erasing parts of the different layers. Sanjay started by creating a low-res version of the image to show the client, Adobe Systems, Inc. To build this image, he placed different scanned images of photographs he had taken into layers. The sky, brick wall with ivy, a building with windows and an alley, the inner arch, the outer arch and a car with wheels are all separate layers. To build the final image, Sanjay carefully blended the layers together by hiding or revealing elements from each layer. For more information on blending layers together, see Chapter 12.

Sanjay started with the Background layer, a flat brick wall with ivy on it. To add more ivy to the brick wall, he first selected the ivy using the Select/Color Range command; then he copied and pasted the ivy selection. When editing the sky, Sanjay created a channel, then used the Gradient tool to create a blend in the channel. Next, he loaded the selection from the channel. Then, he darkened and added yellow to the sky with the Image/Adjust/Curves command. Finally, he added motion to the sky by using the Motion Blur filter. The outer arches that appear in the brick wall are really the same arch that was copied and pasted several times. Visible within each arch is another image appearing from a different layer. The wheels were originally part of an image of a road and a car. Sanjay spread out the distance between the wheels by cutting and pasting. Then, he selected the wheels and the road, and pasted them into a new layer in the final image.

**3** Sanjay began this cover for a children's dictionary by creating the three-dimensional interior of the "sky" box from a digitized image of a sky. To create the top, bottom and sides of the box, he copied and pasted the sky, then used the Image/Effects/Scale and Perspective commands. Along the edges and corners, he used the Dodge and Burn tools to add shadows and contrast to enhance the sense of depth.

To increase contrast in the zebra, Sanjay used the Image/Adjust/Curves command. Next, he needed to add detail because the original zebra's underside was too dark. To lighten the dark areas, he copied and pasted different white areas using partial opacities. To lighten the shadow areas in the neck, he used the painting tools. To produce the shadow for the zebra, he first used the Pen tool to create a path around the zebra, then converted the path into a feathered selection. He shifted the zebra selection to the position where he wanted the shadow. Then he darkened the selected area slightly by using the Image/Adjust/Curves command. Next, he silhouetted the apple using the Pen tool. Then, he copied and pasted the apple into the final image. Using the Dodge tool, he lightened the edges of the right side of the apple to simulate a light source. The shadow for the apple was created in the same way as the shadow for the zebra.

The last step was to create the text. The flat planes around the text were created in alpha channels, where they were scaled and rotated. Selections were then loaded from the alpha channels and filled with the appropriate colors to produce yellow and red flat planes around the type. The Dodge and Burn tools were used to produce the beveled edge effect for the type. Both Sanjay and Clifford Stolze worked together on the type usage.

**2**

**3**

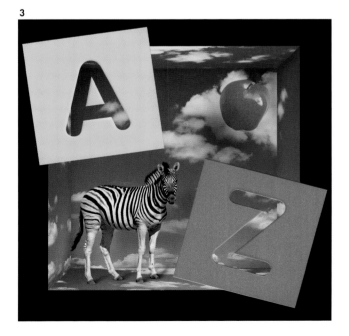

**2**
**Artist:** Sanjay Kothari
**Client:** Adobe Systems Incorporated

**3**
**Artist:** Sanjay Kothari
**Client:** Houghton Mifflin Co.

# The Photoshop Portfolio

**4** Dave started the design for this Alice Cooper CD cover after Alice gave Dave some copies of old sideshow posters. Alice provided the posters to give Dave an idea of the faded yellow look he wanted for the cover. Dave then made several small acrylic paintings, and digitized them into Photoshop. The digitized acrylic images, 19th century letters, along with an inverted version of smoke from one of the old posters were combined to create the final image. When blending the images together, Dave first selected different image elements with the Marquee and other selection tools, then copied and pasted them into the final image. When necessary, he used a selection tool with a feathering option to soften selection edges. To achieve the overlay effect between images, he changed Composite Control settings. To learn more about Composite Control settings, see Chapter 12.

The photograph of Alice Cooper was taken by Dean Karr in Los Angeles. This image was composited with the background using the Lighten mode, so that the lighter burning smoke would show through.

**5** To create this intriguing book cover, Dave started with a 4-by-5-inch transparency of the boy in the chair, the collaged tower, and the puppet. At first, the image didn't look lively enough, so Dave scanned the transparency and about thirty other images along with fragments of photos, textures, and type. Then, he rebuilt the entire image from scratch giving it more of an "out of kilter" feel. When working, Dave used every one of Photoshop's selection tools, copying and pasting the various elements into the final image. To adjust the colors, he used the Image/Adjust submenu commands: Curves, Levels, Color Balance, Hue/Saturation. When blending the different elements together, he changed Composite Control settings so he could control just what range of pixels would appear in the final image. Finally, to add depth and energy, he applied sharpening and blurring filters to different image areas.

Dave says, "Although I love photography, this gravity-less digital space has become my favorite reason to use a computer."

**6** Dave started by making a quick painted version of the face using acrylics and ink. He digitized the painted sketch to rough out where the light and shadow areas would be. Next, he reshot old family photos, using a projected slide as a light source. He then scanned and composited these images into appropriate light and dark areas. While working, he blended the images together by changing Composite Control settings. Occasionally, he would distort the images using various Image/Effects submenu commands—Skew, Perspective and Distort—to suggest contours of the face. The mouth area is a photo of some peeling paint. Very little of the original painting was left visible.

**4**

**5**

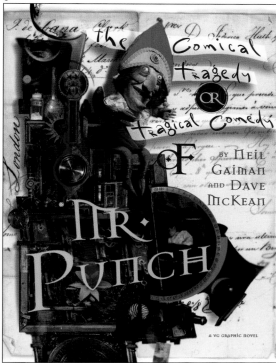

**6**

**4**
**Artist:** Dave McKean
**Client:** Sony Music Entertainment Inc./Epic Records

**5**
**Artist:** Dave McKean
**Client:** Victor Gollancz

**6**
**Artist:** Dave McKean
**Client:** Vertigo/DC Comics

# The Photoshop Portfolio

**7**   The special effects company, Matte World Digital, created this anthropomorphic rock formation for the Hollywood movie "City Slickers II." Digital Matte Artist Chris Evans began the process of creating the Frozen People image by photographing several slides at Arches National Park in Utah. In Photoshop, Chris started by creating a low-res version of the image, primarily by selecting, cutting and pasting parts of the digitized images of the Arches slides. After receiving approval from the film's director, Special Effects Supervisor Paul Rivera rescanned the original images at a high resolution suitable for recording and transferring to film. When working on the high-res image, Chris and Paul zoomed-in to smooth image edges with Photoshop's painting tools. To help blend the rocks together they created masks of the rocks in an alpha channel. Using the Paintbrush tool, they smoothed the mask edges. After fine-tuning the mask edges, they loaded the selection from the alpha channel using the Select/Load Selection command. Once the selections were loaded, they pasted the rock image data into the selection.

When the Photoshop work was complete, the image was exported to a Silicon Graphics computer where animation was added to make the clouds drift by.

**8,9**   "The City of the Future" is a still from Producer/Director Craig Barron's pilot for the television series "Unknown Worlds." The image was created by combining film footage of the Fresno City Hall in California (Image 8) and compositing it with a digital matte painting, a 3-D rotating Earth globe, and a live-action shot of actor James Bozian.

The 35mm footage of the city hall was transferred to Exabyte tape for compositing on a Macintosh computer, using Cosa After Effects. This element was composited with a digital matte painting of futuristic buildings created by Digital Matte Artist, Chris Evans. To smoothly blend the two images together, Digital Effects Supervisor Paul Rivera first created a mask of the image in an alpha channel. After editing the mask in the alpha channel, he loaded it back into the final image. Paul created the holographic globe with image maps made in Photoshop. He then rendered it with a transparent alpha channel in Infini-D, a three-dimensional modeling program. Paul rendered the image as a QuickTime element in an alpha channel, then he imported it into Cosa After Effects to be composited with the painting and the live-action shot. The final image was transferred back to Exabyte tape, then to D1 tape for final editing using Knoll Software's transfer utility, Missing Link. Missing Link allows desktop video users to read and write images to an Exabyte 8mm tape drive in Abekas NTSC and PAL formats.

**7**

**8**

**9**

# The Photoshop Portfolio

**10** This image is a frame from a CD-ROM presentation created to publicize the ABC-TV Miniseries "Stephen King's, The Stand." It was the first Multimedia press kit of its kind produced for an entertainment program. The CD-ROM was created using Adobe Photoshop, Adobe Premiere and MacroMedia Director. At the direction of ABC-TV's Directors of Photography, Peter Murray and Brent Petersen, freelance artist Diane Becker executed the Photoshop work. To begin, Diane scanned a slide of the background, which is a desert scene photographed by Mark Seliger. Next, the logo, "Stephen King's, The Stand," created by Grey Entertainment, was scanned, copied and pasted into the desert background. Diane also scanned the ABC logo and placed it into the background scene. The final items which were needed for the screens were the 3-dimensional buttons. These were created using alpha channels. One alpha channel was used to create the highlight area; another alpha channel was used to create the shadow area. For more information on creating 3-dimensional effects using alpha channels, see Chapter 11. The text in the buttons were created using the Type tool.

**11** Dan created this light-hearted image from photographs he shot that were later digitized onto a Photo-CD. The cats in the window and the footsteps in the sand were photographed (in black and white) in upstate New York. The tuba player was photographed on a busy street in New Orleans. The background image is a photograph of Morro Bay in California. Dan started creating this image by selecting the sand area with a feathered Lasso. Then, he copied the sand and pasted it into the bay image. Next, he selected the tuba player with the Pen tool and copied and pasted him into the scene. He positioned and sized the tuba player to fit in with the shadowy footsteps in the sand, leaving mysterious shadows from where another person once stood on the right. He selected the windows with cats, and pasted them one at a time with the Screen compositing mode, so that the dark parts of the windows would appear primarily transparent. Next, he created an alpha channel to build a selection that would select most of the sky fading out into the tops of the windows. He pasted a new photo with more dramatic clouds into the selection.

**12** Nik started creating this cover by choosing a stock image snow scene from Allstock. In the original snow scene image, photographed by Carr Clifton, snow and melting ice covered portions of the ice surface, and branches from the shoreline were seen in the foreground. Nik removed these by making a feathered selection of the clear ice and then copying it over the area that had the snow, melting ice and branches. Next, he created five Olympic ring paths using the Pen tool. Once he created the rings, he colored the Pen path with a neon glow effect using the Path's palette Stroke command in successive applications. He began with a very wide brush at a very low opacity followed up by narrower brush strokes at heavier opacities.

Oksana was photographed in a studio (not on ice) in Los Angeles, by Philip Saltonstall. When the photo was taken, both of Oksana's skates were protected by blade guards. Since these would be removed in Photoshop, a photo was taken of Oksana's skates without the guards. Later in Photoshop, Nik removed the guards by merging and cloning the different skate images together. When working on the right skate he used the Rubber Stamp's From Saved command to return Oksana's right thumb to the image. After editing the skates, Nick used the Pen tool to silhouette Oksana, converted the Path into a selection and pasted Oksana into the final image.

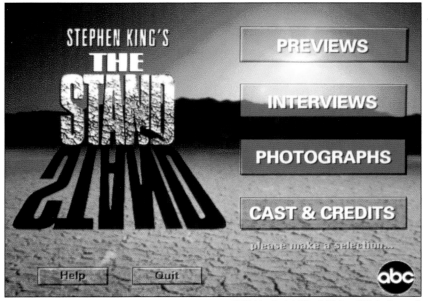

**10**
**Artist:** ABC Television Photo Dept.
**Client:** Capital Cities/ABC, Inc.

**11**
**Artist:** Dan Doerner
**Client:** Self promotion

**12**
**Artist:** Nik Kleinberg
**Client:** Sports Illustrated for Kids

**11**

**12**

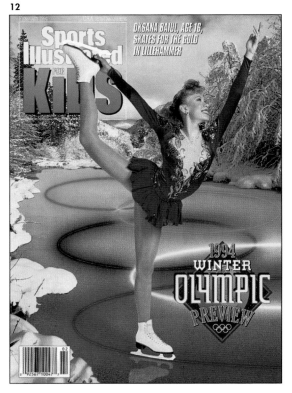

# The Photoshop Portfolio

**13** Bart Simpson and Photoshop were called in to action to create this invitation announcing KTTV's Fox Television fall schedule. Art Director August Santistevan began the image by creating a linear blend in the background using the Gradient tool. After he created the gradation, he added texture to the background by applying the Add Noise filter with the Median setting. Then he applied the Facet filter.

Next, he scanned a black-and-white image of Bart, then converted it to CMYK Color so he could work in process colors. August then used the Magic Wand to select areas, then filled the areas with colors. When Bart was complete, he drew the banners with the Lasso tool. Then he stroked these selections with black. The last step was to create the logos in the banners. He scanned the logos that appear in the banners, then copied and pasted them into the final image. The Married with Children text was created using Photoshop's Type tool.

**14** This Big Apple image was created for the cover of the New York Macintosh Users Group magazine. Wendy started by first creating a pencil sketch of the final image. After the sketch was approved, she scanned it into Photoshop. The image was saved as a PICT file so she could use it as a template in Illustrator. In Illustrator she created the background. She then placed the Illustrator file into Photoshop. The image inside the monitor is a screen shot. It was placed into the monitor using Photoshop's Edit/Paste Into command.

Wendy created the filmstrip and surfer in Adobe Dimensions and then placed it into Photoshop. She created the type, mouse, stem and leaves of the apple, and the surfer in Adobe Dimensions and then placed them into Photoshop. In Photoshop, she created shadows for various elements to give the illustration depth. Several shadows were created by selecting an area, then painting around the object with the Airbrush tool using a 300-pixel-wide brush with an opacity of 8%. As she worked her way towards the object, she decreased the brush size and increased opacity. Other shadows were created using alpha channels. (To learn how to create shadows using alpha channels, see Chapter 11.) To create the bubbles and spheres she used KPT's Lens Flare medium filter.

**15** This wild image is a photograph of model Gregory Melendrez taken by Greg Weiner. To create the unusual mix of colors, Bob Sekelsky first selected various areas of the image. Next, he made color adjustments to these areas using the Curves, Hue/Saturation, and Color Balance commands from the Image/Adjust submenu. To create the unusual color effect, Bob posterized the image using the Image/Adjust/Curves command. (For more information on posterizing using the Curves command, see Chapter 13.)

The glow for the prize was created in an alpha channel, blurred with a filter and feathered. The channel was loaded into the image using the Select/Load Selection command, then filled with yellow. The letters BDA were typeset in Adobe Illustrator and placed over the model's gloves. The static in the sun glasses was a scan of video static. The static was copied then pasted into the lenses, and the numbers "94" were created in Illustrator and placed on top of the static.

13

**13**
**Artist:** August Santistevan
**Client:** KTTV FOX Television

**14**
**Artist:** Wendy Grossman
**Client:** New York Macintosh Users Group

**15**
**Creative Director:** George Pierson
**Designer:** Mark Scheider
**Electronic Retouching:** Bob Sekelsky
**Client:** Broadcast Design Association

14

15

**16** Marc used three layers to create this image. Layer 1 is the manipulated face and fingers. Layer 2 is the computer chip in the upper-left corner. In order to produce the fade-out effect in the computer chip he used a Layer Mask. (See Chapter 12 for a description of how to use Layer Masks.) To create the circle over the fingers, he created a selection and then copied it into a new layer, Layer 3. In this layer, he changed the opacity and mode to produce the transparent effect.

Then he created a rectangular selection over the eyes of the person at the bottom of the image. He copied and pasted the selection. While the selection was in float mode, he added green to the selected area using the Hue/Saturation command in the Image/Adjust submenu.

The numbers at the bottom are from a telephone keypad that was made into a pattern. In order to produce the fade-out effect, he used a Layer Mask. To apply the neon effect to the numbers 0,1 he used KPT's Gradient Path filter. To attain the overall red color of the image Marc used the Indexed Color mode.

**17** James generally starts all his images by sketching his ideas out in pencil on grid paper. After consulting with Art Director Charles Drucker, James turned to the computer to create the Globe image. James created the globes by first rendering each element separately in Crystal Topas against a black background. He used a black background so that he could easily eliminate extraneous edge pixels in Photoshop with the Select/Matting/Remove Black Matte command. (To learn more about the Select/Matting/Remove Black Matte command, see Chapter 3.) In Topas, he rendered each globe using a scanned photo texture map of the computer products seen in the globes. Then, he wrapped the texture maps around the globe models. The tile floor was also created in Topas. The sky was painted in Fractal Design Painter. After creating the separate elements, James placed the images into Photoshop where he carefully trimmed away extraneous black edge pixels. Then, he selected the elements with different selection tools before pasting them into the background image. To soften the image and create an early morning misty effect, he applied the Aldus Gallery Effects Diffuse Glow filter. After applying the filter, he pasted in the globes so that they would remain crystal clear.

**18** James started creating the Droid in the same manner as the Globes image (Image 17), by sketching his ideas in pencil and consulting with Art Director Charles Drucker. Both James and Charles tried out different versions until they arrived at a solution they both agreed upon. When time permitted, color comps were created, but often the colors were discussed on the phone as the image developed. He started the image by creating the 3-D background airport scene in Topas. The sky, the city, and the tarmac were created in Painter X2. Since the Droid was to be the focus of the image, it required the most attention. James started by scanning a sketch, then painted over it in Fractal Design Painter. He dropped the Droid and other images into the background by selecting with the Magic Wand tool with a low tolerance setting. Next, he copied and pasted the Droid into the destination image. To blend extraneous colored pixels James used the Select/Defringe command, then touched up the blending work around image edges with the Paintbrush tool. To learn more about the Select/Defringe command, see Chapter 3.

**16**

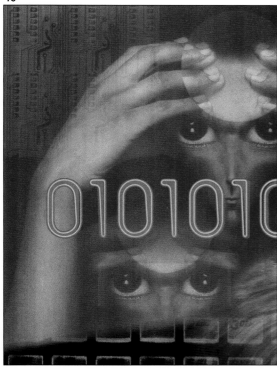

**17**

**18**

# The Photoshop Portfolio

**19** Sanjay photographed this model on a loveseat with a very soft, flat light. When developing the image, he had transparency film processed using color negative chemistry. This made all the colors very saturated. It also, however, added a yellow cast to the highlights and the film grain tended to get a little coarse. After the film was processed, Sanjay scanned the negative on a Scitex scanner. Using the Scitex scanning software and Photoshop, he removed the yellow cast using the Curves command. To reduce the grainy effect, Sanjay used Photoshop's Airbrush tool to soften the skin texture. He then used the Dodge and Burn tools to accentuate the model's eyes and lips.

To enhance the red in the loveseat, Sanjay first created a selection using the Lasso tool. Then, he used the Image/Adjust/Curves command to push yellow and magenta to 100% which removed all of the cyan. The changes applied to the Curves dialog box made the sofa redder. Sanjay also made curve adjustments to lower the black, leaving only enough for the shape and detail.

The background was originally red. Sanjay applied a huge feather radius of 100 pixels to the selection around the sofa. After the selection was feathered, he then used the Hue/Saturation sliders to shift the red color to cyan. What appears to be a glow is merely the red that is left over from the background appearing as it was before the feathered selection was applied. The last step was to add noise to the green background.

**20** Sharon used both Adobe Photoshop and Fractal Design ColorStudio to create this unusual image. She started by picking two stock photos: a tiger and a business forecaster. She masked the tiger's head, copied it, then pasted it on top of the businessman's face. While the tiger's head was still selected and floating, she scaled the head to the proper proportions. She also darkened the red in the tigers head. To create the stormy sky, she used painting tools and color correcting commands.

To create the lamb in the crystal ball, Sharon first drew a lamb on a piece of paper, then scanned the sketch. After the lamb was digitized, she selected it, copied and pasted it into the crystal ball. Next, she created the upside down reflection of the tiger in the crystal ball by first applying the Spherize filter to a duplicate selection of the tiger. Then she used the Image/Effects/Scale and Image/Rotate commands to resize and flip the image before pasting it into the crystal ball at a 40% opacity.

19

20

©Sharon Steuer and ©COMSTOCK

# The Photoshop Portfolio

In both color inserts of this book we've included interesting, diverse and highly professional works of Photoshop art. After you've examined the images and read through the explanations of how the images were created, you might have noticed similarities of approach and execution.

To all of the artists one of the most important stages in creating these images was conceptualization and planning. All of the artists had a central idea or concept they wished to portray in their images. Most of them began developing their ideas with rough sketches on paper. Many times the artists showed and discussed these sketches with clients and art directors.

A crucial step in the planning stage was to ensure that all images needed in the final artwork could be obtained and digitized. Obtaining images could mean searching through stock photo albums and CD-ROM collections or scheduling photography sessions. A few of the artists took the photographs themselves. When the artists digitized their work, all were very careful to ensure that they were digitized at the correct resolution. (To learn more about digitizing your images, see Chapter 7.) As they planned their work, the artists analyzed whether they should be working in RGB or CMYK Color mode. They also kept in mind whether they would be outputting to a transparency, a commercial printing press or video. As part of the conceptualization/design process, some of the artists created low-res versions of their images. By using low-res files, they could work faster, and quickly show their clients "comps" of what the final images might look like.

Following the conceptualization and planning stages, the artists focused on their artistic vision. None of the artists used special effects to make their images as wild as possible. Instead of relying on special effects, they relied on ability, intuition and a firm knowledge of fundamental Photoshop techniques. The artists created selections using the selection tools, the Pen tool and alpha channels. They copied and pasted the selections to blend image elements together. They also used painting/editing modes and changed Composite Control settings to help composite images.

After reviewing the images in the color insert sections of this book, you're certain to agree that Photoshop offers unlimited design possibilities. Yet despite the freedom Photoshop provides don't forget the importance of conceptualization, planning and knowledge of basic Photoshop skills. As you gain more proficiency in Photoshop from reading this book and working on your own Photoshop projects, every now and then, you might wish to return to the color insert sections for inspiration and ideas.

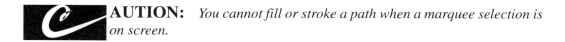

To fill or stroke a path or subpath, use the Fill Path/Subpath or Stroke Path/Subpath command from the Paths palette's pop-up menu. Paths cannot be filled or stroked by Photoshop's Edit/Fill or Edit/Stroke commands.

When you fill or stroke a path, Photoshop fills or strokes underlying pixels *beneath* the path and leaves the path as a separate independent object. This means that you can move the path and execute Fill Path or Stroke Path again, or edit the path—without affecting the filled or stroked images on screen.

**CAUTION:** *You cannot fill or stroke a path when a marquee selection is on screen.*

## How Photoshop Fills a Path

When you choose the Fill Path command from the Paths palette pop-up menu the entire path will be filled—if there are no intersecting or overlapping segments. The illustrations below show how Photoshop fills a path with overlapping or intersecting segments.

When filling paths (including clipping paths, explained later in this chapter) Photoshop uses a Postscript rule called the Even-Odd Winding rule. It's not essential that you understand this rule. But if you are going to create complicated paths, you might wish to read the following explanation.

To understand how the Even-Odd Winding rule works, first pick a point in your image that is within the path, but not on the path. Then draw an imaginary line through any path segments out to the edge of the document window. Now count the number of times a path crosses the imaginary line. If the number is even, the point where the imaginary line starts will not be filled. If the number is odd, the area will be filled.

## Filling a Path Comprised of Subpaths

When filling a path, it's important to remember that Photoshop considers all path segments and subpaths on screen to be one path. Before you fill a path you must deselect, so that no segments are selected. If you select any part of a path, the Fill Path command changes to Fill Subpath in the Paths palette pop-up menu.

To see how Photoshop fills and strokes paths comprised of subpaths, you must have at least two separate path segments displayed. If you deleted the figure-eight path created in the previous exercise, create another closed path now, before beginning the next exercise.

1. Use the Pen tool to create a square subpath to the right of the figure eight (or any other subpath). To ensure that all subpaths will be filled, deselect any path that is currently activated or selected. To deselect, activate the Arrow tool in the Paths palette and click away from the path segments.

2. To fill all paths on screen, click on the pop-up menu and select Fill Path. The Fill Path dialog box appears. The Fill Path dialog box will also be displayed if you press OPTION (PC users: ALT) and click on the Fill Path icon ( ▣ ) at the bottom of the Paths Palette.

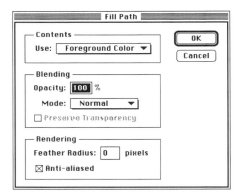

3. In the Fill Path dialog box:

   a. The Use pop-up menu should be set to Foreground Color. This pop-up menu also offers options for filling the path with the Background Color, a pattern, a snapshot version, the last saved version of the image, Black, 50% Gray, or White.

   b. As in the standard Fill dialog box, you can choose an Opacity setting and a painting Mode for blending. Type **50** in the Opacity field and make sure the Mode is set to Normal. The Preserve Transparency check box will be active if you are working in a layer that has a transparent background. If you check this option, transparent areas will not be affected by the Fill.

**c.** As in the Lasso tool's dialog boxes, the Feather Radius and Anti-aliased options are used to soften edges. Feather Radius values can be from 0 to 250 pixels.

**4.** Click OK. Both the figure eight and the square subpaths are filled according to your specifications.

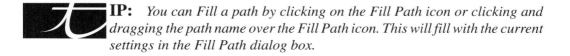

**IP:** *You can Fill a path by clicking on the Fill Path icon or clicking and dragging the path name over the Fill Path icon. This will fill with the current settings in the Fill Path dialog box.*

## Stroking a Path

If you don't have the two subpaths on screen from the previous section, create two subpaths now, then deselect.

Now try stroking the path.

**1.** Change the foreground color to a color that will allow you to see the effects of the stroke.

**2.** To stroke a path, click on the pop-up menu in the Paths palette, and select Stroke Path, or press OPTION (PC users: ALT) and click on the Stroke Path icon ( ⬛ ) at the bottom of the Paths palette.

**3.** When the Stroke Path dialog box appears, open the Tool pop-up menu. You'll get a list of the painting and editing tools that use the Brushes palette.

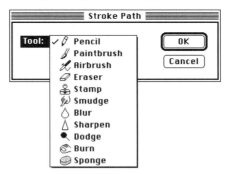

**10**

**4.** Apply an Airbrush stroke to your path. Select Airbrush from the Tool pop-up menu in the Stroke Path dialog box and click OK.

The path is stroked using the current brush size in the Brushes palette and opacity settings for the Airbrush tool. To better control how the stroke is applied to the path, you may wish to first select the tool with which you will stroke the path and choose the specific settings you want in the Options and Brushes palette for that tool. Then click on the Stroke Path icon at the bottom of the Paths palette. Instead of opening the Stroke Path dialog box, Photoshop will automatically stroke with the activated tool in the Toolbox, using its Brushes palette settings.

 **IP:** *You can stroke a path by clicking on the Stroke Path icon in the Paths palette or by clicking and dragging the path name over the Stroke Path icon.*

### Filling or Stroking a Subpath

As stated earlier, if you don't wish to fill or stroke an entire path, Photoshop allows you to fill or stroke a subpath. When you click on a path segment, or SHIFT-click to activate more than one segment, Photoshop considers them to be subpaths.

To see the effects of stroking a subpath, change the foreground color and make sure a selection tool in the Toolbox is selected. Then choose the subpath you wish to stroke by clicking on it with the Arrow tool. This activates the subpath. You do not need to select every anchor point in the path. Next, click on the pop-up menu in the Paths palette. Notice that the Stroke Path command has changed to Stroke Subpath. In the Stroke Subpath dialog box, select a tool; then click OK. Only the subpath you clicked on is stroked.

## SAVING, HIDING, LOADING, AND DELETING PATHS

After you create a path, you may wish to save it; by saving a path you can give it a name and create a clipping path out of it.

When a path is saved, Photoshop saves all path segments as one path on screen, whether they are selected or not. If you edit the path after saving it, or if you add a subpath, the changes to the path will be saved automatically. After you save a path, you can hide it and create more paths. This ability to hide an object is somewhat similar to that of drawing programs that allow you to work in layers. But, unlike drawing programs, or Photoshop's own Layers palette, if you save multiple paths in Photoshop, you cannot view the multiple saved paths simultaneously.

## Photoshop in Action

The background was created by scanning a rough-textured paper.

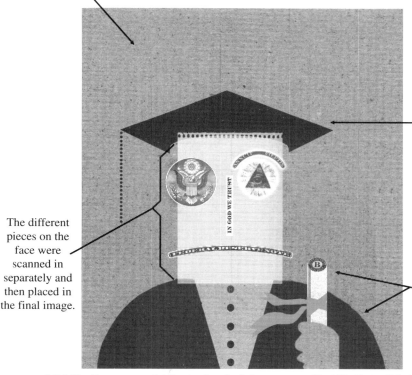

The mortarboard was created using the Pen tool.

The different pieces on the face were scanned in separately and then placed in the final image.

The diploma, hand, and jacket were created using the Pen tool.

Artist: Rico Lins    Art Director: Lucy Bartholomay    Client: The Boston Globe Magazine

**10**

Lucy had Rico create this humorous image for the cover of the *Boston Globe* magazine issue featuring an article on whether a college degree is worth the price.

Rico started the image by first scanning a rough-textured paper that was used as the background. He used the Pen tool to create the mortarboard, jacket, diploma, and hand. Once these shapes were created they were filled using the Fill Path command in the Paths palette.

All the pieces in the face were scanned in separately, selected, and then pasted into the final file.

**N****OTE:** *It's important to understand that a saved path does not receive an assigned disk filename. Rather, you provide a name for the path that will appear in a list in the Paths palette. The path names that appear in this list are only available in the document in which they were created and saved. If you wish to copy a path from one document into another document, you can use the Edit/Copy and Edit/Paste commands. You can also drag a path name from the Paths palette into another open document or drag the path itself into another open document with the Move tool. The path name, as well as the path itself, will be available in the other document.*

In the next exercise, you'll learn how to save a path, hide a path, and then reload the path. Before you begin, make sure that you have one path displayed on screen.

1. After you've created a path, you may want to save it, especially if you are using the Pen tool to isolate an area of a digitized image. Later you can convert the path into a selection to use as a mask. To save a path, click on the pop-up menu in the Paths palette and select Save Path. You don't have to select a path before you select the Save Path command. When you apply the command, all path segments on screen are automatically saved.

**T****IP:** *You can also save a path by dragging the words Work Path over the New Path icon at the bottom of the Paths palette or by double-clicking on the Work Path in the Paths palette.*

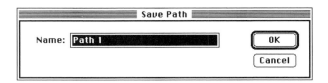

2. In the Save Path dialog box, you can name the path, if you wish, by typing the name in the Name field. Click OK. Notice that the name of the path now appears in the Paths palette.

If you wish to rename the saved path, double-click on the name of the path in the Paths palette. The Rename Path dialog box will appear, allowing you to rename the path.

**3.** Now hide the path you just created, so that you can name and save another path. Click below the name you assigned the path in the Paths palette, or choose Turn Off Path in the Paths palette pop-up menu. The path on the screen will disappear, but the Path name remains in the Paths palette.

**4.** Create another path.

**5.** Choose Save Path from the pop-up menu in the Paths palette. In the Save Path dialog box, Path 2 appears in the Name field; give the path another name if you wish, and click OK to save the path. The name of the path now appears in the Paths palette.

**6.** With two paths now saved, you will be able to see how you can view them independently. To return to the first path, click on the name of the path in the Paths palette. This path now appears on screen. To view the second path, click on the name of the second path in the Paths palette. The area around the path name turns gray.

Continue to experiment, and adjust your saved paths, if you wish. Remember, once a path is saved you can edit it without resaving.

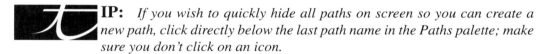

**IP:** *If you wish to quickly hide all paths on screen so you can create a new path, click directly below the last path name in the Paths palette; make sure you don't click on an icon.*

**7.** Before proceeding to the next section, delete the second path you created. First activate the path by clicking on the name you assigned to the second path in the Paths palette. Then select Delete Path from the pop-up menu in the Paths palette. You can also delete a path by clicking on the path name and dragging it over the Trash icon ( 🗑 ) at the bottom-right corner of the Paths palette. When the Trash icon changes colors, release the mouse.

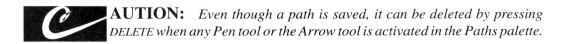

**CAUTION:** *Even though a path is saved, it can be deleted by pressing DELETE when any Pen tool or the Arrow tool is activated in the Paths palette.*

## Duplicating Paths

Now that you know how to save a path, you can create a duplicate of it using the Paths palette.

To duplicate the current path on screen, simply choose Duplicate from the Paths palette's pop-up menu. Alternatively, click and drag the Path name from the Paths palette over the New Path icon ( ▫ ) in the palette. When the Duplicate Path dialog box opens, enter a name for the new path. After you click OK, the duplicate as well as the original path will appear in the Paths palette.

## Exporting a Path to Adobe Illustrator

Exporting a path from Photoshop to Illustrator can be valuable, especially after you've created a path in Photoshop by tracing over a digitized image, and want to use it in Illustrator.

To export the path so that you can integrate it into a design in Illustrator, choose Export in the Photoshop File menu. From the Export submenu, choose Paths to Illustrator. Choose the path name from the Write pop-up menu. Name the file and click Save (PC users: OK). The file can then be loaded directly into Illustrator. To do this in Illustrator, just execute the File/Open command, locate the file, and open it. To activate and select the path in Illustrator, choose Select All in the Edit menu.

If you don't need to save your path, but you do want to export it to Illustrator, select the entire path and then use Edit/Copy in Photoshop and Edit/Paste in Illustrator to drop the path into an Illustrator file. To do this, you must have either Illustrator 5.0 or later on the Mac or Illustrator 4.0 or later on the PC.

If you wish to create a silhouette mask out of a Photoshop image and place only the masked portion in another application (such as Illustrator or a page-layout program), you must create a clipping path, as described next.

## CREATING AND SAVING CLIPPING PATHS

One of the most useful features in the Paths palette is the Clipping Path command. A *clipping path* silhouettes an area, masking an image so that only the portion of the image within the clipping path will appear when the Photoshop file is placed in another application.

Figure 10-5a shows an Alaskan brown bear image before the Pen tool was used to create a clipping path. Figure 10-5b shows the results after the Bear file with the clipping path was placed in Adobe Illustrator. Only the bear was included in the clipping path, so that it could be placed on top of a new background in Adobe Illustrator.

The following exercise walks you through the steps required to turn a path into a clipping path and then to save the file in EPS format so it can be imported into another program.

(a) The original Alaskan brown bear image, before the clipping path was created; (b) Only the image area within the clipping path appears in Adobe Illustrator

(a)

(b)

**10**

**FIGURE 10-5**

1. Open a file that contains an image that you wish to silhouette and export to Illustrator or a page-layout program. If you don't have a suitable image, use the Frames file (PC users: frames.jpg) in the Photoshop Tutorial folder.

2. Create a path around the portion of the image that you wish to include in the clipping path.

3. Once you've created the path, choose Save Path from the pop-up menu or double-click on the Work Path name in the Paths palette. In the Save Path dialog box, enter a name for your path.

4. After the path is saved, choose Clipping Path from the pop-up menu in the Paths palette. When the Clipping Path dialog box appears, click on the Path pop-up menu and select the name of your saved path.

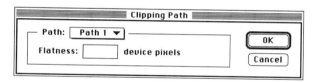

In the Clipping Path dialog box, you can adjust the Flatness value to *flatten*, or simplify, paths that may be too complicated to print. You can leave this field empty unless you receive a PostScript "limitcheck" error when printing the clipping path image in another application. If you do receive this error, you can try entering a number into the Flatness field. A higher Flatness value will reduce the number of straight lines that will be needed to define the curve, thus simplifying the curve. If you flatten the curve too much, however, you will alter the shape of the entire path. Acceptable Flatness values are from .2 to 200 pixels. Try entering a value from 1 to 3 in the Flatness field for low-resolution printers and 8 to 10 for high-resolution printers.

5. To save the path as a clipping path, click OK. Notice that the name of the path will become outlined in the Paths palette. The image on screen will not change. You will see the effects of creating a clipping path only when the file containing the clipping path is placed in another program.

In order to use the clipping path in another program, you must save the Photoshop file in EPS format. To save your clipping path, choose Save As or Save a Copy from the File menu. When the dialog box appears, name your file, choose EPS from the Format pop-up menu, and click OK. The EPS Format dialog box appears.

**OTE:** *If your document contains alpha channels, choose File/Save a Copy so you can save in EPS format without the alpha channels. For more information about alpha channels, see Chapter 11.*

```
┌─────────────────────────────────────────────────┐
│ ═══════════════════ EPS Format ═══════════════   │
│                                                   │
│  Preview: │ Macintosh (8 bits/pixel) ▼ │  ┌ OK ┐ │
│                                                   │
│  Encoding: │ Binary              ▼ │    │Cancel│ │
│  ┌─ Clipping Path ──────────────────────┐        │
│  │  Path: │ Path 1 ▼ │                   │        │
│  │  Flatness: │     │ device pixels      │        │
│  └──────────────────────────────────────┘        │
│                                                   │
│  ☐ Include Halftone Screen                        │
│  ☐ Include Transfer Function                      │
└─────────────────────────────────────────────────┘
```

If the correct path does not appear in the EPS Format dialog box, click on the Path pop-up menu and choose the path. If necessary, set the Flatness value, then click OK to save the file. If you are going to be creating color separations from the image masked by the clipping path, the file must first be converted to CMYK Color mode before you save it. For more information about saving in EPS format, see Appendix A.

**IP:** *If you have problems printing a clipping path, try installing the Even-Odd to Winding Rule optional plug-in. This can help simplify the path, particularly for older imagesetters.*

When the Photoshop document is placed in Illustrator or a page-layout program, only the portion of the image within the clipping path will appear.

**10**

# Photoshop in Action

The background scene was photographed in Florida, then scanned.

Chicago Bulls star Scottie Pippen was photographed sitting on foam stairs. After the photograph was scanned, the Pen tool was used to outline Pippen. This image was later copied and pasted over the bull.

The stuffed bull was shot in California, and then scanned. Once it was scanned, the Pen tool was used to outline it. The bull was later copied and pasted into the final image.

Artist: Nik Kleinberg                    Client: Sports Illustrated for Kids

Nik created this "unbelieva-BULL" image for a *Sports Illustrated for Kids* cover using photographs taken by George B. Fry III.

After all the shots were taken, they were scanned separately. First the background was scanned, then the bull, and then Pippen. After the bull and Pippin were scanned, the Pen tool was used to silhouette (outline) each image. The paths were saved and then turned into selections with the Paths palette's Make Selection command. The selections were copied and then pasted into the final image to make it appear that Pippen was having the ride of his life.

## CONCLUSION

If you've followed the exercises in this chapter from beginning to end, you've progressed to a more sophisticated level of expertise with the Paths palette and the Pen tools. Now that you're familiar with the scope of the Paths palette commands, you'll want to keep the palette handy. As you become proficient at using the Pen tools, very few shapes or objects will be beyond your grasp.

In the next chapter you'll learn how to create masks using the Quick Mask mode and then how to save them.

**10**

# CREATING MASKS AND USING CHANNELS

Before computers came along, the traditional method of isolating parts of an image for color correcting, image editing, and retouching was to create a mask. A *mask* is a type of stencil, often translucent, which is laid over an image to protect certain areas and allow others to be edited. Cutouts in the mask make selected portions of the image accessible for painting and editing, while the remainder of the image is protected by the stencil. Although the process of creating a mask can be time consuming, it allows work on the image to be performed precisely.

In many ways, the selections you create with Photoshop's selection tools are masks. When a selection is on screen, all the painting and editing work you do affects only the area within the blinking selection marquee. Unlike a traditional mask, however, a selection is temporary. When a new selection is created, the previous one disappears. As discussed in Chapter 10, one method of retaining a selection is to create a path with the Pen tool. Unfortunately, the Pen tool can be difficult to master, and creating intricate paths takes time. To meet the need for maintaining multiple reusable selections that are easy to edit, the designers of Photoshop developed an electronic masking capability that surpasses both the Pen tool and the traditional mask. This electronic capability allows you to save a selection as a mask in an extra channel, called an *alpha channel*, attached to your image.

Once an alpha channel is created, you access it through the Channels palette. The mask in the alpha channel is loaded on screen to serve as a selection. Using alpha channels, you can reload complicated selections and easily switch back and forth among selections while working on a document.

If the relationship between a mask, an alpha channel, and a selection sounds complicated, don't worry. The exercises in this chapter lead you gradually from creating simple masks and working with alpha channels to sophisticated commands that let you superimpose channels and files to create exquisite effects.

As you work through the exercises, you'll see a new and powerful facet of Photoshop open up for you. You'll never have to worry about intricate selections disappearing into the digital stratosphere if you inadvertently click on the screen or close your file. Once you learn how to use masks, you'll be able to save, load, and easily edit any selection, no matter how complex. Not only will this be helpful in your day-to-day Photoshop work but you will also gain the skill to create sophisticated three-dimensional effects that require precise control over light sources and shadows.

# WORKING WITH QUICK MASKS

Perhaps the easiest way to understand the relationship between masks and channels is to start by using Photoshop's Quick Mask mode, which creates a temporary mask and a temporary alpha channel. A Quick Mask is similar to a *rubylith,* the red-colored translucent film that is used as an overlay to protect parts of an image in print production.

Like a rubylith, a Quick Mask allows you to view your work through a translucent "overlay." The areas on screen covered by the overlay are protected from image editing; the cutout areas not covered by the overlay are not protected. (If desired, you can change the Quick Mask settings so that the reverse is true.) In Quick Mask mode, the shapes of the cutout areas (the unprotected areas) are easily edited with Photoshop's painting and editing tools. When you exit Quick Mask mode, the unprotected areas are transformed into selections (or one selection).

  Notice the Quick Mask mode icon in Photoshop's Toolbox: The default setting is a shaded square with a clear circle cut out of it. The shaded area represents the translucent mask; the circle cutout is the unprotected area. The Standard mode icon (beside the Quick Mask icon) depicts what you will see when you exit Quick Mask mode: The overlay is gone, but a blinking selection marquee remains on screen.

## Creating a Quick Mask

In this section you'll learn how to create a Quick Mask and use it to edit a selection. If you wish to follow along, load the Fruit (PC users: fruit.jpg) file, an image of fruit on a plate, from the Tutorial folder. (Our example uses an image of a pork chop on a dinner plate.) You'll create the Quick Mask along the rim of the plate, so that you can add variety to it and make it look more interesting.

Begin by creating a small elliptical selection with the Marquee tool in the rim of the plate, as shown in Figure 11-1. Don't deselect.

Clicking once on the Quick Mask mode icon puts you in Quick Mask mode; double-clicking on the icon activates the mode and opens the Quick Mask Options dialog box as well. To view the dialog box options, double-click on the icon. Once the Quick Mask Options dialog box appears, as shown in Figure 11-2, you'll see that a red overlay also appears on screen. If the default settings are in use, the red overlay area represents the protected area; and the area you selected is not covered by the red overlay (this is the unprotected area).

 **OTE:** *If you can't see the unprotected area on screen because the Mask Options dialog box opened in front of it, move the dialog box by clicking and dragging in its title bar (on "Mask Options").*

Selected area

Image before entering Quick Mask mode (photograph courtesy of Stacy Kollar Photography)

**FIGURE** 11·1

In the Quick Mask Options dialog box you can designate what you want the color overlay to indicate: the masked (protected) areas or the selected (unprotected) areas. By default, the Masked Areas radio button in the Color Indicates section is selected. The default color setting for the overlay is red with a 50% Opacity. With the Masked Areas radio button selected, the specified color and opacity are applied to all areas in the image *except* those that were selected before you entered the Quick Mask mode. When the Selected Areas radio button is selected, the translucent colored overlay will appear *over* your selection, rather than around it. (If this is the case now, click on the Masked Areas radio button.)

**IP:** *You can switch between the Masked Areas and the Selected Areas options without opening the Quick Mask Options dialog box by pressing OPTION (PC users: ALT) and clicking on the Quick Mask icon. The Quick Mask icon will change to reflect the option you have chosen.*

Unprotected area          Channel indicator

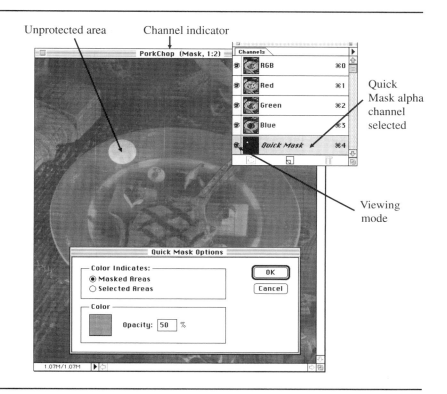

Quick
Mask alpha
channel
selected

Viewing
mode

Image
in Quick
Mask mode
with
translucent
color
overlay
(compare
with
Figure 11-1)

**FIGURE 11-2**

You can change the overlay color by clicking on the swatch in the Color section of the Mask Options dialog box; this opens Photoshop's Color Picker. If you change the percentage in the Opacity field beside the color swatch, the translucency of the overlay is adjusted accordingly. For the following exercise, leave the default Mask Options settings selected (Color Indicates Masked Areas, and the overlay color at 50% red). Click OK to continue.

You are now in the Quick Mask channel overlay. Before continuing, take a moment to look at Figure 11-2 to see how your surroundings have changed. First, examine the document's title bar. You should see "Quick Mask" rather than "RGB."

The Channels palette should now be open; if it isn't, open it by choosing Show Channels in the Window/Palettes submenu. In the Channels palette, notice that a new channel called Quick Mask has been added (this is an alpha channel). Next to the Quick Mask channel, the eye icon (👁) means the channel is visible, and the gray area surrounding the words "Quick Mask" indicates the channel is selected and can be edited. The selected channel is often called the target channel. Notice that there are eye icons next to each of the RGB channels also, but no gray area. Thus, even though you can see your image on screen, any editing changes you make now will not affect it, but rather the mask only.

## Editing a Mask in Quick Mask Mode

To resize and fine-tune the mask, you can paint it. This changes the unprotected and protected areas (which changes the selection marquee on screen after you exit Quick Mask mode). When you paint to edit the mask, you can only use black, white, or shades of gray. Your Picker palette is now restricted to 256 shades of gray. If the Picker palette isn't on screen, open it, and notice that all of the swatches are now shades of gray.

When you paint with white in Quick Mask mode, you add to the unprotected area (the selected area). When you paint with black, you subtract from the unprotected area (and add to the protected area). Painting with gray shades creates a type of "partial" selection when you exit Quick Mask mode. When this selection is filled with an opaque color, the result is a translucent color.

The following table summarizes the effects of painting with white, black, or gray when the Color Indicates Masked Areas radio button is selected in the Mask Options dialog box:

| Painting Color | Effect in Quick Mask Mode | Effect in Standard Mode |
| --- | --- | --- |
| White | Subtracts from colored overlay (protected area); adds to unprotected area | Adds to selection marquee |
| Black | Adds to colored overlay (protected area); subtracts from unprotected area | Subtracts from selection marquee |
| Gray | Adds a partial overlay | Partial selection |

To see how painting in white edits the mask and changes the selection, set the foreground color to white. Select any painting tool, and click on a medium, soft-edged brush in the Brushes palette. (A soft-edged brush will produce a selection with feathered edges; a hard-edged brush will create a sharper selection.) Make sure Opacity is set to 100% in the tool's palette.

Use the Paintbrush tool to paint around the entire rim of the plate. As you paint with white, the translucent overlay melts away. As you remove the overlay, you increase the size of the selection that will appear when you exit Quick Mask mode.

**IP:** *You might want to zoom in and use a smaller brush so that you can carefully select the rim and nothing else. If you make a mistake, just paint with black to add to the overlay.*

Before leaving Quick Mask mode, take a moment to view the Quick Mask channel *without* the composite image displayed. This will give you an idea of exactly what happened in the channel when you painted with white. To turn off the RGB composite display, click on the eye icon to the left of the RGB channel in the Channels palette. The RGB composite image disappears, and you will see the black mask and the white, unprotected area. When you painted with white, you subtracted black from the mask. Only when the RGB composite image and mask appear on the screen together is the mask displayed in a translucent color. Restore the RGB image by clicking on the eye icon next to the RGB channel in the Channels palette.

Now that you have isolated the rim of the plate, you are ready to return to Standard mode, where you can use the selection that the mask creates.

## Exiting the Quick Mask Mode

To exit Quick Mask mode, click on the Standard mode icon in the Toolbox. The selection marquee now appears around the entire plate, as shown in Figure 11-3. Notice that "Mask" no longer appears in the window's title bar. In addition, if you examine the Channels palette, you'll see that the Quick Mask channel is no longer listed. Thus, your selection remains, but the alpha channel containing the mask has disappeared.

**11**

**OTE:** *If you painted with white in several different areas in the Mask channel, several selection marquees will appear on screen when you exit Quick Mask mode.*

Now you can edit or color correct the rim of the plate. Try using the Brightness/ Contrast controls in the Image/Adjust submenu to increase the contrast. As you adjust brightness and contrast, only the selected area of the plate changes. When you're finished, don't deselect.

The selection reflects the area that was painted with white in the Quick Mask channel

**FIGURE 11-3**

As mentioned earlier, your task is to make the rim of the plate more interesting. Suppose you'd like to apply a pattern to enhance the rim of the plate. This creates a problem: You need to create a selection to define the pattern, but if you do this, you will lose the selection around the rim of the plate. The solution is to save the selection. Keep your selection on screen and proceed to the next section.

## SAVING AND LOADING A SELECTION

Any Photoshop selection can be saved, whether it was created in Quick Mask mode or not. When a selection is saved, Photoshop creates a mask from the selection and places it in an alpha channel.

To try this out, make sure you have a selection on screen, then choose Save Selection from the Select menu. The Save Selection dialog box opens. This dialog box allows you to save a selection into a new channel to any open document. In the next section, you'll have a chance to explore the dialog box options. For now, notice that the Destination Document pop-up menu shows the name of your current document. The Destination Channel pop-up menu is set to New. Click OK to create the new channel.

**IP:** *To automatically save an onscreen selection to an alpha channel, click on the Selection icon (⬚) in the Channels palette.*

Notice that the Channels palette now contains a new channel, channel #4. The selection around the rim of the plate, created in the previous section, is now stored in channel #4 so it can be recalled after you define a pattern. (If you were in a CMYK Color file, the first alpha channel would be #5.)

Click on the eye icon column next to channel #4 to see the mask that is stored in the Channels palette. An overlay similar to the Quick Mask overlay appears over your image. Click on the eye icon next to the RGB channel to turn it off. Without the underlying image, the mask now appears in black and white. Return to your composite image by clicking on the eye icon again, and the overlay returns. To hide the overlay from view, click on the eye icon next to channel #4.

**IP:** *You can toggle back and forth between the alpha channel and the RGB composite channel by pressing COMMAND-4 (PC users: CTRL-4) to access alpha channel #4 and COMMAND-0 (PC users: CTRL-0) to access the RGB composite.*

With your selection stored, you can safely select another area on screen and define it as a pattern. Select one of the leaves in the Fruit file with the Rectangular Marquee tool, and choose Define Pattern from the Edit menu.

Now recall the plate rim selection by choosing Load Selection from the Select menu. When the Load Selection dialog box appears, notice that #4 automatically appears in the Source Channel pop-up menu and that the Source Document pop-up menu shows the name of your current document. Other options in the dialog box will be covered in the next section. Click OK to load the selection.

**IP:** *To automatically load a selection from an alpha channel, OPTION-click (PC users: ALT-click) on the name or number of the channel in the Channels palette. You can also drag the name or number of the channel to the Selection icon at the bottom of the palette.*

The mask from channel #4 is placed on the screen as a selection.

**11**

Once the plate rim selection appears, apply the pattern using the Edit/Fill command. In the Fill dialog box, select Pattern from the Use pop-up menu. Enter **20** in the Opacity field and set Mode to Normal; then click OK. Figure 11-4 displays the results of applying a pattern (created from the feather shown in the image) with a 20% opacity to the rim selection.

## Changing Settings in the Save and Load Selection Dialog Boxes

As you've seen from the previous example, the Save Selection dialog box allows you to save selections. The Load Selection dialog box allows you to load a selection from an alpha channel.

In this section you'll explore the options in the Save Selection and Load Selection dialog boxes that allow you to add to, subtract from, and intersect selections stored in alpha channels. To follow the discussion in this section, you should have the file from the previous section on screen with its alpha channel. If you don't have the file

The plate, after the pattern was applied to the selection

**FIGURE 11-4**

on screen, load any image and create a selection. Next, save the selection by using the Select/Save Selection command, then deselect.

To accurately view the effects of the options in the Save Selection dialog box, the colored overlay mask with the cutout area should be displayed on screen. To see the overlay, the alpha channel you just created or any other alpha channel you will be editing should be in view and editable. Also, the other Channels (RGB, R, G, and B) in the Channels palette should be in view. Thus, the eye icon should appear next to the name or number of the alpha channel and all the other channels in the Channels palette. The alpha channel you will be editing should be selected (surrounded by gray). If the alpha channel is not set up this way, click on the alpha channel to select it. To display the eye icons of the other channels, click on the eye icon column of that channel.

Before exploring the Save Selection operation options, you must create a new selection on screen. Create this selection so it slightly overlays the cutout area of the colored overlay on screen. Use any selection tool to create the selection, then open the Save Selection dialog box by choosing Select/Save Selection.

As you saw in the previous example, the New option in the Destination Channel pop-up menu allows you to save a selection in a new alpha channel. By choosing a channel in the Destination Channel pop-up menu, you can alter the selection stored in a pre-existing alpha channel. If you are in a layer (other than the Background), the Channel pop-up menu will also allow you to create a layer mask in a new channel from your selection. Layer masks are discussed at the end of this chapter, and in Chapter 12. When you select a pre-existing channel in the Destination Channel pop-up menu, the dimmed options in the Operations group become active. To see these options in action, choose channel #4 in the Destination Channel pop-up menu. Try out each option by choosing the radio button, then clicking OK. After you see the effects on screen, choose Edit/Undo, then try another option. Before you begin, make sure that the Destination Document pop-up menu is set to the name of your document and not to New. This way, the effects will take place in the document you have open on screen and not in the new document.

**11**

```
╔═══════════════ Save Selection ═══════════════╗
║  ┌─ Destination ──────────────────┐  ┌──────────┐  ║
║  │ Document: [ PorkChop ▼ ]       │  │    OK    │  ║
║  │                                │  └──────────┘  ║
║  │ Channel:  [ #4    ▼ ]          │  [ Cancel ]    ║
║  └────────────────────────────────┘               ║
║  ┌─ Operation ────────────────────┐               ║
║  │ ● New Channel                  │               ║
║  │ ○ Add to Channel               │               ║
║  │ ○ Subtract from Channel        │               ║
║  │ ○ Intersect with Channel       │               ║
║  └────────────────────────────────┘               ║
╚═══════════════════════════════════════════════════╝
```

*New Channel* This option creates a new selection, completely replacing the selection in the channel chosen in the Channel pop-up menu.

*Add to Channel* This option creates another selection in the channel or adds to the selection in the channel.

*Subtract from Channel* If the selection on screen overlaps with the selection saved in the channel, the overlapping area is subtracted from the selection in the channel. If the areas do not overlap, the selection in the channel is not affected.

*Intersect with Channel* If the selection on screen overlaps with the selection saved in the channel, the overlapping area becomes the selection in the channel. If no areas overlap, the selection in the channel disappears.

**IP:** *To automatically add a selection on screen to a selection stored in an alpha channel, press SHIFT, then click and drag the Selection icon (* □ *) over the name or number of the alpha channel you want to add to. To automatically subtract a selection on screen from a stored selection in an alpha channel, press COMMAND (PC users: CTRL), then click and drag the Selection icon (at the bottom of the Channels palette) over the alpha channel you want to subtract from.*

After you're done experimenting with the Save Selection dialog box, change the settings in the Channels palette so you'll be able to see selection marquees on screen. First, turn off alpha channel #4 in the Channels palette by clicking on "RGB." When the gray area disapears from channel #4, it means that editing work will not affect this channel. Turn off the eye icon next to alpha channel #4 in the Channels palette. This removes the overlay from the screen. Now you can take a look at the options in the Load Selection dialog box. To open the Load dialog box, choose Load Selection from the Select menu.

The Load Selection dialog box loads selections stored in an alpha channel onto the screen. Before exploring the different options available in the dialog box, create a selection on screen, then choose Load Selection from the Select menu. In the Load Selection dialog box, the Destination Document pop-up menu allows a selection to be loaded into any open document. Make sure that the pop-up menu is set to the name of your document. The Destination Channel pop-up menu allows you to choose a channel from any open document on screen.

If you are working in a layer, the Destination Channel pop-up menu provides a transparency option. This allows you to load the non-transparent areas of the layer as a selection.

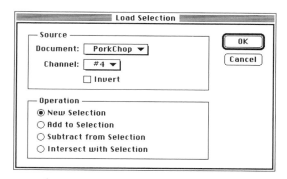

At this point, you can choose how you want the selection stored in the alpha channel to affect the selection on screen. Feel free to try any of the choices.

The four Operation options in the Load Selection are summarized below:

*New Selection* This option creates a new selection, replacing any previous selection on screen.

*Add to Selection* This option adds to the selection on screen or creates an additional selection on screen.

*Subtract from Selection* If the selection in the channel would overlap with the selected area on screen, the selection area from the channel is subtracted from the selection on screen. If the selections do not overlap, the selection on screen is unchanged.

*Intersect with Selection* If the selection in the channel would overlap with the selection on screen, the overlapping area becomes the selection. If no area overlaps, nothing is selected on screen.

**IP:** *To automatically add a selection from an alpha channel to a selection on screen press OPTION-SHIFT (PC users: ALT-SHIFT), then click on the alpha channel name or number in the Channels palette. To automatically subtract a selection on screen from an alpha channel, press OPTION-COMMAND (PC users: ALT-CTRL), then click on the alpha channel name or number in the Channels palette. To change the selection on screen to be the intersection of the selection and a selection stored in an alpha channel, press COMMAND-SHIFT (PC users: CTRL-SHIFT) and drag the alpha channel over the Selection icon. To change the selection stored in the alpha channel to be the intersection of the selection on screen and the alpha channel, press COMMAND-SHIFT (PC users: CTRL-SHIFT) and drag the Selection icon over the alpha channel.*

**11**

Now that you've created and altered selections stored in alpha channels, you may want to copy your alpha channel into another file so it can be used with other documents.

## Duplicating an Alpha Channel

The Duplicate command in the Channels palette pop-up menu allows you to create an exact duplicate of a channel. The Duplicate command can place a duplicate of a channel in an existing file, or in a new file.

The Duplicate command is often used to duplicate channels into new files so they can be deleted from their original file, helping to keep file size to a minimum. By duplicating the channel into a new file, the channel can always be loaded back into the original file with the Duplicate Channel command. It can also be loaded as a blinking selection marquee with the Select/Load Selection command.

To duplicate an existing channel, click on the channel in the Channels palette that you want to duplicate, then choose Duplicate Channel from the Channels palette pop-up menu.

In the Duplicate Channel dialog box, rename the channel, if desired, in the As field. Use the Document pop-up menu to choose the Destination file for the channel. If you wish to place the existing channel into a new channel in a new document, choose New from the Document pop-up menu. Name the new file in the Name field, if desired.

```
═══════════════ Duplicate Channel ═══════════════

Duplicate:  #4                              ┌─────────┐
      As: │#1                          │    │   OK    │
                                            └─────────┘
                                            ┌─────────┐
                                            │ Cancel  │
   ┌─ Destination ──────────────────────┐   └─────────┘
   │ Document:  │ New          ▼ │       │
   │                                     │
   │      Name: │ Untitled-1          │  │
   │            □ Invert                 │
   └─────────────────────────────────────┘
```

The Invert option for the Destination is similar to choosing Invert from the Image/Map submenu. This option changes light pixels into dark pixels and dark pixels to light, producing a negative of your image.

**IP:** *To quickly duplicate a channel from one file into another file, click and drag on the name or number of the channel from the Channels palette into the other document. You can create a duplicate of a channel in the same file by clicking and dragging on the name or number of the alpha channel over the New Channel icon (▣) in the Channels palette.*

## Deleting a Channel

Once you've duplicated a channel into another file or if you're done working with a channel, you may wish to delete the channel from the document it is in. If you still have the rim selection stored in an alpha channel from a previous exercise, delete it to keep your file size as small as possible. If you have any other channels that you don't need, delete them now.

To delete a channel, first select it, then choose Delete Channel from the Channels palette pop-up menu.

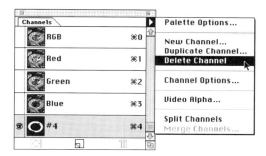

As a shortcut, you can also move the mouse over the channel you wish to delete in the Channels palette. The arrow pointer will change to a pointing hand icon. Click and hold down the mouse button, then drag the channel towards the Trash icon (🗑). As you drag, the pointer will change into a grabbing hand icon. Drag the tiny hand icon over the Trash. When the Trash changes colors, release the mouse and the channel will be deleted.

## CREATING AN ALPHA CHANNEL WITH THE NEW CHANNEL COMMAND

The New Channel command in the Channels palette's pop-up menu allows you to create a new alpha channel. You can then work in the channel and create a mask from scratch using a painting, editing, or selection tool. To utilize the mask as a selection, you will need to execute the Select/Load Selection command.

In this section, continue using the Fruit (PC users: fruit.jpg) file from the Tutorial folder as you learn how to create and edit a channel using the New Channel command. Start with no selection on screen. If the plate rim is still selected from the previous exercise, deselect it by choosing None from the Select menu.

**11**

To create a new alpha channel, click on the pop-up menu in the Channels palette, and choose New Channel. As a shortcut, you can create a new channel by clicking on the New Channel icon (⊡) in the Channels palette. A new alpha channel appears in the Channels palette, and the Channel Options dialog box opens. Name the channel; type **Plate** in the Name field. In the Color Indicates section, choose the Selected Areas radio button. This way, when you paint with black, you will be creating a selection; when you paint with white, you will be subtracting from the selection. Note that this is the opposite of the settings you had when you created the Quick Mask earlier in this chapter. Leave the color swatch set to red and Opacity set to 50%. Click OK.

```
╔══════════════ Channel Options ══════════════╗
║                                              ║
║  Name: │ Plate              │    ┌───────┐   ║
║                                  │   OK  │   ║
║  ┌─ Color Indicates: ──────────  └───────┘   ║
║  │ ○ Masked Areas               ┌─────────┐  ║
║  │ ◉ Selected Areas             │ Cancel  │  ║
║                                  └─────────┘  ║
║  ┌─ Color ──────────────────┐                ║
║  │ ▨▨▨   Opacity: │ 50 │ %   │                ║
║  └──────────────────────────┘                ║
╚══════════════════════════════════════════════╝
```

**𝓃OTE:** *At any time, you can edit the Channel Options settings for a channel by clicking on the channel in the Channels palette, and then choosing Channel Options in the Channels palette's pop-up menu.*

Your screen will now be white because you are in a new, empty channel, and you are viewing only the channel, not the image. Notice in the Channels palette that the eye icon appears beside the new channel (Plate) and that the channel is selected, indicating it is displayed and that you can edit it. At this point, none of the other channels can be viewed or edited.

**𝓣IP:** *You can create a new channel by clicking on the New Channel icon (⊡) at the bottom of the Channels palette. After you click on the New Channel icon, the Channels Options dialog box will appear. If you want to bypass the Channels Options dialog box, press and hold OPTION (PC users: ALT) while you click on the New Channel icon.*

Now you are ready to create a mask. But you'll want to see the mask in relation to the image on screen. To view the RGB image, click in the Eye column next to the RGB composite channel. After you click, all of the channels will be visible, but only the Plate alpha channel will be editable (it's the only one with gray surrounding its name in the Channels palette).

## Creating and Editing a Mask in an Alpha Channel

To create a mask in the Plate channel from the previous section, click on the Default Colors icon to set foreground to black and background to white. Use the Paintbrush to paint the inside of the plate, but not the rim area. You will be painting with the same type of translucent overlay with which you worked in Quick Mask mode. If you make a mistake, you can erase the overlay by simply clicking and dragging with the Eraser. (This works because the Eraser paints with the background color, white.) If you are using the Fruit image, also paint over the large pear in the middle of the plate.

The following table summarizes the effects of painting in an alpha channel when the Color Indicates Selected Areas radio button is selected in the Mask Options dialog box. Remember, this is the setting that is opposite to the one used when you created the Quick Mask earlier in this chapter.

| Painting Color | Effect on Colored Mask Overlay | Effect When Selection Is Loaded |
|---|---|---|
| White | Subtracts from colored overlay (unprotected area); subtracts from unprotected area | Subtracts from selection marquee |
| Black | Adds to colored overlay (unprotected area); adds to unprotected area | Adds to selection marquee |
| Gray | Adds a partial overlay | Partial selection |

 **IP:**  *By using black, white, and gray in an alpha channel you can create a fade-out effect. To learn how to do this, see the section "Creating Fade-Outs" in this chapter.*

After you've painted the center of the plate with the colored overlay, take a look at what appears in the Plate channel. To view the Plate channel as a separate image, turn off the eye icons in the other channels by clicking on the eye icon next to the RGB composite channel. This hides the display of the RGB channels and leaves the Plate channel on screen. Notice that you painted in black.

To load the black area on screen as a selection, first select the RGB composite by clicking on RGB in the Channels palette, or press COMMAND-0 (PC users: CTRL-0). Note that the Plate channel is no longer the Target channel. Then choose Load Selection from the Select menu. If you wish to edit the selected area, try applying the Distort/Twirl filter with a setting of 999 degrees. With the filter applied, the food turns into soup, as shown in Figure 11-5. In the Fruit file, you'll get a similar effect. When you've finished applying the Distort/Twirl filter, delete the Plate alpha channel using the Delete Channel command in the Channels palette's pop-up menu.

After the selection is loaded and the Distort/Twirl filter applied, the pork chop turns into soup

**FIGURE 11-5**

As practice, try using the New Channel command to create an alpha channel to mask a different area of your file so you can safely edit in that area. After you're done, you may wish to save your file with the alpha channel. Proceed to the next section to learn how to do this.

# SAVING ALPHA CHANNELS WITH A FILE

After you've created an alpha channel, you may wish to have it saved with your file so the mask can be loaded as a selection at a later time. If you save your file in Photoshop's native format or in TIFF format, all alpha channels are automatically saved with the file. If you wish to save a copy of an image in another file format without its alpha channels, choose File/Save a Copy. Choose a file format from the Format pop-up menu. If the format will not accept alpha channels, the Don't Include Alpha Channels check box will automatically be selected. For more information about saving in other formats, see Appendix A.

## Using the Color Range Command

Another helpful command that allows you to create masks very quickly is Photoshop's powerful Color Range command. Color Range creates a selection based upon color. In some respects, the Color Range command is like a combination of the Magic Wand tool and the Select/Similar command in that Color Range selects a color range anywhere in an image. When using Color Range, you can choose to have Photoshop select colors according to preset colors, or you can have it create a selection according to the colors sampled in your image. As you'll see in the following example, the Color Range dialog box previews the selection in a mask.

To try out the Color Range command, load an image on screen. If you don't have an image open the Portrait file (PC users: portrait.jpg). To open the Color Range dialog box, choose Color Range from the Select menu. The rectangular preview area in the middle of the dialog box displays either the mask or your onscreen image. Click on the Image radio button and you will see your image in the Preview box. Although you will probably be most interested in monitoring the mask in the Selection preview, choosing the Image radio button is helpful when you zoom into specific image areas. The Image radio button will always show you the entire image or selection, even if you have zoomed into a small area on screen.

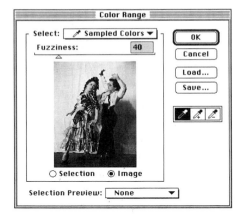

Now click back on the Selection radio button to see the mask. Notice that the mask is mostly black because the Color Range command has not begun its search for colors. Once you specify what color range you want selected, the selection will be represented by light areas in the mask.

To specify which colors you'd like selected, use the Select pop-up menu. The Select pop-up menu allows you to pick from preset colors or colors that you sample with the dialog box's Eyedropper from a gamut of colors. The Select pop-up menu also allows you to select according to shadow, midtones, and highlights. Try a quick test to see how the dialog box can select specific colors for your image.

**1.** From the Select pop-up menu, choose Red.

Notice that an area of the mask gets lighter. This corresponds to the Red areas on screen. This is the area that will be selected when you return to your image.

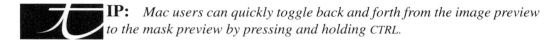

**IP:** *Mac users can quickly toggle back and forth from the image preview to the mask preview by pressing and holding* CTRL.

**2.** Try choosing yellow from the Select menu.

Notice that the areas corresponding to the yellow areas in the image grow lighter.

Next, you'll take a look at how the Selection Preview pop-up menu can help you preview the selection. As you read through a brief explanation of the options in the Selection Preview pop-up menu, try out each one by clicking on the menu choice.

*Grayscale* previews your image in grayscale. The preview on screen appears as it would if it were in an alpha channel. This mode can be helpful when the Select menu is set to Highlights, Midtones, or Shadows.

*Black Matte* displays the mask of the selected areas in color. All other areas are black. This mode is especially helpful in seeing a selection that will be created in dark image areas.

*White Matte* displays the selected areas in color. All other areas are white. This mode is especially helpful in seeing a selection that will be created in light image areas.

*Quick Mask* displays the image using the current settings in the Quick Mask Options dialog box.

Now assume that you want to select only the flesh tones in the image, or any other color area in your image. Before continuing, set the Selection Preview pop-up menu back to None. You can specify this color range by clicking on the image with the Eyedropper that appears in the dialog box. In order to use the Eyedropper, you will need to change the Select pop-up menu. When you use this option, you can extend a selection by clicking on the Eyedropper+; you can reduce the selection by choosing the Eyedropper–.

To select using a sampled color:

1. In the Select pop-up menu, choose Sampled color.

2. Move the Eyedropper over the flesh tones in the image on screen, and select another color you wish to use. Click the mouse.

   Notice that the mask turns lighter in areas corresponding to the color you chose.

3. If you wish to soften selection edges, drag the Fuzziness slider to the right. If you drag the slider very far to the right, the selection will be extended. Drag it to the left to sharpen selection edges.

4. Now, extend the selection by clicking on the Eyedropper+, move it into your image on screen, and select a darker fleshtone or other dark area.

After you click, the white area of the mask is extended to include this color range. To see the actual selection in your image, click OK. When the image returns on screen, you'll see the blinking marquee surrounding the area specified

# Photoshop in Action

The sky was created by using the Gradient tool.

Using the selection tools, the architectural engraving was selected and then saved to an alpha channel using the Select/Save Selection command. Once the channel was created, it was easy to isolate the building and apply color.

The stock certificate was selected and the Perspective command was used to add depth.

A mask of the architectural engraving was created by first selecting the engraving and then executing the Select/Save Selection command.

Using Photoshop's Select/Feather command, the edges of the stock certificate were blurred.

**Artist: Marc Yankus**
**Client: General Electric**

Marc created this cover image for an annual report by scanning black-and-white architectural engravings, a page from the *Wall Street Journal*, a stock certificate, an American dollar, a Japanese yen, a German deutsche mark, and some ticker tape. After the images were scanned, they were placed into a file and different masks were created of the images. The masks were put to use by first executing the Select/Load Selection command. After the selections were loaded, they were edited and colored.

in the mask. At this point, you could either begin to edit the selection using the Quick Mask mode or save the selection to an alpha channel.

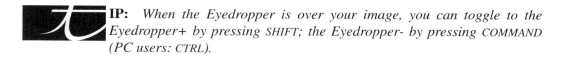

**IP:** *When the Eyedropper is over your image, you can toggle to the Eyedropper+ by pressing SHIFT; the Eyedropper- by pressing COMMAND (PC users: CTRL).*

## ALPHA CHANNEL TECHNIQUES

The following sections provide exercises that will broaden your understanding of alpha channels and put you on the road to creating sophisticated effects with them.

### Creating Fade-Outs

In this section you'll learn how to use alpha channels to make images gradually fade out. Figure 11-6 is an image of a castle fading out. To create the gradual fade-out, a linear gradient from white to black was created in an alpha channel. Then the selection in the alpha channel was loaded and the castle image was pasted into it.

Start by opening the file that you wish to apply the fade-out to. If you don't have a file, use the Tools file (PC users: tools.jpg) in the Tutorial folder.

Image with
fade-out
effect

**FIGURE 11-6**

1. Once your image is on screen, create a new alpha channel by clicking on the New Channel icon at the bottom of the Channels palette. When the Channel Options dialog box appears, make sure that the Masked Areas option is selected in the Color Indicates group. Leave the Name set to #4 (if you are using a CMYK Color file, the Name will be set to #5), the Color to red, and Opacity set to 50%. Click OK to create an alpha channel. At this point only channel #4 is being viewed and can be edited. The RGB channel cannot be edited because the RGB channel is not selected in the Channels palette.

2. Before you create a linear gradient in the alpha channel, make sure that you are viewing all the channels in the Channels palette. That way you can create the gradient while viewing the image and the colored overlay of the alpha channel. In order to do this, click in the eye column next to RGB in the Channels palette. At this point, only alpha channel #4 should be selected in the Channels palette. This means that any changes you make will only affect alpha channel #4.

3. To activate the Gradient tool, double-click on it in the Toolbox. In the Gradient Tool Options palette, make sure that the Mode pop-up menu is set to Normal, Opacity is set to 100%, the Style pop-up menu is set to Foreground to Background, and the Type pop-up menu is set to Linear. Then set the Midpoint slider between 40% and 60%.

4. Before you create a linear gradient, set the foreground to white and the background to black. Then create a linear blend by dragging from the top of your image to the bottom. This will create a linear blend from white to black. To see the white to black linear blend in the alpha channel, without the image, click on the eye icon next to "RGB" in the Channels palette. Later in this exercise, the black areas of the gradient will be the faded out areas of the image, the gray areas will be the translucent areas, and the white areas will be the opaque areas. If you want to reverse the fade-out, create a linear gradient from black to white, or create the gradient from the bottom to the top of your image.

**IP:** *You can alter the effects of the fade-out by changing the length, style, type, opacity, and colors used to create the gradient in the alpha channel. You can alter the fade-out by creating various selections in the alpha channel and applying different gradients or shades of black to the selections.*

5. Return to the RGB composite channel, by clicking on "RGB" in the Channels palette. The RGB channel in the Channels palette will now be surrounded by gray. Turn off the view of channel #4 by clicking on its eye icon.

   Now that you've selected the RGB composite channel, you're going to select and then cut the image into the clipboard.

6. Before selecting your image, set the background color to white. Choose the Select/All command, then choose Edit/Cut. The image is now cut from your file and placed into the clipboard. Your document is now white, the color of the background color.

7. Next, load the selection from the alpha channel by clicking and dragging channel #4 over the Selection icon in the Channels palette.

8. When the selection from the alpha channel appears, choose Paste Into from the Edit menu. Your image that was stored in the clipboard appears in the selection. By pasting your image into the gradient from channel #4 your image gradually fades out.

When you're done, deselect. If you wish, use the File/Save As command to save your file with a new file name.

## Using Alpha Channels to Create Shadowed Text

Now that you possess the power to save and load selections, creating special effects becomes easier. For instance, you can easily create shadowed text, as shown in the following illustration, by utilizing the alpha channel features already covered in this chapter. In this exercise you'll create two alpha channels, one for the shadow area of the text and the other for the text.

1. Create a new RGB Color file 5 inches by 5 inches and then open the Channels and Picker palettes if they are not already open. Set the foreground to a light color.

2.  Next use the Type tool to create some text on screen. For our example we used an Adobe font called Remedy Double Extras. When the text is on screen, move it into the center of your document window. Keep the text selected.

3.  While the text is still selected, choose the Select/Save Selection command to create a mask in an alpha channel (channel #4) of the text floating on screen. In the Save Selection dialog box, leave the default settings; the Destination Document pop-up menu is set to Untitled 1 and the Destination Channel pop-up menu is set to New. Click OK. Don't deselect the text on screen.

4.  Now create another mask in an alpha channel of the text floating on screen. Choose Select/Save Selection. Again, don't change the default settings in the Save Selection dialog box, and click OK. After you have a mask of the floating text in the second alpha channel (channel #5), deselect the floating text.

5.  Click on channel #5 in the Channels palette to activate the alpha channel.

    Next, you will offset the text in channel #5 to begin creating the shadow effect.

6.  To offset the text in channel #5, choose Offset from the Filter/Other submenu. In the Offset dialog box, type in the amount you want to offset the text horizontally and vertically. Type a positive number less than 10 in the Horizontal and Vertical fields to offset the shadow text to the right and down (a negative number offsets to the left and up). Choose the Wrap Around radio button in the Undefined Areas group and click OK.

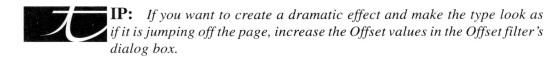**IP:**  *If you want to create a dramatic effect and make the type look as if it is jumping off the page, increase the Offset values in the Offset filter's dialog box.*

7.  If you want your shadow to have a soft-shadowed look, apply the Gaussian Blur filter to channel #5. In the Gaussian Blur dialog box, type in a number between 1 and 10 depending upon how much of a blur you want. If you don't want a soft-shadowed look, skip this step and proceed to step 8.

8. Next, load the selection from channel #4 into channel #5 by choosing Select/Load Selection. When the Load Selection dialog box appears make sure that the Destination Channel pop-up menu is set to #4, then click OK. The selection from channel #4 should now appear in channel #5.

9. Fill the selection in channel #5 with black with the Edit/Fill command. The white area you see in channel #5 will create the drop shadow after you load the selection.

10. Click on the letters "RGB" in the Channels palette to return to the composite image.

11. Now, choose Load Selection from the Select menu. In the Load Selection dialog box, choose #5 from the Channel pop-up menu, then click OK. After the selection appears, fill it with a dark color. Deselect to see the effects.

At this point, both the text and drop-shadow selections are saved in two different alpha channels. This means that at any time you can fill your entire screen with white and then reload the selection in #4 (text), fill it with a color, then reload the selection in channel #5 (shadow) and fill it with a different color. You can also fill either selection with a blend, or apply a filter.

Even though this exercise applied a drop shadow to text, you can apply the same steps to create a drop-shadow on any object. Just skip steps 1 and 2 and, before you start step 3, make sure that your object is selected before you choose Select/Save Selection.

**OTE:** *To learn how to create drop-shadows using layers, see Chapter 12.*

Save your file if you wish and proceed to the next section to learn how to create three-dimensional effects using alpha channels.

## Creating a Three-Dimensional, Raised-Type Effect

You can create endless striking three-dimensional effects by loading and filling selections from alpha channels. You can save even a sliver of a selection that has just the look you want and reload it to be used as a light source or a shadow. The exercise in this section demonstrates how to create a raised-type, or embossed, effect by filling one selection for a light source and another selection for a shadow.

Before starting, examine Figure 11-7. Notice the raised look of the text; it is created primarily from the thin slivers of light and dark along the sides of the letters. The white slivers along the left edges create the illusion of a light source, and the dark slivers along the right edges appear as shadows. Together, they create the depth needed to produce the raised-type effect.

In the exercise, you'll create a separate mask for the light source and another for the shadow. Then the selections are filled with white and black. If you keep these steps in mind as you work through the exercise, you'll have a clearer idea of why you are executing each step. The concepts presented here can be used in other situations where a raised, recessed, or beveled effect is needed.

1. Start by opening any file to which you would like to add raised text. If you don't have a suitable image, load the Fruit file (PC users: fruit.jpg) from the Tutorial folder.

2. Activate the Type tool and click on screen to open the Type Tool dialog box. Type the text to be added to your image and click OK. Once the type appears on screen, move it to the desired position. Then set Opacity in the Layers palette to **1%**. Don't deselect the text.

You're undoubtedly wondering why the Opacity value is 1%. This setting prevents the text from being filled with the foreground color. The

Three-dimensional, raised-type effect (photograph courtesy of Stacy Kollar Photography)

**FIGURE 11-7**

text will be produced by light and shadows, rather than a fill color. The 1% opacity creates a marquee selection of the text that is completely transparent. Later this text selection will be transformed into the two masks for the white edge and the black edge.

**3.** While the text is still selected, choose Save Selection from the Select menu. In the Save Selection dialog box, make sure the Document pop-up menu is set to Fruit and the Channel pop-up menu is set to New. After the alpha channel appears in the Channels palette, double-click on it. In the Channel Options dialog box, name the channel **Black Shadow**; this is the channel you will use to create the shadow for the text. Select the Masked Areas radio button for the Color Indicates option, and click OK.

**4.** In the Black Shadow channel, deselect the text. To lay the groundwork for creating the black shadow slivers, apply the Emboss filter to the entire channel. Choose Emboss from the Filter/Stylize submenu, and in the Emboss dialog box type **135** in the Angle field, **3** in the Height field, and **100** in the Amount field. Click OK to execute the filter.

**5.** Next, duplicate the alpha channel by clicking on it and dragging it over the New Channel icon at the botom of the Channels palette. The second channel will provide the basis for the light source for the raised text.

**6.** To rename the duplicate channel, double-click on it in the Channels palette. When the Channel Options dialog box appears, name the alpha channel **White Shadow** and click OK.

**7.** From the Image/Map submenu, choose Invert to reverse the light and dark areas on screen.

**8.** Next you will isolate the white area of the alpha channel. Choose Threshold from the Image/Map submenu. In the Threshold dialog box, set the slider control somewhere between 200 and 255 and click OK. Before continuing, compare your image with Figure 11-7. Remember that white represents the image area that will become a selection.

**9.** Now isolate the area that will provide the black shadow for the text. Click on the Black Shadow channel in the Channels palette; when the channel is active, choose Threshold from the Image/Map submenu. In the Threshold dialog box, set the slider control somewhere between 200 and 255 and click OK. Once again, compare your image with Figure 11-7. The white area on screen represents another selection that will be loaded into your image. This selection area will be filled with black.

*Photoshop in Action*

Two alpha
channels were
created of the
face of the
text.

Artwork by: Daniel Clark          Client: Dauz Drums

Two alpha channels
were created for
beveled edge.

Daniel started creating this image by setting the type in Freehand, using the typeface Lubilan Graph. After the Type was set, it was imported into Adobe Dimensions in order to create the beveled 3-D perspective. The Adobe Dimensions 3-D wireframe outline was brought into Adobe Photoshop. Once the text was brought into Photoshop, four alpha channels were created: two for the face of the text (for the upper and lower half), and two separate alpha channels for the beveled edge (one for the small beveled edge and another for the large extrusion—the thickness of the letters).

Once the alpha channels are created, Daniel created the chrome effect by using the Gradient tool to create various blends. The foreground color was set to black and the background color was set to white.

**10.** Now you are ready to create the raised-type effect. Select the RGB composite channel by clicking on RGB in the Channels palette or by pressing COMMAND-0 (PC users: CTRL-0).

**11.** To create the shadow portion of the text, load the Black Shadow selection. Choose Load Selection from the Select menu, and select Black Shadow in the Source Channel pop-up menu. Keep the Document pop-up menu set to Fruit. Click OK. When the selection appears, fill it with black. To examine the shadow you just created, hide the selection marquee by choosing Hide Edges from the Select menu.

**12.** To create the light source for the text, choose Select/Load Selection again and select White Shadow in the Source Channel pop-up menu. Keep the Document pop-up menu set to Fruit. Click O.K. When the selection appears, fill it with white. Deselect.

This three-dimensional effect can be applied to any object or shape, not just to text. Also, if you'd like, you can reload the White Shadow and Black Shadow selections and fill them with other colors using various opacities. Try experimenting to create different effects. Fill the Black Shadow selection with white and the White Shadow selection with black, then try filling the white selection with yellow at a 50% opacity.

If you wish to create your own three-dimensional effects, start by analyzing shadow and light sources, and text or object areas. Use the Offset and Emboss filters to help create displacement effects. Use the Image/Effects submenu's Threshold or Invert commands, or the Image/Adjust/Levels command to control the brightness levels. Experiment by filling the selections with the different colors.

Now that you know how to create and use alpha channels, you may wish to explore the other commands in the Channels palette's pop-up menu. But before you go any further, use the File/Save As command to save your document under a new name.

## Using Alpha Channels to Create and Print Spot Colors

In order to print spot colors from Photoshop, you need to use alpha channels. (Spot colors were introduced in the section "Accessing Custom Colors from the Color Picker" in Chapter 4.)

To create spot colors in an RGB Color or CMYK Color file, you first need to select the areas where you want the spot colors to be printed. To easily select the areas, switch to Quick Mask mode, then use the painting and/or selection tools to edit the mask. When you exit Quick Mask mode, these areas will be selected.

Once the areas are selected, choose Save Selection from the Select menu. Click on the New Channel icon in the Channels palette to open the Channel Options dialog box. In the dialog box, enter the name of your spot color in the Name field. The Color Indicates Masked Areas radio button should be selected. Click OK to close the dialog box. On screen, the selected areas are represented by white and the unselected areas are represented by black. This creates a negative plate. If you wish to print a film positive, invert the image by choosing Invert from the Image/Map submenu.

When you wish to print, click on the channel you want to print, then choose Print in the File menu. Do this for each channel.

## Video Alpha Channels

If you are producing Photoshop images for output to video, the Channels palette provides an option for copying the masks you create in alpha channels into a *video alpha channel.* Video alpha channels are often used to overlay titles and graphics in video productions.

Video alpha channels can only be utilized if a 32-bit video card is installed in your computer. These cards are often used in desktop multimedia and videotape production. As discussed in Chapter 1, 24-bit video cards provide over 16 million colors; 32-bit cards such as those manufactured by Radius and TrueVision provide an extra 8 bits that Photoshop's video alpha channel can utilize for storing graphics and titles.

Like all other alpha channels, the video alpha channel allows 256 shades of gray. The brightness values of images and text in the video alpha channel determine the opacity of the image overlaid on the video. The lighter the area, the more translucent; thus, white areas are completely transparent and black areas are completely opaque.

To use an alpha channel as a video alpha channel, choose Video Alpha from the Channels palette's pop-up menu. In the Video Alpha dialog box, click on the Channel pop-up menu to pick a channel, and click OK. When a video alpha channel is created, the eye icon in the Channels palette is replaced with a miniature television (▣).

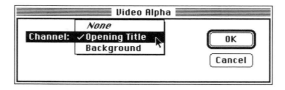

## SPLITTING AND MERGING CHANNELS

A powerful utility offered in the Channels palette allows you to split the channels in a color image into separate files. You can edit an image's separate channels and then merge them back together. In the next section, you'll see how splitting and merging channels can be used to create a colored mezzotint effect.

To split the channels, choose Split Channels in the Channels palette's pop-up menu. The split documents will appear on screen as grayscale images, and the original document is closed.

You can also combine separate channels into a composite image by using the Merge Channels command. To execute this command, all channels to be merged must be open on screen. They must be grayscale images, and their width and height in pixels must be equal. You can merge Photoshop documents together using the Merge Channels command, as long as the documents meet these conditions. In the Merge Channels dialog box, you can specify the number of channels you want to merge and to what mode (RGB Color, CMYK Color, and so forth).

```
╔══════════ Merge Channels ══════════╗
║                                     ║
║   Mode:  [ RGB Color      ▼]   ┌──────────┐
║                                │    OK    │
║   Channels: [3_]               └──────────┘
║                                [ Cancel  ] ║
║                                     ║
╚═════════════════════════════════════╝
```

Click OK, and another dialog box appears where you specify the channels into which you want each open document on screen loaded.

```
╔════════ Merge RGB Channels ════════╗
║                                     ║
║   Specify Channels:        ┌──────────┐
║                            │    OK    │
║   Red:   [ Book Cover.Red    ▼]  └──────────┘
║                            [ Cancel  ]
║   Green: [ Book Cover.Green  ▼]  [  Mode  ]
║                                     ║
║   Blue:  [ Book Cover.Blue   ▼]     ║
╚═════════════════════════════════════╝
```

After you click OK, a new image consisting of the formerly split documents appears in an untitled window.

**11**

## Using Split Channels/Merge Channels to Create a Colored Mezzotint Effect

The Split Channels and Merge Channels commands can be used to create an interesting colored mezzotint effect. First, load an RGB Color or CMYK Color file. Then use the Split Channels command to split the image into separate grayscale files.

Next, create a custom pattern. From the Mode menu, change each file to Bitmap, and choose the Custom Pattern option in the Bitmap dialog box. Click OK to apply the pattern. Do this to every file, and then convert each file back to grayscale.

Next, use the Merge Channels command to merge the channels back together. The color image will reappear, but with a black mezzotint pattern overlaying the colors. The final effect will depend upon the pattern you choose and the colors in the original image.

 OTE: *Photoshop's Mezzotint filter can also create a variety of colored mezzotint effects. See Chapter 8 for more details.*

## CREATING BLENDING EFFECTS WITH THE APPLY IMAGE COMMAND

Once you've learned the fundamentals of creating and using alpha channels, the power of Photoshop's Apply Image command will open a whole new world of design possibilities for you. This command allows you to create exquisite and often striking effects by superimposing channels over other channels. Like Photoshop's Calculations command, covered later in this chapter, the Apply Image command will Add, Subtract, Multiply, and Screen the values of each pixel in a channel with the corresponding pixel values of another channel. The resulting or Target image's channel is changed based upon the calculations applied to the pixel values of the source channels and the target image's channel itself.

Before you begin to use the Apply Image command, it's important to remember the fundamentals of how a digital image is created. As discussed in Chapters 1 and 7, every Photoshop image is created from a grid of pixels. You might think of an image as being created by painting in the rows and columns of grid boxes on a sheet of graph paper. Each grid box is the equivalent of a pixel, and each pixel has a color value from 0 to 255.

When Photoshop executes the Apply Image or Calculations command, it blends channels together by applying calculations to the corresponding pixel values in each channel. For instance, when Photoshop applies the Difference command, it subtracts corresponding pixel values. This means that the value of the first pixel in the first row in one channel is subtracted from the value of the first pixel in the first row of the second channel. The second pixel's value in the first row of the first channel is subtracted from the second pixel's value in row two of the second image, and so on.

It is important to understand that pixel values are measured on a scale of 0 to 255, with 0 representing black and 255 representing white. Therefore, when pixel values increase, the image grows lighter, and when pixel values decrease, the image grows darker.

*n* **OTE:** *When working with a composite image, 0 to 255 represents brightness values of all the RGB channels. If you are a bit puzzled by the representation of brightness values in an image, think of them as a grayscale version of your image. A visual representation of an image's brightness values can be seen by choosing Histogram from the Image menu. For more information about histograms, see Chapter 13.*

Since Photoshop executes the Apply Image command on a pixel-by-pixel basis for channels, it will operate only on images that are exactly the same width and height in pixels. If you wish to use the Apply Image command on channels from two images that are different sizes, you can crop one, or use the Image/Duplicate command to create a duplicate of one image. After the duplicate is created, you can copy and paste the image you need into the duplicate.

*n* **OTE:** *The mathematical formulas for many Apply Image blending options are provided in this section. Undoubtedly, you won't want to keep your calculator accessory open on screen to compute pixel values before applying commands. The formulas are supplied here not so you have to do the math but to help you understand how the commands work and aid you in predicting their outcomes.*

## Using the Apply Image Dialog Box

The Apply Image dialog box allows you to blend a source channel with a target channel. The channels can be in the same document or in different documents. The easiest way to see how Apply Image works is to create a simple blend between an image and a channel with some text in it. This is how the effect in Figure 11-8a was created.

The Apply Image command was applied to the digitized image of the piano in Figure 11-8b and the alpha channel with text in Figure 11-8c to create the effect shown in Figure 11-8a. The Apply Image dialog settings are shown in Figure 11-9. The dialog box settings will be discussed in detail, later in this section.

To complete the following example, load any image on screen. If you don't have an image to load, use the Fruit file (PC users: fruit.jpg). Once the image is loaded, create a new channel by clicking on the New Channel icon (the dog-eared icon in the bottom of the Channels palette). In the Channel Options dialog box that appears, name your channel **Text**. Make sure the Color Indicates Selected Areas is selected

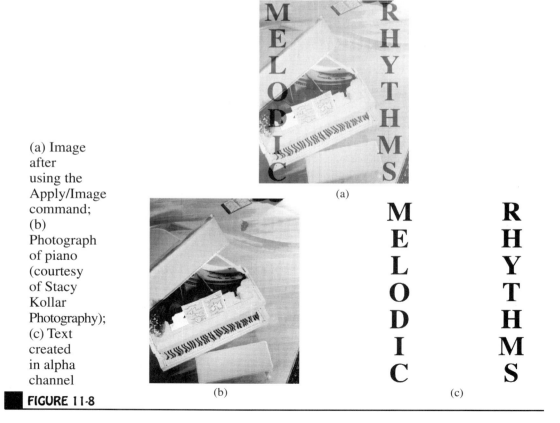

(a) Image after using the Apply/Image command; (b) Photograph of piano (courtesy of Stacy Kollar Photography); (c) Text created in alpha channel

(a)

(b)

(c)

**FIGURE 11-8**

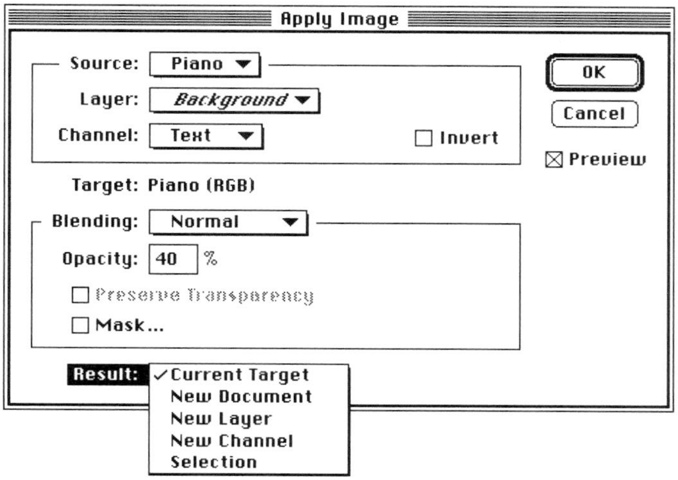

```
┌══════════════ Apply Image ══════════════┐
│  ┌─ Source:  [ Piano  ▼ ]─────────┐   ┌──────────┐  │
│  │   Layer:  [ Background ▼ ]      │   │    OK    │  │
│  │  Channel: [ Text    ▼ ]   □ Invert   └──────────┘  │
│  │                                      ┌──────────┐  │
│  │   Target: Piano (RGB)                │  Cancel  │  │
│  │  ┌─ Blending: [ Normal   ▼ ]──────   └──────────┘  │
│  │  │  Opacity: [ 40 ] %              ⊠ Preview  │
│  │  │  □ Preserve Transparency        │
│  │  │  □ Mask...                      │
│  │  └──────────────────────────────  │
│  │  [ Result: ] ✓Current Target       │
│  │              New Document           │
│  │              New Layer              │
│  │              New Channel            │
│  │              Selection              │
└═══════════════════════════════════════┘
```

The Apply Image dialog box settings for the example shown in Figure 11-8

**FIGURE 11-9**

(this will place a white background in the channel) and click OK. When the channel appears, click on the eye column next to the RGB composite channel in the Channels palette to turn on the view of the RGB composite. This allows you to see the image in the Fruit file while you work in the alpha channel.

Make sure that your foreground color is black. Use the Type tool to add text to the Text channel. After the text appears, position it as desired. Then deselect the text. Before executing the Apply Image command, turn off the eye next to the Text channel. Next, make the RGB channel the target channel by clicking on it in the Channels palette. If you do not select the RGB channel, you might inadvertently apply the Apply Image command to the Text channel rather than the composite RGB channel of the target image on screen.

Now you're ready to open the Apply Image dialog box—but don't choose the command quite yet because there are actually two versions of this dialog box. The version that appears when you choose Apply Image from the Image menu will only allow you to apply the blending effect to the target channel of the active document on screen. It will not allow you to create the effect in a new document. A more versatile version of the dialog box appears if you first press OPTION (PC users: ALT) before choosing Image/Apply Image. This version of the dialog box allows you to choose where you want the Apply Image effect to appear. The examples in this section are designed to work with either version of the dialog box.

**11**

To open the extended version of the Apply Image dialog box, press OPTION (PC users: ALT). Keep the key pressed while you choose Apply Image from the Image menu. At first the commands  you see in the dialog box might seem a little bewildering, but once you understand their purpose, you'll find that Apply Image is actually rather easy to use. Here's a review of the dialog box options.

- The Source pop-up menu at the top of the Apply Image dialog box allows you to choose a document file that you wish to use as one of the blending files. Only documents that have the same width and height in pixels as the active document on screen appear in the Source pop-up menu.

- The Layer and Channel pop-up menus allow you to pick a Layer and a Channel from the source document.

- The Channel pop-up menu allows you to pick a channel from the Source document to use for the blend. If you choose a layer in the Layer pop-up menu (other than the Background), the word "Transparency" appears in the Channel pop-up menu. If you use this option, a mask of the channel is used in the blend. In the mask, transparent layer areas are black, and colored areas are white.

- If your document does not have any transparent layers, the word "Background" appears in the Layer pop-up menu. If your Source image has several layers, the Layer pop-up menu allows you to choose Merged. If you choose this option, the Apply Image command applies calculations to the Source image as if all its layers were merged into one layer.

- The Invert check box adjacent to the Source group allows you to invert the pixel values of the Source pixels. If you click Inverts, black pixels will be read as white, white as black, and pixel values of colors as their complements.

- By default the Target section in the dialog box is where the Apply Image effect will appear. The Target image is always the current active document on screen. The names of the Channel and Layer that the blending effect will appear in are shown in parentheses next to the name of the Target image. The Target channel and the target layer are the currently selected Channel and Layer for the active document on screen. The Target channel and the target layer are both surrounded by a gray shade in the Channels and Layers palette.

The Blending pop-up menu allows you to pick from a group of blending effects. Select the Blending pop-up menu now to see the list of choices. Each choice produces a different effect by telling Photoshop to use a different set of pixel calculations when blending Source and Target pixels. Notice that several of the choices in the pop-up menu are the same names that appear in the Mode menu in different palettes and dialog boxes. These perform virtually the same functions when blending channels as they do when painting.

In the Opacity field, enter the Opacity percentage that will be used when channels are blended together. Low opacities will make the Source channel more translucent. High opacities make the pixels in the Source channel less translucent.

The Mask check box allows you designate a channel in an image to use as a mask. As you'll see later in this section, the dark areas in the mask hide corresponding areas of the source image, allowing more of the target pixels to show through. Light areas in the mask reveal more source pixels and less of the target pixels.

The Preserve Transparency check box only becomes accessible when your target layer is not the background. When the Preserve Transparency check box is selected, transparent areas of the Target image will not be affected by the Apply Image command.

The Result pop-up menu only appears if OPTION (PC users: ALT) is pressed when choosing Image/Apply Image. The Result pop-up menu allows you to choose where you would like the results of Apply Image to appear. The result of Apply Image can be in the Current Target document, a New Document, a New Layer in the target document, a New Channel in the target document, or in a Selection in the target document. If you choose New Layer or New Document, a Name field appears where you can enter the name of the new layer or new document.

Now that you're familiar with the dialog box options, you can try creating a simple blend between the image on screen and the text channel.

1. First, set the Source group. By default the active document on screen appears in the Source pop-up menu. Since it is the only document on screen, no other files appear in the Source pop-up menu. If you are using

**11**

the Fruit file, the word "Background" appears in the Layer pop-up menu. If you are using an image that has layers, you can choose a layer from the pop-up menu.

2. Before you change the Channel pop-up menu to Text, notice that the Target image is your active document. Since you want to blend the Text channel with the document on screen, choose Text from the Channel pop-up menu.

3. Since this is just a simple demonstration of the Apply Image dialog box, leave the Blending pop-up menu set to Normal. Change Opacity to 40%. Then click on the Preview check box. On screen you will see the channel text blended with your image.

4. To create an effect of lighter type blending against the background, click on the Invert check box, next to the Source group. This lightens the text and darkens the background.

Before you proceed to investigate the various Blending options Apply Image has to offer, try changing the Opacity setting. If you lower Opacity, you will see the fruit image becomes more prominent; raise opacity and the text from the channel becomes darker.

If you wish to apply the Apply Image command, click OK, then use the File/Save As command to save your document under a new name. Otherwise, click Cancel and continue to explore the blending options offered by Apply Image.

In the next examples, you will use the Preview check box to examine the different Apply Image options. After you've examined the effect, you can Cancel, or click OK to apply the effect to your target document. If you'd like the blending effect to appear in a new file, choose New Document from the Result pop-up menu, then click OK.

 **EMEMBER:** *If you would like the Result pop-up menu to appear in the Apply Image dialog box, press and hold* OPTION *(PC users:* ALT*) while selecting Image/Apply Image.*

Remember, if you are using Tutorial files, choose File/Save As to rename your document so that you do not overwrite your original files.

## Add and Subtract

The Add and Subtract Blending options add or subtract the values of corresponding pixels in the Source channel and a channel in the Target image. As mentioned earlier, if an image's pixel values increase, the image grows lighter; if the pixel values decrease, the image grows darker. Thus, the Add Blending option can be used to blend and create a lighter Target image, and the Subtract Blending option can be used to blend and create a darker Target image.

Both Blending options allow you to adjust the pixel values of the Target image by entering a *Scale* value and an *Offset* value. To understand these values, let's analyze the formulas Photoshop uses to add and subtract. Here is the Add command formula:

$$\frac{(Source + Target)}{Scale} + Offset = Result$$

This formula adds the pixel values from the Source and Target to produce a brighter Target image. The Scale factor is divided into the sum of the Source pixels; thus Scale can be used to decrease the brightening effect. Scale can be any number between 1.000 and 2.000 inclusive. If Scale is 2, the calculation will result in the average brightness of both images. The Offset factor can be a number between -255 and 255. Adding a positive Offset number lightens the image; adding a negative Offset number darkens the image.

The Subtract Blending option formula uses the same components as the Add formula, except that the Source pixels are subtracted, as is the Offset value.

$$\frac{(Source - Target)}{Scale} - Offset = Result$$

**11**

Here is an exercise to try out the Add and/or Subtract Blending options using the Hands file (PC users: hands.jpg). In this exercise, you'll blend the Hands file with another file created with the Clouds filter. Since both files need to have the same dimensions in pixels, the easiest way to create the Clouds file is to duplicate the Hands file, then create the clouds over the duplicate file.

1. Open the Hands files (or any files in which you want to Add or Subtract brightness).

**2.** To duplicate the file, choose Duplicate from the Image menu. In the Duplicate Image dialog box, name the new file Clouds.

```
═══════════════ Duplicate Image ═══════════════

  Duplicate:  Hands                                 [   OK   ]

        As: [ Clouds                          ]     [ Cancel ]

                  ☐ Merged Layers Only
```

**3.** Before you add color, you'll need to convert the Clouds file to RGB Color. To do this, choose RGB Color from the Mode menu.

**4.** To change the duplicate image into clouds, first change the foreground color to blue and the background color to white. To create the cloud effect, choose Clouds from the Filter/Render submenu.

Now you can blend the two images together—first with the Add command, then with Subtract.

**5.** Choose Apply Image from the Image menu, In the Apply Image dialog box, note that the Target file is the Clouds file because it is the active image on screen.

   **a.** Set the Source pop-up menu to be the Hands file (the Channel pop-up menu is black because the image is a grayscale image).

   **b.** Set the Blending pop-up menu to Add.

   **c.** In the Scale field, type **2**; in the Offset field, type **30**. Set Opacity to 100% . Make sure the Preview button is selected.

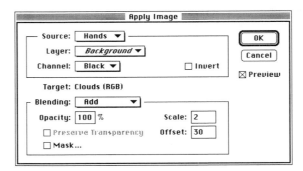

The results will show the Hands file lightened against the Clouds background.

**d.** If you wish to lighten the effect, increase the Offset value.

**e.** Now try the Subtract command by choosing Subtract from the Blending pop-up menu. This will produce results opposite from those of the Add Blending option. The Scale factor should be set to 1. The blended images will be darker. Raise the Offset value if you wish to lighten the image.

## Difference

The Difference Blending option subtracts the pixel values of the Target channel from a channel in the Source image. The results of the Difference Blending option are fairly easy to predict because the calculation is quite simple:

Source – Target = Result

With this formula, if darker Target pixels (other than black) are subtracted from lighter pixels, the blended Target pixels will be darker than the Source pixels and lighter than the original Target pixels. Also, two very bright pixels subtracted from each other will result in a dark pixel. Subtracting from black leaves image areas unchanged. Subtracting from white inverts the color. If a negative number results from the calculation, that number is used as a positive number.

The image in Figure 11-10b was combined with the alpha channel containing black and white stripes shown in Figure 11-10c to create the effect in Figure 11-10a. The dialog box settings for the Apply Image command are shown in Figure 11-11. The Target image shows you that when black is subtracted from the Source, no change is produced (because the pixel value of black is 0). When white (a pixel value of 255) is subtracted from the Source, the result is a negative of those image areas.

If you'd like to see the Difference Blending option in action, load any color image, or use the Fruit file (PC users: fruit.jpg) from the Tutorial folder. Once your file is on screen, select New Channel from the Channels palette's pop-up menu. In the Channel Options dialog box, make sure the Masked Areas radio button is selected, then click OK. In the channel, create a series of white stripes, as shown in Figure 11-10c. After creating the stripes, click on the RGB channel to select it as your target channel. Then execute the Apply Image command. In the Apply Image dialog box, set the Source to the Fruit file, set the Channel pop-up menu to be channel #4 (the new channel you just created), and set the Blending pop-up menu to Difference. Keep Opacity at 100%. Make sure the Preview check box is selected to see the results.

**11**

FUNDAMENTAL PHOTOSHOP

(a)

(a) Image
after
using the
Difference
Blending
option in
the Apply
Image dialog
box; (b)
Photograph
of Aruba; (c)
Black- and-
white stripes
created
in alpha
channels

**FIGURE 11-10**　　　　(b)　　　　　　　　　(c)

## Lighter and Darker

The Lighter Blending option compares the values of every pixel in the Source and Target images. Any pixel that is lighter in the Source channel will replace darker pixels in the Target image. When blending grayscale images, lighter pixel values replace darker pixel values. When blending two composite color channels, Photoshop compares the color value in each channel, then uses the lighter value (higher value in RGB images) to produce the effect. This could mean that the colors in the Target/Result image could be quite different from the Source or original Target pixels. For instance, assume a Source image pixel in the RGB channel is Red 50, Blue 150, Green 200. Its corresponding pixel in the Target is Red 25, Blue 100,

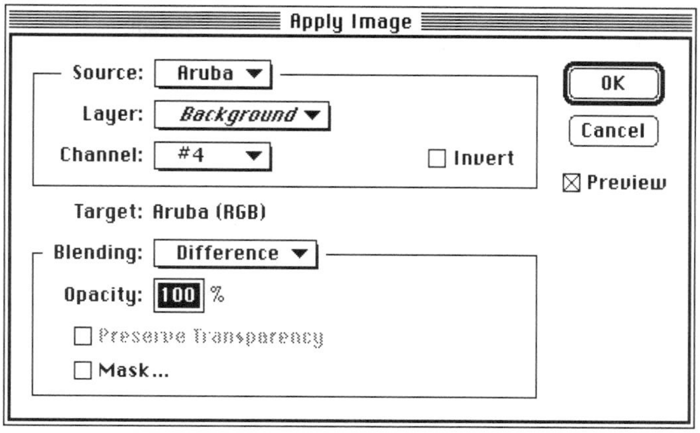

```
┌──────────────────── Apply Image ────────────────────┐
│                                                      │
│   ┌─ Source:  [ Aruba  ▼ ]────────────┐  ┌── OK ──┐  │
│   │   Layer:  [ Background ▼ ]          │  ├ Cancel ┤ │
│   │  Channel: [ #4      ▼ ]  ☐ Invert  │             │
│   │                                     │  ☒ Preview  │
│   │   Target: Aruba (RGB)               │             │
│   │ ┌─ Blending: [ Difference ▼ ]──────┐│             │
│   │ │  Opacity: [100] %                 ││             │
│   │ │  ☐ Preserve Transparency          ││             │
│   │ │  ☐ Mask...                        ││             │
│   └─┴───────────────────────────────────┘             │
└──────────────────────────────────────────────────────┘
```

Apply Image dialog box settings for the example shown in Figure 11-10

**FIGURE 11-11**

Green 75. After Apply Image is executed, with the Lighter option chosen, the pixel values in the Target file will be Red 50, Blue 150, Green 200.

The Lighter Blending option has a similar effect to that created by the Lighten painting/editing mode (see Chapter 5). The Darker Blending option produces the opposite effect: any pixel that is darker in the Source channel will replace lighter pixels in the Target image. In the above example of pixel values, Darker would result in a pixel value of Red 25, Blue 100, Green 75. The effect of this command is similar to that created by the Darken painting/editing mode (also described in Chapter 5).

The Lighter Blending option was applied to the RGB channels of both the Source (Aruba) and Target (Bricks) images shown in Figures 11-12b and 11-12c to achieve the result shown in Figure 11-12a. Notice that the lighter brick mortar pixels appear in the Target (Bricks) image rather than the corresponding darker pixels from the Aruba image. Throughout much of the Target image, the lighter texture of the bricks is also visible. Figure 11-13 illustrates the Lighter dialog box settings for this example. Had the Darker option been applied instead of Lighter, the dark trees would have been more dominant in the Target image.

If you wish to try out the Lighter and Darker Blending options, try blending the Window file with an image created with the Clouds filter. First, load the Window file (PC users: window.jpg). Then use the Image/Duplicate command to create a duplicate of the file and name it Clouds. Set the foreground color to a light blue and the background color to dark blue. Execute the Clouds filter by choosing Clouds from the Filter/Render submenu.

**11**

(a)

(a) Image after using the Lighter Blending option in the Apply Image dialog box; (b) Source: photograph of Aruba; (c) Target: brick wall (courtesy of D'pix Inc.)

(b)

(c)

**FIGURE 11-12**

Execute the Image/Apply Image command. The Target file will be the Clouds file because it is the current active document. Set the Source image to be the Window file. Make sure the Channel pop-up menu is set to RGB. In the Blending pop-up menu choose Lighter. Set Opacity to 100%.

In your Target image, you will see that the darkest areas of the window panes are completely replaced by the lighter pixels from the clouds. Next, choose the Darker option from the Blending pop-up menu. The results will be just the opposite: black window areas will be replaced by the lighter areas of the Target Clouds file.

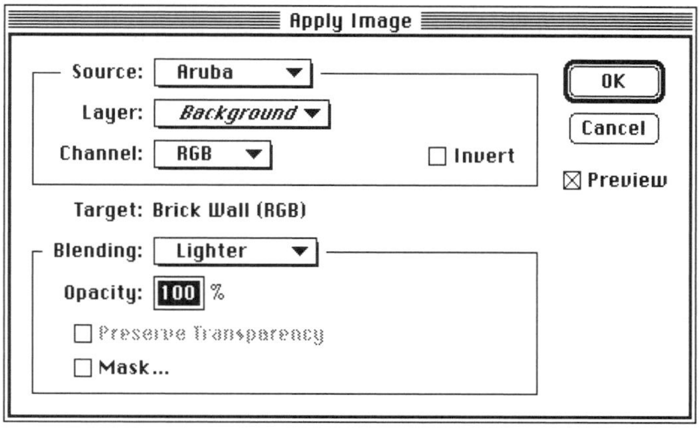

Apply
Image
dialog box
settings for
the image
example
shown in
Figure
11-12.

**FIGURE 11-13**

## Multiply

The Multiply Blending option produces the effect of two positive transparencies placed over each other and viewed over a light table. The effect is similar to that created by the Multiply painting/editing mode (see Chapters 5 and 11).

The Multiply formula multiplies the two Source values and divides the result by the brightness value of white (255). Thus, applying the Multiply Blending option to a dark image and a light image will produce a dark Destination image. Here is the formula:

$$\frac{(\text{Source})\ (\text{Target})}{255} = \text{Result}$$

Using the Multiply Blending option, you can easily create the effect of a portrait emerging out of dark shadows. Try an exercise using the Portrait file (PC users: portrait.jpg) from the Tutorial folder.

First open the Portrait file. Create a new channel and name it "Gradient." Make sure the Masked Areas radio button is selected and click OK. Click on the eye icon column to view the RGB composite channel, so you can see the Portrait image while you work in the channel. Make sure that your Target channel is your Gradient channel.

**11**

Next, using the Gradient tool, create a white-to-black radial blend in the Gradient channel. Make sure the Midpoint Skew slider in the Gradient Tool Options palette is set to at least 50%. With both the Gradient channel and the Portrait file visible, you can easily create the blend in the area over the girl's face. Since you want the blending effect to occur around the girl's face, create the blend by clicking and dragging from the middle of her face to the end of your document window. Turn off editing in the Gradient channel and set the Target channel to RGB by clicking on RGB in the Channels palette. Turn off the eye next to the Gradient channel by clicking on it.

Execute the Image/Apply Image command. The Source pop-up menu will be the Portrait file. Set the Channel pop-up menu to be the Gradient channel. The Target image will be the Portrait file. Make sure the Preview check box is selected, then choose Multiply from the Blending pop-up menu.

Your final composite image shows darker pixels enveloping most of the Portrait image. The girl's face appears through only the very lightest areas of the blend.

## Screen

The opposite of the effect created by Multiply can be achieved with the Screen Blending option: the effect of layering one film negative on top of another and printing the combined image on photographic paper. The result is similar to using the Screen painting/editing mode (discussed in Chapters 5 and 12).

The relatively complicated Screen formula generally ensures that the resulting Target pixel values will be greater than the Source pixel values; thus, the Screen Blending option produces an overall lighter Target /Result image.

$$\frac{255-(255-\text{Source})\,(255-\text{Target})}{255} = \text{Result}$$

The Screen Blending option was used to combine the image of the model in Figure 11-14b with the radial blend in Figure 11-14c to create the final image in Figure 11-14a. The radial blend was created in a new alpha channel in the Model file. Then the Screen Blending option in the Apply Image dialog box, shown in Figure 11-15, was used to blend the Source and Target images together. The resulting effect is a *vignette*; the Screen Blending option used the white pixels in the Gradient channel to overpower the dark pixels in the model image. It also took the pixels in the model image that corresponded to the dark part of the blend and lightened them.

(a)

(a) Image after using the Screen option in the Apply Image dialog box; (b) Photograph of a model (courtesy of Stacy Kollar Photography); (c) Gradient created in an alpha channel

**FIGURE 11-14**

(b)

(c)

You can easily duplicate this vignette effect using the Portrait file (PC users: portrait.jpg) in the Tutorial folder. Follow the same basic steps that you used for the Multiply Blending option in the previous section, except this time use the Gradient tool to create a black-to-white radial blend in the alpha channel, rather than a white-to-black. After you execute the Apply Image command with the Screen Blending option, your final image will show that the white pixels in the blend have more influence than the darker pixels in the portrait file. If you wish to darken the effect, set the Midpoint slider in the Gradient Tool Options palette to at least 50% and the Radial Offset slider to 40% before creating the radial blend. This will produce a large black area in the radial blend.

11

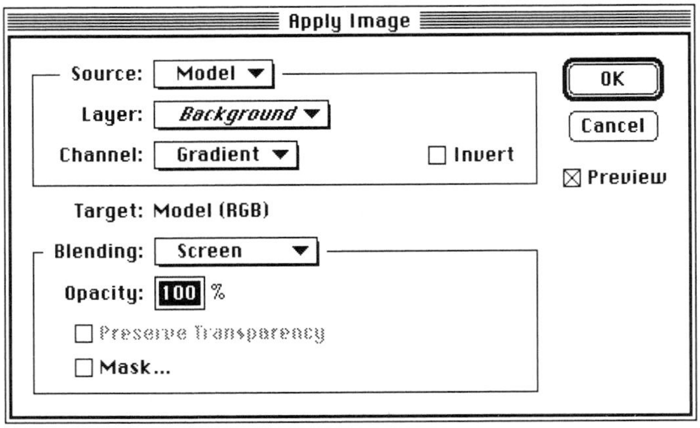

```
┌─────────────────── Apply Image ───────────────────┐
│  ┌─ Source: [ Model ▼ ]──────────        ┌─────────┐│
│  │   Layer: [ Background ▼ ]              │   OK    ││
│  │ Channel: [ Gradient ▼ ]     ☐ Invert  └─────────┘│
│  │                                        ┌─────────┐│
│  │                                        │ Cancel  ││
│  │  Target: Model (RGB)                   └─────────┘│
│  ┌─ Blending: [ Screen ▼ ]                ☒ Preview  │
│  │  Opacity: [100] %                                 │
│  │  ☐ Preserve Transparency                          │
│  │  ☐ Mask...                                        │
└────────────────────────────────────────────────────┘
```

Apply
Image
dialog box
settings
for the
example
shown in
Figure
11-14

**FIGURE 11-15**

## Overlay

Overlay will screen or multiply depending upon the colors in the Target channel. When bright source colors blend with the Target channel, they are screened; when dark colors blend with the Target channel, they are multiplied. The highlights and shadows of the Target channel are always maintained.

To see the Overlay Blending option in action, try blending the Window file (PC users: window.jpg) with a copy of the Fruit file. As explained earlier, when blending two images together, they must have the same dimensions in pixels. Use the Image/Duplicate command to create a duplicate of the Window file, then copy the Fruit file into it.

Here's a brief review of the steps. After you open the Window file, use the Image/Duplicate command to create a duplicate of the file. Name the duplicate **MyFruit**. Open the Fruit file, then use the Select/All command to select the entire image. Then copy and paste the image into the MyFruit window. Deselect. Choose Image/Apply Image to open the Apply Image dialog box. Set the Source image as the Window file, and the Source channel to RGB. The Target file will be the MyFruit file. Make sure the Opacity is set to 100%. Make sure the Preview check box is selected, then choose Overlay from the Blending pop-up menu. The preview image will show the Source and Target files composited together. The bright flowers and the napkin in the image show through a blend of the two files. If you'd like to experiment more with the Overlay Blending option, change the Target file by clicking Cancel to close the Apply Image dialog box. Then activate the Window file instead of the MyFruit file. Reopen the Image Apply dialog box. When you apply the Overlay Blending option, set the Source to be the Fruit file. The results will be completely different because the effect is based upon the colors of the selected channel in the Target file.

## Soft and Hard Light

Now that you've had a chance to try out several of the blending options in the Apply Image dialog box, experiment with the Soft Light and Hard Light commands on your own. Both Soft Light and Hard Light Screen or Multiply depending upon on the colors of the Target image. In both blending modes, if the Source channel pixels are lighter than the Target pixels, the Target pixels are lightened. If the Source channel pixels are darker than the Target pixels, the Target pixels are darkened. Soft Light applies a soft, spread-out lighting effect, while Hard Light applies a harder, more direct lighting effect. If you don't have images to use, try creating a linear blend in one file and blending it with the Fruit file using Hard and Soft Light.

## Using the Apply Image Dialog Box Mask Option

Now that you've examined the options in the Blending pop-up menu, you might wish to try some more sophisticated blending techniques by using the Mask check box in the Apply Image dialog box. The Mask check box allows you to use a channel as a mask for the Target image. By default, darker image areas in the mask will allow more of the Target image to show through the composite. Lighter mask areas hide Target image areas. Thus, in areas that correspond to light pixels in the mask, the Source image is more predominant in the final blended image, rather than in the Target image.

To help you visualize how the Mask option works, suppose you are creating a patriotic image containing images of the president, the vice president, and the flag of the United States. Assume the president is the Source image, the vice president is the Target image, and the flag is the mask. In this case, assume the mask is a composite RGB channel. When the images are blended together, the Source image is more prominent in the lighter areas of the mask, and the Target image is more prominent in the darker areas of the mask. Thus, the image of the president would be more apparent in the areas corresponding to the flag's white stripes, while the vice president would be more apparent in the areas corresponding to the red stripes.

Figure 11-16 shows the results of the Apply Image command when executed with the Mask option. In this case, we used a blend in an alpha channel as a mask, though a separate file could have been used. The piano (Figure 11-8b) was the Source image, the model (Figure 11-14b) was the Target image. The model and a blend

11

Image after using the Mask option in the Apply Image dialog box to combine the piano and model images

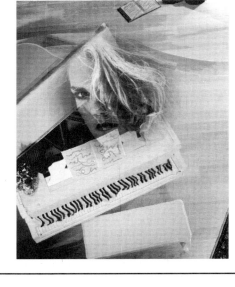

**FIGURE 11-16**

(Figure 11-14a) comprised the mask. The blend was created in a channel in the same file as the model. The Apply Image dialog box settings for this example are shown in Figure 11-17. When the Apply Image command was executed, the piano appeared in areas corresponding to the lighter areas of the mask, and the model appeared primarily in areas corresponding to the darker part of the mask.

If you wish to try out the Mask option, you can work with the Window and Portrait files used earlier in this chapter to create a similar effect. To ensure that both files are the same size and resolution, you'll duplicate the Window file, then copy the Portrait file into the duplicate.

1. Load the Window file from the Tutorial folder, and then use the Image/Duplicate command to create a duplicate of the Window file. Name the file "Girl," then click OK.

2. Next, load the Portrait file. Press COMMAND-A (PC users: CTRL-A) to select the entire file. Then, copy and paste the image of the girl into the Girl file on screen. Deselect. Close the Portrait file to preserve memory.

3. In the Girl file, create a new channel and name it "Gradient." In the Channel Options dialog box, make sure that the Color Indicates Masked Areas option is selected. Click OK.

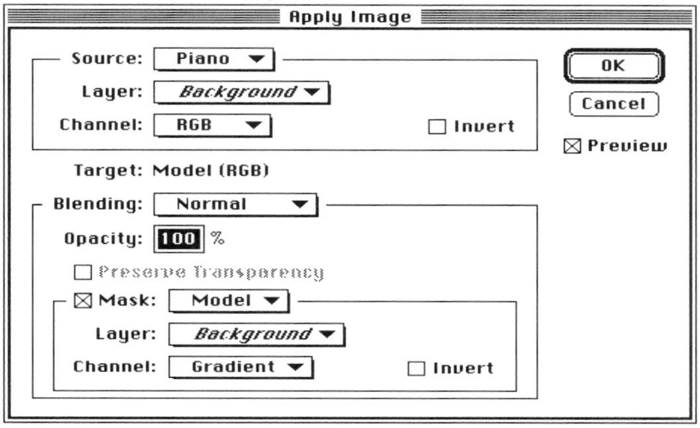

Apply Image dialog box settings for the example shown in Figure 11-16

**Apply Image**

Source: Piano ▼
Layer: *Background* ▼
Channel: RGB ▼          □ Invert

OK
Cancel
☒ Preview

Target: Model (RGB)

Blending: Normal ▼

Opacity: **100** %

□ Preserve Transparency

☒ Mask: Model ▼
Layer: *Background* ▼
Channel: Gradient ▼          □ Invert

■ **FIGURE 11-17**

4. Click on the eye icon column next to the RGB channel. This will enable you to see the Girl image while you work in the alpha channel, but you won't affect the girl.

5. Before creating the radial blend, make sure the foreground is set to black and the background to white. Then double-click on the Gradient tool and set the Type pop-up menu in the Gradient Tool Options palette to Radial. Choose Foreground to Background as the Gradient Style, and set the Midpoint slider value to 50% and the Radial Offset slider to 20. This will increase the black portion in the center of the blend.

6. To create the radial blend, click on the middle of the girl's face and drag past the end of her head, about a half-inch or so. Now click on the RGB Channel and turn off the eye icon in the Channels palette next to the Gradient channel.

   Next, you will use the Apply Image command to blend the Window file with the image of the girl. When the composite is created, the gradient in the alpha channel will mask out everything but the little girl's face. Target image areas corresponding to black areas in the gradient will appear; areas corresponding to white will not appear.

7. From the Image menu, choose Apply Image. Set the Source document to Window and the Channel to RGB. The Target file should be the Girl file. Set the Blending pop-up menu to Normal and Opacity to 100%. Click on

**11**

the Mask check box. Set the Mask pop-up menu to the Girl file, since this is where the blend for the mask was created. Set the Channel pop-up menu to Gradient.

The results will show the little girl's face appearing through the image of the window. Apply Image produces an ethereal fade-out effect in areas that correspond to the gradient alpha channel fading from black to white. To see a completely different effect, click on the Invert check box in the Mask section. The middle of the little girl's face disappears—it's as if an invisible girl in clothes appears on screen. Clicking on Invert created the same effect that would be created with a white-to-black radial blend (rather than a black to white). Remember, when using the Channels Options dialog box, white areas hide the target file, black areas reveal it.

On your own, try out different blending options with the Mask option selected. After you've had a chance to experiment, continue to the next section to explore the Calculations dialog box which also allows you to combine channels together.

## USING THE CALCULATIONS COMMAND

The Image menu's Calculations command provides many of the same features as the Apply Image commands. Both allow you to create blends between channels by choosing a blending option and changing opacity. Both dialog boxes require that all images used have the same width and height in pixels. The primary differences between Apply Image and Calculations is that the Calculations command does not produce its effects in a composite channel. The resulting effect can appear in any channel or alpha channel other than an image's composite channel. The Calculations command can also create the result in a new file with a new channel in it. The result can also be a *layer mask*. A layer mask is a mask created in a new channel that allows you to hide or reveal portions of different layers. After the mask is created, it can easily be edited to reveal more or less of the layer you are in and more or less of the underlying layer.

Since the blending options in the Calculations dialog box are the same as those in the Apply Image dialog box, each individual blending option will not be discussed here. Instead, the following section provides a simple demonstration of how to create a blend between two channels with the Calculations command. This is followed by step-by-step instructions for using the Calculations command to create a layer mask.

Start by loading the Flower file (PC users: flower.jpg) or any other image. Use the File/Save As command to rename the file Myflower. Click on the New Channel icon to create a new alpha channel in the file. Name the channel Text. Make sure the Masked Areas radio button is selected.

Set the foreground color to white. Activate the Type tool and click in the left side of the channel. Select Times or any other serif typeface at a point size between 75 and 100. Enter the word **GROW** in the text area, then click OK. After you position the word in the center of the channel, deselect. Next, click on the New Channel icon to create another channel. Name this channel Radial. Double-click on the Line tool and set the Line Width to 25 pixels.

Next, create a white cross that extends to the edges of the channel. Use the Radial Blur filter to create a blurring effect in the channel. In the Radial Blur dialog box, set the Amount to 25 and Quality to Draft. After the filter runs its course, reselect the RGB channel to make it the target channel.

Set the background color to white. Choose Select/All from the Edit menu. Then choose Edit/Cut to fill the entire screen with white and place the flower image in the Clipboard. Later you will paste the flower back into a selection created by the Calculations command.

To open the Calculations dialog box, choose Calculations from the Image menu. The illustration below shows the settings for the Calculations dialog box that you'll need to complete this exercise.

```
┌──────────────────────── Calculations ════════════════╗
║  ┌─ Source 1:  [ Myflower ▼ ]──────────    ┌─────────┐ ║
║  │     Layer:  [ Background ▼ ]             │   OK    │ ║
║  │   Channel:  [ Text   ▼ ]     ☐ Invert   └─────────┘ ║
║  └──────────────────────────────           ┌─────────┐ ║
║                                             │ Cancel  │ ║
║  ┌─ Source 2:  [ Myflower ▼ ]──────────    └─────────┘ ║
║  │     Layer:  [ Background ▼ ]             ☒ Preview   ║
║  │   Channel:  [ Radial ▼ ]     ☐ Invert               ║
║  └──────────────────────────────                       ║
║  ┌─ Blending:  [ Difference ▼ ]─────────               ║
║  │   Opacity:  [100] %                                 ║
║  │   ☐ Mask...                                         ║
║  └──────────────────────────────                       ║
║  ┌─ Result:    [ Myflower ▼ ]──────────               ║
║  │   Channel:  [ Selection ▼ ]                         ║
║  └──────────────────────────────                       ║
╚═══════════════════════════════════════════════════════╝
```

**11**

> **OTE:** *If you don't have a large monitor, you can open a small version of the Calculations dialog box by pressing* OPTION *(PC users:* ALT*) while choosing Image/Calculations.*

As mentioned earlier, the Calculations dialog box includes the same blending features as the Apply Image dialog box. To see the blending choices, click on the Blending pop-up menu. As in the Apply Image dialog box, Opacity can be set by entering a percentage. Unlike the Apply Image dialog box, the Calculations dialog box allows you to specify *two* sources. The channels in the Source documents contain the data that Photoshop uses when it applies Calculations.

The Source 1 pop-up menu allows you to choose any open document on screen whose pixel dimensions in width and height match the active document's pixel dimensions. In the Layer pop-up menu, you can choose the layer from the Source 1 document you wish to use when blending. The Channel pop-up menu allows you to choose any channel from the Source 1 document that you use wish to use when blending.

At this point, the name of your new document appears in the Source 1 pop-up menu. Set the Channel to the text channel.

The Source 2 pop-up menu works exactly the same as the Source 1 pop-up menu. Only images whose pixel dimensions are the same as the active document's will appear in the pop-up menu. The Layer and Channel pop-up menus refer to layers and channels in the Source 2 document.

At this point, the name of your new document appears in the Source 2 pop-up menu. Set the Channel to the Radial channel since you will be using it as the second source for the effect.

To create the blend effect, you use the Difference Blending mode. This will subtract the pixel values of the Radial channel from the pixel values of the Text channel. To choose the blending mode, select Difference from the Blending pop-up menu.

The Result pop-up menu allows you to choose where the results of the Calculations dialog box will appear. If you choose New in the Result pop-up menu, and New in the Channel pop-up menu, the results of the Calculations command will appear in a new document with one channel in it. You could then duplicate the channel to any document when needed.

In the Channel pop-up menu, you can choose the channel in the Result document where you want the blended channel to appear or you can have the result appear in the Result document as a New Selection. If the Result document has a layer in it, you can set the result channel to be a layer mask.

In this example, leave the result file set to the document on screen, and set the result channel to be a Selection. Later you will paste the flower from the Clipboard into this selection.

Before executing the command, note that the Calculations dialog box includes a Mask option. If you click on the Mask pop-up menu, the dialog box expands to allow you to choose a source document for the mask, as well as the channel and layer that the mask is in. When a mask is used, dark areas of the mask allow more of the document to appear, light areas allow the Source 2 image to appear.

For each of the Source 1, Source 2, and mask channels chosen, an Invert option is available. If Invert is chosen, the channels' pixels are inverted to create a negative of the image.

As in the Apply Image dialog box, the Preview check box is an invaluable aid in predicting blending effects. When using the Calculations dialog box, the preview appears in the active document on screen. Click the Preview check box to preview the Difference effect.

Now execute the Calculations command by clicking OK. On screen you will see a selection. The selection is the result of subtracting one alpha channel from another. Now paste the flower image into the selection by choosing Edit/Paste Into. On screen you'll see the flower image through both the text and the lines created by the radial blur.

## Creating a Layer Mask Using the Calculations Command

The following steps show how to use the Calculations commands to create a layer mask using Adobe Photoshop Tutorial files. Of course, feel free to substitute your own files if you'd like.

Start by preparing Source 1 and Source 2 images. These images will be blended together to create a mask in a third file.

1. Open the Seasons file from the Tutorial folder. Choose Select/All, then Edit/Copy. Close the file. Next, create a new 72ppi file 4.5 by 5.75 inches. In the Name field, enter the word **MySeason**. When the new file appears, choose Edit/Paste. While the Seasons file is still floating, use the Image/Effects/Scale command to scale the Seasons image so that the image extends to the edges of the document. Then deselect.

2. To add texture to the MySeason image, apply the Add Noise filter. In the Add Noise dialog box, set the Amount to 100 and the Distribution radio button to Gaussian.

3. Now create a new alpha channel by pressing and holding the OPTION key (PC users: ALT) while you click on the New Channel icon in the Channels palette.

4. In the alpha channel, use the Marquee tool to create a black and gray checkerboard pattern. Use different shades of gray when you create the checkerboard. Make the squares about 1-inch wide.

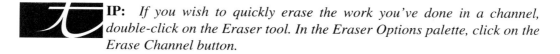

**IP:** *If you wish to quickly erase the work you've done in a channel, double-click on the Eraser tool. In the Eraser Options palette, click on the Erase Channel button.*

Before executing the Calculations command, you need to create a result file with a layer in it. (The layer mask option is not available unless the Result document has a layer in it.) The Result file will be created with the Fruit and Window images from the Tutorial folder.

5. Then create a new 4.5-by-5.75-inch RGB Color file and set the Resolution to 72. Set the background Contents to White. Name this file **Final**.

6. Next, open the Fruit file (PC users:fruit.jpg). After the Fruit file is open, choose Select/All then Edit/Copy. Close the file, then choose Edit/Paste to paste the Fruit image into the Final document on screen. Deselect.

Next you will create a layer in the Final file by dragging and dropping the Window file over it.

7. Open the Window file (PC users: window.jpg). To create a layer in the Final file, use the Move tool to move the Window image over the Final file that has the Fruit image in it. After your layer is created, close the Window file.

At this point, you can't see the entire Fruit image because the Window layer covers it. This was done on purpose in this example to make the effects of applying the Layer Mask more apparent. Later, when the Layer Mask; is created, dark areas in the mask will reveal areas from the Fruit layer, light areas will reveal areas from the Window layer.

**AUTION:** *Do not select the Background in the Layers palette; otherwise you will not be able to create the Layer Mask for Layer 1.*

**8.** To set the dialog box options for the Layer Mask, choose Calculations from the Image menu. In the Calculations dialog box, set the Source 1 document to be the MySeason file. Set the Channel for the Source 1 document to Gray. The Gray option is the composite RGB channel. The Source 2 pop-up menu should be set to MySeason also. Set the Source 2 Channel pop-up menu to #4. This is the channel with the checkerboard pattern in it. Now choose Subtract in the Blending pop-up menu, and leave Opacity set to 100%. Leave Scale set to 1. Set Offset to 100. Set the Result pop-up menu to Final. In the Result Channel pop-up menu choose Layer 1 Mask. Click on the Preview check box.

A preview of the mask will appear in the Final file on screen. When the layer mask is created, the image you see will be copied into a new channel in the Final file.

**9.** To create the layer mask, click OK. To see the effect in the Final file, click on RGB in the Channels palette.

The Final file on screen will suddenly change to reveal a blend between the two layers in the image. Notice that the Fruit layer is more prominent in areas corresponding to the dark part of the mask, and the Window is more prominent in areas corresponding to the light part of the mask. The texture you see is from the noise created from the layer mask. Examine the file to see how the light and dark areas from the checkerboard alpha channel contribute to the final image.

One of the most intriguing features of layer masks is that the image on screen is actually a type of preview of how the image will appear when the layer mask is *applied*. The appearance of the image on screen changed because you are viewing it through the Layer Mask. You can edit the mask without actually changing the pixels in the Result image.

You can access the layer mask through the Channels palette. Notice that the Channels palette now has a new channel named "Layer Mask." If you wish to edit the mask, you could click on the words "Layer Mask." If you paint with a dark color in the mask, you will reveal more of the Fruit layer. If you paint with a light color, you will hide more of the Fruit layer and reveal more of the Window layer.

**11**

# Photoshop in Action

The recessed-type effect was created using alpha channels and the Image/Calculations and Image/Adjust/ Levels commands.

The background image is a photograph of a rock that was scanned.

Artist: Daniel Clark                                  Client: Petersen Publishing

Daniel started creating this calender cover by scanning a photograph of a rock into Photoshop. Next he traced the "4Wheel & Off-Road" logo in Freehand and filled it with black. In the digitized rock file, he created a new alpha channel and placed the logo into it.

While the logo was still floating, he copied and pasted it into two other alpha channels. In each alpha channel, he blurred and then feathered the floating logo. Next he deselected the logo and offset it. The alpha channel that would be used for the highlight areas of the recessed text was offset to the right by using the Filter/Other/Offset command. (The alpha channel that would be used for the shadow areas of the recessed text was offset to the left using the same filter.) After the filter was applied, the logo in each alpha channel was inverted using the Image/Map/Invert command. This produced white type on a black background.

To create a mask for the highlight area of the text, the Image/Calculations command was used with the Darker blending option selected. In the Image/Calculations dialog box, the digitized rock file was chosen in all the Source pop-up menus. The Source 1 Channel pop-up menu was set to the very first alpha channel (containing the text that was not offset). The Source 2 and Destination Channel pop-up menus were set to the highlight channel (the second channel). To create a mask for the shadow area of the text, the Image/Calculations command was also used with the Darker blending option. The same settings were used, except the Source 2 and Destination Channel pop-up menus were set to the shadow channel (the third channel).

Once the masks were completed, Daniel loaded each selection individually and used the Levels command to darken or lighten the selection to complete the recessed effect. For a finishing touch, he exported the file to Fractal Design Painter, where he used a textured airbrush tool to add cracks to the letters.

If you are happy with the effect the Layer Mask produces, you can apply it to your image or you can discard it. Applying it to your image *will* change the pixels in the image. To apply or discard the layer mask, you drag it into the Trash in the Channels palette. Try dragging the layer mask into the Trash now. A dialog box will appear. If you wish to apply the layer mask to your image, click Apply. If you wish to discard the layer mask, choose Discard. To cancel and leave the layer mask on screen, click Cancel.

At this point feel free to experiment with different Sources, Blending options, and Opacities with the Layer Mask option.

**OTE:** *Many layer mask operations can be handled from the Layers palette. For more information, see Chapter 12.*

## CONCLUSION

You've seen in this chapter how valuable channels can be in image editing, creating special effects, and blending images together. In Chapter 12, you'll learn how layers can be used to blend images together and create layer masks.

# WORKING WITH
# LAYERS

Layers open up a new world of artistic freedom and design possibilities. When you start using layers, digital art you imagined but never thought feasible lies within your grasp. Layers set you free from many of the restraints imposed by a pixel-based program. They allow you to experiment with an infinite range of design possibilities without having to spend hours of time selecting, reselecting, or starting over again returning to earlier versions of your files.

When you work in a layer, it's as though you're editing an image on a sheet of acetate: images below the acetate can show through the transparent areas. If you have multiple layers, you can reposition them in any order. If you erase an object on a layer, background images will show through. Move the layer and all objects on the layer move together as a group, independently from all other layers.

This chapter will start with a discussion of layer fundamentals, and then proceed to show you techniques for blending images together. You will learn how to create and delete layers, move objects in layers, change target layers, and rearrange layers. Once you've mastered the technical aspects of creating layers, you'll move on to explore the artistic possibilities opened up to you by the Layers palette. You'll blend images together using the Layers palette's painting/editing modes and explore its Composite Controls, which allow you to specify the pixel range in layers that you wish to blend together.

Toward the end of the chapter you'll learn how to create a layer mask. With a layer mask, you'll be able to gradually wipe away the pixels of one layer so that it seamlessly dissolves into another layer. But before moving ahead to advanced topics, you need to understand the basics of using the Layers palette.

## EXPLORING THE LAYERS PALETTE

The Layers palette is your command center for managing layers. Among the many operations you can perform in the Layers palette are create new layers, reorder layers, select a target layer to edit in, merge layers, create layer masks, and delete layers.

In the following exercises you'll learn how to use the Layers palette by working with a few simple shapes and some text. This will provide you with an in-depth introduction to layer fundamentals. As you work through the following exercises, you'll create a design with a rectangle, a circle, and text, as shown in Figure 12-1.

Each element will be created in a separate layer. Later, you'll blend each element together by changing opacities and using the Dissolve painting/editing mode.

In order to get under way, you'll need to open the Layers palette and a new document on screen.

1. If the Layers palette isn't open, open it now by choosing Show Layers from the Window/Palettes submenu.

2. Start by creating a new RGB Color file, 7 inches wide by 5 inches high at 72 ppi. Set the background Contents to white by clicking on the White radio button in the Contents group, then click OK.

   After the file opens, notice that the word "Background" appears in the top section of the Layers palette. The base layer of any file that is created without a transparent background will appear in the Layers palette designated as the Background. Also notice the eye icon ( 👁 ) that appears to the left of "Background." This indicates that the Background is visible in your document. The gray area surrounding the word "Background" in the Layers palette means that the Background is the current target layer. The target layer is the layer you are editing.

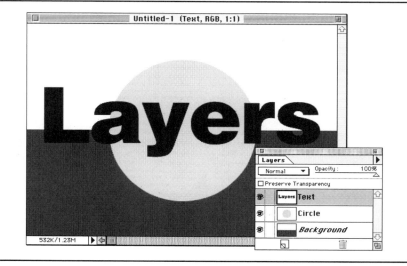

Three layers were used to create this image, as indicated in the Layers palette

**FIGURE 12-1**

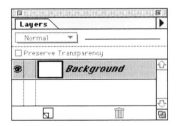

Before adding a layer to your file, create an object on the Background so that you see how it affects the Layers palette.

**3.** Use the Marquee tool to create a rectangle that covers the entire bottom portion of your file and fill it with red, as seen in Figure 12-1. Then deselect.

In the Layers palette, notice that a red rectangle appears in a miniature thumbnail version of the layer. Before continuing, you might wish to change the size of the thumbnail in the palette.

## Changing the Palette Thumbnail Size

By default, the Layers palette shows you a thumbnail of all layers in a document. The thumbnails are a handy reminder of exactly what is in each layer. Keeping an eye on the thumbnails is also a helpful way to ensure that you don't edit the wrong layer. To adjust the size of the thumbnails in the Layers palette, click on the Layers palette's pop-up menu arrow and choose Palette Options from the list of choices. This will open the Palette Options dialog box. In the dialog box, click on the radio button alongside the thumbnail size you'd like on screen, then click OK. We recommend you keep the thumbnails as small as possible so they don't consume valuable screen space. Also, if you pick a large size, you might find that the thumbnails slow down the screen display a bit.

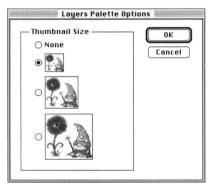

## Creating New Layers

Now, assume that you wish to add a circle and text to your image. If you add them to the Background, the circle and text will be locked down onto it. If you create one layer for the circle shape and one for the text, as shown in Figure 12-1, you will be able to move and edit either the circle or the text without affecting the other layers. In this section you will create a new layer and then add the circle to your image. Later you'll create some text. While the text is still floating, you'll convert it into a new layer.

The simplest way to create a new layer is to click on the New Layer icon (the dog-eared page) in the Layers palette. Another way to create a layer is to click on the pop-up menu arrow in the Layers palette and choose the New Layer command. In Chapter 3, you learned that a new layer can be created by dragging and dropping an image from one file to another. Later in this chapter, you'll learn that a layer can be created from a floating selection, and you'll also create a new layer with the Edit menu's Paste Layer command after copying a selection into the clipboard.

1. Start the process of creating a layer by clicking the New Layer icon ( 🔲 ) at the bottom of the Layers palette. Doing this opens the New Layer dialog box. In it, you'll see options for changing opacity, setting a painting/editing mode, and grouping layers. You'll learn how to use these options later in this chapter. At this point, name the layer by typing **Circle** in the Name field, then click OK.

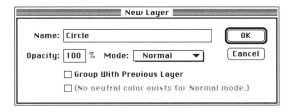

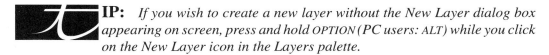

**IP:** *If you wish to create a new layer without the New Layer dialog box appearing on screen, press and hold OPTION (PC users: ALT) while you click on the New Layer icon in the Layers palette.*

**12**

Notice that the word "Circle" appears in the title bar of your document. This indicates that you are working in the Circle layer. It may not seem like it now, but when you have several layers on screen, it's very easy to forget what layer you're working in. So, every now and then as you're working, take a quick glance at the title bar.

≣ Untitled-1 (Circle, RGB, 1:1) ≣

Now examine the Layers palette. At the top of the palette is the word "Circle," which indicates that it's the top layer in the document. In the Layers palette, the layer on top is always the top layer in the document; the layer on the bottom is the base layer of your image. In the Layers palette, you'll see an eye icon to the left of the word "Background" and an eye to the left of the Circle layer. This indicates that both the Background and the Circle layers are visible. Notice that the gray shading appears only in the Circle layer section of the Layers palette. This confirms what the document title bar is telling you—that you are working in the Circle layer. This is your target layer. As soon as you create a new layer, Photoshop automatically designates it as the target layer. Now you are ready to create a circle in the Circle layer.

2. Switch to the Elliptical Marquee in the Toolbox. You can quickly toggle between the Elliptical and Rectangular Marquee by pressing OPTION (PC users: ALT) and clicking on the Marquee tool in the Toolbox or by pressing M on your keyboard. Use the Marquee tool's Elliptical shape to create a circle about 3.75 inches in diameter in the middle of your document that overlaps the rectangle on screen, as seen in Figure 12-1. Fill this circle with yellow color, then deselect.

Now take a look at the memory indicator in the lower-left corner of the screen. In the next section you'll learn how layers increase file size.

## Checking Layer Memory

As you create layers, you should know how much memory the layers are consuming. To find this out, first make sure the memory readout in the lower-left corner is set to show document memory, not scratch disk memory. Check this now by clicking on the pop-up menu arrow in the lower-left corner of your document. The pop-up menu should be set to Document Sizes. If it is not, change it.

As mentioned in Chapter 2, the document size number on the left indicates the size of your image without any layers, while the number on the right indicates the file size with all layers included. When a new layer is created, colored areas in the layer add to your file's size. This is a fact of life with layers that you need to get used to. Fortunately, the transparent area of a layer does not add to document memory.

Later you'll learn how to merge layers to reduce file size and flatten layers so that you can drop the file to its original size.

When working with layers, it's easy for file size to grow quickly. If you do not have extra memory or a lot of free space available on your scratch disk, you'll have to work carefully with layers, possibly merging them as you finish working on different image areas. If you need to keep doing this, though, you're taking some of the versatility out of working with Photoshop. If you want to work with many layers, your best bet is installing more RAM and/or purchasing the largest hard disk you can afford to use as a scratch disk. Once you're free of memory worries, you'll be able to work comfortably with several layers in your document.

Now that you've been cautioned about the memory consumption of layers, you're ready to add another layer to your image. Beware that when you add another layer to the file on screen, the file size could reach over 1MB. The file size will depend upon the amount of information you put in the layer.

## Changing a Floating Selection into a Layer

In this section, you'll learn how a floating selection can quickly be converted into a new layer. You'll use the Type tool to create some text. When the text appears on screen and while the text is still floating, you'll place it into a new layer.

1. Start by setting the foreground color to blue.

2. Activate the Type tool by clicking on the Toolbox, then click anywhere in the middle of the screen.

3. When the Type Tool dialog box appears, pick a font (the font in Figure 12-1 is Helvetica Black), set the Size to 130, Spacing to -3, make sure the Anti-Aliased option is selected, and use a horizontal alignment. Type the word **Layers** in the text box, then click OK. When the text appears on screen, move it to the middle of the document so that it looks like Figure 12-1. Don't deselect. Since a floating selection is a temporary layer, the words "Floating Selection" appear in the Layers palette.

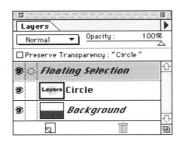

4. To convert the floating selection to a layer, move the pointer to the words "Floating Selection" in the Layers palette, then double-click. The Make Layer dialog box will open on screen.

 **OTE:** *You can also create a new layer out of a floating selection by dragging the words "Floating Selection" in the Layers palette over the New Layer icon.*

5. In the Make Layer dialog box, name the layer "Text." Leave the other settings in the dialog box unchanged. Click OK to make a new layer. If you completed the previous exercises, your image and Layers palette should now look like Figure 12-1.

 **IP:** *You can rename a layer by double-clicking on its name in the Layers palette or by choosing the Layer Options command from the pop-up menu in the Layers palette.*

After the Text layer is created, notice that your file size has increased. Now examine the Layers palette. The new layer appears with the eye icon next to it. Notice that the gray shade surrounds the Text layer, indicating it is the current target layer. Any image editing you do now will affect only this layer. Even though you see the circle clearly on screen, you cannot edit it now, because it is not in the current target layer. Photoshop allows you to have only one target layer at a time. Thus, if you wish to move or edit the circle, you will need to switch target layers.

## Moving Objects in Layers

As mentioned earlier, layers are like sheets of acetate overlaying each other. If you move a Photoshop layer, all objects in the layer move as one, as if they were all on the same acetate sheet. Being able to move layers independently of other layers gives you the freedom to quickly experiment with many design options without worrying about the pixels locking down on the underlying images.

In Photoshop you can move a layer by simply clicking and dragging on it with the Move tool. If you wish to move a layer in one-pixel increments, you can press any of the directional arrow keys on the keyboard. Pressing OPTION (PC users: ALT) while pressing any of the directional arrow keys moves the layer in 10-pixel increments (a 10-pixel increment moves you 1 frame in a Filmstrip file created in Adobe Premiere). Photoshop also allows you to *link* layers together so they can be moved as a unit. In the next exercise, you'll practice moving the Circle and Text layers independently, then link them so they move as one unit.

Before you begin, make sure you have a circle in a layer, the words "Layers" in a layer, and a red and white background, as shown in Figure 12-1.

1. Try moving the text you just created by first activating the Move tool, then clicking and dragging on the text. As you drag the text, the entire layer moves. Move the text to different locations on screen to experiment with image composition.

   If you want to move the circle in the Circle layer, you need to switch target layers. To switch target layers, simply click on the name of the layer that you wish to use as your target layer. Try activating the Circle layer.

2. To set the Circle layer as your target layer, click on the word Circle in the Layers palette. The Circle layer in the palette turns gray and the title bar of your document now includes the layer name.

**12**

Now that you have switched target layers, you can either edit or move the Circle layer and position it independently of the Background and the Text layer.

**TIP:** *You can switch target layers by pressing COMMAND-[ (PC users: CTRL-]) to move down to the underlying layer, or COMMAND-] (PC users: CTRL-]) to move up to the next layer. To move to the base layer, press COMMAND-OPTION-[ (PC users: CTRL-ALT-[). To move to the top layer, press COMMAND-OPTION-] (PC users: CTRL-ALT-]).*

3. To move the yellow circle on screen, use the Move tool to click and drag on the circle and reposition it so that it is placed near the text.

   You might wish to move several layers at a time. Photoshop allows you to do this, as long as the layers are linked. Layers can be linked by clicking on the empty column (*link column*), which appears to the left of the layer name and to the right of the eye column in the Layers palette. After you click, the link icon ( ✛ ) will appear in the column. If you click on the link column, above or below the Target layer, Photoshop links that layer with the target layer. Clicking on the link column next to other layers will add those layers to the layers that are already linked. Step 4 describes how to link the Circle and Text layer.

4. To link the Circle and Text layer, first make sure that the Circle layer is your target layer. Then, click on the link column to the left of the word "Text" and to the right of the eye column in the Layers palette. A link icon will appear next to both the Circle and Text layer in the Layers palette.

5. To move the two linked layers, activate the Move tool, then click and drag anywhere on screen. Both the circle and the text will move together.

Before continuing to the next section, move the text and circle into the middle of your document, as shown in Figure 12-1. To do this, you may need to move the Text and Circle layers independently. To unlink layers, click on the link icon in the link column.

## Viewing and Hiding Layers

If you wish to view only the images in one layer without seeing objects in other layers, you can hide the other layers. To hide a layer, you need only click on the layer's eye icon in the Layers palette. Clicking on the eye icon turns the icon off and hides the corresponding layer. Clicking again in the same place (the *eye column*) returns the eye icon back to the Layers palette and brings the layer into view. If you click and drag over different eyes in the eye column, you will hide all of the corresponding layers. If you click and drag in the eye column again, the layers and their corresponding eyes will return to view.

In this section you'll delete a portion of the circle, as shown in Figure 12-2, then hide the other layers to see how the Circle layer was affected. Before you begin, make sure that you are working with the elements in Figure 12-1 and that the Circle layer is your target layer.

Start by making a rectangular selection in the middle of the circle and then deleting the area inside the selection.

1. Activate the Marquee tool's Rectangular shape; then create a rectangular selection approximately 1/4-inch wide in the middle portion of the circle.

2. To delete this section of the circle layer, press the Delete key. Only the yellow area of the circle is removed, as shown in Figure 12-2. Neither the text nor the Background is affected because each is in other layers. When

When a portion of the circle is deleted, the Background shows through the deleted area

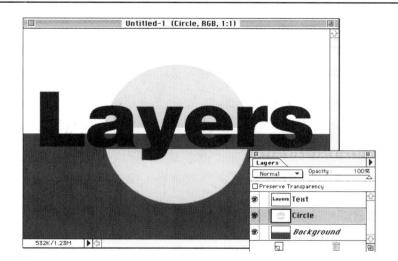

**FIGURE 12-2**

you deleted, you wiped away the yellow pixels of the circle, leaving behind its transparent background. The text and background show through the transparency. You'll be able to see this by hiding both the Background and Text layers.

3. Hide the Background by clicking on the eye column next to the word "Background." After you click on the eye icon, the eye icon disappears from the Layers palette and the white and red Background disappears from the screen. The Circle and Text layer remain on screen. You should now see the familiar transparent checkerboard pattern in the Circle and Text layers. As discussed in Chapter 3, this indicates that the backgrounds of the Text and Circle layer are transparent.

 **OTE:** *If you wish to change the checkerboard pattern of a transparent layer, choose Transparency from the File/Preferences submenu.*

4. Hide the Text layer by clicking on the eye column next to the word "Text," in the Layers palette. Now only the Circle layer remains on screen. In the middle of the circle you see the checkerboard pattern.

 **IP:** *If you OPTION-click (PC users: ALT) on the eye column, Photoshop will hide all visible layers except the layer of the eye you clicked on. If you OPTION-click (PC users: ALT) again in the same area of the eye column, all layers will be visible.*

5. To return the Text and Background layers to the screen, click on the eye column next to the words Text and Background in the Layers palette.

    Before continuing, take a look at your image without the Circle layer.

6. To hide the Circle layer, click on the eye icon next to the circle. The circle vanishes. All you see are the Text and Background layers. It's important to realize that the Circle layer is still your target layer. Notice that the gray shade still surrounds the word "Circle" and the word "Circle" still remains in your title bar. This means that editing the file now will affect only the Circle layer, even though you don't see the Circle layer on screen.

7. To make the Circle layer visible, click on the eye column next to the word "circle." The circle reappears on screen.

## Reordering Layers in the Layers Palette

Now assume that you would like the circle in Figure 12-2 to overlap the text, rather than the text overlap the circle. There's no need to cut and paste between layers. All you need to do is reposition the layers stacking order in the Layers palette by clicking and dragging with the mouse. To make the Circle overlap the Text layer, you can drag the Circle layer above the Text layer. Try it now.

To change the order of the layers in the Layers palette, position the mouse pointer over the word "Circle" in the Layers palette. The mouse pointer will change to a pointing hand icon (  ). Click and keep the mouse button pressed, then drag up. As you drag, the pointing hand will change to a grabbing hand icon (  ), and an outline of the Circle layer will move in the Layers palette. Once the Circle is above the Text layer, release the mouse. On screen, the circle now overlaps the text. In the Layers palette, the Circle layer is now the top layer.

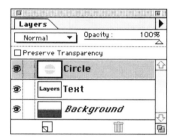

**OTE:** *The Background layer in the Layers palette cannot be moved unless you change its name. The easiest way to change the name of the Background layer is to double-click on the word "Background" in the Layers palette. The Make Layer dialog box will appear and you will see that Photoshop will automatically rename "Background" as "Layer 0." Click OK to activate the change.*

Before continuing to the next section, reorder the layers so that the text is the top layer and the Circle layer is below it.

## Changing Layer Opacity

The Layers palette provides a variety of options that allow you to blend images together and create special effects. The easiest way to blend layers together is to

**12**

change the Opacity setting in the Layers palette. When you change opacity, you change opacity for the entire target layer.

On screen, assume that you would like the red background in Figure 12-2 to show through the circle that overlaps it. One way of achieving this is to lower the opacity in the Circle layer.

1. To lower opacity in the Circle layer, first make sure that the Circle layer is the target layer. Remember, the target layer is the layer that is selected in the Layers palette (surrounded by the gray shade). If the Circle layer is not selected in the Layers palette, click on the word "Circle."

2. To change opacity for the Circle layer, click on the Opacity slider in the Layers palette and drag to the left. Set the Opacity slider to 50%.

**IP:** *If the Move tool, a Selection tool, or the Hand or Zoom tool is selected in the Toolbox, you can change the opacity for a layer by typing 0 to 9 on your keyboard. This changes the Opacity slider in the Layers palette. Type 1 to set opacity to 10%; type 0 to set opacity to 100%.*

3. The Info palette keeps track of the opacity of a layer. To see the opacity readout for the Circle layer, open the Info palette by choosing Show Info from the Window/Palettes submenu. Next, click on the eye icon next to the word "Background" in the Layers palette, to hide the background. Now, move the mouse pointer over the circle and notice that an Op value of 50% is displayed in the Info palette. The Op readout in the Info palette will not appear if the Background is visible.

4. Move the mouse pointer over the text and notice that the Op value is 100%. If you wish, experiment by changing the Text layer to the target

layer and changing its opacity. You won't, however, be able to change opacity in the Background layer, unless you rename it. The Opacity slider in the Layers palette and the Op value in the Info palette are active only if you are in a layer with a transparent background or if a floating selection exists on screen. After you are finished experimenting, make sure that all layers are displayed on screen.

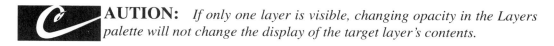**AUTION:** *If only one layer is visible, changing opacity in the Layers palette will not change the display of the target layer's contents.*

Your next step in exploring the Layers palette is to investigate how the painting/editing modes can create special blending effects between layers.

## Blending with the Painting/Editing Modes

Now that you've become familiar with layer fundamentals, you might wish to start exploring more ways to blend images using the Layers palette. One of the fastest ways to create special effects while blending layers is to use the Layers palette's Mode pop-up menu. In order to access the Mode pop-up menu in the Layers palette, you must be in a layer other than the Background, or have a floating selection on screen. Make either the Circle or Text layer from Figure 12-2 your target layer.

Take a moment to click on the Mode pop-up menu. You'll see a familiar list of choices, starting with the word "Normal" and ending with the word "Luminosity." These are the same painting/editing modes described in Chapter 5. They work very much the same way when blending layers together as they do when painting with the painting tools. When used with layers, the painting/editing modes affect the target layer and the layer directly beneath it. Try using the Dissolve mode to break up the colors of the images in the Circle and Text layers:

1. If the Circle layer from Figure 12-2 isn't your target layer, select the Circle layer as your target layer by clicking on the word "Circle" in the Layers palette. If the Circle and/or Background is hidden, click in the approximate area in the eye column to view it.

2. To change painting/editing modes, click on the Mode pop-up menu and choose the Dissolve mode. The Dissolve mode randomly changes the pixels, using the colors of the target layer and the layer below it. Keep the Opacity for the Circle layer set to 50%.

**12**

3. Next, set the target layer to the Text layer by clicking on the word "Text" in the Layers palette.

4. Use the Dissolve mode once again. Set Opacity to 70%. This time, the effect will dissolve pixels from the Text and the Circle layers. After you change the mode to Dissolve, adjust Opacity as desired. Your image should look somewhat like Figure 12-3.

You'll have a chance to practice using different modes later in this chapter when you load different images on screen. For now, if you'd like to experiment, try the Lighten, Darken, and Difference modes.

As you experiment with different painting/editing modes, you might wish to add more colors to the layers on screen. When editing layers, an option that can prove helpful is the Preserve Transparency option that appears at the top of the Layers palette.

**OTE:** *If you create a layer by clicking on the New Layer icon, you can choose a mode for the layer in the New Layer dialog box. When you pick a mode, Photoshop provides a variety of choices for filling in the transparent layer areas with black, white or gray, depending upon the mode chosen.*

## Using the Preserve Transparency Option

The Preserve Transparency option locks in the transparent area of a layer so it can not be edited. This feature can be helpful when you are filling selections in layers

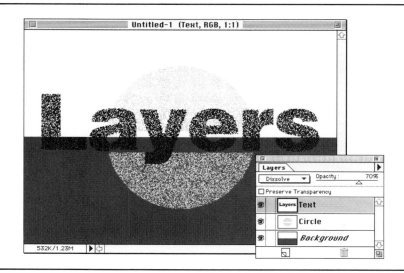

The Dissolve mode applied to the Text layer at 70% opacity

**FIGURE 12-3**

or when you are painting in layers. In the next exercise, you'll try out the Preserve Transparency option with the Text layer from Figure 12-3. Assume that you want to change the colors of the text in the Text layer, but don't want to inadvertently paint over the text. Here's how to do it with the Preserve Transparency check box.

1. Set the target layer to the Text layer by clicking on the word "Text."

2. In the Layers palette, make sure that the Preserve Transparency option is selected.

3. Set the foreground color to the color of your choice.

4. Activate the Paintbrush tool and begin painting over the text with broad brush strokes.

Notice that no matter where you paint on the type, the transparency area of the layer remains transparent. If you'd like to experiment a bit more, use the Gradient tool to create a blend over the text. You'll see that only the letters will be affected by the blend.

**IP:** *On layers other than the background, you can select nontransparent areas by pressing COMMAND-OPTION-T (PC users: CTRL-ALT-T).*

**OTE:** *If you have created some elements in a transparent layer and then decide you want to erase some of them with the Eraser tool, the Eraser will produce slightly different effects depending upon whether or not the Preserve Transparency option in the Layers palette is selected. If the Preserve Transparency option is not selected when using the Eraser, the transparent background will show through the area you erased. If you have the Preserve Transparency option selected, when you use the Eraser to erase the elements in the layer, the Eraser will apply the background color. Both options will not, however, affect the transparent areas.*

The next procedures will describe how to remove the Background layer from your practice image (Figure 12-3) so that you can duplicate the text and circle into another file.

## Deleting Layers

To remove a layer from your image, you must first set it to be the target layer. Once you've set the target layer, you can remove the layer either by choosing Delete Layer from the Layers palette pop-up menu or by dragging a layer into the Trash icon ( 🗑 ) in the Layers palette. Photoshop makes it a bit more difficult if you wish to delete the Background.

Here's how to delete the Background from your file.

In the Layers palette, position the mouse pointer over the word "Background." The icon will change to a pointing hand. Click and drag the layer over to the Trash icon in the Layers palette. As you drag, the icon will turn into a grabbing hand icon. Move the grabbing hand icon over the Trash icon. When the Trash icon changes colors, release the mouse. The red and white background will be removed from your file and from the Layers palette.

**IP:** *If you would like to add a Background layer to a file that does not have one, click on the New Layer icon, then choose Background from the Mode menu in the New Layer dialog box.*

Before you place the circle and text (Figure 12-3) into another file, you're next step is to compress them into one layer by using the Merge Layers command.

## Merging and Flattening Layers

The Merge Layers command found in the Layers palette pop-up menu is used to compress all visible layers into the bottom visible layer of a document. Once you've executed the Merge Layers command, the visible layers are merged into one layer. Hidden layers are not affected. This command can be helpful if you've completed your design work and don't need to make changes in individual layers. By merging layers, you can also keep your file size low.

Try merging the layers in your practice document by choosing Merge Layers from the Layers palette pop-up menu.

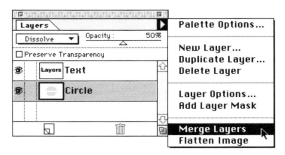

After the layers are merged, the file size is reduced. Notice that transparency of the elements is still intact, even though there is only one layer in the Layers palette.

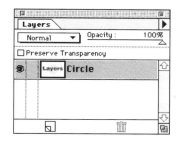

Another option, which compresses visible layers and reduces file size, is the Flatten Layers command. It's important to understand the difference between flattening and merging layers. Unlike merging layers, flattening layers removes all hidden layers from the file. The flattened file has no transparent background. This means it can be saved in a variety of different file formats, not just Photoshop 3.0. Before you save your file, proceed to the next section to learn how to duplicate a layer from one file into another.

## Duplicating a Layer into Another File

Now that you've deleted the Background and merged the Circle and Text layers in your practice file, you can place the merged layers into another file by using the Duplicate Layer command accessed from the Layers palette pop-up menu.

1. Open any file that you wish to use as a new Background file. If you don't have an image to use as a background, open the Frames file (PC users: frames.jpg) from the Tutorial folder. After the Frames file is loaded, activate your practice image by clicking on it.

2. To place the merged Circle layer from your practice file into the Frames file, choose Duplicate Layer from the Layers palette pop-up menu. In the Duplicate Layers dialog box, choose the file that you wish to place the layer into by clicking on the Document pop-up menu and choosing the file. If you are using the Tutorial image, choose Frames from the pop-up menu. Leave the As field the way it is. To copy the layer into the Background file, click OK. Notice that the elements in the Circle layer from your practice file retain their names and transparency.

*n*OTE: *You can also copy a layer from one file to another by dragging the layer name from the Layers palette into an open file's document window.*

12

# Photoshop in Action

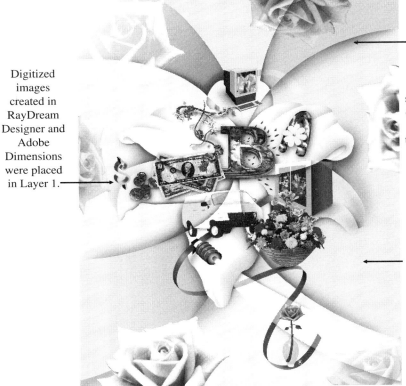

Digitized images created in RayDream Designer and Adobe Dimensions were placed in Layer 1.

All of the shading was created in Layer 2. The shadows were created using the Airbrush tool and alpha channels.

The shapes that were created in Illustrator were placed into the Background layer.

**Artist: Wendy Grossman**          **Client: FTD Florist**

Wendy used various programs to create the different elements in this image. After the separate elements were created, she composited them together using Photoshop's layers.

In Adobe Illustrator, Wendy sketched the background shapes, the computer and refrigerator, and then placed them into the Background layer. In Layer 1, she placed images she created in RayDream Designer (the letters, the basket, the flower vase and stem), the images she created in Adobe Dimensions (the dollar sign and the ribbon), and the images she scanned (the money, truck, and flowers). Wendy added shading effects in Layer 2. To create the shadows for various elements she used the Airbrush tool and alpha channels. In this layer she also created the spotlight.

The final step was to place the scanned flowers along the edges of the image. These were pasted into the image using different opacities and modes.

The Circle layer is duplicated into the Background file and the elements are placed in the center of the background. If your background file is smaller than the elements in the Circle layer, Photoshop will clip the elements in the Circle layer. This means that the portion of the layer that is not visible still exists.

### Saving a File with Layers

If you wish to save your file with all its layers, use the File/Save As command to save the file in Photoshop 3.0 format. In the Save As dialog box, enter a new name for your file so that you don't replace the original version.

As discussed in Chapter 3, if you wish to flatten layers when you save your image, choose the File/Save a Copy command and make sure the Flatten Image option is selected. Once the Flatten Image option is selected, you can click on the Format pop-up menu and choose a file format. For more information on using different file formats, review Appendix A.

Now, that you've learned the fundamentals of using layers, you're probably eager to create special effects using them.

## CREATING SPECIAL EFFECTS USING LAYERS

Now that you've explored the Layers palette, you're ready to create some special effects using layers. In the following sections, you will use layers to create drop shadows, place images into text, and blend images using the painting/editing modes. At the end of the chapter, you'll use layer masks to fade one image into another.

### Creating Drop Shadows Using Layers

In this section you're going to create a drop shadow by duplicating a layer and then applying the Gaussian Blur command to the duplicate layer. The blurred layer will create the shadow effect. By creating the drop shadow in a layer, you'll have complete flexibility as to where the shadow appears and how much of a three-dimensional effect you wish to create. Figure 12-4 shows a drop shadow applied to digitized maple leaf ( 🍁 ) over a background of clouds ( ▦ ).

Before you begin producing the drop shadow, start by using the Clouds filter to create a background for your final image. If you prefer, you can skip steps 1-3 by loading a digitized background image. Start by opening the Layers palette; if it isn't open, open it by choosing Show Layers from the Window/Palettes submenu.

**12**

Leaf
with drop
shadow
created
with layers

**FIGURE 12-4**

1. Create a new RGB Color file, 5 inches by 5 inches, with the Contents radio button set to white. When the new file is on screen you are ready to begin creating clouds.

2. Next, set the foreground color to light blue and the background color to white.

3. Apply the Clouds filter, by choosing Clouds from the Filter/Render submenu. Notice that your file now looks like clouds. The Clouds filter uses the foreground and background colors to create clouds.

4. Open the image that you wish to apply the drop shadow to. The image you apply the drop shadow to should be smaller in size than the background file on screen and have the same resolution. If you don't have an image, you can use the Leaf file (PC users: leaf.psd) in the Tutorial file.

*n* **OTE:**   *Before creating a drop shadow on an image, you may wish to silhouette the image using the Pen tool, the Select/Color Range command, and/or selection tools. By using a silhouetted image as the image you apply the drop shadow to, the shadow will look more realistic.*

Next you'll place the image you want to apply the drop shadow to (the Leaf image, if you're using a Tutorial file) into the background image and create a layer at the same time. You can use several techniques. You could copy the image, then choose the Edit/Paste Layer command in the Background file. Perhaps the easiest way is to drag and drop the leaf into the Background file.

**5.** Use the Move tool to click and drag the Leaf file (if you're using the Tutorial image) into your background image. As you drag out of the Leaf file the pointer will change to a tiny grabbing hand. When the grabbing hand icon enters your file with the background image, a black frame will surround the file. After you see the black frame, you can release the mouse. This will create a new layer over the Background with the leaf in the new layer. Notice that in the Layers palette you now have Background and Layer 1.

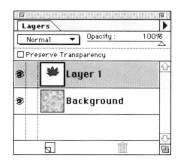

Note that your target layer is the layer that you just created. As mentioned earlier, the title bar and the gray area of the Layers palette indicate the target layer you are in.

**6.** Use the Move tool to position the leaf into the center of the file.

Now you are ready to create the drop shadow for the leaf. To do this first duplicate the Leaf layer you just created, then use the duplicate layer to create the shadow. To duplicate a layer, you can either choose the Duplicate Layer command in the Layers palette pop-up menu or drag a layer in the Layers palette over the New Layer icon.

**7.** To duplicate the Leaf layer, position the mouse pointer over the words "Layer 1" (the layer that you wish to duplicate). The mouse pointer will change to a pointing hand. Click the mouse and drag the layer over to the

New Layer icon. As you drag, the pointer will change to a tiny grabbing hand. Drag the grabbing hand icon over the New Layer icon. When the New Layer icon changes colors, release the mouse. A copy of the Leaf layer is automatically created. To change the name of the layer, double-click on the word "copy" in the Layers palette. This opens the Layer Options dialog box. Type in the words **Drop Shadow** in the Name field, then click OK.

**N**OTE: *You can create a duplicate of a layer by first selecting the layer in the Layers palette and then choosing Duplicate Layer from the Layers palette pop-up menu. You can name the layer in the As field of the Duplicate Layer dialog box, and choose a destination for that layer in the Document pop-up menu. The destination of the duplicated layer can be any open file or a new file.*

At this point you should be viewing all layers (all eye icons are displayed in the Layers palette) and your target layer should be the Drop Shadow layer (this is the layer that is highlighted with a gray bar in the Layers palette. Also notice the words "Drop Shadow" now appear in the title bar of the current document).

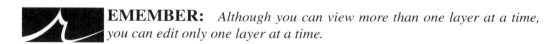

**R**EMEMBER: *Although you can view more than one layer at a time, you can edit only one layer at a time.*

8. With the Drop Shadow layer as the target layer, use the Move tool to move the leaf in this layer so that it is slightly offset from the leaf in Layer 1. Offset it in any direction.

    After you've moved the leaf in the Drop Shadow layer, your next step is to darken the color of the leaf in the Drop Shadow layer to create the shadow effect. It will be easier to do this if the drop shadow layer is the only layer visible on screen.

9. To hide the leaf in Layer 1 and the Background layer, turn off the eye icons for both the leaf in Layer 1 and Background layers by clicking on each layer's eye. Leave the eye icon next to the Drop Shadow layer so that you are viewing only this layer on screen.

Now that you are viewing only the leaf in the Drop Shadow layer, you can fill it with the color you want the drop shadow to be. In the next step, the Preserve Transparency check box in the Fill dialog box will be activated so the Edit/Fill command fills only the image on screen, not the transparent area.

**10.** Set the Foreground color to the color you want the drop shadow to be. Choose either a very dark green or black depending upon the desired effect. From the Edit menu, choose Fill. In the Fill dialog box, set the Use pop-up menu to Foreground Color, set the Mode pop-up menu to Normal, and set Opacity to between 80-100%, depending upon the desired effect. Make sure the Preserve Transparency option is selected. Then click OK to fill the leaf.

To create the soft drop shadow effect, apply the Gaussian Blur to the Drop Shadow layer.

**11.** Choose Gaussian Blur from the Filter/Blur submenu. In the Gaussian Blur dialog box, use a number between 3-10 in the Radius field. The higher the number the greater the blur effect. Click OK to activate the changes.

**12.** To view the leaf in Layer 1 and see the effects, click on the eye icon next to Layer 1. Notice that the leaf in the Drop Shadow layer is on top of the leaf in Layer 1. To place the leaf in the Drop Shadow layer below the leaf in Layer 1, click on "Drop Shadow" in the Layers palette and drag it over Layer 1.

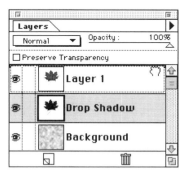

**13.** If you would like to move the shadow closer or further away from the leaf, make sure that the Drop Shadow is your target layer. If you need to change target layers, click on "Drop Shadow" in the Layers palette. Then

**12**

use the Move tool to move the shadow. When you are happy with the position of the shadow, activate the eye icon next to the word "Background" in the Layers palette to see the entire image.

At this point, if you wish to reposition the leaf and the drop shadow together, you will need to link the layers. As discussed earlier in this chapter, the Layers palette allows you to link layers together so you can move more than one layer at a time.

**14.** If you wish to link the leaf and drop shadow so that they can be moved together, make sure that "Drop Shadow" is the active layer. To link the layers, move the mouse into the blank area to the right of the eye icons and to the left of Layer 1 in the Layers palette. Click the mouse. A cross, called the *link icon*, appears next to the Drop Shadow layer and Layer 1. This means that the two layers are temporarily linked and will therefore move together. With the Move tool activated, you can now move both the leaf and the drop shadow together. To unlink the layers, click on one of the link icons in the Layers palette.

To save your file with its layers, save using the Photoshop 3.0 format. Name your file **Shadow**. If you want to duplicate your image and drop shadow, proceed to the next section. Before you proceed, create a duplicate of your file with its layer to work in with so that you won't affect the file you just created. To create a duplicate file and close the onscreen file, choose File/Save As. In the Save As dialog box, type **Shadow2** and set the Format to Photoshop 3.0. Click Save (PC users: OK) to create a duplicate file.

## Duplicating an Image With its Drop Shadow

After you've completed all the steps in the previous exercise, you may want to create yet another leaf (if you're using the Tutorial image) with a drop shadow. The easiest way to do this is to merge the leaf and its shadow together, then duplicate the merged layer. To do this, you need to first hide the Background layer.

 **EMEMBER:**   *The Merge Layers command merges all visible layers.*

**1.** To hide the Background layer, click on the eye icon next to the word "Background" in the Layers palette.

2. To merge the leaf and its shadow, choose Merge Layers from the Layers palette pop-up menu. In the Layers palette, notice that the two layers (Layer 1 and Drop Shadow) are merged into the Drop Shadow layer.

3. After the layers have been merged, you can unhide the Background layer by clicking in the eye column next to the word "Background" in the Layers palette.

4. To duplicate the merged layers, click on "Drop Shadow" in the Layers palette and drag it over the New Layer icon. A new layer, named "Drop Shadow Copy," appears in the Layers palette and becomes the target layer. The Drop Shadow layer with the original leaf image and drop shadow is directly below the Drop Shadow Copy layer (the new layer that was just created).

5. To see the two leaf images with their drop shadows, use the Move tool to drag the image and its shadow in the Drop Shadow Copy layer in any direction. As you drag, you'll see the original leaf image in the Drop Shadow layer. You may also want to move the original leaf image in the Drop Shadow layer. To do so, set the Drop Shadow layer to the target layer and then move the original leaf image with the Move tool.

At this point feel free to embellish the image on screen. You may want to use some of the Image menu commands to scale, rotate, lighten, or color. Figure 12-5 shows two leaves with drop shadows after applying various Image menu commands.

After you've saved your work, close your file and proceed to the next section to learn how the Layers palette can help you place images within other images.

## Placing Images Within Other Images Using Clipping Groups

When you are working with layers, you can create a special layer group in which the bottom layer controls the shape, transparency, and mode of the other group members above it. This type of layer group is called a *clipping group*.

In the next examples, you'll see how clipping groups can be used to place one image into the shape of another image. One image is used as the shape, the other is the background image that is placed into the shape. The image that is used for the shape creates a mask. This technique is often used to place textures or other images into text. The next few examples show you different ways of creating and using clipping groups to place one image into another image.

**12**

Image
after Drop
Shadow
layer was
copied,
scaled,
and rotated

**FIGURE 12-5**

## Using Groups with Previous Layer Option

In this example, you will place an image into a shape, as shown in Figure 12-6. To achieve the effect, you will need two images: one will be used for the shape of the final image; the other image will be placed into the shape. In Figure 12-6, a sailboat was used as the image that was placed into the leaf shape. To create the silhouetted leaf, the Pen tool was used to outline a digitized leaf. The drop shadow behind the leaf was created using the steps described in the earlier section "Creating Drop Shadows Using Layers." When both images were placed in a clipping group, the leaf masked the sailboat image, making it appear as if the sailboat is in the leaf. Try out the following steps to create the same effect with two images. If you don't have images to use, load the Leaf file as your shape and the Portrait file as your image to place into the shape.

1. Start by opening the image that you wish to place into the shape. If you don't have an image use the Portrait file (PC users: portrait.jpg) in the Tutorial folder. Open the Layers palette if it isn't already open.

2. Next, open or create the image you want to use as the shape. If you are going to use a digitized image, use an image that has been silhouetted. If you don't have an image to use, open the Leaf file in the Tutorial folder.

Clipping
group used
to place
sailboat
image from
a layer into
leaf image
in another
layer

 **FIGURE 12-6**

---

**OTE:** *If you wish to design your own shape, first create a new layer in your file, then use the selection tool or the Pen tool to create the shape in the layer. Next fill the shape with color.*

**3.** After you open the file with the silhouetted image, use the Move tool to drag and drop it into the file of the image that will eventually appear in the shape (the destination image). To drag and drop one image into another, place the images side-by-side or so that the shape image (silhouetted image) overlaps the destination image. Activate the Move tool, then click and drag the shape image into the destination file. When the pointer touches the destination image, it will change to a grabbing hand. Position the grabbing hand in the middle of the destination image, and release the mouse. A new layer will be created in the destination image, with the shape image in a layer.

**4.** Rename the layer by double-clicking on the name of the new layer in the Layers palette. Name the layer "Shape."

**5.** If you wish, use the Image/Scale command to enlarge the image in the Shape layer. This will make more of the image show in the shape. (If you wish to review the Scale command, see Chapter 7.)

**12**

To use a clipping group to place an image into the shape on screen, the Shape layer must be underneath the Background layer. Unfortunately, Photoshop won't let you do this if your base layer is named "Background." Try moving the Shape layer underneath the Background layer. You'll see that the layers won't switch positions. Here's a trick that will allow you to switch positions: rename the Background layer.

**6.** The quickest way to change the name of the Background layer is to double-click on the word "Background" in the Layers palette. When the Make Layer dialog box appears, notice that the layer is now named "Layer 0." Click OK. Now move the Shape layer below Layer 0.

Now that you've changed the order of the layers, proceed to the next step to learn how to create a clipping group.

**7.** Move the mouse pointer to the dividing line in the Layers palette that separates the Shape and Layer 0. Press and hold OPTION (PC users: ALT). When the mouse pointer changes to a grouping icon ( ⁀⬛ ), click the mouse button to create a clipping group. After you click, the image changes on screen so that the layer above the shape is seen within the shape. Notice that the Shape layer in the Layers palette is underlined and that the line dividing the two layers has changed from a solid line to a dotted line. This indicates that the layers are in a clipping group with the Shape layer at the base of the group.

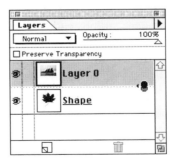

As you just saw, creating a clipping group changes the shape of all visible layers above the base layer in the group to the shape of the base layer. In the example above, you created a clipping group by OPTION clicking (PC users: ALT) between layers in the Layers palette.

Creating a clipping group automatically turns on the Group with Previous Layer option in the Layer Options dialog box. To verify this, double-click on the top layer in the clipping group. In the Layer Options dialog box, notice that the Group with Previous Layer option is selected. You can probably guess that another way to create the clipping group would be to open up the Layer Options dialog box and selecting the Group with Previous Layer check box. You'll probably find, however, that OPTION clicking (PC users: ALT) in the Layers palette is faster.

**NOTE:** *If you wish to remove a layer from a clipping group, double-click on the name of the layer in the Layers palette, then deselect the Group with Previous Layer check box in the Layer Options dialog box. You may also OPTION-click (PC users: ALT) on the dotted line dividing the clipping group members in the Layers palette.*

8. At this point, you can reposition the image in the shape, or reposition the shape itself. If you'd like, you can move either of the layers independently of the other or link them so that they move together. If you wish, you can also use the Image/Effects/Scale command to resize the image that is in the shape. If you rescale the image, sharpen it with a sharpening filter, if necessary. You can also lighten or darken the image in the shape with the Brightness/Contrast command in the Image menu. If you wish, experiment with various opacity settings and modes in the Layers palette. You can also apply a drop shadow to the image in the Shape layer by following the steps in the earlier section "Creating Drop Shadows Using Layers."

9. When you are satisfied with the image's appearance, you may wish to flatten the layers in the image to conserve memory.

If you wish to save your layers with your file, use the Photoshop 3.0 format; otherwise, use the File/Save a Copy command to flatten the layers when you save. After saving your work, close the file on screen and proceed to the next section.

## Placing an Image into Text Using the Paste Into Command

In this section you'll create a fashion advertisement by using the Paste Into command to place an image of a model into text, as shown in Figure 12-7. When you paste an image into a selection, the pasted image is put in Float mode. While the image is

The Paste Into command and layers were used to paste an image of a model into the text (photograph courtesy of Stacy Kollar Photography)

**FIGURE 12-7**

floating, you can reposition it, execute Image menu commands, apply filters, and change the opacity and painting/editing mode in the Layers palette.

1. Start by opening an image of a person. If you don't have an image, use the Portrait file (PC users: portrait.jpg) in the Tutorial folder. If the Layers palette isn't open, open it now by choosing Show Layers from the Window/Palettes submenu.

2. When the image is on screen, choose All from the Select menu, then choose Copy from the Edit menu. When the image is copied to the clipboard, close the file and create a new file. When you choose New from the File menu, you'll see that the settings in the New dialog box reflect the dimensions of the image stored in the clipboard. In the New dialog box, make sure that the radio button in the Contents group is set to Transparent. Click OK to create the new file.

3. When the new file appears, Activate the Type tool; then click in the left side of the image to open the Type Tool dialog box. In the text box, type **WEAR** on one line and press RETURN; then type **IT WELL** in the next line. Choose the following settings: Font, Helvetica; Size, 55; Leading, 45; Spacing, −3; and Style, Bold. Make sure that the Anti-Aliased feature is activated and set the Alignment to Center.

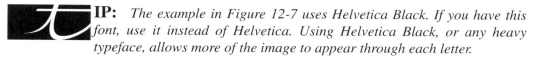**IP:**  *The example in Figure 12-7 uses Helvetica Black. If you have this font, use it instead of Helvetica. Using Helvetica Black, or any heavy typeface, allows more of the image to appear through each letter.*

**4.** Click OK to have Photoshop place the text on screen. If necessary, reposition the text in the middle of the screen. Don't deselect.

**OTE:**  *Notice that the leading setting of 45 keeps the two lines of text close together. If the leading were larger, more space would appear between the two lines. In Photoshop, leading is measured from baseline to baseline. You can enter leading values from 1 to 1,000.*

**IP:**  *Here's a way to quickly select a letter or group of floating letters to be moved either closer together or farther apart. While the Type tool is still activated, press COMMAND (PC users: CTRL). The Type tool changes to the Lasso tool, which you can click and drag over the floating letters to electronically "rope in" the ones you wish to select.*

**5.** Use the Scale command to enlarge the type to the size of your document to allow more of the image to show through the letters. (If you wish to review the Scale command, see Chapter 7.) Don't deselect.

**6.** While the text is still floating, choose Paste Into from the Edit menu. Your image now appears in the text. Don't deselect.

**7.** To place the floating image that is inside the text into a layer, either drag the words "Floating Selection" in the Layers palette over the New Layer icon or double-click on the words "Floating Selection." When the Make Layer dialog box appears, click on the Group with Previous Layer option to select it. If the Group with Previous Layer option is not selected, the new layer will be created without the image in the text. As mentioned in the previous section, Group with Previous Layer creates a clipping group. If you don't create a layer, after using the Paste Into command the image will get locked down after you deselect. If the image locks down onto the background pixels, you won't be able to reposition it.

**12**

*n*OTE: *If you dragged the words "Floating Selection" over the New Layer icon, a Layer Mask is created in the Layers palette. To learn more about Layer Masks, turn to the section "Using Layer Masks to Blend Images Together" at the end of this chapter.*

8. At this point, you can reposition the image in the text or reposition the text itself by moving one layer at a time, or you can move both layers together. If you wish, you can also use the Image/Effects/Scale command to resize the image that is in the text. If you rescale the image, sharpen it with a sharpening filter, if necessary.

9. When you are satisfied with the image's appearance, save your image with both layers by saving your file in Photoshop 3.0 format.

When you're ready, close the file on screen and proceed to the next section.

## Using the Preserve Transparency Option to Place an Image into Text

In this section you'll use the Layers palette Preserve Transparency option to place an image into another image. Although this example places an image into text, feel free to do the example with any shape and an image.

1. Start by opening the file of the image that you wish to place the text into. If you don't have a file, open the Tools file (PC users: tools.jpg) in the Tutorial folder. Then open the Layers palette if it is not already open.

   Your next step is to copy and paste the image into the clipboard. You will use this image to paste over text or a shape you later place on your screen.

2. When the image is on screen, choose All from the Select menu, then choose Copy from the Edit menu. When the image is copied to the clipboard you can close the file.

3. Next choose New from the File menu. Notice that the settings in the New dialog box reflect the dimensions of the image stored in the clipboard. In the New dialog box, make sure that the radio button in the Contents group is set to Transparent. Click OK to create the new file.

4. When the new file appears, use the Type tool to add some text to your file. Move the Type tool into the center of your document and click. In the

Type Tool dialog box, pick Times or any other serif font, set the size to 75, set the leading to 60, make sure that Bold and the Anti-Aliased option are selected, choose center alignment, and type the words **SPECIAL EFFECTS** in two lines in the text field. Click OK to display your text on screen. Don't deselect.

**OTE:** *If you are not using the Tools Tutorial image you may need to use different settings in the Type Tool dialog box.*

5. When the text is in the center of your document, use the Image/Effects/Scale command to expand the text vertically and horizontally so that it's the same size as your document. When the text is in position and the size of your document, deselect it.

6. To place the image that is in the clipboard into your file, choose Paste from the Edit menu. While the pasted image is still floating over the text, change the settings in the Layers palette so that the Opacity is 100% and the Mode is Normal; select the Preserve Transparency: "Layer 1" check box so that it is activated. The screen changes so that the pasted image appears only inside the text and not on the transparent background.

At this point you could end the project by deselecting. If you deselect, the pasted image gets locked down into the text. A more versatile way of finishing would be to place the image into a layer so that you can manipulate the text and image separately. You can place the floating image into a layer by dragging the words "Floating Selection" in the Layers palette over the Make Layer icon or by double-clicking on the words "Floating Selection" in the Layers palette. The Make Layer dialog box will appear with all the settings you set in the Layers palette in step 6. Notice that the Group with Previous Layer option is activated. When you chose the Preserve Transparency option, Photoshop set the check box to Group with Previous layer. Choosing Preserve Transparency essentially created a clipping group (discussed earlier). Click OK to see the new layer in the Layers palette. Notice that the dotted line between the two layers indicates that a clipping group has been created.

If you wish to save your file with its layers, save it in Photoshop 3.0 format; otherwise, save and flatten your image by choosing File/Save a Copy.

Close your file, then proceed to the next section to learn more about blending images together using the Layers palette's Mode pop-up menu.

**12**

# Photoshop in Action

The arcing water was created using R/GA Print's own proprietary 3-D modeling software.

The moon was created by combining a photograph of a clay model of the moon and a photograph of a person

The Squirt can is a product shot. White was added with the Airbrush tool to the area around the base to create a cloud effect

The earth image is a NASA photograph

**Photograph by: Steve Bronstein   Digital Imaging: R/GA Print   Client: A&W Brands/Squirt**

The painting tools were used to create stars over a black background. Next, a digitized image of the earth and a product shot of a Squirt can were pasted into the file. A clay moon with the contours of a face in it was sculpted by a model maker and then photographed by Steve Bronstein. Steve then took a photograph of a person whose round visage would provide a good man-in-the-moon face. Both the moon and face photographs were scanned and combined using Paste Into and Composite Controls. To remove color from the face but leave the gray values the Luminosity mode was used. Then the Rubber Stamp's Cloning option was used to enhance the blending effect. The painting tools and painting modes were used to turn the man in the moon purple.

To complete the image, Steve took a photograph of water squirting out of a hose. The photo was scanned and then warped using R/GA's own proprietary 3-D modeling software. The squirt was then pasted into the final image.

## Blending Two Images Using the Modes in the Layers Palette

Earlier in the chapter you saw how the Dissolve mode created an unusual speckled blend between layers. In this section you're going to add a layer to an image and use the Layers palette's Mode pop-up menu to experiment with different blending effects. By trying out the modes with images, rather than with the simple shapes used at the beginning of this chapter, you will gain a better understanding of the power of the Layers palette's Mode pop-up menu.

If you don't have two images that you want to blend use the Window (PC users: window.jpg) file and the Leaf file (PC users: leaf.pds) in the Tutorial folder. You'll use the Window file as the Background underlying layer and the Leaf file as the target layer. If the Layers palette isn't open, open it now.

1. Open both files that you wish to blend together and place them side by side or so they overlap. If you overlap the images, put the image you wish to use as the overlying, target layer (the Leaf file, if you are using the Tutorial file) over the image you want for your background, underlying layer (the Window file, if you are using the Tutorial files).

2. Once both files are on screen, activate the Move tool and drag the file you wish to place in the target layer over the Background, underlying layer. If you are using Tutorial files, drag the Leaf over the Seasons file. Photoshop will create a new layer with the leaf in it. Position the image in the layer so it is entirely in view.

As discussed earlier in this chapter, you can use the Opacity slider and the Mode pop-up menu in the Layers palette to control how the pixels in the one layer will blend with pixels in the underlying layer. In this situation, the Modes in the Layers palette work much the same way as when a painting tool is activated. (To review the painting/editing modes, see Chapter 5.) The difference, though, is that Photoshop applies the painting/editing modes to the underlying layer based upon the pixels in the target layer, rather than using the foreground color.

**12**

𝓷 **OTE:** *The modes and opacity options will also become active when a floating selection exists on screen. This means that you can change modes and opacity to create the blend effect between the floating selection and the underlying layer.*

Before you begin experimenting, position the image (leaf) in the layer so that it is over light and dark image areas of your background (Window file). This will give you a better idea of how the modes work. If you want, you can use the Image/Effects/Scale command to make the image in the target layer larger.

Now try switching from one mode to another. Here's a brief review of how some of the more powerful modes in the Layers palette work:

- To create a composite where darker pixels in the target layer replace corresponding lighter pixels in the underlying layer, and darker areas from the underlying layer replace lighter pixels in the target layer, choose Darken.

- To create a composite where lighter pixels in the target layer replace corresponding darker pixels in the underlying layer, and lighter pixels from the underlying layer replace darker pixels in the target layer, choose Lighten.

- To blend the Hue and Saturation values of the target with the underlying layer, choose Color. The Luminosity value of the underlying image will not be affected, thus preserving the underlying layer's brightness levels.

*n*OTE: *As discussed in Chapters 7 and 13, a histogram is a visual representation of an image's brightness or gray levels. To prove to yourself that the brightness values of the image don't change when the Color mode is chosen, view the Histogram (Image/Histogram) of your underlying layer with the target layer hidden. View the histogram again (in Color mode) with both layers visible. The histogram doesn't change.*

- To create a darker composite from the pixel values of both the target and underlying layers, choose Multiply. This can produce a result similar to overlaying colored magic markers.

- To create a lighter composite from both the pixel values of the target and underlying layers, choose Screen. This often creates the effect of bleaching out colors from an image.

- To create a random effect from the pixels in both the target and underlying layers, choose Dissolve and use the Opacity slider to adjust the results. As you lower the Opacity, the top layer gradually dissolves, revealing more of the underlying layer.

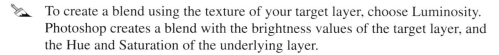 To create a blend using the texture of your target layer, choose Luminosity. Photoshop creates a blend with the brightness values of the target layer, and the Hue and Saturation of the underlying layer.

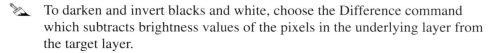 To darken and invert blacks and white, choose the Difference command which subtracts brightness values of the pixels in the underlying layer from the target layer.

 To lighten or screen where light areas overlap, and darken where dark areas overlap, while preserving highlights and shadows choose Overlay. (If you are using the Leaf image, drag the leaf to the right edge of the Window image. The leaf becomes almost completely transparent. When you drag it to a black area in the window image, the leaf completely disappears.)

**CAUTION:** *If you drag a layer so that part of the image is hidden off screen and then change modes, Photoshop will crop the offscreen areas.*

Figure 12-8c shows a backyard scene that was placed in a layer over the waterfall background image, shown in Figure 12-8b, to create the composite shown in Figure 12-8a. After the new layer for the backyard scene was created, the Darken mode was selected in the Mode pop-up menu of the Layers palette. Remember, when the Darken mode is applied, Photoshop compares the pixel values in the target layer to the pixel values in the underlying layer. It then replaces lighter pixels with corresponding darker pixels. Thus, in Figure 12-8c, the lighter areas of the waterfall were replaced by the darker trees and fence from the backyard scene. To make more of the underlying image visible, Opacity in the Layers palette was lowered to 50%.

Now that you've seen the effects of using the modes to blend images, continue to see how the Layer Options dialog box provides even more versatility when blending images together.

## Using Composite Controls to Blend Images Together

The sliders found in the Layers Option dialog box allow you to control exactly what elements from a target and underlying layer appear in the final composite image. With the sliders (in previous Photoshop versions, referred to as Composite Controls), you can pick which pixels in the underlying layer will be replaced by the pixels in the target layer. The Composite Controls sliders can be accessed by first clicking on

(a)

(a) Blend between two layers created using the Darken mode and low Opacity in the Layers palette; (b) Underlying layer; (c) Target layer

(b)

(c)

**FIGURE 12-8**

a layer name, then choosing Layer Options from the Layers palette pop-up menu, or by double-clicking on the target layer in the Layers palette.

The following exercise demonstrates the Layers Option dialog box sliders and its options. For the exercise, you will need two images: one image to be the underlying background image, and another to be the image that will be blended with the overlying target layer.

For example, Figure 12-9c shows an image of a boat in a layer over another layer filled with the textured background shown in Figure 12-9b. The Layer Options dialog box sliders were used to blend the two layers together to create the composite shown in Figure 12-9a. Adjusting the sliders allowed the lightest pixels from the boat layer to be eliminated so that the textured background could show through.

The background image shown in Figure 12-9b was created by applying the Add Noise and Zigzag filters to a Linear blend. (See Chapter 8 for a review of the filter commands and Chapter 5 for a review of creating blends.) If you wish to re-create this background for the following exercise, create a new file, 4 inches high by 6 inches wide. Set the background contents to white by choosing the White radio button in the Contents group.

After you create the new file, choose a dark foreground and a light background color to be the starting and ending colors for the Linear blend. Once you have created the blend, apply the Add Noise filter (in the Filter/Noise submenu) with the Uniform option set to 32. Apply the filter two or three times to achieve a speckled effect. To transform the image into a rippled pond, apply the Zigzag filter in the Filter/Distort submenu. Choose the Pond Ripple radio button and set Amount to 87 and Ridges to 20.

Now that you have created the textured image for the underlying layer (the Background), your next step is to create a new layer. In this layer you will place the image you wish to blend with the underlying layer. Create the new layer by using the Paste Layer command, as described in the following steps:

1. Open a file that you wish to blend with the textured background you just created. If you do not have a file to use, you can open the Window file (PC users: window.jpg) in the Tutorial folder.

2. Select the entire file, or an area of it, that you wish to paste into the Background file (the Window file if you are using the Tutorial file).

3. From the Edit menu, choose Copy, and then close the file.

4. Activate the textured background image. Choose Paste Layer from the Edit menu. When the Make Layer dialog box appears, make sure Opacity is set to 100%, the Mode pop-up menu is Normal, and the Group with

**12**

(a)

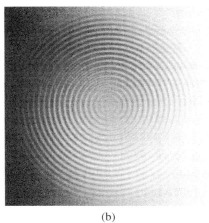 

(b)                    (c)

(a)Composite image created using Composite Controls; (b)Underlying layer created with the Gradient tool and the Add Noise filters; (c)Target layer (photograph courtesy of Jonathan Pite)

**FIGURE 12-9**

Previous Layer is not selected. Name the layer if you wish. Click OK for the Window image to appear in your document in a new layer. Open the Layers palette if it is not already open. Note that the new layer you created is the target layer.

**5.** Choose Layer Options from the Layers palette pop-up menu or double-click on the top layer to open the Layer Options dialog box.

```
┌─────────────────────────────────────────────────────────┐
│░░░░░░░░░░░░░░░░░░░░░ Layer Options ░░░░░░░░░░░░░░░░░░░░░░│
│┌───────────────────────────────────────────────────────┐│
││                                                         ││
││   Name: │Layer 1                    │      ┌────────┐   ││
││                                             │   OK   │   ││
││   Opacity: │100│ %  Mode: │ Normal     ▼│   └────────┘   ││
││                                             ┌────────┐   ││
││          ☐ Group With Previous Layer        │ Cancel │   ││
││                                             └────────┘   ││
││  ┌─ Blend If: │ Gray    ⌘0 ▼│ ──────────  ☒ Preview    ││
││     This Layer:    0      255                           ││
││     ▐▬▬▬▬▬▬▬▬▬▬▬▬▬▬▬▬▬▬▬▬▬▬▬△                          ││
││     ▲                                                   ││
││     Underlying:    0      255                           ││
││     ▐▬▬▬▬▬▬▬▬▬▬▬▬▬▬▬▬▬▬▬▬▬▬▬△                          ││
││     ▲                                                   ││
│└───────────────────────────────────────────────────────┘│
└─────────────────────────────────────────────────────────┘
```

The options in the top of the Layer Options dialog box are already familiar to you from the New Layer dialog box. The options in the bottom of the dialog box, in the Blend If section, are called *Composite Controls*. The Composite Controls feature several options for controlling how pixels in an overlaying layer and an underlying layer will blend together. These options are examined in the paragraphs that follow.

## Composite Controls Sliders

The Composite Controls sliders let you control exactly which pixels to include and exclude from the target layer (the top slider: "This Layer") and underlying layer (the bottom slider: "Underlying"). For both sliders, the black slider control affects dark areas, and the white slider control affects light areas. The range of both sliders is from 0 (black) to 255 (white).

When the This Layer slider's black slider control is dragged to the right, darker pixels of the Target layer will not be included in the composite image. When the This Layer slider's white slider control is dragged to the left, lighter pixels of the target layer will not be included in the composite image. All pixel values designated in the range between the target layer's slider controls will appear in the composite image.

With a little experimentation, the effects of the two sliders will be more apparent to you, so let's continue with the exercise.

**12**

**OTE:** *Before you begin adjusting the sliders, make sure the Preview check box is selected in the Layer Options dialog box, so you can preview the results.*

Try dragging the This Layer slider's black control to the right. This will remove the darker pixels from your target layer. Drag the white control to the left, and you remove the lighter pixels in the target layer from the composite. The results will be more obvious if you drag the black control back to 0 before moving the white control.

Before you begin experimenting with the Underlying slider, reset the Composite Control sliders to their original settings. This will make it easier for you to see the effect of adjusting the Underlying slider controls. To quickly reset all options, press OPTION (PC users: ALT). The Cancel button will change to a Reset button; click this to reset the settings and remain in the dialog box.

Now consider the Underlying slider: when you click and drag the black slider control to the right, dark areas from the underlying image will be added into the composite. As you drag, underlying pixels with values from 0 to the value set by the black slider control will appear in the composite. Clicking and dragging the white slider control to the left will add light areas from the underlying image to the composite. As you drag, underlying pixels with the value from that set by the white slider control to 255 will appear in the composite image. Thus, values between the black and white controls are the pixel values in the underlying image that will not appear in the composite image. These pixels will be replaced by pixels from the target layer in the composite image.

Try clicking and dragging the Underlying slider's black control to the right. As you drag, you add dark pixels from the underlying layer and remove any pixels from the target layer that would have appeared over this area. Move the Underlying slider's black control back to 0 and then move the white control to the left. Notice that as you drag, you are adding light pixels from the underlying layer to the composite and removing pixels from the target layer image in the composite.

## Splitting the Slider Controls

To create a smoother composite effect, you can split each individual slider control ( ) into two parts ( ). To split a slider control, press OPTION (PC users: ALT) and then click and drag on one of the edges of the control. For each slider control that is split you will see two values showing the range between the split controls. The pixels in the range defined by the split slider control will be only partially colored. This can help smooth the blend between the target layer and underlying pixels.

To gain familiarity with how your composite image will be affected by splitting the slider controls, experiment with all four of the controls on both the This Layer and Underlying slider bars.

## Other Composite Controls Options

The remaining options in the Layer Options dialog box allow further possibilities and refinement when creating a composite image.

The Blend If pop-up menu allows you to control the blend based upon the color values of individual color channels. When viewing an RGB image, the word Gray in the Blend If pop-up menu indicates that the Composite Controls affect the luminance or brightness values of the pixels in all channels. In an RGB Color image, Blend If lets you work separately in the red, green, or blue channel of the image. Thus, if Red were chosen in the Blend If pop-up menu, you could control the range of red values (from 0 to 255) for both the target and underlying layers.

You'll also find the familiar Mode pop-up menu and Opacity setting in this dialog box. By entering an Opacity value less than 100%, you can make your target layer more translucent. The Mode pop-up menu offers you the same modes that are available in the Layers palette. These modes work almost exactly as they do when you use the Layers palette to blend layers together (as described in the previous section) but with one major difference: the effect applies only to the pixel values specified by the Composite Controls sliders.

Experiment with the modes and opacities in the Layer Options dialog box until you achieve the effects you desire. Once you are satisfied with the preview of your image, choose OK to activate the changes.

Now that you've explored the Layers Options dialog box's powerful blending options, you probably feel that you've exhausted all of Photoshop's blending features. There's still one very powerful Layers palette option to investigate that allows you to create effects that seamlessly blend images together, Photoshop's *layer masks*. Save your file if you wish. Then close it and proceed to the next section.

## Using Layer Masks to Blend Images Together

Photoshop's Layer Mask option combines the power of layers with the power of alpha channels. Layer masks can be used to help create seamless composites between layers. Unlike the other options you've explored in this chapter, a layer mask allows you to use a painting tool to gradually wipe away or hide image areas from the target layer. This allows images from the underlying layer or layers to appear through the areas you wiped away in the target layer. The result can be a beautiful mix between layers or an ethereal effect where images in one layer gradually fade into another.

When using a layer mask, you can paint only with shades of gray (including black and white). This is exactly like editing an alpha channel, as described in Chapter 11. By using different shades of gray or different opacities of black and

**12**

white, you can control how transparent the target layer becomes, and thus how much of the underlying layer or layers appears through it.

Figure 12-10a shows the results of a layer mask used to gradually blend the Koala bear image seen in Figure 12-10c with an image of the Sydney Opera House, Figure 12-10b.

When working with a layer mask, your image changes on screen according to how you edit the layer mask. It's important to understand, however, that you are not actually editing your layer. You are viewing your layer through a mask. Photoshop is providing you with a preview of how the image will appear once the layer mask

(a)

(a) Two
layers
blended
together
using a
gradient
in a Layer
Mask; (b)
Background
layer; (c)
Koala layer

(b)

(c)

**FIGURE 12-10**

in the Channels palette is applied to the layer. For this reason, working with a layer mask provides you with the ability to always undo any previous changes you make. Once you're satisfied with the onscreen effect of the layer mask, you can decide whether or not you want to apply the effects to the layer.

If this sounds like an elaborate procedure, don't worry. You'll soon see that using and applying a layer mask can be quite simple. The following exercise leads you step by step through the process of creating a layer mask and using the mask to blend one layer into another.

If you don't have two images that you want to blend together, use the Fruit file (PC users: fruit.jpg) and the Flower file (PC users: flower.jpg ) in the Tutorial folder. In this exercise, you'll drag the Flower file into the Fruit file, thereby creating a new layer for the flower in the Fruit file. Then you'll add a layer mask to the Flower layer.

Before you begin, make sure that both the Layers and Channels palettes are open as separate palettes on screen. If these palettes are in a palette group, separate them by clicking and dragging on the Layers or Channels palette's tab and dragging away from the palette group.

1. Open the file that you wish to use as your base layer. If you are using the Tutorial images, this will be the Fruit file. Next open the file that you want to apply the layer mask to. If you are using the Tutorial images, this will be the Flower file. Set up the files on your screen so you can drag the flower into the Fruit file.

2. Next, activate the Move tool and drag the Flower file on top of the Fruit file. Photoshop will create a new layer for the flower. Notice that in the Layers palette you have a Background and Layer 1.

3. Before you create a layer mask, make sure the target layer is the Flower layer (Layer 1). To create the layer mask, click on the pop-up menu arrow in the Layers palette and choose Add Layer Mask. In our example, a layer mask was added to the Koala layer.

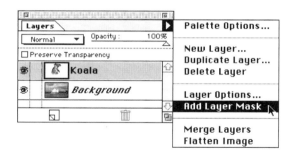

Notice that the title bar now includes the name of your file, the name of your layer, and the word "Mask."

**▤ SYDNEY (Layer 1, Layer 1 Mask, 1:3) ▤**

In the Channels palette, you will see that a new channel appears called "Layer 1 Mask." (If you don't see these words, you'll probably need to enlarge the size of the palette.) Notice that the Layer 1 Mask in the Channels palette is selected. This means that any changes you make on screen will now affect only the mask, not your image.

In the Layers palette, a small white box appears between the words "Layer 1" and the layer thumbnail in the Layers palette. This box is a miniature version of the Layer 1 Mask you viewed in the Channels palette.

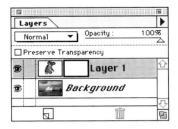

4. To examine layer mask options, double-click on the layer mask thumbnail, the small white box between the words "Layer 1" and the

thumbnail in the Layers palette. This will open the Layer Mask Options dialog box. (You can also access the Layer Mask Options dialog box by double-clicking on the Layer 1 Mask channel in the Channels palette.)

```
┌──────────────── Layer Mask Options ────────────────┐
│  ┌─ Color Indicates: ─────────────┐                │
│  │  ◉ Hidden Areas                │    ┌───────┐   │
│  │  ○ Visible Areas               │    │   OK  │   │
│  │                                │    └───────┘   │
│  └────────────────────────────────┘   ┌─────────┐ │
│  ┌─ Position Relative To: ────────┐    │ Cancel  │ │
│  │  ◉ Layer                       │    └─────────┘ │
│  │  ○ Image                       │                │
│  └────────────────────────────────┘                │
│  ┌─ Color ────────────────────────┐                │
│  │  ┌────┐                         │                │
│  │  │    │   Opacity: [ 50 ] %     │                │
│  │  └────┘                         │                │
│  └────────────────────────────────┘                │
│     ☐ Do not Apply to Layer                        │
└────────────────────────────────────────────────────┘
```

Most of the dialog box options are the same as those in the Channel Options and Quick Mask Options dialog boxes discussed in Chapter 11. By default, the Color Indicates Hidden Areas radio button is selected. This means that when you paint with black, you will be hiding image areas in your target layer. When you paint with white, you will be revealing image areas in the target layer, thus hiding underlying layers. Gray shades will make your image more or less translucent. If you change the radio button to Color Indicates Visible Area, then white will hide areas from your target image, black will reveal areas. As mentioned earlier, by hiding or revealing the image in your target layer, you control what parts of underlying layers appear in the final composite image.

The Position Relative To Layer or Image choices in the dialog box determine the mask position if you move the target layer after the layer mask is created. If Position Relative to Layer is chosen, the mask will always move with the layer, no matter where it is positioned on screen. If Position Relative to Image is chosen, the mask will not move from its original position if the target layer is moved. Normally, you will probably want to leave the Position Relative To Layer option selected in order to always keep the layer and mask together. The Do Not Apply to Layer check box should remain deselected if you want to see how the mask will affect your image. If you select the check box, Photoshop places a red X in the layer mask box in the Layers palette, indicating that you will not be

**12**

able to see the mask's effects. Keep the default settings, then click OK to close the dialog box.

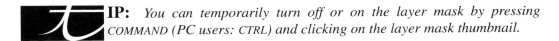

**IP:** *You can temporarily turn off or on the layer mask by pressing* COMMAND *(PC users:* CTRL*) and clicking on the layer mask thumbnail.*

Next you'll have a chance to try out the layer mask by painting over it with the Paintbrush tool. Before continuing notice the black frame surrounding the layer mask thumbnail in the Layers palette. The black frame surrounding the layer mask means that the changes you make when editing will affect the mask. You won't actually be changing pixels in the target layer, even though it appears that they are changing. When the layer mask thumbnail is selected, Photoshop shows you how your image would look if the mask were applied to it. You'll see this in the next set of steps, where you'll have a chance to paint over your image.

If you wish to view the layer mask as it appears in its channel, OPTION-click (PC users: ALT-click) on the layer mask thumbnail. OPTION-click again to return the layers into view.

5. Before you begin editing, open the Picker palette on screen. Notice that your palette of painting colors has changed. In the Picker palette, the color slider now indicates a color range from black to white. When you edit the layer mask, you can paint only in black, white, or shades of gray. As mentioned earlier, when Color Indicates Hidden Areas is selected in the Layer Mask Options dialog box, if you paint with black or darker colors you will hide areas in the target layer; paint with white or lighter colors and you reveal areas in the target layer.

6. Set the foreground color to black.

7. Try using the Paintbrush tool with a soft-edged brush to paint over the image in the target layer. Make sure the Mode pop-up menu in the Paintbrush Options palette is set to Normal and Opacity is set to 100%. As you paint, you will gradually hide image areas.

**EMEMBER:** *When the Layer Mask thumbnail is selected, all painting and editing affects only the layer mask.*

8. Change the foreground color to white.

9. Try painting with white over the areas you just painted. Notice that the portions of the image that you wiped away gradually return (see Figure 12-11). To vary the effect, try changing to different shades of gray in the Picker palette and keep painting or change the opacity in the Options palette.

**𝓃OTE:** *If you wish to temporarily exit the layer mask, click on the thumbnail of your target layer to the left of the layer mask thumbnail. If you do this, colors will return to the Picker palette. Afterwards, any editing changes you make will affect the pixels of your target layer, not the mask. To reenter Layer Mask mode, click on the thumbnail of the layer mask. You can also turn on and off the overlay by SHIFT-clicking on the layer mask thumbnail.*

Now try creating a gradient in the layer mask.

10. Double-click on the Gradient tool. In the Gradient Tool Options palette, set mode to Normal, Opacity to 100%, the Style pop-up menu to Foreground to Background, the Midpoint value to 50%, the Type pop-up menu to Radial, and the Radial Offset value to 50%. Before you use the Gradient tool, set the foreground color to white and the background color to black. Then, move the Gradient tool to the middle of the overlying

Koala and Sidney Opera House images blended together using a Layer Mask

**FIGURE 12-11**

12

target layer (the flower) and click and drag from the center out. Now the middle of the flower is seen overlaying the fruit but the image gradually dissolves into the background (the fruit image).

*n* **OTE:** *If you wish to edit the mask in the mask channel, open the Channels palette on screen. Click on the Eye column to the left of the mask channel. The red overlay (discussed in Chapter 11) appears. You can now use the painting tools to edit the mask by adding to and subtracting from the overlay. When you're done editing, click on the Eye column in the Channels palette again to make the overlay disappear.*

Once you've completed editing the mask, you can decide whether to change your image according to your edited mask or you can discard the mask. To apply or discard the layer mask, choose Remove Layer Mask from the pop-up menu in the Layers palette, or you can drag the layer mask thumbnail in the Layers palette over the Trash icon in the Layers palette. A prompt will appear asking whether you wish to apply the mask to a layer before removing it. If you choose Apply, the layer mask will be applied to your image. If you choose Discard, the layer mask will not be applied to your image. If you choose Cancel, the Remove Layer Mask command will be ignored.

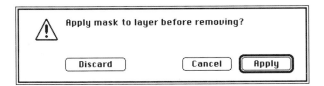

11. Try applying the Layer Mask to the image by choosing Remove Layer Mask from the pop-up menu in the Layers palette. In the dialog box that appears asking whether to apply the layer mask, choose Apply. The target layer on screen is now updated to reflect the changes you made to the layer mask.

After you've applied the layer mask, the layer mask thumbnail disappears in the Layers palette. Any image editing you do now will affect the target layer.

If you'd like to experiment more with layer masks, try dragging another image into your file and creating a layer mask for it. Try using the Leaf file (PC users: leaf.psd), if you are using the Tutorial images.

When you're done experimenting with layer masks, use the File/Save a Copy command to flatten the image to conserve memory and rename the file, or use the Save As command to save the file with its layers under a new name.

## CONCLUSION

As you've seen from this chapter, layers provide numerous ways of juxtaposing and compositing images. Changing opacities and modes, using Composite Controls, and creating clipping groups and layer masks all provide different effects. Once you understand and master the layer options covered in this chapter, the image editing possibilities are endless.

# 13

# RETOUCHING AND
# COLOR CORRECTING

A Photoshop image frequently undergoes numerous transformations before it is finally output to the printed page, to video, or to a transparency. No matter what the project, an essential and often unavoidable step is color correcting or retouching. These steps are critical to making the final design match the Photoshop artist's vision.

*Color correcting* involves changing an image's hue, saturation, shadows, midtones, and/or highlights so that the final output has the most appealing appearance possible. Color correcting is often required to compensate for loss of color quality as a result of digitization. The process of translating your Photoshop image to the printed page often makes color correction a necessity as well. For instance, paper stock, resolution, and impurity of printers' inks may force you to adjust your Photoshop image's colors to produce a suitable printed version. Color correcting is important in making sure that an image's colors conform to those of the original, and may in fact produce an improvement over the original. You may also need to *retouch* an image. In addition to removing imperfections in an image, retouching can even make it appear better than real life.

For example, nature often doesn't cooperate by providing the perfect weather, the perfect setting, or the perfect face. A photo of a beach resort taken on a damp, cloudy day will show the beach and water looking brown, the sky gray, the models pale, and the picnic food soggy and uninviting. Photoshop's color-correcting tools can turn the sky and water magnificent shades of blue, make the models tan, and the sand pearly white. When reality must truly take a back seat to the needs an image must meet, you can summon the magic of retouching.

Retouching can remove little bits of litter and debris from the beach. It can smooth a few wrinkles or clear up a pair of bloodshot eyes in a tired face. Even the picnic food can be made to look more inviting. With Photoshop's Rubber Stamp's cloning option, you can even toss more shrimp on the barbecue and add more strawberries to the shortcake.

Clearly, retouching and color correcting often go hand in hand. To get you started with the fundamentals of these operations, this chapter begins with a discussion of how to improve the tonal qualities of a grayscale image. After you learn how to correct a grayscale image, you'll see how faded, damaged old photographs can be retouched. Next, you'll apply retouching techniques to eliminate wrinkles and blemishes in a face and learn how to improve outdoor scenes. The chapter concludes with the steps for color-correcting images.

Since both retouching and color correcting require the use of many of the tools and techniques discussed throughout this book, you may wish to review some previous chapters. For color correcting, you should be familiar with the basics of color theory (Chapter 4). For advanced color-correction work, you will need to know how to select areas using the Pen tool (Chapter 10), or isolate an area in Quick Mask mode in order to save selections to channels so they can be reloaded later (Chapter 11). For retouching, you will need to know how to use the Eyedropper, Rubber Stamp, Pencil, Paintbrush, Airbrush, Smudge, Blur/Sharpen, and Dodge/Burn/Sponge tools (Chapters 5 and 6). You may also need to know how to use the Dust & Scratches filter (Chapter 8).

Both color correcting and retouching call for some artistic skills that require practice. The more experience you gain with Photoshop's color-correcting commands and retouching tools, the better your skills will be. You'll also be able to save yourself and/or your clients a substantial amount of money if you can correct images and retouch them on your desktop computer. The color examples you'll see in this chapter are from professional work created in Photoshop that in previous years would have required high-end computer workstations or dot etchers, who would edit the individual halftone dots by hand on the film separation.

## BEFORE YOU BEGIN

This chapter won't just introduce you to new Photoshop commands but will also show you how to obtain the best-quality results from your work. With this goal in mind, we must again emphasize the importance of *calibration* before you commence any color-correcting or retouching project. If your monitor is not calibrated, you may well find that your final image is quite different from the one you were working with on screen in Photoshop. Be sure to follow the steps in the section on calibration in Chapter 1.

You might also want to review the File/Preferences/Printing Inks Setup dialog box, which lets you change the display of grayscale images to compensate for dot gain. Although the settings in the dialog box do not affect the display of RGB Color images, they do affect the display of CMYK Color images. For more details, see Chapter 9.

## ANALYZING THE IMAGE

When you start with the best possible original and digitized image, you'll have less retouching and color-correcting work to do. If the original image is underexposed, overexposed, damaged, or has other defects, the digitized version will reflect this.

**13**

Thus, before digitizing, always try to obtain high-quality originals, since corrections are easier if the problems are small. Of course, correcting a bad image may not be impossible, but it could involve completely re-creating parts or most of the original image. You'll have to decide whether it's worth the time to perform major surgery.

After your image is digitized, look carefully for imperfections. Many digitized images may seem near perfect when viewed on screen at actual size, but when magnified or printed, flaws may become apparent. To properly analyze an image, zoom in to different areas and carefully check for noise or *posterization*, which is a lack of sufficient gray levels, and whether the image is sharp and crisp, or blurry and out of focus. Keep in mind that if an image looks flawed on screen, it may be best to redigitize it with better equipment or at a higher resolution before retouching and color correcting.

One of this book's authors, Adele Droblas Greenberg, worked on a project that involved correcting faded and scratched grayscale images for a Reader's Digest book. She digitized the images on a midrange scanner (Agfa Arcus) rather than on a low-end scanner. Images that had been test-scanned on a less sophisticated scanner often exhibited noise and black blotches in shadow areas. The blotches were caused by posterization. The images were eventually rescanned on the Agfa Arcus to ensure that no problems arose during the printing or tonal-correcting process.

**OTE:** *For more information on digitizing your images, review Chapter 7.*

Once you have the best possible digitized image, avoid the temptation to dive right in and start making changes. Take a few moments to identify your objectives. Decide carefully how you want to improve your image. Your goal is obviously to make the final image look as good as, or better than, the original; nevertheless, it should still look natural and believable.

After you've digitized your image, use the File/Save As or File/Save A Copy command to make a backup of your original digitized image. *This is extremely important* because you may find that color correcting or retouching removes details or colors that shouldn't have been replaced. If you need to start again from scratch, or to sample part of the original image so you can clone back the detail you've removed, you can always use the backup. While working with an image, try to save different versions of it as you proceed, or use the Edit/Take Snapshot command. That way you'll always be able to return to a previous version.

Whether you are working on a color or grayscale image, start the correction process by taking readings of the image using the Info palette and the Eyedropper tool. The Info palette assists you in reading gray and color values. When you move the Eyedropper over various areas in the image, the Info palette reads out the exact color or gray values of the underlying pixels. Once you grow accustomed to reading them, you'll learn to rely on the Eyedropper readouts (rather than on your monitor) as a true guide to an image's tones and colors.

**OTE:**  *Before you begin using the Eyedropper tool to gauge grayscale and color adjustments, it's a good idea to set the Eyedropper's sample size to a 3-by-3 pixel sample rather than Point sample, which only evaluates one pixel at a time. This way, one errant pixel won't unduly influence the Info palette readout. To reset the sample size, double-click on the Eyedropper in the Toolbox and choose 3-by-3 Average from the Sample Size pop-up menu in the Eyedropper Options palette.*

## CORRECTING A GRAYSCALE IMAGE

If you wish to learn how to correct the tones of a grayscale image, open any grayscale image, or open the Hands file (PC users: hands.jpg) in the Tutorial folder.

When you make tonal corrections, you increase detail in the shadows, midtones, and highlights of an image. Figure 13-1a displays a digitized photograph that will be used to demonstrate the techniques involved in correcting a grayscale image. The photograph, taken in the late 1800s, is of Medora von Hoffman de Mores, a French nobleman who came to the Dakotas to raise cattle. The problems in the photograph are numerous: Details are faded, the image is too dark, and dirt and dust spots are sprinkled throughout. Ken Chaya, art editor of the Reader's Digest book *Discovering America's Past*, asked Adele Droblas Greenberg to retouch the photograph of Medora. Figure 13-1b shows the photograph after the gray tones were corrected and the image was retouched. The final image was converted to a sepia. (The finished retouched sepia is shown as image 4 in the first color insert of this book.)

### Using the Eyedropper and Info Palette to Take Readings

Once you have a grayscale image on screen and the Eyedropper tool is activated, open the Info palette. Since you are working with grayscale, all you need is one readout in the Info Palette. If you have two readouts, click on the Info palette's pop-up menu and choose the Palette Options command. In the Info Options dialog box, make sure that Show First Color Readout is checked and is set to Grayscale or

**13**

A digitized old photograph of Medora von Hoffman de Mores in the late 1800s (courtesy of the Library of Congress), before and after tonal adjustments and retouching

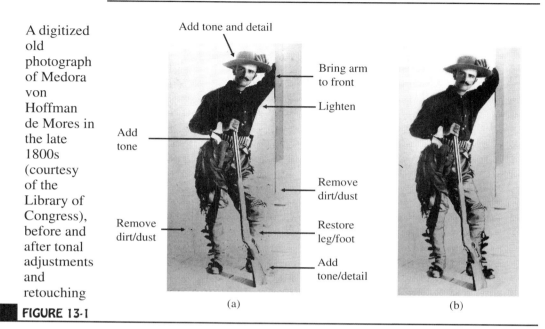

Add tone and detail

Bring arm to front

Lighten

Add tone

Remove dirt/dust

Remove dirt/dust

Restore leg/foot

Add tone/detail

(a)                    (b)

**FIGURE 13-1**

Actual Color. Show Second Color Readout should not be enabled. Leave Show Mouse Coordinates on, and choose the measurement option of your choice. Click OK to activate the changes.

With the Eyedropper selected and the Info palette on screen, move the Eyedropper over different parts of your image. Notice that the K (black) value in the Info palette displays the percentage of black in the area touched by the Eyedropper. Your next step is to take readings of the darkest and lightest points in your image. It's important to do this because areas with less than 5% black tones will often print as white. Dot gain in printing may cause areas with over 95% black tones to look blotchy. If you are outputting to newsprint, dot gain increases, so try to keep the darkest shadow areas around 80%. In Figure 13-2, you can see that the darkest shadow area reads 99% K (black). Soon you'll see how these dark areas were diminished.

 **OTE:**  *The paper, screen frequency, and printing press used all affect the quality of the final output. Consult your print shop if you have questions.*

Once you know the values of your darkest and lightest points, take a reading of the midtones. If the midtone areas are too light or too dark, you'll probably want to adjust these levels during the tonal-correction process.

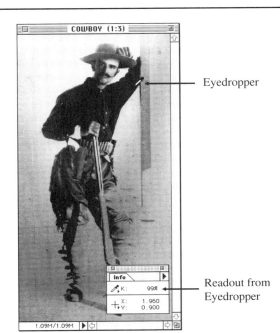

Reading the darkest areas of the image with the Eyedropper tool

**FIGURE 13-2**

13

Since it's impossible to take a reading of every pixel of your image by using the Info palette and the Eyedropper, it's often valuable to view a histogram of the image, as described next.

## Using a Histogram to View the Tonal Range

When you open a grayscale image on screen, every pixel in the image can have a value between 0 (black) and 255 (white). Darker pixels have lower gray values; lighter pixels have higher values. A *histogram* plots the disbursement of the gray tones in an image and gives you a visual sense of an image's tonal range. To display a histogram of your image, select Histogram from the Image menu. If part of your image is selected, the histogram will only chart the selected area.

The Histogram dialog box graphs the number of pixels in relation to the tonal range of all possible gray values in an image. The horizontal (x) axis represents the possible gray values from 0 to 255. The vertical (y) axis represents the number of pixels for each tone/color. Beneath the x-axis is a gradient bar showing the actual gray levels from black to white. Dark image areas are graphed on the left of the graph, midtones in the middle, light areas on the right. The height of each vertical line represents the number of pixels for each tone on the x-axis; the higher the line, the more pixels at that gray level in the image.

If the histogram is weighted predominantly toward the right, your image is probably too light. This is often called a High Key image. If it is weighted toward the left, it's probably too dark. These are called Low Key images. A histogram that bulges in the middle is stuffed with too many midtone values and thus may lack contrast. In general, a well-balanced image will show pixels spread over the entire tonal range, with most in the midtone area. This is often called a Normal Key image.

The Histogram dialog box also displays the following precise statistics of your image:

- The Mean value represents the average brightness.

- The Std (Standard) Deviation value represents the variance of the brightness values in the image.

- The Median value represents the middle brightness value in the image.

- The value in Pixels is the total number of pixels in the image or selection.

When you move the mouse within the graph, the pointer becomes a crosshair. When you move the crosshair over the histogram, the Level, Count, and Percentile values will change, as follows:

Level represents the level of grays at the crosshair location on the graph; 0 is the darkest level (black) and 255 is the lightest level (white).

 Count represents the number of pixels at the crosshair location on the graph.

 Percentile is a percentage based on the crosshair's position on the x-axis, from 0% to 100%.

Move the crosshair from left to right over the histogram. As you do, the Level and Pixels values display brightness values and a pixel count. Next, click and drag in the middle of the histogram. A blue or black bar appears above the area over which you drag, and the Level readout displays the gray-level range.

**IP:**  *As you make adjustments to your image during the correction process, you should return periodically to the histogram to get a sense of how your changes are affecting the tonal range.*

The histogram's crosshair readout in Figure 13-3 shows that at level 255, the pixel count is 0. Thus, there are no white pixels in the cowboy image, and no need to reduce the highlights in the image. Figure 13-4 shows the histogram after very dark values were eliminated to ensure better printing of shadow areas. Notice that the histogram's crosshair readout indicates that at level 0 (black), the pixel count is 0.

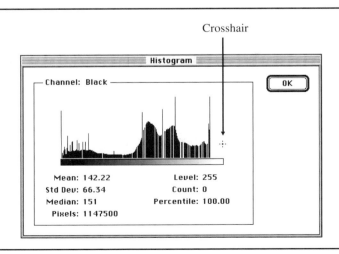

Crosshair

Histogram of cowboy image, before tonal adjustments

 **FIGURE 13-3**

**13**

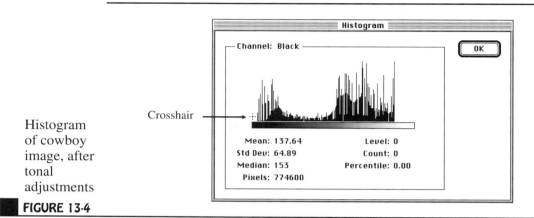

Histogram
of cowboy
image, after
tonal
adjustments

**FIGURE 13-4**

If you are viewing the histogram of the Hands file, notice that the image is weighted toward black pixels; otherwise, the tonal distribution is fairly constant.

When you think you are well acquainted with the tonal distribution in your image, you are ready to make tonal adjustments to that image.

## ADJUSTING A GRAYSCALE IMAGE

What do you do if the shadows in your image are over 95%, the highlights under 5%, and the midtones either too dark or too light? When you make tonal adjustments, you often must increase the brightness or contrast. Sometimes you need to expand the tonal range of an image—the range from the lightest point in the image to its darkest point.

To change the darkest, lightest, and midtone areas in an image, you can either use the Levels, Curves, and/or Variations commands in the Image/Adjust submenu. (You won't use the Image menu's Brightness/Contrast command because it has no controls for adjusting shadows, highlights, and midtones.) The command you choose for adjusting these elements in your image will often depend upon the image itself and on how comfortable you are with the available tools. Sometimes you may need more than one Image/Adjust command to complete the operation successfully. Practice using these commands before you attempt to correct images in a real project.

The next three sections tell you how to use the Image/Adjust Variations, Levels, and Curves commands to improve tonal range by adjusting highlights, midtones, and shadows for grayscale images. All of these commands can be used for correcting color images as well, as discussed later in this chapter.

## Using the Variations Command

The Variations command provides a simple and quick way to visually adjust highlights, midtones, and shadows, using miniature image previews—undoubtedly the most intuitive way to adjust tones in an image. Unfortunately, this method does not provide exact adjustment for the color or grayscale values in image areas. Though you can make an image's highlights, midtones, or shadows lighter or darker by clicking on the thumbnail images, you cannot specify a precise value for lightness or darkness (as you can using the Levels and Curves commands).

 **OTE:** *If the Variations command does not appear in the Image/Adjust submenu, the Variations plug-in has not been installed or was removed from the Filters folder in the Plug-ins (PC users: plugins) folder.*

Open the Variations dialog box by selecting Variations in the Image/Adjust submenu. The original image, before adjustments, is displayed in the thumbnail labeled "Original" at the top of the dialog box. You make your adjustments to the shadows, midtones, and highlights by selecting the appropriate thumbnail. To make image areas lighter or darker, click on a thumbnail labeled "Lighter" or "Darker"; the effects are then displayed in the Current Pick thumbnail. Generally, if you darken shadows and lighten highlights, you add contrast to your image. If you lighten shadows and darken highlights, you decrease the contrast. If you want to revert to the original image, press and hold OPTION (PC users: ALT) while you click on the Original thumbnail.

The Fine/Coarse slider allows you to specify the level of change in brightness that will occur when you click on a Shadows, Midtones, or Highlights thumbnail. When you drag the slider control to the right, toward Coarse, the difference between lighter and darker grows larger. When you drag the slider control to the left, toward

**13**

Fine, the difference decreases. Each increment on the slider is double the previous incremental change.

The Show Clipping option, shown in Figure 13-5, turns grayscale image areas to a white color if making them lighter or darker pushes, or boosts, the area to pure black or pure white. If you're viewing the Hands image, the Darker thumbnail in the Shadows column also reveals the results of having Show Clipping selected. Part of the image is chromed out, and this is a warning: If you darken the image, detail will be lost.

To try out the Variations command, move to the Shadows column and click on the Lighter thumbnail. This tells Photoshop to make the darkest parts of the image lighter. Notice how the thumbnails change to reveal the Current Pick. Try another variation: Move to the Highlights column and click on the Darker thumbnail; this will darken the lightest parts of the image. If you wish, try adjusting the Fine/Coarse slider and then examine the effects on various thumbnails.

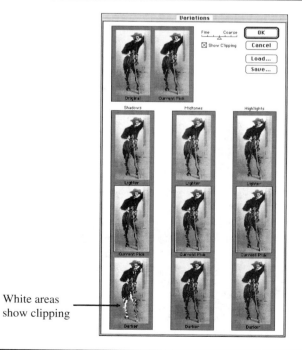

The Variations dialog box with the Show Clipping option enabled

White areas show clipping

**FIGURE 13-5**

**OTE:** *Unfortunately, when the Variations dialog box is open, you can't move the Eyedropper over your image to gauge the degree of change as you can when the Levels and Curves dialog boxes are used.*

Be sure to cancel the adjustments you have made before exiting the dialog box if you don't want to change your image. To cancel your changes, press OPTION (PC users: ALT) while you click on the Original thumbnail.

## Using the Levels Command

With the Levels command, you reduce or increase shadows, midtones, and highlights by dragging sliders. It allows more precision than the Variations command because specific values can be entered in the Levels dialog box. Another advantage to using the Levels command is that it allows Eyedropper/Info palette readings to be taken while you make tonal adjustments. The Info palette displays these readings as "before" and "after" settings.

Select Levels from the Image/Adjust submenu; the Levels dialog box displays a histogram of your image or selection. Directly beneath the histogram, along the bottom axis, is the Input Levels slider, which allows you to add contrast by adjusting shadows, midtones, and highlights. The white slider control on the right side primarily adjusts the image's highlight values. When you move the white slider control, corresponding values—0 (black) to 255 (white)—appear in the right-hand Input Levels field at the top of the dialog box.

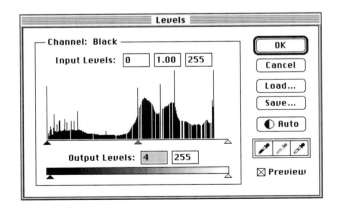

The black slider control on the left of the Input Levels slider primarily adjusts shadow values. Its corresponding values appear in the left-hand Input Levels field

**13**

at the top of the dialog box. The values for shadows, like those for highlights, range from 0 (black) to 255 (white).

The middle slider control represents the midtones, or gamma, in the image or selection. The default gamma setting, which appears in the middle Input Levels field, is 1.00. Moving the middle slider control to the left raises the gamma value and primarily makes midtones lighter; moving it to the right primarily makes midtones darker. When the gamma is set at 1, it's always equidistant from the shadows and highlights.

When you change values for shadows, midtones, or highlights in the Levels dialog box, Photoshop remaps, or shuffles, the image's pixels accordingly. For instance, if you reset the white Input Levels slider control from 255 to 230, values that were 230 are remapped to 255; highlights are thus brightened, and the total number of highlight pixels is increased. The rest of the pixels in the image are reassigned to reflect the new white value. For instance, you'll also see the midtone lightened. The exact number of pixels and how they are remapped is based upon how far you drag the slider control, so be aware that lightening the highlights can cause a rippling effect that partially lightens midtones and shadows.

When the Preview check box in the Levels dialog box is selected, the image or selection changes according to the values in the Input Levels fields. If you wish to see where the highlights and shadows begin in an image, deselect the Preview check box and press and hold OPTION (PC users: ALT). Then drag either the highlight (white) or shadow (black) Input Levels slider control. The screen will show a high-contrast view of your image, indicating the darkest and lightest image areas. (For this to work, the Video LUT Animation option must be selected in the General Preferences dialog box.)

*ᴺ*OTE: *On the Mac, you may find that Photoshop provides a full-screen preview, even when the Preview button is off. This is caused by a Color Lookup Table that dynamically updates your screen when the Video LUT Animation option in the General Preferences dialog box is on. If the Video LUT Animation option is turned on, color and grayscale adjustments appear throughout your entire screen (in every open window) if the Preview button is not selected. For a more accurate preview, click the Preview button, which temporarily disables Video LUT. This will cause the preview to appear only in the active window.*

The Output Levels slider at the bottom of the dialog box reduces contrast by subtracting white or black from an image. Move the black slider control to the right and you will subtract shadow areas from your image, thereby lightening it. Move the white slider control to the left and you will subtract highlight areas, thus darkening your image. When the image is lightened or darkened, Photoshop remaps the pixels according to the new Output Levels values.

For instance, if you drag the white Output Levels control to the left, resetting it from 255 to 200, you remap the image so that 200 is the lightest value. Any pixels with a value of 255 are changed to have a value of 200, and all values are remapped accordingly to make the image darker. The same is true if you move the black control. If the black control is moved from 0 to 50, 50 becomes the darkest value in the image. Pixels that were 0 would now have a value of 50.

At this point, you may be somewhat confused about the difference between the Input Levels and Output Levels sliders. When you drag the left Output Levels slider control to the right, the values increase and the image lightens. But the values also increase when you drag the left Input Levels slider control to the right—yet the image darkens.

Here's the distinction between the two: Assume you change the left (black) Input Levels value to 40. This tells Photoshop to take all the shadow values between 40 and a lesser value and change them to 0 (black). Thus darker pixels are added and the image grows darker. The difference between the lightest and darkest pixels is increased; thus the contrast is increased. On the other hand, if you move the left (black) Output Levels slider control to the right to 40, you are telling Photoshop to take all pixels with values of 0 to 39 and shift them to be 40 and more. Thus darker pixels are subtracted and the image brightens, but the contrast is reduced. Also, remember that the Input Levels slider focuses on highlights, midtones, and shadows; the Output Levels slider adjusts the entire tonal range.

If the shadows in your image are too dark, try dragging the left Output Levels slider control to the right. Figure 13-6 illustrates how this was done to decrease the black areas in the cowboy image. After the blacks were decreased—with the Levels dialog box still open—the mouse pointer (which turns into an eyedropper if CAPS LOCK is not depressed) was placed over the image to measure the degree of change. Notice that the Info palette in Figure 13-6 shows the before-and-after readouts: 99% dark areas were changed to 97%. To avoid lightening midtones and highlights, the shadow areas were not reduced any more in the Levels dialog box; rather, for fine-tuning the shadows, the Curves dialog box was used, as you'll see in the next section. If the white areas in your image are too light, try dragging the white Output Levels control to the left.

If you've moved the sliders too much in your experimentation and you're unhappy with the results, you can reset the image by holding OPTION (PC users: ALT) while you click on the Reset button in the Levels dialog box. (When you press OPTION or ALT, the Cancel button changes into a Reset button.)

**13**

Eyedropper readouts, before and after adjustments

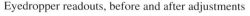

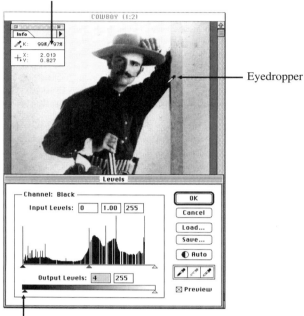

Eyedropper

Slider moved from 0 to 4

Using the
Levels
dialog box
to lighten
shadows

**FIGURE 13-6**

**TIP:** *If you achieve Levels settings that you think you will use frequently, you can keep them handy by clicking on the Save and Load buttons. You can even work on a low-resolution image, save the settings, and apply them to high-resolution files.*

You might have noticed the three eyedropper icons and the Auto button in the Levels dialog box. The white and black eyedroppers can be used to automatically expand an image's tonal range, which can become compressed during the digitization process. The eyedroppers and the Auto button function similarly to the Auto Levels command in the image/adjust submenu. These will be discussed later in this chapter.

Next you will investigate Photoshop's most powerful and precise tool for adjusting colors and tones: the Curves dialog box.

## Using the Curves Command

The Curves dialog box is probably the most versatile and powerful of Photoshop's tone- and color-correcting utilities. It allows the adjustment of any point on an image's tonal curve. By clicking on your image when the dialog box is open, you can also find where that portion of your image is plotted on the curve.

When the cowboy image (Figure 13-1a) was corrected, the Curves dialog box was used to precisely pinpoint shadow areas that were above 95%.

Select Curves from the Image/Adjust submenu. In the Curves dialog box, you see a graph displaying a diagonal line. The x-axis (horizontal) on this graph represents an image's Input values; these are the brightness values in the image when the dialog box opens. The y-axis (vertical) represents the Output values, which will be the new values after the curve is changed. Perhaps it's easiest to think of Input values as the "before" values and Output values as the "after" values. When the dialog box first opens, since no values have been changed, all Input values equal all Output values. This produces a diagonal line because at each point on the graph, the x- and y-axis values are the same. The range of both Input and Output values is from 0 % (white) to 100% (black).

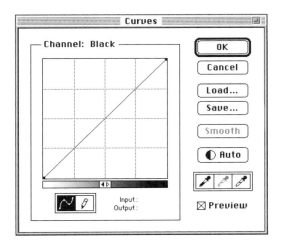

To see a readout of the points on the diagonal line, move the mouse pointer over the graph. The pointer will change to a crosshair. Move the crosshair anywhere on the diagonal line and you will see that both the Input and Output values are displayed at the bottom of the Curves dialog box. Notice that both values are the same. If the dialog box hasn't been changed from its default settings, the gradient bar (under the

**13**

graph) depicting the gray values of the x-axis starts at white and gradually blends to black. If the gradient bar on your screen starts at black and blends to white, click on either one of the arrows in the middle of the bar, or click on the bar itself, to reset the curve to the default settings.

When white is the starting point on the x-axis, the bottom-left corner of the graph—with coordinates of 0%, 0%—plots the lightest possible part of an image. The upper-right corner—100%, 100%—represents the darkest possible area in an image. The slope of the line represents the tonal range, with its bottom depicting the image's shadows and its top the image's highlights. The middle of the slope represents the midtones. The coordinates between the midtones and the highlights are called the *quarter (1/4) tones.* The coordinates between the midtones and the shadows are called the *three-quarter (3/4) tones.*

Since the curve allows you to change an image's tonal range, highlights are adjusted by clicking and dragging on the bottom part of the diagonal line in the graph, shadows by clicking and dragging on the top part of the diagonal line, and midtones by clicking and dragging in the middle of the diagonal line.

If you click on the arrows in the gradient bar to reverse black and white endpoints, the tone curve is also reversed, causing shadows to be represented at the bottom left of the graph and highlights at the top right. This also causes Input and Output levels to be displayed in brightness values from 0 (black) to 255 (white). You may prefer to work using percentage values, since the percentages of black correspond to the percentage values of halftone dots that make up a printed grayscale image.

The curve icon and the pencil icon at the bottom-left of the dialog box tell you what mode you are in. When the curve icon is active (the background of the icon is

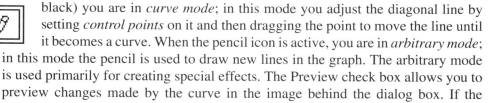

black) you are in *curve mode*; in this mode you adjust the diagonal line by setting *control points* on it and then dragging the point to move the line until it becomes a curve. When the pencil icon is active, you are in *arbitrary mode*; in this mode the pencil is used to draw new lines in the graph. The arbitrary mode is used primarily for creating special effects. The Preview check box allows you to preview changes made by the curve in the image behind the dialog box. If the Preview check box isn't selected, click on it now.

As stated earlier, the Curves dialog box is unique because it can pinpoint any area of an image along the curve's tonal range. When you position the mouse pointer over part of an image and click, a circle appears on the curve, displaying exactly where that image pixel is plotted. All image areas corresponding to that point on the curve are edited by adjusting the point where the white circle appears.

To see this powerful feature in action, move the mouse pointer outside the Curve dialog box and click anywhere in your image. Notice that the mouse pointer turns into the Eyedropper tool and the circle appears on the curve, representing the pixel's exact tonal location. Now click on any dark or shadow area of your image. The circle appears near the top of the curve. Examine the Input and Output values; they should reflect high numbers (75 to 100%). Now click on any highlight or bright area. The circle moves towards the bottom of the curve, and Input and Output values decrease to about 25% or less. Click on the gray or midtone areas of your image. Now the circle is in the middle of the curve, and the Input and Output values are near 50%.

To help you better understand how to use the curve to adjust shadows, midtones, and highlights, let's say you want to lighten the darkest areas of your image and darken the lightest areas. First you must determine where the darkest parts of your image lie on the curve. To do this, move the pointer to the darkest part of your image. The pointer will change to an Eyedropper. Now click the mouse. Immediately you'll see a circle appear on the curve. Note the percentage in the Input Output readout at the bottom of the dialog box. This is the percentage of black for the area you clicked on. Now try decreasing the percentage of black by clicking where the circle appeared and dragging down. As you drag, try to keep the input percentage as close as possible to its original percentage, but make the output percentage lower. As you drag your image becomes lighter.

Dragging the curve tells Photoshop to take the darkest pixels and remap them to make them lighter. This lightens the shadow areas. But because you are clicking and dragging a curve, and not just one individual point, other Input values besides the one represented by the control point now have new values. You can see this by examining the middle point of the curve; it's now lower. When you clicked and dragged on the shadow area of the curve, some of the midtone values came along for the ride. If you truly want to isolate the shadow area and keep other Input values from changing, click on the graph to establish *control points* to serve as anchors on the curve, as described next.

Suppose you wish to darken the highlights in your image, but you want to restrict the change from the midtones. Click on the brightest area of your image to see where this is plotted on the curve. To prevent areas other than the highlights from changing, set a control point. To set a control point in the midtone area, click about halfway along the curve. A small dot will appear, indicating that a control point exists. Create another control point at the beginning of the highlight area. Now position the pointer on the bottom area of the diagonal, and then click and drag up. Notice how the curve bends as you drag the new control point while the other control points serve as anchors. To prevent swaying in the middle of the curve, you can add more control points. If you need to eliminate a control point, click on the point and drag it off the curve.

Figure 13-7 shows the Curves dialog box being used to lighten just the darkest shadows of the cowboy image. Look carefully and you'll see control points applied

Eyedropper readout, before and after adjustments

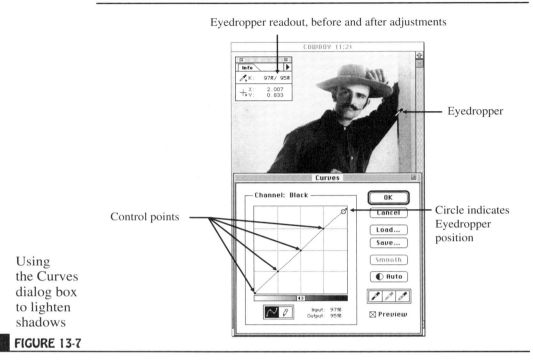

Eyedropper

Control points

Circle indicates
Eyedropper
position

Using
the Curves
dialog box
to lighten
shadows

**FIGURE 13-7**

at each quadrant along the diagonal line, as well as one additional point in the shadow area. This point was dragged downwards to lighten the darkest shadows. Afterward, the mouse pointer, which turns into an eyedropper, was placed over the image to sample the change. The mouse was clicked to locate the adjusted image area on the curve, and a circle appeared in the graph to indicate the area that was clicked on. The Info palette confirmed that the image areas had been changed to the desired percentage, 95%.

To gain more of a feel for using the curves, try a few more tonal adjustments. After you adjust the curve, always examine the Info palette to see the before and after percentages. First, reset the curve by pressing OPTION (PC users: ALT) and then clicking on the Reset button. Assume that you've already adjusted an image's highlights and shadows, yet the image is too dark. To lighten an image overall, set a control point in the middle of the curve and drag the curve downwards. If your image is too light, you can darken it by dragging in the opposite direction.

Reset the slope to the default settings again so that you can create a curve that will be used to bring out the contrast in images that are flat. This type of curve is called an *S curve*. To create it, drag the top part of the slope up to darken shadows;

Create an
*S* curve
to add
contrast to
an image

**FIGURE 13-8**

then drag the bottom of the slope down to lighten hightlights. This creates the *S*-shaped curve shown in Figure 13-8.

With the *S* curve created, move the mouse pointer over your image and examine the Info palette. Notice the readout that shows the before-and-after brightness values.

If you'd like, continue experimenting with the Curves dialog box, making adjustments to the highlights, midtones, and shadows in your image. Remember, if you find a setting for the curve that you will need later, save it by clicking on the Save button. A curve can be reloaded by clicking on the Load button.

**OTE:** *OPTION-clicking (PC users: ALT-clicking) in a white area of the curve will make the grid cells in the curve dialog box a quarter of their size.*

## Using the Curves Arbitrary Mode to Create Special Effects

In both grayscale and color images, you can create special effects by clicking on the Curves dialog box's pencil icon and then dragging it over the graph to create either lines or curves. Before leaving the Curves dialog box, try using the pencil icon in

13

Use the pencil to draw lines along the graph in the Curves dialog box to create a posterized effect

Pencil selected (arbitrary mode)

**FIGURE 13-9**

the arbitrary mode. To switch from the curve mode to the arbitrary mode, click on the pencil icon at the bottom of the Curves dialog box.

One effect you can create is to posterize (reduce the gray levels) of your image. Reset the curve to the default settings, then use the pencil to create some small lines cutting through the diagonal line, as shown in Figure 13-9. The more lines and the longer they are, the greater the posterizing effect will be.

To invert your image to create a negative, click on the top-left corner of the graph; then press and hold the SHIFT key while you click on the bottom-right corner of the graph. This produces a diagonal line from the top-left corner to the bottom-right corner, thus making all black areas white and all white areas black, as shown in Figure 13-10. Creating this slope produces the same effect as executing the Image/Map/Invert command, which is described in Chapter 7.

To create a *solarized* effect, which turns part of your image into a negative, use the pencil to change your graph to look like the one in Figure 13-11. To create this graph quickly, click on the top-left corner of the graph, then SHIFT-click in the center of

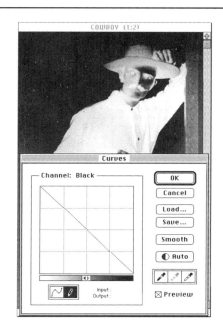

Reverse the slope to create a negative image

**FIGURE** 13-10

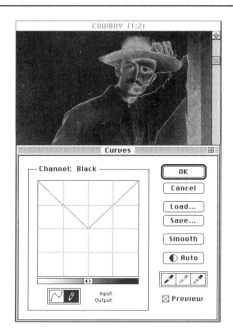

Use this graph to create a solarized effect

**FIGURE** 13-11

**13**

the graph. SHIFT-click again on the top-right corner. The resulting image looks the same as if you had applied the Solarize filter from the Filter/Stylize submenu.

There are many other special effects you can create by using the pencil icon to adjust the graph in the Curves dialog box. For instance, you can use the pencil to create a few individual lines and then join them by clicking on the Smooth button.

## Using the Dodge and Burn Tools to Darken and Lighten Areas

If the areas in your image that need lightening or darkening are small and don't need much tonal adjustment, you might wish to use the Dodge and/or Burn tools for the task.

As discussed in Chapter 6, the Dodge and Burn tools are used to lighten and darken, respectively, portions of an image. Take a moment now, if you need to, and review the Dodge and Burn tools, which can also be used to make tonal corrections.

The Burn tool was used to add tone to the pistol in the cowboy's holster, as shown in Figure 13-12. Here the Exposure value was raised to 25% to add more contrast to the lighter midtones.

Burn ——

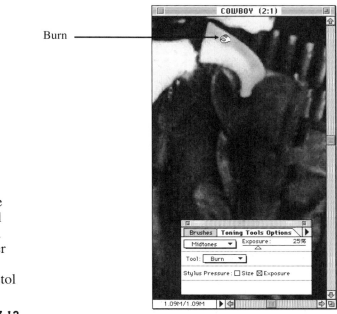

Using the
Burn tool
to darken
the lighter
midtones
of the pistol
handle

**FIGURE 13-12**

# RETOUCHING IMAGES

Once you are happy with the shadows, midtones, and highlights of your image, you're ready to perform any retouching that might be necessary to clean up the image or make it better than the original. Before you begin retouching, you should develop a game plan. Decide which areas you will fix first, and which ones you will do last. To get started and give yourself a better feel for your image, it's often best to begin with the elements that will be easiest to fix, and then proceed to the more difficult ones. Once you have analyzed your image and decided how to proceed, you are ready to begin retouching.

**TIP:** *As you work, it's often helpful to have two windows open, both containing the same image but set to different magnifications. This way you can zoom into a specific area, yet view the results of your work simultaneously at actual size. To open a duplicate window on screen, choose New Window from the Window menu. Also, don't forget that when you zoom in, you can use the Toolbox's Pencil tool with the smallest, hard-edged brush to edit your image one pixel at a time.*

Now continue on to see how the worn and faded cowboy photograph in Figure 13-1a was retouched.

## Retouching Old Photographs

Old photographs often present significant challenges in retouching. The pictures are often marred by spots and scratches, as well as being torn and faded. For very damaged photographs, be prepared to apply some painting and drawing skills to re-create entire sections in your digitized image.

Start by looking for any dust, dirt, scratches, or spots that appear in your image as a result of the digitizing process or due to a flawed original. Spots and scratches can usually be eliminated by using the Rubber Stamp's cloning option to clone background areas over the particles. If you do need to correct spots and scratches, experiment with different opacities until you achieve a soft and natural effect. Another method of removing dirt, dust, and scratches from an image is to use the Dust & Scratches filter. See Chapter 8 for more details.

**13**

# Photoshop in Action

## Before Retouching

Jacket was too light, lacking tone.

Notice the unnatural-looking white brush strokes.

Notice the white brush strokes and that the leg is barely noticeable.

**Photograph courtesy of the Library of Congress**

This picture of hobos taken in the early 1900s was needed for the Reader's Digest book *Discovering America's Past*. Years ago a retoucher began correcting the image traditionally, but stopped in the middle of the job. Notice the white brush strokes on the pants and jacket sleeve of the hobo on the right, and on the jacket sleeve of the hobo in the center. These were painted in by the retoucher. Adele was asked to finish the job so that the picture looked natural.

## Photoshop in Action

### After Retouching

Tone was added to jacket.

The white brush strokes were removed.

The white brush strokes are gone and the leg is more visibly defined.

**Retouched by: Adele Droblas Greenberg**          **Client: Reader's Digest General Books**

Before beginning to retouch the image, Adele used the Eyedropper tool to take readings of the image. Areas that were too dark (in the background) were lightened and areas that were too light (the white brush strokes and the ground) were darkened using the Levels and Curves dialog boxes. In addition, she used both the Dodge and Burn tools to lighten and darken various areas in the image that needed to be corrected.

To add more tone to the jacket of the hobo on the left, Adele used the Rubber Stamp's cloning option. Then she used the Airbrush tool with a soft-edged brush and varied the opacity setting and brush size to create a more natural-looking image. Before activating the Airbrush tool, Adele used the Eyedropper tool to change the foreground color to match the gray tones in the image.

To paint over the white brush strokes on the jacket sleeve and pants of the hobo on the right and on the jacket sleeve of the hobo in the center, Adele used the Airbrush and Rubber Stamp tools. As she worked, she used the Rubber Stamp's Clone options, From Saved and From Snapshot, to complete the retouching process.

**13**

In the cowboy image, the dirt spots in the original photograph and the dust spots introduced by the scanner were cloned away with the Rubber Stamp. After the spots were removed, the hat was the next item to be retouched, since it was the simplest part of the project. A sample from another part of the hat was duplicated over the faded area. The retouching continued from the hat down to the leg and foot—the most difficult area to correct.

Follow along with the techniques used to retouch the cowboy image, and try them in the Hands file (PC users: hands.jpg) in the Adobe Photoshop Tutorial folder or in the image you are using. If you are working with the Hands file, you may wish to retouch the cracks and broken parts of the statue's face. If you have a scanner, you might wish to scan image 3 from the first color insert to practice retouching.

To restore the cowboy's left arm, the Eyedropper, Airbrush, Paintbrush, and Rubber Stamp tools were all put to use. First the Eyedropper was activated to change the foreground color to match the gray tone of the arm. Then the Airbrush tool was selected and used to paint a light outline to serve as a boundary that would not be painted over. The boundary line helped Adele visualize the missing limb while she worked to re-create it.

Airbrush

The area where the limb was re-created was painted using the Rubber Stamp and the Paintbrush, with a medium-sized, soft-edged brush. Although a mask could have been used to isolate the arm, it wasn't necessary. If the area beyond the boundary line were painted over, it could have been easily corrected by changing the foreground color to the correct color and painting with that color.

**EMEMBER:** *If you want to be cautious, or if an area is particularly intricate, you should create a mask and then work in the unprotected (selected) area bordered by the mask. See Chapter 11.*

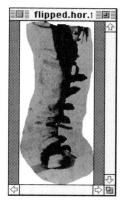

The Airbrush tool was also used to restore detail and tone to the shotgun. The edges of the shotgun's handle were restored with a small, hard-edged brush with Pressure set at 50%.

After the simpler retouching tasks were completed, all that remained was to completely restore the lower part of the left leg. This was more difficult to repair because it required that more details be created. Several steps were involved: First, the Airbrush tool was used to sketch the left leg, as shown in Figure 13-13. Again, the outline served as a boundary line to visualize the missing limb.

Once the left leg was sketched, the Lasso was used to select the lower right leg. This selection was duplicated by OPTION-dragging (PC users:

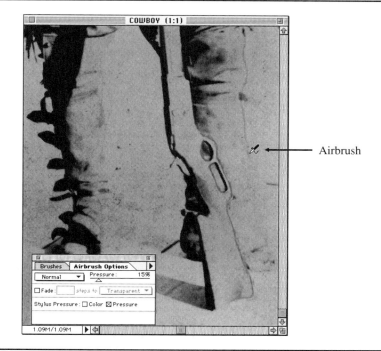

Airbrush

Using the Airbrush to create an outline for the missing part of the left leg and foot

**FIGURE 13-13**

**13**

ALT-dragging) on the selection. The selection was flipped, using the Image/Flip/Horizontal command, and then the leg was cut and pasted into a new file. Remember, when you copy or cut an image and create a new file, the new file settings will be the same size as the cut or copied image.

After the right leg was duplicated, flipped, and placed in a new file, the flipped image and the original one were placed side by side so that the flipped leg could be cloned into the original file. In Figure 13-14, the crosshair indicates the sampled area; the rubber stamp pointer shows the target area where the cloning is being applied.

Before using the Rubber Stamp's clone option, the file was saved so Adele could revert to the last saved version if necessary. As Adele worked, she used the Edit/Take Snapshot command so that she could used the Rubber Stamp's From Snapshot option to revert to the snapshot version of the file. See Chapter 6 for more information on the Take Snapshot command.

After all the retouching was finished, the Unsharp Mask filter was applied to the image to sharpen it and bring out details. Chapter 8 describes how to use Photoshop's sharpening filters.

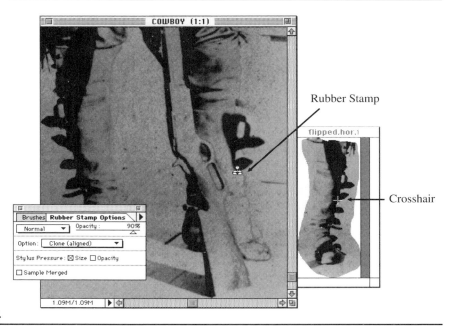

Retouching the lower left leg by cloning the flipped lower right leg

**FIGURE 13-14**

## Removing Wrinkles or Freckles from Faces

Another common task of the retoucher is to eliminate facial wrinkles and otherwise touch up images of people—particularly for advertising projects. Using the Rubber Stamp's cloning feature and the Smudge and Airbrush tools, wrinkles and blemishes can easily be removed.

In the following illustration, the image on the left shows wrinkles surrounding a person's eye before retouching; on the right is the retouched image.

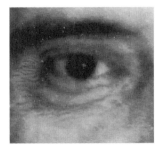

Eye with wrinkles
before retouching

Eye without wrinkles
after retouching

The trick to removing wrinkles or any other facial blemish is to apply a vibrant skin color over that area of the image. Dark skin crevices can easily be blended into lighter flesh tones with the help of the Smudge and Rubber Stamp tools.

Start by using the Zoom tool to magnify the target area. Next use the Eyedropper to change the foreground color to the desired skin color. Then use the Smudge, Rubber Stamp, and Airbrush tools to blend skin tones together in the magnified area. For a gentler, softer effect, use a small-to-medium, soft-edged brush with Opacity in the Options palette set from 2% to 90%.

In our example, the smaller wrinkles were blended into the face using the Smudge tool. To remove the more pronounced lines, the Rubber Stamp's cloning option was used to clone the surrounding tones. The Airbrush tool was then applied to produce a more subtle blend.

If you want to try removing wrinkles from an image, practice on the left hand in the Hands file (PC users: hands.jpg). To experiment with removing freckles, open the Portrait file (PC users: portrait.jpg) in the Tutorial folder. Use the Zoom tool to magnify the girl's nose; then try using the Rubber Stamp, Airbrush, and/or Smudge tools to remove the freckles.

**13**

## Retouching Landscapes

Retouching not only restores old photographs and makes people look younger and more glamorous but it is also used to transform landscapes so that they are more attractive than their real-life originals.

For example, the art director of Reader's Digest General Books, Dave Trooper, wanted the scene for the cover of a proposed book, *Back Roads of America,* to look better than reality. The original image was a near-perfect photograph of a lovely New England scene. Figure 13-15 shows the image before retouching (also reproduced as image 1 in the color insert of this book).

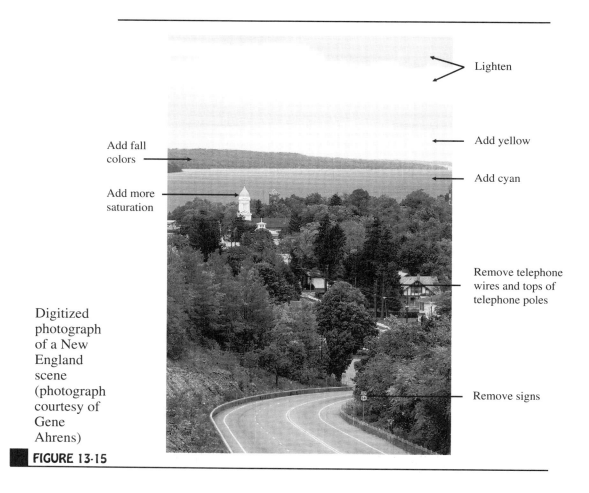

Lighten

Add fall colors

Add yellow

Add cyan

Add more saturation

Remove telephone wires and tops of telephone poles

Remove signs

Digitized photograph of a New England scene (photograph courtesy of Gene Ahrens)

**FIGURE 13-15**

Marring the beauty of the original image were the telephone poles and overhead wires running through the town. For the cover design, Dave wanted to put a map next to the photograph and to remove the road sign for Junction 14. The stop light warning sign, barely visible behind the trees, was also deemed a detraction and needed to be erased. Figure 13-16 shows the final retouched image (also reproduced as image 2 in the color insert of this book).

The Junction 14 sign was the first item to be retouched. The Rubber Stamp's cloning option was used to remove it, with a medium, hard-edged brush rather than a soft-edged brush. A soft-edged brush would have made the cloned area look unnatural because the leaves on the trees were sharp and crisp, not soft and faded. To maintain a natural look, a variety of different leaves from several tree areas were

Proposed book cover after retouching and color correcting

**FIGURE 13-16**

sampled and cloned over the sign. During the cloning process, the Opacity in the Rubber Stamp Options palette was set to varying values between 65% to 85% to blend the leaves into the trees.

To eliminate the stop light warning sign, part of the road was cloned over the sign, and the trees were extended into the road. The Rubber Stamp's cloning feature and the Airbrush were both used to retouch the area. Some of the railing area was re-created with the Airbrush because the cloning tool couldn't create a perfect match between the old railing and the new railing.

Then the Rubber Stamp's cloning option was used again, this time to remove the unwanted wires. For a more natural effect, both a hard-edged and a medium soft-edged brush were used. Opacity was set to about 75% to blend the new leaves with the old leaves.

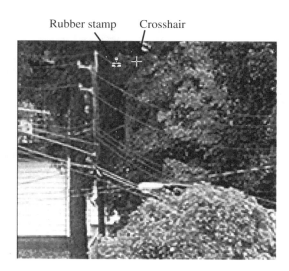

The next section provides an overview of how to undertake a color-correction project, and we will continue using the book cover project as an example. If you have a grayscale image on screen, close it now because you will be using a color file for the remainder of this chapter. If you wish to create another version of your file, use the File/Save As or Save a Copy command. Otherwise, close the file without saving it.

## COLOR CORRECTING

Many of the same issues involved in grayscale tonal correcting also arise when you're *color* correcting. As with grayscale images, it may not be possible to transform an inferior color original or poorly scanned color picture into a perfect image. Exposure and lighting defects found in many grayscale images are also the most common problems in color images. But correcting color is much more complicated than correcting grays because every pixel has the potential of being any one of millions of possible colors, rather than just 256 levels of gray.

The number of colors in an image brings up an important display issue: If your image contains many more colors than your monitor can display, color correcting that image will be difficult. With a video card that only displays 256 colors, you won't be able to accurately judge the colors of continuous-tone images by their appearance on screen. So if you are serious about color correcting, you will want to invest in a 24-bit video card, which can display over 16 million colors.

Even if your system is calibrated and you are working in 24-bit color, you still must be wary of how colors look on your screen. As discussed in Chapter 4, differences between onscreen and printed colors are to be expected. The best way to judge colors is by using the Eyedropper tool and the Info palette. If you are working on color images that will be printed, it's crucial that CMYK colors are displayed in the Info palette. This readout will display exclamation points alongside the CMYK values of any colors that fall beyond the CMYK printing gamut. Remember, the Mode/Gamut Warning command previews out-of-gamut colors. See Chapter 9 for more information.

Always check the Info palette when you're analyzing onscreen colors. For instance, if an apple on the screen looks rich, juicy, and crisp, but the Info palette reading lacks a high magenta percentage, this tells you that your monitor is not displaying the correct colors. For bright red, you should see CMYK values of approximately cyan 20%, magenta 100%, yellow 80%, and black 5%, or RGB values of red 161, green 0, and blue 49.

**13**

To see the Eyedropper and Info palette in action, load an RGB or CMYK file (if you don't already have a color image on screen). For an RGB file, you can load the Truck file (PC users: truck.jpg) from the Tutorial folder. For a CMYK file, load the Café file (PC users: cafe.jpg) from the Tutorial folder.

If the Info palette is not displayed, open it now. If you do not see the RGB and CMYK percentages, click on the palette's pop-up menu in the Info palette. In the Info Options dialog box, make sure that the Mode pop-up menus for First Color and Second Color Readouts are set to RGB and CMYK.

You might wonder why you should keep the RGB values displayed in the Info palette if you are working on a CMYK color file. As discussed in Chapter 4, when you *add* cyan, magenta, or yellow to an image, you *subtract* its complement (red, green, or blue). When you *subtract* cyan, magenta, or yellow, you *add* the color's complement. With both color readouts showing in the Info palette, you'll be able to judge how much of a color or its complement is added or subtracted.

Take a look at the relationship between RGB and CMYK colors in your image. Move the mouse pointer over your image, and notice that any color showing a high RGB value displays a low percentage of its CMYK complement, and vice versa. For instance, a color with a high red value displays a low cyan percentage, and a color with a high cyan percentage displays a low red value. The relationship between RGB and CMYK colors is clearly depicted in a color wheel, as discussed in Chapter 4. Before you start color correcting, you may wish to get a color wheel (such as the one shown on the first page of the color insert of this book) and keep it handy. On a color wheel, each color resides between the two colors that create it. For instance, green is created by adding cyan and yellow. On the opposite side of each color is its complement; for example, opposite green on the color wheel is magenta.

## Color-Correcting Tips

As you work on color-correction projects, here are a few suggestions to keep in mind:

**FASHION**  Work carefully with white and black fabric because it's difficult to maintain detail and definition in very dark and very light image areas. Be careful not to oversharpen or fabric will not look real. Too high a percentage of yellow can make white look dull. Low cyan values will keep reds vibrant; low yellow values will keep blues vibrant. You might wish to obtain fabric samples so you can compare real colors and materials with screen colors.

**PEOPLE**  Strands of hair should be as sharply defined as possible. Teeth should be white rather than dull and yellow, though pure white teeth will look unreal. Consult your print shop concerning the effects of dot gain on flesh tones. Here are some CMYK and RGB values to use as starting points: (C=20%, M=45%, Y=50%, K=0%) or (R=203, G=154, B=125) should be a satisfactory reading for Caucasian flesh tones; for black flesh tones, aim for (C=40%, M=45%, Y=50%, K=30%) or (R=123, G=106, B=93).

**FOOD**   It's often impossible to make all the food in a shot look delicious. For example, brilliant red tomatoes may look delicious, but meat that red will appear raw. Analyze or ask your client what should be the center of attention in the image. Foods that have bland, unrecognizable colors, such as cereals and soup, can be difficult to correct.

**OUTDOORS**   Strengthen greens, blues, and reds with the Sponge tool. Use black to make greens darker, rather than magenta, which will lower saturation. Examine the grays in an image to make sure they are gray and aren't exhibiting color casts. When creating sky, the relationship between cyan and magenta will determine the shade of sky you are creating. For instance, by adding more and more magenta, you can go from bright blue to dark blue.

**SNOW SCENES**   Snow should not be pure white; otherwise, detail will be lost. Concentrate on adding detail to the highlights. Avoid losing detail in darker areas when enhancing whites.

## RGB or CMYK?

A question that many Photoshop users wrestle with is whether to work in an RGB Color or a CMYK Color file. In making your decision, consider the following guidelines.

It is helpful to color correct in RGB because slides and video use RGB colors rather than CMYK. For output to a commercial printing press, you may want to color correct in CMYK so you will be working with the same colors that your print shop uses for your job.

It is helpful to color correct in CMYK colors when you are adjusting blacks in your image. If need be, you can change only the blacks in a CMYK file by making adjustments to the black channel (with RGB colors, no black channel is available).

Since CMYK files are always larger than their RGB counterparts, you may wish to color correct in RGB mode, then output your image to either slide or chrome. You can give a prepress house the slide or chrome to be scanned and converted to CMYK.

**13**

**C**AUTION: *If you are working with an RGB Color file with the Info palette's CMYK reading displayed, be aware that the CMYK Color equivalents reflect the settings in the Separation Setup dialog box. For more information about this dialog box, see Chapter 9.*

If you are correcting an image that was digitized on a high-end scanner, chances are that the image was saved as a CMYK Color file. If you scanned the image yourself on a low-range or midrange flatbed or slide scanner, the file will probably be digitized in RGB rather than CMYK. Digital and video cameras digitize images in RGB rather than CMYK color.

If you wish to work in CMYK mode, you can do so by converting your RGB Color image to CMYK Color. But do not convert to CMYK without first verifying the settings in the Monitor Setup, Printing Inks Setup, and Separation Setup dialog boxes. Before converting an image to CMYK, review Chapter 9. It's important to understand that if you convert to CMYK with improper calibration settings, you may be forced to return to your original RGB file. Once you have reset the calibration options to the correct settings, you'll need to reconvert to CMYK and start color correcting again from scratch.

If your system cannot handle large, high-resolution CMYK Color files, another alternative is to work on a low-resolution color file and save your dialog box settings, or write them down. Then use the Load button in the Levels, Curves, Hue/Saturation, and Variations dialog boxes to apply the settings to the high-resolution version, and make final color adjustments as needed.

## PROCEDURES FOR COLOR CORRECTING

When you are ready to color correct an image, your first steps should be to correct the overall tonal range of the image. Then proceed to correct specific areas.

The New England scene in the Reader's Digest book cover, first discussed in the "Retouching Images" section of this chapter, will be used here to demonstrate the steps involved in color correcting.

The image was scanned by a prepress house on a high-end drum scanner to obtain the best digitization. In the scanning process, the image was converted to a CMYK file and saved in TIFF format. Since the file was over 30MB, it was saved on a Syquest cartridge so it could be delivered to the client.

After examining a Matchprint (a proof made from film separations) from the original scan, it was decided that the clouds should be lightened so that the book title would stand out as much as possible. The decision to color correct was made not because the original image or scan was flawed but because the design of the book cover required it. The art director also decided to enhance the color of the foliage in the town. Additionally, he felt that the colors of the water and church dome were a little light and that the saturation should be increased. Finally, he wanted a more autumn-like look to the hills across the bay.

Before color correcting, the colors in the Matchprint were compared to those on the CMYK Color file on the monitor. After analyzing the two, slight calibration changes were made in the Gray Balance fields in the Printing Inks Setup dialog box. (For more information on calibrating to a proof, see Chapter 14.)

## Taking Readings with the Eyedropper and Info Palette

The next step in color correcting the New England image was to analyze the problem areas as well as the good areas using the Eyedropper and Info palette to carefully evaluate the colors.

Once you know the RGB values or CMYK percentages of the image areas, you can evaluate the colors that need to be added or taken out, and in what percentage. In the photograph for the proposed book cover, readings were taken of the clouds, water, hills across the bay, church dome, and foliage. The Eyedropper readings of some of the foliage showed a predominance of cyan, with little yellow and little magenta. These would obviously need to be boosted to improve the impression of autumn colors.

## Using a Histogram to View the Tonal Range

After analyzing the areas that needed enhancement, the next step was to view the image's histogram. As explained earlier in this chapter, a histogram is useful for examining the tonal range of an image—from its brightest to its darkest points. In a color image, a histogram provides not only a visual impression of the brightness values of the entire image but of the separate channels as well.

The histogram of the New England image before color correcting revealed that the tonal range was fairly broad, with few shadow pixels.

To view a histogram of an RGB image, you can load the Truck file (PC users: truck.jpg) from the Tutorial folder. Or you can load a CMYK file, the Café file (PC users: cafe.jpg) from the Tutorial folder.

With the image file open on screen, choose Histogram from the Image menu. Click to open the Channel pop-up menu. If you are viewing a CMYK image, the Channel pop-up menu allows you to view brightness (luminance) values of the

**13**

CMYK composite (Gray channel) and the color values of the individual Cyan, Magenta, Yellow, and Black channels. For an RGB image, you'll see a Gray channel for the composite brightness values and one for each of the Red, Green, and Blue channels.

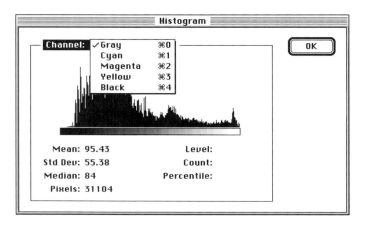

If you are viewing the Truck file, click on the Channel pop-up menu in the Histogram dialog box, and take a moment to view each channel to see the color values. You'll see that the image is lacking in shadow and highlight areas. The image does not have enough contrast. If you are viewing the Café file, you'll see that the image has few shadow pixels, and has only a small spurt of highlight pixels. The image has a washed out look. In the next section, you'll learn how to stretch out the tonal range.

## Setting a White, Black, and Neutral Point

 During scanning, an image's tonal range can be compressed, particularly by low-end scanners that cannot reproduce as broad a range of colors as high-end scanners. The histogram often reveals this compression: Images with compressed tonal ranges often lack shadow and highlight areas. One technique for expanding the tonal range of an image is to set a white (highlight) point and a black (shadow) point. By setting a white and black point, you specify areas in your image that you wish to have as its lightest point and darkest points. The eyedropper icons in the Curves and Levels dialog boxes, described earlier in the chapter, allow you to set these points—as well as a gray point to help eliminate color casts from an image.

The tasks of eliminating color casts and setting white and black points are often handled during the digitization process. If your image was scanned on a high-end scanner and converted to CMYK (as the New England image was), you probably will not need to set a white, black, or gray point. On the other hand, when you work with RGB-digitized images or images converted from RGB to CMYK color, you should be aware of how setting these points can be helpful.

In Photoshop you can set the white and black points automatically, manually, or by setting levels in the Color Picker. Before you work through the following paragraphs describing these methods, load any color image on screen. You may want to use the Truck file or Café file from the Tutorial folder.

## Setting the White and Black Points Automatically

The easiest way to set the white and black points is to have Photoshop do it automatically. If you set the white and black points automatically using Photoshop's default settings, the lightest areas in an image are remapped to white and the darkest areas to black. This often expands the tonal range, providing more contrast in images that are flat and dull.

With your color image on screen, open the Levels dialog box (choose Levels from the Image/Adjust submenu). To have Photoshop set the white and black points automatically, click on the Auto button. Immediately you will see a change in your image, which is reflected in the histogram. In the histogram, you'll often see that the balance between shadows, midtones, and highlights is improved.

To ensure that Photoshop does not use only one tone when it sets the white and black points, a preset *clipping* percentage range is built in when Photoshop adjusts the image. This can prevent very light or very dark areas from overly influencing the tonal change when Photoshop sets the white and black points.

This clipping range can be changed in the Auto Range Options dialog box. To open the dialog box, press OPTION (PC users: ALT) and click on the Auto button. Acceptable values for the Black Clip and White Clip fields are from 0% to 9.99%. The value entered is the percentage that Photoshop will ignore when it automatically sets the white and black points. For instance, if you enter 9% in the Black Clip field, Photoshop ignores the darkest 9% of your image when it redistributes pixel values after you click on the Auto button.

```
╔══════════ Auto Range Options ══════════╗
║                                         ║
║   Black Clip:  [0.50] %      ┌────────┐ ║
║                              │   OK   │ ║
║   White Clip:  [0.50] %      └────────┘ ║
║                              ( Cancel ) ║
║                                         ║
╚═════════════════════════════════════════╝
```

**13**

If you are unhappy with the results of Photoshop's automatic setting of the white and black points, you can return your image to its original settings. First press and hold down OPTION (PC users: ALT); the Cancel button will change to a Reset button. Click Reset to return your image to its original settings, and then try the manual method of setting white and black points. To undo the last step, press COMMAND-Z (PC users: CTRL-Z).

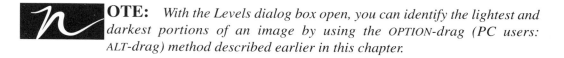**OTE:** *The tonal range of an image can also be expanded by executing the Auto Levels command in the Image/Adjust submenu. This command produces the same effect as the Auto button in the Levels dialog box, and uses the clipping percentage set in the Auto Range Options dialog box.*

## Manually Setting the White and Black Points with the Eyedroppers and Color Picker

If you are color correcting a CMYK Color image, you may wish to gain more control when you set the white and black points to ensure you don't lose detail in highlight and shadow areas. From the Levels and Curves dialog boxes, you can use the eyedroppers to access the Color Picker to set color levels for the white and black points. If you choose this method, you'll first want to take color readings with the eyedroppers to locate the lightest and darkest parts of your image. But don't click on the eyedroppers in the dialog box yet.

First locate the lightest and darkest parts of your image. Move the mouse pointer (which will change to an eyedropper) over the lightest areas of your image, and examine the Info palette readouts as you go. Very light areas will display low values of each CMYK component; high values of each RGB component. Generally, when evaluating an image to set the white point, you should search for highlight areas with detail, not pure white areas.

Next, locate the darkest part of your image and move the eyedropper over it. Dark image areas will display high values of each CMYK component; low values of each RGB component. When searching for the black point, look for shadow areas that are not pure black.

**OTE:** *With the Levels dialog box open, you can identify the lightest and darkest portions of an image by using the OPTION-drag (PC users: ALT-drag) method described earlier in this chapter.*

Now that you've found the lightest and darkest points, you're ready to set a white and a black level. To set a value for the white level, double-click on the white eyedropper in the Levels dialog box. The Color Picker dialog box opens; notice the words "Select white target color" at the top.

Let's assume you want to ensure that the lightest areas of your image are not pure white, not created from the absence of ink on paper. Entering the Cyan values from 5 to 7 with Magenta and Yellow both set from 2 to 3 with Black (K) set to 0 should provide good results. Click OK to close the Color Picker.

Now move the Eyedropper tool over the lightest portion of your image that you identified earlier, and click the mouse. Photoshop automatically adjusts the tonal range so the lightest areas match the white point you set.

The procedure for setting a target value for the black point is virtually identical to that for setting the white point, except you use the black eyedropper. Double-click on the black eyedropper. The Color Picker dialog box opens, and you'll see the words "Select black target color" at the top. The following values should help to ensure detail in shadow areas: Set Cyan to 95, set Magenta and Yellow from 82 to 87, and Black (K) to 80. Click OK to close the Color Picker.

Now move the eyedropper pointer over the darkest portion of your image that you identified earlier, and click the mouse. The tonal range is adjusted so that the darkest areas in the image match the black point you set.

If the results of setting the black and white points are not satisfactory, try setting different points in the image, or slightly adjusting the White and Black point levels in the Color Picker. Also, remember that not all images will improve when setting the white and black points, and that different images printed on different types of paper may require different black and white points.

*𝓃***OTE:** *When you are setting the white and black points of a grayscale image, you may wish to set the white point at 5% in the K field (leave the CMY fields blank) and the black point at K=95% (again, leave the CMY fields blank).*

*𝓃***OTE:** *If you set color levels for white and black points in the Color Picker dialog box, they will be used when you set the white and black points with the Auto button, or use the Auto Levels command in the Image/Adjust submenu.*

After setting the white and black points, you may wish to fine-tune the tonal balance in your image by lightening or darkening it. If so, you can use the Output

**13**

Levels slider in the Levels dialog box to reduce the white and dark values of your image. As described earlier in this chapter, drag the right-hand Output Levels slider control to the left to reduce the brightness in image highlights, and drag the left-hand Output Levels slider control to the right to lighten shadow areas. You may also want to enhance the midtones; do this by clicking on the middle (gamma) Input Levels slider control. As discussed earlier in this chapter, dragging left lightens midtones, and dragging right darkens them.

When you're satisfied with the tonal adjustments in your image, click OK. Your next step is to eliminate any color casts that may exist.

### Adjusting for Color Casts by Defining a Neutral Tone

Color casts can be the result of several factors. Photographs taken in fluorescent light often produce pink color casts. Outdoor images taken with indoor film might display a blue color cast. Indoor scenes shot with daylight film may yield a yellow color cast. Color casts can also be introduced inadvertently during the digitizing process.

Both the Curves and Levels dialog boxes include a gray eyedropper icon that can be used to reduce color casts. Here are the steps: Click on the gray eyedropper in the dialog box and move it over your image to the most neutral, or gray, area. Click, and any color cast should disappear or be diminished. Photoshop shifts the hue and saturation values to match neutral gray and continues to shift hue and saturation values to eliminate color casts. If you wish to specify the gray that Photoshop uses when it sets its neutral gray level, you can double-click on the gray eyedropper. This opens the Color Picker dialog box in which you enter the desired values.

## Creating Masks to Isolate Areas to be Color Corrected

After you have adjusted the basic tonal range in your image and eliminated any unwanted color casts, you can proceed to the tasks of fine-tuning problem areas in your image. To color correct specific areas of an image, you must select them first. As discussed in Chapters 10 and 11, it is often helpful to create masks of these areas in alpha channels or using the Pen tool, since you will likely need to select them again and again. (There are various ways to create and edit a mask in an alpha channel. For more information, see Chapter 11.)

**OTE:** *If you wish, you can use the Pen tool to create a selection. First create a path and then click on the Make Selection icon in the Paths palette. For more information about paths, see Chapter 10.*

In the New England image, five different masks were created in alpha channels: one for the church dome, one for the water, one for the hills across the bay, and two for different parts of the sky. These masks were created so that they could be reloaded in case more changes were needed. Because alpha channels increase file size, only one mask was included in the New England file at a given time. The masks that weren't being used were exported into a new file using the Select/Save Selection command. Masks of the foliage were created when needed using the Lasso tool and the Quick Mask mode. The Select/Color range command could also have been used. These masks weren't saved; they could easily be re-created and they didn't need to be as precise as the others.

## Using the Image/Adjust Commands to Color Correct

Once all of the preparation work has been accomplished, you are ready to begin selective color correction. The same Image/Adjust commands you used to correct grayscale images are also available for correcting color images—except that more options are available. For instance, the Variations command allows saturation to be added and subtracted. The Curves and Levels dialog boxes allow you to work with the individual RGB or CMYK channels.

In color correcting the New England image, a selection was generally loaded before a dialog box was opened. As mentioned earlier, to work more efficiently, Adele had previously duplicated channels into separate files. When she needed to load the mask selection, she opened the file containing the alpha channels with the masks. Then she chose the Image/Load Selection command to copy the selection into the New England image file. She loaded the dome selection using the Select/Load Selection command in the Select menu and used the Variations command to color correct the dome.

### Using the Variations Command

Often it's a good idea to begin correcting specific selections with the Variations command because it's the easiest and most intuitive color-correction tool to use. As described in the grayscale portion of this chapter, the Variations dialog box features thumbnails that preview how your image will be changed.

If you'd like to experiment with the Variations command, start by selecting an area of your color image, or load another selection you want to work with.

Choose Variations from the Image/Adjust submenu. When you are working with a color image, the Variations dialog box also allows you to adjust the saturation of a color, in addition to shadows, midtones, and highlights. Strong, full colors are

**13**

saturated; pale colors are undersaturated; neutral tones, such as black, white, and gray, contain no saturation. In most instances, fully colored, saturated images are preferable—but too much saturation can also make an image look unreal, gaudy, or blotchy, which can also cause printing problems.

In the New England image, the Variations command was used to add a touch of yellow to the midtones of the church dome. Figure 13-17 shows the church dome selected; in the Variations dialog box, the Midtones radio button was chosen. After the midtones were enhanced, the Saturation radio button was selected, and the More Saturation thumbnail was clicked to boost saturation. The changes transformed the dome from looking flat to full-bodied. The Sponge tool with its Saturation option could have also been used. If you oversaturate you can use the Sponge tool's Desaturate option.

## Using the Color Balance Command

The next step in correcting the New England image was to add fall colors to the foliage in the town using the Color Balance command. This command allows you

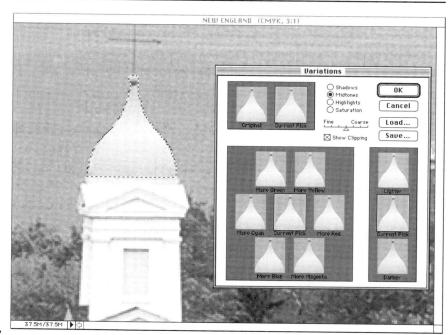

Using the Variations dialog box to adjust the saturation in the church's dome

**FIGURE 13-17**

to mix colors together to improve the color balance in an image. If you have a sense of color theory, you will find the Color Balance dialog box to be very intuitive.

Before the Color Balance dialog box was opened, Eyedropper/Info palette readings of various selections of the foliage were taken and written down. During the correcting process, the Lasso tool and the Quick Mask mode were used to isolate the background trees that would be corrected.

Choose Color Balance from the Image/Adjust submenu. In the Color Balance dialog box you will see radio buttons for selecting Shadows, Midtones, and Highlights, and three color sliders. The first slider ranges from Cyan (on the left) to Red (on the right). The second slider ranges from Magenta to Green, and the third ranges from Yellow to Blue. If you move a slider control to the right, you add that slider's RGB color to your image. Move the slider control to the left, and you add that slider's complement (a CMYK color) to your image. By clicking and dragging the slider controls, you can move through the range of each RGB color and into the color range of its CMYK complement. RGB values go from 0 to 100, and CMYK colors are measured in negative numbers from 0 to -100.

Keeping the Preserve Luminosity check box selected helps ensure brightness values don't change while you adjust color balance.

The slider triangles turn black, gray, or white depending upon whether the Shadows, Midtones, or Highlights radio button is selected.

In the New England image, the various selections of trees were made to look more autumn-like by adjusting the Color Balance sliders and selecting the Shadows, Midtones, and Highlights radio buttons. Most selections required adding more magenta and yellow and decreasing cyan. As the colors were changed, the Eyedropper tool and Info palette were used to compare the old CMYK values to the new settings to ensure that they were the right color.

After the foliage was corrected, the hills selection was loaded to receive the same color correction. Red, magenta, and yellow were added to the shadows, midtones, and highlights. Besides providing fall color, the change also enhanced the detail in the hills. Figure 13-18 shows the selected hills and the red, magenta, and yellow values added to the midtones.

## Using the Levels Command

The next step in color correcting the New England image was to add cyan to the water. To do this, the Image/Adjust/Levels command was used because it allows more precise control than the Variations command. The Levels dialog box, like the Curves dialog box, gives you access to individual color channels for color correcting.

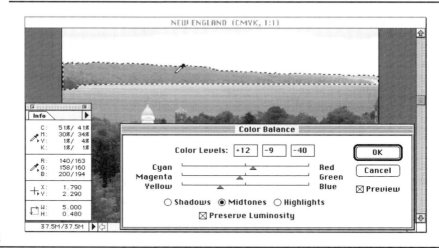

Using
the Color
Balance
dialog box
to add fall
colors to
the hills
across
the bay

**FIGURE 13-18**

To add more cyan to the water, the Cyan channel was selected from the Channel pop-up menu in the Levels dialog box. The right-hand Output Levels slider control was dragged to the left to 236, as shown in Figure 13-19. This took the lightest cyan value over 236 and remapped it to 236, making the cyan level darker; all values over 236 were remapped accordingly. (If the left-hand slider control had been dragged

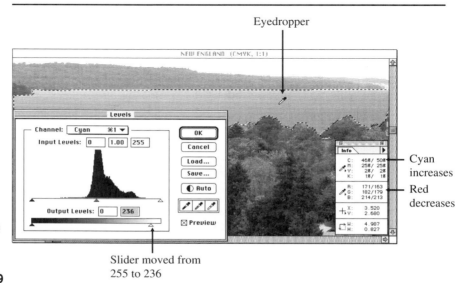

Using
the Levels
dialog box
to add more
cyan to
the water

**FIGURE 13-19**

instead of the right, cyan would have been subtracted and red, cyan's complement, would have been added.) Notice that the Info palette in Figure 13-19 shows that when cyan was increased, the level of red displayed in the Info palette decreased.

If you'd like to try your hand at color correcting a CMYK file, open the Café file (PC users: cafe.jpg) in the Tutorial folder. Then open the Levels dialog box and switch channels in the Channel pop-up menu to Cyan. Click and drag on the right Input Levels slider control to reduce cyan. To color correct an RGB file, open the Truck file (PC users: truck.jpg) in the Tutorial folder. Select a red area on screen; then open the Levels dialog box and switch channels in the Channel pop-up menu to Red. Click and drag on the left-hand Output Levels slider control. Notice that as you drag to the right, red is added. If you drag the right-hand Output Levels slider to the left, cyan is added. For each RGB and CMYK channel, the sliders will move from one color to its complement. The left-hand Output Levels slider control is always an RGB color and the right-hand Output Levels slider control is its CMYK complement. The left-hand Input Levels slider control is always a CMYK color and the right-hand Input Levels slider control is always an RGB color.

## Using the Curves Command

The next step taken in the New England image was to lighten the clouds in the sky using the Image/Adjust/Curves command. As discussed earlier in this chapter, the Curves dialog box allows a specific area to be corrected precisely by pinpointing the area on the curve, and so it was the best tool to use to correct the clouds. Before the correcting process began, the cloud selections were loaded as needed with the Load Selection command.

Like the Levels dialog box, the Curves dialog box allows entry into channels for correcting. Unlike working in an RGB image, when color correcting CMYK images, Photoshop only plots image points on the curve when you work in a channel other than the Composite channel. When working with a CMYK color file, if a channel is chosen in the Channel pop-up menu, dragging upwards on the curve will add the channel's color (when the gradient bar is set for light to dark); dragging downwards will add its complement. If you click on the gradient bar so that it changes from dark to light, the directions for dragging the curve are reversed. When the gradient bar is set for light to dark, the Input and Output Levels are measured in CMYK percentages; otherwise, input/output is displayed in brightness values from 0 to 255. When working with an RGB Color file, if a channel is chosen in the Channel pop-up menu (and the gradient bar is set for light to dark), dragging downwards on the curve will add the channel's color; drag up, and you add the channel's complement.

Since the easiest way to lighten the dark clouds in the New England image was to remove black from the selection, the Black channel was chosen in the Curves dialog box. Next, the Eyedropper was used to click on the middle of the dark area in the cloud selection. A circle appeared on the curve showing the precise point that represented the cloud's color. To lighten the image, the part of the curve where the circle appeared was dragged downwards and to the right. This lightened all areas in the same tonal range within the selection that corresponded to the curve value.

After the blacks were reduced in the cloud area, the Cyan channel was selected so that cyan could be reduced in the darkest parts of the light clouds. To reduce cyan and add a bit of red, the part of the curve representing only the darkest part of the cloud was dragged downwards. The Info palette in Figure 13-20 shows the change in the cyan (14% to 8%) and red (224 to 237) after the Eyedropper was clicked to resample the corrected area. When cyan was reduced, its complement, red, was added automatically.

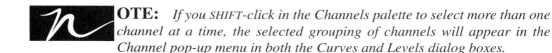 **OTE:** *If you SHIFT-click in the Channels palette to select more than one channel at a time, the selected grouping of channels will appear in the Channel pop-up menu in both the Curves and Levels dialog boxes.*

To complete the correction of the clouds, a sensation of sun and warmth was added by adjusting the Yellow channel's curve upwards.

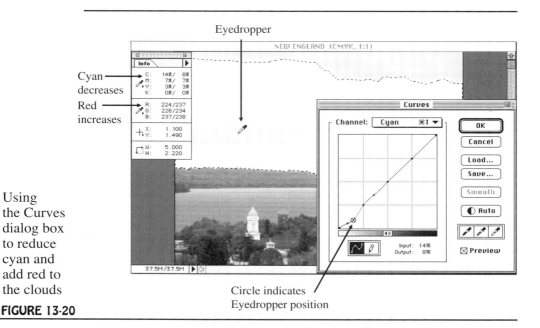

Eyedropper

Cyan decreases

Red increases

Using the Curves dialog box to reduce cyan and add red to the clouds

Circle indicates Eyedropper position

**FIGURE 13-20**

After each of the above corrections, the Eyedropper was used to sample areas that were changed. By keeping an eye on the Info palette, it was possible to gauge the amount of each change.

Once all color correcting was done, the Unsharp Mask filter was applied to sharpen the image. (For more information on the Unsharp Mask filter, see Chapter 8.) The image was then saved on a Syquest cartridge and delivered to Reader's Digest General books, and from there to the prepress house that had scanned the image. Using the retouched and color-corrected image file, the prepress house produced a Matchprint, which was used as a proof before printing the image. A color print of the final image is reproduced as image 2 in the first color insert of this book.

If you wish to experiment with the Curves command using an RGB image, load the Truck (PC users: truck.jpg) file from the Tutorial folder. In the Curves dialog box, set the Channel to Red. Then click and drag downwards to add the red to the image. If you wish to experiment further with this image, reset the image to its original state by holding down OPTION (PC users: ALT) while clicking on the Reset button. To use the curve to increase contrast in the overall image, click on the middle of the curve to set a control point, then drag up on it at about the three-quarter point towards the top of the curve to create an S shape, as shown earlier in this chapter. More contrast is created because you've increased the highlights and darkened the shadows.

If you wish to work with a CMYK file, try experimenting in the Cyan channel of the Café image. Dragging the curve downwards adds red, cyan's complement; dragging upwards adds cyan. As with the RGB Truck file, creating an S curve in this image in the Composite channel will also add contrast to the image.

 **IP:** *Use the Curves for individual channels to help eliminate color casts.*

## Using the Hue/Saturation Command

Even though the Hue/Saturation command was not used to color correct any part of the New England image, this dialog box can be very helpful when you wish to focus on changing the hue, saturation, or lightness values of colors. The Hue/Saturation dialog box features a color sample that helps you preview exactly how a color is being changed.

If you want to test the Hue/Saturation color-correction controls, first use the Eyedropper tool to click on a color in your image that you wish to adjust. This changes your foreground color to the image color that will be displayed in the dialog box. Next, choose Hue/Saturation from the Image/Adjust submenu.

**13**

In the Hue/Saturation dialog box you will see color swatches representing the additive (RGB) and the subtractive (CMY) colors. The Sample swatch at the bottom of the dialog box indicates the color that you clicked on with the Eyedropper. The sliders adjust the hue, saturation, and lightness of an image.

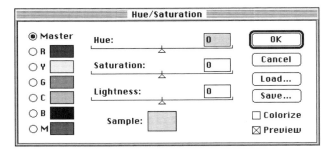

When you select the Master radio button, the Hue slider will move you through the colors on a color wheel, letting you adjust all of the colors in an image. If you click on a radio button for a particular color (rather than Master), you can change the hue, saturation, and lightness of the color by clicking and dragging on the appropriate slider control. Try clicking on the R (red) radio button. The Hue slider will change, showing an endpoint for M (magenta) and for Y (yellow). You can adjust the red levels by dragging the slider control to add and subtract magenta or yellow. In many respects, this is a linear representation of the color wheel: On the color wheel, red is between magenta and yellow. When you click and drag with the R (red) radio button selected, you change only the red values in your image.

Here is a list of the Hue/Saturation radio buttons and how the sliders change when you click on the buttons:

| Radio Button | Slider Colors |
| --- | --- |
| R (Red) | M/Y |
| Y (Yellow) | R/G |
| G (Green) | Y/C |
| C (Cyan) | G/B |
| B (Blue) | C/M |
| M (Magenta) | B/R |

Try selecting one of the radio buttons, and then click and adjust the Hue slider control to see how it changes the color. Try clicking and dragging on the Saturation and Lightness slider controls, too, to see how changing these settings affects your color. Drag the Saturation slider control to the right and the colors get more intense; drag to the left and the image becomes grayer as you remove saturation. Drag the Lightness slider control to the left and the color becomes darker.

If you select the Colorize check box option, the colors in the image change to one color. In this case, adjusting the slider controls lets you tint the image with the color controlled by the Hue slider. To review image colorization using the Hue/Saturation dialog box, turn to Chapter 9.

## Replacing Colors with the Replace Color Command

Another helpful color-correcting option that works hand in hand with the Hue, Saturation, and Lightness sliders is the Replace Color command. You might think of this command as being a type of Search and Replace feature for color. The command will create a mask around a specified color, then allow you to change the hue, saturation, and lightness of the areas within the mask.

To try out the Replace Color command, load any color image, or try using the Truck file from the Tutorial folder. After the image is loaded, choose Replace Color from the Image/Adjust submenu.

To view your image in the Replace Color dialog box, click on the Image radio button. You'll use the Selection radio button to see the mask Photoshop creates in the image. Currently there is no mask.

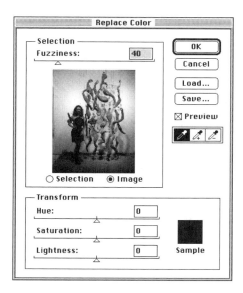

**13**

To start creating the mask, you must choose a color in your image that you want masked. Start by clicking on the first Eyedropper in the dialog box. Move the Eyedropper tool over a color in the image you wish to replace—such as the red on the truck's fender (if you are using the Tutorial file). Click on the Eyedropper in the image. To see how Photoshop creates the mask based on the color, click on the Selection radio button in the Replace Color dialog box. The white area in the Preview box is the area within the mask.

You can expand or contract the mask by clicking and dragging on the Fuzziness slider, or by entering a value between 0 and 255 into the Fuzziness field. The fuzziness slider extends the edges of the color range within the mask.

If you wish to add colors, click on the plus or minus Eyedroppers, then click on the mask in the dialog box or in the image. Try extending the range of the mask by clicking on the Eyedropper+ and then clicking on another color in your image. After you click the color will be added to the mask.

**IP:** *When the Eyedropper is selected, you can switch to the Eyedropper+ by pressing SHIFT; switch to the Eyedropper– by pressing COMMAND (PC users: CTRL). Mac users can temporarily switch between the mask and the image in the Preview area of the dialog box by pressing CTRL, regardless of whether the Selection or Image radio button is selected.*

Once the mask shows the desired area of your image, use the Hue and Saturation sliders to correct or alter the colors. Notice that the sample color swatch previews the colors you create.

If you wish to use your settings again so that they can be reloaded at a later time, click on the Save button so that you can name your settings and save them to disk. The Load button will allow you to load the settings when you need them again.

If you're happy with the changes you made, click OK to close the dialog box; otherwise, choose Cancel.

## Changing Ink Percentages with the Selective Color Command

Once you begin to work with CMYK colors, you may wish to fine-tune color correcting by using Photoshop's Selective Color command which allows you to add or subtract the percentage of inks used in colors. For instance, you could make an apple redder by removing a percentage of cyan, red's complement and/or add magenta.

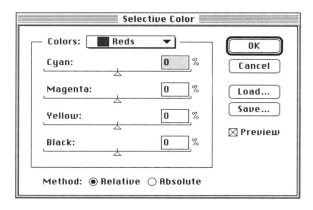

*OTE:* *When using the Selective Color command, you might wish to set the Eyedropper so it displays Total ink percentages. To do this, click on the Info palette's pop-up menu and choose Palette Options. In the Info Options dialog box, set First or Second color to Total ink. After you make changes in the Selective Colors dialog box, move the Eyedropper over your image to view the total percentages for all CMYK inks.*

Before trying out the Selective Color command, load an image on screen.

To use the Selective Color command, choose Selective Color from the Image/Adjust submenu. In the Selective Color dialog box, click the Preview button so you will be able to see the changes in your image as you experiment with the Selective Color command. Next, choose a color from the Colors pop-up menu. This is the color in your image that you wish to change. Note that you can also change whites, grays, and blacks.

The percentage of ink added or subtracted is calculated differently based upon whether you select the Relative or Absolute radio button. Relative applies the percentage based upon the percentage of the original ink. Absolute adds the percentage to the original ink. For instance, assume you are adding color to a 50% Cyan pixel. If you add 5% Cyan in Relative mode, Photoshop will compute 5% of 50% (.05 * .5) which produces a 2.5% increase. Thus, the Cyan ink will be changed to 52.5%. If you add 5% of Cyan in Absolute mode, Photoshop simply adds 5% to the 50%, which results in 55% Cyan.

**13**

Try clicking on the Absolute radio button, then watch how your image changes when you drag the sliders to adjust the colors. When you're done experimenting click Cancel or OK to accept the ink changes. If you'd like you can also use the Save and Load buttons to Save and Load settings for use on other images.

**OTE:** *A variety of third-party vendors have created plug-ins which can speed up and simplify the task of color correcting images. Prepress Technologies' Spectre Plug-ins sets up a color-correction table that can quickly be applied to images. DPA Software's Intellihance can sharpen and despeckle as well as adjust brightness, contrast, sharpness, and saturation in one click of the mouse. Both Intellihance and Monaco Systems' MonacoCOLOR feature batch processing. This allows many images to be corrected automatically while the computer is unattended. MonacoCOLOR also features scanner calibration options and provides many image correction features that can be run with one keystroke.*

## CONCLUSION

As you've seen, Photoshop provides enormous possibilities and many different options when you need to retouch or color correct an image. As you gain more experience with retouching and color correcting, you'll be better able to predict how changes in the relevant dialog boxes will affect your image on screen. You'll also be better able to judge the best retouching and/or color-correcting tool for the job at hand.

# CALIBRATION AND OUTPUT

No matter how exquisite your Photoshop images, all of your design and image-editing work may be in vain if the final printed (or other) output does not match the onscreen image. To get sharp and vibrant printed images, you need to have a clear understanding of how they are produced and how system calibration affects output quality.

This chapter focuses on two subjects: the printing process and system calibration. Most Photoshop users do not need to have a thorough knowledge of the printing and calibration processes because the prepress house or print shop can take care of these complicated issues. On the other hand, even if you don't output your own proofs and film separations, and even if you don't have to set screen frequency in the Halftone Screens dialog box, understanding the prepress concepts covered in this chapter will make for a smoother and more efficient production process. With that goal in mind, this chapter provides an overview of the printing process, explains how proofs can be used to predict color accuracy, and shows you how to calibrate your system to a proof. It concludes with step-by-step instructions for printing separations, and a brief look at how to output to produce slides, chromes, and video images.

Once you grasp the printing process, you'll understand how output resolution, screen frequency, paper stock, and halftones affect the output quality of your images.

## THE ROLE OF HALFTONES IN IMAGE OUTPUT

When an image is printed on a printing press, it consists of many small dots called *halftones*. The size and shape of these dots and the angle at which they are printed create the visual illusion of continuous grays or continuous colors. In traditional printing, halftones are created by placing a glass or mylar screen containing a grid of dots between an image and the film or negative paper on which the image is printed. This photomechanical process re-creates the image as a pattern of dots. Dark areas have large dots, and light areas have small dots.

In color publishing, cyan, magenta, yellow, and black screens are used in the traditional halftone process. The print quality depends on how close together the lines are. The finer the lines, the better the quality. The final result also depends upon the screen angles at which the halftones were created. Specific angles must be used in order to provide clear and consistent color. The traditional screen angles are 105 degrees for cyan, 75 degrees for magenta, 90 degrees for yellow, and 45 degrees for black. When screen angles are not corrected, a mottled and undesirable pattern, called a moiré, may appear. (An example of a moiré pattern can be seen in Chapter 8, Figure 8-1a.)

Commercial printers use the halftone screens to create plates for each of the four process colors. In the printing process, paper is printed with patterns of different-sized cyan, magenta, yellow, and black dots to create the illusion of countless colors. Take a magnifying glass and look closely at a printed color image, and you'll see the pattern of dots in various colors and sizes.

## Digital Halftones

As in traditional printing, digital images that are output to a printer or imagesetter are also separated into halftone dots. The output device creates the halftone dots by turning groups of smaller dots, often referred to as pixels, on or off.

If the output device is an imagesetter, it can output to film as well as paper. An imagesetter producing output at a resolution of 2,450 dpi creates over 6 million dots per square inch. At 300 dpi, a standard laser printer creates images with 90,000 dots per square inch. The more dots an image has, the better its resolution and the higher its printed quality.

It's important to remember that these pixels are *not* the halftone dots. In the printing process, the pixels are organized into a system of cells, and it is within these cells that the halftone dots are created. For instance, the dots from a 1,200-dpi imagesetter might be divided into 100 cells per inch. By turning the pixels off or on inside each cell, the printer or imagesetter creates one halftone dot.

The number of halftone dots per inch is called the *screen frequency*, *screen ruling*, or *line screen* and is measured in lines per inch (lpi). A high-screen frequency, such as 150 lpi, packs the dots very closely together, producing sharper images and distinct colors. When the screen frequency is low, the halftone dots are spread out and produce coarser images with less refined colors.

**EMEMBER:** *For the highest-quality reproduction of digital images, image file resolution generally should be twice the screen frequency. To review the relationship between image resolution and screen frequency, see Chapter 7.*

## Calculating Gray Levels

The number of pixels that the imagesetter turns off or on to create a halftone determines the maximum number of gray levels that can be printed in an image. The number of gray levels determines the quality of continuous-tone images, and whether a gradient blend prints properly. If you print at a screen frequency of 150 and a resolution of 2,450 dpi, you produce output with the maximum number of grays possible (256). Most continuous-tone images require at least 150 shades of gray for acceptable printed results.

**IP:** *To help eliminate banding due to insufficient gray levels in a blend, apply the Add Noise filter to each channel containing color in your CMYK Color image. Filters are explained in Chapter 8. Selecting the Dither check box in the Gradient Tool Options palette can also eliminate banding.*

In order to ensure the image quality you desire, you can calculate the number of gray levels (including white) that will be printed, using this formula:

$$\text{Number of Grays} = (\text{Output Resolution} \div \text{Screen Frequency})^2 + 1$$

On an output device printing at 1,200 dpi and with a screen frequency of 100, each cell is a 12-by-12 matrix of pixels ($1,200 \div 100 = 12$). The pixels in each cell produce one halftone dot. In this 12-by-12 cell, the different combinations of pixels being turned on or off produce 145 levels of gray ($12^2 = 144 + \text{white} = 145$).

Figure 14-1 illustrates how a halftone is created from pixels, and how the number of pixels in the cell determines the number of gray levels. In a 5-by-5 cell, 26 combinations of gray ($5^2 + \text{white}$) are possible. White is created when no pixels are truned on, 50% black is created when half the pixels are turned on, and 100% black is created when every pixel is turned on.

Conversely, if you know your output resolution and the number of grays desired, you can compute the required screen frequency with the following formula:

$$\text{Screen Frequency} = \text{Output Resolution} \div \sqrt{\text{Number of Grays}}$$

If more grays are desired, the screen frequency can be reduced. For instance, if the screen frequency drops to 80 lpi and the resolution remains at 1,200 dpi, the

Pixels
turned
off and
on create
halftone
dots and
determine
gray levels

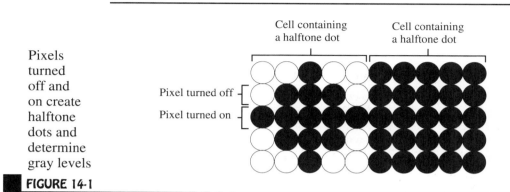

**FIGURE 14-1**

halftone cell size is increased to a 15-pixel square ($1,200 \div 80 = 15$), which produces 226 grays ($15^2 + 1$). This can create a dilemma: the greater the number of grays, the lower the screen frequency; the greater the screen frequency, the sharper the image; yet, the fewer the gray levels. The simple solution to this predicament is to always print at the highest resolution with the highest screen frequency, assuring sharp images, crisp colors, and 256 shades of gray.

Unfortunately, printing at the highest possible resolution and screen frequency may not always be possible, because of two factors: paper stock and printing presses. Not all printing presses can handle high-screen frequency output, and not all paper is suitable for high-screen frequency printing. For instance, when you print at a high-screen frequency on newspaper stock, it absorbs the dots, causing too much ink to spread and produces a muddy output. Thus, paper stock is often the determining factor in deciding what screen frequency to use. Magazines printed on coated stock often use a screen frequency of 133 or 150 lpi. A glossy magazine or art book may be printed at 200 lpi. Newspapers are usually printed at 85 lpi.

Resolution, screen frequency, and paper stock are all issues that should be discussed with your print shop, prepress house, or service bureau. You should also decide whether you want your output on paper or film. Although film is more expensive than paper, it provides sharper output, which is especially important at screen frequencies over 100 lpi. This is the reason color separations are output to film.

If you are producing color separations, the imagesetter will produce four different film separations. The four pieces of film will not be in color, but rather four grayscale versions of the cyan, magenta, yellow, and black components of your image. The print shop will use the four pieces of film (for each of the four process colors) to create plates for use on a printing press.

## PRINTING PROOFS OF YOUR IMAGES

Before you actually go to press with a Photoshop project, you should view a printed sample, or *proof,* of your image. The proof will help you judge the anticipated quality of the final printing job. Proofs can warn you that colors will not print correctly, that moirés may appear, and tell you the degree of dot gain to be expected. (*Dot gain* is the expansion or contraction of halftone dots usually due to ink spreading on paper.)

If you are printing a grayscale image, you may feel that your 300- or 600-dpi laser printer output is sufficient as a proof. If you are creating color images, there are a variety of choices available for color proofs: digital proofs, off-press proofs, and press proofs.

 **OTE:** *No matter how good your proofs look, various problems can occur onpress that affect the quality of your images.*

### Digital Proofs

A *digital proof* is output directly from the digital data in your Photoshop file. Most digital proofs are created by printing to a thermal-wax printer, color laser printer, dye-sublimation printer. Digital proofs can also be output on high-end inkjet printers such as a Scitex IRIS, or other high-end printers such as the Kodak Approval Color Proofer. Digital proofs are often very helpful as the design process proceeds.

Because digital proofs are not created from an imagesetter's film, color output may not be highly accurate, although high-end printers from Kodak, Scitex, and 3M can come close to matching film output. Commercial printers generally will not accept a digital proof as a *contract proof* that they will contractually agree to match.

 **OTE:** *If a service bureau will be creating a digital proof of your image, you may be asked to save your file in EPS format. For more information, see Appendix A.*

## Off-Press Proofs

These proofs are created from the imagesetter's film that will eventually be sent to the print shop. Thus, an off-press proof is considered more reliable than a digital proof as an indicator of how the image will print. The two major types of off-press proofs are *overlay proofs* and *laminated proofs.*

The overlay proof comprises four different images exposed on acetate sheets that are overlaid. An overlay proof is generally considered not as accurate as a laminated proof, where each colored layer is developed and laminated to a base material. Apart from providing a reliable indication of color, laminated proofs can be very helpful in predicting if moirés will appear in your final output. Dupont's Chromalin and 3M's Matchprint are two well-known laminated systems. When analyzing a Matchprint, be aware that it can make colors look more intense than actual colors produced by inks on a printing press.

## Press Proofs

A press proof is considered the most accurate proof because it is made from the actual plates the printer will use, and it is printed on the stock that has been chosen for the job. Thus, the press proof will be a good indicator of dot gain, as well as provide an accurate assessment of final color.

Bear in mind that press proofs are often printed on sheet-fed presses, which may be slower than the press used for the actual print job. The cost of creating printing plates and inking the press make the press proof the most expensive proofing process. For this reason, most clients opt for off-press proofs.

## WHY YOU SHOULD CALIBRATE YOUR SYSTEM

Of course you will want to proof your images as often as possible during a project—the earlier you catch problems with color and design, the easier and cheaper it is to fix them. Another way to avoid problems in attaining color accuracy is to properly *calibrate* your monitor and system. Calibration helps ensure that the image you see on screen portrays your final output as accurately as possible. Calibration is necessary because monitors, scanners, printers, and printing presses vary in the way they render color.

## Monitor Calibration

Calibration is discussed in several places in this book. In Chapter 1, instructions for monitor calibration were included to emphasize the importance of calibrating your monitor as soon as possible before you start using it for color image work. Ideally, you've been working through the exercises in this book with your monitor already calibrated and the options in the Monitor Setup dialog box properly set.

Nonetheless, before you incur any printing expenses, you should ensure that your monitor is properly calibrated. If you don't, you may be working with onscreen colors that are tainted by color casts. Images may appear lighter or darker on screen than they will print. Also, don't forget that the settings in the Monitor Setup dialog box are used when Photoshop converts from RGB Color to CMYK Color.

If you have not calibrated your monitor or selected appropriate options in the Monitor Setup dialog box, return to Chapter 1 now and follow the instructions there, or refer to the Photoshop "User Guide" before continuing. Once your monitor is calibrated, you can fine-tune it further using a printed proof as a guide.

# CALIBRATING TO A PROOF

The Photoshop "User Guide" recommends that you use a press proof to fully calibrate your system. If you can't afford a press proof, it's still advisable to calibrate using an off-press proof, such as a Matchprint. The following sections give an overview of calibrating a system to grayscale and color proofs. If you have questions regarding calibration, consult your prepress house—many use Photoshop every day and may be able to help out.

## Calibrating to a Grayscale Proof

If you are printing a grayscale image, calibrating to a proof is quite simple. When calibrating, you can compensate for dot gain that occurs "on press." (As mentioned earlier and discussed in detail in Chapter 9, dot gain is a change in the size of a halftone dot, usually caused by ink absorption. Dot gain may also be caused by a miscalibrated imagesetter.)

Your first step in calibrating to a grayscale proof is to obtain a proof of a grayscale image that is printed at the resolution, screen frequency, and (hopefully) on the paper stock you will use for printing. Try to use an image that spans a large tonal range from highlights to shadows. You might wish to add an 11-step gray bar in an area in the image. Also, be sure to have your prepress house or commercial printer output the image with a grayscale calibration bar, which steps through grayscale levels. For more information about printing calibration bars, see the section, "The Page Setup Dialog Box" later in this chapter.

When you are ready to calibrate to the proof, open the grayscale image from which the proof was created. To compensate for dot gain, you use the Printing Inks Setup dialog box, accessed by selecting Preferences from the File menu and then choosing Printing Inks Setup. From the Ink Colors pop-up menu, choose the printer or inks that you will be using, and a corresponding percentage is automatically entered into the Dot Gain field. Make sure the Use Dot Gain for Grayscale Images check box is selected. This means that the display of your image on screen will reflect the Dot Gain percentage specified in the dialog box. Click OK to see the effects in your image.

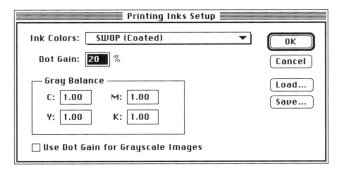

**EMEMBER:** *For grayscale and Duotone images, the settings in the Printing Inks Setup dialog box only affect screen display when the Use Dot Gain for Grayscale Images check box is selected. This will not affect the data in the grayscale image itself.*

If the image on your monitor is lighter or darker than the proof, you may want to reopen the Printing Inks Setup dialog box and change the percentage in the Dot Gain field so that the display matches your image. Before you make changes, however, be sure to consult with your commercial printer and find out if Photoshop's default Dot Gain setting is sufficient. If you do wish to change the value in the Dot Gain field, entering a higher percentage will make your screen display darker, and a lower percentage will make it lighter. Click OK to see the results in the image on screen. Once your screen image matches the printed proof, click the Save button so that you can name and save your Printing Inks Setup settings.

When you work on a grayscale image, load the saved Printing Inks Setup settings. Then use the Image/Adjust command's Curves and Levels dialog boxes to lighten or darken your image. Since the Printing Inks Setup settings only affect screen display in a grayscale image (when Use Dot Gain for Grayscale Images is enabled), changes in the Curves and Levels dialog boxes will compensate for dot gain. (To review the Curves and Levels dialog boxes, see Chapter 13.)

## Calibrating to a Color Proof

For printing a color image, the calibration process is a bit more complicated. If you will be converting images from RGB Color to CMYK Color, your calibration settings will affect the color data in the CMYK Color file. As discussed in Chapter 9, when you switch RGB Color to CMYK Color mode, Photoshop utilizes the settings in the Monitor Setup, Printing Inks Setup, and Separation Setup dialog boxes to create the color data for the CMYK Color image.

When you calibrate to a color proof, you attempt to match screen colors in a CMYK image to printed color output. To begin the calibration process, use a CMYK Color image as your proofing image—it should not be an image that you converted to CMYK Color from RGB Color. The Photoshop "User Guide" includes instructions for creating a proofing image from CMYK color-swatch combinations, but it's probably easiest to use the calibration file that is provided with Photoshop. This is the Olé No Moiré file in the Calibration folder (PC users: testpict.jpg in the calibrat folder).

Once your prepress house or commercial printer creates the proof, load the image from which the proof was created on screen. Your first step is to make adjustments to compensate for dot gain.

### Compensating for Dot Gain

To compensate for dot gain, open the Printing Inks Setup dialog box (File/Preferences/Printing Inks Setup). In the Ink Colors pop-up menu, shown in Figure 14-2 , choose the correct printer or ink colors. The Dot Gain percentage will change according to your choice for Ink Colors, and represents expected dot gain in image midtones. Photoshop uses the Dot Gain percentage to create a dot gain curve for the entire image's tonal range, from highlights to shadows. (As mentioned earlier in this chapter, the Dot Gain field in the Printing Inks Setup dialog box changes the image display to compensate for dot gain on press.)

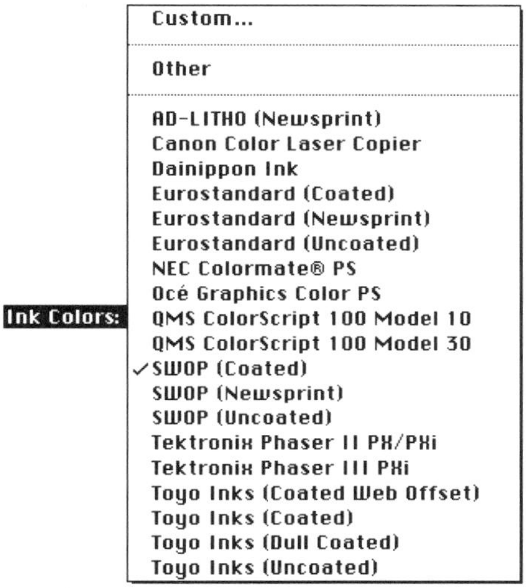

Ink Colors:

| Custom... |
| Other |
| AD-LITHO (Newsprint) |
| Canon Color Laser Copier |
| Dainippon Ink |
| Eurostandard (Coated) |
| Eurostandard (Newsprint) |
| Eurostandard (Uncoated) |
| NEC Colormate® PS |
| Océ Graphics Color PS |
| QMS ColorScript 100 Model 10 |
| QMS ColorScript 100 Model 30 |
| ✓SWOP (Coated) |
| SWOP (Newsprint) |
| SWOP (Uncoated) |
| Tektronix Phaser II PX/PXi |
| Tektronix Phaser III PXi |
| Toyo Inks (Coated Web Offset) |
| Toyo Inks (Coated) |
| Toyo Inks (Dull Coated) |
| Toyo Inks (Uncoated) |

Ink Colors
pop-up
menu

**FIGURE 14-2**

Adobe recommends that you use a densitometer to take a reading on the proof's calibration bar (a color bar of CMYK colors and CMY combinations). A *densitometer* is a device that measures densities of colors and can provide a precise reading of dot gain. If you don't want to incur the expense of purchasing a densitometer or don't know how to use one, your next best choice is to adjust Dot Gain so that the image on screen looks like the proof. The higher the percentage you enter in the Dot Gain field, the darker the image will become. Click OK to see the results on screen. Once you have found the best setting, return to the Printing Inks Setup dialog box so that you can name and save your settings. To save your settings, click the Save button.

**OTE:** *If you are uncertain about the effects of changing the Dot Gain setting, consult your commercial printer.*

As mentioned earlier, dot gain can also occur because of a miscalibrated imagesetter. Photoshop allows you to compensate for miscalibration in the Page Setup dialog box. Nevertheless, when dot gain appears in film separations due to miscalibrated equipment, compensating for it is probably better left to service bureau or prepress professionals. See the "Transfer Functions" section later in this chapter.

**14**

## Adjusting for Custom Ink Colors

In addition to adjustment to Dot Gain, the Printing Inks Setup dialog box allows you to adjust for custom ink colors. This might be necessary when you use ink sets that do not appear in the Ink Colors pop-up menu.

To adjust for custom inks, choose Custom from the Ink Colors pop-up menu. An Ink Colors dialog box will open. The values you see for the different CMYK color combinations are x and y coordinates based upon internationally defined standards (the captial Y stands for lightness). The Photoshop "User Guide" suggests taking a color reading of your proof using a *colorimeter* to enter the correct values. If you do not have color reading equipment, you can click on the color swatches and adjust the colors to match your proof. When you are finished, click OK. Save your settings in the Printing Inks Setup dialog box by clicking the Save button, and then click OK to exit.

| | Y | x | y | | |
|---|---|---|---|---|---|
| | | | | | Ink Colors |
| C: | 26.25 | 0.1673 | 0.2328 | | OK |
| M: | 14.50 | 0.4845 | 0.2396 | | Cancel |
| Y: | 71.20 | 0.4357 | 0.5013 | | |
| MY: | 14.09 | 0.6075 | 0.3191 | | |
| CY: | 19.25 | 0.2271 | 0.5513 | | |
| CM: | 2.98 | 0.2052 | 0.1245 | | |
| CMY: | 2.79 | 0.3227 | 0.2962 | | |
| W: | 83.02 | 0.3149 | 0.3321 | | |
| K: | 0.82 | 0.3202 | 0.3241 | | |

Your next calibration step is to adjust for possible color casts, which may appear when one of the process inks produces a higher dot gain than the others. Color casts can also be caused by incorrect screen angles and the order in which the different plates are printed.

Examine the gray areas of your proof for color casts. If a color cast appears, you can compensate by adjusting color levels. To do this, select Image/Adjust/Levels to open the Levels dialog box. Drag the Input Level slider's gamma control to adjust the screen display until it matches the proof. Adjust the gamma level for each channel, as necessary. (Refer to Chapter 13 for details on using the Levels dialog box.) After you adjust the gamma levels, write down the value for each channel, because you will use it to change the entries in the Gray Balance fields in the Printing

Inks Setup dialog box. Once you have recorded the channel values, click Cancel. (Since these settings are for a systemwide correction, you do not need to click OK, which would change the gamma levels for the proof image only.)

Return to the Printing Inks Setup dialog box so you can enter the numbers that you recorded for each color channel into the appropriate Gray Balance fields. If the value in a Gray Balance field is not 1, take the number that appears there and multiply the gamma setting by it; then enter this number in the Gray Balance field. Raising the value in any of the fields will decrease that color's percentage on screen; lowering the value will increase the color on screen. After you have entered the Gray Balance values, save the Printing Inks Setup settings and then click OK. When you wish to work with an RGB Color image that you will be converting to CMYK Color, load these saved settings.

**EMEMBER:** *As discussed in Chapter 9, changes made in the Printing Inks Setup dialog box do not affect the color data in a CMYK file, but only the screen display of the image; the settings are used when Photoshop converts from RGB Color to CMYK Color. The settings in the Printing Inks Setup dialog box do not affect the display of RGB Color images.*

**OTE:** *A new product which is sure to prove helpful when calibrating is Light Source's Colortron, which will be sold for about $1,000. This hand-held device for measuring color can serve as a monitor calibrator, file/ink densitometer, or a light meter. Accompanying software can determine a match of a sample color to a color matching system such as PANTONE, and can determine the best CMYK approximation of a sample color.*

## Saving Separation Tables

Now that you have compensated for dot gain and adjusted for custom ink colors, your system is calibrated. If you need to convert an image from RGB Color to CMYK Color, your next step is to ensure that the proper settings are entered into the Separation Setup dialog box. Once the information in the Monitor Setup, Printing Inks Setup, and Separation Setup dialog boxes is correct, you can save the settings as a separation table. Open the Separation Setup dialog box (with the File/Preferences/ Separation Tables command), and click on the Save button; name your table after Photoshop creates it. When you wish to use the separation table, open the Separation Tables dialog box and load the table by clicking on the Load button. Photoshop will use this table when you convert from RGB Color to CMYK Color.

For more information about using the Separation Setup and the Separation Tables dialog boxes, see Chapter 9.

## Calibrating with EfiColor Works

If the previous sections on calibration seem somewhat daunting, you may wish to investigate using a color-management software package to aid in calibrating your system. EfiColor Works, by Electronics for Imaging, Inc., is designed to provide consistent color based upon the color properties of specific output devices. It provides a pack of core color profiles and separation tables for various output devices as well as an application that creates scanner profiles. If necessary, the dot gain and GCR levels in the printer and separation table profiles can be fine-tuned for specific printing devices. The package even allows you to convert an image that has already been separated for one printing system so it can be output correctly on another. For instance, you can transform a CMYK image separated for high-end printing so that it prints correctly on a dye-sublimation printer.

Calibration in EfiColor Works is handled in a few simple steps. Once the EfiColor software is installed and Photoshop is opened, you load the Efi Calibrated RGB monitor table by selecting the Load button in Photoshop's Monitor Setup dialog box. Next, you load a separation table for a specific output device using the Load button in Photoshop's Separation Tables dialog box. Once the separation table is loaded, you can convert from RGB Color to CMYK Color using commands in the Mode menu. The following illustration shows the Separation Tables dialog box, after loading Efi's SWOP-Coated separation table.

```
╔══════════════ Separation Tables ══════════════╗

  ┌─ To CMYK ──────────────────────────┐      ┌──────────┐
  │  ○ Use Separation Setup            │      │    OK    │
  │  ● Use Table:   SWOP-Coated.P075   │      └──────────┘
  └────────────────────────────────────┘      ┌──────────┐
                                               │  Cancel  │
  ┌─ From CMYK ────────────────────────┐       └──────────┘
  │  ○ Use Printing Inks Setup         │       ┌──────────┐
  │  ● Use Table:   SWOP-Coated.P075   │       │  Load... │
  └────────────────────────────────────┘      └──────────┘
                                               ┌──────────┐
                                               │  Save... │
                                               └──────────┘
```

**n OTE:** *If you output Photoshop files in QuarkXPress, you may wish to use Daystar's ColorMatch. This color matching system saves Photoshop files with special colorimetric tags in order to provide consistent color when images are imported into a program, such as QuarkXPress, that uses Kodak's Color Management System (KPCMS).*

## TRAPPING IN PHOTOSHOP

When calibration is completed and you are ready to produce your output, your next consideration is whether you'll need to correct for registration problems that might occur during the printing process. Photoshop's Image/Trap command can help.

As paper passes through a printing press, misalignment or movement of the printing plates may cause thin white gaps or color halos to appear around adjoining areas of colors. *Trapping* fixes these discrepancies by slightly overlapping the colored areas so that the gaps won't appear during on-press printing.

When Photoshop traps, it spreads lighter colors under darker ones. Pure cyan and pure magenta, however, spread equally under each other.

*n* **OTE:** *Before you begin to adjust trap settings, bear in mind that trapping is primarily needed when solid tints adjoin. Since most Photoshop images are continuous-tone images with gradual color transitions, trapping is usually unnecessary.*

To trap, you must be in a CMYK Color image. After consulting with your print shop on the width of the trap adjustment, select Trap from the Image menu. In the Trap dialog box, select a measurement unit from the pop-up menu, and in the Width field enter the width for the trap.

```
┌─────────────────────────────────────┐
│ ═══════════════ Trap ═══════════════ │
│                                      │
│  Width: [1    ]  [ pixels ▼ ]  ( OK )│
│                                ( Cancel )│
│                                      │
└─────────────────────────────────────┘
```

Here's an example of how trapping works: Suppose you entered a value of 2 pixels for the trap width. When a portion of an image with a high percentage of yellow adjoins a dark color, the yellow (because it is the lighter color) will spread out 2 pixels. Thus, if a gap existed between the two plates that was 2 points or less, the yellow ink would fill the gap.

If you wish to see the Trap command in action, create a CMYK file with a swatch of a dark color overlapping a swatch of yellow. Execute the Trap command. Then use the Channels palette to view only the yellow channel. To see the difference—before and after applying the Trap—use the Edit/Undo command.

**14**

**CAUTION:** *Discuss trapping issues with your prepress house, which may use a specific software package to trap before outputting your image to film.*

# PHOTOSHOP'S PRINTING OPTIONS

Now that you have an understanding of the printing and calibration processes, you'll probably want to explore all of the options available in Photoshop's Page Setup and Print dialog boxes. The Page Setup dialog box provides numerous output features, several of which fall into the realm of the prepress house or service bureau. If you are not printing to a color printer or imagesetter, you may never need to access these options; nonetheless, getting familiar with them will help complete your knowledge of the printing process.

## The Page Setup Dialog Box

As discussed in Chapter 2, the Page Setup dialog box allows you to specify whether labels, registration marks, and crop marks will be printed on a page. As you'll see in this section, this dialog box also contains prepress options that govern screen frequency and halftone angles.

Figure 14-3 shows a composite output of an image with a label, crop marks, registration marks, calibration bars, a caption, and a 1-pixel-wide border around the image.

To access the Page Setup dialog box, choose Page Setup from the File menu. PC users will choose a printer from the Page Setup dialog box. Mac users will pick a printer using the Chooser in the Apple menu; the Chooser cannot be accessed while the Page Setup dialog box is displayed.

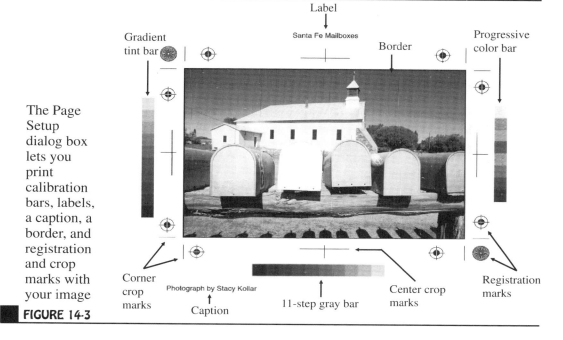

Label

Santa Fe Mailboxes

Gradient tint bar

Progressive color bar

Border

The Page Setup dialog box lets you print calibration bars, labels, a caption, a border, and registration and crop marks with your image

Corner crop marks

Photograph by Stacy Kollar

Caption

11-step gray bar

Center crop marks

Registration marks

**FIGURE 14-3**

Here is an overview of the Page Setup dialog box:

- For both Mac and PC users, the Paper and Orientation settings work much the same as in any Mac or Windows program.

**IP:** *In Photoshop, it's faster to use the Image/Rotate command to rotate an image before printing, rather than changing orientation when printing.*

- *Calibration Bars* This option prints an 11-step gray bar, a progressive CMYK color bar and CMY gradient tint bar (if the image is a CMYK Color image) on each page. The calibration bars are used to match a proof to the screen image; you can see how closely screen grays or colors match the printed output. The gray bar on the page prints from 0 to 100% gray in 10% increments. The progressive CMYK bar prints the following colors or color combinations: yellow, magenta-yellow, magenta, cyan-magenta, cyan, cyan-yellow, and black.

**14**

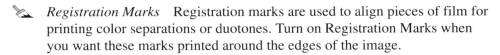 

*Registration Marks*   Registration marks are used to align pieces of film for printing color separations or duotones. Turn on Registration Marks when you want these marks printed around the edges of the image.

*Corner Crop Marks*   Crop marks indicate where paper should be trimmed. Turn on Corner Crop Marks to print these marks at the edges of your image.

*Center Crop Marks*   Select Center Crop Marks to place crop marks around the center of your image.

*Labels*   Select Labels to print the document name and channel name on the page with the image.

*Negative*   Negatives are often used for film output. Most commercial printers in the United States require a film negative to create plates, although other countries create plates from positives, rather than negatives. Ask your printer whether a film positive or negative is required. If you are printing to paper, do not select the Negative option.

*Emulsion Down*   Both film and photographic paper have a photosensitive layer called *emulsion*. When examining film, the emulsion side is the dull side. When the emulsion side is up in a film negative, type will be readable and not reversed. Your print shop may require the emulsion to be up or down. Usually, printing on paper is Emulsion Up; this is Photoshop's default setting.

*Interpolation*   Some PostScript Level 2 printers can improve the appearance of low-resolution files by interpolating pixels when printing. If you do not have a PostScript Level 2 printer, this option will not change output quality.

The Page Setup dialog box also includes buttons that open up additional dialog boxes with more printing options; these buttons are described in the paragraphs that follow.

## Printing with a Border

Select the Border button if you wish to have a black border printed around your image. In the Border dialog box, you select a unit of measurement and a width for the border.

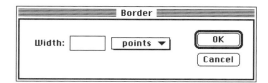

## Printing with a Caption

Select the Caption check box if you wish to print the information entered in the Caption field of the File Info dialog box. To acess the File Info dialog box, choose File Info from the File menu. If the caption information does not appear in the dialog box, choose Caption from the Section pop-up menu. For more information about the File Info dialog box, see Appendix B.

 **OTE:**   *Captions entered in the File Info dialog box can be searched by image database software such as Aldus Fetch.*

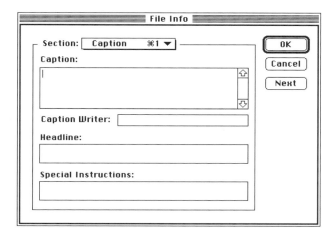

## Printing with a Background Color

If you are outputting to slides, you may wish to have a colored background printed to fill in the area surrounding the image. When you select the Background button, Photoshop's Color Picker will appear. Choose the color that you wish to have as your background and click OK.

**14**

## Transfer Functions

As mentioned earlier in this chapter, when an image is output to film, dot gain can occur due to miscalibration of the imagesetter. The Transfer Functions are used to compensate for this.

To open the Transfer Functions dialog box, click on the Transfer button. In the Transfer Functions dialog box, you enter compensating values in fields that correspond to the dot gain percentages in the image. For instance, if dot gain is higher than it should be, you subtract the desired dot value from the dot gain caused by the miscalibration, then enter the value in the appropriate field. Here's an example: Assume that an imagesetter is printing halftone dots at 60%, when they really should be printed at 50%. The difference between the two figures is 10%. Subtract 10% from 50% and you get 40%. Thus, you enter 40 in the 50% field of the Transfer Functions dialog box.

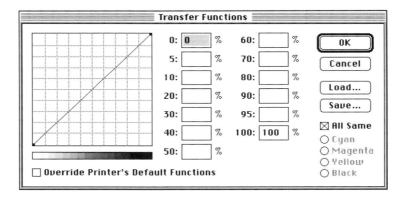

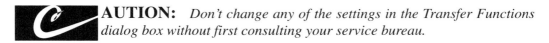**OTE:** *If you check the Override Printer's Default Functions option in the Transfer dialog box, and you export an EPS file with the Include Transfer Function selected in the EPS Format dialog box, the transfer information is used in the exported file.*

**AUTION:** *Don't change any of the settings in the Transfer Functions dialog box without first consulting your service bureau.*

## Setting Halftone Screens

The Screen button presents a Halftone Screens dialog box, in which you can specify elements such as screen frequency, screen angle, and halftone dot shape.

```
┌──────────── Halftone Screens ────────────┐
│  ☐ Use Printer's Default Screens          ┌─────────┐
│  ┌─ Ink: [ Cyan      ⌘1 ▼]               │   OK    │
│  │                                        └─────────┘
│  │ Frequency: [47.4      ] [lines/inch ▼] ┌─────────┐
│  │                                        │ Cancel  │
│  │   Angle: [108.4  ] degrees            └─────────┘
│  │                                        ┌─────────┐
│  │   Shape: [ Diamond    ▼]              │ Auto... │
│  └──────────────────────────────         └─────────┘
│                                           ┌─────────┐
│  ☐ Use Accurate Screens                   │ Load... │
│  ☒ Use Same Shape for All Inks            └─────────┘
│                                           ┌─────────┐
│                                           │ Save... │
│                                           └─────────┘
└──────────────────────────────────────────┘
```

 **AUTION:** *Before changing the default settings in the Halftone Screens dialog box, consult with your service bureau or print shop.*

🖌 *Use Printer's Default Screens option*   If you select this option, any dialog box settings are overridden, and output will be based upon halftone screen settings built into the printer. When this check box is selected, most of the options in the Halftone Screens dialog box are disabled.

🖌 *Ink pop-up menu*   If you are working with a CMYK Color image, click on this pop-up menu to select the channel. Enter the screen frequency and angle for each channel. If you are printing color separations, the angle for each screen must be set properly to prevent the appearance of moiré patterns.

🖌 *Auto button*   If you wish to have Photoshop calculate the screen angles, click the Auto button. In the Auto Screens dialog box, enter the printer resolution and screen frequency. Click OK to have Photoshop calculate the best screen angle for all four halftone screens.

```
┌──────────── Auto Screens ────────────┐
│                                        │
│  Printer: [2400    ] [dots/inch  ▼]  ┌──────┐
│                                       │  OK  │
│  Screen:  [133  ] [lines/inch ▼]     └──────┘
│                                       ┌────────┐
│  ☐ Use Accurate Screens               │ Cancel │
│                                       └────────┘
└────────────────────────────────────────┘
```

🖌 *Shape pop-up menu*   This pop-up menu in the Halftone Screens dialog box offers a list of custom halftone shapes that you can select from to create

**14**

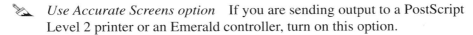
various printing effects. If you wish all four inks to have the same halftone shape, select the Same Shape for All Inks check box.

*Use Accurate Screens option*   If you are sending output to a PostScript Level 2 printer or an Emerald controller, turn on this option.

*Save and Load buttons*   Use these buttons to store and use your halftone screens settings. If you wish to change the default settings, press OPTION (PC users: ALT), and the Load and Save buttons will change to Default buttons. To create new default settings, click the ->Default button; to return to the original default settings, click <-Default.

## Producing a Bleed

The Bleed button allows you to print crop marks inside your image. These crop marks provide the printer with a guide for trimming so that the image can extend (or bleed) to the edge of the page.

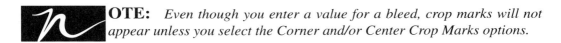

**OTE:**   *Even though you enter a value for a bleed, crop marks will not appear unless you select the Corner and/or Center Crop Marks options.*

After you click on the Bleed button a dialog box appears allowing you to enter a value up to 3.18 mm (.125 inches). This is the distance from the edge of your image that will be trimmed away.

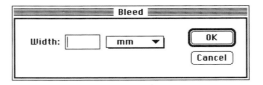

## The Print Dialog Box

After you have selected all the desired options in the Page Setup dialog box, your next step in printing an image is to open the Print dialog box by choosing Print from the File menu. Most of the options in the Print dialog box will be familiar to Mac and Windows users, except for the options at the bottom of the dialog box. These options vary depending upon the image mode (RGB, CMYK, etc.). The following options are important to understand when printing Photoshop images:

🖌 *Encoding*   Binary is Photoshop's default encoding format for outputting files. However, some networks and spoolers will not process binary data. If this is the case for your spooler or network, select ASCII. Bear in mind that an ASCII file is approximately twice as large as a binary file, so transferring data to the printer will take longer. The JPEG encoding options should only be used with PostScript Level II output devices. JPEG Encoding compresses output files which means data is downloaded faster. When outputting using JPEG Encoding, Photoshop utilizes the highest quality compression. Nevertheless, since JPEG is a "lossy" compression format, output quality may be reduced.

🖌 *Print Selected Area*   If you wish to print an area you have selected on screen, choose Print Selected Areas. (This option is always available no matter what image mode your file is in.)

🖌 *Print In Gray, RGB/Lab, or CMYK*   If you have a PostScript color or Quickdraw printer, you can print a CMYK or Grayscale version of an RGB Color, Lab Color, or Indexed Color file. To print a Grayscale version of your image, select the Gray option. Select RGB or Lab if you wish to print neither a Grayscale nor a CMYK version of your image (if you are in a Lab Color image, there will be a radio button for Lab rather than RGB). When you choose CMYK, Photoshop will convert the colors to produce a CMYK composite version of the image. For proper colors, make sure your system is calibrated. The following illustration shows the Print dialog box when you are using an Indexed Color or RGB Color file.

Printer: "LaserWriter II NTX"  8.1.1   [ Print ]

Copies: **1**   Pages: ⦿ All   ○ From: [   ]   To: [   ]   [ Cancel ]

Paper Source
⦿ All  ○ First from: [ Cassette ▼ ]   Destination   [ Options ]
Remaining from: [ Cassette ▼ ]   ⦿ Printer   [ Help ]
○ File

☐ Print Selected Area   Encoding: ○ ASCII ⦿ Binary ○ JPEG
Print in: ○ Gray ⦿ RGB ○ CMYK

**14**

*Print Separations*  Select this option when you are printing separations. This option will only be available when you are working with a CMYK Color or Duotone image. The following illustration shows the Print dialog box when you are using a Duotone or CMYK Color file.

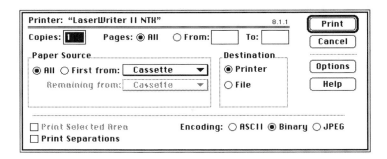

**N**OTE:  *Photoshop will only print one image per page. However, NIQ's Image Up printing software allows multiple Photoshop images to be printed on a page.*

## PRINTING SEPARATIONS

This section leads you step by step through the process of printing a CMYK separation. Even if you're producing output to a 300-dpi laser printer, you may find it educational to see the separation process in action.

To print separations, you will need a CMYK Color image or an RGB Color image converted to CMYK Color. When converting, Photoshop uses the settings in the Monitor Setup, Printing Inks Setup, and Separation Setup dialog boxes. Before you convert an image from RGB Color to CMYK Color, make sure these settings are correct. And always use the File/Save As or Save a Copy command to rename your file before converting, so you'll have a copy of your original image. After converting to CMYK Color, apply the Unsharp Mask filter to sharpen your image. For a complete discussion of converting from RGB Color to CMYK Color, see Chapter 9.

Suppose you want to print your CMYK Color image with registration marks, the image's filename, and crop marks. Follow these steps:

1. From the File menu, choose Page Setup.

# Photoshop in Action

A linear blend from dark to light violet was created with the Gradient tool.

To create the spheres, the Elliptical Marquee, Gaussian Blur filter, Fill command, and an alpha channel were used.

A scanned photograph of the World Trade Center was selected with the Marquee tool. Then Kai's Power Tools were applied to create the fisheye effect. It was then copied and pasted into the final image.

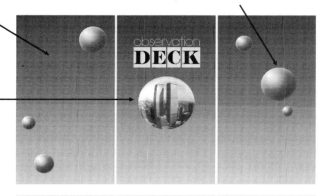

The New York city skyline was created in Adobe Illustrator and then placed into the final image in Photoshop.

Artist: Loren Ruderman          Client: The Port Authority of New York and New Jersey

Loren created this image for the panels in the Observation Deck elevator in the World Trade Center in NYC. The image was separated and output onto film. The film was given to a porcelain enamel fabricator who output the image on porcelain enamel sheets. Loren started by making a rectangular selection with the Marquee tool, filling it with a blend using the Gradient tool, then duplicating it twice. After all three linear blends were completed, he proceeded to make the largest shaded sphere by creating a circular selection with the Marquee tool in a black alpha channel. After the circular selection was created, he filled it with white. He then created a smaller circular selection in the top-left side of the circular selection and filled it with black. Then the Gaussian Blur filter was applied before filling the circular selection with black. Next, the spherical selection was loaded onto the final image and filled with black using a low opacity setting. In order for the sphere to have four rings (four levels of shading), Loren repeated these steps three more times, but each time he increased the size of the circular selection and increased the opacity value. By duplicating the large shaded sphere five times and scaling each duplicate, Loren created the smaller shaded spheres. The final step was to apply the Add Noise filter to each channel in the file to compensate for banding.

2. In the Page Setup dialog box, select the Registration Marks, Labels, and Crop Marks check boxes. Click the Screen button.

3. In the Halftone Screens dialog box, click the Auto button to have Photoshop automatically set the halftone screen angle.

4. In the Auto Screens dialog box, enter your printer's resolution. If you are printing to your laser printer, type **300**. Enter **53** as the screen frequency, make sure lines/inch is set in the corresponding pop-up menu. If you are using a PostScript Level 2 printer, select the Use Accurate Screens option. Click OK to return to the Halftone Screens dialog box.

5. Select the Use Same Shape for All Inks option. Click OK.

6. In the Print dialog box, select Print Separations and click OK.

When the separations print, four images will be output, one for each of the CMYK colors.

 **OTE:** *Second Glance LaserSeps Pro is a Photoshop export filter that creates process separations without halftone screens. It creates the separations using a process called stochastic screening.*

## PRODUCING OUTPUT TO A FILM RECORDER

Film recorders are RGB devices and will not output CMYK files. Thus, if you are producing output to a film recorder for slides or chromes, do not convert RGB Color images to CMYK Color.

For images that will be output to a slide recorder, the gamma of a film recorder is higher than that of the standard gamma setting of 1.8 for images that will be printed. Since the gamma of most film recorders is 2.2, Mac users should recalibrate their monitor with this setting, using the monitor calibration Control Panel device discussed in Chapter 1. Both Mac and PC users should change the Gamma setting in the Monitor Setup dialog box, accessed from the File/Preferences submenu.

When working with a service bureau that outputs transparencies, ask the service bureau for the resolution used by the film recorder. Film recorder resolution is measured by the width and height of the pixels in an image. Many film recorders can output at various resolutions; for instance, two typical resolutions of a film recorder would be 2,048 by 1,366 pixels and 4,096 by 2,732 pixels. When you output to a film recorder, the pixels in your image should fit within the film recorder's grid

# Photoshop in Action

Different views of a miniature quarry were shot on 35mm film, then scanned into Photoshop.

The shoes and the quarry workers were shot on Hi-8 video tape against a blue-screen background.

Director: Craig Barron    Digital Effects Supervisor: Paul Rivera    Production Design: Sean Joyce
Client: The Filmmakers Partnership

This scene from the TV series in development, *Unknown Worlds*, is an example of a Photoshop image that was transferred to video tape. To create this sequence showing an actor looking down into a quarry, Director Craig Barron shot live action scenes against a blue-screen background on Hi-8 video tape. On a ledge below were Special Effects Supervisor Paul Rivera and Production Designer Sean Joyce dressed as quarry workers. The actor's shoes were shot in the foreground.

Later Paul and Craig shot the rocky face of a miniature quarry from different angles. The quarry shots were scanned into Photoshop. Using alpha channels, the Rubber Stamp's Cloning option and the Lasso tool, Paul cut and pasted the different angles to form one long canyon below the actor's shoes. This created the exaggerated forced perspective point of view. Paul combined the foreground and background elements, then added the live action shot using Cosa After Effects. The shot was transferred to Exabyte tape using Knoll Software's Missing Link and sent to the lab for transfer to D-1 digital tape.

**14**

of pixels; otherwise, the image size will be reduced. Remember to consult your service bureau about the resolution you should use when creating your Photoshop file.

If you are designing in Photoshop for clients, find out if they will accept your completed work output on a 4-by-5-inch or 8-by-10-inch chrome from a film recorder. Your client can then have the transparency digitized on a high-end scanner and separated into a CMYK Color file for printing.

## PRODUCING OUTPUT TO VIDEO

If you plan to output your Photoshop images to videotape for multimedia presentation, Photoshop images can easily be exported into animation and video programs such as Adobe Premiere, Macromedia Director, and Avid VideoShop. To calibrate your monitor to video, Gamma should be set to 2.2. See the previous section, "Producing Output to a Film Recorder" for instructions on changing gamma.

Adobe Premiere, Macromedia Director, and Avid VideoShop will all accept Photoshop files saved in PICT format. Photoshop files can be loaded directly into Premiere without changing file formats. From Premiere, images can be output directly to videotape by choosing the Print to Video command from the File/ Export submenu. As discussed in Appendix A, (Premiere) Filmstrip files can be opened, edited, and resaved in Photoshop. Premiere accepts image resolutions of 72 ppi; thus, if your images are intended for video, there generally is no need to create large files in Photoshop at higher resolutions.

For information about importing Premiere files into Photoshop, see Appendix A.

## ON YOUR WAY TO THE PHOTOSHOP FUTURE

This chapter has shown how Photoshop allows you to enter into a technical realm once open to prepress professionals only. Undoubtedly, many Photoshop users would rather not worry about calculating gray levels, compensating for dot gain, and choosing between GCR and UCR (covered in Chapter 9). Although these prepress tasks can be avoided to some degree, you'll find that the more you work with Photoshop, the less daunting they will become. If you establish good relations with prepress houses and commercial printers, you'll have an easier time overcoming problems and getting your questions answered.

Whether you're a novice, intermediate, or advanced Photoshop user, stick with it. We hope this book has truly opened up the wonders of the Photoshop world to you. Now that you've worked through the chapters, examined the beautiful images in the Photoshop Portfolio color inserts, and studied the excellent Photoshop in

Action examples, you'll have learned that Photoshop offers you almost unlimited design choices. We hope that you've already begun to use the examples in this book as a springboard for your own creativity and design ideas, and are planning projects that might once have seemed difficult or even impossible. We're sure that you already agree that after you've experienced the magic of Photoshop, you'll never want to turn away from it. The future's more powerful computers and improved versions of Photoshop are sure to be even more exciting and enticing. We hope this book will help bring you into that future.

If you have comments about the book, or suggestions for subjects and/or artwork to be included in future editions, please write us at this address:

*Fundamental Photoshop*
P.O. Box 3117
Westport, CT 06880

We hope you've enjoyed your journey through *Fundamental Photoshop.*

Adele and Seth

# IMPORTING AND
# EXPORTING FILES

You will often use Photoshop as part of a team of graphics applications. This appendix discusses file formats and the techniques for exporting files created in Photoshop to other programs, and importing files created in other programs into Photoshop.

## USING FILE/SAVE AS AND FILE/SAVE A COPY

When you need to save a file in another format, you can use the File/Save, File/Save As, or File/Save a Copy commands. If you've already saved the file, you must use File/Save As or File/Save a Copy to switch formats. Both the Save As dialog box and the Save a Copy dialog box allow you to pick a specific format from the Format pop-up menu. Figure A-1 shows the Format pop-up menu that appears in both the Save As and Save a Copy dialog box. (PC users will choose from the Save File as Format Type menu.) However, if you've created layers in your document, you will only be able to save in another file format by using the File/Save

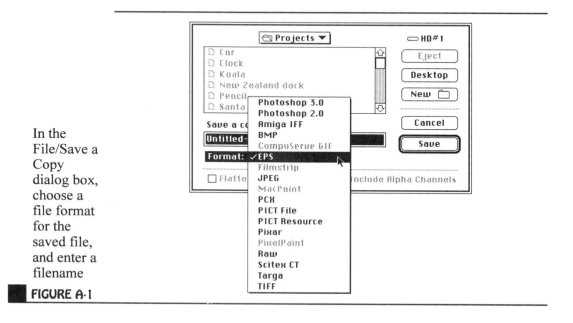

In the File/Save a Copy dialog box, choose a file format for the saved file, and enter a filename

**FIGURE A-1**

a Copy command. File/Save a Copy allows you to flatten any existing layers of an image. If layers are not flattened, you can only save in Photoshop's native format, Photoshop 3.0. File/Save a Copy will also allow you to save an image without its alpha channels. This is necessary when you wish to save in EPS, JPEG, and Scitex CT formats.

After you choose a new file format and click the Save button (PC users: OK), a File Format dialog box often appears, which allows you to specify conversion options.

 **EMEMBER:** *After executing the File/Save As command, you will be working in the document you just saved. When you execute File/Save a Copy you are not working in the file you just saved.*

## WORKING WITH EPS FILES

The EPS (encapsulated PostScript) format is widely accepted by graphics and page-layout programs in Mac and PC environments. The format was originally created as an output format for printing graphic images. If you need to output your files to programs such as QuarkXPress, Adobe Illustrator, or Aldus PageMaker, you can use the EPS format.

The EPS format is often used to export CMYK separation files from one computer application to another. If you are producing your file to be output by a service bureau, you may need to convert your file to EPS format.

If you are working in a bitmap mode file, the EPS format also allows you to save white areas of your image as transparent areas.

### Saving an EPS File

To save a file in EPS format, you choose Save As or Save a Copy from the File menu.  If you choose Save As and your image has alpha channels, you will not be able to access the EPS file format. If you choose Save a Copy instead, and select the EPS format, Photoshop will automatically turn on the Don't Include Alpha Channels check box. If you are using File/Save As, rename the file so that you don't overwrite the previous version. In the Format pop-up menu (PC users: Save File as Format Type drop-down list), choose EPS. (PC users will see the filename extension change to .EPS.) To continue the conversion process, click the Save button (PC users: OK).

Photoshop next opens the EPS Format dialog box. The dialog box that appears depends upon the mode of the file you are exporting (CMYK Color file, RGB Color file, and so forth). If you are exporting a CMYK Color file, for example, the EPS Format dialog box you see looks like this:

```
┌──────────────────────── EPS Format ────────────────────────┐
│                                                             │
│    Preview: [ Macintosh (8 bits/pixel) ▼]     ( OK )        │
│                                                             │
│       DCS: [ Off (single file)        ▼]      (Cancel)      │
│                                                             │
│  Encoding: [ Binary                  ▼]                     │
│                                                             │
│   ┌─ Clipping Path ──────────────────────────────────┐     │
│   │   Path: [ None ▼]                                 │     │
│   │   Flatness: [    ]  device pixels                 │     │
│   └───────────────────────────────────────────────────┘    │
│                                                             │
│   ☐ Include Halftone Screen                                 │
│   ☐ Include Transfer Function                               │
└─────────────────────────────────────────────────────────────┘
```

Many programs, Adobe Illustrator included, allow previews of the EPS file. If you choose the 1 bit/pixel option in the Preview pop-up menu, the preview will be in black-and-white. The 8 bit choice allows 256 colors or shades of gray. Mac users can create previews for the PC by choosing either the TIFF (1 bit/pixel) or TIFF (8 bits/pixel) option. Mac users can also choose Macintosh (JPEG) to save the preview using the JPEG compression format.

The Encoding pop-up menu options allow you to choose whether the EPS file will be a binary or ASCII file or compressed using the JPEG compression format. JPEG removes image data from your file, which can produce a loss in quality. The binary and ASCII formats do not remove data from your file. A binary file is more compact than an ASCII file. Photoshop provides both formats because some applications cannot read the binary format.

In general, you will want to avoid using the Include Halftones Screens and Include Transfer Functions check box options; both of these options may override the settings of an imagesetter or a page-layout program. *Check with your service bureau before you turn on these options.* Here is what they do:

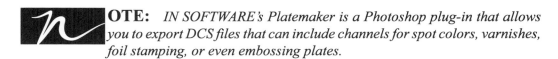 With Include Halftone Screens enabled, Photoshop sends the halftone screen angles and screen frequency settings that are entered into the Halftone Screens dialog box (accessed from the Page Setup dialog box). Enabling this option may override an imagesetter's or other application's halftone screen settings.

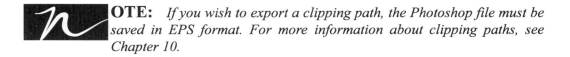 With Include Transfer Functions enabled, Photoshop sends its Transfer Functions information to the EPS file. The Transfer Functions dialog box (accessed from the Page Setup dialog box) allows you to specify dot gain settings to compensate for miscalibrated imagesetters. A well-run service bureau keeps its imagesetters properly calibrated, thus, any Transfer Functions settings you make can adversely affect the quality of the final color separations.

The DCS pop-up menu shown in the previous illustration allows you to create separate EPS files for use with programs that utilize Quark's Desktop Color Separation (DCS) format. When you choose one of the "On" choices in the pop-up menu, Photoshop creates a file for each CMYK component. A fifth file, called a master file, contains a preview of the composite image. If you want a color preview file, choose the 72-pixels/inch color option; for a gray scale preview, choose the 72-pixels/inch gray scale option. If you choose the no composite PostScript option, you cannot print a composite from the file. Note that all five DCS files must be in the same folder if you wish to reload the composite file.

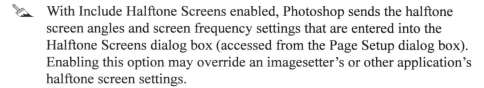

**OTE:** *IN SOFTWARE's Platemaker is a Photoshop plug-in that allows you to export DCS files that can include channels for spot colors, varnishes, foil stamping, or even embossing plates.*

The EPS Format dialog box also allows you to choose a path to use as a clipping path and enter a Flatness value for the clipping path.

**OTE:** *If you wish to export a clipping path, the Photoshop file must be saved in EPS format. For more information about clipping paths, see Chapter 10.*

**A**

## Opening an EPS File

This section explains how to open an Adobe Illustrator file into Photoshop. Photoshop's EPS format is designed to read files created by Adobe Illustrator and Adobe Dimensions. If you are using Freehand, you can convert your files to an Illustrator format by using Altsys' file conversion program, EPS Exchange.

1. To open an EPS file created in Adobe Illustrator or Dimensions, choose Open from the File menu. If you don't see the file, click on the Show All Files check box.

2. Select the file you wish to open. Notice that the file format name is displayed in the File/Open dialog box. Click OK.

   The EPS Rasterizer dialog box that appears next aids you in converting from a drawing or vector program to Photoshop's pixel-based or raster format. In the dialog box, you can change the image's Width, Height, Resolution, and Mode. You can also choose whether to use anti-aliasing. If you want Photoshop to soften the edges of the imported file, click the Anti-aliased check box.

   Turning on the Constrain Proportions option ensures that Width and Height will remain at the same ratio in the converted file. When Constrain Proportions is enabled, a change in either the Width or Height measurement forces a proportional change in the other dimension.

**3.** When you're ready to load the file, click OK. In a few moments, the file opens into Photoshop.

Although the EPS file is now open in Photoshop, it has not been converted to Photoshop's native format. If you intend to edit the file and save and reload it, it's best to convert (save) the file to Photoshop 3.0 format. Otherwise, you will be met by the EPS Rasterizer dialog box each time you load the file.

**4.** To save the file in Photoshop format, choose either Save, Save As, or Save a Copy from the File menu. Before continuing to save the file in another format, Mac users should rename the file; this prevents overwriting the previous file on the disk. (On the PC, when you change file formats, Photoshop changes the filename extension of the file to .PSD; thus, the original file is not overwritten. It's a good idea to rename the file anyway, however, to avoid confusion between versions.) To switch to Photoshop 3.0 format, choose Photoshop 3.0 from the list in the Format pop-up menu. Click Save (PC users: OK) to execute the conversion.

## Placing an EPS File into a Photoshop Document

At times you may want to place an Adobe Illustrator document into a file that is already open in Photoshop. If you want the image to be anti-aliased, select the Anti-alias PostScript check box after clicking the More button in the General Preferences dialog box. This dialog box is accessed by choosing General from the File/Preferences submenu.

Here are the steps to place an Illustrator EPS file into a Photoshop file:

**1.** Open the Photoshop file into which you intend to place the Illustrator file.

**2.** From the File menu, choose Place.

**3.** From the list of files that appears, select the file that you wish to place, and click Open (PC users: OK).

**4.** The Illustrator file appears as a boxed, floating selection on screen. If you wish to move the imported image, position the mouse pointer on the border of the floating box. (The selection pointer should be the arrow pointer.) Click and drag the image to the desired location.

5. If you wish to resize the image and change the width-to-height (aspect) ratio, press and hold down COMMAND (PC users: CTRL) while you click and drag the mouse. If you wish to change the image size but maintain the aspect ratio, press SHIFT and then click and drag the mouse.

6. Once you are satisfied with the size and placement of the imported image, position the mouse pointer over it; when the pointer changes to a gavel icon, click to lock the image down.

## WORKING WITH TIFF FILES

The TIFF format is frequently used for both Mac and PC graphics files. TIFF stands for "tagged-image file format" and was introduced by the Aldus Corporation as a format for saving scanned images. Although the format is used by most page-layout programs, it is not accepted by all drawing programs.

TIFF files can be loaded directly into Photoshop. When you save a TIFF file in Photoshop, the TIFF Options dialog box appears:

```
╔══════════ TIFF Options ══════════╗
║                                    ║
║  ┌─ Byte Order ──────┐  ┌──────┐  ║
║  │  ○ IBM PC         │  │  OK  │  ║
║  │  ● Macintosh      │  └──────┘  ║
║  └───────────────────┘  [Cancel] ║
║                                    ║
║  □ LZW Compression                 ║
║                                    ║
╚════════════════════════════════════╝
```

Here you can specify whether the document is for the Macintosh or IBM PC-compatible computers. Just choose the appropriate radio button under Byte Order.

One valuable feature of exporting files in TIFF format is that TIFF files can be compressed. In the TIFF Options dialog box is a check box you can select to enable LZW (Lempel-Ziv-Welch) Compression. LZW is a "lossless" compression format; the file is compressed without removing image data from it. Most page-layout programs can read compressed TIFF files.

If you have created alpha channels in your Photoshop file, the alpha channels will automatically be saved with the file. Alpha channels are generally used to save selections, as explained in Chapter 12.

 **OTE:** *If you wish to open a TIFF file using File/Acquire/Quick Edit, do not save it with LZW Compression. For more information about Quick Edit, see Chapter 6.*

# WORKING WITH PICT FILES (MACINTOSH ONLY)

PICT is one of the most common data-file formats available on the Macintosh. Most Macintosh graphics applications, such as MacDraw and Claris Draw, can save files in this format. Some PC programs, including CorelDRAW, also accept the format. Both PICT and PICT2 (colored PICT) images can be loaded directly into Photoshop.

When saving files in PICT format, the PICT File Options dialog box appears, which allows you to designate the Resolution (pixel depth) of the image. The dialog box you see will depend on whether you are saving a grayscale or color file.

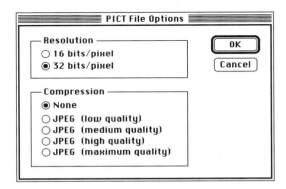

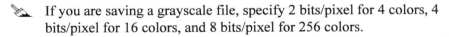 If you are saving a grayscale file, specify 2 bits/pixel for 4 colors, 4 bits/pixel for 16 colors, and 8 bits/pixel for 256 colors.

The choices for color images are 16 bits/pixel or 32 bits/pixel. If you are exporting a 24-bit color image, choose the 32-bits/pixel option. This 32-bit option appears because the Macintosh includes an extra 8-bit channel (an alpha channel). Most software and video cards do not use this extra 8 bits of information, so if you are not using 24-bit color in Photoshop, choose the 16-bits/pixel option; this keeps file sizes smaller.

When QuickTime is installed, the Compression section allows you to reduce file size with JPEG compression. (See the section, "Compressing Files Using JPEG" later in this appendix.)

 **OTE:** *You cannot save CMYK Color or Lab Color images in PICT format. You can't save images with more than one alpha channel in PICT format.*

# Photoshop in Action

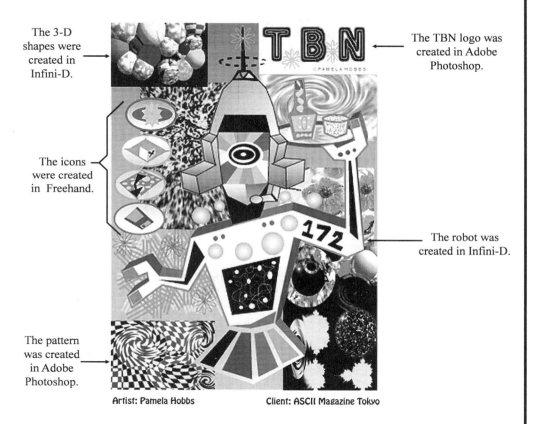

The 3-D shapes were created in Infini-D.

The TBN logo was created in Adobe Photoshop.

The icons were created in Freehand.

The robot was created in Infini-D.

The pattern was created in Adobe Photoshop.

Artist: Pamela Hobbs          Client: ASCII Magazine Tokyo

Pamela created this magazine cover using Adobe Photoshop, Freehand, and Infini-D (a 3-D program). She started by creating the TBN logo and patterns in Photoshop. Once these images were completed, she saved the files as EPS images so they could be placed into Freehand.

The 3-D shapes in the top left-hand corner of the cover and the robot were created with Infini-D. Once these images were completed, she saved the files as EPS images and placed them into the final image in Freehand. With Freehand, she created the icons on the left side of the cover.

## Importing PICT Images Using the Anti-Aliased PICT Command

Although PICT images load directly into Photoshop using the File/Open command, you may prefer to use the File/Acquire command to import PICT images. With File/Acquire, you can select the Anti-Aliased PICT option; this activates a plug-in that offers options similar to those in the EPS Rasterizer dialog box. (See "Opening an EPS File" earlier in this appendix.)

```
═══════════════ Anti-Aliased PICT ════════════════

  Image Size: 2.2 Mb                    ┌──────────┐
                                        │    OK    │
       Width:  1024   (pixels)          └──────────┘
      Height:  768    (pixels)          ┌──────────┐
                                        │  Cancel  │
   Mode:              ⊠ Constrain Proportions  └──────┘
     ○ Gray Scale
     ⦿ RGB Color
```

The Anti-Aliased PICT dialog box lets you change Width and Height proportionally and choose to open the document as a Gray Scale or RGB Color file. When you execute the Acquire command and import the PICT file, Photoshop uses anti-aliasing to soften image edges.

## COMPRESSING FILES USING JPEG

The JPEG file format is used to compress files to make them smaller. JPEG (Joint Photographic Experts Group) is a "lossy" standard, which means information is removed from the file during the compression process. Usually the absence of the subtracted information is not noticed if the image is compressed using a high-quality setting. When the file is reopened, the lost information is not returned to the file. If you've opened any of Photoshop's tutorial files, you may have already worked with JPEG files. JPEG files can be opened directly into Photoshop.

When saving a file in JPEG format, use the File/Save As or File/Save a Copy command and choose JPEG from the Format pop-up menu. The JPEG Options dialog box appears, allowing you to choose an Image Quality option. Remember, JPEG files cannot contain alpha channels.

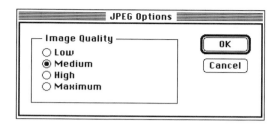

## Exporting and Acquiring Files with Storm JPEG

If you've purchased a Photoshop accelerator card, it may have been bundled with Storm Technology's JPEG Plug-in, which offers additional compression settings and options. The plug-in is accessed through the File/Acquire and File/Export submenus. You can specify different compression settings for selections. It also creates thumbnail previews of the images that you compress.

**OTE:** *If you wish to export an EPS file using JPEG compression, choose Export from the File menu, then select Compress EPS JPEG (PC users: EPS JPEG Export).*

## SCITEX CT FILES

Scitex workstations are often used at prepress houses for image editing and color-correction. Files created by Scitex workstations using the Scitex CT (continuous tone) format can be loaded directly into Photoshop and can be used with Photoshop's File/Acquire/Quick Edit command.

Only Grayscale, RGB Color, and CMYK Color Photoshop files may be saved in the Scitex CT format. Also, you can't save a file with alpha channels in Scitex CT format. If you have a Scitex system, you need special utilities created by Scitex to complete the transfer process.

# PHOTO CD FILES

Photo CD files can be opened directly into Photoshop. Version 3.0 of the program includes Kodak's CMS CD plug-in, which was designed to increase the color range and fidelity of Photo CD images that are loaded into Photoshop. The plug-in helps color reversal or slide film formats look similar to their appearance when viewed on a light box.

You can open Photo CD images from the Open dialog box.

After you execute the Open command, a dialog box appears. You'll need to make the following settings:

Specify the desired Resolution for the file to be imported.

Click on the Source button to open a dialog box where you can choose a Precision Transform option for conversion—Ektachrome (color reversal/slide); Kodachrome (color reversal/slide); or Photo CD Color Negative. If the film "term" is not known but the medium is color reversal/slide, choose Ektachrome. Choose Kodachrome only if K-14 film processing was used to create your negatives. Click OK to accept the Source setting.

To specify the Destination color space, click the Destination button to open another dialog box. In the Device pop-up menu, select Adobe Photoshop

CIELAB if you wish to have images opened in Lab color mode. Images that will later be converted to CMYK Color should be opened in this format. To open an image in RGB Color mode, select Adobe Photoshop RGB. You will see the words "RCS to Adobe Photoshop" or "RCS to Adobe RGB." Don't be confused by the abbreviation RCS, which stands for Reference Color Space. This is an interim color space used in the conversion from Photo CD color space to the destination color space. When you're ready, click OK to accept the settings.

To load the image, click OK in the dialog box.

If you are working on images that will be converted to CMYK, check with Kodak to see whether you can use one of their profiles that converts a file from Photo CD's color space (Photo YCC) into a CMYK color file.

For more details on using Photo CD technology with Photoshop, refer to Chapter 7.

**OTE:** *Photoshop cannot save files in Photo CD format.*

## FILMSTRIP FILES

Filmstrip files are used in animation programs such as Adobe Premier. Filmstrip files can be loaded into the Macintosh version of Photoshop and resaved using Filmstrip format. You cannot, however, convert a file created in Photoshop into a Filmstrip file.

## FROM MAC TO PC AND BACK AGAIN

If you are using a Mac and wish to load a Photoshop file created on the PC, or vice versa, you need only use the standard File/Open command. No special conversion procedures are necessary to load and save files between these two platforms.

To use a PC file on the Mac or to save a file on the Mac for use on the PC, you need to save the file on a medium formatted for the PC (a disk or removable hard drive). Several utility programs, including Dayna's DOS Mounter, Insignia's Access PC, Dataviz's MacLink Plus, Apple's PC Exchange, and Apple File Exchange, allow PC files to be displayed on the Mac. If you are using DOS Mounter or PC Exchange, Adobe recommends saving the file first to your Mac's hard drive and then drag-copying the file to the DOS-formatted medium. This has proved more reliable than saving directly to a DOS disk from Photoshop.

**OTE:** *Many Macintosh computers manufactured earlier than the Mac IIcx are not equipped with drives that read DOS-formatted disks.*

If you are saving a file on a Mac that will be loaded onto a PC, you must give the file a name that is no more than eight characters long and contains no spaces. When you name the file, include a period at the end, followed by a two- or three-letter filename extension. The extension is a "code" that alerts Photoshop for Windows what file format to expect. The following is a list of acceptable file formats and their filename extensions.

| Format | Filename Extension |
|---|---|
| Amiga | .IFF |
| CompuServe Graphics | .GIF |
| Encapsulated PostScript | .EPS |
| Illustrator/ASCII EPS | .AI |
| JPEG (Compressed) | .JPG |
| MacPaint | .MPT |
| PC Paintbrush | .PCX |
| Photoshop standard | .PSD |
| Pixar | .PXR |
| PixelPaint | .PXI |
| Raw | .RAW |
| Scitex CT | .SCT |
| Targa | .TGA |
| TIFF | .TIF |
| Windows Bitmap | .BMP |

The following is a list of PC-compatible filename extensions for palettes and settings:

| Palette/Setting | Filename Extension |
|---|---|
| Arbitrary | .AMP |
| Brushes palette | .ABR |
| Color table | .ACT |
| Colors palette | .ACO |
| Curves | .CRV |
| Custom filters | .ACF |
| Displacement maps | .PSD |
| Duotone options | .ADO |
| Halftone screens | .AHS |
| Hue/Saturation | .HSS |
| Levels | .ALV |
| Printing inks | .API |
| Separation setup | .ASP |
| Separation table | .AST |
| Transfer functions | .ATF |
| Variations | .PSV |

## Saving PC Files on Mac Disks

Many service bureaus accept data on Syquest removable hard disks. If you use Photoshop for Windows and need to format disks in Mac format, use a formatting utility such as Pacific Micro Electronics' Mac-in-DOS Plus for Windows. This program will format both Syquest cartridges and disks.

# USING THE FILE INFO COMMAND

Adobe Photoshop allows you to tag image files with captions, descriptions, and photocredits. Photoshop uses a format, adopted by The Newspaper Association of America and the International Press Communications Council, to identify images. Although this section of the program is primarily designed for the Press, other users can take advantage of the entry screens to enter historical information about images. You might even include a brief description of how your images were created, and what (if any) stock images appear.

To enter identifying information about an image, choose File Info from the File menu. In the File Info dialog box, use the Section pop-up menu to navigate through five different screens: Caption, Keywords, Categories, Credits, and Origins. You can either use the pop-up menu to navigate through the different sections or click on the Next button. The following is a brief description of each section.

## Caption

The Caption section allows you to enter a caption of up to 2000 characters. The name of the caption writer, a headline, and special instructions can also be entered into this section.

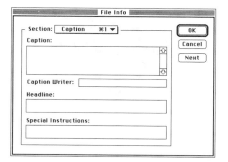

**OTE:** *To print the Caption field beneath an image, select the Caption option in the Page Setup dialog box (choose File/Page Setup). Then choose File/Print.*

## Keywords

The Keywords section allows you to enter different search categories for images.

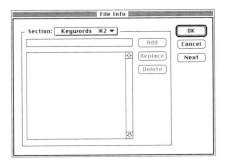

The Keyword field allows up to 31 characters. After typing the word, click the Add button which will add the word to the Keyword list. You can enter as many keywords as you like. If you wish to delete a keyword, select the word by clicking on it, then click on the Delete button. To replace a keyword, enter a new word in the Keyword field, then click on the Replace button.

 **OTE:** *Both the Caption and Keyword entries can be searched with third-party image database software such as Fetch.*

## Categories

The Categories section allows you to enter a category code, supplemental categories, and tag the file with an Urgency value.

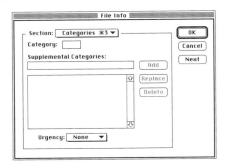

The Category field is designed to hold a three-digit Associated Press category code. To add supplemental categories, enter a word in the Supplemental Categories field, then click on the Add button. After supplemental categories are added, they appear in a list in the middle of the screen. To delete a category, click on it; next, click on the Delete button. To replace a supplemental category, enter a new supplemental category, then click on the Replace button. To set editorial urgency, click on the Urgency pop-up menu, and choose from the list of choices. The lower the value, the higher the Urgency.

## Credits

Use the Credits section to enter a byline, a byline title, a credit, and source information.

## Origin

Use the Origin section to enter historical information about the image. In the Object Name field, type a description of the image. To enter the date, click on the Today button. Enter information in the appropriate fields for City, State, Transmission Reference, and Country.

# INDEX

**J**

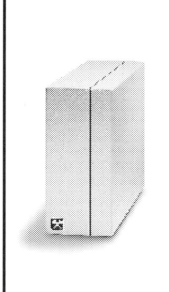

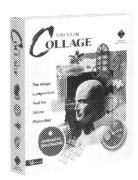
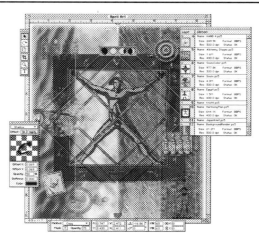

# Disk Offer

*Fundamental Photoshop* was carefully designed so that you can easily re-create the sample projects in the book using your own images or Adobe Photoshop Tutorial files. For more practice, you may wish to use some of the images that appear in the book. If so, you can send for two high-density disks containing 20 color images that appear in black and white in the book. Make your check or money order for $12.95 payable to "AD. Design" and send it to:

**Fundamental Photoshop**
**P.O. Box 3117**
**Westport, CT 06880**

Please specify whether you would like a Mac or PC disk.

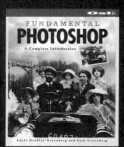

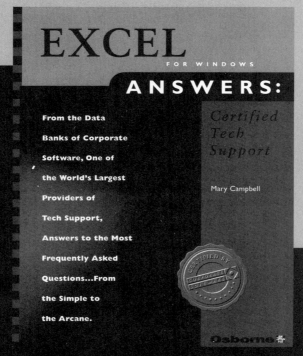

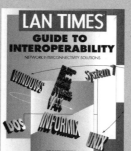

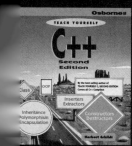

# ORDER BOOKS DIRECTLY FROM OSBORNE/MC GRAW-HILL.

For a complete catalog of Osborne's books,  call 510-549-6600 or write to us at 2600 Tenth Street, Berkeley, CA 94710

**Call Toll-Free:** *1-800-822-8158*
*24 hours a day, 7 days a week*
*in U.S. and Canada*

**Mail this order form to:**
McGraw-Hill, Inc.
Blue Ridge Summit, PA  17294-0840

**Fax this order form to:**
**717-794-5291**

**EMAIL**
*7007.1531@COMPUSERVE.COM*
*COMPUSERVE GO MH*

**Ship to:**

Name _____

Company _____

Address _____

City / State / Zip _____

Daytime Telephone: _____
(We'll contact you if there's a question about your order.)

| ISBN # | BOOK TITLE | Quantity | Price | Total |
|--------|-----------|----------|-------|-------|
| 0-07-88 | | | | |
| 0-07-88 | | | | |
| 0-07-88 | | | | |
| 0-07-88 | | | | |
| 0-07-88 | | | | |
| 0-07088 | | | | |
| 0-07-88 | | | | |
| 0-07-88 | | | | |
| 0-07-88 | | | | |
| 0-07-88 | | | | |
| 0-07-88 | | | | |
| 0-07-88 | | | | |
| | *Shipping & Handling Charge from Chart Below* | | | |
| | *Subtotal* | | | |
| | *Please Add Applicable State & Local Sales Tax* | | | |
| | *TOTAL* | | | |

## Shipping & Handling Charges

| Order Amount | U.S. | Outside U.S. |
|--------------|------|--------------|
| Less than $15 | $3.45 | $5.25 |
| $15.00 - $24.99 | $3.95 | $5.95 |
| $25.00 - $49.99 | $4.95 | $6.95 |
| $50.00 - and up | $5.95 | $7.95 |

*Occasionally we allow other selected companies to use our mailing list.  If you would prefer that we not include you in these extra mailings, please check here:* ☐

## METHOD OF PAYMENT

☐  Check or money order enclosed (payable to Osborne/McGraw-Hill)

☐ AMERICAN EXPRESS    ☐ DISCOVER    ☐ MasterCard.    ☐ VISA

Account No. [ ][ ][ ][ ][ ][ ][ ][ ][ ][ ][ ][ ][ ][ ][ ][ ]

Expiration Date _____

Signature _____

*In a hurry?  Call 1-800-822-8158 anytime, day or night, or visit your local bookstore.*

## Thank you for your order

Code BC640SL